The COMMUNIST SUCCESSOR PARTIES of CENTRAL and EASTERN EUROPE

The COMMUNIST SUCCESSOR PARTIES

of CENTRAL AND EASTERN EUROPE

ANDRÁS BOZÓKI

JOHN T. ISHIYAMA

EDITORS

M.E.Sharpe

Armonk, New York

London, England

The EuroSlavic fonts used to create this work are © 1986–2002 Payne Loving Trust.
EuroSlavic is available from Linguist's Software, Inc.,
www.linguistsoftware.com, P.O. Box 580, Edmonds, WA 98020-0580 USA
tel (425) 775-1130.

Library of Congress Cataloging-in-Publication Data

The communist successor parties of Central and Eastern Europe / edited by András
Bozóki and John T. Ishiyama.
    p. cm.
Includes bibliographical references and index.
ISBN 0-7656-0986-X (alk. paper)
    1. Communist parties—Europe, Eastern. 2. Europe, Eastern—Politics and
government—1989–. 3. Communist parties—Former Soviet republics. 4. Former
Soviet republics—Political and government. I. Bozóki, András. II. Ishiyama, John T.,
1960–.

JN96.A979 C664 2002
324.2′175′0947—dc21   2001058179

Printed in the United States of America

The paper used in this publication meets the minimum requirements of
American National Standard for Information Sciences
Permanence of Paper for Printed Library Materials,
ANSI Z 39.48-1984.

∞

MV (c)   10   9   8   7   6   5   4   3   2   1

Contents

List of Tables and Figures

Tables

Figures

About the Editors and Contributors

Michael Bauer is assistant professor at the Institute for Political Science, Eberhard Karls University, Tübingen, Germany. His main fields of research are comparative politics, democratization, and parties and party systems in post-communist countries. His recent publication, "Die Aussenpolitik Russlands" (Russia's Foreign Policy), appeared in *Der Bürger im Staat, Russland im Umbruch*. Landeszentrale für politische Bildung, Baden-Württemberg 51 (2–3).

Nick Biziouras is a Ph.D. candidate in the Department of Political Science at the University of California at Berkeley. He has published on the politics of foreign direct investment in Asia, including: "The Last Fane to Asia: Volkswagen and Peugeot in China" (co-author), in Aggarwal, ed., *Winning in Asia, European Style* and "Asia Beckons America: The Case of the Automobile Industry" in Aggarwal, ed., *Asia Beckons America: American Firms in Asia*, (forthcoming) (co-author). He is currently investigating the relationship between economic liberalization and the propensity for ethnic conflict in multiethnic societies.

András Bozóki is associate professor of political science at Central European University, Budapest, Hungary. His main fields of research are comparative politics, democratization, political ideas, and political and cultural elites. His publications include three books in Hungarian, and *Post-Communist Transition: Emerging Pluralism in Hungary* (1992) (co-editor); *Lawful Revolution in Hungary, 1989–94* (1995) (co-editor); *Intellectuals and Politics in Central Europe* (1999) (editor); and *The Roundtable Talks of 1989: The Genesis of Hungarian Democracy* (2002) (editor).

Srbobran Branković is a research fellow at the Institute for Political Studies, and professor at the Alternative Academic Network (parallel university during the Milosevic era) both in Belgrade, Yugoslavia. He is also director and co-owner of Medium-Index–Gallup International, a public opinion, market and media research company. His main fields of research are voter behavior, public opinion, interethnic relations, political values and attitudes in Yugoslavia. His publications include *Serbia at War with Itself: Political Choice in Serbia, 1990–94* (1995), and *Electing the Lesser Evil* (1996).

Valerie Bunce is professor and chair at the Department of Government of Cornell University, Ithaca, NY. She is also an outgoing vice-president of the American Political Science Association and current president of the American Association for the Advancement of Slavic Studies. Her main fields of research are comparative democratization, ethnic conflict and East European politics. Her recent publications include *Subversive Institutions: The Design and Destruction of Socialism and the State* (1999) and "Postsocialisms" in Antohi and Tismaneanu, eds., *Between Past and Future: The Revolutions of 1989 and Their Aftermath* (2000).

Barbara Chotiner is professor of political science at the University of Alabama, Tuscaloosa. Her research interests have included innovation and change in the Communist Party of the Soviet Union and its successors as well as their organizational capacities to contribute to systemic evolution. Her publications include *Khrushchev's Party Reform* (1984); "Creating Political Capital," in *The Legacy of the Soviet Bloc* (1997); and "The Communist Party of the Russian Federation: from the Fourth Congress to the Summer 1998 Government Crisis," in Ishiyama, ed., *Communist Successor Parties in Post-Communist Politics* (1999).

Sharon Fisher is an economist at DRI-WEFA Inc., Washington, DC. Her main fields of research are economic and political transformation, post-communist politics, and national identity. Her publications include *The 1998 Parliamentary Elections and Democratic Rebirth in Slovakia* (1999) (co-editor); "Representations of the Nation in Slovakia's 1998 Parliamentary Elections," in Williams, ed., *Slovakia after Communism and Meciarism* (2000); "The Rise and Fall of National Movements in Slovakia and Croatia," *Slovak Foreign Policy Affairs*, 2000.

Anna Grzymala-Busse is assistant professor at the Department of Political Science, Yale University, New Haven. Her research interests include political parties, the state and corruption, and nationalism. She has published several articles on successor parties, post-communist party politics, and the state as well as a book, *Redeeming the Communist Past: The Regeneration of Communist Successor Parties in East Central Europe* (2002).

Sean Hanley is lecturer in politics at Brunel University, West London. His research has focused principally on the formation and institutionalization of political parties in post-communist Central and Eastern Europe. He has a special interest in the politics of the Czech Republic and has published a number of academic articles on Czech and Central European politics. He is currently researching the comparative politics of center-right parties in the region.

John T. Ishiyama is associate professor of political science at Truman State University, Kirksville, MO. His main fields of research are post-communist party politics, institutional development, and ethnic politics in Eastern Europe and the former Soviet Union. His recent books include *Ethnopolitics in the New Europe* (1998) (co-author) and *Communist Successor Parties in Post-Communist Politics* (1999) (editor). He has also published numerous journal articles on post-communist politics.

Diana Janusauskienė is assistant professor and Civic Education Project scholar at the Department of Political Science, Lithuanian University of Law, Vilnius, Lithuania. Her main fields of research are democratization, political participation, and elite change in the post-communist countries. Her dissertation, "Post-Communist Democratization in Lithuania: The Rising New Elites," was completed at the Graduate School for Social Research, Polish Academy of Sciences, in 2001.

Herbert Kitschelt is professor of political science at Duke University, Durham, NC. He has published on political parties and party competition in advanced industrial democracies and post-communist polities. His recent publications include *The Radical Right in Western Europe* (1995); *Post-Communist Party-Systems: Competition, Representation and Inter-Party Cooperation* (1999) (co-author); and *Continuity and Change in Contemporary Capitalism* (1999) (co-editor). His current research focuses on the interface between political institutions, party competition, and political/economic reform across regions and on evolving patterns of party competition in Latin America.

János Ladányi is professor of sociology at the Budapest University of Economics and Public Administration, Hungary. His research focus includes social policy, urban poverty, and ethnic conflicts. His publications include three books in Hungarian and, more recently, "Class, Ethnicity and Urban Restructuring in Post-Communist Hungary" (co-author), in Enyedi, ed., *Social Change and Urban Restructuring in Central Europe* (1998); and "The Hungarian Neoliberal State, Ethnic Classification and the Creation of a Roma Underclass," in Emigh and Szelényi, eds., *Poverty, Ethnicity and Gender in Eastern Europe during the Market Transition* (2001).

Radoslaw Markowski is head of the Electoral Studies Division at the Institute for Political Studies of the Polish Academy of Sciences, and director of the Polish National Election Survey, both in Warsaw, Poland. His main fields of research are political behavior, party systems, and comparative politics focusing on Central and Eastern Europe. His publications include *Predictions and Elections: Polish Democracy* (1995) (co-editor); *Post-Communist*

Party-Systems: Competition, Representation, and Inter-Party Cooperation (1999) (co-author); and *Transformative Paths in Central and Eastern Europe* (2001) (co-editor).

Jeffrey Stevenson Murer is an assistant professor of political science at Swarthmore College, in Swarthmore, PA. His research focuses on the political responses to the political and economic transition in Central and Eastern Europe. His recent publications include "Challenging Expectations: A Comparative Study of the Communist Successor Parties of Hungary, Bulgaria and Romania," in Ishiyama, ed., *Communist Successor Parties in Post-Communist Politics* (1999) and "The Clash Within: Intrapsychically Created Enemies and Their Roles in Ethno-Nationalist Conflict," in Worcester, Ungar, and Bermanzohn, eds., *Violence and Politics* (2000).

Alina Mungiu-Pippidi is professor of political science at the Romanian National School of Government and Administration and director of the Romanian Academic Society, a public policy institute, in Bucharest, Romania. Between 1997–99 she served as news director at the Romanian Television. Her main fields of research include elite change, political culture, public policy and journalism. Her publications include *Die Rumanen nach '89* (Romanians after 1989) (1996); *The Evangelists: Modern International Drama* (1996); *Subjective Transylvania: Social Representations of an Ethnic Conflict* (1999), and *Romania after 2000* (forthcoming).

Richard Sakwa is professor of Russian and European politics in the Department of Politics and International Relations at the University of Kent at Canterbury. His recent publications include *Russian Politics and Society* (1993, 1996, 2002); *Soviet Politics in Perspective* (1998); *Postcommunism* (1999), and *The Rise and Fall of the Soviet Union, 1917–1991* (1999). He has also written numerous articles on contemporary Russian affairs. His main research interest at present is the development of democracy and the state in Russia, in particular the evolution of political institutions and regime types.

Dieter Segert is a researcher at the Faculty of Cultural Studies, European University Viadrina, Frankfurt (Oder), Germany. His main fields of research are comparative politics, party politics, and democratic transitions in Eastern Germany and Central and Eastern Europe, and the history and legacy of state socialism. His publications include *Parteien in Osteuropa: Kontext und Akteure* (Parties in Eastern Europe: Context and Actors) (1995) (co-author); and *Die Grenzen Osteuropas. 1918, 1945, 1989: Drei Versuche im Western anzukommen* (The Borderlines of Eastern Europe. 1918, 1945, 1989: Three Attempts to Catch up with the West) (2002).

Iván Szelényi is William Graham Sumner Professor of Sociology and professor of political science at Yale University, New Haven. He is fellow of the American Academy of Arts and Sciences, ordinary member of the Hungarian Academy of Sciences, and vice president of the American Sociological Association. His research interests include classes and elites, social change, urban sociology, and ethnicity. His books include *The Intellectuals on the Road to Class Power* (1979) (co-author); *Urban Inequalities under State Socialism* (1983); *Socialist Entrepreneurs* (1988); *Making Capitalism without Capitalists: The New Ruling Elites in Eastern Europe* (1998) (co-author); *Poverty, Ethnicity and Gender in Eastern Europe during the Market Transition* (2001) (co-editor).

Daniel F. Ziblatt is a Ph.D. candidate in the Department of Political Science at the University of California, Berkeley. He has published several articles on ex-communist parties that have appeared in *German Politics and Society*, and *Communist and Post-Communist Studies*. He is currently writing a comparative historical dissertation on the politics of federalism in Italy and Germany. He has a forthcoming article on German federalism in the German Political Science Association's journal *Politische Vierteljahreszeitschrift*.

Part I

Approaches

1

Introduction and Theoretical Framework

András Bozóki and John T. Ishiyama

Since 1991, the communist successor parties (those parties which were the primary successors to the former governing party in the communist regime and inherited the preponderance of the former ruling parties' resources and personnel) have undergone a considerable transformation (Bozóki 1997, Ishiyama 1995). Contrary to early expectations that the organizational successors to the communist parties would disappear into the ash can of political history, the successor parties have proven quite durable. Indeed, in most all countries in Eastern Europe and the former Soviet Union, there is at least one active communist successor party.

The study of the development of communist successor parties offers a unique opportunity. For comparativists working in the area of party development and area studies experts interested in linking studies of the post-communist ménage with mainstream western political science examing the sucessor parties the allows for the investigation of something akin to real parties. Unlike so many parties with few organizational resources and little in the way of established social roots, the communist successor parties are not merely clubs of notables or "couch parties" (where all members could fit on a single couch). They have a long political tradition and an organizational history, as well as an internal structure that sets them apart from most other political parties in the region. They are distinct organizations, and by any definition represent "real" political parties. However, they are parties that have suffered the strains of rapid social and political transformation associated with the democratic transition, and have had to change in order to meet these new challenges. Thus, the study of the successor parties allows comparativists to bring to bear some long-standing theoretical propositions regarding party development in investigating the political impact of the democratic transformation in post-communist politics as these changes occur. Indeed, the experience of the communist successor parties offers a unique opportunity for scholars to test first-hand the long-standing theories of party development painstakingly based upon western historical experience. In addition, for area studies scholars, a focus on communist successor parties not only allows the opportunity to integrate the study of this area into the mainstream of political science inquiry, but also to significantly alter existing theory in light of new evidence.

Of special interest, at least from the perspective of this chapter, is how the communist successor parties have adapted to changed circumstances. The collapse of communism in Eastern Europe and the transformation of the formerly dominant communist parties provide an opportunity to test further the propositions regarding party identity change. Indeed, there has been quite a bit of variation concerning how the communist successor parties have adapted to the fundamentally altered political environment of the post–cold war era. Some have changed their political identities and embraced markets, capitalism, and democratic competition, rather than state ownership and democratic centralism. Others continue to cling to ideological purity and Marxist-Leninist values.

What varies among the countries is not so much where the communist successor parties have survived, but how they have survived. The primary purpose of this chapter is to provide a theoretical framework by which we might be able to identify the various adaptation strategies the communist successor parties have persued and to investigate the causes and the extent to which these strategies have changed over time. To do this, we first outline a typology of different adaptation strategies. Second, we develop a theoretical framework by which to explain party change, a framework derived from much of the existing literature on party development.

Characterizing the Communist Successor Parties' Adaptation Strategies

A considerable amount of literature has already examined the development of the communist successor parties since 1991. However, most of the literature thus far has focused on why these parties made a political comeback in the 1990s rather than on how these parties adapted and changed in the face of new political circumstances (Orenstein 1998, Ishiyama 1997a). Several explanations have been put forward as to why the communist successor parties were able to successfully return to the political scene (Ágh 1995, Waller, 1995, Evans and Whitefield 1995, Zubek 1994). These include an argument that characteristics of the previous authoritarian regime were crucial in explaining the return of the successor parties, as well as the degree of competition the successor party faced from other left-wing parties (Ishiyama 1997a, Kitschelt 1995a, Ágh 1995, Waller 1995). Some scholars have further argued that the existence of lingering social constituencies (such as the elderly) facilitate the political success of the formerly dominant communist parties. Others have pointed to the existence of issues which the successor parties can capitalize upon that affect whether or not they are politically successful (Waller 1995).

Yet despite the attention paid to explaining the success (or lack thereof) of the successor parties, relatively little work has been done that identifies the factors that might affect the extent to which the communist successor parties alter their political identities. Among those few works that have dealt with the identity change of the communist successor parties, most have examined early adaptation strategies when confronted with the first competitive elections as opposed to later changes (Ishiyama and Shafqat 2000, Oates 1999, Ziblatt 1998). Further, these studies examined the identity change during the period when the successor parties were reasserting themselves (from 1992–1996) not during their period of relative decline (1996–2000).

To examine the adaptation strategies exhibited by the successor parties following the "second generation elections" (those in which successor parties faced either significant challenges from opponents or were defeated altogether), we begin with the work of Daniel Ziblatt, particularly his study of successor parties in former East Germany (the Party of Democratic Socialism-PDS) and in Hungary (the Hungarian Socialist Party) (Ziblatt 1998). Arguing against the fairly common tendency to equate "successful adaptation" with the "social democratization" of the successor parties, Ziblatt argues that there were at least two strategies available, both of which could have proven politically successful: the strategy of *leftist-retreat*, which involves the successor party embracing its Marxist traditions (rejecting the free-market), repudiating western influence, and adopting the status of an "anti-system" opposition party. This pattern was exemplified by both the PDS in Germany and the KSCM in the Czech Republic, and, as Anna Gryzmala-Busse points out, these parties continue to attack "bourgeois democracy" and "capitalist exploitation" (Gryzmala-Busse 1999). In Hungary and in Poland, by contrast, the leadership of the parties, aside from marginal leftist factions, have followed a strategy of *pragmatic-reform*, attempting to distance themselves from "dogmatic Marxism" and redefining the party as a quasi-European social democratic party of experts, technocrats, and pragmatists. Between these two poles are intermediate positions such as those taken up by the Bulgarian Socialist Party (BSP) and the Socialist Party of Albania (SPA). The leaderships of both have professed the "social democratization" of their respective parties but have had to rely heavily on political nostalgia to mobilize electoral support (which has also been the case for most of the successor parties in the former Soviet Union) (Ishiyama 1997a, 1996a).

In addition to these two strategies, a third can be identified: the *national-patriotic* strategy, which is common to states in the Balkans and the former Soviet Union (Ishiyama 1998a). This strategy, like the "leftist retreat" strategy is characterized by a continued embrace of Marxist-Leninist traditions (rejecting the free-market). However, unlike the leftist-retreat strategy, it does not wholly embrace the Marxist-Leninist legacy. For instance, a central part of the Communist Party of the Russian Federation (KPRF) program is the critical re-evaluation of the past (Chotiner 1999). In particular, the party's program distinguishes between opportunists within the party who corrupted the teachings of Marxism-Leninism, and the party of Soviet patriots. According to the KPRF, the current leadership of the Russian government are the intellectual heirs of this "party of opportunists"—the party of Trotsky, Beriya, Gorbachev, and Yeltsin who have historically plundered Russia. The KPRF itself, however, identifies itself with the so-called patriotic elements within the old CPSU—the party of Soviet heroes, the cosmonaut Yurii Gagarin, Marshal Georgii Zhukov, and author Mikhail Sholokhov. Further, this party claims that socialism is wholly compatible with the primordial collectivist sentiments of the Russian people, and the promotion of socialism necessarily involves the defense of Russian culture and traditions.

While critical of Marxist-Leninist dogma, the *national-patriotic* strategy, unlike the *pragmatic-reform* strategy, does not involve the attempt to redefine the party as a European social democratic party made up of experts (Ishiyama 1998b). Although there is pressure to alter the image of the party, the party leadership does not embrace social democratic principles and capitalism. National patriotism seeks to associate the party with nationalism, a modern ideological alternative to communism which in Eastern Europe is also historically anti-capitalist and anti-west (Szporluk 1988; Gerschenkron 1979). This strategy often involves the formation of "red-brown" coalitions or so-called "national-patriotic" or "fatherland fronts" which have emerged in countries like Russia and Romania.

Thus far the strategies identified have tended to treat adaptation in linear fashion, either moving progressively toward social democracy or retreating backward toward communism. This of course assumes that the parties either became moderate leftist or far leftist (whatever left or right means in the post-communist context). But clearly, there have been parties that have embraced nationalism and patriotism as their legitimizing ideology, and have sought to break with the past. Thus, we might also distinguish between the parties along two separate dimensions, one which represents the parties' movement from communism to social democracy, and the other representing the parties' movement from internationalism to nationalism. Therefore, we propose two dimensions in categorizing the adaptation strategies of the communist successor parties, distinguishing between *reformed* parties and *non-reformed* parties on one dimension, and, what we would call, *transmuted* versus *non-transmuted* parties on the other. The first dimension refers to whether the party transformed itself into what Ziblatt would call a "pragmatic-reform party" or clung to an orthodox communist identity. The second dimension refers to whether the *transmuted* parties made a (sometimes indecisive and ambivalent) break

Table 1.1

A Typology of (Former) Communist Party Positions in Central and Eastern Europe

	Non-reformed	Reformed
Non-transmuted	Orthodox Communist	Modernizationist, Social Democratic
Transmuted	National Communist	Nationalist Socialist, populist

with their leftist traditions and managed a rightist/nationalist turn in order to cope with the political changes in their country. Table 1.1 highlights the differences between these models.

To sum up and elaborate a bit more on the definitions we have sketched above, the term "reformed," refers to a former communist party that abandoned its communist ideology and moved towards a politically more moderate-leftist position. These parties turned away from the revolutionary tenets of Marxism and/or the orthodox methods of post-Stalinism. Reformed socialists generally accept western liberal democracy even if they sometimes criticize its practice. The word "transmutation" on the other hand refers to a former communist party that moved away from the left and adopted culturally right-wing, nationalistic, or anti-west elements into its ideology. In this situation, the party moved away from the non-democratic left toward the non-democratic right. If reform and transmutation are parallel processes, the identity of the former communist party will remain mixed or unclear.

To locate the communist successor parties along the above two continua, Table 1.2 categorizes particular cases. Since reality is more complex than the abstract, heuristic model, we have left room for less clear, "in-between cases" as well.

Non-reformed parties represent systemic opposition to democracy. If they are not transmuted, they tend to cling to Marxism-Leninism as their justifying ideology. An example of such a party is the Communist Party of Bohemia and Moravia in the Czech Republic, and to some extent the Party of Democratic Socialism in Germany (Grzymala-Busse 1999, Phillips 1994, Thompson 1996, Patton 1998). If they are non-reformed but, transmuted, they behave like semi- or anti-democrats, combining communist methods of power with nationalist ideology. A very good example of this kind of adaptation strategy is represented by the national communist line of the Communist Party of the Russian Federation (KPRF). Partly reformed/renewed communist parties are on the verge of accepting the basic tenants of democracy. If they are partly reformed but non-transmuted, they do accept it in their behavior but present themselves as protest parties (like the German PDS) to the regime. If the parties are both partly renewed/reformed and partly transmuted, they might

Table 1.2

Actual (Former) Communist Party Positions in Eastern Europe

	Non-reformed	Partly reformed	Reformed
Non-transmuted	KSCM (Czech Rep.) KPU (Ukraine)		MSZP (Hungary) SLD (Poland) SDP (Slovenia)
Partly transmuted	PDS (Germany) SPA (Albania)	BSP (Bulgaria) LDDP (Lithuania)	SDL (Slovakia)
Transmuted	KPRF (Russia) PSS (Serbia)	PDSR (Romania)	

present themselves as democrats in theory, but they can sometime abuse democratic norms in practice (such as the BSP in Bulgaria) (Murer 1999). Fully reformed/renewed parties stay completely within the democratic game (such as the Hungary Socialists of the Democratic Left Alliance [SLD] in Poland). In that case, if they are non-transmuted parties, they are social democrats; in the event of their partial or full transmutation, they adopt nationalist or populist politics (as with the Romanian PDSR).

What Affects Party Identity Change?

The above typology should not be taken to mean that once the parties adopt an adaptation strategy, it remains fixed over time. Indeed, especially since the "second generation" elections, there have been great incentives for the parties to alter their political strategies. To what extent have the successor parties altered their 'adaptation' strategies over time? And what factors might have caused these parties to change strategies over time?

In the literature on party identity change, two sets of factors are most often cited as affecting changes in party identity. First as Kenneth Janda (1990), Robert Harmel, Christine Edens and Patricia Goff (1995), and Harmel and Janda (1994), argue, change occurs as the result of environmental influences. Parties are assumed to be conservative organizations that are unlikely to change unless forced. As Harmel and Janda (1994, p. 261) put it, "party change does not just happen." Thus, party change is viewed as a rational and purposeful move by the party in response to specific stimuli. Janda proposed a "performance theory" of party change in which he argued that poor electoral performance is necessary for any party change (Janda 1990). Harmel and Janda later modified performance theory and argued that major change will always be precipitated by poor electoral performance (Harmel and Janda 1994).

Janda et al. (1995) tested the hypothesis that parties will only change if they do poorly in elections. The authors defined five different kinds of elections as perceived by the party's activists: calamitous, disappointing, tolerable, gratifying, and triumphal. They found that generally calamitous or disappointing elections were associated with the greatest degree of change in the themes the party emphasized, indicating that parties try to change their identities when voters reject the policy face they had presented in the previous election. This would suggest that a party's electoral performance should correlate with the degree of change in the party's basic platform.

However, some scholars have noted that other external challenges short of electoral defeat, such as the existence of competition from ideologically similar political alternatives to the party, can cause parties to change their identity (Cox 1987). Positive political theorists working on spatial models of electoral competition have noted that in a multi-party system the presence of several parties may exert a "squeezing out" effect on political parties, compelling individual parties to "jump out" from the "pack" and present a different face to the electorate so the electorate can distinguish them from other ideologically similar parties. This squeezing effect depends to a large extent on the electoral law and the structures of the political system. When there are incentives present to broaden the party's appeal (such as under a plurality electoral rule), there is often a crowding effect which squeezes out smaller or weaker competitors, compelling them to adopt extremist positions in order to differentiate themselves from other competitors.

On the other hand, some scholars have suggested that the more external challenges a political organization faces, the more likely the followers of that organization will seek to reaffirm its ideological purity (Stewart 1991). As the party faces greater external challenges, there is greater pressure to reaffirm the movement's identity because, as Richard Gregg (1971, p. 74) argues, there is a need for followers for "psychological refurbishing" and "affirmation." This usually involves a greater attempt to identify the members of the movement as being different from others. This is a way, as Gregg notes, to establish selfhood by "identifying against another," establishing one's identity through contrast (1971, p. 76). Thus, the greater the external competition, the more likely the party will seek to maintain its ideological roots.

The above approach, which emphasizes external stimuli in effecting party change, tends to assume that parties are merely reactive organizations as opposed to "creative" organizations. However it is quite possible that what parties perceive as a win or a loss depends heavily on the composition of the party. Thus, a second approach to party change focuses more on what happens as result of internal features of the party (Harmel and Janda 1994). John Ishiyama and Matthew Velten suggest that the ability of parties to change in post-communist politics is to a large extent dependent upon whether hardliners in the party act as a brake on reforming the party's image, hence its ability to adapt to new political circumstances (1998).

To illustrate the impact of organizational features of the party on the way it adapts, we shall begin with two ideal types of political party organization: the cadre and mass parties. Both were historical types which do not currently exist in their pure form, nor, as Paul Lewis (1996) notes, are they likely to emerge in Eastern Europe and the countries of the former Soviet Union. However, they do represent useful starting points. The cadre or elite parties of the nineteenth century were basically "committees of people who jointly constituted state and civil society" (Katz and Mair 1995, p. 9). Parties then were merely "groups of men" pursuing the public interest, with little need for highly structured organizations or large formal membership. The parliamentary component or the party in office dominated, and the resources required for election often involved local connections and personal political notability. On the other hand, the "mass party," unlike the cadre party, was characterized by a large, active membership. This is because the mass party arose "primarily among the newly activated and often disenfranchised elements of civil society" (Katz and Mair 1995, p. 10). Whereas the old cadre party had relied on the quality of supporters (personal attributes) the mass party relied on the quantity of supporters, attempting to make up in membership what it lacked in terms of individual patronage. Thus, mass parties were characterized by several features, of which the most notable were their reliance on large memberships and ideological homogeneity which linked leaders with rank-and-file members (Neumann 1956). Thus, mass parties were more likely to have organizational brakes which hindered the ability of party elites to alter the party's identity vis-à-vis a changing political environment.

In the post-communist context, the organizational beginning points are crucial in understanding how the successor parties evolved. Where did they come from? As several scholars have argued, the organizational beginning points of the party are largely a function of both the legacy of the past communist regime and the dynamics of the transition period itself.

A direct connection has been drawn between past regime type and the performance of the successor parties. Attila Ágh (1995, pp. 492–493), in his detailed study of the evolution of the Hungarian Socialist Party (*Magyar Szocialista Párt*-MSzP), has noted that the key variable explaining the party's resurgence in 1994 was the historical legacy of the Hungarian communist regime, particularly via the existence of a "large *'reform intelligentsia'* and also (a) *'mass reform movement'* . . . a characteristic product of the special Hungarian developments, originating from the most liberal version of state socialism." Although Ágh emphasizes the exceptionalism of the Hungarian case, his insights have broader implications for the study of the development of other successor parties and their ability to adapt to new circumstances.

The principal contours of this argument underline the effects of the nature of the previous regime. In the Hungarian case the communist regime was more liberal and internally pluralist: that produced a reform leadership that ultimately took control of the party. Consequently, this party leadership was able to assimilate the finer points of democratic competition and to recruit talented middle-level leaders and candidates who organized a party that could win a competitive election. This would suggest a general link between the degree of liberalness of the previous regime and the communist successor party's political fortunes; i.e., successor parties that grew out of regimes that had a tradition of internal contestation, interest articulation, and bureaucratic institutionalization would be better equipped to adapt to the new competitive conditions of the post-communist era and hence become more successful than those that grew out of less liberal regimes.

Herbert Kitschelt suggests that the more repressive and less open the previous communist system, the more successful are the successor parties who follow in the wake of such a regime. This is because repressive communist regimes were "able to entrench" themselves, and thus effectively preclude the emergence of the "challenge of an independent structure of intellectuals or middle-class professionals" (Kitschelt 1995a, p. 455). This implies that a successor party emerging from such a regime would be more successful in adapting to new competitive conditions, not because of the party's ability to adapt, but because its opponents are initially only weak and disorganized.

Another approach contends that, at least in the initial period of democratic consolidation, the political success of the communist successor parties depends on what happened during the transition process. In particular, the degree to which the communist successor parties are able to adapt depends on whether the leadership was comprised primarily of political pragmatists at the moment of the transition, who were willing to dump the ideological baggage of the past and present the party as a credible alternative. Thus, "who wins" in the internal struggle between reformers and the more conservative elements crucially affects the organizational development and political success of the successor party. As other scholars note, the dynamic of the transition affects the characteristics of the successor party as an organization. In countries where an extended period of bargaining and compromise took place, it was more likely that a trained cadre of politicians within the successor parties was produced—politicians who had learned how to play according to the rules of democratic competition and electoral politics, thus raising the probability that they would create parties that were designed to achieve electoral success (Welsh 1994).

Toward Explaining the Transformation of the Successor Parties

Thus, the evolution of the adaptation strategies of the successor parties can be seen as both the product of the interaction between political performance on the one hand and the internal organizational characteristics of the successor parties, on the other. This would suggest that any discussion of the evolution and development of the successor parties must consider the following three sets of questions (although of course, not exclusively):

1. To what extent did the legacy of the communist past impact on the adaptation strategies adopted by the successor parties? Did relatively more open communist regimes give birth to successor parties that were more apt to adopted a reformist strategy, as opposed to more repressive regimes? Did the legacy of the past impact upon the kind of competition the successor parties faced, which in turn affected the performance of the successor parties?
2. To what extent did the dynamics of the transition process impact upon the composition of the successor parties, and how did this in turn affect the kind of adaptation strategy that was adopted?
3. To what extent did the electoral performance of parties affect the choice of adaptation strategy and subsequent changes (if any) in strategy? Did poor electoral performance result in changes to fundamentally alter the public face of the party, or did poor electoral performance embolden the hardliners within the party?

The following chapters in this book aim to address each of these questions. The authors of the individual chapters assess, in whole or in part, the effects of legacies, transition processes, and political competition upon the development of the identities of communist successor parties in the 1990s. The book's organizing principle seeks to combine separate cases in individual chapters within a volume that offers a comparative perspective. The advantage of the former approach is the in-depth coverage of often idiosyncratic factors that affect the development of political parties, factors too often overlooked in broader comparative works. On the other hand, the comparative approach allows for the spawning of generalizable lessons crucial to the development of comparative theory in political science. Thus, this book is divided into three major sections. In the first section (including this chapter) general principles regarding party development are laid out, particularly the effects of past legacies on both the internal development of the successor parties and the political environment currently faced by them. In the second section, individual cases are investigated, particularly the early evolution of the successor parties after the transition, and the initial strategies adopted by these parties. In the third section, the authors utilize comparisons between many of the cases investigated in the previous section, aiming to produce generalizable lessons in regard to factors affecting the adaptation strategies of successor parties in the latter part of the decade (especially after the "second generation" elections). Based on these comparisons we will be in a position to ultimately identify the most important and common factors affecting both the development of (and change in) communist successor party adaptation strategies in the concluding chapter.

Like most multiauthor volumes, there are a wide variety of themes explored in each of the contributing chapters. Despite an almost bewildering array of potentially relevant factors in explaining the evolution of the communist successor parties, we will attempt to tie the various themes together in the concluding chapter. Although a daunting task, it is a truly a necessary one. Through such efforts, we can begin to truly understand the process of party transformation in post-communist politics.

2

Constraints and Opportunities in the Strategic Conduct of Post-Communist Successor Parties

Regime Legacies as Causal Argument

Herbert Kitschelt

The parties succeeding the former ruling communists after the collapse of their regimes in Eastern Europe in 1989 and in the Soviet Union in 1991 are a highly diverse set of political organizations. Most now operate under different labels, with less than half still advertising the attribute "communist" in the party name. New labels often conceal great diversity among their strategic appeals to voters. Furthermore, the organizational form of post-communist parties varies substantially across the entire formerly communist region; it is not a direct function of their strategic appeals. Finally, the parties' electoral success does not follow directly from either their strategic appeals or their organizational form. Cross-nationally diverse profiles of voter preferences and strategic configurations of competitors mediate the causal impact of post-communist organizational form and programmatic appeal on electoral success.

How is it possible to detect logical order and well-considered calculation by power-seeking politicians in this seeming empirical chaos? In line with previous work (Kitschelt 1995a; Kitschelt et al. 1999b), I propose that the actors' skills, experiences, and expectations, based on past political developments and the resulting distribution of resource endowments, are key for our understanding of the current activities and fortunes of the former communist parties. At the same time, I will argue that the past does not fully determine the future opportunities that present themselves to these parties. Initial instrumental power-seeking strategies, based on experiences and resources bequeathed on such parties by past political-economic regimes, may yield disappointments in a new era of politics that force the actors to learn new strategies. Path dependence explains how communist successor parties find themselves facing specific political predicaments and opportunities in post-communist political regimes, whether they are democratic, semi-democratic, or authoritarian. However, it does not, by itself, account for all of the learning that takes place, once parties encounter new challenges of the post-communist era.

In previous papers and publications on the formation of post-communist party systems, political regimes, and economic reform, I have stated the need for a two-step causal analysis, starting with legacies and then incorporating current opportunities (Kitschelt et al. 1999; Kitschelt 1999b; Kitschelt and Malesky 2000; Kitschelt and Smyth 2000). I have then focused on legacies-based arguments because they invariably provide the best explanation for diversity of post-communist political-economic phenomena in the first decade after the collapse of the old systems. If epistemological criteria for causal explanation require a minimum of temporal causal depth, only institutions, structures, processes, and actions that antedate the "proximate" events of the transition qualify as the ultimate causal variables of regime change. Events and developments during the transition are rather concomitant aspects of the explanandum.[1] Nevertheless, we should not entirely discount the causal efficacy of new exogenous shocks and learning opportunities. In the final section of this chapter, therefore, I offer some concrete hypotheses and illustrative evidence detailing how new opportunities, constraints, and external shocks may affect the processes of political learning that lead beyond a legacies-driven trajectory of communist successor party strategies.

The dependent variables in this chapter are threefold. The first is the strategic appeal of post-communist parties. Do they emphasize policy programs or work through selective incentives disbursed via clientelist networks of exchange between politicians and their electoral supporters on the ground? If they emphasize policy programs, what is their issue content? The second dependent variable is the electoral success of post-communist parties that results from an interplay of background conditions. These contribute to a particular distribution of voter preferences, in interaction with the successor parties' own strategic appeal as well as the conduct of their new competitors. Only these two dependent variables received systematic attention in my previous work. I wish to incorporate in this chapter, as a third dependent variable, certain *organizational* features of communist successor parties. Do legacies affect the organizational size of communist successor parties, as measured by the ratio of party members to the electorate or by party members to partisan voters? And do legacies shape the concentration of power inside post-communist parties?

Legacies as Predictors of Strategic Diversity and Electoral Success of Communist Successor Parties

Causal analysis in the comparative study of post-communist politics should not be so shallow as to blur the distinction between explanans and explanandum, but it should also not be so deep as to evaporate any causal mechanism that could operate through human action, identified by preferences, skills, and expectations (Kitschelt 1999a; 2001). "Long distance" relations of determination hypothesizing linkages stretching over hundreds of years constitute incomplete causal accounts. By contrast, we should take seriously the ability to hand down preferences, skills, and memories (written and oral) between overlapping generations. Nevertheless, not even intergenerational causal mechanisms may be required to accept the plausibility of causal chains affecting post-communist partisan politics that originated some fifty to one hundred years ago. Each successive decade of politics in today's post-communist democracies has left its imprint on people's construction of political reality and political possibilities so as to affect subsequent preferences, experiences, expectations, and ultimately actions.

Starting this analysis with the spread of Western and Eastern Christianity, the advance of the three-field system since the Middle Ages, and the timing of state building in Central Europe, Eastern Europe, and finally Central Asia (following Russian occupation during the nineteenth century) would make for interesting comparative history (Chirot 1986). But it would hardly supply a set of causal mechanisms to account for post-communist regime and party system outcomes, even if this epistemological stricture was liberally applied. I find it epistemologically more reasonable, however, to begin the construction of a causal chain of path dependency that ultimately affects the trajectory of post-communist politics with the decades just before and right after World War I. Configurations of political mobilization and state building in the first half of the twentieth century extend beyond the interwar period and feature communist parties both by their presence and absence from politics in regions that subsequently adopted communist rule. It is critical to account for the extent to which these parties flourished, together with the kinds of opponents (bourgeois urban middle-class and peasant) that mobilized during the same time. The national diversity of communist rule that began to appear after the relaxation of Stalinist uniformity in the years following the Soviet dictator's death can be traced to the presence and absence of different players and state structures before communism barely ten to twenty years earlier.

Two aspects of East Central European political development in the first half of the twentieth century stand out and set the stage for different trajectories of communist regimes and successor parties: the mobilization of political associations and parties, as well as the development of a professional career civil service (bureaucracy). We can nestle in an account of the development or non-development of challenging communist parties before their ascent to power into political-institutional landscapes structured by political regime variance and specific features of democratic institutions.

Moderately systematic evidence is available on the formation of political associations and parties, as well as conditions for their interest representation and participation before communism. Only two countries—the Czech lands, under Austrian rule and the German Empire—had for some time fully developed interest groups and parties, including the entire gamut of bourgeois, socialist, and communist affiliations. In both instances, this political society originated in constrained political participation in the pre-World War I period. In spite of the fascist interruption from 1933 to 1945, and 1939 to 1945, orthodox Marxist socialist and communist parties here were firmly entrenched in a broadly mobilized working-class movement and confronted an array of middle-class and peasant parties. In Germany by 1928 and in Czechoslovakia by 1930, the communist parties were fully Bolshevist-Stalinist (Suda 1980, p. 99). Moreover, socialist parties steeped in a Marxist ideological transition made many of their activists support communist parties after World War II supplemented them.

As a consequence, the ruling communist parties in both Eastern Germany and Czechoslovakia after 1946/1948 had strong organizational capabilities and societal backing, but also confronted the challenge of powerful adversaries with plenty of organizational experience. During this post-1953 thaw, communist strategies evolved that continued a firm repression of bourgeois "deviations" of any sort and resisted a de-Stalinization of the ruling parties, as signaled by the continuity of party leadership throughout the 1950s. Internal innovation inside such communist parties in the 1960s had a purely technocratic economic reform bent, regardless of whether the leaders ultimately could contain the unintended political consequences of such efforts (as in the GDR) or not (as in Czechoslovakia). In these countries, the lack of internal personnel and ideological resources for reform, enforced by an organizational apparatus that suffocated whatever innovative thinking would try to make itself heard, produced extremely rigid party apparatuses. Unable to decipher the early warning signals of the 1980s, they ultimately succumbed to a full frontal attack of opposition movements steeped in the experience of functioning party systems and interest associations throughout much of the first half of the twentieth century. After a transition by implosion, these parties entered into a political ghetto that isolated them from their competitors.

With the disappearance of the German Democratic Republic, the successor organization of the Socialist Unity Party, the Party of Democratic Socialism (PDS), had some unique problems to deal with. German politics in the 1990s had two different party systems, an advanced post-industrial capitalist and a post-communist party system. In the former the competition ran from left-libertarian to right-authoritarian politics, combining questions of socio-cultural life style, political participation, and economic distribution; in the latter economic-distributive issues dominated the agenda and even gave rise to a left-authoritarian constituency that found its home in the post-communist party (Neugebauer and Stöss 1996, pp. 273–97). Other left-authoritarians, particularly among the young and undereducated working class, resorted to racist, xenophobic, and neofascist slogans and engaged in violence outside conventional political parties. Given the conditions of German unification, the PDS could become an amalgam of intransigent communist stalwarts with an emerging East German regional identity set against a "takeover" by the West (Ziblatt 1998). Moreover, its strict redistributive economic agenda featured the search of a "Third Way" beyond capitalism and communism that appealed to those socialist left-libertarians in East and West Germany who felt that the predominantly Western and progressively more moderate left-libertarian Greens betrayed their roots in the anticapitalist opposition.

A second group of countries saw the development of primarily peasant, bourgeois, and some weaker socialist parties before World War I, especially under Austrian control (Slovenia, Galicia-Poland). Such parties also flourished in Hungary, but only to a lesser extent. Even weaker was political mobilization in Hungarian dominated and subordinated Slovakia and in those parts of the Croatian lands that were divided between Austrian or Hungarian control. In the emerging independent East Central European states after World War I, political parties in group II countries engaged in constrained competition under quasi-authoritarian rulers after shorter or longer episodes of full democratization. Within Yugoslavia, democratic interest articulation was limited by the dominant Serbian ethnic politicians who often treated their South Slav brethren (who had been formerly under Austro-Hungarian prewar administration) as losers of World War I who were to be submitted to the dominance of a victorious Serbia. The feature of constrained interwar political interest articulation and competition also applies to the Baltic countries, the party systems of which were quite weak and volatile due to the absence of experience with political interest mobilization under Tsarist rule (Rothschild 1974, pp. 371–72).

Overall, a more detailed ranking of the prior civil and political mobilization in precommunist East Central European countries would place the Czech Republic and Germany first (group I), Hungary, Poland, and Slovenia next (group II a), followed by the Baltic countries (group II b) and maybe even behind that by Slovakia and Croatia as peripheries dominated by Hungary (group II c). Even these latter countries, however, must be separated from a third and fourth group of formerly communist countries to be introduced below.

In all the group II interwar polities, the incoming rulers repressed communist and radical-socialist parties, even though such parties could count on only a limited following among the comparatively small urban working-class and intelligentsia. In some cases, this repression was redoubled by Stalinist efforts to eradicate any stirrings of national communism in the aftermath of the first wave of purges inside the Soviet Union. Stalin's Comintern even went so far as to dissolve the Polish Communist Party in 1938.[2] At the end of World War II, Stalin made an effort to train an entire new generation of munist leaders living in exile in the Soviet Union who were then placed on the ground as the new rulers when the Red Army swept through Eastern Europe. When such externally chosen leaders returned to their native soil, however, they encountered quite a diverse set of conditions in which to assert their regimes. In countries that had a modicum of bourgeois and peasant political mobilization in the interwar period and weakly entrenched domestic communist parties, the hegemon's wavering support for such puppet regimes after Stalin's death provoked a mobilization of noncommunist counterforces. Even though the Soviet Union kept communist regimes in place with military and organizational coercion, local communist rulers everywhere made concessions to the virtual opposition of the 1960s and 1970s in order to stabilize their regimes and limit the need for repression.

It is these economic and political concessions that qualify Hungary and Poland as exemplars of national-accommodative communism, based on an implicit exchange of liberalizing reforms implemented by the rulers to create acquiescence by a potentially powerful anticommunist mobilization. The possible counterforces to communist rule in these Central European countries abstained from an all-out assault on the Soviet-backed institutions. The emergence of such national-accommodative regimes involved new patterns of leadership recruitment and succession that displaced the old Stalinist cadres (Grzymala-Busse 1999). By the 1980s this new generation of leaders had spawned a further successor generation whose members came to realize that the established communist political and economic order was no longer viable and could be overcome only by major concessions to a noncommunist political agenda. Ultimately, these "late communist" leaders made it possible for a democratic opposition to gain momentum and to participate in a regime transition by negotiation with the political incumbents. After 1989, the former communist parties in countries with accommodative-communism could quickly shed their old ideologies and reestablish themselves as liberal democrats with a Western social democratic program, adapted to the unique conditions of a transition from communism to capitalism. A great deal has already been published on this strategic trajectory of what is today known as the Hungarian Socialist Party (MSzP) and the Polish Social Democratic Party (SdRP), so I will not add further details (Tökes 1996; Zubek 1995).

This general template highlighted by Hungary and Poland in nationally specific ways also helps us to understand the transitions by negotiations in other countries belonging to the broader set of polities with comparatively encompassing bourgeois and peasant interwar political participation, but communist repression. A general feature complicates the picture in all of these instances—the Baltic countries, Croatia, Slovenia, and even to some extent Slovakia. Everywhere, we are dealing with newly independent post-communist polities with titular ethnocultural groups that were subordinated to a dominant external ethnic group under the old communist regimes (Russians, Serbs, and Czechs). In these instances, national accommodation meant that communist leaders in the ethnic minority regions and party sections made ethnocultural concessions to the subordinate regional majority community. Where these gestures were credible, such leaders could strengthen their role in negotiated regime transitions and their capacity to acquire a new social democratic post-communist image by joining, if not placing themselves, at the helm of national independence movements and coalitions. The Slovenian trajectory epitomizes this feature (Ramet 1997), just as the career of the former Republic level sections of the CPSU in the three Baltic countries (Krickus 1997; Plakans 1997; Raun 1997).

In Slovakia, the strategic trajectories during the transition from communism were somewhat more complex. Here, elements of national-accommodative communism first surfaced in the aftermath of the Prague Spring of 1968, but were relatively weak, not only because of repression from Prague. We also must keep in mind that Slovakia had a very feeble and narrow pre-communist political mobilization and therefore relatively little oppositional pressure to communist rule. Because the Slovak communist leadership was concerned about the national question and much of the (weak) opposition could be channeled in terms of national demands, the purge of noncommunists was not as deep here and intellectual life was not as tightly controlled after 1968 as in the Czech lands (Wolchik 1997, p. 205). Moreover, the national tendencies in the Slovak ruling party made it possible that many former communists soon after participated in a broad noncommunist front during the transition, the Public Against Violence (PAV). A critical mass of them, under the leadership of Vladimir Mečiar, then created, together with other political activists, the ultra-nationalist Movement for a Democratic Slovakia (HZDS) that dominated Slovakia's politics from 1992 to 1998, creating a regime that threatened democratic political freedoms and organized a crony capitalism benefiting associates of the ruling party. This left the formal successor organization of the communist party, the Party of the Democratic Left (SDL), as an arena for fights between communist stalwarts and liberal-democratic reformers. Both rejected the nationalist agenda. The doctrinaire communists ultimately departed from the SDL and set up their own Workers' Association of Slovakia (ZRS) that supported the Mečiar government. By contrast, within the SDL, the pragmatic liberal-reformist element around Brigita Schmögnerova prevailed, though sometimes contested by more orthodox socialist positions.

The Croatian case adds a further complication. Here in late 1971, the Serb-dominated Titoist regime unleashed a campaign to suppress reformist and nationalist currents in Croatia, suffocating whatever momentum toward national-accommodative communism had existed there inside the ruling party (Cohen 1997, pp. 70–71). The resulting docile regional communist leadership belatedly acquiesced to reform, but was entirely pushed aside by a nationalist party that, like Mečiar's party in Slovakia, incorporated many former communists, including the new president, Franjo Tudjman. These nationalists were definitively not market liberal reformers, but had long broken with Serbia and its communist establishment. Like Mečiar in Slovakia, they set up a semi-authoritarian political regime with crony capitalist economic-distributive features, while the old communist party simply disappeared from the scene.

None of the other countries of Eastern Europe and the European fission products of the Soviet Union, constituting together group III of my typology (see Table 2.1, pages 32–33), developed features of national communism. The weakness of precommunist political mobilization in civic associations and parties, together with the repressiveness of authoritarian regimes throughout much of the precommunist era in countries as diverse as Albania, Bulgaria, Romania, Serbia, and greater Tsarist Russia (including Belarus, the Ukraine, and Georgia) created a void that could be more easily filled by incoming communist rulers than in the countries of Central and Eastern Europe. Similar conditions also apply to the Central Asian colonial periphery of Tsarist Russia, which had a thin layer of Russian state institutions grafted onto a continued, but transformed, tribal and clan organization of society (group IV). In these colonial sub-polities the titular elites did not have the same status as the hegemonic elites (Laitin 1998, p. 62). This set them apart from the Baltic region under Russian administration and also in the Ukraine.

None of these group III and IV countries ever had episodes of serious manifest political opposition to communist rule. These regimes assured that individuals trying to organize opposition to communist incumbents had few skills, resources, and cultural idioms to sustain the early formation of interest groups or proto-parties when communism finally crumbled. At the same time, the communist parties could entrench themselves in the state apparatus and appear as the carriers of economic modernity and social innovation, including whatever modicum of affluence and social welfare these countries could achieve under communist tutelage, to such an extent that their successor parties remained popular with large proportions of the population after the formal end of communist dictatorship. Not surprisingly, opponents encountered great difficulty in attempts to build sustained support around partisan alternatives.

In none of these countries did intransigent communist parties implode in ways equivalent to the GDR or Czech experience. Most of them did not embrace a political and economic reform agenda that would have resulted in a negotiated transition to liberal-democratic capitalism. Instead, ruling communist parties tried to make the minimum in concessions to structural economic and political change through preemptive reform, a gamble they were not always successful at. Such parties promised the continuation of communist statism with marginal infringements on the security of people's jobs and social benefits. With that agenda, they either won or very nearly won founding post-communist elections. Examples are Albania, Belarus, Bulgaria, Romania, and Russia. Even where communists failed to win outright majorities, their detractors often appealed to nationalist and economically anticapitalist agendas. These agendas were far removed from the liberal-democratic consensus that began to emerge in East Central Europe with formerly national-accommodationist communist features almost immediately after the collapse of communism. Nowhere in group III and group IV countries could liberal-democratic parties launch sustained bids for political power over successive elections equivalent to what has become standard practice in East Central Europe. Consequently, communist successor parties rarely encountered the incentives to embrace an encompassing liberal-democratic political and economic reform agenda.

When it comes to the reformist commitments of communist successor parties, the outliers to this general pattern were the new European post-communist independent states of group III. These states had titular ethnic groups that had been subordinated under Russian or Serbian ethnocultural hegemony before the demise of communism, including Armenia, Georgia, Macedonia, and Moldova. Here, local elements of the ruling regional communist party sections belonging to the subordinated ethnic groups in the final stages of communist decomposition switched over to a nationalist independence, democratization, and economic reform appeal. All three agenda items were intertwined; national autonomy could be secured only by finding protectors beyond the old Russian or Serbian hegemons. To attract Western support, however, the new rulers had to demonstrate a willingness to embrace economic and political reform. Thus, the strategic appeal of communist successor parties in these group III countries tends to have some resemblance to that of successor parties emerging from national-accommodative communist patterns. At the same time, we must keep in mind that in these group III countries, resources and capabilities for noncommunist political mobilization in groups and parties were weaker without substantial precommunist civic and political society than in group II countries. Akin to the nationalist parties in the weakest members of group II, Croatia and Slovakia, these post-communist successor parties in group III countries, or their eventual challengers, have a propensity to promote clientelist practices and crony capitalism with partial economic reform.

The Ukraine constitutes a complicated case that was closely aligned with the dominant Russian ethnicity, but regionally subordinated under the Russian and later the Soviet empire. Laitin (1998, pp. 34; 60–61) quite appropriately refers to the Ukraine as having had a "most favored lord" status inside the empire. Ukrainians were not considered very different from Russians and communicated on an equal footing with Russians. Moreover, the languages are sufficiently similar to prevent their differences from acting as potentially high barriers of social mobility. These factors mitigating interethnic differences of interests, together with the large size of the Russian speaking minority in the Ukraine, tend to diffuse ethnocultural conflict potentials. Yet they also reduce the support level for Ukrainian independence, as well as the incentives for communist successor parties to embrace liberal democracy and market reform as a way to assert Ukrainian independence against the former Russian hegemon. Even though Ukrainian politicians may wish to diversify their geopolitical options by furthering economic and political reform, with few exceptions they consider this less an imperative of independent survival than politicians in the smaller and ethnically more distinct fission products of the former Soviet Union, including politicians in communist successor parties of such newly founded countries.

More generally, what cuts across the logic of internal domestic legacies in shaping post-communist regimes and successor party strategies—the nature of precommunist political society and the professionalization of the state apparatus—is the geopolitical situation of the newly founded independent countries after the end of communism. Akin to arguments advanced by Lijphart (1977) and Katzenstein (1985) for the conduct of small Western countries in open world markets, the imperatives of domestic self-governance in an uncontrollable international environment with much more resourceful and potentially hostile external actors induces domestic players to embrace consensual strategies that, in the case of ethnocultural divides, may at some point result in *consociational pacts* in the way described in Lijphart's work (over-sized majorities, minority vetoes, proportional representation on government executives). Neither former communists nor their challengers engage in zero-sum strategies to destroy their adversaries. All actors realize that such strategic aspirations pursued in a situation characterized by the structural payoffs of a chicken game are likely to result in disaster for all parties involved.

The propensity to consociational accommodation between communists and their challengers, combined with a compact among different ethnocultural groups, also applies to group IV countries of Central Asia emerging at the colonial periphery of the former Soviet Union. However, with the partial exception of Kyrgyzstan between 1992 and 1995, this propensity articulates itself in very different actor strategies and institutional compacts than in the small group III fission products of the Soviet Union and Yugoslavia. This difference is indeed due to the legacy of patterns of state formation under communist rule, associated with regional and clan-based modes of political interest intermediation and representation (Jones-Luong 2000). Furthermore, the countries' large distance from Western markets and networks of communication made it unattractive for the incumbent communist rulers to adopt broad political and economic reform strategies (Kopstein and Reilly 2000). The absence of opposition skills and experiences virtually assured the continuity of rule by the old communist apparatchiks, even though their rhetoric now switched from Marxist formulae to nationalist slogans. The "old-new" rulers govern through metamorphosed communist state parties, and a nationalist appeal that emphasizes what is now the titular ethnicity. At the same time, in pursuit of the maintenance of domestic tranquility, they are willing to extend side-payments to minority ethnicities, particularly to members of the former dominant Russian ethnic minority, as well as Islamic interests.

Kyrgyzstan is a partial exception because the country's old communist ruler Askan Akayev, reemerging as national president, initially appeared to promote civil and political rights together with a vigorous promotion of market-liberal policies and institutional reforms. However, from the very beginning, this strategy failed to be accompanied by the formation of independent, pluralistic political parties. Internationally, it took place in an environment of neighbors that stuck to unbending authoritarianism and pursued only minimal economic reforms (Kopstein and Reilly 2000). The inability of domestic actors to take advantage of political openness through party formation and the remoteness of the country from Western supporters made Kyrgyzstan quickly return to techniques of economic and political rule peculiar to other group IV countries of the Soviet colonial periphery.

Surveying the regime structures, communist successor party strategies, and political support of all four groups under discussion, it becomes clear that legacies account for most of their observable diversity, modified by the size and geopolitical position of the post-communist polity. Both patterns of continuity and discontinuity in political mobilization and leadership of communist parties and their adversaries before and after World War II are critical in accounting for the beginning of the national-regional diversification of communist rule in the late 1950s and 1960s. It is this diversification that ultimately yielded contrasting patterns of regime transition in the late 1980s and the successor parties' strategic appeal in the 1990s. But there is a second and empirically more intractable side to historical legacies that reinforces the already observed patterns of cross-national variance and allows us to predict features of post-communist political appeal and party organization. It has to do with the availability of the state apparatus as a resource for parties and political leaders as a way to reward constituencies for their political support ("clientelism").

Where a professional civil service did not exist and political parties were created inside a predemocratic regime that later incorporated initially disenfranchised and weak challengers, an advent of democracy enables the initially dominant inside parties to take advantage of state resources to build clientelist networks disbursing selective incentives to their supporters. By contrast, where predemocratic rulers are displaced from the levers of political power by parties that had to mobilize outside the state and where such outside parties encounter a professional civil service, political competition configures around programmatic alternatives (Shefter 1994). Applied to strategy and organizational practices of communist successor parties, the less communist ruling parties could rely on and modify a precommunist professional civil service and be challenged by independent political organizations during the breakdown of communist regimes, the more likely they could rely on clientelist linkage-building to societal constituencies as their dominant organizational and electoral strategy. Such parties often experience considerable programmatic "drift" in the sense that they fail to embrace a full-blown reform program. Instead, they display programmatic incoherence that, by default, yields a strong tendency to cling to the political-economic status quo in practical politics, whatever the programmatic rhetoric of individual party leaders might be. By contrast, when communist leaders are placed in an environment with a more professional civil service *and* resourceful new competitors created by anticommunist adversaries, successor parties are not only likely to be more displaced from power in the new regimes, but also to resort to more programmatic politics to regain electoral competitiveness.

Given current historical research, it is not always easy to precisely determine the nature of precommunist civil service development across Eastern and Central Europe as well as Central Asia. It is also difficult to identify different pathways of bureaucratic metamorphosis under communist rule that would be necessary to assert the causal efficacy of civil service legacies for the diversity among post-communist party strategies and regime features. However, in the comparative politics literature such arguments are currently not unprecedented. Thus, in a global comparison of patterns of corruption, Treisman (1998) finds a robust linkage of low corruption with British colonial heritage as one of several critical causal variables. This variable, in turn, is highly collinear with the extent to which political elites practice the rule of law. Both corruption and compliance with legal universalism are empirical tracers of a professional public administration.

Applied to post-communist polities, we do not have a convenient shortcut to measure civil service professionalism as a colonial heritage precedent. What comes closest is prolonged pre–World War I political rule by Prussia/Germany (Western Poland, small parts of Lithuania) and by the Hapsburg state machinery, subdivided into the more bureaucratic-professional Austrian lands (i.e., Bohemia/Moravia, Slovenia, parts of Croatia) and the lesser bureaucratic professionalism of Hungary (and the subordinated areas of Slovakia; parts of Croatia). The Baltic countries with their historically Germanic administrative background, as well as their comparatively advanced educational systems in the first half of the twentieth century, may represent borderline cases also boosting administrative professionalism beyond what prevailed in the rest of Tsarist Russia and its Central Asian colonial fiefdoms. In this regard, it is important to realize that uniform Russian state formation began very late in the nineteenth century. Until then the Baltic region enjoyed tolerance of its peripheral languages as well as its advanced Germanic educational system that had supplied many leading administrators of Tsarist Russia (Laitin 1998, pp. 38–43; 66). "Russification" of language and state was really the project of the Soviet period (ibid., pp. 43–49), part of which the Baltic region experienced as independent states.

In contrast to the Baltic region, indigenous patrimonial administrative practices, intertwined with high levels of corruption in the Russian heartland (Belarus, Russia proper, and much of the Ukraine), the Central Asian colonies of Russia (with an imperial patrimonialism grafted onto non-professional tribal administrations), as well as the independent Balkan states that Ottoman Turkey left behind, characterized whatever state development took place until the advent of communist rule.[3] While the incoming communist apparatchiks surely transformed bureaucratic practices in all polities after their takeover, comparative cases studies lend plausibility to the claim that these transformations took place in a locally and regionally path-dependent fashion and did not wipe out diversity of administrative professionalism altogether. Consequently, in the 1980s the Baltic Soviet Republics displayed much higher levels of administrative professionalism than the Ukraine and the latter again higher professionalism than the Central Asian republics.

The cross-national distribution of civil service professionalism is highly collinear with the diversity of precommunist experiences to political freedoms and associative mobilization. Nevertheless, we need the bureaucracy variable to define critical mechanisms that result in specific organizational features and strategic appeals of post-communist successor parties. High civil service professionalism and the strength of noncommunist outside political mobilization made patronage strategies unavailable. Communist successor parties then had to concentrate on programmatic politics either of a more traditional Marxian socialist type (in group I countries) or a social-democratic type (in group II countries). By contrast, in group III a and group IV countries, a weak mobilization of market-liberal democrats, in turn, fosters not only programmatic status-quo orientation, but also a clientelist politics that renders programmatic appeals less decisive for the parties' electoral fortunes and ultimate control of state power. This clientelist politics may also mar group III b's small, new ethnoculturally plural polities with unfavorable precommunist legacies (weak political society and administrative professionalism) and define the specific consociational strategies of the successor parties in such polities.

More generally, the following qualification is in order for newly founded ethnoculturally pluralist countries that were formerly dominated by Czech, Serbian, or Russian minorities. Here, communist successor parties with a nationalist appeal, just as nationalist parties that developed separately from the successors to the old ruling parties, may seize upon opportunities to craft clientelist politics. The formation of a new state creates new bureaucracies unprotected from political patronage appointments by professionalized cadres; relying on impartial achievement-based criteria of recruitment and promotion. Of course, where bureaucracies were patrimonial under the old imperial ethnic Russian or Yugoslav ruler, the development of clientelist politics is all the more likely.

Legacies and the Organization of Communist Successor Parties

I have detailed predictions for the strategic appeal, electoral success, and citizen-elite linkage strategies of communist successor parties based on an argument derived from legacies of political mobilization and state formation. I have also tried to incorporate the importance of ethnocultural divides and new polity formation in a geopolitical context. I would now like to briefly specify possible consequences of these patterns for important aspects of communist successor parties' organization, particularly their membership base and internal power centralization.

Let us distinguish three classes of communist party members under the old system: political leaders in core positions (politburo, central committee, cabinets, and regional leadership positions), salaried middle- and lower-level apparatchiks, including those in ancillary organizations (trade unions, youth, women), and finally the vast mass of simple "amateur" members, many of whom might have joined only in order to benefit from the vast patronage of the demised ruling party. These three groups encounter rather different payoff structures from economic and political reform. We might generate predictions about the organizational shape of communist successor parties based on a closer scrutiny of the benefits and costs such actors are likely to experience contingent upon different strategies of post-communist regime change.

The fortunes of the leadership stratum depend entirely on the parties' strategic appeals, in interaction with prevailing mass preferences for reform or the status quo. Some older leaders will inevitably retire. However, for those in their core years of office-holding; say between age 40 and 55, payoffs will vary dramatically across the different sets of polities and strategic options I have distinguished. In bureaucratic-authoritarian regimes, former communist leaders have no public credibility and reputation for reform. This strategy is therefore unavailable to them. In order to maintain positions of power within their parties, their dominant strategy is to maintain an orthodox or only mildly reformist programmatic appeal. In contrast, as a consequence of national-accommodative communism (groups II a and II b) and even in newly founded polities with a patrimonial communist background now governed by a titular ethnic group (group III b), communist party leaders can expect that political and economic reforms will have considerable popularity and that change-oriented former communists might credibly lead such reformist drives. A significant segment of the ruling communist party leaderships may therefore find it imperative for their political survival to advance reformist positions. In contrast, party leaders in the remaining patrimonial communist regimes (groups III a and IV) might find that they continue to pursue their political ambitions with a conservative neocommunist or only incrementally reformist program that would keep them in power for two reasons: large proportions of their local populations are predisposed toward political-economic conservatism and their market-liberal opponents are weakly organized and divided. Moreover, the patrimonial state apparatus made clientelist linkage strategies available to the leaders of communist successor parties. The disbursement of selective incentives to popular constituencies is particularly important with the failing appeal of old communist doctrines, and may be only partially replaceable by a collectivist-nationalist-authoritarian rhetoric.

The middle- and lower-level apparatchiks have nothing to gain from political and economic reform under any established communist system. Almost by definition, political and economic reform implies the dissolution of repressive security services and the dismissal of the vast stratum of intermediate bureaucrats in the economic and political administration. They are rent-seeking groups that have lost any economic and political justification. After the end of bureaucratic-authoritarian communism, they may as well stay inside the communist successor party because they are in full alignment with a conservative leadership and cannot hope for mercy from vigorous anticommunist market liberalizers. In the final stage of national-accommodative communism (groups II a and II b), as well as during the independence struggles of ethnocultural minorities subjected to patrimonial empires (group III b), middle- and lower-level apparatchiks are likely to fight reformist leaders and leave successor parties dominated by reformist leaders in favor of newly founded orthodox alternatives, even if such splinter parties remain unsuccessful. Finally, under patrimonial communism that undergoes incremental preemptive reform (group III a), or continuous established patterns of rule with only cosmetic and semantic modifications (group IV), middle- and lower-level apparatchiks may feel quite at home in their old parties and see little reason to exit, at least as long as these parties remain in power.

For the mass audience of amateur members in formerly ruling communist parties, the material, social, or purposive incentives of party membership are sharply reduced everywhere compared to the old days of communist authoritarian rule. Nevertheless, those incentives for membership vary across political settings. In formerly bureaucratic-authoritarian systems, social and purposive motives are dominant. Older nostalgic communists are likely to remain in the party, but everyone with career ambitions will abandon the organization. In national-accommodative communism, the incentives might be just the reverse. Reformists cannot offer the sentimental bonds and traditions of symbolic proletarianism. Technocratic careerists who wish to seize on the political and economic opportunities of the new regimes, by contrast, may find communist successor parties attractive channels for their ambitions. While communist successor parties after national-accommodative communism might thus shed their mass membership base, there is likely to be one exception to this pattern. Where reformist-communist leaders participate in national independence fronts, they often generate a new purposive enthusiasm that does not depend on communist doctrines. Moreover, many independent-minded citizens might consider it less risky to mobilize for independence under the shield of the communist successor party than as members of a new opposition group. Such popular considerations enable communist successor parties to attract a large number of new amateur members and activists that replaces old socialist-minded individuals.

Among polities with contrasting legacies, successor parties after patrimonial communism provide the broadest range of incentives for amateur party membership. They still have sentimental social and purposive appeal. Furthermore, many citizens expect them to remain venues for upward social mobility, given the extensiveness and intensiveness of their patronage networks. Because of their continued popular electoral support, they may thus display high member/citizen as well as member/party voter ratios.

In terms of member/citizen ratios, communist successor parties are likely to shed the greatest number of amateurs and lower/middle level professional cadres after national-accommodative communism. Here, technocratic-reformist leaders will in fact do everything to force sentimental amateurs and lower-salaried cadres out because they constitute direct impediments to the new reformist agenda of the parties. As indicated above, this may not apply to successor parties that rally to national-independence demands. They exchange their old careerist and Marxist ideological amateurs for new nationalist mass support. Communist parties after bureaucratic-authoritarian communism are likely to shrink slower than in formerly national-accommodative communist regimes that cannot thrive on the independence issue. Their orthodox leaders do not mind continued incorporation of the traditional salaried cadres or of nostalgic amateurs with purposive motivations. At the same time, many former members turn away because the party cannot furnish material incentives.

The differences in member/partisan voter ratios across former communist systems may be even more dramatic. After national-accommodative communism (net of independence appeal), the reformist post-communist parties not only have a small member/citizen ratio. Because their reformist appeal makes them electorally quite attractive, their member/voter ratios tend to be tiny. National-accommodative successor parties with national-independence appeal will definitely do better in that regard, but within limits because their electoral popularity depresses their member/partisan voter ratio. Bureaucratic-authoritarian successor parties, in contrast, tend to lose most voters and a great deal of members simultaneously. Consequently, even a drastically shrunken membership may give them a solid member/voter ratio. Successor parties following patrimonial communism are also likely to have also robust member/voter ratios for precisely the opposite reasons that apply after bureaucratic-authoritarian communism. They lose both members and voters at a relatively lower rate than their counterparts in other post-communist polities.

In addition, authority patterns inside post-communist parties are likely to vary across systems characterized by different legacies. Where there is a reinforcing alignment between orthodox leaders, professional cadres and sentimental amateurs after bureaucratic-authoritarian communism, leaders can afford to dare more intra-party democracy without risking to be upstaged by their rank and file. They can employ the idioms of intra-party democracy and decentralization for symbolic purposes to claim a democratic disposition while maintaining an orthodox socialist program. In contrast, the tension between technocratic-reformist leaders, status quo-oriented middle- and lower-level professional cadres, and sentimental amateurs in the final stages of national-accommodative communism yields a "centralization of power in a small elite of reformist executive and legislative party leaders" (Van Biezen 2000). It is these reformist leaders who did everything to accelerate the process of shrinking party membership that helped tilt the balance of power inside the successor parties in their favor. With some modifications, the same logic of power-centralization also applies to newly founded countries where elite factions find a commitment to fundamental economic and political reform through communist successor parties both feasible, credible, and electorally profitable (group II b and III b countries). Here, however, leaders may not be so keen on shrinking the membership as accelerating the replacement of communist hardliners with nationalist supporters of independence who see support by the capitalist West as the only way to free their country from the embrace of the former communist hegemons Serbia or Russia.

In all other cases of successor parties after patrimonial communism (groups III a and IV), the lack of willingness to engage in reform and the opportunities to find comparatively broad backing for non-reform appeals and clientelist patronage machines yield mass parties with a modified continuation of Leninist "democratic centralism." De facto, small cliques of leaders make all relevant strategic decisions within continuously authoritarian, centralist party structures. The docile conduct of lower- and middle-level professional apparatchiks and the sentimental dispositions of the amateur rank and file, together with their material compensation through clientelist networks, ensures the perpetuation of old communist party structures.

I have focused on membership and internal authority relations of communist successor parties. Another dimension concerns the linkages between parties and interest associations, particularly labor unions. Orenstein (1998) claims that close links to such unions are an important ingredient of the Hungarian and Polish successors to the ruling parties. I am not convinced that this is theoretically compelling or empirically borne out in a broader comparative framework. While external "transmission belts" certainly help to turn out the vote, degrees of unionization tend to be high just in those economic sectors that have a great deal to lose from market liberalization, such as manufacturing and more specifically heavy coal and metals industries. Unions can therefore become as much an impediment to electorally advantageous economic reformism as a catalyst of political mobilization for the parties.

It is probably important to keep union members and leaders out of the decision-making arenas of reformist post-communist parties, while simultaneously drafting them as external supporters of the parties. This works best where, as in Hungary, no competitor to the communist successor party constitutes a credible representative of labor interests. The inclusion of labor is already more problematic in Poland, where unions can turn to other parties, such as Solidarnosc or the Workers' Union (UP), that may serve as mouthpieces of those whose wages and labor conditions are unpromising in a market economy and who therefore have an interest in the slow down of market-liberalizing reforms. For this reason, I wish to remain agnostic here about the specific patterns and comparative advantages of close union-party linkages for communist successor parties placed in different legacy environments and opportunity structures.

Legacies-Based Typology and Predictions About Post-Communist Successor Fortunes

Table 2.1 summarizes the theoretical discussion of the preceding sections. I would like to contour the predictions quite sharply so as to discuss disconfirming anomalies in the next and final section of this chapter. In the rows of the table, I distinguish groups of post-communist countries with Roman numerals as before. In terms of legacies I have divided newly independent countries with national-accommodative legacies into subgroup II b and II c in order to signal that Croatia and Slovakia represent borderline cases for reasons indicated above.

The first three columns of the table provide the predictor variables for party strategies and organizational bases. Columns 1 and 2 give values for the main domestic legacy variables, the pre-communist development of political society (political rights and freedoms; mobilization of bourgeois and socialist/communist movements and parties) and of a professionalized civil service. The third variable constitutes what is both a historical legacy as well as a contemporary post-communist geopolitical opportunity structure opening up after the collapse of multicultural regional empires with dominant majority ethnicities (Serbia, Russia). Special opportunities and incentives to embrace reformist, liberal-democratic, and market liberalizing programs for

Table 2.1

Precommunist Legacies as Predictors of the Strategies and Organizational Form of Communist Successor Parties, 1990–2000

Communist countries	Strength of precommunist political society?	Professionalization of the state apparatus	Newly independent country seeking Western protection?
Group I: Bureaucratic-authoritarian (Chech Rep., former German Democratic Rep.)	Strong	Strong	No
Group II: National Accommodative Communism			
a. Always independent countries (Hungary and Poland)	Medium	Medium	No
b. Newly independent countries: (Baltics, Slovenia)	Medium	Medium-low	Yes
c. Borderline cases (Slovakia, Croatia)	Medium-weak	Weak	Yes
Group III: Paternal Communism			
a. Independent countries and core regions of empires (Albania, Belarus, Bulgaria, Romania, Russia, possibly Ukraine, Serbia)	Weak	Weak	No
b. Newly independent countries (Armenia, Georgia, Macedonia, Moldova, possibly Ukraine)	Weak	Weak	Yes
Group IV: Central Asian Periphery (Azerbaijan, Kyrgyzstan, Tajikistan, Uzbekistan	Weak	Weak	No

Source: Author's compilation.

Table 2.1 *(continued)*

Programmatic or clientelist linkage linkage strategies?	Programmatic cohesiveness and party ideology?	Electoral support levels?	Mass party base? member/ voter? member/ citizen?.	Internal party centrali- zation
Programmatic	Socialist orthodox	Low	M/C: low M/V: medium	Limited
Programmatic	Reform: social democratic	High	M/C: low M/V: very low	High
Programmatic mild clientelism	Reform: social democratic	High	M/C: medium M/V: medium	High
Programmatic clientelist	Reform: social democratic	High	M/C: medium-low M/V: medium	High
Predominantly clientelist	Diffusely orthodox socialist and nationalist	High	M/C: medium M/V: high	High
Clientelist more than programmatic	Diffusely social democratic and reform	High	M/C: high M/V: high	High
Predominantly clientelist	Diffusely nationalist and anti- reform	Authori- tarian regimes	M/C: high M/V: high	High

communist successor parties exist where there are newly independent countries with titular ethnic majorities that were formerly subjected under an imperial majority ethnicity. This applies, however, only if those new countries have historical legacies that are somewhat promising (due to Soviet state formation) and are not geopolitically too far removed from a Western support infrastructure of trading partners and transportation venues.

Columns 4 through 6 present predictions for the external strategic approach and success of communist successor parties in the different subgroups. The mix of programmatic and clientelist linkage strategies to electoral constituencies shifts gradually in favor of the latter, as precommunist political society mobilization and civil service professionalism decline from group I to group IV. Whatever programmatic orientation can be detected varies with the political society and civil service variables as well, qualified by the impact of new state formation governed by titular majorities formerly subjected under imperial-domination. This allows some new countries with generally inauspicious domestic legacies to embrace reformist politics (group III b). Column 6 advances a hypothesis about the likely average electoral success of parties choosing the appeal specified in columns 4 and 5. In communist successor parties emerging from authoritarian communism, that success rate is generally weak (below 15 percent electoral support), in contrast to just about every other configuration. The assumption is this: As long as successor parties choose "equilibrium" optimal linkage patterns and programmatic appeals, their strategies will convert to reasonable electoral success, yielding popular support of at least one quarter of the national electorates.

Columns 7 and 8 summarize my arguments about the inclusiveness of party membership, captured by member/citizen (M/C) and member/partisan voter (M/V) rates, as well as organizational party centralization. In general, M/C and M/V ratios go up as we move from legacies-favorable to reformist liberal-democratic communist successor parties (group II), or those with unfavorable domestic conditions (groups I, III, and IV). Only elites in the orthodox, but isolated post-communist parties after bureaucratic-authoritarian communism encounter few imperatives and incentives to centralize power because they have virtually no chance of becoming governing parties and as such distributors of scarce economic resources.

Limits of Legacies-Based Explanation: Empirical Anomalies and Political Learning

A close examination of Table 2.1 and consideration of empirical evidence shows that there are anomalies not accounted for by the legacies-based theoretical framework. They are due to exogenous "shocks" not explicable in legacies terms or to learning processes over time that affect both the structure and the strategy of post-communist successor parties. In this final section, I would like to discuss a few individual cases that illustrate the limitations of legacies-based accounts of communist successor parties. As time elapses since the disintegration of communist rule in 1989/91, such anomalies should become more numerous and the explanatory power of legacies-based explanations of party structures and strategies should therefore gradually decline.

Empirical Anomalies Disconfirming the Theoretical Argument

There are a variety of empirical anomalies about the legacies of precommunist political society and the extent of professional civil service development during critical eras of state building that cannot be accounted for in theoretical terms. I have tried to address the biggest class of anomalies through a more systematic conceptualization of ethnic relations in the old multi-ethnic empires (Yugoslavia, Soviet Union). A legacies-based argument, in contrast, would predict diffuse orthodox socialist and nationalist doctrines as well as a strong propensity toward clientelist linkage-building in communist successor parties emerging from patrimonial communism. In newly emerging independent countries where communists threw in their lot with nationalist state builders (group III b), the outcomes of regime transition and communist party metamorphosis look more like those obtained after national-accommodative communism with reformist and electorally popular successor parties. It is the new opportunities of disintegrating empires that open up the option for politicians in communist successor parties to grow beyond the bounds of what domestic legacies alone would have made feasible.

Other empirical anomalies, however, result from unique exogenous historical shocks, idiosyncrasies of timing and particular leadership choices that no broad-based theoretical argument could model in a satisfactory fashion. In Croatia, for example, a legacies-based potential for a national-accommodative arrangement between communists and the overall population could never be realized because the hegemonic Serbian socialists essentially repressed and disorganized whatever reformist potential existed there before 1971. In a similar vein, the historical fact that many national communists and separatists in Slovakia left the old ruling party and the anticommunist umbrella organization in order to found a populist-nationalist party, rather than return to the post-communist party and take it over, has as much to do with unique intricacies of timing as with leadership. A counterfactual may also highlight that other countries with national-accommodative communism, such as Hungary, could have experienced a similar trajectory with the equivalent consequence of creating a strong cronyist-populist-nationalist party outside the reach of the conventional communist network of successor parties, if only key politicians had made slightly different choices. Had the leader of the nationalist-reform communists in Hungary, Imre Poszgay, thrown in his towel and left the Hungarian Socialist Worker's Party in the fall of 1989 rather than in the spring of 1990 and joined the newly emerging Hungarian Democratic Forum (MDF) early, a split similar to Slovakia's might have resulted between a relatively weak reformist post-communist successor party and a nationalist-populist alternative. Conversely, in Slovakia, had Vladimir Mečiar, like Poszgay, stayed inside the reformist post-communist successor party beyond the first free election, the Slovak post-communists might have never had to later tolerate a strong nationalist-populist party and thus have grown into the dominant party of the new independent republic.

A further historical anomaly is seen in the initial economic and political reformism of Kyrgyzstan's president Askar Akayev, who initially courted the West in the expectation of major material aid, but then abandoned his policies when this help was forthcoming to a lesser extent than desired. True, domestic legacies of political society and professional state development never let one expect a different outcome. Nevertheless, here a politician at least tried to break out of a legacies-constrained opportunity structure.

A more important set of historical anomalies has to do with party organization. According to the framework outlined above, communist successor parties after national-accommodative communism in traditionally independent countries should have low organizational density (in terms of member/citizen and member/voter ratios). Intermediate levels should be found after bureaucratic-authoritarian communism (and newly independent countries with formerly national-accommodative communism), and high levels in formerly patrimonial communist countries that had been always independent. Empirically, the argument is more or less borne out for the first several types of legacies, but not in the case of patrimonial communist countries. Bulgaria and Romania confirm the prediction of high organizational density, but Russia and the Ukraine disconfirm it with member-voter ratios of only .02 and .03 (Ishiyama 1999a, p. 97).

While in all formerly patrimonial communist countries the old ruling parties had sufficient electoral support to stay in political power after the formal end of communist rule and reinforce their clientelist support networks, it is historically contingent (to confirm the prediction of high organizational density) whether or not such parties actually did manage to stay in power or were replaced at the helm of the state. In Bulgaria and Romania they stayed in power until at least 1996, whereas in Russia and the Ukraine they did not. In the latter cases, therefore, middle-level apparatchiks in control of local clientelist networks found it disadvantageous to be still affiliated with the old communist parties. Instead, as an empirical case study of Russian local politics shows, such local "bosses" and their local clients often dropped out of the communist successor parties and built and maintained non-partisan localist clientelist networks (Gosolov 1997). The crucial event of losing political power over time thus yields much lower member-voter ratios in Russia and the Ukraine than the general predictive framework would have anticipated.

Political Learning Beyond Legacies

Legacies yield distributions of material resource control between political parties, but also cognitive skills and expectations as well as normative policy preference distributions. Where these configurations lead to the adoption of corresponding post-communist political institutions, they "lock in" legacies within the new regimes. For example, where successor parties after patrimonial communism are electorally popular and conservative, but liberal-democratic challengers weak and/or incapable to build sustained party organization (countries groups III a and IV), it is probable that the actor with the greatest political bargaining power, the successor parties, will successfully obtain constitutions enshrining strong independently elected presidential offices. Strong presidencies, in turn, reinforce clientelist patterns of citizen-politician linkage-building (Kitschelt 2000).

In general, as we move from post-communist polities in group I through groups II a, b, and c, group III b, then group III, a and finally group IV, presidential powers become increasingly pronounced in post-communist constitutions (Kitschelt and Malesky 2000). There are, however, outlier cases where this logic is disconfirmed because of exogenous shocks at the time of constitutional bargaining. A prominent one is the Bulgarian Communist Successor Party (BSP), which lost its popular candidate for a strong independently elected presidential office when a videotape of November 1989 established that he had had a desire to crush the demonstrations of democratic challengers through military repression. The BSP then had no popular presidential candidate and consequently agreed to a parliamentary form of government, something that the initially weak liberal-democratic Bulgarian opposition had wanted all along.

As a consequence, however, Bulgarian democratic institutions are not endogenous to communist legacies. This, in turn, affects politicians' best ("equilibrium") strategies to gain political office. Whereas legacies would lead us to expect clientelist voter-politician linkage strategies pursued primarily by the communist successor party, the realities of nonendogenous democratic institutions endowed with electoral rules that favor ideological party competition rather than clientelism may force power-seeking politicians to build party organizations and linkage strategies that differ from what the pure legacies model would predict. In this case, a former patrimonial communist country may ultimately produce ideologically disciplined parties that build citizen-politician linkages through policy platforms. The legacies argument would have led us to expect programmatically diffuse, clientelism-based parties that are suboptimal given exogenously determined Bulgarian democratic institutions. Initially, politicians may in fact pursue such party formation (Kitschelt et al. 1999, chapters 5 and 6). However, they then learn that these strategies are suboptimal in light of newly installed democratic institutions. By contrast, in Russia, where democratic institutions are endogenous to historical legacies of patrimonial communism, politicians' best strategies may indeed result in programmatically diffuse parties with strongly clientelist linkage strategies (Kitschelt and Smyth 2000).

The general lesson from this example is that politicians learn to adjust their best strategies in terms of contemporary institutional constraints and opportunities that do not necessarily result from political legacies. Politicians may still initially pursue legacies-based strategies of mobilization, but then adjust them when they yield dissatisfactory results. Legacies-based explanations thus find their outer limit in the interaction of exogenous "shocks" with endogenous learning processes of ambitious politicians.

The same sort of learning may also affect the predictive power of legacies arguments for the strategic stance of communist successor parties. As will be recalled, patrimonial communist regimes give rise to successors of the ruling party with programmatically diffuse, yet generally conservative, status quo and anti-liberal market-reform oriented policy predispositions. Yet countries that failed to engage in painful, drastic economic reforms in the first several years of postcommunism have not performed better, but progressively worse, relative to the intensive reform countries throughout the 1990s (EBRD 1999, p. 58, chart 3.1). It may therefore be only a matter of time until even communist successor parties in formerly patrimonial communist regimes will embrace fundamental market-liberal reform programs when coming to political power. They are compelled to learn that alternative heterodox economic policy visions simply do not provide economic results and ultimately weaken the reelection chances of those politicians who preside over economic decline. Again, political learning and not simply legacies is the shaping factor of communist successor parties. A test of this expectation may well be provided by the defeat of market-liberal reformers in the 2000 parliamentary and presidential elections in Romania; a feat that is likely to be repeated in 2001 in Bulgaria, if popular sentiments in that country in late 2000 persist throughout the subsequent year.

Conclusions

In this chapter I argued that historical legacies have provided powerful predictors of communist successor party strategic behavior and organizational reform since the collapse of the old systems in 1989 and 1991.

Precommunist political society and state formation, embodied in more or less professional civil service administration, play a critical role and are intermediated by the post-Stalinist diversification of communist regimes. In this vein, historical legacy arguments do not have to assume long-distance causality even over the relatively short historical period of forty to seventy years. The trajectory of communist rule itself, embodied in more bureaucratic-authoritarian, national-accommodative, patrimonial and ultra-patrimonial, colonial regime forms, creates the bridge between precommunist and post-communist modes of political mobilization and regime institutions.

This chapter then advanced three qualifications to a purely legacies-based explanatory account of communist successor parties. First, the formation of newly independent states based on titular ethnic groups that were formerly subjected to a hegemonic imperial-colonial ethnic group (Serbs and Russians, maybe even Czechs) creates a new dynamic of political mobilization in which communist successor parties may defy domestic legacies-based predictions of their strategic trajectory. This applies in particular to newly independent states with formerly patrimonial communist structures, but situated beyond the colonial periphery of Central Asia. It also includes countries such as Armenia, Georgia, Macedonia, and Moldova.

Second, historical exogenous "shocks," such as external intervention in domestic political structures (Serbs in Croatia in 1971) or the capabilities, tactics, and fortunes of individual leaders of post-communist parties (Petur Mladenov in Bulgaria, 1989–90) sometimes yield a strategic party conduct not anticipated by legacy-based predictions. Third, exogenous democratic institutions, as well as the results of economic reform processes, may convince politicians in post-communist successor parties to pursue different strategies and organizational forms than those adopted in the immediate aftermath of communist collapse. Whereas the latter are most closely shaped by political legacies, learning processes prompted by the experience of electoral victory or defeat within the new systems of democratic institutions as well as national performance in response to varying economic reform programs enable politicians to grow beyond the determinative power of the past and find creative ways to establish and maintain their positions of political power. Thus, while historical legacies are an exceedingly powerful analytical concept for understanding the politics of post-communist regimes in the immediate aftermath of the old regime breakdown between 1989 and 1991, the successive performance of new polities and the political actors embedded within them can be explained progressively less in terms of a path-dependency argument that goes back to "ancient" history, even if this history encompasses barely 100 years.

Notes

1. For a discussion of causal depth, see Kitschelt (1999; 2001) and Pierson (2000). Katz et al. (1992) are careful to distinguish these two ratios. A post-communist successor party may end up with high member/voter ratios simply because it lost a great deal of members and most voters. For some purposes, ratios of party members to the entire electorate are more meaningful coefficients of cross-national comparison.

2. The physical continuity of leadership across the wars cannot be a critical criterion to determine whether there is a mechanism of transition from one period to the next, as Grzymala-Busse (1999, pp. 28–29) claims. Skills, resources, experiences, and expectations are dissipated through the wider constituency of mobilized political currents. Leaders can easily be replaced. Only the physical liquidation of entire population segments, akin to the Nazi holocaust, could eradicate the transmission of such patterns from one generation to the next.

3. The detailed histories of East Central and Southeast Central Europe before World War I and in the interwar period written by Jelavich and Jelavich (1977) and Rothschild (1980), for example, yield copious narrative support for the regional differentiation of administrative capacities I have just sketched.

3

Prospects and Limits of New Social Democracy in the Transitional Societies of Central Europe

János Ladányi and Iván Szelényi

The Hegemony of New Social Democracy During the 1990s in Advanced Western Societies

The electoral victories of Bill Clinton and Tony Blair (and the electoral successes of left-wing parties in France, Germany, Sweden, Israel—just to mention the more important ones) rewrote the political map of the advanced world. During the late 1970s and the 1980s neoliberal political regimes were hegemonic around the advanced world. It appeared that 1989 did not merely end the experiments with state socialism but may have initiated the decay of social democracy as we knew it. Soon we learned, however, that it might be too early to believe in the "end of history." First Bill Clinton, and following him a number of other social-democratic politicians, found the political program which could bring back the electorate to the center-left. There may not have been another time in history when so many social-democratic parties were in government in the North Atlantic region. Arguably, this is simply the result of the move of the political pendulum. The citizenry became exhausted by the decade-long rule of neoliberalism, and in their search for an alternative they did not have much else to do but elect social democratic parties.

The first decade of the twenty-first century may follow a similar logic and this time return the neoliberals to governmental power. This is certainly possible. Nevertheless, it requires an explanation why social-democratic parties were in government for such a long period of time and in so many countries. What explains the relatively brief rule by neoliberals? Traditional social democracy shaped Western politics for decades; neoliberals got only about 8–12 years.

We are inclined to believe that a new chapter opened in the political history of the advanced Western world and what is usually referred to as "new social democracy," or the "New Democratic Party," may deserve the attention of political theorists and commentators.

The New Democratic Party and the American
Economic "Miracle"

By the end of the 1980s it appeared that the United States had lost its economic and political hegemony in the world. The "empire" appeared to be in decay, and it was a safe bet to assume that the "American" twentieth century would be succeeded by an "East-Asian" twenty-first century. Nevertheless, the 1990s proved to be one of the most successful decades in American history.

During the presidency of Bill Clinton the American economy experienced the longest boom in its history. Economic growth was annually around 3–5 percent, inflation and unemployment hit lows not seen for decades, investments and productivity grew. Economic growth became dynamic enough to result in increases in real wages, and by the second half of the decade the growth of incomes began to "trickle down" to lower-income groups as well. The proportion of the population dependent on welfare handouts declined, as did the crime rate, drug consumption, and out-of-wedlock birth. The budget deficit was eliminated, and probably for the first time in its history the U.S. government arrived in a position to repay its debt. The stock exchange broke records year after year, and the number and the proportion of people who owned stocks and bonds skyrocketed. Given these facts, it is not surprising that during the last month of his presidency, Bill Clinton's job approval rate was still around 60 percent, though the majority of Americans—given the turbulent nature of his personal life—did not think much about the moral character of the president.

Yet, by the second half of the year 2000 it became apparent that the American economic boom was coming to an end, and the year 2001 casts doubt on whether this can be a soft landing.

Social scientists undoubtedly will debate it for years to come; what was behind the boom of the 1990s and the burst of the bubble in 2000–2001? Did the policy of the "New Democratic Party" in any way contribute to this economic success? Was the abandonment of these policies in any way responsible for the economic downturn? In this chapter we cannot attempt to give an answer to these questions. There can be little doubt that the long boom of the 1990s was the outcome of many factors, including economic restructuring, the rise of the so-called "new economy," and earlier neoliberal policies followed by the Thatcher and Reagan administrations, which helped to create the grounds for a new wave of economic prosperity. Nevertheless, it is difficult to accept that eight years of economic expansion, which followed twelve years of rather poor economic performance, had nothing to do with the policies of the New Democratic Party. It is also likely that the abandonment of these policies by the Bush administration could at least be partially responsible for the deepening of the unfolding economic crisis. One needs a more careful, balanced analysis to answer how these three factors—economic

restructuring, neoliberalism, and the policies of the New Democratic Party—
shaped the economic outcomes of the 1990s (Quirk and Cunion 2000); however, there is enough prima facie evidence to indicate that the policies of new
social democracy did play some role in the recent economic history of the
advanced capitalist world.

What is New in the Economic Policies of the New Social Democracy

In this chapter we use the terms New Democratic Party, New Labor, or New
Social Democracy of the Schröder type interchangeably. Is there anything
new in the new social democracy, and if yes, what is it? It is not easy to
answer this question. The notion of new social democracy is a broad concept, which often includes very different policies. Schröder's party is not the
same as the New Democratic Party, and of course the French socialists, if
they deserve the label "new social democracy" at all, are very different from
the American, English, and German version of the movements. It is a further
complication that practice and rhetoric are as distant from each other in the
new social democratic movement (Gamble and Wright 1999) as they are in
any other political movement. With a great deal of simplification we will try
to contrast the political packages of the classical social democracy,
neoliberalism, and new social democracy the following way.

1. *The New Social Democracy Claims to Transcend the Dichotomy of Demand and Supply-Side Economics*

   Classical social democracy is the politics of the "demand side." Its
   economic theory follows Keynes's—market failures are believed to
   be caused on the demand side, which must be corrected by government intervention. This is achieved by high levels of taxation, which
   results in large state budgets, used for the generation of consumer
   demand to fight the dangers of crisis by overproduction.

   Neoliberalism follows the opposite economic philosophy. Guided
   by the principles of the doctrines of Milton Friedman (1962), the
   economic policy of neoliberalism believes that "the smaller the state,
   the better it is." The central aim is tax-cuts and the encouragement
   of private investments and savings. In the short run it can even result in a budget deficit increase (as happened in the United States
   during the 1980s). Neoliberals hope that the enrichment of the
   wealthy will eventually "trickle-down." The savings from tax-cuts
   go to investments, these lead to economic growth and eventually to
   the growth of employment opportunities and real wages as well.

   The main aim of the economic policy of new social democracy is
   to put the economy on a growth trajectory. For this purpose the new

social democrats are willing to accept even a reduced level of taxation (this is the reason why Left critics ridicule the new social democrats as "supply side socialists"). But they cut taxes only in order to stimulate economic growth, and they promise that the reduction of taxes will be complemented with a governmental industrial and employment policy. Whether the new social democrats ever did deliver on this promise is and remains hotly contested, but the fact is that they at least differ in rhetoric greatly from neoliberals. Furthermore, in principle the neoliberals operate only with monetary instruments, while the new social democrats claim that they have an industrial and employment policy.

2. *The Promise of the New Social Democracy: An Empowering State*

Traditional social democracy offers governmental solution to most social and economic problems. Its opponents dismiss old-line social democrats as "statist" or proponents of the "tax-and-spend" government. The growth of social democracy between 1930 and 1970 was indeed followed by increases in government budgets and taxes. The political defeat of governments with such policies was the outcome of a tax revolt by the electorate.

The goal of neoliberalism is the "de-etatization" of the economy and society. Neoliberals believe that deregulation of the economy will offer sufficient stimulus for economic growth and will eventually solve specific social problems, such as poverty or environmental degradation.

The new social democrats do not believe governmental policy can solve all problems, but they believe that some problems call for governmental intervention (Giddens 1998). They intend to replace the "tax-and-spend" state with an "investor state." As a result, the new social democrats often are even more conservative in fiscal policy than the neoliberals. They even give higher priority to a balanced budget than neoliberals. This is one of the main reasons why they are so reluctant to cut taxes. And if and when economic growth takes off as a result of moderate tax-cuts, the eventual budget surplus is not used by the new social democrats for further and sharper tax reduction. Those budget surpluses are instead "invested" the following way:

- High priority is put on the reduction of national debt which assumedly will eventually increase governmental resources for future investments;
- The budget surplus is used for the stabilization of the pension system, if necessary, with some reluctance, even the partial privatization of the social security system; thus investment of some

of the pension funds on the stock exchange may be considered
by the new social democrats
- New social democrats "invest" into education, environment, infrastructure, research—generally in those areas where short-term
profits are not likely to occur, thus the marketplace does not guarantee dynamic investments.

The sharpest debate between neoliberals and new social democrats focuses on whether the budget surplus should be used for
tax-cuts, or on repayment of the national debt and other governmental investments.

3. *New Social Democracy Moves from the Welfare State Toward the
Workfare State.*

The new social-democratic welfare reform promises to invest in job
training and conducts a proactive governmental employment policy.

The neoliberals and the new social democrats do not believe that the welfare
state, which was created by traditional social democracy, can be sustained in the
long run. These two schools of political thought also agree that universal insurance systems tend to be too expensive and are likely to lead to negative redistribution, thus they increase rather than decrease social inequalities.

The most often cited example is free tertiary education for all. Given the
high costs of tertiary education and the fact that children of higher income
groups are grossly overrepresented among university students, free tertiary
education represents a massive redistribution of income from the poor to the
rich. Therefore both neoliberals and new social democrats believe that those
who have enough income should meet their needs in the marketplace and
not be eligible for welfare benefits.

There are, however, fundamental differences between the welfare policies of neoliberals and new social democrats. The neoliberals place emphasis on individual responsibility. They believe that once people are freed from
"welfare dependence" they can take care of themselves. Those who cannot
learn how to look after themselves shall be aided by charity. In contrast the
new social democrats promise a more active governmental policy. They suggest using increased tax revenues for training programs, which will remove
people from the welfare roll and bring them back into the workforce. Their
main objective is not to increase employment by the expansion of the public
sector—rather they retrain people and "empower" them this way to enter the
job market (Ladányi and Szelényi 1996). They do not leave it to market
forces and individual responsibility to solve the problems that arise from the
weakening, or elimination, of a social safety net. "It takes a village to raise a
child" is the slogan of Hillary Clinton. One needs social solidarity and gov-

ernmental policy to solve the most burning social problems. Thus the aim of new social democracy is to move toward a smaller, but ultimately more effective state.

New Social Democracy in Transitional Societies

New social democracy is a response to neoliberal excesses in the scaling back of the traditional social-democratic welfare state. Therefore, one may argue that the policies of new social democracy are irrelevant under the conditions of transitional societies. State socialism neglected the welfare institutions, it failed to create an adequate housing system, its educational institutions were not up to the tasks of post-industrial society, and its healthcare system was both expensive and inefficient. The so-called "social policy" of state socialism did not reduce economic inequalities; in fact it contributed to those inequalities (Szelényi 1983). Arguably, this was not "social policy" at all; it was rather an excessively overgrown system of "collective consumption," a paternalistic assemblage of fringe benefits. Socialist collective consumption served economic policy aims; it helped to maintain the myth that state socialism was egalitarian, since it helped to sustain a very inegalitarian system with nominal wage differentials. The high cadres lived better, since they received all sorts of "fringe benefits" ordinary workers were deprived of: special healthcare facilities and schools for their children; free, higher-quality housing; subsidized vacations; and special shops where they could obtain scare commodities, from bananas to Western cigarettes, clothing, and even cars.

Socialist redistribution operated under the conditions of full employment, relative price stability, and economic shortages (Kornai 1980, 1992). The institutions that were created under the system of state-socialist redistributive policy, from public housing to healthcare facilities and childcare institutions, collapsed in the epoch of high inflation, increased unemployment rates, impoverishment, homelessness, and increasing ethnic conflicts.

Arguably, the most urgent task ahead is to build on the ruins of state socialism a modern welfare system, functioning pension scheme, and adequate healthcare and educational institutions. The neoliberal argument that this will all be provided by the invisible hand of the marketplace does not sound persuasive. After decades of neglect a new infrastructure for social welfare has to be created. The neoliberal policy, which was inspired by the social philosophies of Thatcher and Reagan and which cut back the "overgrown" socialist welfare state appears to be ill-conceived in societies that are hit with the worse economic and social crises of recent times. The American social policy model, which is recommended by some welfare reformers to the postcommunist world, does not function that well in the United States either. A depressingly high proportion of the population of the United States is left without health insurance or an adequate pension, while far too many children attend underfunded schools where they do not receive an education needed to function in a modern society and economy. The adaptation of such a policy in societies of transition could have devastating consequences and may even undermine the democratic achievements of the postcommunist world.

Under these circumstances traditional social democracy can perform useful functions in transitional societies. The most urgent tasks in postcommunist societies is the shaping of functioning pension systems as well as educational and healthcare institutions. It is difficult to see how this can be achieved in countries with low real incomes without an active government role.

At the same time transitional societies ought to learn from the lessons of more advanced Western societies. When new welfare institutions are created, postcommunist societies should be aware that universal insurance systems may not always be the best solutions and in the long run may not be sustainable. In the epoch of transition a traditional social democratic policy, corrected by the lessons learned from the new social democracy, could produce a political coalition, which may have a chance to win elections and govern effectively. The political successes of successor parties in Poland in 1993 and in Hungary in 1994 illustrated this well.

In those transitional societies where the communist parties were reformist their successors (primarily in Hungary and in Poland) may have a good chance of presenting themselves as authentic social democratic parties after the fashion of Willy Brandt (Szelényi et al. 1997). These parties do have a chance to be effective and attract electoral support especially as long as the older generations, former communist party members, are still alive. The main dangers for the successor parties is that their electoral base is aging and so far—with the partial exception of the victory of the Polish SLD in September 2001—there has been little evidence that the successor parties can reach out to the younger generations. Thus, in the long run no left-wing policy can rely exclusively on the successor parties of former reform communists. This has created a political opportunity for "liberal" parties, for example the Alliance of Free Democrats (SZDSZ) in Hungary. During the late 1990s the liberal parties faced a substantial crisis in the region. In 1998 the Hungarian SZDSZ suffered a humiliating electoral defeat, which simultaneously brought down the left-wing governing coalition and paved the way for the rise of the right-wing nationalist parties to political power.

A key hypothesis of this chapter is that the liberal parties suffered such a setback as a result of adopting one-sided pro-multinational, antiworker neoliberal policies, which could have been implemented by the conservative parties as well. The political right did steal the economic policy of postcommunist liberalism, and its human rights policy was not enough to distinguish the liberals from the successor parties of the reform communists, which have a credible human rights record by now.

The future of liberalism in the postcommunist world depends on whether the liberal parties can invent a new political package for themselves—and new social democracy offers itself as such a policy package. With the policies of the new social democracy liberal parties would be able to keep the electoral base in a transitional epoch among the anticommunist middle classes and intellectuals who are reluctant to vote for the successor parties. In the short run a coalition of old-style social-democratic successor parties and new social-democratic liberal parties could offer a viable alternative to the conservative right-wing movements. Given the current urgency of creating a modern welfare state the successor parties will inevitably be the "senior partner" in this coalition. As their electoral base weakens due to demographic change and their social function becomes less prominent with the consolidation of market economy and accumulation of middle-class wealth, the liberal parties are likely to become the dominant force of the center-left in the former communist countries.

The liberal parties of the postcommunist region would be better served if they could be "liberal" in the sense of the Democratic Party, in particular the New Democratic Party of the United States. They would flourish if they could leave the neoliberalism of Margaret Thatcher and Ronald Reagan to their conservative opponents.

The crisis of the Left during the 1990s in Poland and Hungary was induced primarily by the inability of the liberals to position themselves on the political map of postcommunism. If the liberals fail to follow the lead of Bill Clinton and Tony Blair to form alliances with the successor parties (which can cast themselves as Willy Brandt-type traditional social democratic forces), the conservative right-wing may move even further to the right, potentially establishing an Austrian-type coalition between conservatives and far right-wing forces. In Hungary in 2002, the socialist and liberal parties (MSZP and SZDSZ) together won an absolute majority and averted a center-right and far-right coalition.

The second half of the 1990s in Western Europe was an epoch of the crisis of the political Right. The Christian Democratic and/or conservative parties lost the elections to "new social democrats" while in postcommunist Central Europe the last years of the century represented a crisis of the political Left. Ironically this crisis, however was not fueled by the loss of the successor parties—they held their electoral support reasonably well—but was the outcome of the decay of liberal parties. This chapter's main hypothesis is that liberalism can have a future in the postcommunist world, but only if it does not cast itself as "neoliberalism," but rather accepts its place to the center-left of the political spectrum, where the new social democracy is located.

Part II

Case Studies

4

The Polish SLD in the 1990s

From Opposition to Incumbents and Back

Radoslaw Markowski

The aim of this chapter is to explain the phenomenon of the growing importance of the Polish communist successor party, the Social Democracy of the Republic of Poland (SdRP) and its parliamentary-electoral coalition, Democratic Left Alliance (*Sojusz Lewicy Demokraticznej*, SLD).[1]

What follows is divided into several sections. In the first section, I briefly comment on the main theoretical arguments concerning the fate of the communist successor parties. Section two is devoted to the idiosyncrasies of Polish socialism and the peculiarities of the Round Table talks. Next, I briefly present the transformative path of the Polish United Worker's Party (PZPR) into the SdRP and then the SLD coalition. Section four focuses on the nature and outcomes of the democratic elections since 1989. In the fifth section, a brief overview of the organizational, programmatic, and ideological features of SLD (SdRP) is presented. In the sixth section, I try to explain the changing social bases of SLD support and its considerable increase in the 1990s. The chapter concludes with general remarks on the fate of SLD in the late 1990s.

Theoretical Arguments

The extensive literature on Eastern European polities, including their institutional design and party systems, can be divided between approaches that lean toward a belief in the existence of rational actors, deliberative decisions, and well-designed, programmatic plans, on the one hand, and those who claim that path-dependent, interactive, short-term decisions, as well as incremental and tactical changes, created the new democratic reality of these polities, on the other. In other words, is the current "state of democratic art" in these countries more a result of a choice or of fate? And more specifically, are the fortunes of political parties determined more by fate, or choice-driven mechanisms? Historical legacies are crucial to many scholars: grand-modernization processes, types of socialisms dominant in particular countries, and transformative paths

51

(i.e. modes of authoritarian exits). Others point to actors' strategic decisions during the formative period and, finally, institutional design choices.

Attempts at testing which of several plausible phenomena are the best explanatory factors remain inconclusive. In my view, attempts at finding a macro-explanation that would explain the divergent fortunes of communist successor parties are, in a way, fated to fail, primarily because there is simply too much variation among the independent macro-variables and too few cases. Numerous scholars who depict the development of communist successor parties use the term "adaptation strategies" (Bozóki and Ishiyama 2002) or the like, to indicate—as I suspect—that they were not the sole or even most important creators of this new reality and that they had to adjust themselves to whatever turned out to be the product of the transformation. However, without going into analytical details, I am inclined to believe communist successor parties' activities should rather be specified as "adaptation tactics," the latter term pointing to a shorter and less comprehensive impact on the political environment. In my view, a few choices deserve to be dubbed "strategic choices." These are decisions concerning:

(a) whether to remain an active political player in the new reality,
(b) whether to claim personal and organizational continuity with the former communist party,
(c) whether to switch from an orthodox Marxist programmatic appeal to a reformist one, leaning towards social-democratic ideology.

Other choices were, in my view, far from strategic; some of these deeds could hardly even be considered choices. Many of the accomplishments are simply effects of complex changes occurring on the Polish political arena, some clearly unintended side effects of strategic choices made by the Polish right. Of course, each of these strategic choices had been constrained by many exogenous factors, which can plausibly be considered real causes (Kitschelt 2001; Kitschelt this volume chapter 2). In this chapter however, it is not the main theme.

Thus, I concentrate on the interplay between the dramatically shifting socio-political reality of the first years of transformation and the decisions made by the Polish SdRP/SLD. Most of them are unlikely to be understood without proper contextualization—a detailed description of other political actors' deeds and their interactive effects.

Setting the Stage: Idiosyncrasies of Polish Socialism and Peculiarities of the Round Table

This section very briefly recollects peculiarities of the historical legacies of contemporary Poland. A number of phenomena deserve emphasis. First, I do share Linz's and Stepan's (1996) point that the totalitarian phase in postwar Poland was either totally missing and/or its manifestations marginal and short lasting. Polish communists, unlike their comrades from other Soviet satellite countries, ultimately did behave in a more civilized way, refraining from drastic solutions and deeds.

Second, there was the role played by the Catholic Church. Under socialism the Church enjoyed stunning popularity and prestige. Its very existence ensured a legal, recognized alternative to the authoritarian ideology, and consequently the survival of an interparadigmatic dialogue at the macro level, contributing to the questioning of the dominant socialist orthodoxy. Stereotypical ideas of Polish religiosity confuse its depth with its breadth; contrary to this stereotype, it is rather shallow, anti-intellectual, and unpersonal in nature, yet widespread if one concentrates on its everyday manifestations. These traits and its highly social character have contributed to the ease with which the Church has coordinated opposition as well as to its declining popularity, once it decided to enter the mainstream of politics at the beginning of 1990s. The role of this institution will proved to be crucial in explaining SLD's fate.

The post–World War II period in Poland was also marked, in contrast to the other bloc countries, by the existence of private land-ownership in agriculture (and limited privatization in other sectors), resulting, among other things, in an independent alternative economy and a widespread spirit of self-reliance. This resulted from an "early Gomulka" idea of a specific, "national road" to socialism. Relative political liberalism, freedom of mass-media, science, and culture are thoroughly described in the literature, yet deserve mentioning as a permanent phenomenon of Polish socialism.

On the other hand, extremely poor economic performance, both in absolute and relative terms, appears to be another one of the peculiarities of Polish socialism. Practically all of the Eastern European Soviet satellite parties could, at least partly, derive their legitimacy from either relatively efficient macroeconomic performance[2] or notable social developments in the areas of education, mass culture, health, and social security. However, the PZPR could do this only to a very limited extent.

Results of numerous sociological projects have demonstrated that citizens' ties with "official" institutional infrastructures in Poland are extremely weak or non-existent, pointing to the fragility of the official intermediary institutions. This, however, should not mislead us to believe that civil society was weakly developed. Polish society of the 1970s and 1980s in fact manifested a relatively developed and self-organized civil society. Almost all spheres of societal activities were covered by the grass-roots, informal institutions of the alternative, "second society" and "shadow economy." Contrary to the experience of stable democracies this infrastructure falls short of meeting the formal legitimacy criteria. But it is exactly this latter trait (lack of a formal yet strong social legitimacy), that proved to be a source of its viability and political power and crucial at times of authoritarian backlashes (i.e. under earlier martial law).

Finally, the relative liberalism of the internal life of the Polish United Workers Party should be considered. Among the compelling facts that ought to be mentioned are some important ones:

(1) none of the party leaders had lost his life in communist trials and purges;
(2) almost until the very end of communism a collective leadership existed, and separation of the functions of the party leader, the prime minister, and the president (head of the State Council);
(3) the existence of internal fractions, surfacing during frequent anti-socialist revolts, contributing to the strengthening of the opposition ranks by PZPR "converts";
(4) contrary to the sovietologists' over-generalized wisdom concerning the region, PZPR's satellite parties, ZSL in particular, enjoyed certain policy-independence, especially in agrarian and local matters, which encouraged weak, semi-open, and pluralist decision-making procedures in selected domains.[3]

These "merits" of PZPR's internal life also have to be relativized; the above description obviously does not meet even minimum standards of real democratic pluralism.

Lack of space forces us to ignore other phenomena, such as a relatively free official, party-controlled press, including its official periodical *Nowe Drogi*. Ideological-free semantics of PZPR's public debates and appearances of their politicians; words like "communism," "communist," and "comrade" were deliberately replaced by "society based on social justice," "party member," and similar equivalents, to soften the alien expressions.

The above description does not by any means permit us to claim the existence of real pluralism, democratic procedures, a free press, and the similar attributes of democracy and democratic parties. In the East European context however, these minor departures from orthodoxy mattered a lot, if not in other respects, they indicated a lack of confidence in Polish communists' own ideology.

From PZPR to SdRP and the Formation of the SLD Coalition

Let me start with quoting a knowledgeable author of East European politics:

During the five years from 1989 to 1994, a series of parties in East-Central Europe moved from enjoying a monopoly of power in single-party states to standing on the threshold of recognition as social-democratic parties in a context of competitive party politics. . . . The evolution of former communist parties . . . presents the political analyst with quite a remarkable series of cases of adaptation of political parties to changes in their environment. (Waller 1995, p. 473)

And additional introductory sentences of yet another area specialist:

It has been five years since the demise of Communist rule in Eastern Europe. Nonetheless, the collapse of the Communist systems did not necessarily lead to the demise or disappearance of the Communist parties. (Ishiyama 1995, p. 47)

Both authors (and many others) seem to assume continued existence of the "communist party" and its adjustment to the new context. This is what occurs in the initial paragraphs of numerous articles, and although some scholars convincingly elaborate on the complexity of the phenomenon, it nevertheless points to the fact that, from a phenomenological perspective, continuity seems to dominate over change for most authors. Limited space again does not permit an in-depth analysis of the dynamic concept of political party; however, what is worth emphasizing is the difference between the operational definition of party change compared to change within a party. It is about clarifying the functional requisites of a party. A party's identity can be traced at various levels:

(a) normative—manifestoes and programs,
(b) personal/biographical continuity versus change among the membership and/or leadership,
(c) the organizational extent to which "new" entities inherit real-estate, funds, and equipment. These factors are quite obvious. More demanding, yet more debatable indicators of party identity are:
(d) stratificational—the profile of their supporters,
(e) external factors, among them the relationship with the international political community, in Poland's case the Socialist International,
(f) deeds and policies implemented while in power.

What follows is a brief recollection of the way one formal entity, the Polish United Workers Party (PZPR), has ceased to exist and a new one, Social democracy of the Republic of Poland (SdRP) was established. SdRP formally came into being in January 1990, preceded by an important constitutional amendment abandoning the provision of the "leading role of PZPR." SdRP inherited most of the real-estate, funds, and logistical apparatus of the former party. The SLD was formally established in July

1991, and it included numerous branch trade unions, associations, and leftist parties.

Assessing the extent of personnel continuity of the leadership is difficult, as it raises several questions. What should in fact be evaluated—their previous biographies or their current political outlooks? Do we simply look at individuals or at their political profile? Indeed, most of the new leaders happened to be relatively young people who joined the party in the last decade or so; nevertheless, representatives of the older fraction of PZPR activists were present among broad SdRP leadership as well. Many of them contributed both to the Round Table talks and the economic reforms strived for in the 1980s. True, with one or two exceptions, none of the SdRP leaders could be classified as PZPR "ideologue"; most of them were pragmatic, nonideological technocrats in desperate search of a new identity.

In terms of mass membership, just like in the other countries of the region, the decrease of the successor party proved to be substantial. Its membership went from almost two million PZPR members to about 20,000 right after the establishment of SdRP and then to 60,000 by 1993.[4] SdRP has been the major political party constituting the Democratic Left Alliance (SLD); in fact SdRP never contested an election alone. Finally, two phenomena should be emphasized here: (a) contrary to the experience with Solidarity trade union and its political umbrella coalition Solidarity Election Action (AWS),[5] the SLD is dominated by the political entrepreneurs of SdRP; and (b) the electoral debate and public discourse is about the political stances and policy deeds of SLD rather than of SdRP.

Polish Democratic Elections Since 1989

Four parliamentary and two presidential elections were held[6] between 1989–1997 in Poland. The first parliamentary election of 1989 was in fact a semi-democratic one; free elections to the Senate were accompanied by "compartmentalized" (Olson 1993) elections to the Sejm, with only 35 percent of the seats freely contested. The result: an overwhelming victory for the Solidarity party wherever free rules were applied. The overall message has been meaningful in yet another way, it proved to be at odds with rational-choice reasoning concerning democracy, which emphasizes the importance of stable rules of the game and a certain level of uncertainty in its outcomes (Przeworski 1991). The post-1989 experience in Poland demonstrates that in a period of accelerated, multidimensional change, the stability of the rules is not necessarily conducive to successful democratic consolidation. Higher levels of uncertainty in the Polish transition as compared to elsewhere, contributed to its institutional design at the outset of the transition.

The presidential election of 1990 has been thoroughly described in many works (Jasiewicz 1993; Grabowska, Krzeminski 1991). Its main lessons were that: (a) leaving a charismatic leader outside institutionalized political structures is a mistake, and (b) Walesa's comeback destabilized the fragile elite consensus, allowing room for unknown political entrepreneurs.

In the three parliamentary elections of 1991, 1993, and 1997, SLD has been respectively supported, by 11.99, 20.41, and 27.13 percent of active voters; a steady growth in support.[7] Meanwhile, in 1995, a presidential election took place in which, in the second round, SLD's candidate and its parliamentary caucus chairman, Aleksander Kwasniewski, received 51.7 percent of the vote in a runoff against Lech Walesa. In the 2000 election, Kwasniewski won in the first round with almost 55 percent of the vote.

Organizational, Programmatic, and Ideological Features of SLD

The political program and ideological orientation of a party depends on many factors. In a new democracy "historical" parties can simply, with minor modifications, adopt the program of whatever existed prior to the introduction of the authoritarian regime. New parties are tabula rasa entities able to virtually adopt any plausible program. The situation of the communist successor parties is more complicated; they are both historical and newly established. They are historical in at least two ways: (a) communist, socialist, and social-democratic parties in the region have existed prior to World War II; selected aspects of their legacies became important for the new parties after 1989, (b) the legacy of the postwar socialist period. My basic point here is that the legacy of PZPR is complicated—on the one hand, and from an absolutist perspective, it quite clearly performed as an agent of Moscow's geopolitical concerns. On the other, its evolution via crises (1948–90), showed the extent to which national-adaptive socialism and certain semi-freedoms were in fact possible in the region. However, in contrast to the Hungarian communists, PZPR was clearly unsuccessful in its economic reforms policies.

In sum, at the beginning of the transformation the PZPR and subsequently the SdRP were weakly legitimized entities, with no positive records in the economic domain and a mixed legacy in the socio-political sphere because of the temporal proximity of martial law. However, both the Round Table Accord and the peaceful power transfer of 1989 pointed to the flexibility and potentially successful democratization of these successor parties.

In the aftermath of the presidential election of 1990, SdRP launched activities aimed at organizing a broader leftist coalition of forces, disappointed with the changes. In mid-1991 a coalition named Democratic Left Alliance or *Sojusz Lewicy Demokratycznej* (SLD), came into being, with SdRP as its dominant actor. Among sixty-one SLD deputies elected to the 1991–93 parliamentary term thirty-nine were SdRP members; in the 1993–97 term eighty-six out of one hundred seventy-three were SdRP members.

If there were any major fault lines within the successor party, these ran along the economic policy dimension rather than along sociocultural issues. This is true for most of the post-1991 period and on both mass and elite levels (Wiatr 1993). After the 1991 election both the parliamentary caucus of SLD and SdRP as a party behaved clearly in accordance with the norms of a disciplined democratic opposition. Their main objective in that period was to gain recognition among broader society, as well as attract voters among important social strata.

The organizational structure of the SdRP can be easily derived from their statute, however because of the confusion arising from the parallels with SLD, the evaluation of the working of this structure has been widely debated in Poland. At this point, a concluding quotation from Ewa Nalewajko's (1997) book will suffice.

> SdRP is distinguished by its hierarchical structure and homogeneous orga-
> nization at the national level. The power in the party is concentrated and
> exercised in an oligarchic manner. This oligarchic group can be easily traced
> by simply following the list of names, which systematically reappear in the
> leadership circle, comprising the president, deputy presidents and secre-
> tary general of the party. The relative weakness of the institution (that is
> SdRP-RM) arises from its underformalization, partial decentralization of
> decision-making and blurred boundaries of the organization, accompanied
> by a restriction of its autonomy. . . . Internal integration is cultural rather
> than bureaucratic in character. Closed oligarchic procedures, accompanied
> by a controlled members' mobilization, decide leadership recruitment out-
> comes. Choice of the leader is based . . . on the consensus among party
> elite, which contributes to his strong position within the party as well as
> outside it. Party leadership is of a transactional character with few transfor-
> mative traits. . . . Previously mentioned cultural integration is warranted by
> adherence to collectivist norms and a relative proximity of power, as well
> as poor tolerance of uncertainty by the leadership."

Among other, democratic-friendly paragraphs of SdRP's platform, one finds provisions permitting:

(a) intra-party fractions,
(b) referenda,
(c) horizontal structures in the party,
(d) decision-making autonomy of the lower organizational units,
(e) freedom of economic activity of the local units.

Between 1991 and 1994 several changes occurred in SdRP's platform, among the most important being a strengthening of the middle levels of its organizational structure (party's district units), a more open, grass-roots leadership recruitment, as well as the organizational strengthening of factions. However, irrespective of the formal decentralized structures, the practice of decision-making revealed the existence of a tendency for the party's central apparatus to exert strong control over the party's affairs. Further, although there appeared on the surface to be an emphasis on collective decision-making, this was not really the case. Indeed, among all Polish political parties, SdRP presents various party leaders, of moderately different political options, contributing to an image of a multi-oriented political organization. However, when it came to political deeds, including roll call voting behavior and campaign activities, SLD/SdRP proved to be a highly disciplined body.

Finally, since 1990 the SdRP has been headed by three leaders (Kwasniewski, Oleksy, and currently Miller). However, change at the top on no occasion led to an overhaul of the party leadership. The leadership group has consisted of the very same personalities over time.[8]

Social Bases of SLD Support

There are many ways of measuring the links between social structure and political support. Alford's index is one of the best known indicators of class voting (Alford 1963), although it is a viable and relevant tool primarily in two-party systems.[9] For the sake of simplicity, I will present here on the one hand the extent to which SLD has been able to "encapsulate" a particular socio-economic group, i.e. to persuade its members to support them, and, on the other, the extent to which SLD has been dependent on the support of each group. The latter is exemplified in the upper rows of Table 4.1; one may plausibly argue that SLD's support in the 1990s has considerably changed over time and the change indicates "condensation." In 1991, two groups, the intelligentsia and "white-collars," disproportionately contributed to SLD's support—12.7 and 12.1 percent respectively.[10] In 1993 the two dominant groups were "white-collar" and "pensioners." In the 1997 parliamentary election 42 percent of SLD support came from the latter group, with an additional 25 percent from white-collar supporters. This means that only about one-third of SLD's support can be attributed to all other groups, a phenomenon which I refer to as "condensation."

From the other perspective, social group encapsulation, i.e. the extent to which groups were captivated by SLD's appeal, no dramatic changes were visible throughout the 1990s. In the three electoral events of the 1990s approximately a quarter of white-collar respondents and pensioners regularly supported SLD; in 1997 almost a third of the former group voted for the party. It is worth emphasizing that SLD recently became more attractive to

Table 4.1

Social Bases of SLD Support

	1991	1993	1997
Size of SLD support derived from a given socio-professional group	12.7 (INT)* 12.1 (W-C)	25.2 (PEN) 23.4 (W-C)	42.1 (PEN) 28.6 (W-C)
Percentage of a given socio-professional group voting for SLD	26.3 (PEN) 25.8 (W-C)	26.0 (W-C) 23.7 (INT)	29.4 (W-C) 26.5 (B-C) 25.9 (PEN)

Source: Data for 1991 and 1993 come from exit polls conducted by INFAS/OBOP and OBOP, respectively. The 1997 data come from Polish National Election Survey.
Notes:
*Letters in brackets stand for:
INT   —intelligentsia, university degree professionals, civil servants, etc.
W-C   —white-collars, (usually) secondary education, administrative staff, employed mainly in non-private sector.
PEN   —pensioners; retired people and/or health pensioners.
B-C   —blue-collars, manual workers irrespectively of educational level as well as branch or sector employed in.

"blue-collar" respondents, a new, ideologically important phenomenon for the future of any leftist party.

Another way of depicting SLD's support is to look at the ideological profile of its electorate. Before presenting these profiles and their changes between 1992–1997, attitudinal developments among the Polish public as a whole should be discussed. In fact, detailed subhypotheses were already presented and tested a few years ago (Markowski and Tóka 1995). Let me briefly repeat them; hypothetically, several phenomena might prove responsible for SLD's growth:

(i)   distinct levels of electoral mobilization by supporters of particular parties;

(ii) political preferences of the electorate at large might have changed in favor of leftist parties;

(iii) specific changes in issue preferences of the leftist electorate;

(iv) a general growth of confidence in SLD unattributable to any specific changes in attitudinal preferences or mobilizational behavior of any particular social groups; should this be the case one will not be able to reveal the reasons for this growth.

In Table 4.2, fully comparable data on opinion/attitudinal preferences of Poles is presented;[11] for the entire active electorate as well as for SLD voters (the latter for only 1993 and 1997).

Table 4.2

Selected Opinion/Attitudinal Duty as Percentage of Active Voters in Poland

		1992	SLD voters 1993	1993	SLD voters 1997	1997
C	(agr)	State should provide jobs for everyone	81	88	90	79	81
D	(dis)	Reducing income differences is harmful to economy	43	37	50	32	46
E	(agr)	Economic situation of the country is poor	79	80	87	50	44
F	(dis)	Privatization of state enterprises will help the country's economy	45	56	81	35	56
G	(dis)	Unprofitable enterprises should be unconditionally closed down	54	71	81	50	59
H	(dis)	Atheists should not hold public offices	82	80	93	72	92
I	(agr)	Nationalism is harmful for the country	66	60	66	54	72
K	(dis)	People like me have a good chance of getting ahead in life	77	83	93	54	63
M	(dis)	Politicians should care more about crime than about human rights	23	23	28	17	19
N	(agr)	Woman should have the right to abortion, if she decides so	74	73	92	60	92
O	(dis)	Politicians should rather be experts than patriots	45	37	48	32	42
P	(dis)	Church in our country is too influential	78	79	96	60	92
Q	(agr)	Students and their parents should have free choice concerning religious instruction at school	88	88	96		
R	(dis)	The president should be granted extraordinary powers to combat crime and disorder	28	30	55		
		Declared membership in OPZZ	3	2		8	
		Declared membership in NSZZ "S"	7	6		5	
		Declared former membership in PZPR	12	13		12	
		Weekly church attendance	58	54		60	
		Young (18 to 30 years of age)	18	15		—	
		Old (61 and over)	—	—		30	

Source: Data for 1992 and 1993 come from CEU longitudinal project "Party Formation and Electoral Alignments in East Central Europe"; data for 1997, from Polish National Election Survey.

Note: dis=disagree, agr=agree.

Let us start with an effort aimed at explaining the 1993 SLD victory in general, and its almost 10 percent increase in popular support growth between 1991 and 1993. Among the attitudinal changes that may have contributed to this victory was an increase in economic populism and paternalism/egalitarianism (items F,G, and C, D). In previous work (Markowski and Tóka 1995, p. 84), we estimated this growth in leftist attitudes and calculated exactly the influence of attitudinal change (Table 4.3). This led us to conclude that:

> the shift in politically significant attitudes and the social position of the individuals is responsible for the 2.4 percent increase of the total of SLD voters. If the overall increase is estimated at 5 percent,[12] then our analysis still does not explain the remaining 2.6 percent increase in SLD support. In other words, half of the SLD popularity increase should be attributed to: (1) changes in the social base of its electorate and/or (2) the general increase in SLD popularity, which took place between 1992 and 1993.

Turning to Table 4.4,[13] we noted that the support for the SLD increased by 7 percent for two groups: the leftist and the liberal. In the remaining two groups virtually no increase was visible. This configuration leads us to the following conclusion: since the leftist and Christian-national groups were similar with respect to economic issues and substantially different from the liberal and rightist groups in this respect, it seems clear that the SLD's increase in support cannot be attributed to the impact of economic factors. The increase came from the opponents of the Christian-national ideology. In other words, SLD's increase in popularity came mainly from the shift in Poles' attitudes on one dimension— liberalism versus Christian-national "antiliberalism."

One should, however, bear in mind the working of institutional electoral rules. An example of this is the introduction of thresholds; almost 28 percent of the rightist vote was wasted, which resulted in a highly disproportional parliamentary seats allocation, with 171 seats (37.2 percent) for the SLD and 132 seats (28.7 percent) for PSL, the two forming the new governmental coalition which lasted four years.

The SLD in Power

Before depicting the deeds of the SLD/PSL coalition—an uneasy coalition from the beginning—it is useful to recall the main electoral appeals of the 1993 SLD campaign. It proved to be one of the fiercest critics of the proposed economic reform (Balcerowicz Plan) of 1989, pointing to the plan's allegedly dire results—high unemployment, widespread pauperization, decrease of real incomes (of white-collar workers) in particular, bankruptcy of the agricultural sector due to a lack of agricultural and industrial policies. SLD's manifesto opted for more state intervention, internal market protectionism, and higher taxes for the wealthy. Both SLD's manifesto and campaign favored general privatization policies, but with explicit substantial amendments aimed at more employee-friendly solutions. Their electoral slogan: "Things need not be like this," indicated both general support for marketization and associated policies on the one hand, and a promise of a more sophisticated way to combat the negative side effects of the reforms. Emphasis on market-reform was unavoidable by 1993 when it became clear that SLD attracted substantial support among the winners of the transformation (*Biuletyn CBOS*, 1993). Only a tiny fraction of them could be labeled former *nomenklatura*, who switched from "apparatchiks to entrepreneurchiks." Their message in the sociocultural domain was quite apparent—a secular state and limited role of the Church, accompanied by a promise of a review of the abortion law and a move towards pro-choice provisions. Prior to 1993, the SdRP and SLD's foreign policy stands seemed to be marked by significant reservations concerning a "western opening," be it NATO or EU membership.

To what extent have these promises been accomplished? Before we move to evaluate them, a few caveats should be noted:

(a) implemented policies, passing of bills in the parliament, and finally, the real outcomes, all resulted from interactive games between SLD and PSL. The 1993–97 government was a coalition;

(b) the election platform of parties are one thing and implemented policies quite another,[14] especially in new democracies. One of the most important factors contributing to such incongruence—apart from the low costs of departing from political pledges—was the impact of external factors, the International Monetary Fund and World Bank in particular;

(c) in the short run and in unstable times there is an additional problem of discriminating between the effects of the first "great push" (i.e. the Balcerowicz Plan) and the effects of subsequent amendments.

Turning the evaluation of the regime's performance, a major Polish weekly, (*Polityka* 1997, pp. 3–6) summarized the coalition government's deeds on the eve of the 1997 election in a special report entitled "Four Weddings and a Funeral," pointing to the four relative successes and one failure in the economic policies of 1993–1997. The four accomplishments were:

(a) an annual inflation down from 34 to about 14%,

(b) a budget deficit kept at below 3% of GDP,

(c) public debt down from 86% of GDP in 1993 to below 50% in 1997,[15]

(d) an unemployment rate decrease to below 12% from over 16% in 1993.

Table 4.3

The Model of SLD Support Determinants in 1992, 1993, and 1997

Set of independent variables	B	SE	Beta	T
1992 (N=672)				
Young people (below 30 years old)	−0.09	0.03	−0.10	−2.65
Membership in PZPR	0.11	0.04	0.11	2.82
Weekly religious practices	−0.09	0.03	−0.14	−3.44
Membership in OPZZ	0.39	0.07	0.21	5.50
Disagreement with the following statements:				
Privatization of state enterprises will help the country's economy	0.06	0.03	0.09	2.15
Unprofitable enterprises should be unconditionally closed down	0.05	0.03	0.07	1.80
People like me have a good chance of getting ahead in life	0.06	0.03	0.08	2.08
Agreement with following:				
Abortion rights should be guaranteed	0.05	0.03	0.07	1.70
Constant	0.03	0.04	—	0.74
Variance expained = 13%				
1993 (N=666)				
Former membership in PZPR	0.19	0.04	0.17	4.66
Membership in "Solidarity" TU	−0.11	0.06	−0.06	−1.73
Urban residence	0.09	0.03	0.10	2.66
Weekly religious practices	−0.13	0.03	−0.16	−4.26
Employed in own company	−0.07	0.04	−0.08	−1.94
(dis) People like me have a good chance of getting ahead in life	0.06	0.04	0.06	1.64
(dis) Privatization of state enterprises will help country's economy	0.08	0.03	0.09	2.47
(agr) Church in our country is too influential	0.12	0.04	0.12	3.27
Constant	0.05	0.06		0.80
Variance expained = 15%				

The main failure was the trade deficit, which by 1996 had increased to 4.5 times the size of 1992. By the end of 1997 indisputable symptoms of economic overheating were taking place.

Accomplishments were less pronounced and included the liberalization of the abortion law and the slowing down of the concordat's ratification; second, although hardly attributable exclusively to SLD, the new Constitution was finally adopted in 1997. Third, during the SLD/PSL government Poland moved toward integration with the West. It joined OECD and was invited to NATO and to EU membership negotiations. Although it is difficult to judge to whom the credit lies, contrary to both the SLD's campaign announcements and the policies of their coalition partner, the process of integration was not hindered.

Turning to the failures. In the first place, numerous intercoalitional conflicts between PSL and SLD either impeded or slowed down many crucial

Table 4.3 *(continued)*

Set of independent variables	B	SE	Beta	T
1997 (N=1054)				
Intelligentsia	–0.09	0.02	–0.10	–3.61
Weekly religious practices	–0.10	0.03	–0.11	–3.78
Urban residence (except Warsaw)	–0.07	0.03	–0.07	–2.58
Membership in "Solidarity" TU	–0.15	0.05	–0.08	–2.86
Former membership in PZPR	0.21	0.04	0.16	5.83
Employment in non-private sector	0.07	0.03	0.08	2.69
Per capita household income below 270 PLN	–0.05	0.03	–0.05	–1.71
(dis) privatization of state enterprises will help country's economy	0.09	0.03	0.11	3.74
(agr) economic situation of the country is favorable	–0.12	0.02	–0.13	–4.77
(dis) Atheists are unfit for public office	0.05	0.03	0.05	1.69
(agr) Church in our country is too influential	0.14	0.03	0.15	4.87
(agr) Abortion rights should be guaranteeed	0.11	0.03	0.12	3.77
(constant)	0.13	0.04		3.18
Variance explained = 23%				

Source: Data for 1992 and 1993 come from CEU longitudinal survey, "Party Formation and Electoral Alignments in Central and Eastern Europe"; data for 1997 are from Polish National Election Survey.

Note: All variables recoded into dummies.

Wording of all opinion/attitudinal items in the three surveys are exactly the same.

The OLS Regression After the Initial Logistic Regressions; All Variables Dichotomic, the Dependent Variable Codes: 1 - Would Vote for SLD, 0 - Would Vote for Other Party.

Dis=disagree, agr=agree.

changes, including health and social-security reforms, as well as administrative reform of the country. PSL's agricultural policies clearly resulted in the freezing of backward rural structures. "Soft" financial constraints in selected crucial branches: metallurgy, mining, rail, telecommunications, transportation, and shipyards, to name the most important ones, contributed to poor economic performance. The toleration of unprofitable industrial giants, the creation of numerous ineffective holdings (oil, sugar), statism, and the over-regulation of economic life are further examples of failed policies.

Both parties in the coalition, especially PSL, contributed to economic protectionism, paternalization of the economy as well as patrimonial recruitment, and promotion in the administration. The following example illustrates the growth of regulatory, statist measures as implemented by PSL/SLD coalition. Before 1993 there were eleven domains under governmental licensing; in 1996 economic activity in fifty domains required licensing.[16]

Generally, inefficient state companies benefited the most from the "generosity" of the PSL/SLD government, although economic growth was created mainly in the private sector. Poor redistribution of growing fiscal revenues was striking. This resulted in almost unlimited availability of funds for the state sec-

Table 4.4

Distribution of Select Political Party Support in Poland, 1992–97
(in percentages)

Profile of attitudes	Leftist	Liberal	Christian-national	Rightist	Total
October 1992 (N=1149)					
Political orientation (vote)					
None	39	39	53	51	46
Post-Solidarity	27	37	23	29	30
PSL	9	9	8	8	8
SLD	15	6	8	3	7
Other	10	9	8	9	9
Total	16.3	27.7	15.2	40.8	100.0%
August 1993 (N=1469)					
Political orientation (vote)					
None	30	35	37	45	39
Post-Solidarity	23	36	28	31	30
PSL	12	9	16	12	12
SLD	22	13	9	4	11
Other	13	7	10	8	8
Total	20.0	19.4	22.2	38.4	100.0%
September 1997 (N= 1054)					
Political orientation (vote)					
None	44	35	44	24	38
Post-Solidarity	13	9	35	39	20
PSL	5	1	3	4	3
SLD	26	23	4	11	18
UW	7	21	4	9	11
UP	2	5			2
ROP		5	7	6	4
Other	3	1	3	7	4
Total	31.6	31.6	21.4	15.4	100.0%

Source: as in Table 4.2
Note: For detailed description of the four "ideological groups," see note 17, pg. 87.

tor and consequently directed investment to branches of strategically secondary importance. Diverging economic policies towards the two sectors—market and non-market—became increasingly noteworthy (Wilczynski 1996).

For many interested observers however, policies of this coalition ought to be evaluated separately, and much credit for the successes was attributable to SLD-controlled branches. The three ministers of finance happened to be SLD representatives or prominent economists supported by it. All of them were eager—irrespective of tactical criticism—to continue Balcerowicz's reforms and assure sound fiscal policies. When the ambitious Grzegorz Kolodko revealed his "Strategy for Poland" in 1995, it became clear that the revolutionary rhetoric of the campaign had been substituted by economic "real politics" aimed at controlling the budget deficit, combating inflation, cutting down expenditures, and opening the economy to foreign investment. Extremely sound policies of the truly independent Polish National (Central) Bank, helped accomplish these tasks in times of growing populist pressures.

Thus, in sum, the 1993–97 parliament was a highly unrepresentative one, with 34 percent of votes wasted and an extremely high deviation from proportionality which created an artificial situation of "empty political space." The missing part of the space: in the sociocultural domain the rightist Christian-conservative representation, and in the economic domain the promarket liberal one. In such circumstances real politics forces the remaining parliamentary parties to fill this space. PSL was eager to switch to an all-national Christian-Democracy, remaining at the same time populist, statist, and protective in economic domain. SLD on their part has moved towards the promarket pole. They have embarked as well on a path towards pro-western, pro-European foreign policy, irregardless of some eastward-oriented rhetoric. In these two domains there appears to be more continuity than change in comparison to the Solidarity governments of the early 1990s. Contrary to the dire predictions of many observers in late 1993, budget deficits did not emerge.

Finally, apart from the substance of politics, what matters are technical and procedural skills as well as effectiveness in policy implementation. Public opinion surveys in 1997 showed Poles to be notably more satisfied than in 1993. The "Consumers' Optimism Indicator," surveyed regularly for the *Rzeczpospolita* daily, was highest (exceeding 100 points) in 1996–97 and lowest during ten months of 1993–94. Another longitudinal survey of CBOS (Public Opinion Research Center) showed that in 1997 almost the same proportion (25–30 percent) of adult Poles did evaluate the economic situation as good and bad, compared to about 5–7 percent and 55–60 percent, respectively, in 1993. A basic indicator of diffuse political support, assessing satisfaction with democracy, reveals this type of satisfaction to have doubled between 1993 and 1997, from around 20–25 percent in 1993 to about 40–55 percent from 1995–97 (as of 2000, the figure is down to about 30 percent). In terms of the average evaluation of "household financial condition" nearly 33 percent of respondents claimed it to be "good" and slightly above 20 percent to be "poor." The same figures for 1993 were 15–17 percent of the first opinion group and 40 percent of the second. The Central Statistical Office's hard data on households displayed a similar picture: wealth, real incomes, and consumption grew considerably compared to the early nineties. It should be noted however, that these positive trends were attributed almost exclusively to one of the coalition partners—the SLD.

A certain degree of political "cartelization" took place as well, but only some aspects of the phenomenon (Katz and Mair 1995) actually occurred, such as the "capital-intensive campaigns" and "blurred relationship between members and non-members" (Mair 1997, p. 113). The capital-intensive campaign was clearly visible during the presidential election of 1995 as well as the 1997 parliamentary election. The blurred relationships, although not easy to explain, derive from the legitimacy deficit of SdRP and SLD in the early 1990s. Apart from the strong and stable position of party leadership, many publicly known (semi-partisan) figures were invited to play the role of consultants or representatives of SLD. Finally, the SLD proved very successful in political statism and mixing party apparatus with the state civil servants. They also turned out to be successful in promoting their image as professionals and skilled managers.

To what extent can SLD be labeled as a modernizing agent? The issue has been raised on several occasions by András Bozóki (1997) in relation to both the Polish SdRP/SLD and the Hungarian Socialist Party (MSP). Two interesting questions arise: to what extent were these parties "forced" to embark on modernization policies (Bozóki 1997, p. 61) and in which policy areas did they perform as modernizers? After winning the 1993 election, the SLD inherited an economy growing at 4 percent per annum that displayed other initial signs of recovery. The main question at that time was whether to continue the sound macroeconomic policies of Balcerowicz and if yes, how to justify this dramatic policy switch. Fortunately for SLD, by the end of 1993 the debates over sociocultural issues, the role of the Church, the abortion law, and religious instruction at public schools were heated enough to drive away immediate attention from economics. In 1994 a certain duality emerged—the public rhetoric of SLD elites remained favorable towards egalitarian, welfarist policies on the one hand while tough yet tacit liberal macroeconomic policies were implemented on the other. With the passing of time SLD's economic policies became even more explicitly promarket and liberal, because of two factors: a "contextual," one, i.e. extreme populist policies pursued by their coalition partner, PSL, and the existence of "empty political space" in parliament which called for political representation.

Thus, the modernizing policies of SLD in power were more likely to be found in the sociocultural policy domain, rather than in the economic one. What is clear from the 1997/98 macroeconomic indicators is that SLD did contribute to a classical social-democratic consumerism. The extent to which they might have been forced to pursue modernization policies is twofold, they seemed to be deliberate and conscious modernizers in the sociocultural sphere, but semi-forced modernizers the economy. Had 1994 not been the third year of substantive economic growth—evidence that the liberal package launched by Balcerowicz worked—an incentive to try their "third way" ideas in practice would have likely surfaced. The SLD's economic modernization thus involved promoting consumerism accompanied by "social welfare generosity."

The SLD Out of Power: The Message of the 1997 Election

It is important to note that the vote totals for the PSL/SLD coalition in 1993 and 1997 were comparable—36 and 35 percent of the vote, respectively. Both parties' contribution to the former figure were relatively equal, between 15 to 20 percent respectively in 1993. However, this changed dramatically four years later, when the SLD received 27 percent of the vote to the PSL's 7 percent. This phenomenon shows sophistication of the average Polish voter— the governmental coalition has not been treated *en bloc* as an indistinguish- able entity—voters have been able to evaluate the deeds of both parties separately and act accordingly.

To understand the causes of the growth in the popularity of the SLD party, one has to turn back to the data in Tables 4.1 through 4.5. First, the simplest explanation is that the growth in SLD support might have been due to the general growth of leftist attitudes and opinions among electorally active Poles. Table 4.2, indicative of attitudes towards salient public issues, are divided into four groups:

(1) items C, D, F, G are indicative of the economic promarket versus state protectionist/redistributive dimension,[17]
(2) items H, N, P cover the religious-secular divide,
(3) items I, M, O are indicative of a nationalist/authoritarian versus cos- mopolitan/libertarian dimension,
(4) items E and K are general evaluations of the economic situation, the first stands for macro-conditions, the second, for microprospective conditions.

Growth of support for a leftist party could have come about due to the following changes:

(1) growth in antimarket sentiments,
(2) growth in secular preferences,
(3) growth in cosmopolitan/libertarian predispositions,
(4) increase in pessimism concerning the economic situation.

However, comparing column figures of Table 4.2 for 1993 and 1997 re- veals exactly the reverse picture—a clear growth of promarket attitudes, es- pecially towards privatization and company closure issues (by 21 percent) and, though less pronounced, of anti-egalitarianism and a decrease of state paternalism. What is even more striking is that SLD voters have changed considerably in the same direction, in some respects even more so than the general public (SLD voters are included into the general active voters group).[18] This applies for "proprivatization" as well as "acceptance of unprofitable companies closures," certainly not an indicator of a leftist ideological profile. If one traces changes in the religious-secular divide, one finds that Poles' attitudes have become more antisecular and more pro-Church (see the evaluation of the "influence of the Church" and "prolife stances on the abortion issue"). Yet the SLD voters did not change in the same direction, with the minor exception of their attitudes towards influence of the Church a change hardly favorable to the growth of the leftist party. In the nationalist/authoritarian versus the cosmopolitan/libertarian dimension, change seems to be more ambiguous and definitely less spectacular than in the economic one. Finally, the subjective evaluations of the macroeconomic situation and microeconomic prospects show—just as other public opinion data—that Poles has become increasingly optimistic. Good prospects of "getting ahead in life" and perceptions of the "economic situation of the country as not poor" has jumped by some 30 percent among adult Poles, and by 43 percent among SLD voters. Briefly, the analysis of attitudinal profiles among electorally active Poles does not permit us to claim that a leftist-favorable change has occurred—this cannot be the reason for the SLD's success.

Another hypothesis contends that the growth in SLD support can be attributed to differential levels of mobilization of the electorate. A glance at Table 4.4 shows that:

(a) the general size of the four ideological camps has changed substantially: leftist (for exact meaning see note 17) has grown by 12 percent and liberal by 13 percent, Christian-national has remained the same, and rightist has declined by 18 percent.

(b) The above observation might seem contradictory to the findings in Table 4.5, but this is only if we neglect the nonvoters row in Table 4.4. What happened over the four years is a tremendous growth of leftist nonvoters, although the leftist group has grown by 12 percent, the active voters within this group have in fact decreased by 2 percent, because the nonvoters subgroup has grown by 14 percent.

(c) The 13 percent increase in the liberal camp between 1993 and 1997 has all been channeled into the electoral arena, i.e. the nonvoters subgroup among liberals has remained high though the same. Quite the reverse story applies for the Christian-national party (ZChn), the general size of the group has remained the same (21%), yet those who withdrew from participation grew by 7 percent. Still another change occurred in the rightist group: a dramatic decrease of support in the population at large, is to a certain extent, counterbalanced by a relatively considerable change in their participatory mobilization.

(d) What do all these trends mean for SLD's electoral performance? First of all, as predicted by the analysis of Table 4.5, the leftist ideological group remains, in absolute terms, the one that contributes to SLD's support the most; nevertheless in the last four years it has grown by only 4 percent. The relatively highest growth in SLD support came from party orientation change in the liberal camp, by 10 percent. If we measure the liberal camp's support for SLD over three consecutive points in time (which correspond roughly to the elections of 1991, 1993, and 1997) comparing it to leftist support, one arrives at the following respective ratios: 2 : 5, almost 1 : 2, and almost 1 : 1. In other words, during the democratic transition in Poland an ample part of SLD's support was attributable to their persuasive skills towards individuals of liberal (i.e. promarket and secular) outlook.

(e) The most dramatic, and unexpected, change in SLD's support between 1993 and 1997 was their ability to attract Poles of rightist ideological orientation. Since the only ideological camp where SLD had lost support was the Christian-national one, it is clear that sociocultural issues worked for or against SLD depending on whether they were accompanied by pro- or antimarket economic outlooks. Growth in both liberal and rightist groups clearly indicates that promarket attitudes favor SLD voting, and that even sociocultural conservatives, if accompanied by promarket orientation, are favorably disposed towards the SLD.

The above findings lead us to speculate whether or not the SLD should still be treated as a leftist party. Let us begin with an examination of the population's general perception (by the society at large) of the SLD's position on a left-right scale. In 1991 about 77 percent labeled SLD as a leftist party, in 1993–78 percent, in 1995–76 percent, in 1996–74 percent, and in 1997–76 percent.[19] In short, virtually no change occurred in the general public's perception of SLD's leftism. In addition, no change in perceptions occurred between 1995 and 1997 of the SLD's position by SLD voters. In both cases about 82 percent labeled the party as leftist. In addition, there was a great deal of fluidity between the years 1995–1997 in SLD voters' self-identification; 58, 91, and 74 percent, respectively, referred to themselves as leftists in these years. And finally, leftist self-identities among adult Poles were fluctuating over the years: between 1990 and 1997 they fell below 13 percent and did not rise above 26 percent, within the 1993–97 period (around 20 percent plus/minus 4, on average). What is worth mentioning however, is the steady growth, since mid-1994, of definitely-rightist[20] self-identities, from about 10 to 20 percent. During the same period the definitely-leftist identities remained stable, at approximately a 10 percent level.

In other words, the SLD's image has remained leftist irrespective of the following:

(a) growth of rightist and liberal groups comprising SLD's electorate,
(b) an increase in promarket, sociocultural conservative attitudes among both Poles in general and SLD voters in particular,
(c) growth of overall rightist and strongly rightist self-identities among adult Poles. Symbols and political semantics seem to be extremely resistant to empirical reality.

A complete explanation of the growth in the SLD's support thus remains elusive, since examing attitudinal, sociodemographic, and symbolic-ideological factors in contextual design allowed us to exclude certain factors (Christian-nationalism) as determinants of this phenomenon. A final attempt has been designed to trace the direct determinants of SLD support. In Table 4.5, a set of selected factors were analyzed using the SLD vote as the dependent variable, yielding the following results:

(a) Compared to an analysis of previous (i.e. 1992 and 1993) SLD vote determinants, the model for 1997 explains much more of the variance: 23 percent, compared to 13 and 15 percent, respectively;
(b) The primary determinant of the SLD vote in 1997, after accounting for all other influences, was former PZPR membership. In 1992 and 1993 this factor was important, though we note its steady impact increase. Two remaining affiliative factors—trade union membership and Church attendance—continue to exert a direct, net effect on SLD vote. Rate of Church attendance contributes to explaining SLD vote, however a considerable part of its gross effect disappears when analyzed in a multifactoral design (its gross effect explains 6.3 percent of the dependent variable variance, its net, only 1.2 percent);
(c) A new factor that contributed notably to the SLD vote was the affective-cognitive opinion that "currently the economic situation of the country is favorable" for a respondent' s family. Several things are worth mentioning at this point: first, in 1997 the winners of the transformation contributed to the SLD's support. In previous elections, quite the opposite was true. Second, this positive evaluation of macroeconomic conditions directly impacted the SLD vote, almost entirely independent of other influences.[21] Third, this positive evaluation of the results of the economic transformation was not, however, associated with the main cause—privatization of state-owned property; the SLD vote was influenced by antiprivatization attitudes;
(d) Sociocultural issues did influence the SLD vote in the same way as they did at the beginning of the transformation. Support for the SLD depended considerably on their pro-choice abortion policy

stance, and their effort to constrain the Church's influence. Both factors were highly correlated, so their gross effect (r= .28 and .30, respectively) disappeared and the direct one proved to be mŕod-est, although important (see 'beta' standardized coefficients in Table 4.5). Noteworthy is the fact, however, that in 1997 the im-pact of these factors on the SLD vote was even more prominent than before;

(e) Finally, there were less salient structural factors—not belonging to the "intelligentsia," employment in a non-private sector, residence in urban areas, though not in Warsaw—which contributed in 1997 to the SLD's support.

In conclusion, formal social ties—organizational affiliations indicative of the "regime divide" and historico-symbolic links—matter most. These fac-tors, accompanied by a clear mixture of secular attitudes and a satisfaction with the economic situation, contributed to greater votes for the SLD. Its electorate were found mainly in urban areas, among medium-ranked white-collars with a secondary education (variables missing in the final model, though important), and state or public employees. This is where the SLD's appeal was most successful in 1997.

In Table 4.5 a dynamic regression model is applied. The model presented is aimed at revealing this dynamic phenomenon of growth in SLD support.

From these results, the message is relatively clear—apart from certain constants in SLD support, there are a few specific factors responsible for the growth of SLD support between 1993–97. The crucial ones were the attitu-dinal stances on the issue of abortion and evaluation of economic conditions. Slightly less—though worth mentioning—are two socio-demographic fac-tors: living anywhere outside medium-size towns (fifty to one-hundred thou-sand inhabitants) and higher than average per capita household income.

The model explains 6 percent of the change in SLD support between 1993 and 1997. Affiliation factors and trade union membership did not account for SLD growth in the latter period, nor did some of the indicators of "au-thoritarian/nationalist" orientation. The growth did not come, as in 1993, from the public sector employees (see Table 4.5), although they still remained an important support group (see Table 4.2). The real growth of support came from those satisfied with the condition of the economy.

In the final part of this section, I would like to address another set of issues. Since support for SLD more than doubled between 1991 and 1997, and data shows that newcomers to the SLD's camp are not necessarily from a classical leftist electorate, it is plausible to expect that this new electorate will be more heterogeneous and/or feel less identification with the SLD. This might contrib-ute to the parts of the spectrum by the placement of SLD into different places in the Polish electorate. Table 4.6 presents the mean location of SLD voters in a

Table 4.5

The Model of Determinants of SLD Support Growth in 1992–93 and 1993-97

Set of independent variables	B	SE	Beta	T
a) 1992-93				
(dis)President granted extraordinary powers	0.11	0.03	0.15	4.49
Membership in NSZZ Solidarity	−0.11	0.05	−0.07	−2.19
Membership in OPZZ	−0.32	0.08	−0.14	−4.18
(agr) Church is too influential	0.08	0.03	0.10	3.01
Public sector employee	0.08	0.02	0.12	3.59
(dis) Politicians should rather be experts				
than patriots	0.05	0.02	0.07	2.21
Constant	−0.13	0.03		−4.49
Variance explained = 7%				
b) 1993–97				
Residence in towns between 50–100 thousand	−0.11	0.03	−0.13	−4.05
Per capita household income over 500 PLN	0.05	0.03	0.07	2.02
(agr) Abortion rights should be guaranteed	0.12	0.02	0.15	4.79
(dis) Economic situation of the country is	−0.12	0.02	−0.15	−4.75
favorable				
Constant	0.08	0.03		3.24
Variance explained = 6%				

Source: subtable (a) from CEU data; subtable (b) from Polish National Election Survey data; for details see table 4.2.
Note: Regression Analysis, Dependent Variable - Change in SLD Support.
   dis=disagree, agr=agree

three-dimensional political space at four points in time.[22]

The first hypothesis concerning the growing diffuseness of the electorate is not confirmed. The standard deviations of religious fundamentalism–secularism [R-S] dimension support the prediction (if the comparison starts in 1992), however the nationalist/authoritarian–cosmopolitan/libertarian [N/A-C/L] divide unveils a change to the contrary. The economic promarket liberalism–redistributive state paternalism [EL-SP] dimension simply did not change.

The second hypothesis predicted change in the mean location of the growing size of the SLD electorate towards, and in accordance with, the general trends of society at large (see Tables 4.2 and 4.4). The data makes it clear that SLD supporters occupied an apparently secular position in 1992, which shifted from extremely radical to less radically secular position. No significant change, however, has occurred in the last four years. No other Polish party's electorate came close to SLD voters' secular-radicalism. Next, between 1993 and 1995, SLD voters became, on average, more centrist on the economic dimension [EL-SP], moving away from a redistributive state-protectionist po-

Table 4.6

Location of SLD Voters in the Polish Political Space, 1992–97

	Dimensions						
	R–S*		EL–SP**		N/A–C/L***		N
SLD voters:	x	SD	x	SD	x	SD	
1992	−0.81	0.50	0.27	1.08	−0.05	1.31	30
1993	−0.67	0.66	0.33	0.98	0.27	1.31	47
1995	−0.63	0.54	0.03	1.50	0.12	1.09	178
1997	−0.69	0.69	0.07	1.04	0.05	1.03	278

Source: Data for 1992, 1993, 1995 – from CEU longitudinal project "Party Formation and Electoral Alignments; data for 1997 – Polish National Election Survey
Notes: Entries of column "x" are means of factor scores (varimax rotated) created on the basis of the list of items presented in Table 4.2; entries of column "SD" are their standard deviations.
  *religious fundamentalism—secularism
 **pro-market liberalism—redistributive state paternalism
***nationalism/authoritarianism—cosmopolitanism/libertarianism

sition. This change has not been accompanied by an increase in diffuseness, thus making it more likely that the switch from leftist-protectionist, populist policies is a real and stable change.

Finally, the interactive effect between the mean position and heterogeneity of the N/A-C/L dimension, reveals that SLD voters have moved from a moderately nationalist/authoritarian position to a moderately cosmopolitan/ libertarian one. Coupled with a notably decreasing diffuseness of this dimension among a considerably larger electorate seems to indicate a consolidation of their cosmopolitan/libertarian profile. Overall, there occurred a substantial change in SLD's electoral position in the political sphere. Taking into account its decreasing heterogeneity, this suggests that the SLD's electorate is becoming crystallized and is likely to remain durable.

Since one of the major concerns of the present volume is whether and to what extent successor parties adopt nationalistic policies, we need to look in more detail at the policy stances indicative of nationalism. Table 4.2 indicates that the view "nationalism is harmful for the country" was shared by 66 and 72 percent of SLD's electorate in 1993 and 1997, respectively, indicating a noticeable overrepresentation of this viewpoint by SLD voters as compared to the general public. Disagreement with another statement indicative of nationalism ("politicians should rather be experts than patriots") reveals a 10 percent difference with the general adult population of Poles and a change in time; SLD's voters are less nationalistic than voters of other parties and they became even less so in 1997.

Now, if we turn to the political elites' (party leaders) judgments (Kitschelt,

Mansfeldova, Markowski, Tóka 1999), a clear issue indicative of the nation-alist–cosmopolitan divide[23] shows SLD's mean location (on a twenty-point scale) is at point 13.5 (an average judgment of juries from all relevant par-ties), closer to the cosmopolitan edge; only Polish Democratic Union (UD) (15.9) and Liberal Democratic Congress (KLD) (18.0) proved to be more cosmopolitan. The other pole is occupied by Christian National Union (ZChN) (3.4). To summarize, there is virtually no evidence that SLD seeks a nation-alist appeal; quite to the contrary, SLD elites should be labeled "cosmopoli-tan." The same message comes from an analysis of SLD's popular images (CEU project, data not shown) and their manifestoes (Materska-Sosnowska 1997; Slodkowska 1997), especially after the party's 1994 switch towards a western-orientated foreign policy stance.

Let us now check the impact of the "communist legacy" factor; i.e. exam-ine whether the affective and policy proximity indicators are aligned or dis-torted. The results indicated by columns 1 and 3 of Table 4.7 are quite straightforward. The affective component of the interparty relationship ex-hibits some ideological and/or programmatic ordering. Indeed, SLD elites' sympathy for UP and PSL, as well as for UD, can be easily explained by a mixture of programmatic or tactical factors. The reverse—other party elites' sympathy for SLD—reveals a more complicated picture. Apart from UP elites, virtually all others display strong or moderate antipathy towards SLD. If we look at this data in a different way, another conclusion can be drawn; "sym-pathetic fits" are more likely to be found between the SLD and parties of the so-called Polish "right" than between the SLD and their immediate neigh-bors on the left of the political spectrum (with the exception of UP).

The analysis of "sympathetic fits" calculated on the basis of subtracting absolute differences between the affective reciprocity of all Polish parties reveals that:

(a) the net negative fit, that is absolute antipathy toward SLD, is defi-nitely highest compared to all other Polish parties (–2.69) and
(b) the asymmetrical, that is nonreciprocal relationship, is highest as well (3.39).

The numerical expressions in brackets are highly abstract and have only relative meaning, either as measures of distance to the other parties in the same party system or compared to other post-communist parties of the region vis-à-vis their party competitors. In comparison to other post-communist "sister parties" of the region, SLD's relationships with other po-litical entities appear reasonably rational—that is, moderately biased by emotional residuals. By comparison: the negative fit of the Bulgarian So-cialist Party is more than twice as high (–6.23) and the affective asymmetry almost twice as large (6.23). The affective–rational relation to Czech/Moravian

Table 4.7

Affective-Programmatic Distances Between SLD and Other Relevant Parties in Poland, 1993–94

	Elites				Masses	
	SLD's sympathy for other parties	Weighted issue-distances (ideological placement)	Other parties' sympathies for SLD	SLD's repre-sentativeness for other parties	Issue-distance (ideological placement)	Representativeness of the other parties for SLD voters
UP	6.24	202	4.24	5.14	1.08	4.37
PSL	5.57	293	0.76	5.65	1.29	4.74
UD	3.32	288	-3.14	4.79	1.45	3.73
KLD	1.57	419	-3.99	3.32	1.60	3.73
BBWR	0.51	383	-6.47	2.83	2.40	2.82
"S"	-6.09	414	-6.08	5.31	1.57	3.77
KPN	-7.09	417	-5.28	2.80	1.08	3.71
PC	-7.09	459	-7.61	2.53	1.41	3.50
ZChN	-7.26	517	-6.66	2.09	2.49	3.33

Sources: The elite data come from the project, "Party Formation in Eastern Europe," headed by H. Kitschelt, conducted in 1993/94; the masses data—from CEU longitudinal survey.

Note: Entries of columns are presented in raw (unstandarized) form and are not comparable across elite-mass columns. Entries within each column are comparable, though only relatively.

post-communists reveals a figure of –4.64 for the negative fit and 4.64 for asymmetry. In Hungary, the same figures are –3.49 and 3.50, respectively. In brief, the hypothesis that a communist-legacy factor strongly influences interparty affective relations is clearly supported by the cases of intransigent Communist Party of Bohemia and Moravia (KSCM) and partially recycled Bulgarian Socialist Party (BSP), in both the Czech Republic and Bulgaria. Where real programmatic and policy implementation changes have occurred, for the Polish social-democrats and Hungarian socialists, the affective symmetry is more pronounced.

To show the broader picture of distances between parties as perceived by elites and masses, correlations between policy distance and sympathies/representativeness scores were calculated. The results are compelling—on the mass level the correlation between the representativeness of other parties for SLD voters and issue-distances between those parties is much higher (.73) than between the representativeness within the SLD for other parties' voters and issue-distances (.57); the latter being a statistically insignificant coefficient. On the elite level this difference is absent; sympathies of SLD politicians towards other parties, sympathies towards the SLD among politicians of other parties, and issue-distances are almost equal (correlations of .87 and .89, respectively).

Recent Developments and Trends, 1997–2001

In April 1999 the SLD transformed itself into a unitary party, with the former leader of SdRP, Leszek Miller, as its first president. Almost all of the previously allied thirty-two organizations (most of them trade unions and associations) decided to unite their forces and create a single political party.

By the end of 1999, the SLD's assets looked impressive, it contained roughly 80,000 members (SdRP could barely claim 40,000). About one-third were young people (below thirty) and an equal amount were recruited from "newcomers to politics." There was also an impressive enrollment of former communist party members. The new SLD program and their congressional declaration reveal further efforts to distance the party from the communist past, condemning its atrocities and economic ineffectiveness. Future policies promised attractive accomplishments in many domains; although education, agriculture, and construction were at the fore. Significant new policies were also devoted to corruption, justice and cuts in the administration. On the other hand, the role of the state was expected to increase, both economically and in the social welfare domain. No hints at lowering tax burdens or boosting privatization were present in the documents.

The years 1997–2000 showed further growth in SLD's support. Opinion polls recently indicated stable support of about 40 percent of the electorate. To be sure, provided that only several negligible parties contest the forthcoming election, and given that the electoral law retains its 5 and 8 percent entry thresholds for parties and coalitions, it is very likely that SLD will be able to form a single-party majority government in the next election.

Who are the new 10-plus percent supporters of the SLD? Survey results indicate that the new SLD supporters are:

(a) more centrist in many detailed policy/issue areas;
(b) considerably younger;
(c) less educated;
(d) poorer;
(e) living in smaller cities and villages;
(f) more religious;
(g) less interested in politics, more politically apathetic.

This profile also tells us that they are more optimistic about the future, leaning towards liberal solutions in the economic domain, and more politically neutral (i.e. evaluating the reforms in an independent manner; assessing more equally the leftist and rightist politicians).

With the passing of time and the broadening of the social base of support for SLD two observations can be made: first, this support can be explained by both sociodemographic and issue stances,[24] and second, the number of important explanatory factors decreases. After 1997, formerly important variables like education, place of residence, and age become much less significant in explaining SLD support than prior to 1997. During this time two issues contributed most to the explanation of this support: attitude towards religion and the Church (in 1997 in particular) and attitudes towards decommunization. During the nineties however, the single most important factor was "left-right self-identification," which in the year 2000 became more important than in the early 1990s. If one examines the expanded SLD electorate via issue/policy preferences, it is clear that the bigger part of this new electorate is made up of Poles of a centrist and center-right orientation. A logical consequence would be to see the mean self-identification of the SLD's electorate move in a more rightist direction. This, however, did not occur. The party maintains a strong leftist image, and those who switch to support the SLD change their left-right identification in accordance with the party's label, not the other way around.

Finally, Table 4.8 attempts to depict the dynamic nature of the SLD's support. Socio-demographic and issue factors turn out to explain about 7 percent of the SLD's growth in support. The most significant increase in support comes from the less educated, the young, and those not interested in politics. In addition, there are a number of policy preferences expressed by these voters that clearly do not belong to the traditional leftist repertoire: rejection of the state's social safety net and decreased emphasis on unem-

Table 4.8

The Model of Determinants of SLD Support Growth in 1997–2000

Set of independent variables	B	SE	Beta	T
Level of education: (lower)	-0.08	0.04	-0.09	-1.87
Age: (young people below 30)	-0.10	0.04	-0.10	-2.31
Not interested in politics	-0.13	0.06	-0.11	-2.29
Agreement:				
Church is too influential	0.08	0.04	0.09	1.90
Nationwide redistribution is always unfair	0.01	0.01	0.08	1.69
Reduce state's involvement in the economy	0.01	0.01	-0.09	-0.1.86
Poland should be governed by eminent leader	-0.02	0.01	-0.13	-2.84
The economy should be state-controlled	0.01	0.01	0.08	1.69
Unemployment is less important than other policy areas	0.02	0.01	0.11	2.26
State should take care of citizens social safety net	-0.02	0.01	-0.10	-2.06
Constant =	0.27	0.09	—	3.00
Variance explained =	7%			

Note: Regression Analysis, Dependent Variable - Change in SLD Support.

ployment as a major policy area. What is new, compared to the previous stages (1991–93 and 1993–97), is the decreased importance of religious factors and attitudes towards a communist past. The latter phenomenon seems a logical consequence of four years of practical reforms implemented in Poland. Economic issues have finally gained importance after nearly a decade of emphasis on sociocultural issues. One caveat, however, is that this message applies only to the determinants of the dynamic variable-growth of SLD support during their period as an opposition party (1997 to present).

This phenomenon would not have been possible had it not been for the extremely poor performance of the rightist parties after 1997. The reforms implemented appeared unplanned and ill prepared. Briefly, the growth of SLD support is attributable equally to the failures of the rightist government as well as to the "procedural correctness" of SLD's public behavior. Contrary to its major rightist counterpart, AWS, SLD is a disciplined parliamentary entity, with effective organization at the local level, and behaves in accordance with democratic procedures and rules.

The SLD has learned the lesson of democratic politics very effectively, with a little help from their rightist rivals. In my view, the classical explanatory variables of their party strength such as organizational capacity and material or human (membership, activists) assets contributed only to a limited extent to their political success. I also find no indication that their political success was linked to effective management of the relationship between their apparatus and activists. The latter has been an important issue, significant for PZPR/ SdRP decision-makers during the heated period of 1989–1990. As long as high levels of uncertainty remained constant, the role of the former activists and apparatchiks diminished. Virtually no indication of any grass-roots pressure or revolt was registered in the 1990s. No SdRP/SLD Congress or any other formal meeting has witnessed an attempt by the grass-roots activists to contest the leadership, which remains stable and cooperative. The party has noticeably become a hierarchical top-down organized structure. The point that I question is whether the SLD's organizational superiority inherited from communist times was a crucial factor in explaining its later success (Rivera 1996). Had this been the case, their superiority over their political rivals would have been most apparent at the beginning of the transformation, when the difference between SdRP and other political entities in organizational capacity and material assets was greatest. This, however, was clearly not the case.[25] As the transformative time passes these assets became more equally distributed among political parties. Thus, Poland seems to be an exceptionally plausible case for the argument I have made. Indeed, the relatively poorest electoral outcome of SLD in 1991 occurred exactly at the time when both (relative to other parties) their assets were impressive and when the euphoric, protective mechanisms of the first period, which might have contributed "artificially" to the success of the noncommunist parties, was over.

Conclusions

From the above chapter, several conclusions can be drawn:

(1)   There were constant structural determinants of voting for SLD in the1990s. Their supporters were more likely to be found among the following: middle-ranked state sector employees, retired people and pensioners, those employed outside the private sector, former PZPR, current OPZZ members, and those who were unlikely to be frequent churchgoers. Supporters were generally negatively disposed towards liberal economic policies; however this was more likely to be the case at the beginning of the transformation than by the end of the decade.

(2)   Apart from static determinants of SLD support there are factors that contributed to the dynamics of the change. The growth of SLD support in the early 1990s can be attributed to the effectiveness of their appeal to OPZZ trade union members and public sector employees. Clear stances on a set of sociocultural issues concerning the Church, nationalism, and the extraordinary powers of the president have also advanced SLD growth. The increase of SLD support between 1993 and 1997 is of a different origin; their accomplishments proved attractive to residents of villages and small towns as well as urban areas and those with a relatively high per capita household income. Yet these two groups were overrepresented among the "converts" to SLD. Newcomers to the SLD camp between 1997–2000 were more likely to be optimistic about future prospects and definitely pro-choice on the abortion issue. The latter indicates that an anti-clerical mood among a sizable segment of Polish society in the 1990s has been a rich source of SLD recruitment.

(3)   These new supporters of SLD are more likely to be present among people of relatively good standing, and although this factor does not contribute notably to overall SLD performance (it is missing from the static model of SLD support), it did affect the 1993–97 growth in support. Earlier supporters were to be found mainly among two groups outside the leftist ideological camp: the liberals and rightists. Indeed, SLD attracted 11 percent of those who are believed to be adherents of the opposite ideological camp.

(4)   On the one hand, from a purely sociological point of view, SLD remains popular among the likely losers of the transformation (retirees, trade union members, state employees of medium-rank positions; those of lower-medium per capita income). On the other, the "ideological" and attitudinal profile of this electorate, especially during

and after 1997, reveals that SLD supporters are fairly satisfied with their future individual and economic prospects. Although apparently contradictory, I submit here that current SLD support comes mainly from those representatives of the "would-be loser groups" who are, as individuals, actually doing quite well. Such a configuration—a leftist collective identity coupled with relative satisfaction with reforms—clearly favors the SLD. Moreover in the last three years, the majority of the population has further become dissatisfied with both the content outcomes of reforms launched by the AWS-dominated government and by the way procedural politics has been managed by the rightist incumbents. This in turn has contributed—via a different mechanism—to further growth in SLD support performance.

(5)   The interpretation of the 1993–97 SLD fate and support plausibly fits the descriptive part of the economic-redistributive deeds of the SLD/PSL government. Soft budgetary constraints, "cheap credits," generous welfare benefits, and similar policies of 1993–97 were welcomed by and benefited those oriented towards immediate consumption; that is, the majority of the population. The very same policies proved troublesome for economists concerned with the condition of the Polish economy in the new millennium. Public finances in 1997 were in poorer condition than the Polish economy. The scope of "mandatory expenditures" and public debt's technical costs obstruct finding funds for developmental objectives. A general abandonment of reform turned out to be a comfortable and politically beneficial way of "staying" in power. It proved wise from a socio and psychological standpoint to introduce a period of calm (i.e. 1989–93).

The new rightist government installed in 1997 offered four major reforms (of the pension-system, healthcare, education, and bureaucracy), tough fiscal policies, and many austerity measures which were quite unpopular. In politics one can distinguish between mechanisms that attract voters and mechanisms that repel them. In real political life the two coexist and impact reality simultaneously; but, in the case of the last three years, the electoral success of SLD can be mainly attributed to the negative experiences with the AWS/UW government. In Poland we have entered, perhaps permanently, a specific political-business cycle in which the role of the unpopular and politically costly great reformist plans are assigned to the post-Solidarity camp while long-term beneficial results are likely to be "consumed" by the post-communists and their allies.

(6)   Another meta-factor present in the 1993–97 period which contributed to SLD's popularity was the external situation. One might say

their "foreign policy." The real influence of any Polish govern-ments' foreign policy on the external world is limited. The Slovak case exemplifies the ample effects of embarking on internationally unaccepted policies. In this sense, SLD did follow the norms of the international community and did not obstruct the clearly prowestern aspirations of the majority of Poles. SLD politicians were both effective in achieving the main goals of Polish foreign policy and were even more effective at presenting them as their exclusive successes.

(7)   SLD politicians turned out to be capable of convincing the general public of their meritocratic and professional skills; to a relative extent they were less agents of "substantive" as opposed to purely "procedural" democracy, as is also the case with Hungarian MSZP elites (Bozóki 1997, p. 72). The successful passage of many bills and the implementation of policies can clearly be attributed to their procedural competence. In the long run, an image of the SLD as an effective party has been shared by many Poles. This phenomenon has been both conducive to the "cartelization" process and benefi-cial to the party in the electoral realm.

(8)   The SLD's modernization drive ought be labeled "followers' mod-ernization"; even the slightest classically social-democratic policy—ideas in improving, for example, employment or social welfare policies, were in reality missing from the SLD's program, except for boosting welfare "generosity." The SLD's position on economic issues has been more vague than on sociocultural ones; in the lat-ter domain SLD established itself as a serious advocate of secular policies. Thus, if one believes that secularization is an attribute of modernization, SLD is a champion of this trend. This seems to be the main reason why, irrespective of the changes in the SLD's ef-fectiveness in attracting rightist and liberal ideological groups, their public image remains clearly leftist.

(9)   Attracting adherents of ideologically distant groups did not alter the SLD's leftist public image, but contributed to its new inclusive image. The overall range of political alternatives for SLD voters did not change between 1993 and 1997. All this seems to indicate a clear solidification and support of elite mass, as well as develop-ment of a party identification among SLD supporters.

(10) The above review of their deeds, followers, and organizational changes forces one to reconsider whether SLD/SdRP can still be labeled a postcommunist party. The merits of their policies, in-cluding the failures, resemble what one can find in any socialist or social-democratic package. Their "procedural correctness" and ob-servation of the democratic rules of the game is clear. True, the

special links some SdRP politicians appear to have retained with their Russian counterparts might seem troublesome, yet are again hardly specific to the former dominant ideology.

(11) The crucial meta-factor influencing the successful outcome of the Polish SLD/SdRP appears to lie in the peculiarities of the Polish "national adaptive" version of "real" socialism. This eclectic reality consistently fostered unintentional tolerance, self-reliance, individual freedom, and self-organization—relatively to the regional norm, of course. By the end of the 1970s, a well-organized alternative society with its own institutional infrastructure, independent norms, and rules of conduct contributed to the conviction that political sphere could be ignored. The combined existence of alternatives, tolerance, and flexibility towards neutrality and ignorance ultimately played a key role in the SLD's acceptance among voters. The protracted agony of socialism in Poland as well as its pioneering transformative status have created a mood of "relativeness." This phenomenon and its relationship with SLD's fate is hard to trace in empirical projects based on sociological surveys; fortunately its impact can plausibly be unveiled in comparative designs—an initiatory of this sort is presented elsewhere (Kitschelt, Mansfeldova, Markowski, Tóka 1999). The consequences of specific configuration at the Polish Round Table and the initial years of intra-Solidarity camp struggles coupled with SLD's procedural correctness have clearly been profitable electorally.

Finally, it is apt to paraphrase SLD's own electoral slogan: "it could have been better." In this historically important time of modernization or "catching up" with the rest of Europe, the four years (1993–1997) could have been spent more effectively. In brief, the SLD's tactical success was achieved at the expense of real strategic, policy-oriented achievements. Nonetheless, the SLD has survived and flourished, and maneuvered itself to the brink of power. Indeed, these tactical successes, coupled with the failures of the post-Solidarity camp (1997–2001) greatly contributed to the SLD's triumphal electoral comeback in the fall of 2001.

Notes

1. In the remainder of the chapter I will refer to SLD as a political party, though for most of the nineties it has been a coalition of numerous entities (details further on in the text). Yet from the electoral point of view—dominant in this chapter—there are good reasons to treat SLD as a party, as it is the only parliamentary and electoral entity that exists for voters. The same reasoning applies to the governmental and parliamentary deeds; rarely, if ever, has SdRP played any role as a distinct actor in

these two institutional domains. Finally, in April 1999 a new party under the logo of SLD was officially registered; consequently SdRP ceased to exist.

2. Especially in the fifties and sixties, and in some countries (Bulgaria, Romania) more than in others.

3. This interpretation of the satellite parties' role should be understood precisely as follows: satellite parties (ZSL, SD, and other "Christian" organizations) had virtually no say in strategic issues, foreign policy alliances, macro-economic policies, and similar matters. But precisely because of this, as well as the lively ideas of the "national way" (proclaimed by Gomulka in the early years of socialism), and the rebellious mood of the Polish society, several policy niches were created. These domains were more open to pragmatic, non-ideological rationality, aimed at pursuing sectoral interests, which promoted a very particular type of controlled pluralism. Ultimately it led to a notable acceptance of innovation, clearly visible only after the collapse of the socialist experiment.

4. See: *Biuletyn Informacyjny SdRP*, 1995 nos. 1 and 2, pp. 1–2.

5. AWS stands for *Akcja Wyborcza "Solidarnosc"* ("Solidarity" Electoral Action).

6. In 1989 the president was elected by the General Assembly.

7. Since 1997 public opinion polls show continued support of SLD; in 2000 the average figures fluctuated between 37 and 44 percent.

8. These are: Leszek Miller, Jozef Oleksy, Jerzy Szmajdzinski, Izabella Sierakowska, Marek Borowski, Aleksander Kwasniewski (active in SdRP only until the presidential election of 1995), and Krzysztof Janik.

9. For an in-depth discussion of the topic see: Sarlvik and Crewe 1983; Scarbrough 1987; Dunleavy 1987; Denver 1989; Heath et al. 1991.

10. The official electoral result of SLD was 11.99 percent, however in the 1991 exit-poll by INFAS/OBOP (just as in most other public opinion polls of early 1990s) SLD was underrepresented by almost 3 percent; the figure amounted to only 9.1 percent. It is thus plausible to assume that the real vote of the two most supportive groups was slightly higher than indicated in Table 4.1.

11. The 1992 and 1993 data are from Central European University's longitudinal project entitled "Formation of Party Systems and Electoral Alignments in East Central Europe," headed by Gábor Tóka; the 1997 data are from the Polish National Election Survey (PGSW), headed by R. Markowski. All remaining tables in the text, except if otherwise indicated, come from these two projects.

12. The 5 percent derives from an assumption that the 1991–93 growth was a steady one. Since our data-gathering starts only in the fall of 1992, we submit the figure equals about half of the overall growth between the two elections. The 2.4 percent figure was obtained by multiplying the impact (B coefficient value) of three important determinants of SLD support (see Table 4.2; namely attitudes towards privatization and company closures as well as a general growth in economic pessimism) by the size of change that occurred between 1992 and 1993, which gave us a figure equaling 1.8% [(11% * .06) + (17% * .05) + (6% * .05) = 1.8%]. The remaining .06% comes from an estimation of the change in the socio-demographic variables that influenced SLD support in 1992 (see Table 4.3) and at the same time did change between 1992 and 1993 (see Table 4.2).

13. Explanation of the exact content of the "ideological groups" is due. The very basis are two dimensions each composed of different attitudes/stances: (a) first, indicative for pro- vs. anti-market attitudes: items F and G, representative of privatization and unprofitable companies and (b) for, a depiction of pro- vs. anti-liberal sociocul-

tural views, at least two of the following items: P (influence of the Church), R (extraordinary presidential powers), H (atheists in public office). Next, four combinations of the two dimensions create the four "ideological groups," i.e. the leftist ideology consists of anti-market economic and liberal sociocultural attitudes; liberal—of promarket economic and liberal sociocultural attitudes; Christian-national—of anti-market economic and anti-liberal sociocultural attitudes, and rightist—of promarket economic and anti-liberal sociocultural attitudes. The ideological labels are thus obviously simplified approximations of otherwise complex, multi-dimensional connotations of the concepts used; nevertheless the variables used seem to cover the central traits of these political ideologies.

14. Even the most promarket, cosmopolitan party, accused by many of rigid liberal ideologization of the economic policies—KLD (Liberal-Democratic Congress)—came forward with several electoral promises, which easily could be classified as "populist."

15. The public debt went down from 86 to 70 percent in 1994 alone; mainly due to the previous government's agreement with the London Club on Polish debt reduction. In 1995, it decreased to 58 percent.

16. In fact, if one adds the licensing requirements at the local and district levels the number goes up to almost a hundred in 1996.

17. Grouping of the items presented here corresponds to the dimensions obtained empirically when factor analysis is applied; three of them almost exactly resemble the three dimensions presented in Table 4.6. Among the items/statements of the first (economic) dimension, the three crucial items are C, F, and G. Item D (egalitarianism) in the factor analysis, quite often, depending on the year, weakly stresses this dimension or constitutes the nationalist/authoritarian versus cosmopolitan/libertarian dimension.

18. For the sake of comparison I present here data for all active voters; it serves the regression analysis estimations, as well as a description of a general public mood in the 1990s. Nevertheless, one ought be aware that were we to exclude the SLD voters from the general electorate for 1993 and 1997, the difference between SLD voters and the remaining politically active Poles (that is electorates of all other parties) would have been even more significant.

19. The data for 1992, 1993, and 1995 comes from the Electoral Studies Division of the Institute of Political Studies surveys, for 1996 from CBOS omnibus surveys (see Pankowski 1997), and for 1997 from the Polish National Election Survey.

20. "Definitely-rightist" is not an evaluative term here, nor does it denote the phenomenon of rightist extremism; it simply means that more Poles than ever identify themselves as definitely being on the right side of the political spectrum, i.e. on a seven point left-right scale chose point seven.

21. Simple correlation between this factor and the SLD vote is: –.14 and the standardized 'beta' coefficient –.13, which means that the gross and net effects are virtually the same.

22. The three dimensions are a result of factor analysis (with Varimax rotation) of the attitudinal/opinion items presented in Table 4.2. The three dimensions are labeled as: [i] religious fundamentalism, i.e. secularism (most of the time based on high factor loadings of items H, N, P), [ii] economic pro-market liberalism and redistributive state paternalism (items C, F, G; rarely D), and [iii] nationalism/authoritarianism—cosmopolitanism/libertarianism (items I, M, O). The acronyms for the three dimensions are: "R-S," "EL-SP," "N/A-C/L." All presented factors, at all points in time reveal eigenvalues greater than 1 and explained variance over 10

percent. The entries in Table 4. 6 are factor scores' means and standard deviations for locations of SLD voters.

23. The wording of the quoted question was: "Please place each of the parties on a scale, one end of which stands for/and indicates the necessity for pursuing a historical and cultural Polish distinctiveness and the other, a strong drive towards cosmopolitan interdependencies and the opening of Poland to Western Europe and global development."

24. In the early 1990s OLS regression models show approximately a 10–12 percent deviation of this support being explained by a set of variables. In 1997 the same figure goes up to 26 percent.

25. The same mode of reasoning applies to another, post-communist party which was successful in transferring their material assets from the 1980s into 1990s, namely former ZSL (currently PSL). The support they enjoy shows little logical relationship to the relative magnitude of their organizational assets.

5

The Hungarian Socialists

Technocratic Modernizationism or New Social Democracy?

András Bozóki

The purpose of this chapter is to discuss the question: What kind of change in identity is needed for a former communist party to reform itself toward social-democratization and become a successful successor party at the same time? What are the changing and continuous elements of its identity and policies? Which factors of its social context shaped most the party's adaptation process? These questions will be investigated through a case study of a decade-long history of the Hungarian Socialist Party (*Magyar Szocialista Párt*, MSZP).

The MSZP was born on October 7, 1989, as a legal successor of the communist Hungarian Socialist Worker's Party (*Magyar Szocialista Munkáspárt*, MSZMP) which had monopolized power in Hungary for over four decades. Now more than a decade after, the MSZP is a respected member of the Socialist International and has transformed itself into one of the most popular parties in the country. The party returned to power in 1994 and stayed there until 1998, and was in opposition until their successful comeback in the elections of 2002. How can we explain and evaluate these changes?

Looking at the literature, it seems taken for granted that the MSZP represents a success story as far as a communist successor party transformation is concerned (Ágh 1995, Mahr and Nagle 1995, Waller 1995, Szelényi, Fodor and Hanley 1997, Orenstein 1998, Racz 1999, Ágh, Géczi and Sipos 1999). The different forms and meanings of social democracy and the ideology of the Left in the context of postcommunist democracy, however, still need to be explained.[1]

The concept of social democracy went through substantial changes in the international political scene, from Eduard Bernstein to Willy Brandt; from Jean Jaures to Francois Mitterrand (Bernstein 1961, Pelinka 1983, Goodwin 1987, Kitschelt 1994). In more than a century, it changed from a major political force of class struggle (Bartolini 2000) to a broader, reformist movement of materialist, and later also post-materialist values. During the second part of the twentieth century, important debates occurred over the nature of democratic socialism, the possibility of market socialism, or the attractivity of "humanized socialism," and their relations to both communism and social democracy (Hegedüs, Heller, Márkus and Vajda 1976, Markovic 1982, Bobbio 1987, Estrin and LeGrand 1989, Bell 1993). Social democracy's change of identity went continuously on, and still it goes today, when various European politicians, like Amato, Blair, Delors, Fabius, González, Jospin, Lafontaine, Prodi, Rocard, and Schröder gave it a more modern, "professional," multifaceted, flexible, and sometimes contradictory meaning. The political wrestling between representatives of old and new values of socialism and social democracy was further colored by the decline of Marxism, the disintegration of communism (Tismaneanu 1988, Taras 1992), and the appearance of ex-communist (sometimes self-proclaimed) Social Democrats in the new Europe.[2]

In sum, I argue that in the postcommunist context, the Hungarian socialists became a modernizing-privatizing, "managerial-capitalist" political party in the early and mid-1990s, under the banner of social democratization. They practiced a politics "with a Janus face": the Socialist Party maintained its official rhetoric toward the "man-of-the-street," while the party elite and supporters close to the leading circles benefited from the privatization and capital accumulation process. The party had many voices to reach different groups of voters: one was to speak the nostalgic language of the working class, the language of the losers, while the other talked about modernization and the project of "catching up" to Europe. For the Socialists, "modernization" and "Europeanization" became catchwords in the 1990s and these notions were understood as "social democratization" of the party. They proved to be successful, but the task to build strong, credible social democracy is still ahead of them.

In our introduction to this book,[3] we proposed a terminological distinction between reformed parties on the one hand, and transmuted ones on the other. Former communist (now socialist) parties reformed themselves on the Left and caught up to democracy, while the transmuted ones made a (sometimes indecisive and ambivalent) break with their leftist traditions and managed a rightist turn in order to cope with the political changes in their country.

By reformed parties, we mean former communist parties which abandoned their communist ideology and moved toward a culturally more moderate, leftist position. These parties are not communist anymore; they turned away from the revolutionary tenets of Marxism and/or the orthodox methods of post-Stalinism. Reformed socialists accept Western liberal democracy even if they sometimes criticize its practice.

By transmuted, on the other hand, we mean former communist parties, which moved away from the Left and adopted some or more culturally right-wing, nationalistic, or anti-Western elements in their ideology. Reform matches democratic conditions while transmutation alone does not. The latter might indicate a move on the authoritarian scale away from the non-democratic Left toward the non-democratic Right.

Non-reformed parties represent an ideological or practically systemic opposition to democracy. If they are not transmuted, they are still Marxist-Leninist, like the Communist Party in the Czech Republic (Grzymala-Busse 1998, 1999). If they are non-reformed but transmuted, they behave like semi- or antidemocrats, combining communist methods of power practices with nationalist ideology. Partly reformed communist parties are on the verge of accepting the framework of democracy. If they are partly reformed but nontransmuted, they do accept it in their behavior but present themselves as protest parties to the regime, just as the Party of Democratic Socialism did in Germany (Minnerup 1994, Phillips 1994, Thompson 1996, Barker 1998, Patton 1998). When reform and transmutation are parallel processes, as has happened in many cases, party members might present themselves as democrats in theory, but can sometime abuse democratic norms in practice (Harsanyi 1999, Murer 1999). (In these cases, the identity of the former communist party will remain mixed or unclear even if it matches the democratic conditions.) Only reform presupposes to take democratic rules more or less seriously. Table 5.1 highlights the differences between these models.

In this typology, the MSZP clearly does not belong to the group of transmuted successor parties, which produced a variety of political stances and values on the "dimension of transmutation," from communism to nationalism. During the last decade, the MSZP moved away from its rather weak communist position toward a "modernizationist" understanding of social democracy, so it moved on the "axis of reform." It remained antinationalistic and pro-European, while becoming a democratic political party (with sometimes, elitist tones) both in its values and organizational structures.

The Hungarian and Polish ex-communist parties surprised the international public with their spectacular political comeback in the second free elections which occurred in Poland in 1993 and in Hungary in 1994. These changes provoked many students of postcommunism to start examining the communist successor parties and the secret of their success. These parties—together with their Lithuanian and Bulgarian counterparts—were able to win decisively in free elections just a few short years after the collapse of communism (Ishiyama 1995, 1999, Markowski and Tóka 1995, Wade, Lavelle and Groth 1995, Bukowski and Racz 1999, Wrobel 1999). To lose elections in 1989–91 and return in four years' time was rightly seen as a bigger achievement than staying in power continuously. (On changes of "government-opposition" positions within the ex-communist parties see Appendix 1 on page 473.) They differed from most of the former communist parties in the new Yugoslavia and Romania, because they had not turned to nationalism—they opted for modernization.

Table 5.1

Ideological Positions of Communist Successor Parties in Central and Eastern Europe

Party Positions	Non-Reformed	Reformed
Non-Transmuted	orthodox communist	modernizationist, social democratic
Transmuted	national communist	nationalist, populist, Christian-socialist

The "Modernizationist" Idea: From Theory to Ideology

The "modernizationist" political parties are trying to apply a former reform-ist line deprived of its ideology in a democratic context. In Hungary, the leaders of the Hungarian Socialist Party combined the promise of social pact and corporatism (to ease social conflicts) with neoliberal economic policies of crisis adjustment. They spoke in different voices at the same time. The concept of modernization is not the same as modernity.[4] The slogan of mod-ernization is used to control the political, social processes from above, by a group of technocrats, as opposed to supporting the spontaneous processes of the formation of civil society. Thus, there are the "modernizers" and those "to be modernized." Modernizers tend to view their policy as representative of a "synthetic," "competent," "ideology-free," modernist-pragmatic line. The term pragmatic is applied here to illustrate that they are unable to follow a policy of welfarist social democracy while an economic restructuring is going on, therefore they have no choice but act as modernizers.

The theory of modernization was originally a by-product of American sociology and political science of the late 1950s and 1960s (So 1990). Its main theorem was the concept of a linear economic-political development, applicable to all the countries of the world, which followed different stages with different but decisive effects on the opportunities of political democ-racy. A division of the countries of the world into "developing" and "devel-oped" nations originated in the above terminology. In the Cold War period, the political application of the theory of modernization successfully proved the superiority of the Western world over countries of the Soviet system. The latter, however, tried to represent an alternative theory of development al-though they refused to use Western terminology. "Even if modernity was strangely incomplete, missing some of its crucial political and economic com-ponents, even if it was only a 'fake modernity' (Sztompka 1993, 1996), yet 'changes, sometimes dubbed as modernization, produce fundamental shifts in people's values and behaviors'" (Reisinger et al. 1994, Tóka 1994a, 1994b). After all, the idea of modernizing societies was originally an inherent part of

Table 5.2

Modernization Theory and Modernization Ideology Contrasted

Major elements of modernization theory (1960s)	Major elements of modernization ideology (1990s)
Industrialization	Europeanization
Urbanization	Westernization
Nuclear family	Individualism
Evolutionism	Radical design
Stages of development	Shock therapy
Economic growth	Budget balance
Sustainable growth	Crisis management
Universalism	Beyond left and right
Functional differentiation	Pragmatism
Democracy	Technocracy
High literacy rate	Internet
Experts' influence	Expert rule
Low-risk society	High-risk society
Historical optimism	Relative gratification
Linear development	Linear development
"End of ideology"	"End of history"

Note: Elements of modernization theory have been identified from the vast academic literature of the field,[1] while elements of modernization ideology have been formulated by using sources as party programs, manifestos as well as political speeches. For modernization theory see Apter (1965), Black (1967), Eisenstadt (1966), Lerner, Coleman and Dore (1968), Levy (1966), Parsons (1964), and Weiner (1966).

the Marxian revolutionary agenda (Tucker 1969, pp. 92–129). Modernization, therefore, was familiar and could easily be used by the ruling communist elite, even after they had lost their faith in the fast implementation of Marxist tenets (Lagerspetz 1999, Guilhot 2001).

When, in the 1980s, the Hungarian reformist economists and reform-minded new political scientists employed the terms of modernization, they meant to utilize the critical function of both its terminology and contents against the existing dictatorship, i.e. to obtain an ideological meaning. With the changing face of "feasible socialism," from totalitarianism to authoritarianism, and its subsequent disintegration, modernizationism substituted the ideology of the Left. No wonder that the idea of Europe and modernization became core references to the paradoxical "non-ideological ideology" of the Socialists later on.

In the 1970s, the classic theory of modernization was sharply criticized and became increasingly obsolete in the international social sciences.[5] Hungarian reformers, however, were still under the influence of the classic modernization approach and were quick to discover the advantages of its political usage. In the late 1980s, political rhetoric that emphasized the need to catch up with Europe and modernize successfully won over the arguments of hard-line politicians trying to withstand change. In this way, it played an important part in not only breaking up the system but also in convincing the old elite that there was no alternative to a peaceful transition. On the other hand, reformers realized the historic possibility of converting their political capital into economic capital (Hankiss 1990).[6] Legislation dealing with economic change, favoring the Socialists even before the Round Table Talks with the opposition in 1989, made it possible to keep them inside the game of democratization. This was the price to pay for a peaceful regime change (Urbán 1992, Bozóki 2000). The argument of the modernizers at the same time reassured the technically competent members of the old elite that they had nothing to fear, since their professional skills would be needed in the new regime as well. It was strongly inferred that while regimes could change, an enlightened "modernizing elite" would retain its place.

In the 1990s, antinationalistic, ex-communist political parties were characterized by a "modernizing" social democratic line. They were not classical Social Democrats since they represented more than one social class and more than simply the interests of the losers. They no longer believed in the leading role of the welfare state. They were not only the parties of workers—of those living on their wages—but also of middle-class urban settlers, younger people, and largely the technocrats who started their career in the old regime and could be considered winners of the transformation. A heterogeneous "coalition" of voters was cemented by a secular, nonconventional ideology, which is based on the catchy but empty slogans of competence and modernization. Patrick O'Neil makes a point when he observes that in 1994 "the population, increasingly weary of the costs of economic transition, found the MSZP's social market ideology, based on its image of political experience and technocratic expertise, more attractive than the opposition promise of further radical reform" (O'Neil, 1998, p. 197). However, the idea of a "social market economy" was already in use by the center-right MDF-led government, which they referred to as part of the political heritage of an Adenauer-type of Christian Democracy. What mattered more was the return to expertise. They promised to form a "government of experts" as their campaign slogan claimed: *"Let Competence Govern!"*[7]

Epochs of Change: The Hungarian Socialist Party in the 1990s

Prehistory

Concerning the prehistory of the Hungarian Socialist Party, one should note a strong continuity in personnel with the previous communist party, MSZMP. The reasons for this lie in the fact that the MSZMP was already a more open, comparatively reform-oriented communist party, which allowed more technocrats into its ranks than any other party in the Soviet bloc. Moreover, the regime change of 1989 was preceded by a change of the dominant political formula, a change in the nature of dictatorship, and, as a consequence of these factors, a generational and professional change in the political elite (Machos 1997, Pop-Eleches 1999).

The prehistory of MSZP goes back to the 1960s, when communist party leader János Kádár initiated a cautious, but noticeable economic reform process, acquiring some of the lessons of Hungary's Revolution of 1956. He was able to implement a Khrushchevist-style political formula, which emphasized economic growth, technological innovation, and the importance of reforms to prove the supremacy of the communist system over capitalism. The Hungarian version of this formula was the separation of economy and politics, offering some freedom to citizens in the former area in order to keep a monopoly in the latter one. Thus, the regime was able to reestablish and maintain social peace, to produce some economic prosperity and a limited cultural diversity. The regime was flexible enough to co-opt technocrats, experts, degree-holders, and intellectuals into its ranks; thus the communist party increasingly became a mass party of intellectuals and technocrats who remained the "vanguard party" of the workers (Konrád and Szelényi 1979). In a way it was a paradoxically successful adaptation of Leninist revolutionary theory within a postrevolutionary and posttotalitarian dictatorship.

Although Kádár himself managed to survive the antireform turn of Soviet politics after 1968, he was still forced to sacrifice a reform process that led to more inequalities between the more or less competent segments of the elite. This campaign was a revenge of the bureaucracy against a previous advance of the technocrats. A neo-Stalinist demagoguery halted the reform process of the 1970s and finally made clear the inability to achieve serious economic innovation under communist regimes. The long-lasting crisis of the communist regimes was a structural one stemming from the very nature of those systems.

In the 1980s, the "relative deprivation" argument increasingly became the political formula used in Hungary for "legitimizing" the regime. There was no more promise of catching up to the West; it was rather a cynical, informal propaganda which claimed that Hungary was still better off than its "brother" countries, including Poland, Czechoslovakia, Romania, and the GDR, not to mention the Soviet Union. By that time, Kádár turned out to be an old, conservative communist, who disliked Gorbachev's desperately last minute attempts for "progressive" change. In Hungary, the reformers of the 1960s, and the young, pragmatic modernizers of the 1980s both had to realize that their historic task was crisis management, a rational operation in an irrational regime. Therefore, they were socialized for the role of "supreme rationality" in the chaotic period of deideologization and disintegration. They did not care about ideological notions, such as communism, dictatorship, or freedom and democracy, because they wanted to introduce a more rational regime, be it democracy or not, and make it work. Some of them even admitted to approval of the Chilean and South Korean models of economic growth, arguing that economic transformation should precede political democratization. No wonder that nonideological, technocratic, "expert" knowledge was highly valued, even overvalued, in this context of increasing social anomie.

However, reformers had no time to rationalize the authoritarian communist regime, because it collapsed quickly and completely in 1989. The gravely ill patient died before the life-saving operation. To their major embarrassment, these technocrats were even stamped by the emerging, morally driven democratic opposition groups as communists, as immoral servants of the old regime. It is true, as ideological pagans, they were never communists. But neither were they Democrats. With the collapse of the regime, they were temporarily marginalized in politics by heavily politicized groups of humanistic intellectuals. The latter led the two major parties of the regime change, the Hungarian Democratic Forum (*Magyar Demokrata Fórum*, MDF), and the Alliance of Free Democrats (*Szabad Demokraták Szövetsége*, SZDSZ). These parties navigated the transition to democracy by performing the tiring job of party formation, dominating the freshly liberated media, and negotiating the constitutional issues of the emerging democracy at the historic roundtable talks (Bozóki and Karácsony, 2001). It was the intellectuals who gave identity, morality, and an ideology of change to the new democracy. The technocrats of the late Kádár era returned to the semiprivate sphere and took advantage of spontaneous privatization. Many of them, however, remained disappointed, because they felt that their historic project for "rational change" had been interrupted. They did not calculate the occurence of a democratic revolution. After 1989, communist reformers were seeking political representation, looking for the next chance to grasp. They looked like a natural new elite for a reformed and renewed Socialist Party (Szalai 1990).

Table 5.3 summarizes the major changes of the political elite that occurred in the post-totalitarian period of communist rule.

As we shall see in the following, the legacy of the pretransition period shaped the character of the Socialist Party substantially. Being a "reformer" was not simply a political tactic for them but slowly became an inseparable part of their identity. This was backed by a movement of reform-minded local party members, pushing for political change in 1989 (O'Neil, 1998). Top reformers viewed themselves with high self-esteem as the only ones who knew what to do. Reformism, however, may have been more associated inside the party with elite-driven expert politics than classic social democracy based on the defense of the lower and lower-middle classes.

Table 5.3

Changes in Hungary's Political Elite, 1965–89

Time period	International context	Internal politics	Dominant political formula	Way of elite change	Composition of new elite
1965–72	Cold War; competition and co-existence	Economic reforms; political neutralization of citizens	Economic modernization Khrushchevist plan for "catch up"	Co-optation of "experts" to the decision-making	A mix of technocrats and apparatchiks
1973–79	Cold War; détente	Anti-reform wave	"Social justice"; equality	Reversing the influence of experts (but the mixed elite remains)	Advance of the apparatchiks
1980–88	Cold War; slow disintegration of the communist bloc	Economic reform attempts; crisis management	Relative gratification	Convergence; co-optation on a broader scale	Technocrats take over
1989	The collapse of communism in Central and Eastern Europe	Caretaker cabinet; roundtable negotiations; peaceful, revolutionary change	Democracy and civil society	Rapid elite settlement (negotiations) supported by urban masses	Former marginal elite groups, mostly intellectuals

In the more than decade-long history of MSZP (1989 to 2001) four major periods need to be identified. These are the following:

1. The victory of the reformist communists, the foundation of the new party and its subsequent electoral defeat, which latter provoked change in the leadership (1989–90)
2. The formation of leftist social coalitions and the period of political growth from a minor opposition party to a senior governing party (1991–94)
3. Reaching absolute majority, dominating the socialist-liberal government coalition (1994–98)
4. Following electoral defeat, the search for a new identity (1998–present)

To cut a long story short, I will concentrate only upon the major characteristics of MSZP in each period.

Building a Democratic Political Party: The Beginning (1989–90)

The Hungarian Socialist Party was established in October 1989, as an alliance of different platforms. According to an observer of the time, the supporters of change included a platform called Alliance for Reform (*Reformszövetség*) that included reform-socialists, and some radical reform-communists.[8] On the other hand, the influential, less progressive, Popular Democratic Platform (*Népi demokratikus platform*) included the more cautious reform-communists, "idealist bolsheviks," the apparatchiks of the former state and party administration who maneuvered between the lines, as well as corporate managers who represented a "liberalized and rationalized form of Kádárism" (Bihari 1990). It was not obvious that the party would be able to reform itself.[9] However, an important decision was made: Membership in the old party automatically came to an end when the MSZMP changed itself to MSZP. Those who wanted to become members of the new party had to join. This was a risky choice, Socialists risked losing political significance completely. In early October, the old MSZMP had 700,000 members, while a month later, the new MSZP had only 30,000. A crucial step toward democratic reform was taken.

Despite the change of its name, membership card, and also its self-imposed moral and political purge, the Socialist Party lost heavily in the first free elections, where voters declared the "last judgment." Capturing little more than 10 percent of the seats, as opposed to 90 percent given to the former opposition parties, was a referendum over socialism with clear results. (See Appendix 2, page 474.) The MSZP spent the 1990–94 period in opposition. Retrospectively, 10 percent was not a particularly bad result for the Socialists. They were legitimized by the popular vote and had enough seats and time to start rebuilding their party. The May 1990 party congress and its effects had already played a major role in identifying the MSZP's profile. Rezsö Nyers, the first chairman of MSZP,[10] was replaced by Gyula Horn, the foreign minister of the last communist cabinet. A former gray figure in diplomacy, Horn, by that time, became known for his more marked Western orientation. Together with the then Prime Minister Németh, he played a major part in dismantling the Iron Curtain and allowed East German refugees to leave for the West. He also urged the MSZP to approach the Socialist International (they gained full membership by 1996). Horn astonished political observers when he stated, despite Hungary's then current Warsaw Pact membership, that the country was to join NATO as soon as possible (Hungary officially joined NATO in March 1999).

The party program adopted by the congress was closer to social democratic than reform communist. In addition to a demand for full support of political democracy, it expressed the party's endeavors to establish a democratic society. The internal rules of the party, which were worked out in detail between October 1989 and May 1992, became as democratic as those of the former opposition organizations (Machos 1999). Later on, while other parties moved toward an increasingly authoritarian leadership style and internal structure, the MSZP, untouched by the immediate chance to get to power, could afford to remain internally democratic (Machos 2000). Ironically, but understandably, the former communists were more eager to prove their democratic credentials in everyday practice than those who saw themselves as "natural born" democrats. In this way, the MSZP could appear as the critic and engine of democratization in a period when other parties were mainly concerned with building up an institutional-procedural democracy; talking less about the social context of it. Moreover, the MSZP was the only party in the Parliament that represented leftist values, with 10 percent of the seats, defending some of the results and social groups of the old regime. Together with the liberal parties, it strongly opposed the legislation of "decommunization" (González Enriquez 1998).

Growing Big (1991–94)

The MSZP was able to leave its "political ghetto" in 1992. That was the year when a soaring unemployment rate reached the limits of social tolerance. It was a year of strikes, hunger strikes, popular initiatives, and was one of the worst years in the deep and long-lasting transformation crisis. To some extent, it was also the year of the radical Right, when István Csurka, then vice-president of the senior governing party, MDF, attacked his own leader, the moderate Prime Minister, József Antall, and even threatened the consolidation of democracy. Liberal and leftist intellectuals formed a social movement, the Democratic Charter (Bozóki 1996), which gained significance as a sort of new "popular front" by standing up against the rising radical Right.

This served the political interests of the MSZP very well, because they had already claimed in their 1990 program that: "The Socialist Party . . . is the only political force that can prevent a take-over of the extreme Right" (MSZP 1990). The increasingly visible Left-Right divide forced many centrist and liberal opinion makers to re-evaluate their attitude to the Left. Thus, the "heirs of communism" were quickly seen in a more positive light and became the "defenders of democracy" in three short years.

Voters tended to shift to the Left from 1993 for a number of reasons (Bozóki and Lomax, 1996). It became apparent at the municipal elections of social security deputies in May 1993, which won in a landslide victory by the successor union of the former communists, the National Alliance of Hungarian Trade Unions (MSZOSZ). People found it hard to accept that unemployment soared from zero to 13 percent in two years. Although the center-right government declared its commitment to a "social market economy," it did little, despite its sincerely best wishes, to ease social tensions or to achieve a more proportionate contribution to public expenditure. In addition, people were irritated by the official, ideological "lessons in history" repeatedly issued by the government. Political life was ideologically driven, and public debates were full of symbolic politics. Public opinion turned unambiguously in favor of an anti-ideological Left, which promised a better life and more competent government.

Among the reasons of the MSZP's electoral victory in May 1994 (see Appendix 2) one can mention the following points:[11]

1. The burden of simultaneous transition. Voters suffered from initial political instability and had to pay the costs of the economic transformation. The first years of the post-election period were the years of anomie in the Durkheimian sense of the term. Legal rules were viewed as transitory, and people lacked clear legal guidelines in their economic (and other) activity. People became tired of halfway solutions, temporary guidelines, and a lack of security.

2. The growing expectations of the voters. People expected more and got less in the first four years of the new democracy. Despite the center-right government's moderate measures, people wanted a less painful transformation. Foreign and domestic experts who had promised earlier and faster recovery also underestimated the difficulties of the economic transformation.[12]

3. The unpopularity of identity politics. Disillusionment was fostered by the increasing identity politics of the Antall cabinet, which utilized an overdose of symbolic-ideological, history-based metaphorical politics. As a result, people tended to prefer parties with pragmatic political behavior.

4. The high volatility of the voters. Postcommunist politics is characterized by an unreliability of voters and what is termed an index of elusiveness; it was measured as close to 30 percent in the case of Hungary's voter behavior (Tóka 1994a, 1994b). Lacking firm attachments, the unstable mass of voters within the new parties did not stick too long to their first choice. Unlike the unreliable majority of the voters in other parties, the MSZP had a firm base of voters, loyal to the party, disciplined, and quite numerous, containing mostly former MSZMP members and their families (Angelusz and Tardos 1995, Higley, Kullberg and Pakulski 1996). This "hard core" played an important role in maintaining political activity in the local opposition and later in winning over undecided voters.

5. *The internal weaknesses of the regime-changing elite.* The intellectuals, who were in the frontline of the regime change, proved to be good "moral politicians" for the radical change but less able pragmatic politicians for the task of institution-building. Voters had to realize that a large part of the regime-changing elite was not competent enough to manage the horrendous task of the transformation. Socialists, who failed to convince the voters in 1990, could successfully picture themselves as political experts and became increasingly convincing with this rhetoric (Bozóki 1999).

6. *The political "infrastructure" of the Socialists.* In the communist period only socialist connections could be utilized in the national network, since social integration was restricted to relatives, friends, and close acquaintances. One of the bases of this national network was the Communist Youth League (KISZ) and relationships inside the MSZMP. They gained special significance in the period of spontaneous privatization, which made former party connections invaluable in the postcommunist times. It was also important that sympathizers of the Socialists occupied strategic positions in the media. They controlled the daily *Népszabadság* (People's Freedom), the former party daily newspaper which was privatized just before the first free elections. That newspaper, unlike former communist dailies in other countries, soon became the most popular one.

7. *The well-chosen socialist campaign strategy.* The socialist political strategy was based on two pillars: first, a widespread nostalgia among older people toward the Kádár era, when bread was cheap and they felt secure; second, upon the belief that the Socialists, and only the Socialists, were able to run the country competently. They played upon an increasing myth of the last communist government that those politicians made up "the government of experts." Since politics as such became rather unpopular, by 1994, ironic as it was, Socialists could successfully sell themselves not as politicians but experts. Being a technocratic modernizer, an economic winner of the postcommunist transition and also the defender and speaker of the losers, perhaps, sounds incoherent and self-contradictory. This incoherence was the exact secret of the success of the Socialists' campaign strategy. They could speak in different voices and could reach different types of voters. Socialist party-chairman Gyula Horn was particularly adept at bridging this gap, he committed himself to modernization and "Europeanization" on the one hand, but in his everyday communication he behaved like the best pupil of Kádár and convinced elderly voters of his leadership potential.[13]

8. The characteristics of the Hungarian electoral system. Finally, one should mention that one of the unusual features of the Hungarian electoral system, characterized by two rounds and two votes; mixed, is that it increases the number of the governing party's mandates (and only the governing party) out of proportion to ensure stable governing. In 1990, after the MDF won a 25 percent party list victory, it gained 42 percent of the parliamentary mandates. This proportion of the Socialist Party mandate was 33:54 in 1994.

In sum, most people in 1994 voted for the MSZP not primarily because of their socialist image, although those votes should not be underestimated either. Voters thought that the MSZP would neither jeopardize the already victorious democracy or the continuation of the "humanistic" Kádárist traditions of postcommunist times. People hoped that the MSZP could simply turn "soft-communism" into "soft-capitalism." The MSZP won because it could harmonize and utilize its own contradictions in the political arena.

Dominating the Government (1994–98)

Comparing the socialist-led MSZP-SZDSZ coalition government headed by Prime Minister Gyula Horn with its predecessor, one conspicuous difference soon became clear. While the Antall cabinet pursued a *Weltanschauung* style of politics, it had a vision of the future of Hungary (social market economy and Christian-Conservative identity), however, they were not able to obtain social support for it. The Horn cabinet initially had no such grand vision but enjoyed greater popular support. By placing modernization in the limelight, however, the Horn cabinet could hide for awhile a lack of government philosophy.

Relying on modernization-ideology (see Table 5.2) was ambiguous because the modernization process, in a sociological sense, had already taken place in Hungary before, even if not as successfully as in the West. Place of residence and of work got separated, the process of urbanization accelerated, and the agricultural labor force transferred itself to industry. Women became part of the labor force *en masse* (even if in a forced way) thereby creating the condition for their financial independence. Multigenerational family models were replaced by a two-generation model. Even if less developed than the Western countries, Hungary is a modern country. If something is modern, it can hardly be "modernized." If it can be, modernity, just like communism was, must be a never-ending project.

Naturally, the ideology of modernization was used by the socialist majority government for political not theoretical reasons. This malleable notion was used only to give mixed signals to the reformers of the 1980s and the middle classes socialized in the Kádár era. The message to the former was that the government needed their expertise and wanted them back. For the latter, it suggested that no radical change conducive to anomaly would be instituted and that the time of overheated symbolic-ideological politics was over. Modernization ideology was also used to serve a third purpose, i.e. as a panacea to cure the identity crisis of the Socialist Party, which had come about because the classical redistributive social-democratic policy could not be pursued during the time of shock-ridden transformation.

When defining their economic policy the parties in the governing coalition started out on the basis that the country was in a deep crisis. With a worsening balance of payment and a growing budget-deficit in view, the parties concluded that the crisis was not a simple recession but "a general crisis of transition." The economic policy makers of the two parties (MSZP and SZDSz) shared the view that this crisis was deeper than the Great Depression of 1929–32. They pointed out that the primary task of the government should be to manage the crisis and, at the same time, put an end to squandering at the big distribution systems, with a particular emphasis on the reform of social insurance. The rhetoric was similar to the rhetoric of the technocratic elite in the late Kádár era (in 1987–88), which also began from the premise that there was a general crisis and proposed to initiate a monetary crisis management policy by cutting down on consumption for the sake of recovery. In both cases the two aims, i.e. to achieve economic growth and to restore a balanced budget were defined as two opposite goals. The economists of the Socialist-led government were inclined to consider the economic growth of 1993 to be detrimental and to respond to the general crisis with general restrictive measures. "Crisis-mongering" was not only dominant in the vocabulary of government but also, generated by the government, common to the general public talk about politics.

Parallel to this propaganda, the leading Kádár-era economists and radical reformers also returned. The already existing suspicion was strengthened and confirmed that the rhetoric was inspired not only by the actual conditions of the postcommunist economy but also by the professional socialization of the returning economists. What these economists learned in the 1980s was that "irrational" processes of a disintegrating economy can only be fought by means of a restrictive monetary policy conducted from the enlightened center. It seemed as if they had known only one possible economic policy and that they had considered it equally suitable for handling the difficulties of both the disintegrating communist economy and the developing market economy. The cure they suggested for the 1994 "market chaos" was similar to the cure for the central redistribution chaos in 1988: "modernizing rationality." It is not by chance that in the fall of 1994 they also proposed to work out a three-year modernization plan which, however, was removed from the agenda. The economic program of the Socialists was nothing else but the completion of the "modernization project," which was interrupted by the regime change of 1989. It was a call for the technocrats of the period of

1980–88 to come back and complete their half-finished job. The composition of the elite of 1994–98 was indeed, similar to the younger generation of the elite groups of the 1980s.

March 12, 1995—the day when the infamous "Bokros-package," an austerity program that was introduced in a putsch-like manner—was a major turning point in the history of modern Hungarian socialism. With the approval of Horn (and in collaboration with the Chairman of the Bank of Issue, György Surányi) Finance Minister Lajos Bokros implemented a neo-liberal/monetarist program of crisis-adjustment and introduced a "shock-therapy" package which probably saved the country from a threatening debt-trap but impoverished many people by reducing their real wages by 12 percent in a year. (A drop of living standard, comparable to this, last happened in Hungary in 1952.) The stabilization package's measures decreased budget expenses, devalued the Hungarian currency, and imposed a customs surcharge on imported goods. A new policy was also announced, i.e. the "planned" crawling-peg devaluation of the forint in order to cool the ever increasing inflation-related expectations. The "Bokros-package" was also meant as an attempt to initiate state administration reforms, such as narrowing family allowances, introducing tuition at the higher educational institutes, and narrowing the range of free medical services. Although by the summer of 1995 the Constitutional Court ruled a great number of measures in the package unconstitutional and actually cancelled them, the restrictive policy remained intact enough for the Socialist-led coalition to champion it as its greatest achievement (Bauer 1996), and its final break with the paternalist Kádár regime.

This moment brought the victory of not only a new financial practice but a framework of interpreting social changes (Eyal, Szelényi and Townsley 1998).[14] Monetarism was seen as the proper "technology of government"[15] as well as a neutral governing philosophy, which had no alternative. Modernization ideology was at that time seen as an effective course between Marx and Friedman, a common denominator for social change followed by a design of "enlightened" leaders with "educational" purposes. They wanted to be more than reformers but less than revolutionaries. They considered themselves radical reformers or the designers of economic transformation. Kádárist "reform economics" of the 1980s reinvented itself as a new, "transformist economics" in the 1990s (Böröcz 1999). In many ways, Hungarian socialists could be compared to their French counterpart who "generally . . . claimed that their own project represented a 'third way,' distinct from both Soviet-style communism and reformist social democracy" (Bell 1997, p.16). The Hungarian socialists argued that they represented a transitory way between Soviet-type communism and reformist social democracy, which should be the antithesis of the former, a fast and successful "transformist strategy" that used monetarist, modernizing measures.

The populist-unionist old left within the party suspiciously watched the capitalist transformation, taking place under the Socialist Party government. On the one hand, using modernization talk pacified the populist left-wing by diverting their attention from capitalism. On the other hand, it encouraged the technocrat elite by letting them know that they could go on benefiting from privatization. So modernization-ideology, in a broader sense, served to bridge the gap between the party elite, the winners of the transformation, and the Socialist voters that were mainly recruited from the losers.

It was a period when the concept of modernization as used by the Socialists and the notion of "Europeanization" (which can also be understood as the Hungarian version of the concept of globalization) became entangled and therefore richer, including notions such as integration, Westernization, "catching up," and internationalization at the same time. At this point, the governing behavior of the Hungarian socialists offers some comparisons with the French socialists of the Mitterrand era. As a scholar has noted: "Indeed, 'Europe' came to replace 'socialism' as the provider of a sense of purpose in Mitterrand's scheme of things" (Bell 1997, p. 40). For Mitterrand's modernizing Prime Minister, Laurent Fabius, who turned to "the new culture of managerialism" and forgot the old socialist goal of a break with capitalism,

> the new priorities were "modernization" and *"rassemblement"* (the rallying for broad support). Modernization implied restructuring and rationalizing industrial structures to achieve greater competitiveness, at the costs of massive layoffs in unprofitable firms. . . . Competitiveness also meant giving priority to the reduction of inflation and wage restraint. Social redistribution was no longer the mainspring of policy. . . . *Rassemblement*, a term borrowed from Gaullism, implied the abandonment of any reference to class in future socialist strategy (Bell 1997, p. 41).

In Hungary, modernization ideology became a way of thinking to justify both the neoliberal policies of 1995–97 and the departure from neoliberalism to a more social-democratic direction later on. Representatives of the Hungarian Socialist Party argued that they had had to be privatizers and economic liberals in order to construct capitalism. They asserted that the faster the process the least painful it would be for the citizens. They argued, paradoxically, that they had had to introduce capitalism in order to be "real Socialists" later on.

Ironically, when the Hungarian Socialist Party made its definitive turn toward monetarism and neoliberal policies in 1995, it was finally admitted to the Socialist International (in 1996). In the years 1995–97 the modernizing leadership of the Socialist Party also quickly completed a privatization process unprecedented in Hungary's history. By selling out state assets, including electric power plants, Socialists moved far away, not just theoretically but practically, from the position of the old Left.

In a coalition government, the use of modernization ideology was a suitable way for the ex-communist reformers to cover up the economic and political discrepancies of the governing parties. It served as both a political common denominator between the economic reformers of the coalition parties and as a cohesive force to the heterogeneous internal coalition of MSZP. It bridged the former fault line between the Communists and anti-Communists as it aimed toward the future and not at the past. As a matter of fact, the idea of modernization has always had some affinity with the theory of convergence between different political-economic regimes. This convergence theory had an actual message in the mid-1990s, which was the following: It is not a question of choosing between liberal capitalism and democratic socialism but it is a question of the future of modernity. Defenders of modernity should, therefore, come together against the politics of antimodernists. In that sense, the heirs of the former democratic opposition (members of the Free Democrats) and the former reformers of the Communist Party (members of the Socialist Party) should, indeed, govern together, because it was seen as a natural consequence of their prehistories and ideas. By the year 1998, the modernizationist turn was completed, the state-run properties were privatized (with the silent support of the trade unions, whose representatives were sitting in the Socialist benches of Parliament), and the carefully planned and conspiratorially implemented "Bokros-package" brought its first result. The economy started booming, and the rate of inflation and unemployment both began to decrease. Hungary had thus completed one of the greatest social transformations in its history.

Nevertheless, the Socialists lost the 1998 elections and were replaced in power by their major opposition, the Fidesz-Hungarian Civic Party (*Fidesz-Magyar Polgári Párt*, Fidesz-MPP). The main reasons of their defeat (see Appendix 2.) were, briefly, the following:

Elitist Politics. Although, they were ready to give up their socialist commitments to represent the losers (workers, teachers, pensioners, employees in the state sectors, etc.), they abandoned, at least temporarily, earlier appeals to moderate reformism wit the introduction of shock-therapy measures (Bokros-package). This monetarist version of modernization was too quickly adopted to speed up economic transformation. Due to this fact, the right-wing opponents of the Socialists could utilize some of the arguments of economic populism and make themselves quickly attractive to the less educated and less well-to-do voters.[16]

Corruption Scandals. While in power, the MSZP party had produced some corruption scandals which left their socialist credentials substantially shaken. The biggest one was the so-called Tocsik Affair of 1996, in which they forced local officials to kick back hundreds of millions of forints to the agents of government parties in order to receive more grants from the State Property Agency.

Problems of Leadership. Gyula Horn's old-school Kádárist style of politics lost its popular appeal in the shadow of the Bokros-package and the Tocsik Affair. His originally modest, down-to-earth political style promised solid reformist politics with incremental changes, and also political Puritanism with "clean hands." In addition, by interfering with some identity issues of the liberals (making a bilateral treaty with the Vatican, playing with the idea of rebuilding the infamous Dam on the Danube at Nagymaros, etc.), he alienated the voters of SZDSZ, the most important political ally of the Socialists. Moreover, Horn had unexpectedly under-performed in the 1998 campaign, suffering a stunning defeat by the "mixed-bag campaign" of the young, energetic Viktor Orbán, leader of Fidesz-MPP.

The Skillful Campaign Strategy of the Center-Right. Realizing that the rhetoric of expert-led politics, pursued by the Hungarian socialists while in government, fell short of meeting the popular expectations, the opposition was able to act in concert in coming up with more popular promises. The winning ticket of Fidesz-MPP was a politics of contradictory promises, an unusual, but widely accepted package of pro-Western yet anti-globalist sentiments and pro–middle class economic policy with leftist-populist slogans. Post-socialist neoliberalism was thus overtaken by radical conservatism.

The Characteristic Features of the Hungarian Electoral System. The defeat of the Socialists was not devastating at all. In fact, they received more popular votes than their opponents in the first round of the elections, which followed the logic of proportional representation. (See Appendix 2.) But in the second round of the elections, which followed the logic of "winner-take-all" by law, they lost in too many constituencies. That situation offered a chance for the opposition to win if they could temporarily eliminate their internal divisions. The most apparent reason for the Socialists' defeat was finally due to József Torgyán, chairman of the Smallholders Party. Torgyán had realized the logic of the electoral system and withdrew FKGP candidates in 82 electoral districts in the second round. By doing so, he made sure that the candidates of Fidesz-MPP won in most of these districts as the candidates of the "united opposition."

In sum, the Socialists lost the elections of 1998 to the united center-rightist forces, whose platform fiercely opposed neoliberal crisis-adjustment and promised sensible, down-to-earth economic development accompanied by leftist social policy. The latter rejected the "Grand Design" of elite-driven modernization and promised equal opportunities for the embourgeoisement of (almost) every citizen. Thus, two major political blocs in Hungary confronted each other. The Socialist Party brought a basket of political values in which the economic Right was mixed up with the cultural Left. Its major opposition was the Fidesz-MPP, which combined the economic Left with the cultural Right. The two blocs fought hard, and the victory of Fidesz-MPP was finally due to the support of the old Right, the agrarian-populist Smallholders Party (FKGP). Curiously, but not surprisingly, the Socialist Party was beaten by leftist values and populist rhetoric, because the center-right parties adopted a leftist economic program to counter the neoliberal policy of the socialist led Left.

Back to Opposition: In Search of a "Local Tony Blair" (1998 to 2002)

By losing the 1998 elections this way, the Socialists were not really forced to fundamentally revise their previous governmental policies and practices. They failed to draw from the political consequences and just blamed their own campaign mistakes for the defeat. Secondly, they sensed the lost charisma and popularity of the former Prime Minister, Gyula Horn, the chairman of the Socialist Party. In September 1998, László Kovács, former foreign minister of the Horn cabinet, was elected as the new chairman of the Socialists. Yet, none of the above mentioned reasons for their defeat forced them to urgently revise their elitist, and sometimes arrogant, government policies. It took the Socialists awhile to distance themselves from their recent past.

This was the time when the idea of "Blairism" came into the picture as an increasingly standard reference of Hungarian socialists. I have already compared some policies of the Hungarian socialists to those of their French counterpart in the Mitterrand era. The similarities between those two policies were not publicly recognized by the politicians of the time; they seem to be noticeable in retrospect only. However, the political "love affair" of the Hungarian socialists with the British Prime Minister, Tony Blair, was a different phenomenon. Blair scored a spectacular victory for the British Labour Party in May 1997, by breaking the bloc-vote of the labor unions, thereby bringing Labour back from the old Left to a moderate center-left position. To copy the "New Labour" model, or, at least, to learn from its success, became a common wish for the Hungarian socialists, and even for the Free Democrats. Blair defined himself as a modernizer and observers also saw and described him that way (Sopel 1995, Perryman 1996). His new, non-dogmatic approach to modernization was the ideology that brought down neo-liberal Thatcherism and also its post-Thatcher variants (Giddens 1994).

The Hungarian socialists were already modernizers even before Tony Blair started to dominate the British political scene and make an impact on European politics. For them, modernization ideology was used to justify different, contradictory actions, whether those increased or decreased social inequalities.[17] They simply wanted to get out of their post-1989 political ghetto as fast as possible. Many analysts, and so the voters, saw the MSZP's defeat in 1998 as a well-deserved warning for their "betrayal" of leftist values. Hungarian socialists, facing these charges and the parallel success of Blair, tried to respond in a way that would point to Blair as a justification and defense of their own centrist policies. They knew their ideas had come earlier and that they were more "Blairists" than Blair himself.

In that context, the Blair phenomenon served three purposes for Hungary's Socialists, who were losing political ground after their electoral defeat. First, realizing the initial high popularity of Blairism, the Hungarian socialists claimed that "new social democracy," however it was defined, belonged to them, to the Left. By asserting this, they wished to dispel the new neo-conservative Prime Minister Viktor Orbán's likening of himself to Blair. The Socialists feared that the Blair phenomenon was about to be stolen by the Right and tried to prevent this dangerous move.

Secondly, the Socialists wanted to justify retrospectively their previous departure from classic social democratic values. As they claimed, they were "always Social Democrats in their heart" but during the mid-1990s it was an "unavoidable historical necessity" to modernize their country during the period of capitalist transformation. According to them, it was still better for society that a socialist party had installed capitalism, because, after all, they were more than just theoretical privatizers, but rather "reformers with results."[18] Blair's message was understood in Hungary by the Socialists as a justification of the inevitable departure from the welfare state model by taking the global, competitive market economy more seriously.

Third, the Blair phenomenon fueled the party's needs for new, more credible and self-conscious leadership after the lost elections. Old-style leadership by Horn was undisputedly one reason for defeat. Blairism had a message in Hungary that socialism was renewable along modernizationist lines. It was understood that modernizers were actually not destroying socialism, but offering it a last hope for renewal. Besides the replacement of Horn with Kovács in the position of party chairman, Miklós Németh, the head of the (retrospectively popular) caretaker cabinet of 1988–90, also returned to Hungarian political life. He arrived at the MSZP in 2000, after serving nine years as vice-president of the London-based European Bank of Reconstruction and Development (EBRD), in the hope of being nominated by the MSZP as the party's next candidate for prime minister. Although Kovács was re-elected as party chairman in November 2000, personal tensions have remained one of the constant characteristics of the MSZP leadership (Kóczián 2000). Corruption had eroded the cohesiveness of the party, and voters expected not just ideological but moral and intellectual renewal as well. The socialist leadership, while wishing to keep their positions, needed and searched in vain for young representatives from the new generation who had no political ties to the old regime. This led to further tensions between socialist intellectuals and politicians (Gyurcsány 2000, Ripp 2000) concerning the best possible strategy and finding a candidate for the position of prime minister. Finally, the party decided to nominate Péter Medgyessy, a technocrat, who was the former minister of finance in the Horn cabinet between 1996–98, a former banker, and also a former communist politician.

The philosophy of "Blairism" has been, perhaps, most clearly summarized in a programmatic book on the idea of the "Third Way" by Anthony Giddens (1998). The book was translated into Hungarian immediately after its first English publication, and published there a few months later, as well. Obviously, ideological-programmatic texts are always more coherent than complex policy decisions in a democratic society. The latter processes are always influenced by short-term political calculations as well. To be sure, I do not claim that the essential elements of *The Third Way* necessarily became the policies of "New Labour." But this was the blueprint Blair decided to adapt onto his political values. *The Third Way* model included the following elements: radical political center, new democratic state, active civil society, democratic family, new mixed economy, equality as inclusion, positive welfare, social investment state, cosmopolitan nation, and cosmopolitan democracy (Giddens 1998, p. 70). That was the new, post–welfare state lesson to be learned by the "new Social Democrats" in Europe (Blair and Schröder 2000).

Contrasting this to the conflicting views and alternative programs of the Hungarian socialists (MSZP 2000, MSZP Left Wing Platform 2000), we find hardly any reference to positive welfare, the democratic family, and the social investment state. They mix new cosmopolitanism with old internationalism, sometimes supporting a radical political center, but sometimes a civil society. In the area of the economy, the Socialists originally supported a mixed economy, but, in fact, they went far beyond that. In terms of economic radicalism, or the introduction of new measures from the top down, the MSZP leadership was more radical than Blair, Fabius, or Rocard ever were. Their economic radicalism was rooted in the former Kádár regime in which they played the role of "devil's advocate" but were frustrated by the half-hearted reforms of the old-fashioned communist leadership. Abandoned by them by the 1990s, the socialist technocrats felt free to initiate radical economic changes which gradually led to their increasing unpopularity and subsequently to their electoral defeat in 1998.

Table 5.4 demonstrates the rise and fall of technocratic, modernizing socialists in the broader sense of the transformation of elites.

Conclusions

As mentioned in the beginning of this chapter, international social democracy has a long history of changing its character and even identity. Now, it appears to be entering its third historical epoch of development. The first period can roughly be called the epoch of the Erfurt Program, which lasted from the Erfurt Congress of 1891 until the late 1950s. The declaration of the Erfurt Congress, formulated by Kautsky, was based on classic social

111

Table 5.4

Changes in Hungary's Political Elite, 1990 to Present

Time period	International context	Internal politics	Dominant political formula	Way of elite change	Composition of new elite
1990–94	Post-Cold War; disintegration of the Soviet Union and Yugoslavia; associate membership to the EU	Foundational matters; dealing with the past; economic privatization	Constitutional democracy and national identity	Free elections	Ideologically divided intellectuals (cultural "tribes")
1994–98	Partnership for peace; bilateral treaties with the neighbor states; decision on the NATO extension	Economic shock therapy; crisis-management; completion of privatization	"Post-ideological" modernization; consolidation by "experts"; elitism	Free elections	Technocratic modernizers
1998–	NATO membership; negotiations begin with the EU over Hungary's admission	Re-mobilization against "the communists" to combat the former elite	Anti-communism; embourgeoisement; political populism	Free elections	New contenders coming from intermediary groups or local elites

democratic principles of class struggle, anticapitalism and the representation of working-class interests. Socialist revolution was regarded as the
final goal of the movement, which should be reached in the distant future
only. (That is why Communists stamped that approach as "opportunistic.")
The principles of the Erfurt Program made working-class fights for better
wages and working conditions as inherent parts of the capitalist order (Szabó
2001, pp. 163–68).

The second historical epoch of social democracy was the period of the
Bad Godesberg Program of 1959, which lasted from the late 1950s until the
late 1990s. According to this approach, the final victory of socialism, as a
political and ideological goal, became irrelevant, and a more practical goal
of the welfare state came to the forefront of social democracy. Social Democrats gave up the idea of state ownership of the means of production, instead,
they focused on the high proportion of state-controlled redistribution through
progressive taxation. The welfare state, namely the broad system of state-
controlled/redistributed social services and social benefits, became the order
of the day. It tried to embrace all citizens, not just members of the working
class. An acceptable standard of living became a social issue not just a class
issue, so Social Democrats could broaden their electorate significantly. By
the 1980s, the welfare state model of social democracy found itself in crisis,
both economically and politically, and was pushed into the defensive by
emerging neoliberal and neoconservative philosophies.

In the third era, roughly from the mid-1990s, a "new social democracy"
(Gamble and Wright 1999) has emerged as the response of the broadly understood Left to neoliberalism. The "Blairist Manifesto" of Giddens (1998)
intended to mark the beginning of a new epoch, whereby the project of social democracy is less concerned with economic growth and classic modernization understood mainly as economic growth. Rather, it presents a softer,
alternative, ecologically more conscious "Third Way," in which part-time
work becomes more frequent than welfare dependency, and the results of
feminist and other civil rights movements are fully incorporated into social
democracy. Old school modernization is to be replaced by the more liquid
notion of "reflexive modernization."[19] While the welfare state was a project
of the nation-state, the idea of the new social democracy is a project, which
intends to go beyond the nation-state in two ways: toward supranational political organizations and also toward a direction of international (or global)
civil society.

In this quickly changing political landscape, Hungarian socialists face
difficulties catching up to Western social democracy, which looks like a moving target for them. It is clear that the postcommunist MSZP never wanted to
revert to the old social democracy. It could not credibly refer to the idea of
class struggle, because, as an umbrella party, it consisted of both proletarians
and new capitalists. In the spirit of "spontaneous" privatization, the MSZP

also could not turn to the welfare state model either, despite its attractiveness for some leading intellectuals surrounding the Socialists, and despite the fact that the Swedish model was clearly present among the ideas of 1989. The previous Soviet-type state in Hungary never was a welfare state, despite some efforts to make it appear like that. Finally, "new social democracy" sounded too new, too premature, too much a risky option for the Hungarian socialists in the traditionalist, male-dominated, politically precorrect world of Hungarian politics. At the turn of the century, people in Hungary are still preoccupied in dealing with material gains and economic survival. New social democratic post-materialism, a value that successfully represents the generation of Joschka Fischer and Gerhard Schröder in some Western societies, is still a possible losing card in the postcommunist democracies.

Having no clear identity, the MSZP is navigating between old, half-old, and half-new values of Western social democracy, using them pragmatically according to its needs. In short, MSZP follows a politics of inconsistency. It might be disappointing for intellectuals, analysts and all those observers who expect some consistency in politics between ideas and deeds, between policies of different fields. But it very well may be the case that the reason for the successes of Hungarian socialists is their inconsistent politicizing. Only inconsistency can adequately respond to the incompatible demands of their electoral constituency. The common denominator of all paradigms and policies of social democracy is modernization, therefore this ideology is used constantly by the excommunist MSZP to bridge differences in electoral constituencies, political philosophies, coalition parties, and old and new social democracies. However, the electoral defeat of 1998 showed that the modernizationist coalition cannot endure for long in a new and relatively poor democracy. The MSZP lost in 1998 because its opponent, the Fidesz-MPP, could successfully combine the elitist rhetorical elements of modernization with a new populist political discourse. The recipe for an MSZP comeback was exactly this: a more balanced presentation of elitist and populist arguments inside the framework of democratic discourse. By doing so they managed to win in the April 2002 elections and Medgyessy became Hungary's new prime minister.

In many ways, Hungarian socialists can learn a lot from the "new Social Democrats," the story of the political turn of the British Labour Party, as well as the old Western Left in general (Földes 2000). It is important to note, however, that the MSZP, sociologically speaking, never was a labor party. During the 1990s, it was the party of experts, party of managers and different kinds of political entrepreneurs. They will learn to adapt postindustrial political values to their policies in a few years time, but they do not need to start learning the values of modernization. When they search for a new Tony Blair in Hungary, they are not searching for a modernizer. Instead, they are searching for charisma, credibility, and rejuvenation.

Notes

1. There is, however, important new research, including work by Kitschelt (1995), Rose (1996), Ishiyama (1997), Markowski (1997), Kitschelt, Mansfeldová, Markowski and Tóka (1999), Lipset (2001), and a chapter by Ladányi and Szelényi in this volume.

2. Such politicians like Horn, Iliescu, Kovács, Kučan, Kwasniewski, Mesić, Németh, Roman, Weiss, Zeman, and others.

3. But also elsewhere, as in our jointly written paper. See Ishiyama and Bozóki (2001).

4. In a different analytical context, Peter Wagner distinguished between modernist and modern theorizing, whose distinction can be enlightening here as well. As he wrote: "This theorizing is *modernist* rather than modern, because it builds on the double notion of autonomy and rationality, which are key characteristics of modernity, but it also turns this notion into an unquestioned and unquestionable assumption for theorizing in the social world" (Wagner 2000).

5. See for instance, Desai (1976), Dos Santos (1976), Gunder Frank (1978), Lehman (1979), and Smith (1976).

6. Hankiss (1990) especially the chapter on the "Grand Coalition." For a more detailed analysis of regime change and elite change, see Tökés (1996).

7. This was the leading MSZP slogan on giant posters all over the country during the spring 1994 electoral campaign. This slogan was used as a subtitle under the photo of Gyula Horn, party chairman, who, with his rhetoric, fit into the political culture characteristic of the Kádár era. In his case study on the Hungarian reform-communists, Patrick H. O'Neil mentions that with the 1994 victory of the MSZP, "the goal of the MSZP to portray itself as a modern, Western-style social-democratic party . . . was finally achieved" (O'Neil, 1998, p. 198). My approach is more skeptical than this, because being in power, the MSZP opted for a neoliberal, shock-therapy policy in 1995 to manage the economic crisis. This was presented by them as an economic "reform package," a "final break" with Kádárism. The applied policy of "Washington consensus" became a substitute for modern social democracy. After all, modernization was being taken seriously by the MSZP leadership while the idea of a social market economy was not.

8. On the history of reformist circles see Ágh, Géczi and Sipos (1999). The reformist circles regarded themselves as a "mass movement" and they also liked to compare themselves to the Polish Solidarity movement. Both of these statements were, at best, exaggerations. On the ideology of Solidarity and other groups, see Zielonka (1989).

9. Ágh (1995) emphasized the uniqueness of the Hungarian socialists in the communist world, because they renamed and reformed their party before the regime change, and not after it. True, the reform of the communist party occurred before the free elections. But it happened after the National Roundtable Talks of the summer 1989, which had clarified the inevitability of the democratizing process by setting up almost all institutions for the regime change. The September agreement announced the beginning of free and fair elections in the near future, and it was signed by the Communist Party (MSZMP) representatives as well. Therefore, by October 1989, the Communist Party had only two options left: either to reform itself to gain some popularity among the voters, or to reintroduce dictatorship by police and military forces. Since

international actors (most notably Soviet President, Mikhail Gorbachev) were strongly against the use of force by the authorities against the citizens, leaders of the Hungarian Socialist Worker's Party had virtually no other choice to ensure political survival but internal reform.

10. Rezsö Nyers was originally a Social Democrat but joined the communists in 1948. Having been close to Kádár (who came to power with the Soviet suppression of the 1956 revolution), he served in the Politburo for two decades after 1956, which included participation in the morally suicidal decision to execute Imre Nagy, the leader of the revolutionary government. From the mid-1970s onwards Nyers did not have a high party position, although he remained a member of the Central Committee, which gave him an opportunity to rediscover his "social-democratic roots" and commit himself to reformist ideas. In the October 1989 Party Congress, he was elected to be the first chairman of MSZP because he could bridge the gap between two major opposing factions, the Alliance for Reform, and the Popular Democratic Platform. For more details, see Nyírö et al. (1989).

11. I discussed these points earlier in detail (Bozóki 1997).

12. Paul Marer, Professor of Economics at Indiana University, who was an active member of Hungary's Blue Ribbon Committee (a think-tank on economic policy in 1989–90) admitted this in his presentation to a conference on Hungarian transition. Bloomington, Indiana, USA, April 1–2, 2000.

13. At one point Prime Minister Gyula Horn promised that pensioners would fly for free on MALÉV (Hungarian Airlines) flights. As a pragmatic politician, Horn sometimes made astonishingly populist statements, but then he went "back to business" and accepted shock-therapy measures.

14. See especially chapter 3, "The Ideology of the Post-Communist Power Elite" (Eyal, Szelényi, and Townsley 1998, pp. 86–112).

15. This monetarist mindset was elegantly reconstructed by Eyal (2000), in his Foucaultian analysis of the Czech case.

16. The strong and immediate social impact of the Bokros-package made József Torgyán, a populist leader of the Smallholders Party who had been a marginal figure in Hungarian politics, a major political player and (temporary) leader of the opposition.

17. Modernization was an equal panacea to cure the illnesses of the state-controlled economy by privatization, as well as the "digital divide" in society (a gap between social groups created by unequal access to the internet and other new information technologies). At one stage it looked like the revolutions of 1989 represented not just a temporary interruption of the process of modernization. Much of the discourse of the Socialists relied on that assumption (Lagerspetz 1999).

18. They referred to the achievements of the Németh cabinet in 1989–90. They even tried to create a myth of the Németh cabinet as "the government of experts." Some Socialists were convinced, already at the Roundtable Talks in 1989, that they were the only ones who really knew what to do with the stagnating/declining economy. For more details see Bozóki and Karácsony (2001). On the Hungarian Roundtable Talks in detail, see Bozóki (2000), and Bozóki et al. (1999–2000).

19. For the origin of the term, see Beck, Giddens and Lash (1994).

6

The Troubled Evolution of Slovakia's Ex-Communists

Sharon Fisher

The development of Slovakia's political scene during the 1990s was in certain respects unique, and the evolution of the former Communist Party was no exception. As in the case of its Hungarian and Polish counterparts, Slovakia's communist successor party, the Party of the Democratic Left (SDL), gradually transformed itself into a modern social democratic party, as demonstrated by its admission into Socialist International in September 1996. However, unlike the Hungarian Socialists and the Polish Social Democratic Party, the SDL has never managed to win more than 15 percent of the vote in elections and therefore has never been the major player in any government.

A number of factors have influenced the SDL's lack of success in elections. The first relates to the more hard-line nature of the communist regime in Czechoslovakia than in Poland or Hungary. The repressive nature of the communist regime did not prevent a reform-oriented leadership from taking control of the SDL in the early 1990s, and unlike their Czech counterparts, the Slovak communists managed to transform themselves into social democrats within a few years. Nonetheless, the previous regime did have an impact on public support for the party, as many Slovaks continued to be skeptical of the SDL's aims and to accept the party as "communist," despite efforts by the party's leadership to distance itself from its past. By early 1996, the SDL was the party for which Slovak citizens felt the greatest degree of sympathy; however, only about 10 percent of those planning to take part in elections said they intended to vote for the SDL (Butorova et al. 1996, pp. 56–60). Although other parties on the political scene were more polarizing, the population was apparently reluctant to vote for the successor of a party that had supported repressive policies in the past, particularly given that the country is overwhelmingly Catholic.

Another key factor influencing the success of the SDL in elections in the 1990s was that elements of the left-wing platform were adopted by other Slovak parties. In fact, the emergence of competing parties with similar pro-

grams has represented a much greater danger to the SDL than has its communist legacy. If the SDL were the only party in Slovakia promoting leftist
values, many Slovaks might be inclined to overlook its past or to support the
party out of nostalgia. Unlike the Polish and Hungary communist successor
parties, however, the SDL has been unable to keep the left united, and that
has been the SDL's biggest failure. The SDL's first serious competition on
the left side of the spectrum emerged in April 1991, with the establishment
of Vladimir Meèiar's Movement for a Democratic Slovakia (HZDS). While
the HZDS has been a dominant player on the political scene ever since, a
number of other parties have also adopted leftist ideas and rhetoric, also
taking potential support away from the SDL.

Internally, the SDL has experienced several periods of change and introspection since the fall of the communist regime as it has struggled to find its
identity and define itself within Slovakia's complicated and unstable political scene. The first and most dominant approach was one of pragmatic reform, as the SDL gradually transformed itself into a modern social democratic
party. That phase began with the collapse of the communist regime in November 1989. It was basically completed when the party joined several center-
right opposition parties in March 1994 by dismissing a Meèiar government
and subsequently formed a transitional cabinet until the next parliamentary
elections. The SDL's pragmatic-reform strategy was influenced by the party
leadership's desire for international acceptance and recognition, and that acceptance was sometimes gained at the expense of public support at home as
the party overlooked the needs and interests of its domestic constituency and
therefore lost its ability to unify the left.

The SDL's poor results in the 30 September–1 October 1994 parliamentary elections served as a wake-up call to the party, influencing the leadership to launch a period of introspection during which its reform course was
called into question as it tried to distinguish itself from its political allies on
the center-right. That period lasted until the Meèiar government's illegal
thwarting of a referendum on direct presidential elections in May 1997, after
which the SDL went firmly back into the opposition camp.

The SDL fared surprisingly well in the parliamentary elections of 25–26
September 1998 by presenting itself as a European-style social democratic
party of experts, and following the elections, the party again rejoined the
center-right in government. Nonetheless, the SDL did not become the dominant party in the cabinet, and the party's participation in a government that
has presided over a period of difficult economic reforms has once again given
the impression that the SDL is failing to protect the interests of its constituency. A new shift in the party's approach began in late 1999, not as the result
of election failure but rather after the establishment by an SDL rebel of a
new political alternative that led to a significant drop in the party's public
support. The new party, called Smer ("Direction"), is led by the young lawyer

Robert Fico, who by the time of the 1998 elections had become the SDL's most popular politician.

These two periods of introspection brought to the forefront several conflicts within the SDL. On the one side are the "moderates," who have striven to continue leading the SDL on its course toward Western-style social democracy, while the other group, the "pragmatists," have preferred a more leftist approach and aimed to bring the party back to its roots. Several recurring themes have divided the pragmatists and moderates since 1989. One controversy that has emerged during both of the SDL's terms in office has revolved around economic reforms, and some representatives from the pragmatic wing appeared not to comprehend the necessity of making deep structural changes before a strong social welfare system could be introduced. Another major point of discussion within the SDL during much of the 1990s was the question of whether and to what extent the party should cooperate with the HZDS, with the pragmatists generally favoring closer ties with that party. Nonetheless, the two sides have generally been united in a pro-Western stance on questions of democracy, human rights, and foreign relations, and that in the end has always led the party to reject deeper cooperation with the HZDS. The SDL has been even stronger in its criticism of the radical right-wing Slovak National Party (SNS), which in the past has served as a junior coalition partner of the HZDS.

While both pragmatists and moderates have shown occasional signs of populism and nationalism, these approaches have not been of overriding importance during any phase of the party's development. Nonetheless, in 1992 the party joined the HZDS and SNS in voting for a declaration of sovereignty and the new Slovak constitution, thereby contributing to the breakup of Czechoslovakia. Moreover, the SDL's pragmatists have been inclined on occasion to imitate the HZDS in using the national card against Slovakia's ethnic Hungarians, thus giving the impression that the party has in certain respects broken with its leftist internationalist traditions and become transmuted toward a more nationalistic approach.

Since the establishment of Fico's Smer party, public support for the SDL has been hovering around the 5 percent threshold needed to enter the parliament. Thus, more than a decade after the fall of the communist regimes across Central and Eastern Europe, it appears that the SDL is in danger of extinction, as other alternatives have emerged to compete for the same political space. The pragmatists now have control of the SDL, and their efforts to reaffirm the party's leftist orientation and rebuild its support have failed to attract the wider public. It remains to be seen whether the SDL will manage to regain public confidence by the time of the next parliamentary elections, scheduled for September 2002.

This chapter examines the SDL's rocky evolution from communist to democratic left and beyond, beginning with an investigation of the party's efforts to separate itself from its communist past and to remove the hard-line elements. Next, it looks at the SDL's first period of introspection, when it tried to promote itself as an "independent opposition party." Following a brief look at the party's structure, the chapter continues with an exploration of the SDL's relatively successful results in the September 1998 parliamentary elections. It then moves on to an analysis of the SDL's role in the government that has held office since 1998, including its second period of self-analysis. The chapter closes with a discussion of the party's future prospects.

From Communist to Democratic Left

The hardline nature of Czechoslovakia's communist regime clearly had a significant effect on the evolution of the SDL, which was quick to distance itself from the crimes of the past. In the months after the so-called "Velvet Revolution" of 17 November 1989, which led to the collapse of the Communist Party's "leading role in society," the first step in transforming the Slovak communists was to rid the party of its previous structure and controversial personalities. Thousands of members abandoned the party, and some of the most conservative forces were expelled, with younger, proreform members taking control. In an emergency party congress on 18 December, the Communist Party of Slovakia (KSS) changed its structure, abolishing its presidium and replacing it with an executive committee. The dominance of the younger generation was demonstrated by the selection of Peter Weiss, who was born in 1952, as party chairman on 20 January 1990. A former employee of the Institute of Marxism-Leninism of the KSS's Central Committee in Bratislava, Weiss specialized in the political and scientific problems of society.

Serving as chairman of the KSS and later of the SDL until April 1996, Weiss symbolized the young, intellectual, and democratically minded orientation of the new leadership and played a key role in the KSS's transformation. From the beginning, Weiss proved successful in relations with the media, which was crucial in building a new image for the party. One analyst noted that Weiss, whose presentations in the press and on television were generally thoughtful and well prepared, was one of the few Slovak politicians who knew how to build his image in the media and to create relationships with journalists. As a result, the Slovak press was for the most part quite favorably inclined toward him (Chelemendik 1996).

Despite the initial changes that were implemented in the KSS, the population's anticommunist mood meant that the party performed relatively poorly in the 8–9 June 1990 parliamentary elections, winning only 13.34 percent of the vote and 22 of 150 seats in the Slovak National Council. At its congress on 20–21 October 1990, the KSS approved a new temporary name: the KSS-SDL. The party fared slightly better in the 23–24 November 1990 local elections, winning 13.6 percent of the seats in local councils and 24.2 percent of all mayoral posts.

While the KSS was pushing forward with reforms, the Communist Party of Czechoslovakia (KSC) was more problematic. Pavol Kanis, who had worked with Weiss at Bratislava's Institute of Marxism-Leninism, served as the KSC's last chairman. Born in 1949, Kanis was just a few years older than Weiss, and he also represented the younger, reformist stream within the party.[1] Kanis pointed out in November 1990 that a split had emerged between the Slovaks, who were quick to implement democratic structures into the party, and the more hard-line Czechs. By late 1990, the Slovak communists reportedly no longer had "any communist ideas" but backed "principles of pluralism, democracy, and the social market economy" (Kanis interview, *Der Standard*, 24 November 1990). Still, the KSS became part of the federalized Communist Party of Czechoslovakia (KSCS) in November 1990. Although the KSS was transformed into the SDL on 26 January 1991, thus dropping the word "communist" from its name, its formal split with the Czech Communist Party did not occur until the first SDL congress in December 1991.

In the early 1990s, the SDL consistently struggled to put forward a democratic-left ideology as Weiss and other party representatives repeatedly stressed the party's discontinuity with the ideas of the past. As a demonstration of his party's reform efforts, Weiss pointed out that since the SDL's transformation, two new communist parties had been established, both of which criticized the SDL for separating itself from the KSS program and ideology. One commentator stressed that although Weiss and other SDL representatives continually tried to argue that the party was "a modern, European-style leftist party" that did not have anything in common with the communists, Slovak citizens still accepted the SDL as a continuation of the KSS. He added that it was exactly this "nostalgic longing for the good old days" that was helping the SDL to increase its popular support (Lukac 1992).

While some voters were drawn to the SDL because of its predecessor's commitment to social equality, the SDL remained unacceptable to others simply because it was the communist successor party to the KSS. In former Czechoslovakia, which had one of the most repressive communist regimes in Eastern Europe during the "normalization" period from 1969–89, it would be hard to imagine a communist successor party—no matter how reformed it might be—gaining equivalent support that was received in the elections of ex-communists in Poland and Hungary.

The disdain of many Slovaks for the former Communist Party did not mean that popular politicians from other parties were not ex-communists. Most of Slovakia's major parties, with the exception of the right-of-center Christian Democratic Movement (KDH) and Democratic Party (DS), were dominated by individuals who were at one time members of the Communist Party. Seeing the unfairness of being blamed for past evils, Weiss stressed that "nine-tenths of former KSS members are [now] in other political parties and movements." He alleged that Mečiar's HZDS had "many more former communists than the SDL" and asked "who has the right to judge whether those in the SDL are worse than those in the HZDS?" (Weiss interview, *Plus 7 dni*, 10 March 1992). Along the same lines, SDL representative Milan Ftacnik pointed out that "it is difficult to say whether I am more responsible for the past than is a former member of the Communist Party of Czechoslovakia who switched to another party" (*Plus 7 dni*, 7 April 1992). Likewise, Kanis claimed that the HZDS included "many more" highly placed members of the former communist nomenklatura than the SDL (Kanis interview, *Narodna obroda*, 14 June 1993). Despite such arguments, the HZDS was generally not regarded as "communist," since Mečiar and other party members were "cleansed" by joining the anticommunist umbrella movement Public Against Violence (VPN) after the 1989 Velvet Revolution and gaining the initial approval of its former dissident leaders.

One analyst commented that by attempting to create a Western-style social democratic party, Weiss overestimated the theoretical abilities of potential voters and underestimated the pragmatism of his competitors (Chelemendik 1996). Although the SDL had a practical monopoly on the left side of the political spectrum following the changes in November 1989, the party gradually lost its chance to become a major political force because, unlike his counterparts in Poland and Hungary, Weiss was unable to gather all the ex-communists into a single party. In trying to appear "West European" rather than "communist," the SDL lost its identity and forgot its roots, which was especially apparent in its failure to keep up with its main constituency: the workers. As one analyst noted, in devoting their attention to "foreign political factors," the SDL leaders failed to take into consideration—even in the formation of their own discourse—the domestic electorate as well as "the history, mentality and traditions of Slovak society" (Minar 1994). Seeing an obvious niche, Mečiar adopted many traditional leftist ideals, at least in rhetoric, thereby helping the HZDS to "steal" leftist ideas and voters, while at the same time attracting members of the old business elite. Although workers should have been natural supporters of the SDL, Mečiar managed to attract the backing of a significant portion of them.

Economic reform and the future of Czech-Slovak relations were the major campaign themes of the 5–6 June 1992 parliamentary elections. The SDL emerged as the second biggest force, with 14.7 percent of the vote and 29 seats in the Slovak parliament; however, it was far behind Mečiar's HZDS, with 37.26 percent and 74 seats. In its campaign, the SDL criticized the quick economic reforms advocated by the pre-election government, particularly since the effects of the transformation process proved more difficult for the Slovaks than for the Czechs. Nonetheless, the party repeatedly rejected allegations that it favored halting reforms altogether. Although it may have appeared logical for the SDL to support coupon privatization since it was considered socially just, the party expressed a preference for standard methods, characterizing coupon privatization as a political move aimed at creating the illusion that people could get rich quickly (Kubin et al. 1993, pp. 40, 54). Weiss argued that although the SDL did not oppose privatization as such, it was against coupon privatization becoming "a tool for a part of the current state bureaucracy to seize economic power by using its monopoly on information" (Weiss interview, *Plus 7 dni*, 10 March 1992).

The SDL position on the national question also evolved prior to the 1992 elections, and the party shifted from the communist position of "proletarian internationalism" toward a more nationalistic stance (Lukac 1992). When asked in late 1990 about possible cooperation with the pro-independence Slovak National Party (SNS), Kanis replied "they have the radically thinking Slovaks on their side. We do not support their goal of an independent state" (Kanis interview, *Der Standard*, 24 November 1990). By early 1992, however, the party's stance had changed. It rejected the government-supported 1991 Milovy Agreement on federal Czech-Slovak relations in February 1992, and most SDL deputies backed an unsuccessful declaration of Slovak sovereignty in May 1992. At the same time, however, the party sometimes stressed that the future form of Czechoslovakia was not a top priority. In a party advertisement, one candidate emphasized that "it is rather enough for me that I am able to help simple people who are tormented not by the state arrangement but by economic and social concerns" (*Pravda*, 2 June 1992).

The SDL was sometimes criticized for its vague position on the future state arrangement, and it appeared that the party was keeping its options open and trying not to offend anyone. In its election program, the SDL stressed that the common state "must be built only as an expression of the will of the citizens of both republics, which is why we will support the kind of state arrangement that the people choose in a referendum." The party stressed its conviction that the will of most Slovaks was to live in a common state with the Czechs, and the SDL called for the expression of that desire to take the form of a treaty between the two republics, characterized as a "voluntary alliance of equal and strong national states." The party also emphasized the right of each nation to self-determination and called for the approval of a Slovak constitution, which it saw as "the culmination of Slovak statehood in the spirit of the message of the Slovak National Uprising" (Volebny program SDL, 1992).

After the 1992 elections, the HZDS was just short of a parliamentary majority; however, Mečiar chose not to form a coalition government, noting that his two most logical choices were "ex-communists or nationalists. . . words [that] do not generate a favorable impression" (Slovak Television, 4 December 1992). Nonetheless, Weiss was elected deputy parliament chairman in apparent appreciation of his party's backing of the government on several crucial issues that required a constitutional majority, including the declaration of sovereignty and constitution. At first glance, the SDL's decision to side with the HZDS and SNS in supporting Slovak independence was puzzling since the party had never formally advocated an independent state, particularly without a referendum. However, given the differing election results in Slovakia versus the Czech Republic, the SDL apparently believed that there was no other choice but to back Mečiar's proposals.

Although in one sense the SDL had adopted a nationalist approach, the party still retained certain elements of openness and tolerance. For example, the SDL's views on the World War II Slovak state and the Slovak National Uprising were much like those of the civic right parties, considering the former as a "a fascist political regime that sent tens of thousands of its citizens to death in concentration camps" and the latter as an expression of "the national and democratic consciousness of the Slovak nation," with a message that had "antifascist, national, democratic, as well as Czecho-Slovak dimensions" (*Smena*, 11 May 1992). In trying to appeal to leftist voters from the Hungarian minority in the 1992 election campaign,[2] the party produced radio spots for the Hungarian audience and Hungarian language campaign posters. Moreover, during the 1990s, the SDL included two ethnic Hungarians in its leadership: Alzbeta Borzova, who served as deputy chairwoman for economic and social policy until the 1995 congress, and Jozef Zselenak, who was deputy chairman for local and regional policy between 1996–1998.

Following the Czech-Slovak split on 1 January 1993, public attention was increasingly focused on the HZDS's domestic policies, and as the economic situation deteriorated throughout that year, opinion polls showed that Slovaks were gradually losing trust in politicians. Nonetheless, while the SDL had 45,000 members when it was founded in early 1991 (representing about one-tenth of the KSS's former membership), that figure grew slightly to 47,000 by late 1993.[3] Although a September 1993 opinion poll put the SDL in front of the HZDS by a margin of 10.8 to 10.2 percent,[4] the SDL's support still had indicated a drop from its 1992 election results. As a leftist opposition party, the SDL should have been able to capitalize on the HZDS failure and pick up that party's supporters as its popularity fell. However, one analyst noted that although the SDL had accepted leftist values in its program, the party lost contact with voters and allowed the personal ambitions of individuals to start shifting the party toward the liberal center (Juza 1994).

No one challenged Weiss for the post of chairman at the SDL's second party congress on 22–23 May 1993, and he was reelected with more than 90 percent support. At the same congress, a group centered around Kanis worked into the foreign policy agenda a discussion about the advantages of Slovakia's membership in NATO. Kanis threatened to resign from his position as deputy chairman should the congress reject the proposal (Kanis interview, *Narodna obroda*, 14 June 1993).

By late 1993, analysts were pointing to a split between Weiss and Kanis,[5] accompánied by warnings that Mečiar was aiming to deconstruct the SDL along those lines. When asked about the conflict, Weiss protested that "we are a real democratic party, and we know how to work out differences of opinion." (Weiss interview, *Narodna obroda*, 15 November 1993). At the same time, a third power center appeared around the party's representative in the Council of Europe's parliamentary assembly, Lubomir Fogas.

During the parliamentary crisis in February and March 1994 caused by the defection of a number of HZDS and SNS deputies, the SDL was reluctant to join the other opposition parties in a no-confidence vote, stressing that early parliamentary elections would first have to be scheduled. The SDL and HZDS were neck and neck in opinion polls, and the SDL apparently favored new elections so that it could gain more parliamentary support. The party even offered to form a coalition with the HZDS on the condition that the SNS be excluded and that Mečiar step down as prime minister. Only after Mečiar rejected that offer did the SDL agree to join the other opposition parties in dismissing the Mečiar government on 11 March 1994, inadvertently helping to perpetuate Mečiar's image as a "victim." After the cabinet's dismissal, HZDS support shot up to 26.4 percent.[6]

Following Mečiar's removal, the SDL joined the left-right government of his successor, Jozef Moravcik, a decision that was made by the SDL parliamentary caucus without the approval of any party organ. The largest party in the cabinet, the SDL was given seven out of eighteen posts, including several risky ones involving economic policy. Nonetheless, the SDL ministers were limited in implementing leftist policy both by their coalition partners—the conservative KDH and centrist-liberal Democratic Union (DU)—and by general economic constraints. Brigita Schmognerova, a former employee of the Economic Institute of the Slovak Academy of Sciences, was named deputy prime minister for economy, and she was responsible for working out loan agreements with the IMF and other international financial institutions as well as writing the cabinet's 1995 budget draft. The policies she endorsed were far from being "leftist," but she has remained one of the party's top personalities and a respected politician. Another key SDL minister was Economy Minister Peter Magvasi, who had strong ties to the industrial lobby and was one of the main sources of contention within the government. Although other SDL representatives had come out in support of coupon privatization, with Weiss telling journalists in late March 1994 that coupon privatization "enables those citizens to take part in the privatization process who otherwise do not have the money to do so," Magvasi favored conducting privatization through sales to managers and employees. He represented a fourth power center within the party, referred to as the "privatization group"; however, that alliance did not have much influence on party structures or on the wider electorate because of insufficient time in government (Juza 1994). Aside from its economic policy, another area in which the SDL left its mark during the Moravcik government was through its reluctance to fire HZDS appointees for fear of being accused of political purges.

The SDL's move toward the center by entering the Moravcik cabinet contributed to the creation of a splinter group in April 1994, when SDL deputy Jan Luptak expressed dissatisfaction with his party's participation in the government and transformed the Association of Workers of Slovakia (ZRS) civic movement into a political party. Thereafter, he refused cooperation with the SDL. The emergence of Luptak, a former worker who was sometimes called a "crypto-Bolshevik," was in some senses a natural reaction to Weiss's intellectualism, something for which many Slovak voters were unprepared. The ZRS positioned itself on the far left of the political spectrum, alongside the KSS, which was established in March 1991, shortly after the SDL dropped "communist" from its name.

Following Luptak's departure, internal struggles continued, and the SDL Party was divided over whether to cooperate with the HZDS following the next parliamentary elections. In a May interview, the young lawyer Robert Fico stated that the SDL would not have a problem cooperating with the HZDS if that party would adopt a similar program to the one it had had in 1992. Fogas and Kanis also hinted that they might support forming a coalition with the HZDS after the elections. Weiss, however, argued that there was a difference between the HZDS election program and its concrete policies. Noting that the SDL Republican Council had recently agreed that the decision to dismiss Mečiar's government was correct, Weiss added that "we have stepped out against demagogic, populist politics." Weiss also stated that the HZDS's new election campaign was aimed at creating an "enemy" by positioning "Slovaks against Hungarians, against Czechs, and against each other," and he stressed that unless the HZDS changed its policies, there would be no basis for post-election cooperation (Weiss interview, *Slovensky dennik*, 24 May 1994).

Prior to the fall 1994 elections, the SDL united in a coalition with three smaller left-wing parties to ensure that they would make it to the parliament and no leftist votes would be lost. The Common Choice coalition was formed in May 1994, grouping together the SDL, the Social Democratic Party of Slovakia (SDSS), the Green Party of Slovakia (SZS), and the tiny Movement of Peasants (HP). By adding the Greens to the coalition, the SDL hoped to gain support from young voters, while the HP would help secure the backing of rural leftist voters. Partnership with the SDSS was especially strategic because of that party's membership in Socialist International, and the SDL hoped to improve its own chances of gaining membership in that organization by association. Nonetheless, critics questioned the SDL's decision to form the coalition without sufficient planning or explanation. All three of its partners were in debt and were unable to finance even a minimal campaign, leaving the responsibility with the SDL. Mistakes made in the election campaign included a program that was not properly clarified, the replacement of the SDL's commonly recognized acronym with that of the new coalition, the insistence on putting party chairmen rather than experts at the top of the lists, and the failure to show on the ballots which party a particular candidate represented. One analyst noted that the decision to form the coalition was one of a narrow elite within the party, in which narcissism and personal ambitions prevailed (Juza 1994). There were numerous conflicts over the coalition's formation within all parties except the HP, which led to splits within both the SDSS and SZS.

The Common Choice electoral platform was based on the values of "social justice and solidarity, democracy and human rights, peace and good relations with neighboring countries, the coexistence of ethnic communities, environmental renewal and responsibility toward nature." The coalition voiced support for Slovakia's transition to a market economy but noted that it could not allow for "the constant fall in wages, rising unemployment, and a feeling of hopelessness at a time when a sliver of society lives in luxury." Privatization was considered "an important and unavoidable element of economic change, but it had to be transparent and serve to improve companies' competitiveness." The coalition also favored more power for regional administrative bodies, a fight against crime, and NATO membership following a referendum. In pre-election interviews, Weiss said the elections were giving the population a chance to decide between "politics of controversy, revolving around the image of an enemy and made-up stories about conspiracies against the young Slovak republic" or politics "based on professionalism and cooperation." Also at stake was whether Slovakia would "pursue a rational economic policy or rely on improvisations, whether we will have a stable constitutional system or a tendency to change the existing regime... to kindle nationalistic passions into flame or to encourage national reconciliation."[7]

Although opinion polls prior to the 1994 elections predicted results as high as 19.3 percent for the Common Choice, the coalition performed extremely poorly, winning only 10.41 percent of the vote and 18 seats, barely surpassing the 10 percent barrier needed for four party coalitions. Of those 18 seats, the SDL gained just 13, while the remaining were divided among its coalition partners. Weiss had clearly miscalculated by speculating that the coalition would attract all the votes of its component parts. Instead, it gained significantly less support than what the SDL alone had had in most polls shortly before the coalition was formed.[8] As leftist voters looked for alternatives, the ZRS and KSS won 7.34 and 2.72 percent of the vote, respectively, and although the latter failed to enter the parliament, the former gained 13 seats.

The composition of the parliament after the elections made Luptak the kingmaker, allowing him to support either the Mečiar or the Moravcik camp.

Luptak initially refused to join either side, but in December the ZRS finally joined a new Mečiar government. Although the party at first continued with extreme leftist rhetoric, speaking out against international organizations and privatization,[9] before long it had almost completely lost its character and was transformed into a virtual HZDS puppet. The party supported numerous policies that were in clear contradiction with its original goals, and several of its representatives were believed to have made significant personal monetary gains from the privatization process. The ZRS's only major impact on policy was in the establishment of the Construction Ministry, and its public support remained below 5 percent almost throughout the election term. The ZRS began to crumble in April 1995 when one deputy left its parliamentary caucus, while several more deputies quit the party in 1998.

The SDL as an "Independent" Opposition Party

After the 1994 elections, the SDL went through a troubled period, during which many predicted that the pro-HZDS wing of the party would take control from Weiss, Ftacnik, and Schmognerova. According to a report prepared by Schmognerova after the elections, entering a HZDS coalition government would present unacceptable risks for the SDL in light of the types of policies that such a cabinet could implement. Her analysis predicted "a substantial slowing of the transformation process, antidemocratic methods of governing, the instigation of ethnic intolerance, a slowdown in the flow of foreign capital, a deepening of social tension, complications in relations between the government and the trade unions," as well as other problems (Meseznikov 1997a).

At the same time, Kanis sent warning signals when he openly expressed regret that the SDL had supported the dismissal of Mečiar's cabinet in March 1994. Mečiar waited anxiously for the results of an SDL Republican Council session on 15 October 1994, hoping that the outcome would be in his favor. Although observers predicted that the party leadership would be changed, Weiss was retained as chairman, crushing Mečiar's hopes of gaining the SDL's support. Afterward, Weiss issued a list of conditions for joining a HZDS cabinet and said that the SDL would only consider participation in a wide coalition government, implying that the DU and KDH would also have to be included. The HZDS formed a majority government in December with the SNS and ZRS, but the coalition was seven seats short of the ninety votes needed to change the constitution. Although pressure continued to be applied on the SDL, none of its deputies chose to switch sides.

In the local elections of 18–19 November 1994, the SDL was boosted by a win of 15.87 percent of the votes and 17.87 percent of the mayoral seats. Still, the party's third congress on 18–19 February 1995 was devoted to a discussion of its poor parliamentary electoral results. Despite criticism, Weiss was reelected as party chairman with 53.9 percent of the vote while Fogas, who represented the wing leaning toward cooperation with the HZDS, gained 33.7 percent, and Ftacnik was third with 12.3 percent. Ftacnik, Schmognerova, and Kanis were chosen as deputy chairmen, but Fogas refused to take on a post because of his disagreement with Weiss's leadership. Despite the negative mood within the party, the congress reaffirmed the positions of those opposed to cooperation with the HZDS and supported the SDL's development as a party of social-democratic orientation, seeking membership in Socialist International.

After the congress, the party repeatedly attempted to stress its "leftist" orientation, with Weiss arguing that the SDL stood between the nationalist-populist ruling coalition and the center-right opposition. Although the SDL backed the HZDS on a number of issues, including a constitutional law on conflicts of interests that the two parties co-sponsored in May 1995 as well as a controversial state language law of November 1995, SDL criticism of certain government policies grew stronger, particularly concerning the ruling coalition's attacks on President Michal Kovac, changes in the media, and privatization policies.

In May 1995 the SDL established a sixteen member "shadow cabinet," headed by Juraj Hrasko, who had served as Environment Minister in Moravcik's cabinet. After his appointment, Hrasko stressed that the SDL would remain an opposition party since the "current style of governing is not in harmony with the SDL's program, which seeks national understanding and concentrating the strength of all wise people of this nation for the fulfillment of a positive program" (Hrasko interview, *Sme*, 25 May 1995). Hrasko was later replaced by Kanis.

Despite the results of the 1995 party congress, Weiss's opponents, united in the "pragmatic" wing, did not give up the idea of adopting a different party line that would be more amenable to cooperation with the HZDS. Pointing to the SDL's drop in support, which in September 1995 was down to around 8 percent, the "pragmatists" criticized the group around Weiss for its inability to renew party structures and for other organizational problems. They stressed that their views were not an expression of personal ambition but rather a reflection of the mood of the party membership. For Fogas, the key task the party faced was the strengthening of its regional structures and the improvement of finances. Because the HZDS privatization policy discriminated against firm managers who were oriented toward the SDL, those managers were reportedly pressuring SDL leadership to change its critical attitudes toward the government (Meseznikov 1997a).

In October 1995, the SDL attracted distrust from other opposition parties when it refused to participate in a joint opposition meeting following an extraordinary parliament session dealing with the case of the abduction of the president's son. Explaining the SDL's need to hold a separate meeting with its Common Choice partners, Fico argued that the party wanted to conduct "its own opposition policy." Seven of the thirteen Common Choice deputies present at the meeting approved a statement blaming not only the ruling coalition but also the opposition KDH for increasing political tensions. Later, the SDL's Republican Council stated that the party had the potential to become an alternative to the policy that was prevalent at the time, and "for that reason it does not want to and cannot be in a united opposition camp" (Melis 1995). The SDL's insistence on forging an "independent opposition policy" eventually led to the collapse of the Common Choice coalition.

Continued internal conflicts combined with low public support led to Weiss's surprising announcement in November 1995 that he would not run again as chairman during the fourth party congress, scheduled for 27–28 April 1996. The SDL's membership fell from an estimated 40,000 in 1995 to just 25,000 in 1996. It was widely expected that the young Fico would take over Weiss's position; however, just before the voting took place, Fico gave up his candidacy and encouraged his supporters to elect Fogas. Fogas received only 37.2 percent support and was beaten by the unknown Jozef Migas, with 62.8 percent of the vote. Migas, who at the time was serving as Slovakia's ambassador to Ukraine, was seen as a compromise candidate between the two wings of the party. Weiss remained deputy chairman, along with Schmognerova, Fico, Fogas, Magvasi, and the Hungarian Zselenak. Although Migas criticized the government and stressed that the SDL would remain in opposition until the 1998 elections, he also hinted that his party's participation in the Moravcik cabinet was a mistake. Migas displayed his leftist views during May Day celebrations, when he called for "taking Marx off the shelf and dusting him off" (CTK, 1 May 1996).

The SDL's leadership change and its newly adopted general principles represented an effort to revitalize the party, improve its organization, and strengthen its internal unity and identity, steps that were to be accomplished in part based on Socialist International's "Declaration of Principles." The SDL also aimed at stabilizing its local structures in light of plans for the country's new administrative division. Although the party reaffirmed its desire to follow a leftist-oriented independent opposition policy, it said it would cooperate with the right-wing opposition in defending democracy and the constitutional state.

Despite those signs, some believed that Migas's election would finally bring an alteration in the party's stance on the ruling coalition, and Mečiar himself noted that "we assume that the changes in the SDL leadership will cause the party to stop demonizing the HZDS and its chairman and open the way for normal conditions for cooperation" (Slovak Radio, 20 June 1996). Migas and other SDL representatives came under considerable criticism in June 1996, when the government was threatened by a conflict over privatization. At a time when the ruling coalition seemed near collapse, Migas naively offered his party's tacit support for a HZDS-led minority government, failing to consider Mečiar's ability to outmaneuver him. The SDL strongly opposed early elections, partly because of waning support but also because it wanted Mečiar to serve out his four-year term and suffer the consequences of any unpopular decisions. In the end, the ruling coalition stayed together, and although the SDL took credit for averting the fall of Mečiar's government, the party came under serious attack from the other opposition parties and from journalists, who have since remained skeptical of the SDL's intentions toward the HZDS (Fisher 1996).

The SDL's "independent" opposition policy continued over the question of direct presidential elections, which the other opposition parties favored in an effort to prevent Mečiar from increasing his powers once President Kovac's term ended in March 1998. In December 1996, SDL deputies rejected an opposition proposal for a constitutional amendment on direct presidential elections, arguing that it opposed constitutional changes at that time. In early 1997 the SDL refused to join its opposition partners in a petition campaign for a referendum on direct presidential elections, questioning whether it was possible to change the constitution through a referendum. Once opinion polls were published showing high popular support for direct elections, the SDL was in a difficult position. After the necessary signatures were collected and President Kovac called the referendum for 23–24 May 1997, the SDL recommended that its supporters vote "yes." Regarding the three questions on NATO that the ruling parties proposed as part of the same referendum, the SDL recommended that its supporters vote "yes" to Slovakia's entry into the organization, "no" to having nuclear weapons on Slovak territory, and that they ignore the question about having military bases stationed in Slovakia. Migas was the first Slovak politician to express concern about the nuclear weapons issue, noting shortly after his election as SDL chairman that while he generally supported NATO membership, his party would oppose NATO enlargement if it meant the deployment of nuclear weapons on Slovak territory.[10] After Interior Minister Gustav Krajci took the question on direct presidential elections off the ballot, the SDL considered the referendum to be "illegal and chaotic." Although the party put some of the blame on President Kovac and on the opposition parties that initiated the referendum, the ruling parties' obvious breach of the constitution led to increased cooperation between the SDL and the rest of the opposition. The SDL was the only party that took the subsequent attempts to elect a new president through the parliament seriously, trying to find individuals who might attract broader support. Nonetheless, the party eventually gave up since no candidate was able to muster the necessary three-fifths majority.

Migas in some respects turned the SDL in a different direction than Weiss; however, he did manage to bring the party into Socialist International in

September 1996. Although differences of opinion continued to exist, Migas succeeded in bringing more unity to the party, with a continued balance between the more moderate, intellectual group around Weiss versus those who sided with Fogas. SDL representatives clearly realized that a split would mean disaster for the party.

The SDL's Structure

According to SDL party literature published in 1996 while the party was in opposition, the SDL's highest party body is the congress, which meets at least once every two years. The congress elects the party chairman, deputy chairmen, Republican Executive Committee, and Republican Council and adopts the party's constitution and program. The Party Leadership, which consists of the chairman and deputy chairmen, the heads of the "shadow cabinet,"[11] the parliamentary caucus, and the chairman of the Committee for Local and Regional Policy, meets weekly. Meanwhile, the Republican Executive Committee holds sessions each month and decides on the main political issues. The Republican Council, which is the highest body between meetings of the congresses, consisted of sixty-five members in 1996: the Party Leadership, Executive Committee, parliamentary caucus, and regional representatives (SDL brochure 1996).

Concerning its extra-party ties, the SDL cooperates with three main organizations: the Young Democratic Left, the Union of Democratic Left Women, and the Ladislav Novomesky Foundation. The latter, named after one of Slovakia's popular communist-era writers, is "committed to study, discuss and spread leftist values in culture, science, education, and politics." The SDL also stresses the importance of cooperation with trade unions and civic associations. Although the party does not have formal ties to trade unions, relations improved in the years prior to the 1998 elections. In the SDL's 1998 election program, the party included a section on ties with trade unions, criticizing the Mečiar government's neglectful stance toward unions and noting the importance of cooperation. In light of the Mečiar cabinet's refusal to continue to cooperate with the unions through the approval of an annual tripartite agreement between the government, trade unions, and employer organizations, the SDL called for "the basic principles of tripartism to be declared in the constitution" and protected by law. At the same time, the SDL expressed respect for the impartial character of the Slovak Confederation of Trade Unions (KOZ) but added that "impartial" does not mean "apolitical." Moreover, the party noted that the KOZ's social program was "very close" to that of the SDL. At the SDL's fifth congress on 25 April 1998, which was focused on preparing for the upcoming elections, there was discussion about placing KOZ Chairman Ivan Saktor on the SDL's election lists; however, Saktor was reluctant to be associated with any one political party.

The SDL's Entrance into Government

Throughout 1996 and 1997, the SDL's support was fairly steady at about 10 percent, and in the months before the elections some polls put the party as high as 14.3 percent. The party's electoral prospects were improved by the decision of its former coalition partners—the Social Democrats and the Greens—to join the KDH, DU, and DS in the newly formed Slovak Democratic Coalition (SDK), while the HP merged with the HZDS. By presenting itself as a leftist-democratic alternative to the HZDS, the SDL expected to attract voters who were frustrated with their economic situation. Importantly, the SDL was the party for which Slovaks felt the least antipathy; according to a February 1996 opinion poll, only 17 percent of citizens were resolutely opposed to the SDL (Butorova et al. 1996, pp. 56–60).

In October 1997, the SDL voter profile was fairly balanced according to age, work status, and income, and in most cases it corresponded roughly to the break down of the population as a whole. The vast majority of SDL supporters claimed to have a leftist orientation, while more than 80 percent supported Slovak membership in the European Union (EU) and about 50 percent favored the country's entry into NATO. Over 60 percent of SDL voters had a "democratic" orientation concerning basic political principles, while less than 10 percent were "undemocratic" (Butorova 1998, pp. 42–53). Although some analysts pointed out that SDL and HZDS voters were similar in terms of economic orientation, a February 1996 poll showed that while SDL supporters considered the center-right parties constituting the SDK as being at a "mid-range distance," the ruling parties and the Hungarian coalition were seen as being at a "far distance" (Butorova et al. (1996, pp. 72–73).

A major problem for the SDL was that consolidation had yet to take place on the left end of the political spectrum. A large number of political parties continued to be relevant; in the 1998 elections, left-leaning voters had seven major choices: the SDL, SDSS, Greens, HZDS, ZRS, KSS, and the new Party of Civic Understanding (SOP), which was established in April 1998. Although the parties offered voters varying messages, they were all competing for the left-wing vote and—with the possible exception of the HZDS—all considered themselves to be left-of-center parties. On the far left were the KSS and ZRS, neither of which managed to surpass the 5 percent barrier for entry into the parliament, while the SDSS and SZS moved toward the center of the political spectrum by joining the SDK.

The SDL was largely responsible for the dispersion of the left, and the SOP's establishment was particularly worrisome to it, especially since the latter party emerged in a position in which the SDL wanted to be. The SOP's main personalities did not hide the fact that they were ex-communists, and they tried to promote themselves as a party of reconciliation between the anti-Mečiar and pro-Mečiar forces. Through such rhetoric, the party consistently gained about 15 percent in opinion polls and was able to appeal to segments of the business elite who were concerned about Mečiar's inability to lead Slovakia into the EU.

As the elections approached, the four major opposition parties—the SDK, SOP, SDL, and the Party of the Hungarian Coalition (SMK)—held a series of round-table discussions together with representatives of the trade unions, non-governmental organizations, the Association of Towns and Villages, and the Council of Youth of Slovakia. Agreeing on a "fair approach" toward each other in the elections, they also decided to work together in filling the polling station commissions and preparing a constitutional law on direct presidential elections, among other issues.[12] The SDL's participation in those meetings signaled that it would cooperate with the center-right democratic forces after the elections because of their common view of the need to bring Slovakia closer to Europe, to renew democracy, and to restore rule of law.

Despite some doubts on which direction the party would take under Migas's leadership, the 1998 election campaign presented the SDL as a Western-style social democratic party made up of experts. The SDL concentrated its election campaign on addressing social problems, and its main election slogan was "To live better." The party's television ads drew attention to the professional qualifications of the party's top candidates, pointing to problems in society and ways to resolve them. The main issues of the SDL campaign were increasing wages and pensions; improving Slovakia's image abroad and ensuring membership in the EU; rejuvenating the economy by putting a halt to partisan privatization and guaranteeing state participation in strategic firms and financial institutions; creating new jobs; securing accessible and quality health services for all; allowing each citizen free access to education; ensuring the construction of apartments for young and socially weak families; fighting crime, and securing the renewal of democracy and rule of law. The SDL campaign focused on its eight election leaders, each of whom was presented as an expert in a given area. These were (in the order they appeared on the SDL's election list): Migas, Schmognerova, Fico, Kanis, Weiss, Fogas, Magvasi, and Ftacnik. The party's campaign was influenced by that of the British Labour Party, and candidates distributed cards with their pictures on the front and a list of promises on the back. During the campaign, Schmognerova presented her "Black Book of Governing," which discussed numerous controversial policies implemented by the Mečiar cabinet.

In the elections, the SDL won 14.66 percent and 23 seats, becoming the third strongest parliamentary party after the HZDS and SDK. The SDL's results were considered a great success, particularly because of its surprising appeal to young voters, with more than 18 percent of its constituency consisting of citizens aged 18–24 (Gyafarsova et al. 1999). The SDL made an effort in its campaign to put forward its young representatives, particularly Fico, who at the time of the elections was 33 years old, but also journalist

Milan Istvan and party spokesman Lubomir Andrassy, who were just 23 and 25, respectively. All three became parliamentary deputies, and after the elections Fico was elected SDL first deputy chairman, while Andrassy became one of the party's deputy chairmen. Fico's role in bringing support to the party was demonstrated by the fact that he received the most preference votes of any candidate, moving him up from third to first on the party list, while Migas fell to fourth, behind Weiss and Schmognerova.[13]

An exit poll showed that the SDL electorate had a higher than average education level and tended to live in bigger towns and cities. The party's support in Slovakia's regions was fairly evenly dispersed, ranging from 10 percent in the Nitra region to 16 percent in Zilina. In terms of professions, the SDL attracted 24 percent of all students, 21 percent of office workers and professionals, and 14 percent of laborers and the unemployed. The HZDS remained the party of workers, with 29 percent of voters in that category giving it their support, while even the SDK won the backing of 6 percent more workers than the SDL.[14] Only 22 percent of SDL supporters had voted for the Common Choice in 1994, while 18 percent had supported the HZDS, 11 percent were first-time voters, and 9 percent had been non-voters.[15]

The SDL managed to win considerably more than the SOP in one of the biggest election surprises; the latter gained just 8.01 percent and 13 seats, making it the smallest of the six parliamentary parties. While state-run Slovak Television had run a smear campaign against the SOP before the elections, the station had carefully avoided attacking the SDL, signaling that the HZDS saw the party as a potential coalition partner.[16] Voters may also have rejected the SOP since it ran the most negative campaign of all the major parties, indicating that it had moved away from its earlier aim of promoting reconciliation.

Because the HZDS emerged as the biggest parliamentary party, with one more seat than the SDK, parliament chairman Ivan Gasparovic gave the HZDS the first chance to form a cabinet. The SDK, SMK, and SOP immediately rejected talks with the HZDS, leaving the party with the SNS and SDL. While the former welcomed the HZDS efforts, the SDL said it would only discuss the transfer of power and not the possibility of setting up a government. Although the SDL and the three other opposition parties announced their intention on 27 September to create a cabinet of their own, the HZDS gave the SDL an offer inspired by the "Czech model,"[17] according to which the SDL would form a one-party government with tacit support from the HZDS and SNS. The SDL, however, resisted the proposal, emphasizing that Slovakia needed a strong government because of the difficulties it was facing. Clearly, the party realized that it would have been political suicide to form a minority cabinet after having won less than 15 percent of the votes, particularly since it would then take full responsibility for the economic problems that were awaiting the country. Moreover, the fact that the four opposi-

tion parties combined had won a constitutional majority gave the SDL striking evidence of the population's desire for a real change, and if the party had
acted against such signals, unrest could have ensued. Finally, the SDL's cooperation with the HZDS would have endangered the party's hard-won membership in Socialist International and would have likely caused a split within
the party. The SDL's decision to enter a cabinet with the other opposition
parties was formally supported by an SDL congress on 24 October.

Although it was clear that the SDL would join the other opposition parties
in a new government, the SDL was criticized for using its offer from the
HZDS to obtain more cabinet positions than its election results warranted.
Moreover, the SDL tried to decrease the influence of the two small coalition
parties, and some SDL representatives even argued against the SMK's inclusion in the cabinet since the other three parties would have a parliamentary
majority without it. Some SDL representatives expressed concern about the
Hungarians' differing approaches to the Benes decrees[18] and the Gabcikovo-
Nagymaros Dam case. While the SDK and SOP generally considered the
Hungarians' participation important to guarantee political stability and enhance EU entrance talks, the SDL was accused of following Mečiar's lead in
playing the "Hungarian card." Some analysts believed the SDL feared the
public's reaction to the Hungarians' inclusion in the government, but others
thought the party wanted to increase the power of the leftist elements in the
ruling coalition by leaving out the SMK, which was likely to side with the
SDK on economic policy. SMK representatives, who in the past had provided tacit support to several minority governments, warned that failure to
include ethnic Hungarians in the cabinet would send them into "strong opposition." The SDL eventually backed down, but its actions did not set a
positive tone for cooperation between the two parties.

The SDL's Role in Government

The four parties signed a coalition agreement on 28 October, and Migas was
elected parliament chairman during the opening parliament session the next
day. Appointed on 30 October, the new twenty member cabinet was led by
Dzurinda as prime minister and four deputy prime ministers. The breakdown
of posts by party was: nine for the SDK, six for the SDL, three for the SMK,
and two for the SOP. The SDL got the positions of deputy prime minister for
legislation (Fogas), finance minister (Schmognerova), defense minister
(Kanis), agriculture minister (Pavol Koncos), education minister (Ftacnik),
and minister of labor and social affairs (Magvasi). The SDL's feeling of con-.
fidence was strengthened in the local elections on 19–20 December 1998.
With the parties constituting the SDK running separately, the SDL came in
second place, behind the HZDS.

Among the first issues addressed by the new cabinet was the presidency.

While the SDK preferred direct presidential elections, the SDL viewed the absence of a president negatively and favored electing one in the parliament given the new government's constitutional majority. According to the SDL, direct presidential elections could take place following a normal five-year presidential term. Nonetheless, the government eventually agreed to keep its promise by holding direct elections in May 1999, and SOP Chairman Rudolf Schuster became Slovak president.

Most of the battles among the four government parties pitted the SDL against the SMK or SDK. While some were personality conflicts, others were based on policy, particularly relating to the economy. The deteriorating economic situation after four years of Mečiar's government meant that the new cabinet was forced to take many unpopular steps, and the SDL was uncomfortable taking part in a cabinet that could be blamed for social problems. The first policy-oriented conflict emerged in February 1999 over the state budget, centering on the differing approaches of Schmognerova and Deputy Prime Minister for Economy Ivan Miklos, an SDK representative who had served in the VPN government before the 1992 elections. After a number of domestic and international analysts evaluated Schmognerova's budget proposal critically, expressing doubt that the goals set forward were reachable, Miklos suggested raising the minimum level of VAT (Value Added Tax) to ensure additional budget income. Schmognerova and other SDL representatives countered that they preferred alternative measures that would have a less negative effect on Slovaks living in poor social conditions, and tensions between Schmognerova and Miklos reached such a high that Schmognerova stated in March 1999 that it was necessary to "build barriers against the renewed influence of former prominent figures from the VPN, who with their neo-liberal ideas about economic development caused deep social trauma in the early 1990s." After several months of delay and a drop in the Slovak crown's value, Miklos's proposal won, and the SDL's image was harmed by perceptions that the steps would have been less harsh had the cabinet acted sooner.

In February 1999, the SDL and SMK embarked on a long-running public dispute over who would head the Land Fund, which administers state land and land of unknown ownership. Although the post was initially promised to the SMK, the SDL put its own candidate in the position, and Agriculture Minister Koncos threatened to resign should it be given to the SMK. The two parties also clashed over funding for minority culture in the 1999 state budget. Additionally, the SDL clashed with all three of its coalition partners over the privatization of strategic enterprises as well as over plans to approve a treaty between Slovakia and the Vatican.

Echoing the deficiencies of the Mečiar regime, the SDL was the first government party to be accused of promoting clientelism. In March 1999 media revealed that Schmognerova had retained Slovakia's Devin banka as the financial mediator in the repayment of Russian debt to Slovakia, even though the Mečiar cabinet's use of the same bank for that purpose had been the subject of controversy. The bank was chosen without any public tender, and Schmognerova argued that it was the state-owned utilities firm Slovenske Elekrarne (SE) rather than the ministry itself that had chosen the bank. It was later revealed that Devin banka's new head, Lubomir Kanis, had close ties to the SDL.

In March 2000 the SE again became embroiled in a controversy between the SDL and its coalition partners, starting with the dismissal of the firm's head, Stefan Kosovan, an SDL appointee. Kosovan was fired after an Economy Ministry audit of the firm revealed several inconsistencies. The Economy Ministry, led by Lubomir Harach of the SDK, held over 95 percent of SE shares, giving it legal authority over the firm. While some SDL representatives accepted Kosovan's recall, Migas took a strong stand against it, leading journalists to argue that Migas's insistence on retaining Kosovan stemmed from personal interests rather than those of Slovakia as a whole.

Following Kosovan's dismissal, Migas vowed to reevaluate the coalition agreement, while the other ruling parties opposed the move, arguing that it could cause instability. In the midst of a coalition crisis, the opposition called a special parliament session in April 2000 in an attempt to dismiss the cabinet in a no-confidence vote. Although the government survived, Migas's vote against the cabinet caused considerable commotion. Migas claimed that he wanted the coalition to continue, but he demanded the cabinet's reconstruction and proposed the merger of several posts, while criticizing some of the SDL's own ministers, particularly Schmognerova and Kanis. Migas also suggested the possibility of replacing Prime Minister Dzurinda because of the unclear situation within the SDK. Although the cabinet appeared near collapse in spring 2000, the situation calmed after the SDL dropped its demands. Nonetheless, Migas's actions prompted a wave of criticism. One commentator speculated that Migas's main aim in proposing a cabinet reshuffle was to appoint one of his allies as the new SE head, which he planned to achieve by removing SDL rebels from the government and giving Magvasi the economy minister post, which would also shift responsibility for high unemployment away from the SDL. Other commentators stressed that Migas was pushing for Russia's interests, while some media pointed to his drinking problems and claimed that he was intoxicated while voting against the cabinet. By calling attention to his faults, Migas's idea of rebuilding the cabinet harmed the SDL more than its coalition partners.

Although Migas argued that his efforts to distinguish his party from its coalition partners were based on falling public support for the SDL resulting from the cabinet's economic policies, it appeared more likely that the drop in popularity was actually based on Fico's decision in December 1999 to create a new SDL splinter group, Smer ("Direction"). Despite Fico's contribution to the

SDL's electoral success, he was not given any cabinet post, which could be considered a big mistake of the party leadership. Smer was set up as an untraditional party focused on the ideas of order, justice, and stability, and opinion polls showed that the party had 10–15 percent support, taking votes from both the SDL and SOP. After Smer's establishment, SDL's support dropped to around 5 percent, while the SOP's backing was even lower. Fico, who according to opinion polls had emerged as the country's most trusted politician, was balancing himself between the opposition and coalition in the apparent hope that he would become kingmaker after the next elections. Dissatisfied with the government's privatization policies and its "servility" toward the West, Fico called for the creation of a new cabinet consisting of two or three parties and for the emergence of a new generation of politicians.

In 2000, the SDL had about 22,000 members, while the Young Democratic Left had 2,000 (Nicholson 2000). By the summer of 2000, Migas's position within the SDL appeared uncertain, and his role as party chairman was challenged during an SDL congress on 8 July 2000 by the moderate education minister Ftacnik, whose reputation was untarnished by corruption scandals. In a speech before the congress, Migas blamed Kanis, Weiss, and Schmognerova for some of the party's problems, claiming that they had brought internal party conflicts to the public. Nonetheless, Migas was reelected by a margin of 52 to 41 percent. The deputy chairman posts went to Ftacnik, Andrassy, and the 27-year-old former television anchor Brano Ondrus, while Weiss's bid for reelection was rejected. Despite ideological differences, Ondrus supported Migas because of his willingness to promote the party's young generation (Nicholson 2000). The results clearly represented a victory for Migas's wing, and one analyst commented that Weiss had lost the battle to create a Western-style social democratic party (*Sme*, 11 July 2000). Nonetheless, the party's Republican Council later expressed support for Schmognerova, who threatened to quit her ministerial post if she did not have the party's backing. Schmognerova's position was strengthened in September 2000, when the British *Euromoney* magazine named her best finance minister of the year; she was the first woman to win the prize. During the first two and one-half years in office, the only SDL minister to lose his post was Kanis, who was forced to resign following complaints over personnel policies at the Defense Ministry and his construction of a luxurious villa. The SDL nominated Slovakia's ambassador to the Czech Republic, Jozef Stank, to replace him, and Stank has been pushing forward quickly with reforms needed for Slovakia's NATO accession.

Prospects

Shortly after the 1998 election results were announced, SDL representatives declared that their next major goal was to win the 2002 parliamentary elections. After several years of internal chaos, however, that prospect now appears highly unlikely. By sabotaging the work of the cabinet, certain SDL representatives have harmed the party's image and increased the divisions between the two wings of the party. Although the SDL's entrance into government after the 1998 elections as the second strongest ruling party could have provided a solid basis for its future development, the continuing internal and external battles have caused its public support to dwindle. At the moment, not only its future orientation but also its very existence are in question. If the party continues suffering from allegations of corruption, struggling with internal conflicts, and threatening the stability of the ruling coalition, its support will continue to remain low.

As a left-wing party, the SDL obviously stood to lose the most from the effects that the government's economically restrictive policies have had on the population; however, when it entered the ruling coalition, the party was well aware of the kinds of problems that the cabinet would face. Because the SDL made the decision to join the government, it now has no choice but to remain there, at least until the economy improves significantly. Although the SDK will probably get more of the credit for any improvement in the economy, since its representatives have been pushing harder for change, support for the SDL could go up as well. The SDL could also be boosted if it manages to integrate the left side of the political spectrum; however, that prospect seems unlikely with the emergence of Smer, and more unlikely if Migas and other middle generation politicians intend to stay in power. In June 2001, Migas announced that he will not serve as the party's election leader for the 2002 parliamentary elections, although he would like to remain in the post of SDL chairman. That step is unlikely to help the party significantly unless an election leader emerges who can bring together leftist forces and attract the confidence of the electorate.

Throughout the 1990s, the inability of the SDL to keep the left united represented the SDL's greatest failure; however, it was not until recently that the emergence of left-wing alternatives has threatened the existence of the party. As the next elections approach, the pragmatists in the SDL will likely attempt to look to the party's leftist roots in attempts to attract more public support. Nonetheless, as part of the current ruling coalition and a continuing ally of the center-right, the SDL has little choice but to present itself as a modern social democratic party. If it moves to revamp its leftist elements, the party will distance itself from its coalition partners and cause more interparty conflicts, which would only serve to bring more disdain from the electorate.

Notes

1. At the time of the "Velvet Revolution," Kanis was working on a controversial analysis of the position of the KSC within society. See interview with Kanis, *Der Standard*, 24 November 1990.

2. None of the three major groups representing the Hungarian minority, which in 1998 merged into the Party of the Hungarian Coalition (SMK), advocated leftist views.

3. See interview with Weiss, *Narodna obroda*, 15 November 1993; and SDL brochure (1996).

4. Journalist Study Institute poll, reported in *Narodna obroda*, 20 October 1993.

5. Some claim that this conflict had existed since the SDL's beginnings, when Weiss won the post of party chairman; however, Kanis said that this was a "myth." See interview with Kanis, *Slovensky dennik*, 17 January 1994.

6. Slovak Radio poll published in *Pravda*, 23 March 1994.

7. TASR (News agency), "1994 Parliamentary Elections in the Slovak Republic," 27 September 1994 and interview with Weiss in *Parlamentny kurier*, September 1994.

8. According to a Slovak Statistical Office opinion poll conducted in early May, the SDL had the support of 16 percent of respondents, the Greens had 4 percent, and the SDSS had 3 percent.

9. Just after the presentation of the government's program declaration, which expresses support for the "continuation and acceleration" of privatization, EU and NATO membership as well as cooperation with the IMF, on 14 January the ZRS issued a statement declaring privatization to be "the foundation of a speculative economy" and said "we are obliged to tell governments, the IMF, the World Bank and the European Union, it is not possible to continue further with this policy which is leading the whole world to barbarism." *Sme*, 16 January 1995.

10. CTK, 30 April 1996. The party's program recommends that Slovakia should have a similar position within NATO as Denmark or Norway. See http://www.sdl.sk/dok_politicky.htm#bezpecnost.

11. Obviously, the shadow cabinet does not exist while the party is in government.

12. See *Plus 7 dni*, no. 24 (June 15, 1998): p. 15; CTK, 24 June 1998.

13. Voters were allowed to circle a maximum of four names on the party list of their choice, and Fico received 194,519 preference votes from the SDL's 492,507 voters, compared with 164,619 for Weiss, 149,830 for Schmognerova, and 92,807 for Migas. See *Pravda*, 30 September 1998.

14. Exit poll conducted by the Focus agency and the International Republican Institute (IRI), 25–26 September 1998.

15. Focus/IRI exit poll, 25–26 September 1998.

16. See, for example, the Osservatorio di Pavia's assessment of the Slovak media during the election campaign, conducted for the OSCE (Organization for Security and Cooperation in Europe).

17. Although during the campaign preceding the last Czech parliamentary elections parties were extremely vocal about whom they would not cooperate with, after the elections the Social Democrats (CSSD) managed to forge an agreement with its long-term "enemy," the right-of-center Civic Democratic Party (ODS) whereby the ODS would "tolerate" a one-party CSSD minority government.

18. The Benes decrees, proclaimed after World War II by Czechoslovak President Eduard Benes, declared collective guilt for ethnic Germans and Hungarians living in Czechoslovakia.

7

The Communist Party of Bohemia and Moravia after 1989

"Subcultural Party" to Neocommunist Force?

Seán Hanley

While scarcely "the last Communist Party in Europe" (Novák 1992), the Communist Party of Bohemia and Moravia (KSČM) is nevertheless a relatively isolated exception within East Central Europe. Unique among major successor parties KSČM sought to maintain and renew a communist identity. In the mid-1990s, this unusual choice seemed to have allowed the "historic" Czech Social Democratic Party (ČSSD) to emerge as the principal party of the democratic left. However, in 1998–99, against a background of economic stagnation and growing public disenchantment with ineffective minority governments, KSČM experienced a rapid increase in popularity, suggesting that its "neocommunist strategy" was paying unexpected political dividends.

Much earlier comparative writing stressing the "social democratization" (Waller 1995) of successor parties or the dichotomous alternatives of postcommunist technocratic modernization versus patronage-based chauvino-communism (Ishiyama 1997a; Bozóki 1997) made it difficult to incorporate an "orthodox" communist party such as KSČM, strongly profiled in terms of egalitarian, statist antimarket attributes (Kitschelt et al. 1999), into comparative typologies. Recent, more sophisticated typologies, however, have enabled the party to be defined more accurately as a "radical socialist" (Bigio 1998) or "non-reformed, non-transmuted" (Bozóki and Ishiyama 2001) ex-ruling party characterized by a rejection of both "chavino-communism" and social democracy and the presence of an anticommunist historic, social-democratic party. However, KSČM's comparatively unreformed and orthodox character compared to other ex-ruling parties in Eastern and Central Europe, coupled with a lack of research, has often led the party to be dismissed as a political holdover whose politics are unchanged from the undemocratic "Marxism-Leninism" of the pre-1989 Communist Party of Czechoslovakia

(KSČ), "a real 'dinosaur' of Leninism which has no future . . ." (Nagle and Mahr 1999, pp. 179–80).

In this chapter tracing KSČM's development, I will argue that this view is an oversimplification and that that the "neocommunist" strategy embraced by KSČM since 1993 is a more sophisticated attempt to reinvent the party than simple revanchism, conservatism, or nostalgia and includes innovative and democratic elements. I will go on to argue that KSČM's development into such a party was a contingent, if predictable, outcome of internal political struggles over the party's adaptation to competitive electoral politics, and an outcome strongly influenced by the specific traditions and history of Czech communism. I will suggest throughout that for most of the first postcommunist decade it can be usefully understood as a neocommunist "subcultural party" (Enyedi 1996), whose strategy was driven by a "logic of constituency representation" rather than a "logic of electoral competition" (Kitschelt 1989, pp. 1–74). Finally, in exploring the growth of KSČM support in the late 1990s, I will suggest that the possibility of significant political and electoral success may be more destabilizing to it than its established role as a "subcultural party" appealing to a limited core constituency.

The Communist Tradition in the Czech Lands

The historical peculiarities of the Czech Lands offer a number of clues to the specificity of Czech and Czechoslovak communism, including its post-1989 development. First, we should note that, historically, communism and the Communist Party in the Czech Lands enjoyed significant, though varying, levels of mass support. The Czech Lands are unusual in Eastern and Central Europe because of their high degree of precommunist socioeconomic modernity (Rothschild 1974; Kitschelt 1995b; Kitschelt et al. 1999). As the most highly industrialized region in the Austro-Hungarian Empire in the late nineteenth century, the Czech Lands developed a large labor movement and Social Democratic Party (founded in 1878) relatively early on, a movement which, as elsewhere, split into reformist and communist wings in the wake of the Bolshevik Revolution.

The Communist Party of Czechoslovakia (KSČ), founded in 1920, existed throughout the democratic interwar Czechoslovak Republic (1918–38) as a legal political party, which remained in opposition and enjoyed electoral support of 10–15 percent, evenly distributed between Czech and Slovak regions. After 1945, boosted by the ignominious collapse of the prewar democratic regime following the 1938 Munich Agreement (and the support of the USSR), the KSČ successfully harnessed the appeal of left-wing social and economic policies and resurgent anti-German Czech nationalism to emerge as a newly dominant mass force. In the 1946 elections it polled 38 percent of the vote in Czechoslovakia as a whole, and 40 percent in the Czech Lands, where it was the largest party. Given such mass support the Communist Party was able to take power in February 1948 in a coup that outwardly respected legal forms and constitutional procedures (Kaplan 1987). However, their popular support and legitimacy varied, and indeed oscillated historically. While in certain periods communism can be seen as a distinct subculture, isolated from broader Czech society (Paul 1979), as for example in the interwar period (Rupnik 1981) or after post-1968 "normalization" (Williams 1997), at other times, the Communist Party was capable of acquiring broader legitimacy, as in the immediate postwar period or during the "renewal process" of the 1960s (the so-called "Prague Spring"). Finally, there was also a historical duality within the party itself, between an understanding of socialism and the party's role in terms of loyalty to the USSR on the one hand, and a reformist national-democratic communist tradition on the other. Thus, although strongly influenced by its Austro-Marxist and social-democratic roots, the party underwent "Bolshevization" at the behest of the Comintern in 1929, establishing its ultra-loyal pro-Moscow orientation. This process was facilitated by its existence as a legal mass organization (Rupnik 1981.) It readopted a national-democratic identity in 1945–48.

In the 1950s, the party reverted to pro-Soviet loyalism, implementing some of the most uncompromisingly Stalinist policies of socioeconomic transformation and political repression seen anywhere in Eastern Europe (Lewis 1994). This occurred before radical-reform communism gained ground in the party in the 1960s and briefly took control of it in 1967–68. This inner duality was finally eliminated when the post-invasion "normalization" regime of the early 1970s systematically expelled and excluded reformers from the party en masse (Kusin 1978). Although, reformist pockets later re-emerged in the party whose monolithic rigidity was, in hindsight, overestimated (Grzymala-Busse 1998a), pragmatists in the leadership such as Ladislav Adamec and Lubomír Štrougal sought unsuccessfully to promote limited economic reform in the late 1980s. Until the regime's collapse in November 1989 the party followed a "normalization" strategy of repressing and containing society.

"They Fled from Power Like A Bunch of Hooligans": The Communist Party in the Velvet Revolution

In the "Velvet Revolution" of November 1989, the Communist Party of Czechoslovakia was wholly unprepared both for transition and the onset of competitive pluralistic politics. Having decided against a Chinese-style "solution" to the crisis, the party leadership was politically paralyzed, and responsibility for transition negotiations thus passed by default to Ladislav Adamec, the Federal Prime Minister. By the time the Communist Party convened an Extraordinary Congress on 20–21 December 1989, the key mechanisms of the country's transition had already been agreed upon with leaders of the Civic Forum and Public Against Violence movements. Hastily devised stratagems such as attempts by communist deputies to have the president directly elected or instructions that communists infiltrate local Civic Forum organizations were wholly ineffective. In the words of the exiled former reform communist Zdeněk Mlynář (1996, p. 9) the communists had simply "fled from power like a bunch of hooligans."

The December 1989 Extraordinary Congress represented a belated, desperate and largely incoherent attempt to come to terms with the party's sudden loss of power and to formulate a response, which would allow it to recuperate some support and legitimacy. The congress swept away the entire pre-November leadership (most of whom had already resigned and some of whom, such as former General Secretary Miloš Jakeš, were later expelled), reelecting only four members of the 200-member Central Committee to a slimmed down successor body (Obrman 1990). The new echelon of leaders were drawn from lower down or outside the Communist Party power structure, often from the normalization era academia. Miroslav Štěpán, the former head of the Prague Party organization in November 1989, for example, told one interviewer in May 1990 that "of the current KSČ Executive Committee I only know Mr Adamec and Mr. Mohorita personally," adding of the then Federal Party chairman, "I've never seen or heard Mr. Machalík. I just know he was a lecturer somewhere at a university. . ." (*Svobodné slovo* 1990a). Resolutions passed at the Extraordinary Congress included a blanket rejection of the doctrines of the normalization period; an apology for wrongdoings of the Communist Party since 1948, an acceptance of the loss of its "leading role"; general endorsements of the rule of law of a "socialist market," human rights and democracy and a commitment to become a "modern political party." However, while littering their program with previously taboo phrases borrowed from either the dissident opposition ("democracy for all") or the reform communist era ("Action Program," "deformations," "Stalinist models," "renewal"), the KSČ set out no clear future direction for the party. The most concrete changes made by the Extraordinary Congress were measures to democratize and decentralize the party organization, including formal recognition of the role of "platforms" (factions) and the federalization of the Communist Party of Czechoslovakia into two autonomous national parties. Although the Communist Party of Slovakia (KSS) had formally existed since 1930, in the Czech Lands a "new" party had to be created, the Communist Party of Bohemia and Moravia (KSČM), formally established on 31 March 1990.[1]

Despite the de facto collapse of the regime, the opposition elites heading Civic Forum sought to follow a "pacted" model of transition based on "round tables" and a Government of National Understanding, including communist representatives. From spring 1990, however, a growing mood of anticommunism took hold in the Czech Lands, leading to strikes and demonstrations for special measures against the Communist Party and its property, and even the party's banning (Pehe 1990a; Martin 1990). The unexpectedly high rate of 14 percent of Czech Communists polled in the June 1990 elections suggested that, as in other postcommunist states, the former ruling party had some underlying bases of support. This situation reinforced the anticommunist feelings of a public increasingly concerned with the (supposed) role of "nomenklatura brotherhoods" in the economy and state apparatus. In October 1990, ill-judged remarks by federal Communist Party Chairman Vasil Mohorita provoked uproar. Mohorita, a politician with a hitherto reformist reputation, urged communists to retain their workplace cells and prepare for the end of "national understanding" and the onset of an uncompromising political struggle (Pehe 1990b). However, in hindsight the incident is perhaps best seen as indicative of communist leaders' inability to define the party's role in competitive politics and contrasts markedly with the relatively coherent projects of other former ruling parties at this stage.

Neocommunism or "Democratic Socialism": The Struggle over the Character of the Party Between 1990–1993

Despite the disorientation and paralysis within the Communist Party of Czechoslovakia in 1989–90, the period did see a flourishing of communist discussion clubs, forums, and platforms. These highly visible, but politically ineffective, "platforms" not only marginalized reformers—preventing them from launching an early preemptive strike to transform the party along postcommunist lines (as occurred in Slovakia) (Grzymala-Busse 1998a), but also highlighted a range of alternatives that the Czech communists as a party would ultimately choose from. One speaker at the January 1990 meeting of the Democratic Forum of Communists (DFK) group, for example, spoke of clearly identifiable "democratic socialist," "reformist" anti-Stalinist, and "neo-Stalinist" currents (Vilhelm 1990).

At the first KSČM congress, held in Olomouc in November 1990, Jiří Svoboda, a film director and unconventional left-wing intellectual who had briefly participated in the founding of Civic Forum, was elected chairman, defeating the more conservative Jan Machalík by 387 votes to 248 (Pehe 1990c). Despite his lack of political experience, Svoboda had a clear objective for KSČM: to make it the basis of a solid, well-organized Left acceptable to a large part of Czech society by salvaging the democratic and progressive aspects of its communist tradition and distancing the party from its totalitarian past. This would entail dropping the word "communist" for the label "democratic socialist" or "Radical Left." Resisting radical demands by small postcommunist groups within the party (such as the Democratic

Left), for KSČM's immediate social democratization,[2] Svoboda and his allies adopted an evolutionary approach, initially seeking to change the party's
name at the Olomouc Congress to a transitional double name: "Communist
Party of Bohemia and Moravia: Party of Democratic Socialism" (*Svobodné
slovo* 1990). However, while delegates approved a democratic socialist program they rejected the name change.

Despite outward unity in 1991–92, factional conflicts slowly accumulated
within KSČM. The formation of the social-democratically oriented Democratic Left faction by younger communist deputies was paralleled by the
increasing assertiveness of conservative communists, including the neo-
Stalinist Marxist-Leninist Clubs that were increasingly vocal in criticizing
Svoboda (Svoboda 1993i). On the party's other wing, the Democratic Left
and other reformers successfully called for a referendum of members to
change the party name. However, the referendum held in 1992 voted by a
75.94 percent majority to retain the existing name[3] (*Naše pravda* 1992).
Frustrated at the slow pace of reform, the Democratic Left had already
broken away from KSČM in December 1991 to form the short-lived Democratic of Labor (DSP).

In January 1992, KSČM formed the Left Bloc (LB), an electoral coalition
linking it in the Czech Lands to a number of tiny left-wing groups[4] and prominent left-wing independents, such as the flamboyant Marxist philosopher
Ivan Sviták. In the June 1992 elections the Left Bloc polled 14 percent in the
Czech Lands, emerging as the largest opposition party. However, despite
this relative success, LB remained politically isolated and lacked sufficient
influence to prevent either the dominance of the Right in Czech politics or
the division of Czechoslovakia agreed upon by the right-wing Czech Prime
Minister Václav Klaus and his Slovak counterpart Vladimír Mečiar.

The second KSČM congress, held at Kladno in December 1992, indicated the growing strength of conservatives in the party. It passed resolutions
reinterpreting the 1990 Olomouc program as a starting point for KSČM,
rather than a definitive statement of a postcommunist orientation (KSČM
1992). However, in a highly charged emotional atmosphere, Svoboda, who
was hospitalized and unable to attend the congress after a near fatal assault
by a presumed anticommunist extremist, was overwhelmingly reelected.
Nevertheless, in January 1993, a number of prominent figures in the pre-
November 1989 regime who had been readmitted to the party, including
former Prague party leader Miroslav Štěpán and former Interior Minister
Jaromir Obzina, formed the "For Socialism" platform, which called
unashamedly for the wholesale restoration of the pre-November 1989 regime (*Haló noviny* 1993a). This display of open communist revanchism led
Svoboda to intensify his campaign to reform the party. He demanded the
immediate expulsion of the "For Socialism" leaders, an immediate change in
the party's name, and the adoption of an unambiguously postcommunist ori-

entation. However, on 10 March 1993, when the majority of the KSČM Central Committee offered him only lukewarm support and excised the concept of democratic socialism from its declaration, Svoboda announced his resignation as party chairman (*Haló noviny* 1993b). His resignation was soon withdrawn after the Central Committee passed a motion stating that it did not consider the "For Socialism" leaders to be members of the party and called for the party's third congress to be moved to June 1993 to resolve the issues of party name and identity.

Svoboda (1993e) viewed the choice facing KSČM as one between nostalgic neo-Stalinist obscurantism or postcommunist "democratic socialism." However, from 1992 onwards a third, "neocommunist" alternative emerged in KSČM. "Neocommunists" sought a middle way which would retain the communist character of the party in some form other than crude antidemocratic neo-Stalinism. Neocommunist ideas were elaborated in greatest detail by Miroslav Ransdorf, a Marxist intellectual with a critical and reformist bent, well before 1989. However, neocommunist arguments were employed by a number of communist leaders, including KSČM Deputy Chairmen Miroslav Grebeníček, who emerged as Svoboda's main rival in 1993.

As pre-congress district party conferences took place, it quickly became apparent that Svoboda's strategy would be heavily defeated, approximately two-thirds of KSČM district organizations supported retention of the party's communist name and only one-third Svoboda's postcommunist option. A small number favored the compromise double name suggested by a group of Left Bloc deputies (KSČM 1993). Facing a humiliating defeat, Svoboda declared that he would neither seek reelection as chairman, nor attend the congress, adding that he would not remain a member of an unreformed KSČM (Svoboda 1993i). As expected, the congress, held in the town of Prostejov, produced a clear victory for the neocommunists and their conception of the party.[5] It rejected the idea of a name change and elected Grebeníček chairman with Ransdorf as one his deputies. The congress also voted to expel the leaders of the "For Socialism" platform (whose politics and support Grebeníček and other neocommunists had consistently rejected), and abolished any formal role for platforms in the party on the grounds that they gave too much influence to minorities lacking real grassroots support. Delegates from the postcommunist minority led by Central Committee member Josef Mečl then left the congress to found a postcommunist breakaway party, the Party of the Democratic Left (SDL).

Space precludes detailed consideration of the organizational changes within KSČM. However we should note a number of points. First, the extensive post-November 1989 democratization and decentralization of communist structures gave district organization substantial autonomy from the center, making radical any reorganization dictated by the center difficult and later unfeasible. Second, Svoboda seems to have underestimated the importance of ideology and identity to KSČM members, an impression reinforced by his frequent assertions that rank-and-file communists were decent people who joined the party from essentially public-spirited motivations which could be divorced from the party's record in power (Svoboda 1993h; 1993i). Finally, Svoboda's tactics of seeking a rapid resolution of the 1993 issue concerning the symbolic issue of the party name, although perhaps a product of desperation, weakened his position and mobilized opposition against him. Thus, while the neocommunist outcome was, given the preferences of the KSČM membership, most likely, there was a substantial minority in KSČM for the "postcommunist" course championed by Svoboda; it was not inevitable or uncontested.

Postcommunist vs. Neocommunist Strategy

Postcommunists and neocommunists agreed over many important issues: the idea of democratization after 1989 as a free-market "property putsch" (*majetkový puč*), the key tenants of the party's social and economic policy (egalitarian, statist interventionist, nationalistic), the nature of the party's social constituency (losers in transformation), and the need to reject neo-Stalinism. However, the conflict over the apparently symbolic issue of the party's name concealed both different assessments of the party's past and present and different strategies for its future. With the exception of 1968, for postcommunist reformers communist rule was largely a period of crimes and "inexcusable violations of human rights" (Svoboda 1993a), which had collapsed in November 1989 because they had rightly been rejected by the people (Svoboda 1993b). "Real socialism" would, reformers argued, always be an unattractive political model and one indelibly associated with communism and the Communist Party (Svoboda 1993d). The label "communist," Svoboda (1993f) argued, reinforced the ghettoization of the party and was "a kind of burden, which drives both our deputies and our party as a whole into a corner." The party's isolation and identification with a stigmatized past, reformers asserted, made it naive to imagine that in any social crisis voters would automatically move left and turn nostalgically back to the communists (Masopust and Mečl 1993a; Svoboda 1993b). Moreover, having, as they saw it, adopted a noncommunist "democratic-socialist" program (at Olomouc), KSČM had already ceased to be a communist party and should have signalled this to the Czech public logically by changing its name (Svoboda 1993c; 1993d). Opposition to a name change was "nothing other than a sign of a lack of faith in the substance of the party's policies and a clinging on to outdated symbols" (Masopust and Mečl 1993a).

At the tactical level, Svoboda and his supporters noted that the split of Czechoslovakia at the end of 1992 had removed the potential for a left-wing federal coalition with left-of-center Slovak parties, leaving the KSČM and the Czech Left in a new, more right-wing dominated Czech party system (Masopust and Mečl 1993a). However, when the policies of the Czech Right floundered, opportunities for the Left could open (Mečl and Masopust 1993b).

Despite being the largest opposition party, reformers argued KSČM was too weak on its own to constitute a viable Left. It was, however, excellently placed to form the nucleus of a new left-wing alliance, if it could make itself acceptable to potential partners and articulate the interests of newly emerging social groups (Svoboda 1993a; 1993f). Without such an alliance, neither KSČM nor the Left would ever realistically be able to challenge the Right or exercise political influence and "it is to this that it is necessary to subordinate our activity" (Svoboda 1993d). The creation of the Left Bloc in 1992 was thus intended as a step towards the creation of a postcommunist electoral alliance subsuming the former ruling party in a manner similar to the Polish Democratic Left Alliance. In Svoboda's view (1993b; 1993e) the Left Bloc was "in embryonic form the cooperation necessary to achieve social change . . . [and] the overcoming of the traditional contradictions between the communist, social-democratic and Christian-social left." To make such an alliance viable KSČM should not only change its identity but also "gradually seek the outline of a common minimum program" capable of "uniting the opposition (from center to radical left)" (Svoboda 1993e). Thus, in April 1993, Svoboda offered to allow Left Bloc's participation in the "Realist Bloc" of left-wing parties proposed by newly elected Social Democrat leader Miloš Zeman. However, the social democrats and all other potential participants rebuffed the offer. (Vachudová 1993).

Reformers saw the reform of KSČM as a race against time. If KSČM missed the "historic opportunity that social development will undoubtedly offer" to form the nucleus of a powerful left-wing bloc (Svoboda 1993d), then other left-wing forces would ultimately take that role, leaving the communists an isolated, declining political sect. As Svoboda told one party meeting "time is not working for us but against us. . . . The program adopted at the Kladno Congress [1992] is acceptable to a huge majority of the membership and many outside the party. However, the membership is aging, many basic units are disintegrating and there is a minimal inflow of new members" (Svoboda 1993d). Thus, reform rather than a distraction was the only way the party could become an effective political force (Svoboda 1993d).

Neocommunists, by contrast, saw the issue of the party name as a "substitute problem" imposed on the party from outside which was distracting it from real political tasks (Grebeníček 1993a). A name change, they argued, would be cosmetic and unnecessary, given that any successor party would always be associated in the public mind with its communist predecessor, (Novák 1993). For neocommunists, retaining a communist identity was important as "a symbol that we have not gone down on our knees" (Ransdorf

1993a). Neocommunists also saw Svoboda's project as both undemocratic and dangerous because it sought to impose a change from above rather than seeking an orientation that commanded majority support, thus risking a disastrous split which might destroy the party (Ransdorf 1993s; 1993b; Grebeníček 1993c). Neocommunists also saw democratic socialism as a social-democratic program of ameliorating capitalism, rather than a communist program seeking a systemic alternative to it. This, they argued, was not only a denial of the party's identity and *raison d'être* but also no real alternative given the crisis and apparent exhaustion of West European social democracy after 1989. Finally, neocommunists questioned the strategic assumption that it would be possible to create a single, broad-based left-wing bloc, primarily because communist and social-democratic programs were incompatible, and secondly because the center-left was already occupied by the Social Democratic Party (ČSSD). While postcommunists cited the success of postcommunist parties in Poland and Lithuania, neocommunists countered with the examples of the French Communist Party and the Italian "Communist Refoundation" (Grebeníček 1993b). Rather than risk alienating the party's loyal electorate (Novák 1993), "it would be rational to appeal to those citizens social democracy cannot catch" (Ransdorf 1993a).

As an alternative to Svoboda's project, Ransdorf (1993c) offered his own ideas to an "expansive transformation" of KSČM resting on a very different strategic rationale. While considering communist isolation overstated and partly surmountable by local activism, Ransdorf and other neocommunists were aware of their strategy's costs and implications that in the immediate future the party would become isolated and restricted to a defensive role. Ransdorf (1992, Part 5), for example, wrote of "the defense and development of elements of civil society and the principles of the social state and the rule of law" as a "line of defense for the movement and the rights of working people" (Ransdorf 1992, Part 6). Communists, Ransdorf argued, should adopt a long-term perspective and "not fear years in the wilderness and have the courage to swim against the tide (*jít proti proudu*)" (Ransdorf 1993a). In summary, neocommunists thus viewed their strategy as both more principled and more realistic than the postcommunist alternative given the "real waterline of opinion" in the party (Grebeníček 1993a) and the competitive context of Czech politics.

KSČM Policy and Ideology

Although one survey has suggested that the underlying values of Czech Communist supporters are similar to those of postcommunist successor parties (Evans and Whitefield 1995), qualitative analysis of KSČM programmatic documents (KSČM 1993; 1995a; 1996; 1998; 1999) suggests that its supporters and leaders understood transformation politics quite differently from postcommunist social democrats. In its 1996 election program the party depicts politics as based on class or social conflict between a popular constituency of "ordinary people," who have lost out in the transformation, and privileged elites and foreign interests. Economic transformation since 1989 is seen as a "property putsch" which has "brought only negative results" (KSČM 1996, p. 15), a restoration of capitalism "ruthlessly dividing society into a small group of nouveaux riches (*zbohatlíků*) and an ever more impoverished majority. Foreign capital and its domestic lackeys (*přisluháčů*), including the state bureaucracy and other top administrators, are acquiring an extraordinary position in this country" (KSČM 1996, p. 16).

Resistance to capitalist restoration is also linked to resistance to foreign and Western influence. The party speaks of a need to "protect the national cultural heritage from devastation or sale abroad" and to prevent "the Americanization of our public life" via subsidies to culture and measures such as a language law to enforce the use of correct Czech with foreign neologisms in advertising and broadcasting (KSČM 1998). The party has also campaigned vigorously against such traditional foreign enemies as the Sudeten Germans, the Catholic Church, or the Czech aristocracy and their supposed claims for the restitution of property confiscated between 1945–48. It is resolutely opposed to Czech membership in NATO, which it considers an unnecessary and expensive "leftover of the Cold War . . . misused in the interests of the USA and in Europe the FRG" (KSČM 1998). However, it takes a more ambiguous, if highly skeptical view of the EU, rejecting "unconditional and rushed entry . . . under conditions which would put our republic in the position of a colony, viewed by other stronger countries only as a market open for their surpluses and a source of cheap labor" (KSČM 1998). It nevertheless, favors European integration in some form, advocates the incorporation of certain EU norms, such as the European Social Charter or Charter on Local Self-government into Czech law. It does not oppose the Czech Republic's current "associate" links with the EU, and anticipates EU membership in many of its political calculations.[6]

While not opposed to private ownership per se, KSČM economic policy favors the development of a strong state sector, the transformation of the Czech privatization agency (the National Property Fund) into an agency for "strategic planning," and an interventionist industrial policy. It also advocates heavy investment in public services, increased index-linked pensions and social benefits and public subsidies of rent and utilities. The party also seeks to encourage employee shareholding, enterprise leasing, as well as cooperative and municipal ownership. Such policies would be combined with protectionist measures and stricter limits on foreign investment and foreign control of Czech industries (KSČM 1996). KSČM says it does not seek to renationalize privatized industries across the board. However, it does wish to halt privatization, investigate "disputable privatization decisions," and "revise" the restitution of property to the Church and "persons with problematic claims" (KSČM 1998). The party does not state whether it would then restart or continue with privatization. Such a vision of a market economy based on diverse forms of (mainly public) ownership embodies KSČM's concept of "modern socialism" as a systemic alternative to capitalism. More broadly, the party defines socialism as a socially just and essentially noncapitalist society in which parliamentary democracy is heavily supplemented by elements of direct democracy, corporatist mechanisms, and industrial and other forms of "self-management" (Ransdorf 1992, Part 6).

It is central to KSČM ideology that its policies offer the prospect of system change or a systemic alternative (as opposed to the vaguer idea of the leftist "civilizational alternative" promoted by Svoboda). Thus, suggestions in the party press of 1993 that such policies in fact amounted to no more than a radical, if peculiarly expressed, form of social democracy (Schwarz 1993) were angrily rejected (Hába 1993). As a long-term goal, the party also commits itself to "communism" understood in conventional Marxist terms as a classless society (KSČM 1996).

KSČM is keen to project itself as a normal legitimate party. Its leaders and documents have repeatedly stressed the party's internally democratic character and its acceptance of parliamentary democracy, political pluralism, private property, the market, and the rule of law. In particular, KSČM leaders emphasize that the party does not wish to return to pre-1989 "real socialism," is committed to legal and peaceful means, and makes no special claim on power. In the words of Party Chairman Grebeníček, "we do not aspire to have an article in the Constitution about the leading role of the party. We know that would be the road to self-destruction and to the loss of people's trust . . . we do not want any going back" (*Mladá fronta Dnes* 1997). In spite of the persistence of nostalgia and revanchism among part of the party's membership and voters (26 percent of whom favored a return to the pre-1989 regime according to a 1998 poll) (*Mladá fronta Dnes* 1998b), there seems no real reason to doubt the substance or sincerity of such claims. KSČM has made sustained efforts to reformulate its ideology in democratic, but nevertheless communist, terms and despite its lack of political influence, has consistently devoted considerable efforts to researching and drafting policy and legislation. Moreover, as Grebeníček notes, any suggestion of revanchism would be deeply politically damaging to the party, reinforcing its pariah status and risking a possible ban under current Czech legislation on political parties.

Nevertheless, finding an interpretation of the period of communist rule (1948–89) which is both plausible and acceptable to its supporters has proved difficult for KSČM. In general, while prepared to accept that "real socialism" was deeply flawed and a historical failure, KSČM is reluctant to concede that the post-November 1989 system represents any overall improvement, and is grudging even in its acknowledgement of those areas where it recognizes that improvements have taken place (the rule of law, civil liberties, and pluralism). The party's 1996 election program, for example, characteristically asserts that "we will not allow the repetition of past mistakes, which led to stagnation and defeat" (KSČM 1996, p. 6), but blandly depicts the 1948–1989 period at some length as "one of the greatest periods of social and economic growth," which despite "serious internal and external problems" compares favorably with both prewar and postcommunist Czechoslovakia (KSČM 1996, p. 12). However, nowhere are the "mistakes" and "inadequacies" specified, and KSČM's 1998 election program simply ignored the issue altogether (KSČM 1998).

A paper prepared as a 1995 congress resolution (KSČM 1995b), which has been publicly endorsed and cited by party leaders (Grebeníček 1999), does address the issue at length. The paper highlights the party's underlying, deeply contradictory and ambivalent attitude to the past. It explains the collapse of "real socialism" mainly as a consequence of a lack of democracy and self-management creating privileged and self-seeking bureaucratic groups. However, while effusive about the progressive character and economic achievements of the 1948–89 period, it is evasive and euphemistic about the repressive character of the regime, referring only to "unacceptable forms of conflict resolution," "insensitive administrative approaches to private peasants in the collectivization of agriculture," "the disproportionate repression of active opponents," and "excesses," and argues that even in the 1950s "not all trials were show trials" (KSČM 1995b, p. 6). Assessing 1968, the paper accepts the normalization doctrine that "procapitalist forces" exploited the Prague Spring and that the 1968 invasion "prevented counterrevolution." It criticizes the invasion only as politically clumsy because it delegitimized the regime and blocked the subsequent prospect of reform (KSČM 1995b, p. 9), not because it was politically or morally wrong. Similarly, the regime of the 1970s and 1980s is not rejected per se, but because the "undifferentiated use of repressive measures" increased the influence of "right-wing, antisocialist dissent" (KSČM 1995b, p. 10). However, even this paper proved so controversial that the Congress shelved voting on it in 1995 and did not discuss it in 1999.

The Czech neocommunist ideology is something of an eclectic synthesis. Certain themes—"bureaucratic deformation" as the cause of "real socialism's" failure; socialism as self-management plus multiple forms of ownership; European integration reducing Eastern Europe to dependency upon the West— echo the thinking of the Western far Left and, by a historical irony, the ideas of 1960s East European and Czechoslovak reform communism and revisionist Marxism. Elsewhere, reinterpretations of key themes of the official ideology of "normalization" also emerge. Other themes such as anticlericalism or anti-German chauvinism are artifacts of traditional Czech nationalism taken up by the Communist Party after 1945. Sociological notions of post-industrialism and post-capitalism borrowed from Western thinkers are also featured in the writing of party intellectuals as a ways of stressing the party's historical relevance.

Party Organization

To a significantly greater extent than other former ruling parties in Eastern and Central Europe, KSČM has a mass membership and organization. As elsewhere in the region, early 1990 saw the Communist Party of Czechoslovakia's vast monolithic organization disintegrate, with most party property being voluntarily divested or confiscated. However, by late 1990 the KSČM had succeeded in re-creating a central apparatus and a nation-wide organizational network, albeit on a greatly reduced scale, based on territorial (basic and district) rather than a workplace basis. Since 1990, district and local organizations have been conceived of in party statutes as autonomous and "self-managing" (*samosprávní*) units, with the authority of central bodies carefully delineated and limited. Such autonomy, although reduced after 1993, does have substance, given that the party's mass membership allows some KSČM district organizations to be largely self-financing, rather than dependent on state-funding redistributed from the center as is the case with many other Czech parties (Šimíček 1995).

Estimates and internal party data suggest that after post-transition losses and further decline in the 1991–93 period, KSČM membership stabilized at approximately 160,000 (see Table 7.1). The party currently claims to have 5,700 local branches (basic organizations), figures broadly confirmed by the party's electoral activity at a local level (Kostelecký and Kroupa 1996) and its reported income from membership dues (Matoušková 1995a; 1995b). Since 1990, the KSČM membership has rapidly become one largely composed of retired people, a fact reflected in a steady decline in membership (approximately 5 percent a year) to the current figure of 136,000. There has also been a related shrinkage in its organizational network and a decline in the number of communist local councillors. For this reason, networks of branch chairpersons, councillors, and district party organizations are increasingly replacing local branches as the effective organizers of local activity (KSČM 1999). However, despite this, KSČM is still numerically by far the largest political organization in the Czech Republic; its nearest rival, the Christian Democratic Union (KDU-ČSL), has only 60,000 members.

KSČM has attracted few new members—figures from 1992 suggested that only 0.5 percent of party members joined after 1990 (KSČM 1992, p. 17). The party has also had little attraction for young people; the KSČM youth organization, the Communist Union of Youth (KSM), reportedly had only 250 members in 1998 (*Lidové noviny* 1998b).

Table 7.1

KSČM Membership, 1990–99

	Total membership	% aged over 60	% of workers	No. of basic organizations
1990 (30 June)	562,529	39.8%	29.9%	?
1991	355,045	51.6%*	21.0%*	?
1992	354,500	?		10,669
1993	317,100	?		8,530
1995	195,443	?	?	7,030
1997	154,900	?		5,826
1998	142,500	70% (est.)	?	5,545
1999	136,500	?		5,406

Sources: Dokumenty I. Sjezdu KSČM, p. 10; Dokumenty II Sjezdu KSČM, pp. 16-17; IV Sjezdu KSČM, p. 36; *Lidové noviny*; "Draft report of the Central Committee of the Communist Party of Bohemia and Moravia (KSČM) on the Party's work in the period between the 4th and 5th Congresses," www.kscm.cz.

Note: *Projection based on 12 districts (58,000 members)

Despite its impressive size, the real effectiveness of the party organization is patchy, with marked variations between regions, localities, and organizational units. KSČM Congress reports repeatedly bemoan the failure of members to take an active interest in party activities, "self-government," and policy discussion (KSČM 1995a; KSČM 1999). KSČM Congress reports speak of many members,

> suspiciousness and lack of trust . . . passive reactions; [and] tendency to wait for the views of the leadership and approve them without discussion"; ignorance of party policy and absorption in local affairs (KSČM 1995a, pp. 38–44); "inadequate dialogue and . . . confrontation and pedantry" in internal discussions; and failure to engage in any political activity not strictly internal to the party (KSČM 1999, pp. 6, 12).

The mass character of the party also imposes substantial organizational costs and coordination problems. Despite limited investment in computer technology, elite-mass links are mainly organized through a hierarchical chain of command, face-to-face contacts and meetings, and to a lesser extent via the party's loss-making daily newspaper *Haló noviny* (circulation 30,000–40,000) and weekly *Naše pravda*. The party newspapers thus fulfill the contradictory role of being the main internal channel of communication to the rank and file and the party's main chosen means of informing the wider public of its views and policies given the "information blockade" it sees as imposed by a hostile media.

Social Constituencies

KSČM has defined itself as a "party of the underprivileged" and of "ordinary people" (KSČM 1996, p. 1). It defines its assumed constituency in broad populist terms as "working people" (*lidé práce*) and groups "whom the capitalist system existentially threatens, pushes out to the margins of society, and offers no real chance of change" (KSČM 1996, p. 60), "social groups who derive their living from the results of honest work, in either the past or present, and from deserved social benefits . . . industrial and agricultural workers . . . farmers in transformed cooperatives . . . and other employees" as well as ". . . intellectual workers, linked with the lives of ordinary working people (teachers, doctors, workers in social services, lower officials)," small businesspeople, the self-employed and "socially weak and threatened groups" such as young people, pensioners and women (KSČM 1995a, p. 61).

How did KSČM's real social base compare with this imagined constituency? Polling from June 1996 showed communist supporters were, compared with those of other parties, disproportionately likely to be over age sixty (47 percent), retired (51 percent), on a low income (54 percent), or resident in small or medium-sized towns (40 percent). Economically active communist supporters were more likely to be industrial and agricultural workers or members of the police and armed forces (Machonin et al. 1996, pp. 122–25; *Svobodné slovo* 1998a; 1998b). Survey evidence also showed KSČM supporters to be an unusual and distinct group significantly to the left of the Czech median voter in terms of "economic ideology" (Evans and Whitefield, 1998), a trend which strengthened throughout the 1990s. Research on economic attitudes showed 35.2 percent of KSČM supporters with a "clear left" orientation in 1992, in contrast to 43.9 percent in 1996 (Večerník 1996, p. 255).

For a clearer picture of KSČM's real social constituency, such data must be considered in conjunction with the nature of the party organization, as well as historical factors and political geography. First, we should note the remarkably high ratio of KSČM members to voters: approximately 1 : 4.[7] In other words, to a considerable extent, the party's members and sympathizers were its electorate. Second, opinion poll findings have consistently shown that KSČM has a high percentage of core voters and relatively little "marginal" support. An April 1998 STEM poll, for example, found that 83.5 percent of KSČM supporters had voted for the party in 1996 (*Právo* 1998) and that 77 percent felt strong or relatively strong attachment to the party, the highest such figures for any Czech party (*Lidové noviny* 1998e). Finally, ecological analyses of spatial voting patterns revealed both the remarkable geographical stability of the communist vote after 1989 (Kostelecký 1995) and a close correlation of post-1989 distributions with historical (1946) patterns of communist support (Kostelecký, Jehlička and Sýkora 1993;

Kostelecký 1994). KSČM support thus appeared based on a distinct historical and generationally defined group, an impression reinforced by internal
party data. A 1992 KSČM Congress report based on an extensive membership survey, for example, showed that 37.4 percent of members had joined
the Communist Party in the 1945–48 period, compared to 18.2 percent at the
height of "normalization" (1971–80) (KSČM 1992, p. 17). As sociologists
have noted, it is precisely this communist-oriented generational group, for
whom the war and immediate postwar years were formative political reference points, who were most favored by "real socialism" in terms of social
mobility and, later, by structures of remuneration and social benefits (Večerník
1996, pp. 49–50). However, we should note that while a majority of KSČM
supporters are elderly, this does not mean that the majority of this generation
are KSČM supporters. In the June 1998 elections, for example, exit polls
suggested that only 18 percent of those over age sixty voted Communist
(*Mladá fronta Dnes* 1998c).

The Position and Strategy of the KSČM Since 1993

From 1993 onwards, KSČM has been internally stable and its leadership
secure and solidly supported by its members and voters. Polling in early
1998 showed that only 13 percent of KSČM supporters were dissatisfied
with the leadership of Grebeníček (*Týden* 1998). Electorally, the Communist
Party maintained its relatively strong position in local politics in two sets of
communal elections (1994 and 1998). Against expectations, the party also
managed to gain two representatives in the Czech Senate, elected in 1996
and 1998 (on a first-past-the-post basis), successfully mobilizing its support
in a generally low turnout. However, in the (list-based) parliamentary elections the party's electoral vote dropped from 14 percent to 10 percent in
1996, losing 13 of the 35 seats won by Left Bloc in 1992; the greatest loss
for any party. In June 1998, KSČM made a modest recovery, polling just
over 11 percent of the vote, rising from 22 to 24 seats in Parliament and,
gaining 30,000 extra votes despite a reduced overall turnout.

KSČM's neocommunist leaders have faced no serious challenges from
within the communist camp. The Party of the Democratic Left (SDL) and a
second postcommunist party, the Left Bloc Party (SLB), created in December 1993 by Left Bloc deputies, failed to attract much of the Left Bloc/KSČM
electorate, polling only 0.13 percent and 1.3 percent respectively in 1996,
before merging in early 1998 to form the tiny Party of Democratic Socialism
(PDS). In May 1995, Miroslav Štěpán and other expelled "For Socialism"
leaders founded the neo-Stalinist Party of Czechoslovak Communists (SČK).
However, SČK's main rationale was to influence and reintegrate with KSČM.
Some small Stalinist groupings such as the magazine *Dialogy-otázky-odpovědi*
and its readers circles have continued to function within KSČM (*Lidové noviny*

1998c) and the party's tiny youth organization, the Communist Union of Youth (KSM), also appears revanchist in outlook (*Lidové noviny* 1998c).

KSČM has consistently aimed at participation in a coalition government, either of the center-left or a Grand Coalition. The 1995 KSČM congress defined the party's medium-term goal as the formation of "a broad left-wing, patriotic, anti-right-wing grouping" (KSČM 1995a, p. 72) and a coalition government of the Left. However, after the experience of the Left Bloc, KSČM was suspicious of electoral coalitions which might subsume the party's identity or allow smaller groupings to profit at its expense. In 1995, it thus envisaged such an "anti-right-wing bloc" more in terms of ad hoc local or issue-based cooperation than electoral pacts (KSČM 1995a, pp. 53–54). More recently, KSČM leaders such as Vojtěch Filip, chairman of its parliamentary group, have advocated the notion of a "Government of National Accord" based on the "widest possible consensus," and if possible, uniting all parliamentary parties with a "minimum common program" (Kalenská 1998). From 1992, however, KSČM tried to extend its influence "downwards" into society by developing into a locally based left-wing social movement, a "civil society in miniature" (Grenbeníček 1993b) based around the party's organizational network. This was embodied in the Program of Active Social Self-Defense (PASS), adopted in 1992, which sought to establish links between the party and relevant civic initiatives and organize a range of nonpolitical activities and services of practical interest to the KSČM target constituencies (e.g. legal advice, social events, and "popular" business ventures [*lidové podnikaní*]) (Votova 1993).

Although KSČM largely maintained its position in Czech politics, its efforts to extend its influence have met with scant success. Other parties and important political actors such as President Havel continue to regard KSČM as an extremist pariah party. The Czech Social Democrats (ČSSD), which emerged as the main party of the Left in 1996, repeatedly ruled out any cooperation with KSČM despite showing a pragmatic attitude towards cooperation with the Right after inconclusive election results in 1996 and 1998 (see below). Despite a more left-wing public mood in the Czech Republic during the mid-1990s (Večerník 1996, pp. 217–39; Matějů and Řeháková 1996; Matějů and Vlachová 1998), KSČM has gained little support. Moreover, in 1998 as the pre-election polls of the populist Pensioners for a Secure Life Party (DŽJ) (*Lidové noviny* 1998f) showed, the Communist Party made few political inroads, even among those social groups such as those over age sixty where left-wing values and nostalgia for the pre-1989 regime were highest. The party's efforts to build up a left-wing civil society also floundered. As internal party material concedes, efforts to influence key groups such as working-class youth, students, and workers, as well as attempts to build up locally based "anti-right-wing groupings," all took place "without any great result" (KSČM 1995a, p. 32). Nor was KSČM able to influence many "civic initiatives" other than a small group already closely aligned with the party, such as the anti-German Club of the Czech Borderlands (KCP) or the Clubs of Left-Wing Women. While the Program of Active Social Self-Defense was "relatively successful" in organizing social activities, it was also admitted to have been incoherent and lacking in political impact (KSČM 1995a, pp. 32–33).

A Neocommunist "Subcultural Party"

Evans and Whitefield (1995) suggest that rather than KSČM supporters' distinct "economic ideology," it is their distance from the promarket majority of Czechs that explains KSČM's politically isolated position. However, the party's continued isolation must to a large extent be seen as the effect of the conscious collective choice for a neocommunist strategy, rather than a sociological reflection of the distribution pattern of left-right preferences concerning economic ideology in Czech society. This impression is reinforced by the fact that the leftward shift of Czech public opinion and electoral support from the mid-1990s on failed to benefit the communists. How then can we understand KSČM's neocommunist orientation? Public choice and party competition theory has long shown that the institutional dynamics between internal party actors can lead parties to adopt electoral strategies that are collectively "irrational" (Tsebelis 1990; Dunleavy 1991; Kitschelt 1994). It is thus tempting to see Svoboda's strategy as a vote maximizing "rational" course and the neocommunist outcome as an irrational or "sub-optimal" deviation from it produced by a combination of strategic miscalculation, internal institutional dynamics, and the weight of traditional communist core support. However as Kitschelt (1994) notes, there are often a number of potentially rational strategies open to parties and it is in fact hard to assess whether the assumptions of the neocommunist or postcommunist alternatives were more realistic or more rational.

In an earlier work, Kitschelt (1989) distinguishes between two fundamental and conflicting logics that parties in competitive multiparty systems may follow: "a logic of constituency representation" in which party "organization, strategy and progress are derived from the ideology of their core support groups in society" and a "logic of electoral competition" in which parties "adapt political stances to appeal to their marginal sympathizers in order to maximize electoral support" (Kitschelt 1989, p. 48). In this light, the neocommunist orientation, by giving priority to the demands of the party's historic core constituency and loyal mass membership, can clearly be seen as following a "logic of constituency representation" at the expense of the party's chances of gaining real political influence. By contrast, in Svoboda's strategy of transforming KSČM into the Party of Democratic Socialism or a broad Left Bloc, "a logic of electoral competition" (vote maximization) had prevailed. A "logic of constituency representation" is usually characteristic of newly formed parties with highly mobilized, ideologically motivated support, interested in wide-ranging policy change and the intrinsic rewards of participation—an example being the Green parties which emerged in Western Europe in the 1970s and 1980s (Kitschelt 1989). However, KSČM cannot really be considered a newly formed party. Neither does its rank and file seem to have been strongly policy oriented. Rather than substantive policies, KSČM membership and core support seem motivated more by a sense of tradition and identity—what Panebianco (1988) terms "identity incentives." As with many other Eastern and Central European parties, in the case of KSČM the conceptual tools of Western-based party literature do not seem fully adequate. However, applicable here is the notion of the "subcultural party" developed by Enyedi (1996) and used in a case study of the Christian Democratic People's Party (KDNP) in Hungary. The subcultural party is defined as a type of party based on a distinct, culturally defined segment of society with similar lifestyles, "common norms, values, and convictions," "feelings of solidarity and loyalty to each other" which is organizationally expressed by the party and affiliated organizations (Enyedi 1996, p. 379).

While echoing the "encapsulation" strategies of historical mass parties, such a strategy need not imply mass organization, but merely the "building up organizational networks . . . able to provide their adherents in diverse, not only political, spheres of life," ". . . social organizations that claim to represent the values and interests of a culturally and ideologically well-defined group" (Enyedi 1996, p. 378). It thus represents a low-yield, low-risk strategy, the main risk to which is not electoral competition, but rather, the possible erosion of the subculture.

KSČM and its neocommunist strategy and aspirations to become a left-wing "civil society in miniature" of the 1990s appeared to fit the pattern of the subcultural party, a position that recalled Czech communists' earlier historical experiences of political isolation in interwar Czechoslovakia. However, while the subcultural party of Hungarian political Catholicism, the KDNP, seemed able to reproduce itself through, for example, Catholic schools and youth organizations, the Czech communist KSČM subculture, while numerically larger, appeared stagnant and narrowly defined generationally. As Svoboda had feared, other forces appeared to usurp the role of an active and relevant postcommunist democratic Left.

Instead of a Postcommunist Party? The Fall and Rise of the Czech Social Democrats

In the Czech Republic, it was not a reinvented Communist Party that formed the basis of this postcommunist democratic Left but a reinvented and resurgent "historic" Social Democratic Party (ČSSD). Despite being outpolled by the communists in both 1990 and 1992, the social democrats emerged in 1996 as the dominant force of the Czech Left with 26 percent of the vote. From July 1996 until December 1997, the social democrats "tolerated" the Klaus-led coalition as a minority government before polling 32 percent to become the Czech Republic's largest party. It then formed a single-party minority government in July 1998 based on institutionalized cooperation agreements with Klaus's Civic Democrats.

In many ways, the development of the social democrats in the 1990s mirrored that of the Communist Party. In the early 1990s, the social democrats, like the communists, were a marginal party with an elderly membership undergoing divisive debates over their party's identity and place in the emerging party system (Lindstrom 1991; Vermeersch 1993; Kunc 1996; Mitrofanov 1998). Elderly former emigrants such as party leader Jiří Horák viewed ČSSD as a "center-left" party that would join a governing bloc of democratic parties extending from center-right to center-left, as it had once done in interwar Czechoslovakia. This strategy reflected the belief that the economic transformation policies carried out by Václav Klaus were proving highly successful (ČSSD 1995, pp. 13–15).

However, a faction of "radicals" within ČSSD, including a number of former left-wing Civic Forum MPs and members of the *Obroda* club of ex-reform communists which merged with ČSSD in October 1991, disagreed. Rather than a politics informed by anticommunism and the experience of interwar Czechoslovakia, they argued that the social democrats could and should become a broad party of democratic opposition able to defeat the Right and replace it in government with an alternative model of transformation (ČSSD 1995, pp. 132–35; 64–83). This, however, entailed not dialogue or cooperation, but "getting the government by the throat" (Zeman 1993). In their view, Horák's attempts to build bridges with the Right to win ČSSD a place in government or posts in the state administration destroyed ČSSD's very *raison d'être* as an opposition party. At the Twenty-Sixth ČSSD Congress of 27–8 February 1993, the social democrats narrowly elected the leading "radical" Miloš Zeman as party chairman.

Although Zeman's initial plan of forming a "Realist Bloc" of the left and center-left parties around ČSSD (*Rudé právo* 1992) quickly foundered due to the instability and internal fractiousness of these parties, ČSSD itself proved well placed to absorb both their electoral support and their political elites. In addition to many ex-reform communists still involved in politics, ČSSD steadily attracted leaders from former parties, including the defunct social-liberal Civic Movement, the ex-satellite Czechoslovak Socialist Party (ČSS), and the Moravian regionalist party, as well as would-be "postcommunist" groups, such as the Party of the Democratic Left (SDL) and the Democratic Labor Party (DSP). In 1997, even Jiří Svoboda joined ČSSD as a rank-and-file member (*Svobodné slovo* 1997). At the same time, ČSSD built an electorate which was not only large but diverse and representative of all regions and age groups in a way that KSČM had not been (Machonin et al. 1996, pp. 122–23, 125). ČSSD itself thus proved able to become a broad opposition alliance by shifting from a strategy based on historic identity and a "logic of constituency representation" towards one based on a "logic of electoral competition." This "radical" strategy was similar in many ways to that advocated by the reformers in KSČM which was abandoned in 1993.

Given the failure of reformers in KSČM, ČSSD became in effect the functional equivalent of a broad-based social democratic ex-ruling party. Not only did the party absorb what remained of the Czech reform communist tradition, but from the mid-1990s onwards it also took up elements of the discourse of technocratic efficiency, modernization, and managerial competence (Machonin et al. 1996; Machonin 1996) championed elsewhere by postcommunist "social democrats"; a discourse which up to that time in the Czech Republic had been associated with Václav Klaus right-wing Civic Democratic Party (ODS) (Hadjiisky 1996). Moreover, since 1998 the Czech Social Democrats have also faced a range of typical postcommunist dilemmas, centering on reconciling the roles of being both a broad populist party of "losers" in the transformation and agents of technocratic modernization (Machonin et al. 1996, pp. 87–88, 110–12).

The Dynamics of Breakthrough? KSČM's Surge in Support 1999–2001

Although the absence of a stable majority government and the tense relationship between ODS and the Social Democrats since 1996 made communist voters and deputies, for the first time since 1989, a factor to be reckoned with when calculating political outcomes, the communists' position in the late 1990s did not seem likely to outgrow that of a successful "subcultural party." However, to almost universal surprise in late 1999, as the tenth anniversary of Czechoslovakia's "Velvet Revolution" approached, KSČM found itself poised on the threshold of a breakthrough in its political support. In 1998–99, against a background of economic stagnation and growing public disenchantment with both the minority social democratic government and the right-wing parties of the former coalition, the communists experienced a sudden and rapid increase in popularity, overtaking both the incumbent social democrats and Václav Klaus's center-right Civic Democratic Party (ODS), to become the most popular Czech party. According to the IVVM polling institute, KSČM support had risen from the 10 percent it had received in June 1998 to a peak of 23 percent of potential voters in October 1999 (*Lidové noviny* 1999a; *Mladá fronta Dnes* 1999a), before falling back to 15–20 percent in 2000.

In electoral terms the significant factors benefiting KSČM seem to be the disappearance of the far-right Association for the Republic-Republican Party of Czechoslovakia (SPR-RSČ) as a political force in 1998 (some of whose voters gravitated towards KSČM) and the disappointment of many left-wing voters with the performance of the minority social democrat government and the "Opposition Agreement" it concluded with Klaus's ODS. In more general terms, however, there was a sense of wider malaise in Czech politics, which brought the communist rhetoric of "crisis" closer to the mainstream, and, despite deep public division on the issue, fostered a tendency to view KSČM as a "normal" party, which need not be boycotted (according to 47 respondents in one survey) or prevented from entering government (*Právo*, 11 January 2000).

The rapidity and scale of the party's rise in opinion polls seems to have taken communist leaders by surprise. Speaking to a party Program Conference in January 1999, Grebeníček argued that after a period of "temporary turning inwards" KSČM had established itself as a "renewed party" which could move onto a third phase: that of seeking to win a share of political power. In the speech he set the party a goal of winning 20 percent support of the vote and entering government within ten years (Grebeníček 1999, p. 3). Most communist leaders were deliberately muted in their reactions and, despite earlier hints of a rethink in party strategy, the resolutions adopted at KSČM's Fifth Congress in December 1999 contained little that was new. Indeed, in effectively abandoning the grander vistas of the Social Self Defense Program, the long-prepared congress reports and resolutions painted a relatively pessimistic picture of an isolated but "consolidated" party, in which many of the problems identified five years previously remained unresolved (KSČM 1999). Even in purely ideological terms, despite incorporating the notion of globalization (Ransdorf 2000) and a slight softening of the language used concerning Czech EU accession, there were few detectable shifts. Perhaps significantly, however, early 2000 did see a campaign by KSČM leaders to rid the party of neo-Stalinist "dogmatists" by the deregistering of a number of local branches in Prague (Götzová 2000a, 2000b). However, this campaign, heralded a year previously by the verbal attacks of Party Chairman Grebeníček against unrealistic "older members" of the party who "make a lot of noise, [but] may end up devaluing the self-sacrificing work of KSČM members of all ages" (Grebeníček 1999, p. 2), provoked criticism from the more conservative figures within the party leadership, such as Václav Exner, one of the party's deputy chairmen. At present, therefore, KSČM leaders seem unwilling or unable to entertain any realignment going beyond the neocommunist strategy of the 1990s.

Conclusions

The Communist Party of Bohemia and Moravia's unwillingness to assume the role of a postcommunist party after 1989 reflected both the strength of a specific communist tradition in the Czech Lands and the early demise of its reform communist wing after 1968. A number of contingent choices in Czechoslovakia's transition and early post-transition politics favored the emergence of an organizationally and politically intact, but politically unreformed, non-social democratic Czech successor party. Key among these were the attitude of transitional elites, the tactics adopted by the relatively weak reformist forces within the party, and the strength of anticommunism and hostility to the old regime in the Czech Republic after 1989. Two further interrelated sets of contingent outcomes to internal struggles within KSČM and ČSSD in 1991–93 marked the final stage in KSČM's development: the victory of the communists' neocommunist faction and the involvement of social democrat "radicals" in internal party struggles in 1993. A critical factor in both cases was the ability of the successful faction to articulate a strategy, which was both politically coherent in itself and capable winning majority support within the respective party. KSČM's decision in 1993 to adopt a neocommunist rather than a postcommunist strategy can, however, can be seen as a relatively rational adjustment to democratic politics. Although it provided opportunities to the "historic" social democrats denied to them elsewhere in Eastern and Central Europe, it preserved KSČM organizationally and politically and averted a split that might not have yielded significant political returns.

KSČM's neocommunist adaptation to democratic politics has, nevertheless, been a complex one. Much of the party's identity, ideology and support are rooted in the 1948–89 communist regime and its statist, *dirigiste* vision is in many ways a conservative "counter-transformational" strategy (Machonin et al., p. 100) reacting against processes it did not initiate and has been largely unable to influence. Its assessment of the period of one-party rule is, moreover, deeply ambiguous, and the concept of "system change" at the heart of KSČM ideology appears to represent an ambiguity towards liberal democracy. Nevertheless many democratization theorists would argue that democratic consolidation requires less a "democratic culture" on the part of political actors than their day-to-day acceptance of democracy as the "only game in town" (Linz and Stepan 1996, pp. 143–46). Despite playing the role an "antisystem party" within the Czech party system and a political home for the revanchist moods of its membership, KSČM has in practice scrupulously conformed to democratic norms since 1990. Thus, despite their conservatism and orthodoxy in comparative terms, its politics do nevertheless represent a significant move away from those of its totalitarian predecessor party.

While it would be an exaggeration to speak of "a stunning comeback" (Mudde 2000), KSČM's success in maintaining its organizational and electoral base allowed it to benefit from subsequent instabilities in the Czech party system. However, its continued lack of coalition potential, reflecting a broader lack of acceptability and legitimacy in Czech society, remains a fundamental problem for the party. Nevertheless, KSČM's survival as an established party in Czech politics as well as the extraordinary surge in its popularity in 1999–2000 call into question many received wisdoms about the party's prospects. Reports of the party's "dying off" seem greatly exaggerated. Indeed, perhaps the most immediate danger facing it may stem from possible growth in its electoral support. By increasing the attractiveness and viability of a "logic of electoral competition," the surge of support in 1999–2001 seems to have brought to a head internal tensions echoing those of the 1991–93 period. The dilemma of choosing between a "logic of constituency representation" versus a "logic of electoral competition—a dilemma faced by many left-of-center parties in both Western and Eastern Europe—therefore seems likely to reassert itself. In the case of KSČM, such dilemmas will be thrown into still sharper relief by the recent reforms of the Czech electoral system, which have introduced a much less symmetrical form of proportional representation and favor larger, more popular parties at the expense of smaller, minority groupings (*Central Europe Online* 2000).

Notes

1. The "federated" Communist Party of Czechoslovakia existed until December 1991, when national and political differences led the Slovak party, renamed Party of the Democratic Left (SDL), on 1 February 1991 to cut formal ties with the Czech communists.

2. This group left the party to form the Democratic Party of Labor (DSP) in December 1991. The title "Democratic Left" was used by a number of distinct postcommunist organizations in the years 1990–93. See Grzymala-Busse (1998a, pp. 453–57, fn29).

3. Of 291,783 votes (an 82.3 percent turnout), 221,575 opposed changing the party name; 69,007 were in favor.

4. The largest being the Democratic Left of Czechoslovakia led by Lotar Indruch, itself an early breakaway from the Communist Party. At a federal level the Left Bloc was a coalition of KSČM and the Slovak communists are now renamed Party of the Democratic Left (SDL).

5. The label "neocommunist" was used by the party in its 1993 congress documents, but dropped in 1995 after criticism of an implied break in communist tradition.

6. Grebeníček, for example, anticipated KSČM deputies working with other communist parties in the European Parliament (Grebeníček 1999).

7. 626,136 votes in 1996 compared to an estimated 160,000 members; 658,550 votes in 1998 compared to the party's own figure of 136,500 members in 1999.

8

The PDS

Regional Party or a Second Social-Democratic Party in Germany?

Dieter Segert

The adaptation strategy of the Party of Democratic Socialism (PDS) appears at odds with previous theoretical attempts to understand party change. Even though the PDS is the successor party to one of the most conservative and least pluralistic political regimes in Soviet-dominated Eastern Europe, its leadership is on the way to a moderate leftist understanding of postcommunist realities, similar to the Hungarian and Polish Socialists. Although the PDS could have freed itself from its own hard-liners at the very beginning of its transition period in 1990 much more quickly, and even radically, than other successor parties, the public image of the party still wavers between reformist and hard-line orientations.

Further, in opposition to certain theses, the PDS experienced a sudden identity change just after a relatively good election performance by the party. For example, after the elections in 1994 and 1998, the conservative orientation gained broader influence within the membership. In the struggle for alternative adaptation strategies the most influential actors are not conservatives and reformists within the elite-stratum of the PDS, but rather there is a contest between the mainly reformist and pragmatic leadership, on the one hand, and the more conservative-oriented membership, on the other.

The aim of this chapter is to critically assess the PDS. It seems fruitful in this way to stress the differences between this East German successor party and all other former communist parties in the region. The most important difference stems from the fact that the PDS has had to compete within the setting of a stable post-communist German democracy. Thus, what does "success" for the PDS really mean in this context? This paper will also address the conditions of success, and, finally, analyze the main direction of the identity change of the party. In the end, the question will be answered whether and to what degree the party has transformed and/or transmuted itself.

The PDS in Comparison with Other Successor Parties

With regard to national election results, the PDS is one of the least success-ful communist successor parties in Eastern Europe. While others have earned shares of between 15 and nearly 40 percent of the electorate, the German postcommunists were only able to pass the 5 percent threshold in 1998. In 1990, the PDS only competed in the East German constituency. In 1994, the party came to Parliament thanks only to its three direct mandates in East Berlin, a rule that is a sort of gratification for strong regional actors embed-ded in German electoral law (see Table 8.1). Surpassing the 5 percent thresh-old led, nevertheless, to the end of public isolation. A member of the parliamentary party of the PDS was elected as one of the deputy speakers of the Bundestag. The PDS Foundation for Civic Education (called "Rosa-Luxemburg-Stiftung") was subsidized by Parliament in 1999, following eight consecutive years of being denied funding. In Mecklenburg-Western Pomerania, the party built a coalition government together with the stronger Social Demo-cratic Party of Germany (SPD). The chairman of the PDS, Lothar Bisky, pointed out at a conference after the elections that "something changed . . . we are now regarded by others as quite a normal party" (Bisky 1998, p. 11).

The PDS remains the smallest parliamentary party in the Bundestag. How-ever, it was able to raise its influence both in relative and in absolute terms through three elections. The size of its share of the vote has more than doubled since December 1990 (up 223 percent). The PDS has gained votes both in the East (where its stronghold lies) and in the West, but in the West, the increase has not been very visible (see Table 8.2).

Every successor party has to overcome a transitional crisis after losing power. What is the place of the PDS within this special group of political parties? How can we compare them to each other? One possible way is to ask how long these parties have stayed in power after the institution of free elections (Segert 1995). The first type of party was able to stay in power over several successive elections (e.g., the socialists in Serbia); another type lost power in the first free elections but was able to return to it soon afterward (e.g., successor parties in Hungary, Poland, and some other countries); a third type remained politically isolated to a high degree, regardless of stable support from parts of society (e.g., communists in Czech Republic). For a long time the PDS belonged to the last type of successor party.

What are the reasons for these different types of party developments after state socialism? There are several explanations for the different paths fol-lowed by the successor parties. One prominent argument (see Linz and Stepan 1996) is that the legacy of the previous authoritarian regime has a great influ-ence on postcommunist development, an argument which was also applied to political party development (Kitschelt 1995a). There is also a thesis that combines both the dynamics of the transition process with the early adapta-

Table 8.1

Electoral Results of the PDS to the German Parliament (Bundestag), 1990-98

Year	Size of mandates	Second votes (in millions)	Second votes (in percent)
1990	17	1.13	2.4
1994	30	2.07	4.4
1998	36	2.51	5.1

Note: The shares of East and West votes were the following: 1990—1m to 126 thousand. 1994—1.7 m to 369 thousand. 1998—2.1 m to 461 thousand (See Brie 2000, p. 5). In the West, it was an increase of 265%; in the East of 110%.

tion strategy (the kind of political competition faced when confronted with the first free elections) that is key to understanding the subsequent evolution of the successor parties (Ziblatt 1998).

The kind of pretransitional regime influences the level of differentiation within the elite of the former state party. This is important in explaining the differences between the second (Poland, Hungary) and the third types (GDR, Czechoslovakia) of successor party development. The protopluralist institutional environment in communist Hungary and Poland led to the early pluralism of the respective state parties prior to the transition. In contrast, in the GDR and Czechoslovakia, the differentiation in the state party (between reformers and conservatives) took place only after the political crisis that led to the transition. The earlier the differentiation started, the more the reformers became the driving force in the transformation (Ishiyama 1997a). In the case of the first type (such as Serbia), the Serbian communists were split much earlier than the communists in Romania and Bulgaria, but their electoral success story was similar to those countries.

One can compare the different cases by their political programs as well. The different programs could be explained as specific strategies of adaptation to a radically changing political environment. The defense of traditional communist values, e.g., in the case of the communists of Bohemia and Moravia (KSČM), would be a special type of adaptation. There are, first of all, two groups of programmatic orientations among the postcommunist parties: pragmatic modernizers and nationalists. Bozóki (1997, p. 11) has emphasized that these two "ideal types" of successor parties are diametrically opposed: "Anti-nationalistic ex-communist parties are characterized by a modernizing social democratic line." There are some intermediate positions as well. The PDS, for example, holds a somewhat mixed position, clearly not nationalistic, but clearly not modernizationist either. However, despite evolving from one of the most conservative state parties in Eastern Europe, the PDS shows certain similarities, both in the areas of its programmatic politics and of its

Table 8.2

PDS Results in the Old (West) and New (East) Lands Since 1990
(in percentages)

Year	West	East
1990	0.3	11.1
1994	19.8	36.4/31.5
1998	21.4	4.4/19.8

Source: Author's compilation.

electorate, with the most reform-oriented parties in the region of Eastern Europe (MSzP, SdRP).[1]

Third, there are some other features of PDS caused by a very specific situation the party faced after the unification of Germany. It is the *only* successor party that has had to adapt to a stable democratic environment. In addition, the divide between East and West continues to be manifested in two different regional political cultures in the united Germany. The PDS has until the present been rooted only in one of them. Indeed, in contrast to other parliamentary parties, the PDS has been simply unable to gain majorities at the national level.

Another special feature is connected to the fact that the successor party of the SED has had to compete in the field of left-oriented voters with other political parties, including the Social Democrats (SPD), and the German Greens (B´90/G).

Thus, in many ways, the PDS should be regarded as an exception when compared to other communist successor parties.

Three Different Explanations of PDS Electoral Success Since 1994

How are the electoral successes of successor parties usually explained, and to what extent are these arguments valid for the case of the PDS? I use the "second winner" argument, the argument of "important organizational assets," and the "recovering after crisis" argument. Although the PDS has neither preserved power nor returned to it through elections, it has been unexpectedly successful. Indeed, early on, serious observers declared it nearly dead (Moreau 1992; Neugebauer and Stoess 1996).

First, in Central and Eastern Europe, there is an electoral phenomenon that is known from other transitions to democracy—too much is expected from the winner of the first free elections and invariably these expectations are not met. As a result, the first winner loses the second (or one of the following) elections. The winner of the second election is generally in a better situation than the first winner. There are two obvious reasons for the unfortunate situation of the first winner: the high degree of volatility of the voters after the collapse of authoritarian regimes (based mainly on the low development of voter-party ties), and the unrealistic claims of the first winners which cannot be met, which in turn provokes mass frustrations afterwards. The political group that was able to present itself as the most important political opponent of the first winner is thus most likely to win the second election. The *second-winner* explanation is valid for several victories or defeats in different frameworks and environments, e.g., the Spanish PSOE vs. UCD (in the elections of 1982), the Hungarian MSzP vs. MDF (in 1994), and the Polish SLD vs. AWS (in 1993). In the post-communist examples, there is a difference from the Spanish case—the second winner was not able to enjoy its victory for long.

Concerning the elections in East Germany, this thesis fits the explanations of the relationship between the conservative Union of Christian Democrats (CDU) and SPD better than those between them and the PDS. The PDS is a kind of a second "second winner." Though it also profited in 1994 and 1998 from the frustrations of the voters towards the CDU government, it did to a lesser extent than the SPD. The explanation may be due to the fact that the PDS was not able to present itself as the strongest opponent of the winner of the first or second elections, the CDU[2] (see Table 8.3).

In East Germany, the fact that there were two strong competitors in the same political niche (SPD and PDS) was used to great advantage by the CDU. A famous CDU campaign poster in 1994 showed "red socks" warning against the return of the "communists" to power if the Left won. In this way, the PDS was depicted as nothing more than the old state party. There was also the underlying message that only the CDU would be able to defend the country against that antidemocratic danger. To understand the political aim of the "red-socks campaign" more clearly, one has to keep in mind that it started just after a minority government of SPD and Greens (*Bündnis 90, Die Grünen*) was tolerated by the PDS in the Federal Land Saxony-Anhalt in 1994. The attack against the PDS was, therefore, also an attack on the SPD.

The PDS was the outcast of the German party system in the first half of the postsocialist decade. Thus, the electoral second-winner model, which was based on voters easily floating from one party to another, became less relevant. Beginning in the year 1993 the postcommunist vacuum in Eastern Germany was partly filled by the East-West cleavage. The outcast image even helped—the PDS now became the representative of a growing segment of East Germans who felt discriminated against by the way the power resources were distributed in the new Germany.

Indeed, beginning in 1993, two tendencies led to this political result. First, a common identity for the inhabitants of the East emerged, a kind of special consciousness (*Sonderbewusstsein*) of not truly being a German but an *East*

Table 8.3

Election Results of the Parliamentary Parties in the Bundestag in the New Lands, 1990–98; Compares National Elections with East Germany (second votes, in percentages)

Party	1990 National	1990 East	1994 National	1994 East	1998 National	1998 East
CDU	43.8	41.8	41.5	38.5	35.2	27.9
SPD	33.5	24.3	36.4	31.5	40.9	34.5
PDS	2.4	11.1	4.4	19.8	5.1	21.4
FDP	11.0	12.9	6.9	3.5	6.2	3.3
B'90/G	5.1	6.1	7.3	4.3	6.7	3.7

Source: Author's compilation.

German (Koch 1993). Secondly, there was a strong tendency towards a three-party system in the East (the Greens and the Free Democratic Party (FDP) lost their political importance). The CDU, SPD, and PDS remained, and among them, only the latter could be identified as a specific East German party (see Table 8.4).

Sonderbewusstsein is not only based on interests but also on values. The specific value orientation of the population in the Eastern Federal Lands was characterized by Neugebauer and Stoess (1996, p. 275)—using a theoretical model of Herbert Kitschelt—as being more orientated towards social justice (vs. free market) and authoritarianism (vs. liberalism) in comparison to the Western part. On the level of political actors, it favors the PDS as the only relevant party that is rooted, first of all, in the East and represents similar preferences in its leadership. The East German members of the other two parties represent this value orientation as well, but as political institutions (at the level of elites), they are dominated by their Western majorities.

The second kind of explanation for electoral success is the *organizational assets* argument, which contends that important organizational resources, or assets, of the successor parties after the transition contributed to their political rehabilitation (Waller 1995, p. 481). Those resources included, first of all, the membership, the network of basic organizations, the party-owned newspapers, the party´s financial assets, and the relationships between the party and interest organizations. In fact, the PDS has remained the party with the biggest membership in the New Lands.[3]

The size of PDS membership was about 91,000 in summer 2000, of which 3,300 are in the West (Neu 2000, p. 16). In the New Lands, the party has far more members than other parties. For its capacity to act, it is important that many members of the PDS are already retired. More than 50 percent of them are above the age of 60 (Neugebauer and Stoess 1996, p. 149; Gohde 1997, p. 2). A large proportion of them support the activities of the local branches of the party as volunteers, especially during election campaigns.[4]

Table 8.4

Election Results to the Parliament of the New Federal Lands (second votes, in percentages)

Federal	1990					1994				1998/1999			
Land	CDU	SPD	PDS	FDP	Gr.	CDU	SPD	PDS	Others	CDU	SPD	PDS	Others
MV-Pom.	38	27	16	—	—	38	30	23	—	30	34	24	—
Brbg.	29	38	13	7	6	19	54	19	—	27	39	23	5DVU
S-A.	39	26	12	14	5	34	34	20	—	22	36	20	13DVU
Thu.	54	19	10	5	6	43	30	17	—	51	19	21	—
Sax.	45	23	10	9	7	58	17	17	—	57	11	22	—

Source: Author's compilation.
Note: MV-Pom: Mecklenburg-Western Pomerania; Brbg.: Brandenburg; S-A.: Saxony-Anhalt; Thu.: Thuringia; Sax.: Saxony; Gr.: Greens, i.e., the party "Buendnis 90," which later merged with the Western Greens; DVU: German People's Union, an extremist right-wing party.

The PDS publishes one of the few national newspapers (the *Neues Deutschland*), with about 70,000 subscribers (Lang et al. 1995, p. 46). In contrast to many other successor parties, the PDS does not have a specific relationship with the Federation of Unions (because there is no successor to the former GDR unions). However, there is an umbrella organization of organized interests (*"Ostdeutsches Kuratorium der Verbaende"*), which is close to the party. This umbrella organization assembles the most important East German interest groups and organizations.

The assets of the party also include very active politicians at the local level. In March 2000, the PDS had six thousand seats in localities but only 87 in the western part of Germany. (*Kommunalpolitik* 2000) In 1998, the party received 17.3 million DM in membership fees, 7.4 million in private donations, and 12.5 million from the state budget on the basis of its electoral performance. All in all, the PDS is neither the strongest, the richest, nor the party with the deepest roots in Germany, but it is strong in comparison with other parties in the eastern part of the country.

The importance of the organizational resources of the PDS becomes clearer if one tries to answer the question why the party was able to transfer its doubtlessly huge resources from the old system into resources that were also usable in a democratic political system. This process is linked to the *third* argument. Every communist successor party must go through an identity crisis; the faster it is mastered, the faster it can exchange prior organizational assets into assets useful in democratic political competition (Segert and Machos 1995). In order to address this issue it is necessary to analyze some aspects of the history of PDS, mainly the question of why and how the party survived the fall of 1989 and the winter of 1990.

After the loss of the monopoly on power, each successor party had to go through a deep political crisis. There were many reasons for this crisis but one of the most important was that the successor parties had lost their capacity to distribute offices to their followers. In addition, membership in the successor party could cause difficulties for individual professional careers following the transition. Due to that, the primary motivation for elites and activists to associate with the communist parties disappeared.

Generally, the political crisis facing the former state party began with a dramatic drop in its membership figures. The SED/PDS lost about 80 percent of its former members between October 1989 and the summer of 1990 (Wittich 1995, p 60). Similar to the other successor parties, some groups of activists even questioned the very existence of the party, especially during the extraordinary party congress in December 1989 and during the open discussions in the second half of January 1990 (Gysi and Falkner 1990).

Why was the party, nevertheless, able to consolidate? A partial explanation was the performance of the PDS in the first free elections to the East German Parliament (or *Volkskammer*), on 18 March 1990. The party won about 16 percent of the votes and became the third strongest faction. The reason for its success was the sentiment against a rapid unification of the two German states, which created an issue upon which the PDS could capitalize.[5] The segment of the population that was against rapid unification regarded a strong PDS as a guarantor of their interests. One half of this part of the population voted for the PDS, while the other half was attracted to different smaller parties, like B´90 (at that time a coalition of several smaller groups), UFV (Independent Women Union), DBD (Democratic Farmers Party), the Greens of the GDR, and others. Nevertheless, opponents of rapid unification were in the minority among voters in the GDR in the spring of 1990—about two-thirds of valid votes tallied on 18 March were in favor of parties that favored joining the Federal Republic of Germany quickly.

During the following months, and especially after unification in October 1990, the number of opponents to unification shrank. So did the percentage of East Germans who voted for the PDS—only 5 percent supported the PDS in the East at the end of 1991.[6] In the beginning, the East Germans enjoyed the advantages of the currency union and the open borders to Europe. The difficulties connected with this new way of life were not yet apparent. The PDS suffered further internal problems during this period—a crisis of confidence connected with financial scandal in the fall of 1990 which led to the resignation of the deputy chairman responsible for the finances of the party. The party recorded an additional drop in membership during that crisis. From the summer of 1990 to May 1991, the PDS membership dropped from 400,000 to 240,000[7] (Wittich 1995, p. 59). Other crises stemmed from the connection of leading politicians of the party to the State Security Service in the GDR. The most important was the crisis centered in Berlin (East), the electoral stronghold of the PDS. In 1991, two chairmen who were elected chairmen of the local party branch were forced to resign in succession. Thus, at the beginning of 1992, there were many who predicted the approaching political death of the party.

The PDS, nevertheless, was able to survive. It gained popularity throughout the whole of 1992, and it became even more prominent at the beginning of 1993. (Segert and Machos 1995, pp. 227–30). The weekly *Spiegel* created an accurate term for it: the "new wall" within Germany (*"die Mauer in den Koepfen"*) (*Spiegel* 1993). A new common East German identity had emerged—77 percent of East Germans (in contrast to only 30 percent of West Germans) agreed with the statement that former GDR citizens would remain "second class citizens" in the united Germany for a long period of time. More importantly for the PDS was that its own political isolation within Western-dominated German politics symbolized for a growing number of East Germans their own inferior existence within Germany. This was reflected in the election performance of the party, which in 1993 (in local elections) and in 1994 especially, exceeded all expectations. In the East, the PDS not only won the same number of votes as in the elections of March 1990, but was especially successful compared to the previous state elections (see Tables 8.3 and 8.4). From the opinion polls, it was clear that the party was regarded more as the "party of the East" (*Ostpartei*) than as a leftist actor (Table 8.5). Some authors ascribe responsibility for the rise of the PDS to both the SPD and the CDU. "The West never did understand the phenomenon of the PDS, because it failed to understand the East" (Bortfeld 1999, p. 1).

The social composition of the membership also reflected the deep changes through which the party had evolved on its way from a mighty state party to a (marginalized) political party within the framework of the established German democracy (Table 8.6). The most interesting trends in the occupational structure between 1989 and 1990 were a decreasing share of blue-collar members and an increasing share of white-collar employees and members with college and university diplomas. Of special importance was the growing share of retirees within the membership, which rose from 17 to 42 percent during this period (Wittich 1995, p. 62; Neugebauer/Stoess 1996, p. 151).

The age structure of the membership also changed considerably—in 1989 over half of the membership (56 percent) was below the age of 50. At that time, 40 percent was between the ages of 31 and 50. In 1991, the respective figures lowered to 39 and 28 percent. That means the membership of the party became older on average. But more important was the fact that the PDS lost most of its influence upon the most active parts of the employed population.[8] Blue-collar workers and farmers voted less often for the party while white-collar workers, especially the "intelligentsia," were clearly over-represented among the supporters of the party (See Table 8.7).

In the last elections to the German Parliament (1994, 1998), voters for the PDS were slightly younger than the population's average. In the East, more than a quarter of the women between 18 and 34 voted in favor of the PDS (the average was 21.5 percent). In the West, most of the voters were under age 44; the elderly were much more poorly represented among the voters (Neu 2000, p. 27). Brie, underlining this trend, noted that in the West the PDS was becoming the "party of the youth" (Brie 2000, p. 25).

Who remained a member of the PDS and why? There are different possible explanations. Neugebauer and Stoess (1996, p. 251) argue that the PDS can be regarded as a political representation of the former ruling class (or using Michael Brie's term, the "Dienstklasse" of the GDR). Another, and in my opinion, more adequate explanation can be found in analyzing the program of the PDS.

Contradictions in the Party Program and its Historic Roots

Neugebauer and Stoess (1996, p. 238) ask what type of party is the PDS? Is it an East German oriented interest party (*Interessenpartei*), or an ideologically

Table 8.5

The Political Image of the PDS (in percentages)

Do you think the PDS is basically a left party or the party of the East?

	In whole country	In the East	In the West
Is mainly leftist	26	23	36
Is mainly party of the East	63	65	55
Do not know	11	12	9

Source: Author's compilation.

oriented party (*Weltanschauungspartei*)? They argue that it is both a type of protest party (*Protestpartei*) and a kind of interest-oriented party, based on East-West contradictions, which makes it only a temporary formation. "Related to the future decline of the East-West conflict and the diminishing of its special social background, the party will have less and less importance. Even if this process lasts one decade, its death as a relevant party is, therefore, inevitable. . ." (Neugebauer and Stoess 1996, p. 306).

However, far from dying, the party has grown. This is because the PDS understands itself as a party that is able to connect three functions, namely to fight for the socialist option throughout all of Germany, to realize the authentic representation of East Germans and their interests, and to possess the political competence necessary to present alternative policy solutions (Schulze-Lessel 1998, p. 1). These different tasks are, in the opinion of the party leadership, closely connected with each other, especially the first and the second ones. That is because the leadership is convinced that the specific problems of Eastern Germany are intertwined with and influenced by a long tradition in German politics; namely the predominance of a neoliberal understanding of politics. In this sense, the most effective way to achieve East German interest representation would be in the fight for a general change of political preferences in all of Germany (Bisky 1998, p. 14). However, as we know from polls concerning the image of the party, the public's preferences are different from the party leadership's (see Table 8.5). Within the party, there are three different groups of actors: the hegemonic "modern socialist" group, the more or less traditional "old Left" membership with its speakers (mainly "communist platform" and "Marxist forum"), and the bulk of pragmatic activists in between. After the consolidation of the party in 1994 and the partial victories in the elections of 1998 and 1999, the quarrel, mainly between modernizers and traditionalists, intensified.

These differences were first publicly apparent during early 1995. They were first described by the scholar Michael Brie (the brother of the electoral manager of PDS André Brie also known as the "grey emininence"). In his view, there is a small but influential group of middle-aged "reformers," the

Table 8.6

Social Composition of the SED and PDS Membership, 1989–90 (in percentages)

	SED: October 1989			PDS: June 1990		
	All members	Employed members	Retired members	All members	Employed members	Retired members
Blue-collars	43	40	53	25	14	41
White-collars	22	24	19	38	40	35
Intelligentsia*	26	28	15	32	42	21
Farmers	5	5	5	3	3	2
Craftsmen	1	1	3	1	1	1
Total	100	80	17	100	56	42

Note: *employees with college and university diplomas.

Table 8.7

Share of PDS Voters in Different Occupational Groups, 1994, 1998
(in percentages)

	1994		1998	
	Germany	New Lands	Germany	New Lands
Average	4.4	19.8	5.1	21.4
Blue-collars	5	15	6	17
White-collars	6	26	6	25
Public servants	3	35	3	15
Self-employed persons	3	17	4	17
Farmers	3	10	3	8

Source: Brie, 2000, p. 17.

so-called "modern socialists," in the party (Brie 1995, p. 28) who were until that year able to exercise hegemonic influence upon programmatic questions within the party. Another group consists of a majority of the mainly retired rank and file, which are oriented towards the arguments of the old Left but bound to the reformers by their traditional understanding of discipline within the party (a kind of "silent majority"). The real convictions of this part of the membership, however, were better expressed by a small faction within the party, the "Communist Platform." Brie underlined the existence of a third group that was decisive in the day-to-day political activity of the party, which consisted of the younger, pragmatic, functional elite, who exercised power at the middle and communal levels of the party organization[9] (Brie 1995, p. 9).

After the party's successful performance in the elections of 1994, the situation changed in one important respect: the "silent majority" of the PDS became represented by a group of known GDR intellectuals from the party organized within the "Marxist forum." Their style of action was highly defensive as seen in an attempt by the "reformers" to reopen a programmatic discussion within the party. The first such attempt consisted of a paper published on the eve of the Fourth Party Congress in January 1995, which became known as the "Ten Theses." This was followed by a book, stating the reformers position that commented on the party program (*Kommentar* 1997). After the elections of 1998, the "reformers" again called upon the party to discuss the long-term prospects of the PDS and, therefore, to open a debate about the party program. The representatives of the "silent majority," on the other hand, were oriented towards the maintenance of the program that was adopted in 1993. Their slogan consisted of the expression that the next (January 1999) party congress must not become the "Bad Godesberg" of the PDS (Bericht 1998, p. 5). In November of 1999, the majority of the program-committee published a document on the further discussion (Thesen 1999). A minority voted against it and published its own statement, with a recommendation to restore the old communist program, especially in its understanding of capitalism and socialism, thus a blow to the modernizers (Benjamin et al. 1999, pp. 3–4). The discussion afterwards led to a further strengthening of the conservative position. In April 2000, a majority of the Party Congress of Muenster postponed a decision on the question of whether a new programmatic document would be necessary for the next round of discussions, which were to start in October 2000 during the Congress of Cottbus.

The 1993 party program was characterized by some important inner contradictions. It was the result of a compromise between the then-active currents in the PDS. There was a consensus that the identity of the party should remain socialist, but at the same time, there were different interpretations of socialism itself. There are also very different understandings of capitalism, and the question of property on the way to a better society in the program. For instance, "capitalism" is defined in both a traditional and modern way in the program. In the first, "anachronistic" (Neugebauer and Stoess 1996, p. 92) understanding, it is an economic structure which should be destroyed completely by a revolution on the way to a better society. Thus, the program proclaims: "We all agree that the rule of capital should be overcome." (*Programm* 1998, p. 1). This could mean that society as a whole should be "destroyed" or "transformed." In the second interpretation of capitalism, there should be something preserved from that society in the change. The program term for that "something": "achievements of the civilization" (*"zivilisatorische Errungenschaften"*) (*Programm* 1998, p. 3). That idea is backed by another understanding of the present dominant societal structure—capitalism is regarded partly as a modern society with a lot of potential for the people. From this point of view, the task of future development is different. The given structure has to be both maintained and destroyed. While the first understanding of capitalism (which is seen as a "source of evil" in the Federal Republic and other Western countries) was an indispensable part of Marxist-Leninist ideology, the second understanding reflects an attempt by a group of intellectuals within the SED to get rid of that old style of thinking.[10] That attempt was undertaken by the so-called "modern socialists," scholars who were mainly inspired by reformist movements in other countries of the Soviet bloc in the second half of the 1980s.[11] There is a certain continuity to the new leadership of the PDS—two members of its executive committee, André Brie and Dieter Klein, took part in the work of that group. It is not by accident that the commentary of the program, which was to a large degree influenced by Dieter Klein, referred to capitalism as equivalent to modern society (*Kommentar* 1997, pp. 25–42, 135–42).

One of the main reasons why the reformers urged the party to change the program had to do with the so-called "private property of means of production" (*Privateigentum an den Produktionsmitteln*) (*Programm* 1998, p. 8).

The "question of property" was the cornerstone of a traditional Marxist program of socialism. The fact that it was being discussed reflected a theoretical crisis of sorts. Another discussion emerged about the extent to which private property should be reestablished within a renewed socialism. There was also a theoretical discussion about the advantages of private property for different purposes. The "modern socialists" started a discussion about the means of socialization and a way to avoid too much centralization of property and power in the hands of the state apparatus. A sign of the contradictions within the PDS in 1993 was illustrated by the fact that the reformers were urged to make a compromise regarding this question.

It was not by accident that the question of property was again the focus of discussion around the Party Congress of Münster. The first indication was a minority statement opposing the theses of the majority of the program committee in November 1999 (Benjamin et al. 1999, p. 3). In an appeal placed as an advertisement in the PDS newspaper *Neues Deutschland* shortly before the congress opened (31 March 2000), the Marxist forum claimed to preserve a thesis in the party program stating that the dominant capitalist property should be destroyed on the way to socialism. The Marxist forum also attacked the reformers for their attempt to break the basic socialist consensus in the party (Joseph 2000). On the other hand, in his Münster speech, former Party Chairman Gregor Gysi attacked the Marxist understanding of capitalist property. The core of the problem in the present should no longer be the question of how to change ownership of the means of production, but rather how to promote the socially and ecologically responsible use of all kinds of property. He added: "We do not live anymore in the era of the Villa-Huegel capitalism, i.e. the capitalism of the big firms owned by families like Krupp or Thyssen (Gysi 2000).

The program also dealt with other traditional themes in contradictory ways. One example is the interpretation of the Russian Revolution and socialism in the Soviet Union. It is, on the one hand, celebrated as an event that caused several "favorable major developments of the twentieth century," which also recalls an old expression about the October Revolution as being the most important event of the epoch (*Programm* 1998, p. 6). However, on the same page, it is written that the influence of Stalinism deformed in principle the construction of socialism.

The language in which the program is written also wavers between different styles. In many places, it is written in quite modern and precise language; in others, East German resentments dominate. Sometimes, one can find the term *anschluss* (affiliation), which refers to the "Anschluss" of Austria in March 1938, instead of unification (of Germany). In other places, it is pointed out that the actions of citizens towards a "better society" in the past should never be regarded as something that needs to be excused.

Some, including Neugebauer and Stoess (1996, p. 117), argue that these contradictions reflect the existence of a deliberate plan by party leaders to avoid the breakup of the PDS as a result of a struggle between different factions (see also Lang et al. 1995, p. 147). In my opinion, however, it is possible to make another argument. The length of the period in which fundamental questions remain unsolved could be understood as a sign that the leadership is unable to force its favored solution upon the membership of the party. That is not caused by its political weakness but is a result of a deliberate shift of the inner decision-making process towards decentralization. The PDS is no longer a traditional, strictly organized, and centralized party run according to Leninist principles. This programmatic incoherence could be interpreted as a product of the real changes occurring along the way from SED to PDS.

This interpretation corresponds with the self-image of the party: "The PDS understands itself as an alliance of different leftist forces. Its support of a democratic socialist order is not bound to a certain world view, ideology or religion" (*Programm* 1998, p. 25). The reaction of the party leaders to the disputes of 1995 and 2000 was, in that sense, to seek a compromise. After the party congress in Münster, the PDS "Commission on Fundamental Principles" (*Grundsatzkommission*), led by the refomer Dieter Klein, passed a reconciliation paper entitled "Out of the Trenches!" ("*Heraus aus den trennenden Graeben!*"). The document called for the re-establishment of communication and confidence between the different factions of the party. The nomination and election of politically neutral Gabi Zimmer (until then the leader of the party branch in Thuringia), to the post of new party leader is another sign of an attempt at compromise.

Past experiences greatly affected these internal developments. In part, the hegemonic position of the reformers within the PDS can be understood as a heritage of the politics of Mikhail Gorbachev. Since the very beginning of his time in office as general secretary, Gorbachev gained much sympathy, especially among the rank and file of the SED. That was mainly a result of his political aims, such as an end to the Cold War (connected with terms like the search for "new thought" and a "common European house"). To a certain extent, sympathy also stemmed from the new Soviet leader's lively manner of communication, which was so different from the usual clumsy language of the party apparatus.

In contrast to other state parties in the SED, a pro-Gorbachev faction within the party elite did not emerge during the late 1980s. There were individuals, and, especially in 1988 and 1989, even some well-known organizations, that posed critical questions about the conservative policies of the SED, sometimes in the form of internal letters of protest. A prominent task was, in that respect, the protest against the prohibition of the monthly Soviet press digest *Sputnik* in November 1988. But these disputes remained mainly within the party, hidden from the public. Only among different unions of artists and writers had the protest gained, to a certain extent, broader publicity from 1987 on.[12]

This incomplete and diffuse kind of movement reached its zenith in the fall of 1989. The key events of the "revolution" in the GDR were the spontaneous demonstrations, first in Leipzig and Dresden, and then in nearly all towns. There were some organized actions as well, conducted by small groups of dissidents ("under the roofs of the churches," i.e. protected by the churches and strictly observed, but more or less tolerated, by the state) and some groups of intellectuals, mainly artists and writers. In September 1989, a professional association of writers from the GDR and the official Union of Rock and Light Musicians demanded publicly the beginning of the democratization of the society and state. The theaters in Berlin and other towns (among the latter, mainly the "state theater" in Dresden) became politically active as well. The biggest political demonstration in the history of the GDR occurred on 4 November and was organized by these artists (Hasche, Schoelling, and Fiebach 1994, pp. 143–44; Bahrmann and Links 1994, pp. 77–80). The last influential political initiative of that heterogenous but influential group (*Fuer unser Land*) ("In Favor of Our Country") occurred on 26 November 1989 in which, instead of fast German unification, they demanded the renovation and radical democratization of the GDR (Jarausch 1995, pp. 119–27).

Coinciding with the perestroika-related activities of groups of artists and other intellectuals in the SED, there emerged in the party a grassroots movement which later led to the PDS. In October 1989 the "modern socialists" began to publish their papers, which stemmed from discussions held since 1988. Impressed by the level of popular unrest, different basic and regional organizations of the SED organized their own demonstrations. Subsequently, this reform movement demanded an extraordinary party congress in December 1989 and prevailed over the objections of then Party Chair Egon Krenz. Thus, there had emerged a reformist movement within the SED. In this sense, the PDS is the heir, or successor, not of the SED as a whole, but of that part of the SED and GDR population (mainly intelligentsia) that sympathized with the ideas of perestroika. Most party members, however, were passive observers of this process, which was fueled by the controversial politics of Gorbachev and the end of the SED-dominated GDR. Thus, the PDS was from the very beginning, a heterogeneous party. Within the leadership there were a tiny group of "reformers" supported by a diffuse and weak pro-perestroika movement within the GDR intelligentsia.[13] In contrast, a "silent majority" represented the membership of the old party.

The group of pragmatic politicans on the level of municipalities and federal lands came from the lower ranks of the former nomenklatura. Members of this group possessed great administrative experience, at least more so than many other politicans in East Germany had at the beginning of the systemic change. Hence, contrary to the beliefs of Neugebauer and Stoess (1996), the PDS does not simply represent the failed political class of the GDR. Nor does the party represent the elite but more specifically, little parts of the sub-elite of the GDR. In this sense, only tiny sections of the former political class survived in the PDS, namely those personalities who were intellectually and politically capable of learning in a basically changed environment and were young enough to do so.

The Future of the PDS: A Declining Regional Party or Germany's Second Social-Democratic Party?

The PDS has clearly broken with the communist SED and has adapted to new circumstances. At first glance, it seems that the party had partly reformed towards a more moderate leftist image, and it has partly transmuted itself by becoming a representative of East German minority interests. But the continuous struggle over its political program has made it clear that the party remains, more than ten years after 1989, in the middle of an identity crisis. Two political alternatives lay before it. The first is that it can become the main representative of the special regional interests of East Germans. The other would be its transformation into a second, more left-oriented, social-democratic party in Germany. This means that the party could move forward either by transmuting or by reforming itself. In my opinion, the decision depends mainly on the respective opportunity structure within the contest for political power in Germany, and less on the balance of power within the party itself.

As a regional party the PDS has to function as the main political representative of the losers of the transition. This is a responsibility of the party brought about by the way in which the GDR joined the Federal Republic in 1990 and resulting in deep social and cultural conflicts. Until now, the voters (as well as the members) of the PDS in Eastern Germany came from the losers of the unification process, although not necessarily the financial losers. Indeed, there are important groups of members and supporters of the PDS who have done well financially. By losers I mean those who suffered damage to their self-confidence and self-esteem. This feeling of inferiority is, by far, shared not only by that part of the GDR-elite who really lost power, but by a much broader section of East Germans. It was produced by the unprecedented unification of two societies that were previously separate camps during the Cold War. It was reinforced by certain practices that made many in the former GDR, in particular the intelligentsia, "second class citizens" within a united Germany.

The social stress of unification and the need to adapt to unchallenged institutions of West German society nearly overnight produced nostalgic feelings among the East Germans. Neugebauer and Stoess quote from typical opinion polls regarding the GDR: "Not everything was bad or wrong!" (1996, p. 285). It was a feeling the authors referred to as "partial nostalgia" (*Teilnostalgie*), because it included criticism of some parts of the GDR but not others. The nostalgia is, in their opinion, primarily a reaction of the former political class in order to avoid having to admit their own political failure.

However, the orientation the PDS takes in capitalizing upon these resentments will also produce certain problems. The strategy chosen will be dependent on the area in which those problems are relevant, in other words the East. The PDS could remain a (fairly left-oriented) regional party and strengthen its image as the original "Eastern party."[14] As an expert from the Adenauer Foundation recently observed, the party could be forced to exercise two different roles within two constituencies, in the East as a slowly declining "milieu-party" and in the West as the remaining protest splinter-party (Neu 2000, pp. 44–45).

The second alternative (*second social democrats*) is based in general upon the strategic options of the reform-oriented and pragmatic leadership of the party. The real chance for this to occur will come mainly from external circumstances. If the SPD needs political cooperation from the PDS, the door to participation as a reformed successor-party in power could open. That was the case after the last elections in Mecklenburg-Western Pomerania. In that way, the PDS resembles other small parties. It has to react to the moves of others. However, to make such a breakthrough at the state level, it is necessary to overcome the stereotypes of the Cold War within the broader West German public. There have already been some signs of change: namely, a kind of symbolic politics; several meetings between PDS leaders like Gysi, Bisky, Holter, and members of government and the SPD-leadership, even the chancellor, and leading politicans from the CDU. Within the PDS, there was recently some discussion on whether the party could be prepared for a coalition government in 2006 or earlier (Bisky 2000).

Perhaps a possible future coalition in the Federal Land of Berlin will produce such a breakthrough. Since 1990, there have been three so-called "large coalitions," representing fewer and fewer voters mainly due to the shrinking electoral influence of the SPD (see Table 8.8). There are two quite different constituencies in the city: in the Western part a strong CDU, gaining around half of the votes; in the Eastern part a strong PDS, gaining, in the last elections, between 35 and 45 percent.

A coalition between the CDU and PDS seems unthinkable due to the political differences stemming from the time of the Cold War. For the SPD, cooperation with the PDS remains difficult for the same reasons, but the party has only a few alternatives. It must either stay in the trap of "large coalitions" and lose still more influence within the electorate, or it could shift and try to search for ways to form new kinds of coalitions that represent both West and East. There are, at present, two possible scenarios: a red-green coalition tolerated by PDS (as in Saxony-Anhalt in 1994) or a red-red coalition (as in Mecklenburg-Western Pomerania in 1998). There was even an idea in the media that in the latter case, the

Table 8.8

Electoral Results in Elections to the Parliament of the Federal Land of Berlin Since 1990 (second votes in percentages)

Party	1990	1995	1999
CDU	40.4	37.4	40.8
SPD	30.4	23.6	22.4
Greens	9.4	13.2	9.9
PDS	9.2	14.6	17.7
FDP	7.1	*	*

Source: Author's compilation.
Note: *below 5 percent

former leader of the PDS-parliamentary party, Gregor Gysi, could become a member of the state government. The question remains whether the majority of West Berliners are able to tolerate the influence of PDS in "their" town. But Gysi as a person is also well-known and respected in Western public circles.

A red-red government in Berlin could pave the way to normalization for the whole country. Both the prejudices towards the party and the political orientations within the PDS could change—and the party would be free from some obsolete stereotypes. It should further adapt to the changed reality. By becoming a smaller, more leftist social-democratic party in Germany, it could participate in a free and open democratic contest in order to create a new political majority within Germany.

Notes

1. For a comparison of successor parties by the author, see in more detail Segert (1995), Segert/Machos (1995), and Segert (1997).

2. In Germany, in the elections to Parliament, every voter has two votes at his disposal, the second is on a party list. The share of second votes determines the size of the parliamentary faction of each party.

3. At the end of 1995, PDS had about 100,000 members in the five new Federal Lands. The CDU had at the same time about 80,000, SPD; about 30,000; FDP, about 26,000; B´90/G, less than 3,000. See Neugebauer (1996, p. 55).

4. Though the PDS contains only about 155 full-time employees, it has at its disposal about 4,000 honorary assistants. See Lang et al. 1995, p. 36.

5. Another reason was likely the modern style of the election campaign of the PDS (Bortfeldt 1992, p. 189, Neugebauer/Stoess 1996, p. 162), but one should not overstretch this argument. The GDR parties that were close to the established political actors in the Federal Republic of Germany (SPD of GDR, CDU, BFD—the partner of the FDP) had, without doubt, much more experience and resources for the organization of election campaigns.

6. The figure was measured from a team at the University of Mannheim (the

famous "Forschungsgruppe Wahlen," which produces the TV program "Polit-barometer"), here quoted from Neugebauer/Stoess (1996, p. 159).

7. The membership-size was developing in the following way. See Neu 2000, p. 17:

> 12–31–1991: 171,800 in the East; 800 in the West.
> 12–31–1993: 130,200, in the East; 1,200 in the West.
> 12–31–1995: 113,000 in the East; 2,400 in theWest.
> 12–31–1997: 96,100 in the East; 2,500 in the West.

Nearly 20 percent of all members had joined the PDS since the end of 1989 (Pressedienst 1998). In October 1997, the PDS started a campaign in order to recruit new members "PDS 2000." The result as of April 1999 was that 2,045 people joined the party (Pressedienst 1999). In a branch of the federal state Thuringia in 1999, more than 200 people became new members for the first time since 1990 (Pressedienst 2000).

8. The drop in the number of the members that are employed as blue-collar workers needs a special interpretation, the group of employed party activists (so-called "*Parteiarbeiter*") in the party and state apparatus, which comprised nearly one-third of the membership (Wittich 1995, p. 63), had substantial numbers of SED members.

Secondly, in the old regime the workers were, due to ideological reasons, the most desirable social group among membership of the SED. That changed immediately after the end of state socialism. The first group of working party activists were more likely to remain in the party after 1990 than the second group of blue-collar workers (though now counted as retired employees).

9. In another part of the article, the same author describes the differentiation in other terms, but intentionally similar: 1) modern socialists 2) political pragmatists, oriented towards a "social and left-liberal pragmatism" 3) a group that leans, in ideological respects, towards a restoration-oriented (mainly in the KPF: "communist platform"), which exercises hugh influence at the grassroots of the party, and 4) an extremely radical, antimarket, and antiparliamentarian group (mainly a representation of the young members; the "AG *Junge GenossInnen*"). Other scholars describe the differences in the PDS similarly, see above all Lang et al. 1995, p. 132; Land/Possekel 1995, pp. 112–13; Krisch 1998, pp. 40. Since the programmatic debate started in the fall of 1999 it seems that the reformers are losing part of their influence and the political pragmatists have gained a much bigger share of power; these personalities include the head of the party branch of Mecklenburg-Western Pomerania Holter and the respective functionary from Saxony-Anhalt Claus. The nominated, and now elected, party leader Zimmer (from Thuringia) is trying to adopt a position in the middle between the different elite groups and the conservative-oriented membership. The turning point was a party congress (the first one in the old federal republic) in Münster at the beginning of April 2000, when at the same time, PDS party leader Bisky and faction leader Gysi declared their intention not to run again in the next respective elections for these offices.

10. It is not by accident that the mainly reform-oriented newspaper *Kommentar* (1997, p. 17) underlines: "our criticism towards capitalism definitely does not stem from the old-styled textbooks of Marxism-Leninism."

11. For the history of this group, see among others, Gysi/Falkner 1990, Segert 1993, and Land/Possekel 1995.

12. See, for example, the speeches of C. Hein and G. de Bryun against GDR censorship at the writers congress in 1987 (Emmerich 1997, pp. 61, 269). For an analysis of dissent within the Union of Painters and Sculptors of the GDR in 1988, see Damus (1991, pp. 346–48). The political influence of perestroika within the GDR theaters is described by Hasche/Schoelling/Fiebach (1994, p. 254). Also see, in this book, the chronicle overview for the year 1989 (pp. 139–46).

13. In a common article C. Machos and I have analyzed the role of party functionaries of the state party in Hungary (MSZP) and Germany (PDS) within the parliamentary parties of the successors. In the MSZP, the size of this special group is much smaller than in the PDS, because the systemic change in Hungary started within the party-elite and, consequently, more persons from that group could survive.

14. Compare the article of Patton, who is of the opinion that the "PDS in the early 1990s most closely fits the pattern of Western regional success" (1999, p. 512).

9

The Romanian Postcommunist Parties

A Story of Success

Alina Mungiu-Pippidi

Students of Romanian communism used to predict very little. At best they expected the obedience of the Romanian people to end one day, especially if Ceauşescu failed to employ means of legitimation more effective than simple propaganda (Fischer, 1997; Nelson 1981). Ceauşescu's successor was supposed to be a member of his family or an heir chosen by Gorbachev. The violent popular upheaval of December 1989 surprised everyone and remains, despite attempts at explaining those events, the most important mystery of Romanian contemporary history. The revolt made Romania, in the course of only a few days, jump through a transformation for which it was not prepared. It created two revolutions, the one of the streets, the students, the intellectuals, and those who wanted reforms to be instituted immediately, and one of the army, the bureaucracy, and the people, who wanted gradual and nonconflictive change. The gap quickly became a chasm, a divide that trapped Romanian society for years to come, making the country lose ground to its Central European neighbors. It is easier for an analyst to explain the slow transition of Romanians towards democracy than it is to understand the Romanian Revolution. Periods of political stagnation alternating with sudden and unexpected developments continued with the forced departure of the Roman government in September 1991 amidst a city besieged by protesting coal miners, and the unexpected victory of anticommunist Emil Constantinescu by November 1996. This is why Romanian postcommunism is such a fruitful topic for journalists and such a poor one for political scientists. Indeed, it is still difficult to penetrate the near total secrecy surrounding Ceauşescu's overthrow. To this day there has been no satisfactory explanation of how nearly 1,000 people died in the upheaval, who the terrorists were who kept Bucharest and other cities under fire just days before vanishing, and why the decision to hide the truth became the common policy of all postcommunist governments (including the anticommunist one after 1996).

These mysteries make it easy to get too deeply entrenched in conspiracy theories and therefore (1) miss the social reality which led to the three victories of the communist successor parties in what can be considered free and fair elections, (2) ignore the connections between the *Securitate*, the new financial oligarchy, and the postcommunist parties. Our difficult task here is to shed some light on the reality of Romanian postcommunism.

Birth of a Political System

Three sets of causes influenced the birth of the postcommunist political system and the evolution of postcommunist parties after 1989. They shaped the system that is still in place today, even after democratic alteration took place, because little was attempted by the new regime to change the fundamentals created by the old one.

Historical Causes

The Lack of a Leftist Urban Intellectual Tradition in Romania

Before World War II, Romania was an agrarian country, with 80 percent of the population made up of peasants. The place of the Left was occupied by the center-left agrarian National Peasant Party. The Romanian Communist Party (RCP) had around 30 members by 1925 and less than 1,000 by the end of World War II (Frunza 1990). The imposition of communism by the Red Army was not popularly supported, since most of the peasants had benefited from repeated land reform and were fearful communists would seize their lands. The Social Democrat Party was almost nonexistent as well, being supported only by a thin stratum of urban workers. Almost every communist leader had come from Moscow with the Red Army in 1945, and these leaders purged the few who had stayed in Romania during the war. Purges inside the Communist Party and participation in the repression of the Hungarian Revolution of 1956 earned leader Gheorghiu Dej the trust of the Soviet Union, which withdrew its troops from the country in 1963. Ceauşescu's independent stand on the occasion of the invasion of Czechoslovakia in 1968 gave even more national legitimacy to the party.

Intellectuals were not traditionally leftist. The best of the Romanian intellectual class before the war had been right-wing. The few leftists were purged by Gheorghiu Dej. The works of the Western intellectual left were not even known in Romania. Therefore neither the RCP nor other organizations such as the Union of Writers developed a tradition of internal discussion on the doctrine of Marxism-Leninism. It was even more difficult later, when Ceauşescu's brand of Asian-style communism allowed only one doctrine, "Ceauşescuism," and even the works of German and Soviet authors were replaced by Romanian nationalist authors. It is significant that the authors of the "letter of the six," the only opposition manifesto from inside the Communist Party, were survivors from the World War II era. Their leader, Salvia Brucan, was one of the last true ideologues left, while another, Alexandru Barladeanu, was an old socialist economist terrified of Ceauşescu's approach to the command economy.

Glasnost and perestroika were also publicly criticized by Ceauşescu and no apparatchik dared to start a pro-glasnost movement in Romania. Thus, the Romanian postcommunist parties had no social-democratic tradition to rely upon and no social democrats to inherit. When having to choose something noncommunist from the political spectrum, they ostensibly chose social-democracy. However, neither Ion Iliescu nor any of his close collaborators ever displayed any knowledge of the doctrine of social democracy, quoted a Social Democrat author, or managed to construct a true social democratic political discourse. Rather, ultimately, they gave in to the temptation of populism and nationalism.

The Absence of Any Organized Resistance Against the Ceauşescu Regime

The National Salvation Front as the principal successor to the RCP, encountered no organized political or civic movement in Romania. One of the reasons was the historical repressiveness of the Romanian communist regime. Around one million people had been imprisoned during the Stalinist years, then released in a general amnesty in 1964. Most of them had been interned in forced labor and re-education camps. The scattered pockets of armed resistance in the mountains and farmers' resistance to collectivization were also liquidated by 1964. Resisters were shot after brief trials and the most stubborn peasants deported to labor camps in Dobrudja. Ceauşescu inherited from Dej a party with no factions left, a society subordinated with no organized opposition, and a rural world in disarray. His own massive industrialization program created no profitable industries, but managed to displace large numbers of people. Economically his plan was a disaster but politically it was a success. As a Romanian sociologist pointed out (Botez 1978), villagers turned town-dwellers soon became the first true supporters of the regime. While peasants increasingly lost the last trace of autonomy they had once enjoyed and became more and more dependent on their state pensions, white- and blue-collar workers enjoyed quite a good life by communist standards until the late 1980s. Thus, in contrast to Poland, unions were not likely to heed a call for revolt in Romania. Indeed, Romania had already become what some labeled as a "society of survival," a society where far from fighting for a better future, people were more concerned about preserving what little they had left (Pasti 1997, p. 37). Survival had become the main value, and this made collective action and civic protest unlikely.

Causes Emerging from the Type of Transition: The Vanishing Party

The Romanian Communist Party (RCP) contained by 1989 about 4 million members out of a population of 22 million. As the Romanian dissident poet Mircea Dinescu pointed out: "to own a party membership card was like owning a driver's license—you couldn't get around without it." The concentration of power in the hands of the Ceauşescus and their clan had considerably weakened the party. Even being personally appointed by the Ceauşescu family as a member of the Political Bureau did not mean that one had a say in important decisions. Indeed, the power of that organization was reduced only to influencing appointments and other distributions of privileges and favors—policy-making was a monopoly of the family, supported by the *Securitate*, Ceauşescu's infamous political police. The penetration of society was not, however, confined to the party—everyone under thirty was a member of the Communist Youth; most people were union members and for nonparty members a Front of Democracy and Socialist Unity (FDUS) was invented a few years before the end of the regime. Of course, participation in all these organizations was compulsory, depending upon the position one held. Thus, the mobilization and control of the society ruled by Ceauşescu was very extensive.

It was a true totalitarian regime by any standard, with a center of power both monistic and monolithic (Linz 1977), where every aspect of life was penetrated by the state (Fischer 1997). The autonomy of Romanians was almost completely gone by 1989—all typewriters were recorded by the police, and everything including bread was rationed. Attempts at building a resistance network were doomed to fail because of the large number of *Securitate* informants (Delletant 1995). Dissidents or opponents were singled out immediately, before being able to recruit others. However, by 1989 poverty was so deep that discontent grew despite the extensive repression.

Had indoctrination not been so intensive perhaps the RCP party could have survived the coup. Guilty of becoming only a personal tool in the hands of Ceauşescu, and deprived of any alternative leadership, the party simply vanished on the evening of December 22. On that night, a small group of people, using their communist connections but also their reputation as dissidents, managed to broadcast live on Romanian television's main channel that Ceauşescu had fled. This small group assumed the mantle of leadership with the help of the army (and probably the *Securitate*). They encouraged people to overthrow both management and party structures and elect leaders of special revolutionary committees. Managers throughout most of the country defected to the National Salvation Front (NSF), as did most party members. By December 23 and 24 delegates at the initial NSF meeting had organized the creation of village, town, and regional NSF committees, and by the beginning of January 1990 a sort of national assembly convened in Bucharest under the leadership of the NSF and the presidency of Ion Iliescu.[1]

Unlike other initial leaders of the NSF, the appearance of Iliescu's name was no surprise. Radio Free Europe had long identified him as the party's only alternative to Ceauşescu. Iliescu was considered an independent, but he had no faction of his own and no followers in the party. However, he enjoyed a good reputation—he had been demoted in the last years of the Ceauşescu regime, which made him a sort of dissident. On December 22, Iliescu was acclaimed by the crowd invading the headquarters of RCP's Central Committee. He displayed authority and self-confidence, and had the support of a group of old apparatchiks who that spring had signed "the letter of the six" and therefore enjoyed a reputation as opponents of Ceauşescu.

Iliescu appointed General Victor Stanculescu, a close friend of the Ceauşescu family, to be part of the government, and appointed as Defense Minister an old friend of his, General Nicolae Militaru, who had been forced into early retirement for his alleged KGB connections. Two obscure characters were also important figures in the new regime—a low ranking *Securitate* officer named Virgil Magureanu was appointed in March as head of the Romanian Service of Information, the official successor of the *Securitate*, and geologist Voican Voiculescu founded a new secret service (known by code name UM 0215), that was subordinated to the Department of Internal Affairs. This new office was involved in the violent June 1990 repression of anti-Iliescu protesters.[2] Stanculescu, Magureanu, and Voiculescu were all central figures that organized the trial and execution of Ceauşescu.

From December 27–29, 1989 two important steps were taken by the NSF Provisional Council following its first "plenary" session: the election of Iliescu as president and the dissolution of the *Securitate*. *Securitate* officers remained an organized structure subordinated by the army until March, when violent ethnic clashes between Romanians and Hungarians in Tirgu Mures provided an excuse to release the *Securitate* from the army's surveillance and transform it into the Romanian Service of Information.

Political parties started to register, taking advantage of the new liberal atmosphere. However, NSF dealt a major blow to democracy when it announced—contradicting previous statements of its leaders—that it would participate in elections itself, not as a party but as a grass-roots civic movement. When this announcement was made on January 3 the country was basically being run from top to bottom by a network of NSF committees previously elected on December 22 and 23. They had replaced the RCP bureaus even at the lowest level. Although many of the people elected had not been former party members, many others were. Most of them were intellectuals educated in the Ceauşescu regime who had been thrust into positions of power and prestige after the regime's collapse. Others had been elected simply because they had enjoyed the sympathy of their colleagues or proved more vocal than them. This heterogeneous mass had much to gain from NSF's participation in future elections—providing Iliescu and his group with a great pool of political talent, while other parties, even the historical ones, had to start from scratch.

From this base the NSF and its satellite parties consolidated a large majority in the constituent assembly, also called the Provisional Council of National Union (CFSN), which passed the first electoral law and organized the May 20 elections. By then Romania had again a single-party state, which officially seized the large properties of the former RCP (45 farms, 55,000 hectares [135 acres] of land, 22 hunting lodges) on January 18. Making the resources of the state their own, including the media, and with the help of a few populist bills (price cuts in energy, increased wages, liberalization of abortion) the victory of NSF was secured. Indeed, on May 20 they crushed their opponents and passed from a government with only revolutionary legitimacy to a democratically elected one. It was the end of the Revolution, but not the end of violence and confusion. In fact, the history of postcommunist parties really only started after May 20; newly elected legislators had very little in common with NSF revolutionaries—they had been selected to fit Iliescu's needs far more than the disorganized, spontaneous mass they had come from.

Structural Causes

Legal Structures

The newly elected Parliament of May 20 had as its main mission the design and adoption of a new constitution. It was, in fact, a Constitutional Assembly. However, less than one month later on June 13 Bucharest was invaded by masses of dissatisfied coal miners. The protest was led by civilians (in some cases identified as *Securitate* officers) and started to methodically destroy all the headquarters of opposition parties and newspapers. When they left by June 17—thanked by Iliescu for their effort to "restore democracy"— the opposition had been completely silenced and the leaders of the spring protest rallies were imprisoned. International protest found Prime Minister Petre Roman more willing to listen than President Iliescu. Gradually, the regime allowed opposition newspapers to publish again, political parties were invited to occupy their few seats in the Parliament, and by the end of the summer even the student leader Marian Munteanu was released from prison.

The coup d'etat against the political opposition is important in understanding the 1990 Parliament. A commission dominated by the NSF investigated the June events and cleared Iliescu and their own party of any wrong-doing. But the main concern of the majority was to build a future to protect them from their own past. It was therefore not by chance that the first important law passed before the constitution was a law on National Safety, granting important powers to the Romanian Information Service, whose boss was responsible only to the President. The same law sealed the *Securitate's* archives for fifty years.

The debate on constitutional matters that followed raised little interest in society. The historical parties fought for the reinstitutionalization of the monarchist Constitution of 1923, not a popular stance in 1991. Romanian lawyers assisted mostly by French experts fought to embody in the new constitution the main centralizing elements of the Communist Constitution of 1964. A touch of nationalism and a mixture of various political systems completed the picture. The main French touch upon the constitution was the addition of a Constitutional Court, which in six years of existence distinguished itself by never ruling against the dominant political power; it even granted Iliescu the right to run for a third term, despite the fact that the constitution limited the number of terms a president could serve to two. The communist remnants survived in preserving the unitary state, with the central and local government fused in the office of the prefect. Appointed by the government, prefects can, according to the 1991 constitution, cancel any decision made by elected local governments. Between 1992 and 1996 this provision allowed the government to dismiss more than one hundred mayors belonging to the opposition parties.

The Constitution of 1991 secured President's Iliescu's power, although the system it created was semipresidential. After personally appointing the General Attorney, the president of the Romanian Information Service, and all judges in the Constitutional and the Supreme Courts, Iliescu could really feel safe. The structure of the political system was set to preserve continuity, although the existence of a new proportional system would do some damage to the National Salvation Front. The state was therefore granted extensive powers, but as time showed, these were "powers over," not "powers to," to use Lukes's famous distinction (Lukes 1974). Collectivism was also embodied in the Constitution, Article 3 proclaiming Romania "a legal state, social and democratic." In the interpretation of its authors this was seen as a "corrective of classical political liberalism," because "freedom is only a metaphor if it doesn't have material support. . . . In the name of public interest the state can—and has to—step in for the leveling of a private monopoly, stimulation or direct support of private sectors, to take over as an administrator of certain sectors, etc." (*Romanian Constitution* 1992, p. 14).

Ironically, another law which helped in the long-term consolidation of the NSF was the Privatization Law of in 1991. The law made the managers of state industry, the main supporting network of NSF, practically unaccountable to the state. It also separated sectors of the economy into the more diffi-cult to privatize "*Regies Autonomes*" (autonomous administrations). The *Regies* included Gas, Electricity, Railroads, Communications, and hundreds of other national companies. The most unusual was perhaps the State Proto-col Regie (RAPS), which took over the fortune of the former RCP and con-tinued to produce special organically grown foods for the restaurant of the Parliament and to administer the vast empire of confiscated real estate by communists.

The law also set up State Privatizing Funds (FPS) to manage the privatization of state enterprises. These were supposed to be run by Boards of Shareholders (AGA) appointed by the Funds. Both FPS and AGA became the targets of NSF politicians and their political clientele. Privatization was slowed down and eventually blocked until 1997, not only for ideological reasons but also due to this network of managers and politicians who took advantage of the law in order to steal state property and businesses. The *Regies* became so autonomous that even today they do not pay taxes, while swallowing huge state subsidies. Thus, an economic and social basis for the postcommunist party's domination was secured; as long as it proved able to keep the state in its grip, it remained in power.

Public Opinion

A reasonable question arising from the above is how the postcommunists managed to remain in power even when corruption and abuses were revealed by the press. How did they manage to win the February 1992 local elections and the September 1992 elections? The answer lies in the absence of a con-solidated alternative—opposition parties did not make their first effective alliances until the local elections of June 1996, but mostly because NSF abuses were hidden by their control over state television.

Polls in Romania since 1990 have indicated a population with strong col-lectivist and authoritarian values. Only in 1994 did a majority of Romanians begin to favor some kind of market shock-therapy—until then the public had supported gradualism. Even today, while two-thirds of the population say that state enterprises must be privatized as fast as possible, when asked if they will work in the private sector in the coming years, two-thirds answered negatively. In fact, a majority still believe the state must set prices and secure jobs for everybody (the *Soros Barometer of Opinion* 1992, p. 117). Between 1990 and 1993 a majority was in favor of a single political party system (according to polls by CIS and Gallup International). The Parliament is the lowest rated institution among the top public institutions, while in a Febru-ary 1998 poll a majority of Romanians expressed their wish that the presi-dent (no longer Iliescu since November 1996) should be more involved in running the country, that is, more involved than constitutional limits allow

(CURS poll, March 1997). Even when postcommunists were voted out of office in November 1996 it was done largely because knowledge of their corruption had become widespread, and not because the ideology of the center-right opposition had more appeal than Iliescu's.

Circumstantial Causes

The Media

When in January 1990, Iliescu explained in an interview with the French daily *Le Figaro* that Ceauşescu had corrupted the otherwise noble ideals of communism, he immediately became the target of anticommunists. From the beginning he had been suspected for his past as an apparatchik, but once he displayed his taste for reformed communism, Iliescu became the enemy of former opponents of Ceauşescu, liberal students, the newly founded independent press, former political prisoners, and the radical revolutionaries of December 1989. He had, however, a formidable instrument on his side—the state-run media—and his decision to use it polarized Romanian political life for the rest of the decade.

When his legitimacy as a nonelected president of Romania started to be contested, especially by the revived historical parties, Iliescu resorted to the state-owned media to make his case. Reformed communist newspapers that had barely changed their title, television speakers who had only a few days before apologized to the public for years of service to Ceauşescu's personality cult, now enrolled under Iliescu's flag. They started a campaign of slander and defamation against the dissidents who had been proclaimed heroes only a few weeks before, against Western-oriented intellectuals, and against the former political prisoners who ran the historical parties. Newspapers such as the NSF's daily *Azi* and the national communist weekly *Greater Romania* were set up for the express purpose of rehabilitating communism, the *Securitate,* and even Ceauşescu in order to build a more legitimate basis for the postcommunist party. In order to discredit its main competitors, the NSF employed a vast apparatus of propaganda to essentially rehabilitate Stalinism. In a memorable letter addressed to Prime Minister Petre Roman, Ceauşescu's chief propagandist, nationalist poet Vadim Tudor applied for funding in order to start a weekly newspaper, *Greater Romania*, to slander the opponents of the regime more effectively than the newspapers already at work. The money was eventually found and Ceauşescu's propagandists were, only a few months after the fall of their protector, in business again.[3]

The propaganda apparatus contributed to the ideology that Iliescu and his group forged. While some in the NSF camp were embarrassed by such propaganda, a number of people who actually held those beliefs joined NSF. They soon became closer to the nationalist communism of Iliescu than pragmatists like Roman.[4] Others, who advocated collaboration with the West and true economic liberalization, also became identified by the propaganda as enemies. Members of the Parliament became closer ideologically to Iliescu and his propagandists than to the technocrats surrounding Petre Roman. On June 1, 1990, they proved it by staging a moment of silence in memory of the wartime dictator Ion Antonescu. The *Greater Romania* weekly had started the rehabilitation campaign of Antonescu, presenting him as an ancestor of Ceauşescu's fight for the independence of Romania against the domination of the Soviet Union. This synthesis of right-wing elements with left-wing ones (*Greater Romania* defended simultaneously the fascist Iron Guard, Antonescu and Ceauşescu, while preaching against privatization and the International Monetary Fund) was particular to Romania. The mixture of nationalism and collectivism proved a success, and a lasting one.

The NSF's propaganda contributed to the radicalization of the country's coal miners. In fact, Iliescu blamed the union leaders of Bucharest, claiming they prevented workers from cleaning up Bucharest, and so the coal miners had to come to the city. President Iliescu said in a speech made on June 14, "We must increase the degree of combativeness of Romanians, especially of the inhabitants of Bucharest, of workers of Bucharest, of union leaders, "union leaders who prevented the workers to fight next to law enforcers" (Press Agency Rompres, "Speech to Welcome the Miners by President Iliescu," June 14, 1990). Victims were denounced as criminals, as was the young hero of the Cluj Revolution, actor Calin Nemes, who had been shot by the army in full daylight on December 21, 1989. The army's official newspaper of 1993, *Armata Poporului*, repeatedly claimed Nemes was an alcoholic who had in fact committed suicide. Yet slander such as this was not the only reason for violence. Undoubtedly the journalists who hailed the miners and published names and addresses where opponents could be found contributed to the problem.

The Presence of a Hungarian Ethnic Party

Another factor was the presence of an ethnic party, the Democratic Association of Hungarians of Romania (DAHR), whose program called for the self-government of the Hungarian minority, which added an important dimension to the political spectrum. Parties aligned either in favor or against Hungarian autonomy. The cleavage line cut across party lines, dividing even the center-right Democratic Convention, the longtime ally of DAHR. The presence of DAHR and its separatist program provided an excuse for the NSF and their right-wing allies in the Greater Romania Party, who used nationalism as a defensive measure directed against the internal territorial fragmentation of Romania. In the elections of 1996 the newly renamed NSF, or Party of Social Democracy of Romania (PDSR), used a campaign poster showing a copy of Samuel Huntington's map from *The Clash of Civilizations* (1996), where Transylvania is separated by the rest of Romania by a line. The text next to the map implied that Western powers had this in store for Romania, especially if the DCR and their Hungarian allies won the elections. This paranoid vision dominated the political debate in Romania and was used by PDSR to play on the fear of Romanians that Transylvania might be lost again (Gallagher 1996).

Although nationalism remained an important issue until the signing of the Romanian-Hungarian treaty that recognized existing borders in 1996, the implications of the PDSR foreign policy dealt a mortal blow to their supposedly progressive electoral strategy. The Romanian voters afterwards considered the matter closed, since Hungary acknowledged in the treaty the present borders of the Romanian state. Thus, social and economic issues ultimately became more important for voters in the 1996 election.

Stages of Development of the Postcommunist Political Movement

Cohabitation

The youngest member of Iliescu's inner circle of 1990 was Petre Roman. His father had a hand in the creation of the *Securitate*. The son studied in France to become an engineer and a lecturer at the Bucharest Technical School. In December 1989 he was designated provisional Prime Minister by Iliescu. On May 20 he was elected NSF deputy of Bucharest, and one month later he was officially appointed Prime Minister. The government he put together was a collection of young technocrats, many of whom had some form of Western education. These politicians had little in common with the NSF clubs in the Parliament.

The government had an agenda of its own that conflicted with that of Iliescu and the Parliament. Bills that were proposed were rejected or delayed despite a general consensus on political matters that existed between Iliescu and Roman. Then Reform Minister Adrian Severin wrote a book using his notes from that time in order to demonstrate how conservative economist Alexandru Barladeanu, who had become president of the Senate (and was supported by Iliescu and the media) managed to delay price liberalization. A law for the restitution of lands up to 10 hectares (30 acres) was eventually passed, but five years later, half of the peasants still did not own land.

In his memoirs, Roman admits that differences between his government and Iliescu developed in time, creating a "cohabitation" regime. It was a shaky alliance between the president, representing a state "which tried to keep a reformed communist system" and a government which was "the only organized and real opposing force to the perpetuation of this system" (Roman 1994).

Unfortunately, Roman did not find a way to cooperate with the political opposition; the popularity of the Roman government soon dropped in the polls, and coal miners again became restive. When, in 1991 Roman refused to continue to grant them subsidies and high wages as he had in the previous year, they invaded Bucharest again, broke the windows of the government palace, negotiated with President Iliescu, and by September, finally obtained the resignation of Roman. President Iliescu claimed there was no other exit from the crisis. The Parliament, including many NSF members, rejoiced that Roman, perceived as arrogant, had lost power. Roman had on his side what was left of the revolutionaries who had joined NSF in December 1989 and the younger generation of managers. The two wings of the party were now in open conflict.

The ground lost in the February 1992 local elections to the opposition became the opportunity for bitter accusations between the two wings of NSF. In the Convention of March 1992, Roman won the contest for leader of the NSF party. The party also gave up on the idea of using Iliescu as a candidate for the next presidential elections. In the following days Iliescu's group split and formed a new party, the Democratic Front of National Salvation (FDSN, later PDSR).

Roman kept the party's name and property; however, he did not keep the constituency, failing to realize how popular Iliescu still was. In only a few months FDSN was running neck and neck with the NSF during the fall electoral campaign. Iliescu took advantage of the fact that presidential elections were simultaneous with legislative ones and became FDSN's front-running candidate.

Restoration

The FDSN won the September 1992 elections. They were indirectly helped by the opposition which once again mismanaged the campaign. The 31 percent share of the vote the FDSN won was not an absolute majority, so the creation of a coalition was necessary in order to form a new government. After formal discussions with all the parties Iliescu decided to form a coalition with two new parties which had won seats in Parliament for the first time: the Socialist Labor Party (PSM) and the Greater Romania Party (PRM). The two were rooted in the RCP—the Greater Romania Party was made up of propagandists and retired *Securitate* officers, while PSM was led by Ceaușescu's former prime minister, Ilie Verdet. Few ideological differences separated the two parties. The alliance was sealed in the autumn of 1992, but another year passed before the two junior parties were actually invited to occupy seats in the government. The coalition that was formed ruled Romania until 1996, when their leaders' personal ambitions and PDSR's concern with its international profile caused it to split prior to the local elections of that year.

From 1995 to 1996 the PDSR increased its membership. According to Adrian Nastase, Executive President of PDSR, membership reached around 250,000 by 1996. Although compared to the old RCP the figure is small, it made the PDSR the largest party by far in Romania. PDSR's recruitment was denounced by the opposition as a blackmail campaign—people were allegedly intimidated into becoming PDSR members. In 1995 and 1996, the PDSR managed to form a real ruling class, which took control of key sectors of the economy and state. Bureaucrats wanted to defend a bureaucratic state in order to maintain their lifestyles by selling their influence, new "capitalists" wanted to keep their monopolies and avoid real competition in a sort of state-favored companies' status (mostly against foreign competitors), and "entrepreneurial" politicians needed a slow, state-controlled privatization because this was the only way to make their fortunes.

Despite this, the postcommunists proved rather pragmatic—their policy of maintaining strong state control was not due to their belief in the beneficial role of the state in leading an economy but rather in its use to embolden the privileges of the ruling class. For instance, the Vacaroiu government, a so-called leftist government, drastically reduced the health and education budgets while granting large state subventions to manager-clients from bankrupt sections of industries (Zamfir 1994).

After the Fall

The total defeat of Iliescu and his party in November 1996 came as a surprise. Most observers had predicted Iliescu would survive a defeat of PDSR, since the DCR candidate, Emil Constantinescu, was considered a weak candidate.

To Iliescu's credit, he was, in fact, the first Romanian leader to leave office in a nonviolent way—other than by death, coup d'etat, or forced resignation—in the whole modern history of Romania. He was, in other words, the first Romanian leader to survive his office to become again an ordinary Romanian citizen. Of course, he again became the leader of PDSR and the leader of the opposition. However, his political behavior remained authoritarian and patronizing towards both the new government and the other parties, which not only led to a split in his party in the summer of 1997, but caused other parties to keep their distance from the PDSR. From a role as the most popular Romanian, a position in the polls he had enjoyed for years, Iliescu fell out of the "top ten" within a few months after the elections (1997 Barometer of Opinion).

Despite this the PDSR kept an important part of its contituency, ranging from 15 to 20 percent of the electorate. Deserters from the party included the opportunist members—the recruits of 1995 and 1996 who had rushed to join the winning parties. The rush to leave was so impressive that the Democrats, for instance, announced after the elections that they would temporarily stop admitting new members into their party. The PDSR was also investigated for corruption, which Iliescu bitterly denounced as political abuse.

Postcommunist Parties and the Postcommunist Party System

Romania has a multiplicity of different parties. In May 1990 more than one-hundred parties were been registered in the country. According to the Constitution of 1991 (Art. 3), parties only had to have 250 members to register, and this was raised to 10,000 by 1996. The proportional representation system was chosen without much debate, and the threshold for admitting a party in the Parliament was set at 3 percent, the lowest of all postcommunist states. With a threshold of 5 percent the 1992 Parliament would have been cleared of the extremist PSM and PRM, who had won only 3 percent of the vote. The combination of a proportional system with party list voting, the laxity of the parties' law, and the absence of a political will to ban extremism from political life combined to create a system characterized by "extreme pluralism" (Sartori 1966). Parties now hold together in coalitions with considerable problems. From its creation in 1992, the Democratic Convention—the main non-communist opposition coalition—suffered two major splits, and in 1998 its leading constituent group, the Civic Alliance, left as well. A government coalition formed in November 1996 by the Democratic Convention, the Democratic Party (led by Roman), and the Hungarian Alliance split in January 1998 when the Democrats pulled out of the Ciorbea government.

The postcommunist coalition, although more stable by comparison, was not without its own internal turmoil. The PSM had in turn been abandoned by a younger, more market-oriented group who in 1994 formed the Socialist Party. PDSR split after the defeat of November 1996, and the group who defected formed a new party, the Alliance for Romania. This group was led by the more reformist ministers of the former Vacaroiu government, while Vacaroiu himself remained with Iliescu. In 1997 the Party for the Unity of Romanians (PUNR) also split, as moderates took control over the party, leaving ultranationalist mayor Gheorghe Funar and his followers powerless.

While the three rounds of elections in the 1990s contributed to stabilizing the existing government at around eight to ten important parties, the centrifugation of the political system continues due to the continuous fragmentation of existing parties. The bipolarity of the system in 1990–1992 was replaced by the current multipolar system. The simple cleavage line separating communists from anticommunists became less visible when Roman's group joined the opposition, although it occasionally surfaced again concerning issues such as the restitution of nationalized estates.

If we consider the Romanian case there are several communist successor parties. The NSF was a populist movement, based to a large extent on revolutionary logic. Although propaganda newspapers started to rehabilitate communism, most members of the NSF did not recognize themselves as successor communists. Iliescu later openly claimed the communist inheritance for his party and had become by 1992 the only real representative of the NSF. This encouraged former CP members with conservative views to join the PDSR.

It is also debatable whether Roman's Democrat Party (PD) can really be considered a successor communist party, although many of its members were former RCP members. Indeed, the PD is very dissimilar in philosophy to Iliescu's conservative line. The Roman government, while showing itself ruthless in preserving its political power, nevertheless promoted a reformist program—they started privatization and price liberalization. Their deceived NSF conservative comrades used to accuse them of neoliberalism. Arguments in their favor, however, point to consistent behavior when it came to decommunization issues; they opposed restitution of nationalized real estate, and they were rather ambiguous about local government autonomy and privatization of the *Regies Autonomes*.

The story is rather different for the other parties. Obviously PSM is a postcommunist party—they even dared to reclaim the fortune of RCP as being the only "legitimate" successor party. The party of Verdet failed to pass the electoral threshold in 1996, as did its dissident wing, the Socialist Party. Both are unsuccessful successor parties at best, because they appeared later than PDSR and tried to compete with it for the same constituency— without having on their side the legitimation of "revolutionary NSF" and the popularity of Iliescu.

The diagnosis is more difficult in the case of PUNR. Their staff is recruited from retired army and *Securitate* officers; however, this alone does not imply PUNR is also a successor party. Rather it is not; its economic policies have been from the beginning closer to the liberal end of the political spectrum (Delletant 1995). It is even difficult to label them as a national communist party, as they display little taste for communism. PUNR is probably the only true nationalist party, and it will remain so with the elimination of its noisy former spokesman Gheorghe Funar. The nationalism of the new moderate leader, Valeriu Tabara, is already focusing on real issues—from the problem of education to that of the self-government of minorities, abandoning Funar's vocal-identity politics and a dispute over national anthems. By doing so they might have abandoned their last weapon in the competition with PDSR, which has long been installed as a moderate nationalist party. Mr. Tabara will soon experience trouble in keeping an identity for PUNR.

The Greater Romania Party is perhaps the oddest case of the postcommunist parties. After Funar lost his party and Iliescu his third term as President, leader Vadim Tudor became quite a prominent character in Romanian politics. Sued for defamation by many Romanian public figures, Tudor's stature rose. In the polls he has surpassed Petre Roman and even Iliescu in terms of popularity. Of course, the difference between Tudor, Constantinescu, and Melescanu is still important. However, Vadim and his private party fill a popular need for a radical challenge to the slow-paced Balkan politics. The rhetoric of the former Ceauşescu propagandist appeals to a part of the former PDSR constituency.

If we examine 1998 polls measuring Romanian voter support for various postcommunist parties, the vote would be equal to that won by the NSF in 1990. The opposition share has stabilized at 25 to 30 percent (including liberals, Christian Democrats, and monarchists) with an additional 7 percent for the Hungarian Alliance. PDSR, PD, APR, and GRP together garnered around 60 percent of the vote, leaving some analysts to fear that a new alliance of the postcommunist parties will someday reconstitute the old NSF. This is, however, extremely doubtful. The postcommunist coalition split in 1996 not only due to competition among leaders for positions and privileges but also due to the constant international pressure on Iliescu to abandon an alliance with extremist parties. The American ambassador to Bucharest, Alfred Moses, wrote a piece in the *International Herald Tribune* in March 1995 explicitly asking Iliescu to give up his allies in order to be accepted by the West. Since NATO and EU integration are the main political goals of all important parties enjoying popular support, it is highly improbable that any of the moderate postcommunist parties will risk an alliance with the anti-American GRP. A more likely development would be the coming together of PD, PDSR, and APR. Ideologies of these parties are not so different, but tensions among leaders which played an important role in their separation still exist.

Conclusions

Despite their temporary loss of political influence, postcommunist parties shaped the current political system and postcommunist Romanian society. The anticommunist victory of 1996 came too late to modify some essential issues necessary for the decommunization of Romanian society. It is important to remember, Romanians would have never given up their support for the postcommunist parties had they not been persuaded that the political opposition would no longer attempt any decommunization. The November 1996 vote was one against corruption and poverty, against the striking inequalities brought about by the party management of the postcommunist transition. The result of all this is the lasting influence of postcommunist ideology (nationalist and collectivist) upon the Romanian society, and a difference between Romania and other ECE countries that can be summarized as follows:

1. *The absence of decommunization and the survival of a communist bureaucracy.* Due to the deep penetration of communist structures in society (over 4 million party members and their families, the large number of *Securitate* informants) attempts at proposing any lustration policy were unpopular. This led to both the survival of the old communist bureaucracy and to the control of important economic positions by former communist elites. The immature opposition was unable to challenge that after coming to power, due to its lack of specialized staff. Typical decommunization policies, such as the opening of the *Securitate* files or the restitution of properties (especially real estate confiscated by communists), could not be passed by 1998. Once the center-right came to power, it was their allies the Democrats who fought against these policies. Romania is the only ECE country where the major political issue was not the restitution of property—understood as a part of the rule of law—but the social protection of tenants currently inhabiting nationalized apartments.

2. *The enhancement of the gap between Romania and other Central European countries by a conservative economic policy, meant to preserve state property.* The main stake of the transition was not the creation of a market economy. For the postcommunist political class it was asserting control over the transformation, mainly of the privatization process, which mattered most. Even in 1998, Iliescu's main condition before he would support Prime Minister Ciorbea's budget was a slowdown of privatization and control over the process by the strongly procommunist Audit Court (*Curtea de Conturi*). The Court, whose president (like all important figures of the judiciary) had been appointed and granted inviolability in the Iliescu era, even tried in 1997 to interfere with the process of determining the value of assets to be privatized, in a purely communist manner.

3. *The creation of a centralized state at the expense of effectiveness and the autonomy of local governments.* Since all parties fear discussing a revision of the constitution, postcommunist propaganda managed to impose a rumor that anticommunists wanted to restore constitutional monarchy—the primacy of the central government's law takes precedence over local laws even in local matters.

4. *The creation of a political system with low accountability and a weak judiciary.* Due to both the constitutional setting and to organic laws, the system suffers most because of a lack of accountability. Elections by party list and the frequent defections of MPs from one party to another—totally disregarding the mandate given by the voters—made Parliament the most unpopular of public institutions. The judiciary, dominated by communist magistrates, also proved

resistant to attempts at reform. Experience measured by years of practice is still the main criteria for being a member of all influential judicial courts, so former communist magistrates dominate the judiciary (IDEA Report 1997). This explains why the campaign against corruption launched by the centrist government stopped short of making an important difference. There is little hope that the present courts can fight corruption effectively. Rather it is privatization that might make a difference by finally separating state from private property, the source of most of the corruption. But to the benefit of whom will privatization finally work? The answer, when known, will finally indicate if postcommunism really lost in November 1996 and free competition really won. Romania's future as a part of the European structure depends on this answer now more than ever.

Notes

1. For theories regarding the Romanian Revolution, see Castex, (1990) and Ratesh (1991).

2. See official reports by members of the Parliament committee charged with the investigation of June 13–15.

3. For an extensive overview on propaganda and specific sources, see Mungiu (1996).

4. For Roman's nationalist rhetoric, see "Proclamatia de la Podu-Inalt," reproduced in Mungiu (1996).

10

The Yugoslav "Left" Parties

Continuities of Communist Tradition in the Milošević Era

Srbobran Branković

The chief successor to the League of Communists of Serbia was the Socialist Party of Serbia (SPS). The party was founded on July 16, 1990, in a merger between the League of Communists of Serbia, the ruling party in the communist era, and the Socialist Alliance of the Working People, one of the satellite political organizations supporting the rule of the Communist Party in the old regime. Slobodan Milošević was elected president of the party, and he kept the leadership position even after the downfall of his regime on September 24, 2000.

The party program worked toward "Serbia as a socialist republic, founded on law and social justice." Although public ownership is the basis of a socialist society, the SPS held that all forms of ownership should be equal in the eyes of the law. The SPS program supports the development of a market economy, simultaneously with "solidarity, equality, and social security" and promotes relations between the Yugoslav peoples and ethnic minorities based on the principles of full equality; it also supports a free and objective press.

The SPS won the elections to Serbian Parliament in 1990, 1992, 1993, and 1997. In the 1992 elections it failed to obtain a majority vote and was thus forced to form a minority government, supported by the representatives of the Serbian Radical Party. In the 1993 elections, the SPS failed, once again, to obtain an absolute majority (winning only 123 of the requisite 126 seats), so the new government was joined by the representatives of the New Democracy. In the 1997 elections, it again failed to obtain a majority vote and was forced to form a coalition with the Serbian Radical Party. In September 2000, SPS suffered a tremendous defeat by the Democratic Opposition of Serbia, a coalition of the Democratic Party, Democratic Party of Serbia, and sixteen smaller parties.

The Yugoslav Left (JUL) was formed in July 1997, as the result of a merger of a series of small communist-oriented parties. The leader of this party was Mira Marković, the wife of Slobodan Milošević. The party claimed to have honored the elements of the communist ideology, but in reality it was a political sanctuary for the nouveau riche who had trouble with the law. The Yugoslav Left has never had significant support from the voters. The political analysts all share a belief that the JUL was not a political party, but rather a political mafia. The subject of this analysis will, therefore, be the Socialist Party of Serbia, as the only party that could be considered the successor of the ruling party of the communist era.

The main opponents to the SPS in Serbia were the parties of the democratic opposition. The most influential opposition parties included the following: First, the Democratic Party (the first leader was first Dragoljub Micunović, and later on, Zoran Djindjić), a party of liberal orientation, supporting substantial economic reforms and civil rights, which, at times, assumed a hard-line nationalistic stand. Second, the Democratic Party of Serbia (the leader was Vojislav Koštunica), founded in 1992 and comprised of the former wing of the Democratic Party, which was in favor of the unification of the opposition. Before the Democratic Opposition of Serbia was formed, which defeated Milošević, the Democratic Party of Serbia had had a nationalistic image, but after it seized power, it became more moderate. It supported the concept of a market economy and privatization. Third, the Serbian Renewal Movement (under the leadership of Vuk Drašković) supported the return of a constitutional monarchy, insisted upon faith and tradition, and claimed to support civil rights and freedom. It failed, however, to substantiate the latter in the local administrations in which it had the majority vote. Finally, the Civic Alliance of Serbia, a rather small party of liberal orientation, supported close cooperation with Europe, civil rights, and freedom.

In addition to the parties that were seen as democratic opposition, there was another significant factor in the political arena: the Serbian Radical Party (under the leadership of Vojislav Sešelj). This party had a radical national-chauvinist orientation, advocating harsh repression against political opponents. It formed a coalition with Milošević's SPS twice: in 1992–1993 and from March 1998 through September 2000. There were about two dozen other parties in Serbia in the 1990s, which had little influence on political matters. However, they contributed to the impression that the opposition was in disarray.

These parties manifested a wide range of ideological differences. Nevertheless, the main cleavage among the participants in the political arena in Serbia was not based upon a program of ideological principles and objectives. The main political cleavage in the last decade of the twentieth century, which determined the position of a party in the political field, was the question: "For or against Milošević?"

The Socialist Party of Serbia: Supporters, Power Structure, Ideology, and Practice

To analyze SPS's rule, it is necessary to divide that rule into three periods: First, from its foundation in 1990 through 1993; second, its heyday from 1994–1997; and finally, from 1998 to its expulsion from power in the autumn of 2000. The distinctive features of each period included (1) the social strata, supporting the party in different periods, (2) the political objectives and the ideology supported by the party, and (3) the basic manner by which the party ruled the country. The characteristics of each of the above-mentioned periods will be discussed further in the respective sections of this analysis.

Supporters and Party Structures: The Social Basis of the SPS

The influence of SPS upon different social strata changed in the course of its ten-year rule in Serbia. It showed significant differences in the three periods mentioned above.

In the periods 1990–1993 and 1994–1997, the Socialist Party of Serbia was mainly supported by the following social strata:

- State administrators at all levels, business management in the state-owned enterprises;
- Employees in the state-owned sector (meaning the majority of the employees);
- Less privileged groups;
- Farmers;
- Dependents (the unemployed and the retired).

In general, the SPS was largely supported by senior citizens (50+ years of age), less educated people (those with elementary and high school educations), and housewives. According to their motivations, these social strata could be divided into two groups. The first group supported the SPS because their own interests prompted them to do so. Members of this group had some social status: a full-time job, stable incomes, and in the case of political and economic leaders, real privileges. This social stratum manifested a considerable fear of any change in the ruling structure, that is, a fear of the loss of what they had. This could be considered the main reason for their progovernment political orientation.

The second group of SPS supporters consisted of people who were attracted to the party for psychological reasons (e.g. senior citizens whose political socialization took place in the communist regime and who internalized basic authoritarian principles, especially, loyalty to the authorities) and desired the existence of an authoritarian political system. This mentality essentially was in sync with Milošević's ruling style. However, this group also consisted of people who were highly susceptible to the influence of political propaganda and media manipulation (such as the uneducated). Various sociological analyses show that support for the SPS in the crisis period (1992–1993) steadily decreased among members of the first group. Indeed, statistical analyses during this period showed a strong correlation between education and age, on the one hand, and degree of support for the SPS on the other.

Over time, the electoral composition in the third period of SPS rule (1998–2000) was reduced to the following social categories:

- The apparatchiks at all administrative and judiciary levels;
- The nouveau riche, whose "business" was founded solely on their affiliation with the regime;
- The top army and police officials and a great majority of the police force;
- Those who were involved, one way or another, in widespread corruption;
- Those whose psychological profile made them loyal to all authorities;
- Those who were attracted to Milošević's ruling style (a paternal leader with an iron-fisted rule).

Concerning policemen, one should mention that, in the late 1990s, their number in Serbia was estimated at 100,000, which was a large number relative to the population. The police had good salaries, far better than army officers, or any other employees. In addition, they had other privileges, such as implicit permission to confiscate goods from the black market, to hold second jobs (as security guards, bodyguards), and the like.

The social support was also generated, reinforced, and maintained through the internal structure of the Socialist Party of Serbia. Here, both formal statutes and informal practices were important. The formal (statutory) organization of the Socialist Party of Serbia was significantly different from the actual internal practices.

The party's formal structure gave its members a key role in setting the party's political strategy, such as defining the program, appointing key personnel, and making important political decisions (e.g. forming coalitions with other parties, reform projects, chief political declarations, etc.). The SPS had a network of local organizations in almost all towns and villages; these local organizations formed the municipal committees; as for Serbia, i.e. the republican level, there was the Central Committee, which formed an Executive Committee. The party program and other strategic decisions were defined by the Party Congress, which was called ad hoc. The Main Committee was the chief party organ in between Congresses. The Congress and the Main Committee's respective decisions were based on a majority vote and they are mandatory for all local committees. The differences in opinion were allowed and the structure was formally based on the local branches and the party members' initiative. In addition, the party had advisory boards for different issues (economic, foreign policy, etc.). These were comprised of experts who were not necessarily members of the party, and their role was to advise on different important resolutions and documents.

The informal relations within the party were very different from the ones defined in the statute. Characteristically, the absolute last word in all important matters rested with the party chief, i.e. Slobodan Milošević. The choice of the top party officials was based on strict principles of loyalty. Any sign of independence led to expulsion from the party. The top officials were subject to dual pressures. On the one hand, they were given the opportunity to get wealthy, but as a rule, they did it illegally. The following example is illustrative: The National Bank kept the foreign exchange rate at a level that was often three times lower than the actual rate, i. e. the one used by the black market dealers. The companies led by those who were affiliated with the regime raised foreign exchange loans from the banks, imported goods, and sold them at the real value, then repaid the loan in dinars using the official rate. This was a source of enormous profit. Similar transactions were practiced even at times of an extremely high inflation rate—people affiliated with the regime would raise dinar loans from the banks, change them into foreign currency, and repay the loans in several months, or several years even, in the original value, irrespective of the inflation rate.

If anyone tried to go against the policy defined by the party leadership, different sanctions would be imposed, depending on the degree of disloyalty. These dual pressures were the main reason for the surprising loyalty, at times, of the people at the top of the regime. It should be stressed that party officials were appointed to high positions in the administration, the judiciary, and the state media and there they kept their loyalty to the regime. The appointments of local party officials were also based on the principles of loyalty. The mechanism to ensure their loyalty was identical to the one applied to the top party leadership, only privileges were derived from the local level. Corruption thus permeated all levels of authority.

A large number of people became members so they could obtain new privileges or keep existing ones—a managerial position, a job in health services, education, or a position in the army, police, judiciary, administration, state or local media, public enterprises, or regime-controlled companies. This group neither identified with the SPS program nor had any illusions regarding the content of that program. They clearly saw that the general principles advocated by the party were seldom put to practice, and, therefore, stayed in the party even at times of dramatic changes in the ideological and political course. Another group consisted of party members who were fascinated by Milošević and his charisma. Still others had joined the party for ideological reasons. This group ultimately departed from the party, when substantial changes occurred in the party policy.

The central principle in the organizational scheme of the internal power structure of the SPS was the authority of the leader; the party was subordinate to him. The second rule was complete loyalty. The breech of this rule was sanctioned in several ways. One type of sanction involved removal from the party although the individual got to keep his/her privileges. This is illustrated by the case of Milorad Vucelić, the former director of the RTS (Radio and Television of Serbia, the state television), who was allowed to conduct a lucrative business in the "gray area" of the Serbian economy, even after his dismissal. Another illustration is the case of one of the Federal Assembly's speakers, who also continued to conduct his affairs after being dismissed from his government job.

A second situation occurred when a disloyal individual was expelled from both the power structure and from the business sphere, but kept some of his/her revenues. The person was not subject to a media witch-hunt, and was not prosecuted. Examples of this situation include Borisav Jović, former member of the SFRY Presidency, and Professor Mihailo Marković, member of the Serbian Academy of Sciences and Arts. Both of the above mentioned groups may have reached an agreement, whether silent or actual, to abstain from criticizing the party and the government.

A third type of situation was when an expelled top member of the party or the administration was not only outwardly critical of his or her former partners but even cooperated with the opposition. Examples of this include, Milan Panić, the first prime minister of the newly founded Federal Republic of Yugoslavia, Dragoslav Avramović, former governor of the National Bank of Yugoslavia, and General Života Panić, former defense minister. In such cases, a violent attack was launched in the state media against these persons; they were placed under police surveillance, and faced arrest. In General Panić's case, a scandal involving his son was made public, causing Panić to stop criticizing the regime.

Finally, the most drastic sanctions occurred when a disloyal member revealed compromising facts and tried to organize an internal putsch of a sort, or caused serious damage to the "business empire" of the ruling family. This was pronounced the most serious crime, and it entailed drastic sanctions. The punishment was, most often, physical elimination. There is a long list of top regime officials or people affiliated with it who were killed, without a single detail of their assassination or the organizers ever being publicly known. This list contains a minister of the interior, a defense minister, one of the leaders from the SPS party ally (JUL), the commander of the most powerful paramilitary forces, and others. It also contains several police inspectors, the nouveau riche (whose power became a threat to the regime), well-known criminals who were affiliated with the regime, and so on.

The Ideology of the SPS

It is important to distinguish between the two aspects of a party's ideology. One is related to the (verbal) proclamations of goals and values that a party advocates (the party program, significant declarations, program speeches by the party leaders). The other is related to the actual political activity of a party. There is always some difference between these two aspects. As for the SPS, the difference between the proclaimed goals and the core of its actual policy was quite considerable.

In addition, the party drastically changed its policy several times, so it has not necessarily been ideologically consistent (Antonić 1993, Mihailovic 1995, Miladinović 1998, Molnar 1998). An analysis of the SPS ideology and policies may benefit from Max Weber's distinction between patronage and ideological parties (Weber, 1990). According to this distinction, the official or effectual orientation of the first type of party is toward gaining power for its leader and securing posts in the administration for its members. The second type of party is orientated toward abstract principles and values (Weber also lists a third type of party whose orientation was toward the representation of interests of a guild or a class, which he called guild parties or class parties). This division is very useful for a perception of the essence of the Socialist Party of Serbia in the period which is discussed here. It is also useful because it allows us to differentiate between the parties that truly honor ideological principles and values from those that use ideology merely in Mosca's sense, as a "political formula" (Mosca 1968), to secure the adherents' support. It is only in the two-dimensional political space, in which the vertical axis would be the "ideological–patronage," or, more precisely, "ideology–demagogy" that the ideological attributes of the SPS could be listed.

The parties using ideological principles as mere verbal declarations, without putting them to practice, would be at the top of a vertical scale. The parties that consistently put their proclaimed ideological principles to practice would be at the bottom of such a scale. As for the SPS, it would be ideal to have a three-dimensional political space, in which, in addition to the vertical axis, there would be two horizontal ones: the "Left–Right" axis, and the "nationalistic–non-nationalistic" axis. The latter one is very similar to the ideological characterization that appears in the introductory chapter of this book. The point is that the party changed its ideology without reforming itself. Due to the difficulty of a three-dimensional presentation, both two-dimensional diagrams will be shown instead of a three-dimensional one.

Concerning the Left-Right axis, one should note that during its ten-year-long rule, the party used a leftist vocabulary, but its policies were totally opposite to its rhetoric. During that time, divisions emerged within the party between two groups: the impoverished majority and the minority who became incredibly rich (the members of the party leadership). The old communist regime in Yugoslavia developed a system of worker participation (the so-called "workers self-management"), which was abolished during the SPS rule. The workers' rights were severely curtailed especially in 1994–1997. In July 1996, new bills on employment and strikes were passed. Even the secretary of the regime's Syndicate Alliance of Yugoslavia criticized the Employment Bill; while an MP in the Federal Parliament he compared it to Mussolini's Labor Charter of 1927.

In the last phase of the SPS rule (in the period of 1998–2000), the SPS returned to the leftist vocabulary, but made no effort to put to practice its rhetoric. Figure 10.1 summarizes the movements of the party in the space defined by the Left-Right scale.

Concerning the "nationalism vs. non-nationalism" axis, the dominant approach of the party in 1990–1993 was nationalistic. At that time, the party had entered into an informal coalition with the ultranationalist Serbian Radical Party (SRS), and was one of the chief promoters of the violent ethnic conflicts in Croatia and Bosnia. In the period of 1994–1997, the SPS broke the coalition with the SRS, detaching itself from the radical leaders of the Bosnian Serbs, even imposing a severe economic blockade against them, as they refused to accept the peace initiatives proposed by the international community. In its public address, the party criticized nationalism harshly. Then came the signing of the Dayton Agreement, and the country entered a stage of peace and tranquility which gave rise to questions regarding SPS responsibility for the previous years' reckless policies. A critical lack of support for the party resulted in the loss of the 1996 local elections. The regime's refusal to admit defeat led to mass demonstrations, which went on for a couple months, and to the deepest crisis of Milošević's rule. Consequently, the regime switched back to a state of emergency. In early 1998, the socialists reestablished a coalition with the SRS and took a fierce nationalistic course, which resulted in the Kosovo war and NATO intervention.

The Attitude Toward the Main Segments of Civil Society

Generally, politics in the SPS was similar to a zero sum game: There was one value, and goods in a society could only be divided in such a way that some gained and some lost. The party never took the initiative to achieve a broad compromise among the major political factors or to provide a social environment that the majority of the social factors could benefit from. The SPS made a sharp distinction between those who supported it and the others, in

Figure 10.1

Positions of the Socialist Party of Serbia on the "Left–Right" Scale

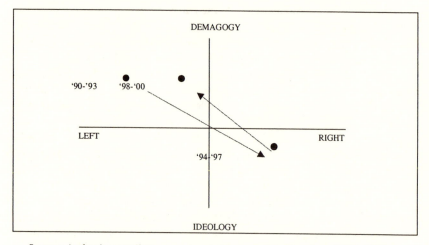

Source: Author's compilations, party manifestos and declarations (1990–2000).

which "the others" were seen as enemies. In a moral sense, the party leaders demonstrated pure Machiavellism: the ruler may use all means to preserve his throne.

An illustration of the way that different segments of civil society were treated in the political sphere is as follows: (when discussing civil society, I am speaking about citizens, respective social groups, opposition parties, nongovernmental organizations, the media, and the unions).

Toward its citizens the general attitude of the SPS was patronizing. The party claimed to be their loving parent, protecting both their interests and themselves from the "wicked" opposition and "assaults from abroad." Those citizens who voted for the opposition parties and took part in the opposition meetings were characterized as brainwashed by the enemy propaganda, their numbers were minimized, and their activity was ignored. It sometimes happened that Belgrade streets were cramped by hundreds of thousands of people, for days at a time, who demonstrated against the regime, without ever being mentioned on state television.

The party posed mainly as the representative of social groups that supported it and in so doing kept the vocabulary of the old regime, creating an impression that the administration promoted the interests of the working class. The social strata that were predominantly antagonistic toward the party (the intellectuals, the students) faced enormous pressure from authorities. For instance, the infamous University Bill of May 1998 was passed, which reduced the rectors, the deans, and the professors to mere administrators ap-

Figure 10.2

Positions of the SPS on the "Nationalism–Non-Nationalism" Scale

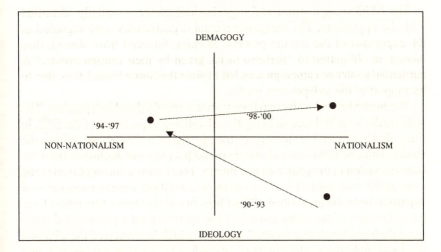

Source: Author's compilations, party manifestos, and declarations (1990–2000).

pointed by the government. In one of the meetings with a representative of the intellectuals, Milošević, who was then the president of Serbia, said that, in his view, a university professor and a farmer were equal, both having one vote according to the law. Consequently, he said, he did not understand why intellectuals insisted on having a special position in society.

Ever since the multiparty system was introduced, the SPS and the institutions it had controlled, regarded the opposition parties as necessary evils. In the media, controlled by the party, the opposition has been portrayed as the exponent of foreign powers, as the public enemy, while the opposition leaders were called mercenaries and traitors. The harsh rhetoric reached its peak right after the war with NATO. As of that time, the use of the term "NATO parties" to describe the opposition became common, conjuring images in people's minds of the bombings of 1998. By that time, more than two-thirds of the population were supportive of the opposition and such an arrogant tone on the part of the SPS only served to enrage people and drive them further away from the party.

In an effort to weaken the opposition parties and their leaders, a complex strategy was designed. In addition to the above-mentioned demonization of the opposition activists in the media, a brutal and systematic repression was applied as well. There was a special riot squad used by the police, and its members applied brutal force against the protestors. The activists of the local opposition branches were frequently arrested, beaten, and imprisoned for their political work. The repression against the opposition increased in the same proportion as the decline of voter support for the ruling party, reaching its peak in the third phase of SPS rule in 1998–2000.

The NGO (nongovernmental organization) sector essentially identified with the opposition. The nongovernmental organizations were regarded as the exponents of the foreign powers, as being financed from abroad, thus having an obligation to "perform tasks, given by their foreign bosses." A particularly intense campaign was led against the Soros Foundation, due to its support of the independent media.

The media had basically two forms: state-controlled and independent. The state media were reduced to being the advertising department of the SPS. In time, all who refused to show favoritism for the SPS were expelled from the media. Thus, in 1992, around one thousand people were dismissed from the state television in the course of one month. Those who were employed in the state media were subject to constant threats, and there were few examples of departure from the proscribed official line. In one incident a film editor from a local branch of the radio and television system aired a prerecorded statement during a break in a football game, in which he criticized the SPS and the local authorities. He was fired immediately, arrested, prosecuted, and sentenced to a long prison term.

The independent media were subject to constant pressure and slander, which gained momentum especially in 1998–2000. The electronic media were denied access to the airwaves, and their equipment was randomly seized with the assistance of paramilitary groups. The independent press waged a constant battle to procure the necessary paper supplies; their editors and journalists were stalked, bugged, and arrested by the police. Later on, when the authorities faced a deep crisis (in the second half of 1998), an extremely repressive information bill was passed, which imposed absurdly high fines upon the independent media. Still later, in April 1999, the owner and editor-in-chief of the most popular daily was killed. Despite all of this, the independent media showed an incredible durability and vitality and they played one of the key roles in the overthrow of the Milošević regime.

As for the unions, the party continued an old union tradition from the communist era of maintaining official unions. They were called "The Independent Unions," but they did not even try to conceal their ties with the ruling parties. During the election campaign, they used to invite their members to vote for the Socialist Party of Serbia. At the end of their mandate, some of their leaders continued their careers in the SPS or in the civil administration. On the other hand, there did exist real independent unions, which the government and the SPS manifested an outright hostility toward. Their activists were arrested and often brutalized by the police while in custody, and their activity was ignored by the official media.

The Basic Characteristics of the SPS Rule

Political analysts, especially those in the Western countries, find it hard to understand how it was possible for the SPS to stay in power for so long. How could they manage to do so while Serbia, after fighting three wars, became one of the poorest countries in Europe? To answer that question, it is necessary to analyze the manner in which the party ruled and the problems that reduced the chances for political change. These included the following features of the party-state:

1. *The SPS was the "party of power."* The SPS was a typical ruling party in Weber's sense. It was a powerful organization, whose one goal was to preserve the positions of power held by its top officials and the privileges enjoyed by its activists.
2. *The party exercised an authoritarian form of rule.* Milošević, his family, and a small circle of his close associates were not interested in just any form of power, but exclusively in authoritarian power. They were interested in such a form of rule that would provide them with unlimited power and privileges.
3. *A social environment that made authoritarian rule possible.* In order to achieve the form of rule described above, it was necessary to create a social environment that would make it possible; and the SPS made a continuous effort to achieve it. Such an environment had the following characteristics: the existence of a criminal economy, and the perpetuation and escalation of conflicts both internal and external.

Criminal economy. The Nietzschean "will to power" shared by Milošević and his family was not quenched by mere political power. As of 1992, especially after the introduction of sanctions, the family became incredibly rich through a series of illegal business transactions in the arms trade, cigarettes, oil, and drugs. A circle of people close to the ruling family also became involved in this trade. Thus a powerful financial oligarchy was formed, which became one of the pillars of Milošević's rule. The SPS conducted a quick redistribution of social power, especially in the second and the third phases of its rule (1994–1997, 1998–2000). These periods coincided with the decline of political support for the SPS. Alongside its traditional strongholds in the repressive state mechanisms and the media, it was building a third one in the new oligarchy.

The perpetuation of conflict. Authoritarian rule, the only form of rule in which the SPS was interested, could be maintained only in an atmosphere of a state of emergency. It soon became clear that the normalization of life in the country placed increasing democratic pressure on the administration. Hence it was imperative for the ruling party to perpetuate conflict in order to secure the conditions for the preservation of its authoritarian rule. Conflicts with the outside world, as a rule, led to a greater homogenization in the country, and thus to a securing of minimal electoral support for the regime, which provided at least the appearance of democratic legitimacy.

Escalating conflict. It became clear that authoritarian rule could be preserved only by perpetuating new conflicts, each new conflict being more severe than the previous one. This was due to several reasons. First, a mode of rule designed to enrich only a few led to the impoverishment of a great number of people, in turn causing increased social discontent. Second, people gradually accepted conflict as a "normal" part of life. These conditions led to the regime's efforts to pursue conflicts in order to distract people from paying attention to increasing social problems, and to escalate these conflicts. In 1991, conflict began in one part of the former Yugoslavia, then it spread to other parts. Later came conflict with the Western countries, and then with the entire international community (UN sanctions). Finally, in the last phase of the SPS rule, a military conflict with NATO occurred.

Isolationism's important role in the SPS policy. Their goals were: a) to limit the information flow from abroad, b) to prevent international law enforcement against war criminals and illegal trade (in arms, cigarettes, drugs, medication), c) to avoid conforming to international democratic standards, d) to keep the opposition from receiving support from abroad, e) to eliminate Serbian Diaspora and its influence. Retreating into isolation seemed to be an option to achieve these aims. The isolationist policy of Milošević was contrary to an anticipation by the international community that the sanctions and isolation would weaken Milošević's position and harm the interests of his ruling oligarchy.

Organized crime was part of the system. In the last phase of the SPS rule, organized crime achieved enormous power; it was directed by the top structures of the secret police and it permeated the entire society. It developed and controlled all lucrative business operations in the "gray" economy. Its members did dirty work for the regime (intimidation of those who disobeyed, blackmail, assassinations, snatching equipment from the independent media). It provided recruits for the paramilitary groups and pressured local Serbian political and military leaders, keeping them subordinate to Milošević, and, upon command from their headquarters, performed ethnic cleansing of different areas. In addition to the nouveau riche, organized crime soon became another pillar of the regime, which served to compensate for a lack of political support for the SPS in the last phase of its rule.

The Difficulties Faced by the Political Alternatives to the SPS

Current political theory suggests at least four preconditions are necessary to induce political change in authoritarian regimes: (1) the discontent shared by a majority of the population, (2) the discontented population must identify the top regime officials as the source of their problems, (3) the discontented population must unify; technically, they must recognize one organization or one person as the leader of their movement for change, and (4) in order to accept the risk of their participation in the movement and in order to be willing to invest their energy into such a political project, people must believe that change is possible.

(1) *The discontent shared by the majority of the population.* The critical point in SPS rule was reached in 1992, when the country engaged in a new war (in Bosnia) and when the UN sanctions were imposed. Since that time, the party failed to obtain a majority vote in the assembly, despite the fact that the party had sought to rig the elections. The seats provisioned for Kosovo in the Assembly of Serbia presented a special difficulty for the opposition parties. The Kosovo Albanians always boycotted the elections in Serbia. Milošević's regime, in turn, controlled all polls in the province. The opposition never succeeded in forming an organization, which would have been able to resist the election forgery, so each time the SPS "won" the majority of seats. Research conducted in December 1998 by the Medium Index Ltd., a public opinion and marketing agency in Belgrade, provided an indicator of the population's discontent. The question asked was: "To what degree are you content with the way Serbia was governed from 1990 to the present?"

As shown in Figure 10.3, 76 percent of Serbia's population was discontent with the way the country was governed from 1990, i.e. the time Milošević seized power (41 percent was very much discontented). By the end of 1999, the financial status of 52 percent of the population got worse, compared to the previous year, 38 percent claimed it remained the same, and only 8 percent claimed it got better. These findings support the notion that the first precondition for political change—the discontentment of the population—existed as early as the mid-nineties.

(2) *The population held the top leaders responsible for the problems of the country.* This issue leads to the heart of the matter. As shown in the graph on page 221, with the outbreak of wars in Croatia and Bosnia (at the end of 1991 and beginning of 1992), the majority of the population of Serbia recognized Milošević as chiefly responsible for the deterioration of the situation in the country. In response to that kind of view of the problems in Serbia, the state propaganda machine launched a wide-scale campaign to introduce the concept of a "New World Order," in which the big countries dominated the small ones, and in which small, independent nations, such as the Serbs, would

Figure 10.3

To What Degree Are You Content with the Way Serbia Was Governed from 1990 to the Present?

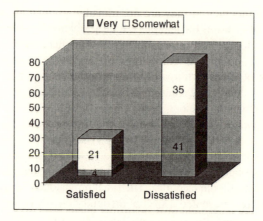

be subjugated. The main theme of the campaign was that the great powers were plotting against Serbia. At first, this concept seemed infantile, and only the hard-line supporters of the SPS believed in it. Around the middle of the 1992, though, the strictest sanctions ever were imposed against Serbia by the UN, due to the former's involvement in the war in Bosnia. This had a devastating effect on the quality of life of the general population, while, at the same time, it fostered an instant accumulation of wealth by the ruling elite. A shortage of fuel, food, and basic medication commenced. In the minds of a large number of people, the above-mentioned idea, infantile at first, started to gain credibility. They reasoned this way: "If the US and the UN really want to remove Milošević, why do they punish little people?"

Figure 10.4 shows how increased outside pressure reduced the number of those who considered Milošević chiefly responsible for the situation in the country, and vice versa. The success in shifting the blame to the international community was one of the main reasons that efforts to change authority failed. The blame, however, was not only shifted to the international community. The regime's propaganda also blamed other culprits for the situation in the country, including other nations from the former Yugoslavia (the official explanation for the war was that they were attacking the Serbian minority, thus pushing Serbia into an armed conflict), and the Serbian opposition, which criticized the administration, thus justifying the outside pressures and the sanctions (See in detail, Brankovic 1995).

(3) *The uniting of the opposition and the creation of a broad movement against the regime.* Since 1992, the opposition parties in total won the majority of votes, as opposed to the SPS, but the latter stayed in power for two

Figure 10.4

Who Do You Think Is Most Responsible for Our Country's Situation?

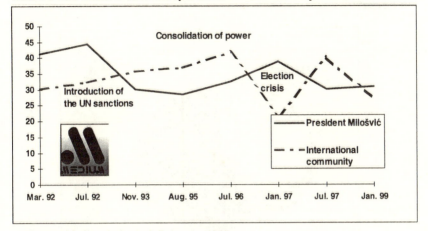

Source: Medium Index Ltd. Belgrade (1999)

reasons: a) the electoral system, created by the SPS, favored the large parties; at the time, the SPS was the only large party and the opposition was
divided into a dozen different parties, hence the latter could not hope to gain
a majority vote in the Assembly, and b) although the SPS failed to obtain an
absolute majority vote, it was always able to find a coalition partner among
the opposition parties to form the government.

The leaders of the main opposition parties could not measure up to their
responsibility, they were too concerned about their own vanity, and they lacked
communication skills in relation to the electorate and to other parties. The
ruling party used the secret police and their "moles" to perpetuate disunity in
the opposition. One of the examples of such strategy was the dissention caused
within the *Zajedno* (Together) Coalition. That coalition was formed right
before the 1996 elections and, despite quite unfavorable circumstances, managed to win the local elections in a great number of cities. The regime tried to
rig the election results, which caused mass demonstrations in those cities.
This was the greatest crisis that Milošević's regime had to face at that time.
He arranged a meeting, via the secret police, with Zoran Djindjić, one of the
coalition leaders and an organizer of the protest. Milošević asked Zoran
Djindjić not to inform his coalition partners about the meeting. The meeting
was not successful, but later on, someone passed on that information to Vuk
Drašković, also a prominent coalition leader. The long concealed rivalry be-
tween Djindjić and Drašković erupted. Alarmed by Djindjić's "treason,"
Drašković broke the coalition and sided with Milošević.

The regime's propaganda completely ignored the opposition leaders

Figure 10.5

"Try to Imagine Serbia in Two Years; Do You Think Milosevic Will Still Be in Power?"

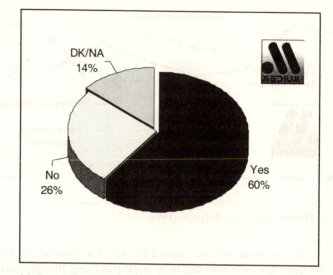

DK/NA
14%

No
26%

Yes
60%

Source: Medium Index Ltd. Belgrade (1999)

anyway. If anyone judged by information acquired from the state television exclusively, it would have seemed that there was no opposition in Serbia. The conflicts between the opposition parties presented an exception to this rule. When they occurred, the state television gave them a lot of attention, passing on the accusations, which the opposition leaders exchanged. This created a sickening impression among the voters who were eager to see some changes, that the opposition parties, already quite feeble, were also hopelessly divided and doomed to lose elections. Both the systematic campaign against the opposition leaders and their interpersonal conflicts led to their bad ratings among the voters. This is illustrated by Table 10.1.

(4) *The belief that change was possible.* Having in mind all the above, it is quite clear why the majority of the opposition-oriented voters did not believe that it was possible to bring about change, as shown in the graph above.

The majority of voters, who did not believe that change was possible, responded by abstaining. From the SPS's point of view, that was as good as votes in its favor.

Table 10.1

Recognizing Somebody Who Personifies Change: "I Would Like to Ask Your Opinion of Some Political Leaders. Please Tell Me Whether You Have a Very Favorable, Somewhat Favorable, Somewhat Unfavorable, or Very Unfavorable Opinion of . . ." (1= Very Favorable ... 4 = Very Unfavorable Opinion) January 1999 [in percentages])

	Favorable	Unfavorable
Vuk Drašković	22	74
Zoran Djindjić	23	71
Vesna Pesic	25	62
Vojislav Koštunica	36	57

Source: Medium Index Ltd. Belgrade (1999)

Conclusions

In the year 2000, the impatience of the voters rose to such an extent that the opposition leaders could not avoid unification any longer. The public pressure by the intellectuals, independent media, nongovernmental organizations, students, and trade unions was so great that the majority of the opposition decided to form a movement, called "The Democratic Opposition of Serbia (DOS)." The turning point was, first, that the voters recognized this group as a real alternative to Milošević, and second, that it was headed by Vojislav Koštunica, a political leader who was not too popular before, but who was also not compromised by either scandal or cooperation with Milošević. That was sufficient to completely defeat Milošević.

Based on the above, the Socialist Party of Serbia preserved a continuity with its communist past when it came to its ruling mode, i.e. curtailment of human rights and freedom, an inclination to dominate all spheres of the civil society, harsh repression, and stifling of the media.

As for ideology, the party made a radical turn in relation to the communist era. The Titoist ideology of "brotherhood and unity," and the idea of proletarian internationalism were replaced by the most rigid nationalism. Some of the ideals of the old regime, i.e. the strife for social equality and workers' participation, have been replaced by the promotion of brutal social stratification and drastic reduction of workers' rights. However, despite the occasional insistence on certain ideologies, the SPS was, and still is, a typical party of power. Its basic goal was to stay in power, while ideology was only the means it used. Hence, the party changed its ideological colors in the last decade with astounding ease.

11

The Metamorphosis of the Communist Party of Lithuania

Diana Janusauskiené

The evolution of the Communist Party of Lithuania (KPL) and its successor, the Lithuanian Democratic Labor Party (LDDP), is a clear example of a successful communist party that was able to adapt to the new political circumstances that appeared after the fall of communism. The KPL, similar to several other communist parties of postcommunist Europe, transformed into a social democratic party able to win the elections and form a government. In comparison to the other communist parties of the exrepublics of the Soviet Union, the KPL occupies a peculiar place. It was the first communist party that broke from the Communist Party of the Soviet Union (CPSU), thus ruining its cohesion. The KPL formed an independent party that gradually transformed its ideology and statute, as well as the title of the party, and refused its political monopoly condemning the communist crimes. All these steps enabled the party to survive and stay an important force in national politics.

The transformation of the KPL underwent several phases. The initial phase was characterized by a struggle for the independence of the party. The beginning of this phase occurred in the late 1960s. According to Lithuanian historian Liekis "at that time [1989] the idea of an independent party had existed for almost a quarter of a century. Such an idea got wings especially in 1968, in the years of the so-called 'Prague spring'" (Liekis 1996, p. 8). The reform-oriented communists of the 1960s dreamed for Lithuania a status equal to that of Poland or Czechoslovakia. However, these aims could only be officially put into an agenda after Gorbachev declared the policy of perestroika. The initial phase of struggle for the independence of the party ended in 1989, when the Twentieth Congress of the KPL declared its separation from the CPSU and the establishment of an independent Communist Party of Lithuania. This phase embraced the internal split of the KPL into reformers (the KPL) and hard-liners (the KPL on the platform of CPSU).

The second phase of the transformation lasted one year (1989–1990) and was signified by the change of name of the party. The internal discussions about the status of the party led to the change of its name, statute, and program. The KPL was renamed the Lithuanian Democratic Labor Party (LDDP). The third phase is characterized by the loss of the first democratic elections, and it lasted until 1992. The fourth phase marked a new era in the development of the party. In 1992, the LDDP won the majority of seats in the Lithuanian Parliament (Seimas), while in 1993 the charismatic leader of the party, Algirdas Brazauskas, became the first nationally elected president of postcommunist Lithuania.

During the fifth phase of its development, the LDDP again experienced a downfall. The party lost the parliamentary elections of 1996. After five years as president, Algirdas Brazauskas decided not to fight for a second term, saying that his communist past negatively influenced Lithuania's image. Emigré Lithuanian Valdas Adamkus, supported by center-right forces, became the new president.

The sixth phase of the evolution is characterized by the rapprochement of the LDDP and the Lithuanian Social Democratic Party (LSDP). Until this phase, the latter had been the chief competitor of the postcommunists on the left wing, and a member of the Socialist International. The LDDP was denied membership in the Socialist International because the LSDP presented itself as the only true social democratic party, which continued the prewar political tradition of Lithuanian social democracy. Under the leadership of Brazauskas, the rapprochement has taken the shape of a coalition during the parliamentary elections of 2000. The coalition won more than one-third of the seats in the Seimas, but was forced into opposition by a broad coalition formed by President Adamkus made up of mostly center-liberal parties with no pre-1989 history. The preliminary agreement to unite the two social democratic parties in the near future was confirmed after the elections, and a merger was completed in 2001.

The Development of the KPL Before 1989

Formally, the KPL was established in 1918 during the first party congress, which took place in Vilnius. The party was formed by a radical group of social democrats (V. Mykolaitis-Kapsukas, Z. Alekna-Angarietis, P. Eidukevicius), who withdrew from the Social Democratic Party, the oldest political party in Lithuania,[1] and joined the Russian Bolsheviks. The KPL was dependent on the Communist Party of Russia (CPR), and it only had rights in the latter's regional committee. However, the program of KPL was much more radical in comparison to the program of the CPR. The communists of Lithuania did not support the right of nations to self-determination, and neglected the peasants (Bloze 1997, pp. 85–86).

Thus, the KPL was a fringe party in by and large a rural country. In autumn 1918, there were 800 communists in Lithuania (Bloze 1997, p. 86).

Many of them were organized by the activists, who were sent to Lithuania by the Lithuanian Bolshevik groups functioning in Russia seeking to establish communist rule.

In November 1918, the Red Army marched into Lithuania. In early December 1918, the KPL proclaimed a government of workers and peasants under the leadership of V. Mykolaitis-Kapsukas. A year later, the KPL tried to unite with the Communist Party of Belarus, however, in 1920 this union collapsed. The KPL did not have much support among the population and, after Soviet Russia acknowledged the independence of the Republic of Lithuania, the KPL went underground. In the interwar Republic of Lithuania the KPL was illegal. In 1921, the KPL declared its independence. However, in reality it was dependent upon the Communist International. In the first parliamentary elections of 1922 the list of communists won five seats in the Parliament. After the coup d'etat of 1926, the communist leaders (K. Pozela, J. Greifenbergeris, K. Giedrys, and R. Carnas) were sentenced to death. Until the Soviet occupation of 1940, the KPL remained an underground microscopic radical party of "professional revolutionaries."

The revival of the KPL came in 1940 when the party became a part of the Soviet Communist Party. At that time, there were only 1,500 communists in Lithuania. The membership of the KPL started to slowly increase after World War II. During 1944–1949, some 0.3 percent of ethnic Lithuanians joined the KPL; their share in the KPL just after World War II increased to about 31 percent (Eberhadt 1997, p. 167), the rest of the members being "the new immigrants." Generally, Moscow's emissaries did not trust their Lithuanian party colleagues. The non-Lithuanian cadres occupied most of the key party positions at all levels. In general, support for the Soviet regime was weak among the Lithuanian population because of the collectivization of land, deportations, administrative domination by non-Lithuanians, and the experience of having been independent. The resistance to the regime was best exemplified by a guerrilla war, which lasted almost a decade. It is estimated that approximately 100,000 people fought against the communist regime between 1945–52. On the other side there were 70,000–100,000 security troops, eight regular divisions and air support, as well as 7,000–10,000 special extermination troops, formed of procommunist Lithuanians (Liekis 1995, pp. 77, 102).

From 1945 to 1965, the number of members of the KPL doubled and increased from 34,500 to 86,400. This reflected the increasing submission and acquiescence of Lithuania to both the naked force employed by the Soviets, and the presentation of new opportunities presented by the post-Stalinist thaw. The "great stabilization" and expansion of the welfare state under Brezhnev drove KPL membership up to 197,000 in 1986. In 1984, communists made up 15.25 percent of the Lithuanian population. The share of Lithuanians in the party gradually increased from 31 percent in 1945, to 38 percent in 1954, 61.5 percent in 1965, and 70.7 percent in 1989 (Eberhadt 1997, p. 167; Keep 1996, p. 145; Misiunas and Taagepera 1993, p. 281).

During the whole Soviet era the KPL was a part of the unitary CPSU and had to implement the policies of the center. Almost 95 percent of the important decisions of the KPL were copies of the decisions taken by the CPSU (Liekis 1996, p. 105). Officially, the KPL had few freedoms, nevertheless, it was able to realize several substantial strategies.

The party leadership promoted the Lithuanization of the party by assuring prestigious but less powerful posts to Moscow's emissaries, and leaving the most important decisions to the native communists. The leadership of the party tried to stop a big flow of Russian immigrants to Lithuania by employing the local rural population in building industries. This is one of the reasons why the ethnic composition in Lithuania is now so different from neighboring Latvia and Estonia.[2]

In the 1970s and 1980s, one of the reasons for entering the KPL was to advance one's career, since there existed strict restrictions for nonmembers on career advancement. In this period the majority of the new members of the KPL were Lithuanians. The result of this was that new people with local roots gradually replaced the old party elite, schooled in Moscow.

After the death of Stalin, the Soviet authoritarian regime in Lithuania was not as rigid as the communists' rule in Romania, for example. On the other hand, society had "assimilated" communism, which led to a perception of the KPL as mostly a native, Lithuanian party. Therefore, during the first years of perestroika, there was no clearly expressed hostility against the KPL, with the exception of some extreme forces like the Lithuanian Freedom League, an underground anticommunist organization. The development of the democratic political party system after the fall of communism in Lithuania clearly showed that the KPL had some troubles remaining in the political arena even though it had wide infrastructural power, political experience and new flexible leadership. Popular national independence movement *Sajudis* was the most dangerous competitor of the KPL even though these two forces were tightly interconnected at the very beginning of the transformation.

The Split from the CPSU

Perestroika brought a great challenge to the KPL. Started in Moscow, "from above," perestroika gradually turned against its parents. In 1988, a nationwide independence movement called *Sajudis* appeared that started to pressure the KPL. The party was forced to adapt to the burgeoning and powerful feeling of national revival. According to Algirdas Brazauskas, who became the first secretary of the KPL in 1988: "there could be no division between the roads of the leading party and the people. Plans of the people had to become plans of the party" (Brazauskas 1999, p. 9).

On 19–23 December 1989, the Twentieth Congress of the KPL decided to separate from the CPSU. Out of 1,038 delegates, 92.5 percent of whom were university graduates (Stuikys 1999, p. 127) and 81.3 percent ethnic Lithuanians (Lapeikis, Masilionis, Paulaskas 1999, p. 9), 1,033 participated in the vote concerning separation from the CPSU. Eight hundred fifty-five (or 82.8 percent) voted for an independent KPL, while 160 (15.5 percent) voted for the KPL as a part of the CPSU.

The results of the national poll taken on the eve of the congress showed that 79 percent of the respondents (85 percent among the ethnic Lithuanians) supported the idea of an independent KPL (Kubilius 1999, p. 122). A similar poll among ordinary members of the KPL showed that 69 percent of the party members were for an independent KPL, 20 percent wanted more autonomy from the CPSU, while 9 percent did not want any changes, and 7 percent had no opinion (Girnius 1991, pp. 62–63).

The independent KPL was registered on 28 December 1989. A day later another party—the Lithuanian Democratic Party—was registered as well. The monolithic party system had finally cracked.

The proreform character of the party leadership played an extremely important role in the transformation of the KPL. The leadership took control over the party, which was not homogeneous in its attitudes. Lithuanian historian Liekis distinguished the following four groups within the KPL: The first was comprised of neo-Stalinists that wanted to strengthen the principal of "democratic centralism" and viewed all changes to KPL's monopoly of power as a disorder. This first group made up 10–15 percent of the KPL members. The second group included the followers of a compromise or those people that understood that while reforms were needed, they wanted the KPL to remain the ruling party. Autonomy, according to them, was possible only in the spheres of economics and culture. There could be no autonomy in politics. The third group consisted of people who understood that the independence of Lithuania could be achieved faster if KPL would not be ruled from the Kremlin. The fourth group included the pessimists, who believed that it was not possible to reform the KPL and achieve Lithuanian autonomy when Soviet troops were still in the country and there existed the KGB (Liekis 1996, p. 35).

The results of the voting during the twentieth congress showed that the hard-liners made up about 15 percent of the delegates. They were not able to stop the split. However, this faction was strong enough to organize itself into a separate political unit; 160 delegates (mostly ethnic non-Lithuanians) declared they were sticking to the CPSU and named their party the Communist Party of Lithuania alongside the platform of the Communist Party of the Soviet Union (KPL/CPSU). In 1990, the KPL/CPSU claimed 35,000 members (Liekis 1996, p. 282). Seventy percent of the party members were non-Lithuanians (Liekis 1996, p. 251). However, the KPL/CPSU had little support among the ethnically Lithuanian population, and many individuals of non-Lithuanian ethnic origin did not support them either. Later, when the KPL/CPSU supported the putsch of 1991 and actively participated in pro-Moscow parallel government (resorting to the use of force), they were viewed as traitors and criminals. Currently, the KPL/CPSU exists underground. Some of the leaders have been sentenced for their antistate activities, while others live abroad, e.g. in Belarus.

The leadership of the independent KPL had trouble defending their position in Moscow at the CPSU conference of June 1990 (Liekis 1996, pp. 67–74). The newly reelected First Secretary Brazauskas justified the split, claiming that otherwise the KPL had no chance to stay in power; the party should lead perestroika to survive. Brazauskas pointed out that "self-care" status meant the implementation of true equality between the communist parties of the Soviet republics. He stressed that the majority of Lithuanian communists wished for independence of the party as well as dissociation and condemnation of the tragic mistakes of the communist party in the past and a turn from centralism to democracy (Liekis 1991, pp. 67–68).

Many scholars and compatriots of Brazauskas pointed to his diplomatic skills—Brazauskas played a twofold game. What he said at the meetings in Moscow were quite different from what was said in Lithuania. This was true even on the question of Lithuanian independence. In Moscow, Brazauskas maintained that independence meant sovereignty within the Soviet Union, while in Lithuania, independence meant much more than the improvement of the Soviet Union (Liekis 1996, p. 75). Brazauskas advocated a "step-by-step" strategy, asserting that further negotiations would be more difficult if they spoiled relations with the center (Brazauskas 1999, p. 13). This moderate position allowed the party leadership to negotiate with Moscow. However, it reduced its public support, which led to the party's loss in the 1990 parliamentary elections.

From the Communist to Labor Party

One year after its declaration of independence from the CPSU, the KPL underwent a second important transformation. The last congress of the KPL, which took place on 8–9 December 1990, decided to change the title of the party and to end its reorganization. Out of 515 delegates, 432 or 83.9 percent voted for a change of the title, 76 delegates voted for the previous one, and 4 delegates abstained. The congress changed the title to the Lithuanian Labor Democratic Party (LDDP) and announced a new social democratic party orientation. The congress confirmed the new party program and statute. The LDDP was reregistered on 19 December 1990.

The transformed LDDP was not the only player on the left wing of the political arena. The Lithuanian Social Democratic Party (LSDP), registered in February 1990, was the biggest political competitor of the LDDP. The Peasant Party was initially weak while other left-wing parties, such as the Socialists, were still too small to be significant competitors. The cooperation between the LDDP and the LSDP was restricted because of the fight for the "social democratic" trademark and electorate. Being accepted to the Socialist International, the LSDP blocked the way of the LDDP to this organization. The LSDP claimed to be the only inheritor of the prewar Lithuanian Social Democratic Party. Meanwhile, the LDDP stressed its affiliation to this tradition as well. The fragmentation of the left wing and the conflict between the LDDP and the LSDP were among the major reasons explaining their loss in the parliamentary elections of 1996 and local government elections of 1997. This loss was a great lesson for both parties, and in the next parliamentary elections of 2000, the LDDP and the LSDP formed a coalition. The coalition united the LDDP, the LSDP, the New Democracy Party (former Women's Party), and the Russian Union, adopted a single list and was titled "A. Brazauskas's Social Democratic Coalition." After the elections (the coalition won 51 seats, but could not form a government because the broader center-liberal "New Politics" coalition got more votes), the LDDP and the LSDP agreed to unite the parties under the umbrella of social democracy. The party congresses devoted to this issue took place in early 2001.

A very interesting example of the survival strategies employed by the LDDP during the "unclear" period in 1990–1992 (the party was in opposition) was the formation of a labor youth union. The LDDP felt that there was a threat that the party would be banned. Therefore, it formed a youth union, which existed under the wings of the party and had the same ideology. It was hoped that even if the party was banned, the youth union would survive and the party could be revived. The original Lithuanian title of the youth organization was *Lietuvos Leiboristine Jaunimo Unija* (Lithuanian Labor Youth Union). Two words, labor and union, used in the title were international, while all words in the title of the mother party *Lietuvos demokratine darbo partija* (LDDP) (Lithuanian Democratic Labor Party) were Lithuanian. In such a way the two titles seemed to have little in common even though they had the same meaning.

One of the leaders of the Labor Youth Union summarized the strategy the LDDP leadership had in mind:

> The initiative group [of the youth organization] appeared in spring 1992. It appeared because at that time the Lithuanian Democratic Labor Party underwent a problem of possible disappearance. It was thought that it might be forbidden and eliminated from politics and Lithuanian life. It was decided to establish a youth organization, which would survive if something happened to "the mother party." It would be a core from which the party could re-group. . . . The title chosen for the organization was "Labor Youth

Union." The title was chosen purposefully in order not to show ties with the party and not to attract attention.[3]

The LDDP won the parliamentary elections of 1992. The threats of banning the party vanished. The youth organization survived and accomplished such goals as preparing the new generation for the party and spreading the party's ideology among the nation's youth.

The internal transformation of the KPL, as well as the appearance of new political parties that attracted some of the members of the KPL, significantly diminished membership in the KPL/LDDP. Before the transformation of the party in early 1989, the KPL had 200,000 members. After separation from the CPSU, only 58,000 members were left (Lapeikis, Masilionis, Paulauskas 1999, p. 44). When the KPL changed its name to the Labor Democratic Party, the number of the party members diminished to 15,000 people. According to the data of the central office of the LDDP, after the establishment of the independent KPL there were no new members from "the outside." Fifty-eight thousand members of the old KPL reregistered into the new independent KPL. The new members started to enter the party only after the party's change of name and statute.

A more detailed dynamics of the membership in KPL/LDDP during the last eighty years is provided in Table 11.1.

According to the data of the central office of the LDDP, party membership has continuously decreased. However, there has appeared a new pattern of participation in the party. The LDDP has numerous supporters who are actively involved in its activities and provide financial support, yet who are not formally members and not officially counted as members of the party. Recently, the party reported having 6,000 such supporters.

The KPL and *Sajudis*—Two Engines of National Independence in Lithuania

The intelligentsia has always played an important role in the modern history of Lithuania. The Academy of Sciences was a place where many important decisions were born. In March 1989, a meeting of the communist party group of the Academy of Sciences analyzed the idea of an independent KPL. This group saw the independent KPL as a political party of independent Lithuania. The party, according to them, had to refuse the priority of any single social class, strata, or group, the dictatorship of the proletariat, or a leading position of the working class (Liekis 1996, p.37). The final decision about the independent KPL was made nine months later. A year earlier, in June 1988, the Academy of Sciences had given birth to *Sajudis*, the national liberation movement. *Sajudis* was established to accommodate perestroika, democratization, and glasnost and grew into a movement for national independence. At the very beginning,

Table 11.1

Membership Statistics of the KPL/LDDP, 1918–2000

Year	Membership (in thousands)
1918	0.8
1940	1.5
1945	34.5
1965	86.4
1986	197.0
1989	200.0
1990	36.0
1991	14.0
1992	12.0
1993	9.0
1994	9.5
1995	10.0
1996	10.0
1997	9.0
1998	8.0
1999	8.0
2000	8.0

Sources: Bloze (1997, p. 86); Eberhadt (1997, p. 167); Keep (1996, p. 145); Misiunas and Taagepera (1993, p. 281); Lukosaitis (1997, p. 108); and data provided by the central office of the LDDP.

Sajudis developed a moderate reform program. The principle aim of this program was to achieve for Lithuania a status comparable to that of "peoples democracies" in Central Europe. However, the moderate program quickly became radicalized and aimed at the complete independence of the country.

Taking into account the further development of the KPL, *Sajudis* and their counter-positions on many questions, it is necessary to point out that at the initial phase of the transformation in Lithuania these two political bodies were highly intertwined. Both of them were extremely important in politics at that time. Sixty percent of the leadership of *Sajudis* in 1988 were members of the KPL (Liekis 1996, p. 28). Many ordinary communists participated in the activities of *Sajudis* as well.

The relations between the KPL and *Sajudis* were consensual though not stable. At the very beginning the KPL was suspicious of *Sajudis*. Later, both organizations proclaimed similar goals, however they spoke more about an improvement of the situation rather than serious change. Both sought to achieve more autonomy for the republics of the Soviet Union and Lithuania, in particular, concerning decisions about economics, social issues, ecology, culture, education, and media questions (Liekis 1996, p. 10). After this initial phase of similarity, however, the positions of the KPL and

Sajudis started to differ. *Sajudis'* rapidly growing popularity radicalized it. The KPL maintained a "step-by-step" position while *Sajudis* began to advocate the idea of complete independence from the USSR. The KPL began to lose its influence and popular support. The transformation of the party soon followed.

The popularity of the KPL and *Sajudis* were highly interchangeable. Just formed, *Sajudis* had wide public support, while the KPL lacked it. However, Brazauskas' participation at the founding congress[4] of *Sajudis*, on 22–23 October 1988, as well as the fact that many documents of the congress showed a similarity in methods and aims between the KPL and *Sajudis*, increased the popularity of the KPL (Liekis 1996, p. 27). In general, connections to *Sajudis* ultimately benefitted the KPL.

An interesting opinion about the popular perceptions of the KPL and *Sajudis* is suggested by the Lithuanian sociologist Gaidys. He believes that people did not separate *Sajudis* and the KPL, therefore when voting for *Sajudis* in the parliamentary elections of 1990, they actually voted for the "left wing" of *Sajudis*, formed of communists.

> At the beginning of 1990 there was no marked differences between *Sajudis* and the KPL. In people's consciousness it was a mass movement. . . . People voted for A. Brazauskas (and his step-by-step policy) and *Sajudis* in 1990.[5] Besides, at that time *Sajudis* included both right and left wings. The empirical data obtained in our 1990 polls could be interpreted as evidence that people voted for A. Brazauskas and the "left" *Sajudis*. The "right" *Sajudis* did not win the elections, but it formed the government. If the results of the 1990 elections are to be interpreted as a "left" *Sajudis* victory, then one could conclude that no particular changes took place between public opinion between 1990–1992[6] (Gaidys 1995, p. 12).

Further development of the KPL and *Sajudis* differed. The KPL turned into a left labor party, while *Sajudis* gave birth to several center-right and right-wing political parties. The Lithuanian Conservatives/Home Union (LC/HU) is the biggest force that emerged from *Sajudis*. The LC/HU was perceived as a continuation of *Sajudis'* tradition. The LDDP and LC (HU) are the starting-point in the measurement of the Lithuanian left-right political scale. They have never formed a coalition. The parliamentary elections of 2000 brought about a major change. Both the LDDP and the LC/HU are currently in the opposition.

The Transformation of the Communist Ideology

During the last decade, the Communist Party of Lithuania has transformed to the Democratic Labor Party and has united with the Social Democratic

Party, thus forming a single Social Democratic Party. The unified party consequently dropped any connection with Marxist-Leninist ideology. Nationalism played an extremely important role in legitimizing the party. The KPL supported the idea of national liberation and the reestablishment of an independent republic of Lithuania. Thus, similarly to other Central and East European excommunist parties, the KPL experienced a movement from communist to social democratic ideology as well as a movement from internationalism towards nationalism.

The LDDP is not homogeneous internally. The party embraced people of both social democratic as well as liberal positions. The policies of the LDDP during the four years of its rule (1992–1996) were defined by opponents as right-wing (reforming the judicial system and economy, continuing privatization, and balancing a foreign policy between the East-West, strengthening national security, and creation of a free-market economy). While stressing its social democratic character, the LDDP asserts free-market economy orientation in the economic sphere and is more market-oriented than the Social Democratic Party. The LDDP promotes Lithuania's integration into the EU and NATO in foreign politics. Meanwhile, the program of the party as well as its electoral program emphasizes social democratic values.

The "Let's act together" program of A. Brazauskas's Social Democratic Coalition during the recent parliamentary elections was clearly social-democratic in orientation. Basic social democratic values, such as solidarity and cooperation, were highlighted while "wild capitalism," conservatism, and libertarianism were denounced. The coalition stressed confidence in national potential and respect for the achievements of the past, asserting independence from foreign economic and political pressure. The key message of the electoral campaign was well-being for all, the fundamental importance of work and work ethics in order to assure social justice, peace, and a clean environment. The coalition expressed pro-NATO and pro-EU views; however, EU enlargement would be supported only if it did not harm the well-being of the Lithuanian people. The program prescribed a "no enemy image" functional foreign policy, focusing attention on Nordic, Baltic, and Central and Eastern European countries, and firm ties with the United States. The coalition took a reserved position towards Russia, pointing to a flexible, but pragmatic relationship of equal partners. The same policy was suggested vis-à-vis CIS countries.

In the economic sphere, the key elements of the policy included preferential treatment of local business (foreign investors could be treated preferentially depending on how many jobs they created); fighting corruption and unemployment; creating jobs; anti-monopoly policies; strict control of state borrowing; stopping "harmful privatization"; and finally, assuring state control over nonprivatized strategic infrastructure objects. The coalition stressed the need for a simpler tax code, a flexible business income tax, and progressive private income tax, while keeping the gross tax burden stable. Concerning the Constitution and laws, the coalition sought to give additional powers to the president[7] in order to assure the independence of courts and the prosecutor's office, and the introduction of the grand jury system.

In general, the Lithuanian population perceives the LDDP as a left-wing party. Nevertheless, a uniform understanding of the party does not exist. According to sociological surveys, there were two opposing assessments of the party in 1996. On the one hand, the party was perceived as representing the workers, while on the other hand, the party was understood as representing large capital. In 1996 the LDDP was most often described from a negative point of view (nomenklatura, Eastern orientation) or by a stress upon its social democratic character (orientation towards the poor, retired, workers, proreform) (Degutis 1997, pp. 145–46).

The Electoral Performance of the KPL/LDDP

In general, the electoral performance of the LDDP has varied considerably since 1990. In the parliamentary elections of 1990, the party lost the elections to *Sajudis*. In 1992, it was the winner and formed the government. In 1996, the LDDP lost again, while in 2000 the social democratic coalition, a part of which was the LDDP, won more than one-third of the seats, but failed to form a government and remained in opposition.

The poor electoral performance of 1990 as well as KPL's defeat in the elections of the Peoples Congress of the Soviet Union in 1988[8] pushed the party towards the internal reforms that ultimately strengthened its social democratic character. In the parliamentary elections of 1990, the KPL won only 46 seats out of 140, and lost the elections. The ratings of the party continued to drop. Eighteen members of the independent KPL withdrew from it after becoming members of the parliament (Lapeikis, Masilionis, Paulauskas 1999, p. 23). The leader of the KPL was not lucky in the elections for chairman of the newly elected parliament of 1990. There were two candidates for that post: the exchairman of the Supreme Soviet of the Lithuanian Soviet Socialist Republic also the first secretary of the independent KPL, A. Brazauskas, and the leader of *Sajudis*, Prof. V. Landsbergis. Ninety-one members of the parliament voted for V. Landsbergis, while 38 members of the parliament voted for A. Brazauskas (Liekis 1996, p. 272). Despite the defeat Brazauskas became the First Deputy Prime Minister.

The elections of 1992 went well for the LDDP. The return of the excommunist party to power was manifested in many postcommunist countries of the Central and Eastern Europe. Lithuanian excommunists were among the first to celebrate such a victory. In general, there were many reasons why the Lithuanian successor party returned to power. The LDDP kept the organizational infrastructures and political capital that it had inherited from the

Table 11.2

The Number of Seats Held by LDDP in the Parliaments of Independent Lithuania

Parliaments	1990–1992	1992–1996	1996–2000	2000–2004*
Seats	46	73	12	51
Percent of all seats	32.85	46.1	8.75	36.2

Source: Lukosaitis, A. (1997, pp. 101, 117).

Note: *In the Parliamentary elections 2000 the Lithuanian Labor Democratic Party entered into a coalition with the Lithuanian Social Democratic Party, the Women's Party, and the Russian Union. The coalition had a single list and was titled "A. Brazauskas' Social Democratic Coalition."

KPL. On the other hand, society was disappointed by the drastic reforms instituted by the *Sajudis* government and the subsequent fall in the standard of living. This was consistent with the argument made by Bielasiak, who contended that: "Choices are not only voluntary and rational, but are often ad hoc responses to crisis in the economy and society or to political challenges from other actors" (Bielasiak 1995, p. 5).

The victory of the excommunist LDDP in the parliamentary elections of 1992 and the presidential elections of 1993 (when A. Brazauskas became the first nationally elected president of postcommunist Lithuania), served as an illustration of the adaptative nature of the successor party, and added to the perception of the postcommunists as a party representing national interests, along with other mainstream political parties.

The electoral performance of the KPL/LDDP is summarized in Table 11.2.

The Constituency

According to sociological surveys taken in 1994 and 1996,[9] the electorate of the LDDP in some respects differs from that of other Lithuanian political parties. The key difference is religiosity (the electorate of the LDDP is by and large nonreligious). Age and education are less important measures of its differences with other political parties. However, one can find that, in comparison to other parties that have the support of the younger generation (the Center Union Party, for example), the electorate of the LDDP in 1996 was rather old. Concerning education, the biggest difference is found among the electorate of the LDDP and the Center Union and Liberal Union, which are supported by many people with university degrees.

An analysis of the electorate of the LDDP is presented in Table 11.3.

Table 11.3

A Description of the Constituents of the LDDP

Description	1994	1996
Age group	Does not differ from the other constituents	People 40-49 years of age and older than 60
Ethic origin	In comparison to other parties' constituents there are more people of non-Lithuanian origin	In comparison to other parties' constituents there are more people of non-Lithuanian origin
Religiosity	Not religious	More people make it a point that they are not religious
Gender	Does not differ from the other constituents	Does not differ from the other constituents
Income	Does not differ from the other constituents	Does not differ from the other constituents
Education	Technical education predominates	In comparison to other parties' constituents, there are many people with professional technical education
Place of residence	Vilnius and rural population	The majority of constituents comprise rural population

Source: Degutis, M. (1997, p. 133).

The data show that the biggest difference in the characteristics of the electorate occurred in the age and place of residence measures. In the parliamentary elections of 1996, the political parties that were formed on an ethnic basis (the Polish Electoral Alliance and the Russian Union) drew their electorate from the LDDP in Vilnius.[10] The second big change is that in the elections of 1996 the LDDP lost the support of the younger generation (Degutis 1997, p. 133).

The majority of the LDDP's electorate, when asked after the elections of 1996 why they voted for the LDDP, said that they did so out of habit (see Table 11.4). This indicates that the party is developing a stable base in the electorate which psychologically identifies with the party.

However, one matter of concern for the party is the fact that 29 percent of the LDDP's constituents in 1992 did not vote in the elections of 1996. Further, 75 percent of the party's voters in 1992 that participated in the elections of 1996 voted for parties other than the LDDP (Degutis, 1997, p. 138).

Table 11.4

Motives of Voting for the LDDP in Parliamentary Elections, 1996

Responses	Percent	Deviation from the mean
I always vote for this party, and I am not going to change my habits	45.0	27.2
I like the leaders of this party	35.4	−4.1
This party could solve my problems the best	17.5	−5.6
Candidates of this party are the most competent	15.2	3.9
I know some members of this party in person	12.7	4.2
I voted for this party only in order not to allow other opposing parties, that I do not like, to get into the parliament	10.1	4.9
This party has helped to solve my problems	6.3	3.6
The parties that were in power did not meet my expectations, thus I voted for those who were not in power yet	3.8	−9.6
I think it is worth to see what this party is able to do. If I am disappointed in this party, next time I will not vote for it	3.8	−11.5
This is the only honest party	3.8	−15.0
This party always keeps its promises; it is responsible for its actions	0.0	−6.0
I am just disappointed in the party I have voted for in the previous elections	0.0	−9.9

Source: Degutis, M. (1997, p. 138).

Towards a Unified Social Democratic Party

During the last decade the LDDP underwent a serious transformation from communist to labor party. The prospects of this situation include a unification with the LSDP and the creation of a strongly unified left-wing party.

Indeed, the LDDP provides an example of a successful communist successor party. In comparison to other communist parties of Central and Eastern Europe (CEE) and the ex-Soviet Union the LDDP occupies a specific place. Separating from the CPSU, the party strengthened its positions in the area of national politics while at the same time it shook the communist ground of the entire Soviet Union. The LDDP was among the first excommunist parties in Eastern Europe to return to power after the fall of communism. The transformed LDDP remains one of the most important political parties in Lithuania and has, indeed, very good prospects for the future.

Notes

1. The constituent assembly of the Lithuanian Social Democratic Party took place in Vilnius on 1 May 1896.

2. In 1989 Lithuanians made up 79.4% (in 1939–41, 69.1–71%; in 1959, 79.3%) of the total population of Lithuania; Latvians made up 52% (in 1935, 75.7%) of the population of Latvia; and Estonians made up 61.5% (in 1934, 88.2%) of the population of Estonia.

3. Source of information is the author's Ph.D. research (Interview No. 3, LLYU).

4. One thousand one hundred twenty-one delegates attended the founding congress of *Sajudis*. More than 77% of the delegates were university graduates, 96% were Lithuanian, 0.8% Russian, 0.6% Jewish, and 0.9% Polish (Vardys 1992, p. 447).

5. The parliamentary elections took place on 24 February 1990.

6. The "left" LDDP won the parliamentary elections of 1992.

7. According to the Constitution, Lithuania is a semipresidential republic. The president has a right to veto the decisions of the parliament; he proposes the candidate for prime-minister, and has additional powers in forming foreign policy.

8. In these elections *Sajudis* won in 36 out of 42 electoral districts. The KPL was forced to adopt a more radical position (Liekis 1996, p. 324). A new consensus between *Sajudis* and the KPL led to the adoption of the laws of legal sovereignty, citizenship and immigration, citizens' rights and freedoms.

9. The data of two sets of research: Lithuanian Political Culture in 1994 and Electoral Behavior of Lithuanian Voters in 1996, was gathered by the Institute of International Relations and Political Science, Vilnius University and the Center of Social Information. The random sample covered 1,203 respondents older then 18.

10. Half of Vilnius' inhabitants are non-Lithuanians, mostly Polish and Russian.

12

The Russian KPRF

The Powerlessness of the Powerful

Richard Sakwa

The Communist Party of the Russian Federation (KPRF) is one of the world's largest nonruling communist parties and exemplifies in extreme form the dilemmas facing communist parties in capitalist democracies, with a few problems added that are specific to Russia.[1] Although the KPRF's obituary has been written many times, it remains a powerful presence in all of Russia's elections, maintains one of the largest blocs in the Russian parliament (the State Duma), acts as one of the poles of Russia's political community by dominating the left and influencing the conduct of politics both at the federal level and in many regions, and influences reintegrative processes throughout the post-Soviet area. This chapter will examine the KPRF's emergence out of the ruins of communist power in the Soviet Union, analyze its electoral performance and political development, and assess its organizational and ideological evolution in the context of its adaptation strategies and relations with the regime.

Parties in postcommunist Russia retain a tripartite character, derived from the ambivalent "transition" out of the old order and the hybrid character of the new. Emerging parties are stamped by a threefold combination of movement (the legacy of the insurgency phase of anticommunist politics), party (representative and electoral), and regime (the "party of power" often fusing political and economic interests). The changed nature of the political system in the exit from communism forced the KPRF to adapt by becoming a parliamentary party, but it did not become a social democratic party (Mahr and Nagle, 1995). Although the KPRF successfully adapted to the "reformist" conventions of parliamentary politics, there remained much that was "revolutionary" in its program and approach to the problems facing the modernization of Russia. Its adaptation was partial; its public political practices conformed to democratic norms while its inner life and ideology retained much that can at best be called suprademocratic. This was to a degree characteristic of postcommunist Russian political development as a whole, and thus we can talk in terms of the KPRF's dual adaptation: to the conventions of parliamentary politics and to the para-political operations of a political regime that itself was weakly accountable to Parliament and the people.

The Logic of Emergence and Development

While the center and right of Russian politics has been occupied by a shifting constellation of quasi- and protoparties, the left is now dominated by the KPRF. This situation was no foregone conclusion; during the early postcommunist period at least half a dozen leftist parties staked a claim as the successor to the Communist Party of the Soviet Union (CPSU). What was to become the KPRF had a head start, however. A separate Communist Party of the Russian Soviet Federated Socialist Republic (CP RSFSR, later to become the KPRF) was established in June 1990 on a par with the other fourteen republican organizations of the CPSU. The establishment of the CP RSFSR reflected Russia's aspirations to be recognized as a separate and equal republic of the USSR, but it was also motivated by a rejection of Gorbachev's humanistic definition of "reform communism." The election of the outspoken Ivan Polozkov as leader of the new organization represented the triumph of those most irreconcilably opposed to Gorbachev's reformism.[2] Thus the emergence of the Russian CP was defined by three features: an antireform ideological orientation, an organizational ethos of intra-elite intrigue, and a protonationalist juxtaposition of "Russia" against the pro-Gorbachev All-Union center. If Biggio (1998) is correct that once the ex-leading parties renounced the plan to accept market democracy "they could evolve toward two alternative extremes: social-democracy, or a hybrid form of nationalism and communism," then the nascent KPRF set on the latter path in the form of "Rossification."[3] The KPRF originated not as an expression of reform communism but as an example of its historical repudiation.

Re-Establishment

The founding moment of the KPRF, as with any other social formation, stamped the character of the movement.[4] The party went on to fulfill its original character by supporting the coup of 19–21 August 1991. Gennadi Zyuganov, who later became leader of the reconstituted party, was one of the authors of "A Word to the People" of 23 July 1991, accepted as the manifesto of the putschists.[5] The election of former CPSU ideologue Valentin Kuptsov to replace Polozkov on the eve of the coup was taken by some as a shift toward a more reformist position, although all it really entailed was the reassertion of the traditional party *apparat* over its regional representatives.

Even before the attempted coup, Boris Yeltsin, elected president of Russia on 12 June 1991, banned the Communist Party from workplaces and gov-

ernment offices.[6] In a series of decrees following the failure of the attempted
restoration, the CPSU in Russia was first suspended and then banned, its
property sequestered, and its organization destroyed.[7] Disoriented by the failed
coup, the party put up no resistance. The legality of the antiparty decrees,
however, was challenged in the Constitutional Court by a group of Russian
deputies, including Sergei Baburin, on behalf of the CPSU. A counter-
petition was filed by a group led by Oleg Rumyantsev and others. The case
raised serious questions about the nature of communist rule in Russia and,
indeed, whether the CPSU had ever been a party, in the strict sense, at all. It
also questioned the legitimacy of the August regime and the legality of Yeltsin's
rule, as it arbitrarily banned a political organization and tried to close down
its newspapers. Yeltsin's supporters, like close legal advisor Sergei Shakhrai,
insisted that the CPSU had in fact not been a public organization but part of
the administrative system and thus properly within the sphere of presidential
directives.[8] In a speech, party leader Zyuganov noted that some 40 million
people had passed through the ranks of the CPSU during its existence: "were
all these linked with an illegal, some argue criminal, organization?"(Zyuganov
2000, p. 18). The party, however, he admitted was not altogether faultless:

> The party is guilty in that for a long period it exercised a monopoly over
> power, losing the experience of political struggle, the ability to evaluate situ-
> ations realistically and to garner support among the masses. Democratiza-
> tion should have begun with the CPSU itself (Zyuganov 2000, p. 19).

The judgement handed down by the Court's chair, Valerii Zor'kin, on 30
November 1992 was a masterpiece of equivocation: the ban on the party's
higher organs (the *apparat*) had been legal, but not the dissolution of the
party's lower bodies.[9] Thus the party had the right to rebuild itself from below, to re-create its network of primary party organizations and to reconstitute itself as a legal entity.

This allowed the convocation of the party's Second (Extraordinary) Congress in February 1993, at which Zyuganov was elected leader. The reconstituted party soon became by far the largest in Russia, with its membership of
over half a million at least double that of all other parties combined. It reestablished a network of some 27,000 primary party organizations,[10] although
its attempts to reestablish a network in factories fell foul of Yeltsin's precoup
departization decree. The party moved from a production-based to a territorial form of organization. The great majority of members at that time and
later were former members of the CPSU.[11] These were not a cross-section of
the former CPSU's membership, however, but its most committed and hard-
line core, and this inherited mass base of the KPRF was to act as a permanent
constraint on the leadership's room for maneuver. While this irreconcilable
mass easily accepted a national-patriotic agenda (Stalin had long ago identi-

fied the fate of communism with that of the first socialist nation),[12] it would be more difficult for historical reasons to smuggle in a social democratic agenda. Many in favor of Gorbachev's reformism had already left the party by 1990–91, when potential leaders of a social democratic alternative within the CPSU, like Aleksandr Yakovlev, demonstratively repudiated his party membership. It was left to the hard-liners to inherit the mantle of party succession, not the reformists. This was not historically predetermined but a result of Gorbachev's failure to split the party in 1990–91 and place himself at the head of an unequivocally social-democratic majority, leaving the fundamentalist rump to its own fate. With a patriotic-conservative KPRF firmly established as the main party on the left, it proved impossible for social democrats later to erode this position.

It proved equally difficult for the KPRF to evolve in a social democratic direction. The KPRF's residual character (as a remnant of the old regime and of the political divisions of the late perestroika period) was both an advantage and a drawback. As the main successor party, the KPRF was able to exploit the legacy of membership, cadres, structures, and loyalty. The KPRF managed to disentangle the fate of the party from the regime's collapse, but in contrast to most Central European successor parties, it featured a less radical programmatic break, stronger organizational continuity, and an inability to find a new social base. The KPRF had few new policies to offer, a notable lack of charismatic leadership, its finances were scarce, and it was threatened by internal splits and external breaks with former allies. Its activity was largely based on the Duma's organizational and material resources, while the leadership problem remains a running sore.[13]

In organizational terms the KPRF largely replicated the former CPSU. The party is led by a Central Committee (CC)—until January 1995 the Central Executive Committee—and old-style institutions, and remains committed to a modified version of democratic centralism. The rhythm of party life reflects that of the CPSU. Between congresses and conferences, plenums of the Central Committee adopt resolutions. For example, the XII Plenum of the CC on 23 January 1999 outlined a plan to draw the country out of economic crisis (*Pozitsiya Kommunisticheskoi Partii Rossiiskoi Federatsii*, 1999). The party owned some 120 newspapers, two journals and dominated the local television stations in some thirty regions.[14] In 1996 the CC had 143 members divided into fourteen working commissions, including economic affairs, women's affairs, and similar others.[15] Following the Fourth KPRF Congress (19–20 April 1997) membership of the CC rose to 221, and the Seventh Congress of 2–3 December 2000 elected 159 members and 56 candidates (*VII s"ezd Kommunisticheskoi Partii Rossiiskoi Federatsii*, 2001), half of whom were new members compared to the usual renewal level of only a third. Instead of a Politburo, current work is managed by a Presidium (17 members were elected at the Seventh Congress in December 2000), while the party leader is officially known as chairman of the

Central Committee. The KPRF restored the whole gamut of raion (local party) committees (*raikom*), district committee (*gorkom*), city committee and *oblast'* committee (*obkom*) regional organizations, with the addition of republican committees (*reskoms*), all reminiscent of what had been thought to be a bygone era.

The view of the KPRF as a party burdened by an aging membership is broadly true, with the average member 52 years old in 1996. There are countervailing trends as younger members trickle in, and internal party accounts suggest that every tenth party member is under thirty. According to Zyuganov at the Seventh Congress, of the 20,000 who join the party every year, half are young people, mainly students, with many taking up leadership positions in the party (VII S"ezd 2001 pp. 28, 71). The social composition of the party is also a matter of considerable controversy, with only 20 percent workers or collective farmers, 23 percent engineering-technical workers, and 31 percent cultural, scientific health, education, and military personnel (Kto est' Chto, 1996). While the communist parties in Ukraine and Belarus remained rooted in the working class, the KPRF gained an increasingly "postindustrial" membership profile, reflecting the shift to postindustrialism in the metropolitan centers. Although the party reestablished itself remarkably quickly, there remained major problems. Having lost almost all of its property in 1991, the party was now beset by financial difficulties and was forced later to woo business and financial structures (as before 1917) and to accept donations from "red" businessmen like the casino owner Vladimir Semago (elected to the Sixth Duma as a communist deputy). The KPRF sought to avoid the mistake of its predecessor in allowing the expansion of the party's administrative staff, recognized now as having encouraged bureaucratization and the sclerosis of the CPSU's political life.

Ideological Contours

Against the background of the almost total disappearance of Gorbachev-style reform communism in the revived party, three ideological groups were identified in the KPRF by Joan Barth Urban and Valerii Solovei: the Marxist-Leninist revivalists, the Marxist reformers, and the left-wing nationalists (Urban and Solovei 1997; Urban 1996). The Marxist-Leninist revivalists were conservatives in the Soviet sense, ideologically orthodox and suspicious of the party's drift toward nationalism while resisting moves toward social democracy. Loyal to traditional notions of class struggle, communist goals and Marxist ideology, the tendency probably reflected more accurately the views of the rank-and-file membership.[16]

Marxist reformers sought to cull a purer socialist tradition out of the past, condemning the monolithic party-state of the Soviet years. Kuptsov, the first deputy chairman of the CC responsible for organizational matters, was a typical representative of this tendency. The approach remained class-based in opposition to Gorbachev's cosmopolitan universalism, but was antibureaucratic and supported inner-party democracy. It was assumed that this tendency would provide the basis for the growth of social democracy in the party, and while in the long term this may indeed be the case, until well into the 2000s they remained committed to a vision of modernized communism.

Although Marxist reformers dominated the proceedings at the Second Congress, a representative of the third tendency was elected leader of the party. Zyuganov is the central figure of what Urban calls the left-wing nationalists, or what the press often calls the national communists, but they might more appropriately be dubbed representatives of the statist-patriotic communist tendency. They are statists (*gosudarstvenniki*) because their allegiance is stronger to the Russian state (not necessarily limited to its present borders) than to the ethnically-defined Russian people (hence they are "Rossifiers" rather than "Russifiers"). They are patriotic rather than nationalist because of a residual commitment to supraethnic internationalist principles and a belief in Russia as a multinational state with equal rights guaranteed to all, although the dominant role of the Russian nation is stressed. And they are communists to the extent that they remain critical of the free market and committed to extended social welfarism. In the Russian context, this adds up to a distinctive type of left-wing conservatism.

Zyuganov was one of the most irreconcilable critics of Gorbachev's perestroika, identifying socialism historically with Russia, and Russia culturally with socialism.[17] He represented a "populist" tendency in the communist tradition, affirming what he calls the "state-patriotic" idea, as opposed to cosmopolitan trends (Zyuganov 1995, p. 125). His CPSU is that of Lenin, Stakhanov, and Gagarin, not Trotsky, Vlasov, Khrushchev, Brezhnev, or Gorbachev. He accepts Stalin's positive role, above all in the Great Patriotic War, while the former leader's crimes are passed over in silence.[18] Zyuganov is a Eurasianist, deriving his ideas from cult historian Lev Gumilev and stressing the role of the *ethnos*, or nation, as the moving force in history. From this comes the idea of Eurasia as a geopolitical entity dominated by the Russian "superethnos," or the fusion of Eastern Slavs and Tatar/Mongols. From this perspective, Russia has allegedly been opposed to the West since 1054, when the great schism took place between Orthodoxy and the Catholic Church (Zyuganov 1995, pp. 10–26). For followers of Gumilev, "modern Russia has more in common with the traditionalist authoritarianism of the Turkic and Muslim world than with the liberal, rationalist humanism of the West."[19] The idea of a distinctive civilizational identity is reinforced by references to Samuel Huntington's notion of "The Clash of Civilizations" (Huntington 1996). Class struggle in Zyuganov's thinking gave way to the contest for civilizational supremacy, with Zyuganov citing Danilevskii, Spengler, Toynbee, and others to support his view of the "decline of the West" (Zyuganov 1995, pp. 24–37; Zyuganov 2000, p. 439). For Zyuganov, Russia was less a nation and more a civilization (Zyuganov 2000, p. 366). Zyuganov is also a National Bolshevik, insisting that the Bolshevik regime fulfilled certain historic tasks for Russia. At the Seventh Congress of December 2000, Zyuganov once again reiterated this point: "Socialism is the contemporary form of Russian and *Rossiiskii* patriotism" (VII *S" ezd*, 2001). In emphasizing patriotism, state-building, and the role of traditional institutions like the Orthodox Church, Zyuganov had moved a long way from old-fashioned notions of class struggle, for which he was condemned by more traditional communists. It is in this context that the KPRF's "nationalization of socialism"—identified as one of the foundations of early fascist ideology—should be considered (Vujacic 1996).

The KPRF's program, adopted by the Third Congress on 20 January 1995 after a tortuous and divisive drafting process, was an incoherent synthesis of these three ideologies, although the influence of the left-wing nationalists was relatively limited. The program's four parts sought to place contemporary world developments into theoretical perspective and then to draw from this a program of action, a program minimum and organizational consequences (*Programma Kommunisticheskaya Partii Rossiiskoi Federatsii Prinyata III s" ezdom KPRF*, hereafter Programma KPRF, 1995). The program was marked by the absence of coherent economic ideas and by a confrontational tone that outlined a radical repudiation of capitalist development, no longer so much for classically socialist reasons than because it allegedly posed a geopolitical threat to Russia's state interests. The Fourth Congress of April 1997 did not come up with much more than some relatively minor amendments to the party's program and statutes. Programmatic documents remained inconsistent, reflecting the party's ideological divisions. The platform for the December 1995 election, for example, called for the return of the USSR, a new constitution, and price controls.[20] Socialism was not mentioned, and there was only one reference to Lenin himself.[21] Zyuganov argued that, as in October 1917, the reactionary-bureaucratic path of development for Russia had exhausted itself, and that Russia should adopt a "revolutionary-democratic path,"[22] although how such a path would look remained unclear.

The KPRF sought simultaneously to be part of the revolutionary left (opposed to certain basic features of modern capitalism like international investment, private ownership of the means of production, the sale of land, and so on) and of the traditional right (above all, messianic interpretations of the role of the nation in historical development). Revolutionary left and radical right positions are obviously incompatible in terms of approaches toward modernization (although not, as we shall see, in attitudes toward modernity) and internationalism, but historically they have shared similar attitudes to politics. Examples of this include the subordination of the state to the political movement, the identification of the aims of the movement with those of a particular group, and a belief that socialism should be "nationalized," and nationalism "socialized." In postcommunist conditions these features were exaggerated by the lack of a convincing developmental model (something that separates it from post-Mao Chinese communism). Socialism in the past, while steeped in the rhetoric of defending traditional but progressive communities, has always projected itself as a modernizing project; whereas the KPRF, other than borrowing the vague notion of "sustainable development," remained locked in regressive policies (*Programma KPRF* 1995, p. 8). The KPRF appeared to concentrate in a single movement the various bloody specters haunting modern European political philosophy: the revolutionist aura of the Enlightenment, the "civil war" politics of class struggle, the rejection of the market of both the revolutionary left and the petty-bourgeois populist right, and the nationalism of national socialism, today combined with the ideological pragmatism and opportunism typical of Stalinism.

Whereas successor organizations in Central Europe typically emerged from the reformist wings of the former communist parties and effortlessly adopted social democratic positions, the KPRF was established to oppose the disintegrative implications of Gorbachev's perestroika and to defend the achievements of "building socialism" in Russia. The CPSU was identified not only with the brutality of the Soviet years but also with the achievements of industrialization, victory over Nazi Germany, superpower status, and the development of a modern, urbanized, and literate society. The KPRF was born out of a fundamentalist protest against communist reformism rather than as a part of its fulfillment. Its evolution conforms to the general pattern that once a communist party is no longer primarily concerned with bringing down capitalism, it tends to find a new role as the defender of traditional national culture against the globalizing effects of capitalism; the KPRF, as we shall argue below, became a *sui generis* conservative party.

Elections and Political Evolution

The KPRF contested the December 1993 elections, took an active part in the work of the Fifth Duma (1994–95), emerged with a plurality of seats in the Sixth Duma (1996–99), and remained the second largest caucus in the Seventh Duma (2000–). The KPRF's leader, Gennadii Zyuganov, was the main challenger to Boris Yeltsin's reelection to a second presidential term in 1996, and was the only serious challenger to president Vladimir Putin's election in March 2000. In purely electoral terms the KPRF can be considered a highly successful party, yet in terms of access to power and state resources the party has been effectively marginalized. How can we explain this paradox?

Elections and Their Results

The KPRF, like all other political organizations in Russia, suffers from the effects of a system of "constrained electoralism" that underpins the "winner takes all" presidential system. The functions of the Duma, while important in legislative, budgetary, and representative terms, are limited when it comes to forming and dismissing governments and initiating policy. The KPRF was able to win itself a powerful presence in the Duma, but Russia's constitutional order is designed to minimize the impact that Parliament can have on the course of politics. This is partially a reaction to the extreme conflict between Parliament and the presidency between 1991–93, culminating in the violent confrontation of October 1993. The constitution of December 1993 permanently embeds some of the "state of emergency" legacies of the October events in the form of executive predominance.

While Zyuganov's plodding leadership is often condemned, he was able to ensure that the KPRF was not destroyed in the fires that consumed the White House (the seat of Parliament at the time). Although a temporary ban was placed on communist papers, it was soon lifted. Zyuganov then waged a bitter internal struggle to convince the KPRF to fight the new parliamentary elections of December 1993.[23] These elections were boycotted by some of the more irreconcilable leftist groups such as the Russian Communist Worker's Party (RCWP), headed by Viktor Tyul'kin, and its Moscow faction headed by the maverick "anarchist Stalinist" Viktor Anpilov, head of the far-left "Working Russia" movement. The KPRF's role in stabilizing the new political order was crucial and endowed the new system with some legitimacy.

The KPRF's acceptance of electoral politics paid handsome political and electoral dividends. Of the thirteen electoral associations standing in 1993, the KPRF was one of only eight whose party-list passed the 5 percent representation threshold needed to enter the Duma (see Table 12.1). Winning 12.4 percent of the proportional vote (32 seats) and another fifteen seats in single-member districts (SMDs), the KPRF, with a total of 47 (10.7 percent) of the 450 seats, emerged as the third largest in Parliament. In the December 1995 elections the KPRF did even better, winning 22.3 percent of the party-list ballot, representing some 15.5 million votes and holding 99 seats. The party was the only one able to nominate its candidates to the majority of SMDs, unlike most other parties, even penetrating rural and nonethnic Russian areas. It won 58 constituency seats to end up with a caucus numbering 157, firmly controlling 40 percent of deputies (Ishiyama 1996a). The strength of the ultraleft was also revealed; the RCWP had lifted its boycott of elections and came close to entering the Duma as a party caucus in an electoral alliance called Communists-Working Russia-For the Soviet Union headed by Tyul'kin, receiving 4.52 percent of the list vote. The group was committed to the destruction of liberal parliamentarianism in favor of the restoration of a unified hierarchy of soviets. The KPRF now faced a serious challenge from the left as well as from the right.

In the presidential elections of June-July 1996, the KPRF's candidate Zyuganov was the main challenger to the incumbent, Yeltsin. The election was bitterly polarized and the contest was effectively as much a choice between regimes as a choice of individuals.[24] The success of the KPRF in the December 1995 elections raised the stakes by making it clear that the communists were the main oppositional body in an effectively bipolar field. With the broad left opposition holding 47 percent of the seats in the Duma, their control of the presidency as well would have entailed a revolution in Russia's political system. In these circumstances, Yeltsin (with his popularity ratings in single figures) came under pressure to postpone or cancel the election, but in the event decided to face the challenge (Yeltsin 2000, pp. 15–24). Zyuganov stood as the candidate of the "popular-patriotic forces" and tried to build an oppositional coalition, which eventually took the form of a "popular-patriotic bloc."[25] All the financial, media, and organizational advantages of incumbency were used to the fullest by the Yeltsin campaign team, but the incoherence of the KPRF's economic program, fears that Russia's precarious stability would be disrupted, and Zyuganov's inappropriate focus on nationalist themes meant that the KPRF was unable to break away from its electoral ghetto.[26] In trying to maximize turnout, the KPRF played to the Kremlin's needs; if turnout had fallen below 60 percent, Zyuganov may well have won. When it came to a straight choice between Zyuganov and Yeltsin, voters preferred the latter (see Table 12.1). Between the two rounds of voting Yeltsin gained an extra 13.5 million voters, rising from 26.7 million (35.3 percent) to 40.2 million (53.9 percent), but Zyuganov attracted only an extra 5.9 million votes to reach a ceiling of 30 million votes. Confronted by strong evidence of vote rigging in some regions, Zyuganov nevertheless faced down demands by radicals in the KPRF to launch a campaign of street protests, and thus for the second time (as in late 1993) helped to stabilize Yeltsin's regime.

Following the election the KPRF sought to make permanent the electoral alliance of leftist and nationalist groups in the form of the Popular-Patriotic Union of Russia (*Narodno-patrioticheskii soyuz Rossii*, NPSR), established at a special congress on 7 August 1996.[27] For Zyuganov, the establishment of the NPSR represented the core of a two-party system, with the "popular-patriotic bloc" now opposing the "party of power." Not all the opposition leaders were convinced by the argument. Baburin's Russian All-People's Union (ROS) had supported Zyuganov in his presidential bid, but now Baburin (a deputy speaker in the Duma and coleader of the Popular Power caucus) subjected Zyuganov's electoral campaign to searing criticism and questioned the long-term prospects of the communist movement in Russia. The KPRF, in his view, "proved unable to reform itself"; it had failed to take into account profound changes in society and had committed crude mistakes in the

Table 12.1

KPRF Election Results

Date and type of election	Percentage of vote	Number of voters (millions)	Single-member seats	Total seats in Duma
12 December 1993, Duma	12.4	7.0	16	47
December 1995, Duma	22.3	15.5	58	157
16 June 1996, first round presidential (Zyuganov)	32.0	24.2	—	—
3 July, second round presidential (Zyuganov)	40.3	30.1	—	—
December 1999, Duma	24.3	13.5	47	88
March 2000, presidential	29.2	21.9	—	—

Sources: Byulleten' Tsentral'noi izbiratel'noi kommissii (TsIK) Rossiiskoi Federatsii, No. (12), 1994, p. 67; *Segodnya,* 27 December 1995, p. 2; *Vestnik TsIK,* No. 14 (34), 1996; *Vestnik TsIK,* No. 16 (36), 1996; *Nezavisimaya gazeta,* 30 December 1999; *Vestnik TsIK,* No. 13 (103), 2000, pp. 63–65; p. 1.

presidential campaign, which were compounded by its goal to remain the "hegemon" in any oppositional coalition. Whatever its failings, the Yeltsin government was more than a "temporary occupational regime." It had conclusively put an end to the Soviet period of Russian history; politics had become parliamentarianized, and there was no longer a direct link between poverty and revolutionism. The great mass of the population had adapted to the new circumstances, whereas the KPRF had not.[28] Baburin later insisted that an opposition headed by the communists stood no chance for success. Scathing about Zyuganov personally, he warned that it would have been disastrous for the KPRF leader to have won the presidential elections.[29]

The NPSR limped on, with a second congress held on 21 November 1998, but in the public mind no clear distinction was drawn between it and the KPRF. There were endless debates over its proper role; whether it should be part of an antigovernment front or a broad coalition of left forces.[30] There were plans to establish its own media presence,[31] but little was done to challenge the KPRF's monopoly on the left. At the same time, attempts to improve links with the trade unions, above all with the ultra-large FNPR (the Federation of Independent Trade Unions of Russia), met with little success, with the latter fearing once again the party's deathly embrace. The FNPR sought alliances with centrist bodies rather than with the KPRF to avert renewed politicization and to avoid displaying undue disloyalty to the regime, which would no doubt provoke the nationalization of its extensive property interests.

In the early 1990s regional governors had been appointed by the president, but from 1996 they were elected. This opened up a new arena for the

KPRF to contest, and by April 1997 Zyuganov claimed thirty governorships, yet party labels often meant less than the personal characteristics of the contestants. Yeltsin's highly personalized style of politics was reproduced at the regional level. Communist candidates, many of whom stood at first under the NPSR umbrella, sought to present themselves as forward-looking professionals and competent managers. On the whole, as might be expected, opposition candidates did better in poorer regions, but this itself only reinforced their dependency on subsidies from federal authorities. The economic crisis in regions where the communists were strongest had a radicalizing effect upon the membership of the party when in opposition; but once in power financial dependency upon the center forced accommodation to the presidential regime. This was markedly true in the "red belt" regions of Belgorod, Lipetsk, Orël, Penza, Smolensk, Voronezh, and others, where formerly oppositional governors reconciled themselves to working with a presidential administration that they had strongly castigated when seeking office.

The KPRF fought the December 1999 Duma election separately and not under the umbrella of the NPSR, and allowed its own radicals (like Albert Makashov and Viktor Il'yukhin) to run on their own. The "For Victory" electoral bloc, established in July 1999, excluded former allies, like the Agrarian Party, to ensure a more disciplined and coherent Duma caucus. The KPRF won 24.29 percent of the party-list vote, giving it 67 seats, and 47 SMD seats. In the Duma a KPRF caucus with 92 members was formed,[32] together with an allied "Agro-Industrial" caucus of 42 members. The KPRF's "go-it-alone" strategy, together with the loss of its former allied Agrarian and Popular Power groups, reduced the left's share of the Duma from 211 (47 percent) to 127 (28 percent).

The 26 March 2000 presidential election was held in a very different context from that of 1996. Yeltsin had resigned on 31 December 1999, allowing Putin to become acting president as well as remaining premier. If the 1996 elections were marked by polarization, Putin's style in 2000 was inclusive to the point of indeterminacy. As incumbent, Putin held himself above the fray, and his espousal of a vague liberal-patriotism brought him support from both the right and the left. In stark contrast to 1996, the anticommunist theme had disappeared, and the media indeed was relatively soft on the KPRF. Although Putin's main rival was Zyuganov, it was clear that some of the communist vote was drifting to Putin.[33] Indeed, many commentators noted, Putin could well have run as the KPRF's candidate. The communists criticized the regime but were careful not to criticize Putin personally. Even the candidate Aman Tuleev, governor of the Kemerovo region, who had stood down in the 1996 election in favor of Zyuganov, stated (in a critique similar to that voiced by Baburin earlier) that in these elections he would throw his support to Putin in the second round as a man of "higher qualities" than Zyuganov, particularly in the areas of "professionalism, statehood, power, and personality."[34]

Improving upon his party's performance in the December 1999 Duma elections, Zyuganov's strong showing in the presidential election (see Table 12.1) meant that he was able to fight off all challengers for the leadership of the left. However, his vote did not match the 32 percent he had received in the first round of the 1996 elections, let alone the 40 percent he won in the runoff, and thus suggested a long-term decline in the communist vote that condemned him forever to second place. In particular, he lost ground in traditional communist strongholds. In the second round of 1996 Zyuganov came first in 32 of Russia's 89 regions, whereas in 2000 Putin came first in 84 regions. In Kemerovo, Tuleev won handsomely, leaving Zyuganov a victor in only four regions (the republics of Adygeia, Chechnya, Altai, and Bryansk region). Great holes had appeared in the communist "red belt," confirming an erosion of positions that had already been evident in the 1999 Duma election.

Of the three functions that can be ascribed to elections: popular representation, government formation, and political socialization, the first and third affected the KPRF most deeply. The party clearly represented an important constituency, but the inability to break beyond a clear ceiling of support limited its ability to engage in government formation, even though its ministers did serve in the governments of Viktor Chernomyrdin and Evgenii Primakov. As for political socialization, the party remained both in the system and opposed to elements of that system, an uncomfortable partial adaptation that vitiated its role in politics. The KPRF has been characterized as "an urban-based program party," adaptive to changing political circumstances, while appealing to a specific constituency. It had the flexibility to modify its program to respond to electoral demands, although the inherent limits to its adaptability might in the long run count against its viability (Ishiyama 1996b). The party did indeed modify its program to broaden its appeal in elections. The party's economic program of 1999 and 2000, for example, was written by the well-known economist Sergei Glaz'ev, and in certain respects it was more "market friendly" than the proposals of some mainstream nationalists (such as Dmitrii Rogozin's Congress of Russian Communities, KRO). This alone, however, was not enough to dilute the KPRF's heavily ideological approach to policy; indeed, constraints on adaptability characterize "ideological" parties like the KPRF.

The Communist Voter and Membership Profile

Who votes for the KPRF? Communists lack a political base among those under 30, and is weak among those between 30 and 40. Despite Zyuganov's denials that the KPRF relied overwhelmingly on the support of the aged part of the population,[35] surveys suggested that this was indeed the case. A poll published in November 1995 found that the KPRF was the most popular party for those over 55 years, but did not rank in the top five for those aged

18 to 24;[36] similar results were found later, although the KPRF gained greater support among those in their forties.[37] The proportion of the Russian population who were pensioners rose from 29.1 percent in 1993 to 38 percent by 2001, representing at that time a constituency of 37 million people. There was evidence to support Zyuganov's assertion that the KPRF was able to broaden its support, in particular among academics, workers in the military-industrial complex, and younger people. The KPRF was able to reproduce its electorate and broaden its appeal, which in geographical terms meant that its weakened position in the "red belt" was compensated by growing support in the Urals, Siberia, and the Far East. Zyuganov argued that the KPRF had overcome its old sectarian approach (which was an attempt to reflect "narrow class interests") and now sought to express the aspirations of the overwhelming majority of the Russian people (Zyuganov 1994, p. 4). These aspirations, however, were only partially reflected in programmatic and organizational changes.

Modern elections everywhere are becoming more capital-rather than labor-intensive. In Russia only the KPRF still relied on traditional methods of agitation, including the widespread use of leaflets, posters, stickers, and doorstep politicking, accompanied by mass meetings. Other electoral associations rely on the media, above all its electronic forms, to put across their message. In the 1990s the media was highly partisan in elections, and thus the party was forced to rely on the activism of its membership. This was particularly important since turnout was a crucial factor determining electoral performance. A feature of the 1995 election, for example, was that the higher the turnout in constituencies, the better the result for the left opposition,[38] a factor that did not operate in the 1996 presidential or gubernatorial elections. As Zyuganov noted after the 1995 elections, for every extra percentage of turnout, the KPRF gained 0.75 percent extra votes;[39] but a different dynamic operated in presidential elections and thus the KPRF's efforts to get the vote out played into Yeltsin's hands.

As for why people voted for the KPRF, it was not simply a matter of the protest vote. The KPRF retained a strong core of committed supporters, joined by a broader group of people willing to vote communist, but the number of these people was limited. As Miller et al. demonstrate, views of the present rather than deep-seated political cultural values determined how people voted. They found that some 20 percent of former members had never believed in communist ideals, another 40 percent of members now repudiated their former beliefs, and in general the values of former members differed little from non-members: "economic complaints were more strongly related to current voting intentions than to past membership" (Miller, White, and Heywood 1998, p. 316). Although there were some protest votes, the KPRF's electorate was a highly ideological one; it had a deep but relatively constricted constituency. Every election demonstrated the limits to the reach of KPRF support.[40]

The deindustrialization of the country undermines the social base for socialist parties in general, with industrial workers now comprising only 22.2
percent (14.3 million) of the total workforce of 64.5 million (*Rossiya v tsifrakh*
2000, pp. 78–79). Zyuganov's electoral base came from rural voters (a rather
paradoxical result given the original communist claim to represent the industrial proletariat), pensioners, long-time communists, and those hit hardest by
marketization, all constituencies that were likely to shrink in the future. The
KPRF appeared to enjoy little room for either organizational or ideological
maneuver. Attempts to broaden the KPRF's constituency either to the left or
right threatened defections to the other side—to rejectionists on the left and
to independent social liberal parties like Yabloko (Apple) to the right. With
the establishment of Unity even the center ground of statist-patriotism was
torn from beneath the KPRF, making its performance in the 1999 and 2000
elections even more impressive. Demographic changes, popular acceptance
of the irreversibility of capitalism, the emergence of elites and groups rooted
in the socioeconomic changes of ownership and incomes, the growing im-
probability of restoring the Soviet Union to anything like its previous form,
the rectification of some of the excesses of the "primitive accumulation of
capital" phase, all challenged the KPRF to rethink its program. The KPRF,
however, is caught in a classic constitutional bind. Like so many Western
European communist parties of the past, the more the party moves to the
center to gain electoral advantage, the more it loses its distinctive constituency; and the more it remains irreconcilably opposed to capitalist democracy, the more enduring its electoral ghetto.

Electoralism and Power

In a presidential system it is difficult to translate electoral support into power,
and more specifically, to translate parliamentary seats into ministerial port-
folios. The KPRF's electoral success in 1995, however, did allow it to take
over the speakership of the Duma and the chairmanship of ten key committees. Gennadii Seleznev, a deputy speaker in the Fifth Duma and from January 1995 a secretary of the KPRF's Central Committee, was elected chairman
of the Sixth Duma. He remained in the KPRF despite calls for him to suspend his membership, and only resigned as a Central Committee secretary
on 20 May 1996. From the moderate wing of the KPRF, Seleznev supported
Zyuganov's line on the need for "constructive" opposition, noting that Russia could learn from the Chinese model of economic reform. He further argued that the Swedish model of socialism was applicable to Russia.[41]
Following the 1999 Duma elections the KPRF kept the speakership and took
far more than its proper share of committee chairmanships (nine, plus two
for its agroindustrial allies) as a result of a deal struck with the new "party of
power," Unity, a deal that unraveled in 2002.

The KPRF proclaimed itself an oppositional party, yet its role in the legislative process rendered it an accomplice of the regime. The party itself gained important institutional benefits by participating in Duma life, which somewhat tamed its oppositionism. The KPRF's organization became dependent on the parliamentary apparatus, with much party work conducted out of the Duma building. The law allows a deputy to employ between one and five assistants; the KPRF established that each communist deputy would have five assistants, one in Moscow and the other four in the regions. The latter are usually full-time party officials, acting as raikom, gorkom, obkom, or reskom secretaries. With their salaries paid from the state budget, the assistants to the communist deputies effectively became the organizational core of the party.[42] Assistants, moreover, have the right to free public transport, offices in the parliament building, and access to working documents and to other state institutions.

Although in formal organizational terms the KPRF was reminiscent of the old CPSU, the leadership's relationship with the rest of the party had changed dramatically. This was most evident in relations with elected governors. Even when nominated by the KPRF, regional leaders were far from obedient clients of the Presidium in Moscow, and at the same time refused to subordinate themselves to the KPRF's national or regional organizations. The KPRF's tendency to favor local candidates in elections, rather than sending functionaries from Moscow, only reinforced the problem of central control. Although the KPRF enjoyed the advantages of a national organization, it was unable to dominate the political life of peripheral, or even red belt, regions. The KPRF is not a source of patronage or advancement even where its governors belong to it. For example, the communist governor of Voronezh, Ivan Shabanov, insisted that "No party will have any privileges in the administration." He admitted that local KPRF officials had expected to fill all the key posts in the regional administration, and were disappointed when Shabanov refused to do this.[43] Similarly, governor Nikolai Maksyuta of Volgograd *oblast'* struggled to free himself from the demands of the regional KPRF organization after his election in December 1996, thus finding himself at odds with the communist-dominated local legislature.[44] In Stavropol the communist Aleksandr Chernogorov was challenged by the head of the regional KPRF organization in the gubernatorial elections of 17 December 2000. Once elected, Chernogorov swiftly moved to oust his rival and bring the KPRF's regional organization under his control.[45] By 2001 only three regions were governed by openly communist governors: Ivanovo (Tikhonov), Kamchatka (Mashkovtsev), and Kursk (Mikhailov). At that time the KPRF and the NPSR had 1,240 deputies in regional assemblies, comprising 33.2 percent of the total (*VII S"ezd*, 2001).

In the national republics the gulf between power and party was even more marked. The leaderships of Tatarstan and Bashkortostan (formerly communist bosses in their respective regions) refused to give up their hard-won sovereignty to the federal authorities, let alone to a resurgent communist ·party. The communist organization in the Republic of Tatarstan was reregistered in November 1993 under the name of the Communist Party of Tatarstan. Like the national party, the communists in Tatarstan called for the voluntary restoration of the USSR in which Tatarstan would enter "on an equal footing with other republics" (i.e. as a union republic). The republican party loyally supported President Mintimir Shaimiev in his struggle with Moscow up to the signing of the power-sharing treaty (*dogovor*) in February 1994, while Shaimiev in return had refused to launch any anticommunist campaign in the republic after 1991 (Zverev 1998, pp. 136–137). In early 1997 Tatarstan's communists rejoined the KPRF.[46]

In the regions and in the Duma the ability of the KPRF to exert power was severely constrained. In the Duma, paradoxically, the larger the KPRF contingent, the more the KPRF feared provoking an early dissolution (and preterm parliamentary elections) by passing no-confidence motions in the government. A repetition of the success of earlier elections was by no means assured, as the presidential administration well knew, and thus the KPRF *de facto* became part of the establishment. Dominance of the Duma in practice endowed the communist with neither power nor authority.[47]

Baburin insisted that the so-called "irreconcilable" parliamentary opposition was more concerned about preserving the Duma than with saving Russia.[48] This was reinforced by the strong personal ties between some prime ministers and the KPRF leadership. Chernomyrdin, for example, was a member of the same nomenklatura elite as the majority of KPRF leaders, and they easily found a common language, as they did with Primakov. The NPSR, indeed, endorsed the decision of one of their five cochairmen, Aman Tuleev, to join the government in August 1996 as minister for CIS affairs, the only oppositionist sponsored by the KPRF to gain a cabinet post at this time. On 23 July 1998, on the eve of the August financial crisis, KPRF deputy Yurii Maslyukov, the former head of Gosplan, joined Sergei Kirienko's government, despite the KPRF's Presidium's unanimous vote against him doing so the previous day. Disciplinary action was preempted by the crash, and the KPRF then approved him joining Primakov's government in September 1998 as one of two first deputy prime ministers with broad responsibilities for trade and industry. The no-confidence vote called by the communists against the government of Prime Minister Mikhail Kasyanov on 14 March 2001, as on other occasions in the past, was largely a bluff since it was clear that the required 226 votes would not be mustered.[49] Also as on other occasions, some presidential advisors (in this case Gleb Pavlovskii) suggested that the bluff should be called. In the event of preterm elections, Pavlovskii insisted, "The new Duma would, without a doubt, be a rightist Duma, a Duma that would contain, once and for all, no more than an isolated communist minority.

That would be the beginning of the end for the Russian Communist Party as a party."[50] This was not exactly the case, since polls revealed the KPRF's support to be running at around 35 percent.[51] Nevertheless, the incident once again demonstrated that, while exerting a powerful influence over parliamentary politics, the KPRF was powerless against a determined presidential regime.

Dynamics of Party Transition

The KPRF under Zyuganov recognized the social changes that had transformed the country and which shaped the party itself, yet sociological determinism does not explain the evolution of the KPRF.[52] The origins of the party, the decisions of its leaders, the balance of political power within the party, and relations with the regime were to prove decisive. If in broad terms there are only two main exit paths out of communism, social democracy or nationalism, for a number of reasons the latter predominated over the former, yet the position in practice is rather more complex. We have already noted three main ideological tendencies within the KPRF, but even these categories have to be modified in the light of changes in strategy and organizational resources. While ideological differences remain important, the evolution of the KPRF was determined more by the varying strategic assets available to elite groups in the party and by the changing configuration of Russian politics. Similarly, while initial starting point is important (in Russia, to use Kitschelt's concept, this was a patrimonial system based on strong hierarchy and low levels of interelite contestation with limited rational-bureaucratic professionalism), path dependency is of only limited help in understanding patterns of institutional and ideological development (Kitschelt 1995a, p. 453).[53]

Just as the live experience of the transition shaped political values so, too, the political exigencies of the period structured political evolution. This was an evolution that proved to be mired in stasis, provoking what some commentators suggested was a full-scale crisis in the KPRF by the turn of the millenium. The view that the KPRF was in crisis was shared by opponents like Oleg Morozov, the leader of the "Russian Regions" caucus,[54] to former allies like Baburin and Aleksei Podberezkin, who argued that "the rotting body of the KPRF fills the whole left flank," preventing any other force developing. The only question, according to them, was whether the KPRF would take five or twenty-five years to die.[55] The crisis was of the type that had afflicted West European parties earlier, characterized in March's words as "an all-encompassing crisis of electoral performance, of ideology, strategy and organization" (March 2000, p. 15). If anything it was even deeper, since many leaders of the Russian party had once enjoyed power and felt that they represented not only an ideological social movement but also the political interests of a great power. The gulf between aspirations and realities, as with Russia's policies in general, was much greater. Equally, the KPRF's crisis reflected the difficulties facing Russian democracy in general, but in that context and from the perspective of party survival, the KPRF was no more crisis-ridden (and in certain respects less so) than most other political institutions.

Political Constraints

The KPRF had taken the door labeled "national-patriotism" out of communism, but what if this path led nowhere? Putin's rise represented in part an acceptance of the patriotic-statist agenda, but in a liberal rather than nationalistic or leftist guise, thus stealing many of the KPRF's best tunes. At the same time, the fall of Slobodan Milošević's regime in Serbia (based as it was on communists-turned-nationalists), in October 2000 revealed the limits of nationalized communism. The overwhelming victory of the Communist Party of Moldova in the parliamentary elections of 25 February 2001 (winning 71 out of 101 seats) was a response to the effective meltdown of the party and political system in the republic, and was based on an internationalist (reintegrationist) rather than nationalist ideology. So why did the social democratic option not beckon more strongly, if only to reposition the party to broaden its electorate? One factor, stressed by the path dependency school, was the monolithic (bureaucratic patrimonial) nature of the old regime and the lack of an autonomous "Eurocommunist" tradition within the CPSU; indeed, after 1968 the CPSU dedicated itself to the eradication of humanistic elements. This does not explain how Gorbachev could place himself at the head of a powerful current seeking to liberalize the regime, applying many of the concepts of the Prague Spring. Despite Zyuganov's assertions, perestroika was more than a conspiracy of renegades within the party in league with foreign powers. Part of the problem, however, was that by the time Gorbachev came openly to espouse social democracy in 1990–91, the regime was crumbling and the country disintegrating, and therefore the concept became associated with failure and was discredited.

Another factor in the early period was the fear of losing the initiative to the orthodox left. This inhibited the KPRF from straying too far toward the social democratic right, while the attempt to maintain the alliance with nationalists (many of whom were anticommunist) restrained the party from moving too far to the orthodox left. The party's marginalized mass base, largely middle-aged and older, constrained the party's room for maneuver yet at the same time forced the leadership to try to insulate itself from its own membership. While the membership sought the expropriation of the "new Russians," the reconstitution of the USSR, and vengeance against the "democrats," the KPRF as a parliamentary party was operating according to another political logic whereby elite pacts, regional governorships, Duma votes, committee chairmanships, and public image were decisive.

Reports on the internal alignment of forces within the KPRF are unreliable and in a sense irrelevant. Tensions are often less ideological (between orthodox communism, right-wing national revisionism and putative social democrats), than between functional interests (the communist elite comfortably ensconced in the Duma, the party apparatus—headed by Kuptsov—regional leaders, and the rank-and-file pressures)[56] and all were equally concerned with party survival. Although the KPRF was far from monolithic, politics at its center could be brutal. The legacy of democratic centralism and the ban on factions lived on. Faced by a loss of identity and direction in the aftermath of the 1999–2000 electoral cycle, the KPRF responded by tightening up internal discipline, dissolving the radical "Leninist-Stalinist Platform," strengthening the grip of Kuptsov's party apparatus, and purging the CC of critics. Although the party's vote in 1999 increased by two percent over that of 1995, the fact that the newly formed Unity party gained only a percentage point less, followed by the disappointing result in the presidential elections, led to a new round of internecine strife. The key issues were ideological, with Marxist-Leninist revivalists (such as Alexander Kuvaev, the head of the Moscow party organization) calling for more emphasis on socialism and less on state patriotism, and organizational, with calls for a separation of the posts of party chairman, Duma caucus leader, head of the NSPR, and head of the Union of Communist Parties (SKP-KPSS), a position that Zyuganov had gained as a result of the ousting of the former hard-line leader, Oleg Sheinin. The call for the separation of posts was directed against Zyuganov's hold over all four postitions.

Following Zyuganov's second presidential defeat in March 2000, pressure for change grew. One manifestation of this was the establishment in May 2000 of the "Rossiya" group within the party by Speaker Gennadi Seleznev. This was less an opening toward social democracy than a recognition of the need for pluralism within the party and an attempt to broaden the party's appeal by creating a center-left force. Although Rossiya's leaders denied any attempt to split the KPRF, its creation clearly represented a challenge to Zyuganov's leadership and his grand geopolitical theories on Russia's destiny. At its first conference on 13 January 2001 Seleznev claimed (incorrectly) that Rossiya had a membership of 600,000 and branches in all of Russia's regions.[57] The aim of the movement, according to Seleznev, was "renewed socialism," which he defined as building a "social state." The movement would back the government to the extent that it pursued this goal. Zyuganov was notable by his absence, clearly disapproving of a body that he feared could provoke a split in the party, while the party's main newspaper, *Pravda*, was closed to Rossiya.[58] Even those sympathetic to social democracy within the party, like representative Ivan Mel'nikov, disapproved of Seleznev's initiative for fear that it could provoke a split. Rossiya represented a direct challenge to the NPSR as a coalition of thirty organizations claiming the left-center spot; and in turn the NPSR was used to undermine Rossiya.[59] Rossiya itself was an unsustainable movement, with no organizational resources or electorate of its own, and was dogged by the impression that its creation was owed to little more than Seleznev's personal ambitions, probably supported by the Kremlin.

Despite much criticism of Zyuganov's style and policies, fear of splits and the legacy of Brezhnevite political passivity inhibited serious challenges to his leadership. There would be no fronde in the KPRF. As his biographers suggest, Zyuganov (and especially his associates) remained stamped by "a nomenklatura communist mentality, developed during the period of the existence of a mass CPSU, and a General Secretary type of leadership."[60] As noted, the separation of the posts of party leader and Duma caucus head were much discussed, including at the Seventh Congress, and represented an implicit attack upon Zyuganov. Once again, as the great survivor of Russian politics, Zyuganov was able to retain mastery of the party, its Duma caucus, the NPSR, and the SKP-KPSS.

There was indeed to be no smooth evolution to social democracy. Urban's suggestion that Putin's rise "may have created an opportunity for incipient social democrats within the KPRF to become the dominant force in the Communist Party, or to create a formation of their own," proved perhaps not unfounded but certainly premature (Urban 2000, p. 14). This was evident at the Seventh Congress in December 2000, when Zyuganov called on the KPRF to move into "irreconcilable opposition" to the regime, a stance clearly to the distaste of Rossiya. The congress once again revealed the obstacles to the social democratization of the KPRF. The moderate ideological secretary, Alexander Kravets, was removed from his post. To some observers it appeared that the KPRF was becoming a marginalized red opposition organ like the French Communist Party (PCF) earlier or was becoming mired in Italian-style *immobilismo*. Such a view, however, underestimates the genuine political constraints limiting the KPRF's room for maneuver, and under the circumstances Zyuganov's leadership and approach were probably the only way to ensure both the unity of the KPRF and its predominant position in Russia's party system.

Dual Adaptation and Organic Opposition

The KPRF moved away from "irreconcilable" hostility to the new order and adopted a stance of constructive opposition within the system. Even opposition under Putin became more muted, despite attempts by the party to flex its muscles and to assert its independence. Its position in the Duma by 2000 had undoubtedly weakened, with its 130 seats (including the Agrarians) far less prominent than its group in the previous convocation, although as the main opposition bloc in March 2001 the KPRF nominated a "shadow cabinet."

The dilemmas of being the main opposition party in a system that does not recognize any power-sharing processes were analyzed by Presidium-member Peshkov in his perceptive study of "opposition and power."[61] There were limits to the degree to which the KPRF could adapt itself to regime politics, even under Putin, as long as the regime remained basically liberal in orientation.

The KPRF adapted to postcommunist democratic conventions but at the same time a second type of adaptation strategy undermined the first; the adaptation to regime politics. The KPRF benefitted from the perilous semiconsolidated nature of Russian democracy, exploiting the political advantages and resources that it offered while fearful of destabilizing the situation. The political system inaugurated in December 1993 limited the opposition's opportunities to shape policies, let alone to modify the constitution; politics was conducted largely on the terrain chosen by the regime itself. The opposition became a symbiotic part of the regime despite itself. After 1996 it appeared that the KPRF had lost all hope of actually winning an election, and Zyuganov's candidacy in 2000 was largely a formality. The regime, it appeared, "needed an opposition that would never have any chance of coming to power";[62] while the KPRF needed a regime that spoke in statist and social terms while doing little to achieve the structural transformation of the economy.

The moderates in the KPRF, like Zyuganov and Kuptsov, March notes, "shared with elements of the regime a cautious, bureaucratic approach and lack of enthusiasm toward mass action and public politics typical of the nomenklatura," rendering it not much more than a "cosmetic opposition" whereby the regime (in 2000) used the KPRF as a "sparring partner" to achieve "electoral victory over a weak opposition" (March 2000, pp. 16–17). The deal cut between Unity and the KPRF following the 1999 Duma elections and Putin's later talk of the need to establish a stable two- or three-party system, with pivotal roles for the KPRF and Unity, all suggested the attempt to create a new hegemonic bloc. We describe this process as the emergence of an "organic opposition," by analogy with the distinction drawn by Gramsci between traditional and organic intellectuals; the former retain a critical independence from a ruling hegemonic bloc, while the latter serve the interests of that bloc. Because of dual adaptation and the emergence of an organic opposition, stability was not a reflection of the consolidation of Russian democracy but of the emergence of a regime appealing to democratic legitimacy while practicing strategies of elite co-optation and pragmatic functional rule. Organic adaptation exposed the KPRF to internal strains as the gulf between elite compromises and membership aspirations widened, quite apart from implicating the KPRF in the policies of the regime that it had little power to shape.

We stress, however, that the adaptation was dual, and the first (to electoral democracy) was as important as the second (to bureaucratic regime politics).

As the only genuine party in postcommunist Russia the KPRF considered itself (not without some justification) the source of a democratic renewal of the system as a whole. While practicing the art of a self-limiting opposition, the party sought to modify the constitution to enhance the accountability of the government to Parliament and to ensure that the regime was held accountable to the people, as in the attempt to impeach Yeltsin in May 1999. The potential of the first adaptation, however, was constrained by the compromises inherent in the second.

The party adapted to regime politics but did not wholeheartedly embrace the logic of liberal democracy. The traditional Leninist attempt of communists in power to depoliticize the political resurfaced in new forms. Baburin in particular was critical of this tendency, denouncing the KPRF's attempts to "grow into power" (*vrastanie vo vlast'*).[63] Viktor Aksyuchits (the former head of the Russian Christian Democratic Movement), too, noted that the communists were unable to transform themselves into a genuine left political force because their "redistributionist mentality and apparatchik experience led them once again to 'inscribe' (*vpisalas'*) themselves into the system of power."[64] This tendency was particularly apparent under the premierships of Chernomyrdin and Primakov, and visible in a different way under Putin's presidency. If ever there had been a "party of power" it was the old CPSU, and now the tendency to replicate this pattern by the regime found its counterpart in the KPRF, constituting itself as a party of power in opposition while organically linked with the regime itself (although certainly not with the presidency under Yeltsin).[65] The system of "elite corporatism" in effect rendered the opposition (both democratic and communist) part of the power system, helping consolidate the ruling group (Shvetsova 1996, p. 83). In conditions where the actual party of power (NDR, followed by Unity) and its oppositional counterpart (the KPRF) were both equally estranged from real power, the KPRF's role became ever more ambivalent.

The party adapted to the formal establishment of democratic political institutions while vitiating its substantive content. If in the Soviet period the Bolshevik party "suffocated" civil society, the KPRF "colonized" modern political society. The KPRF's activities focused on the regime itself while neglecting the development of hegemonic strategies toward civil associations. The party's strained relationship with the trade unions has been noted, while the KPRF's relations with the revived 25,000–strong Komsomol broke down, and on 20 February 1999 a new communist sponsored Union of Communist Youth (SKM) was created, uniting several small organizations.[66] The communists tended to support the government on key votes, giving rise to strains with the more "irreconcilable" part of the opposition. The dilemmas facing the opposition in a system designed to stifle the scope of autonomous political activity were indeed cruel. The KPRF was both a within-system opposition, willing to share governmental responsibility within the framework of the existing constitution, while condemning the system and its policies. As one of Zyuganov's biographers put it, "he was a leader in the name of the state and simultaneously a leader opposed to the existing political system."[67]

This syncretic "communism of transition" was oriented toward the state and had few authentic roots in the transformative processes of society, yet it gave voice to the suffering of millions by grounding its program in an idiom that responded to the traditions and needs of a large part of a disoriented society. To that extent the communist presence played an important part in Russia's political consolidation, preempting the rise of more overtly right-wing authoritarian alternatives. There is much force to the argument that the KPRF, as the only genuinely autonomous serious political actor, was the guarantor of Russia's democratic evolution, preventing the emergence of a personalized oligarchical regime.[68] As part of the existing system, the KPRF ended up defending a constitution of which it disapproved; the KPRF was locked in a dynamic where both power and opposition were degraded. Consolidation in this context was only tenuously democratic and was reminiscent of the "blocked" politics of the First Italian Republic in which, as Urban and Solovei note, "a normal democratic alternation in power of opposing political coalitions was precluded by virtue of the opposition's 'communist' identity" (Urban and Solovei 1997, p. 191). The return of communists to influence *over* but not effectively *within* the new Russian political system revealed not the failure of the democratic transition in Russia but its partial and incomplete nature.

Conclusions

The KPRF's decision to contest the December 1993 elections set the Russian communist party on the path of parliamentary development. The KPRF gained crucial momentum in distinguishing it from other communist parties, allowing it to achieve the domination of the left, thwarting the emergence of a more irreconcilable opposition, and preventing the radicalization of popular protest. The party adapted to the conventions of parliamentary politics and went on in the 1995 election to gain a plurality of seats in the Duma. By the time of the 1999 election the KPRF's predominant position was challenged by what was for the first time an effective "party of power," Unity. The deal struck in the first days of the Seventh Duma between the two parties for Duma committee chairmanships revealed the extent to which the KPRF had become part of an organic opposition, tied to the ruling regime by innumerable ties. The KPRF had adapted to the new political regime in a dual way: accompanying the adaptation to parliamentary politics was an adaptation to the pseudopolitics practiced by the regime. The weakness of political consolidation *within* the Communist Party inhibited its development as an anchor of democratic consolidation in the system as a whole. The KPRF helped consolidate not only Russian constrained electoralism but also those elements of regime politics that inhibited the further development of democracy.

The KPRF today is faced by problems of organizational closure and partial adaptation. The self-limiting nature of the KPRF's opposition was apparent both in Parliament and in society at large. The party adopted a vague and confusing oppositional stance, fearing that too active opposition would provoke confrontation with the authorities and reduce opportunities to benefit from the current regime. Smarting from accusations by the extra-parliamentary left that it had succumbed to "parliamentary cretinism," and fearing that as the dominant party in Parliament it would be held responsible for failing to resolve the country's problems, the KPRF from time to time has radicalized its oppositional stance.[69] Unelectable yet the main electoral alternative, an opposition but an organic one, adapted to both democratic and regime politics, the KPRF remains beset by contradictions. The shape of Russian democratic evolution, however, depends on the manner in which these contradictions in both intraparty development and its relations with the political system as a whole are resolved.

Notes

1. This chapter draws on some of the material of Sakwa (1998). For a useful recent analysis of the dilemmas facing the KPRF, see March (2001). For a useful but flawed general analysis of post-communist communism see Bukowski and Racz (1999).

2. For a discussion of the views of party members in its final days, see White and McAllister (1996).

3. Rossification rather than Russification because of the largely supranational (although Russian-centered) nature of its policies. For a stimulating discussion of the issue, see Sergei Vasil'tsov, "Kommunisty i Russkii vopros," *Sovetskaya Rossiya*, 27 March 1997, pp. 3–4. For the possibility of a socialist political renewal of the party, see White (1994).

4. The point is made in the comparative literature on party development. Angelo Panebianco (1988): p. 50, for example, argues that "the characteristics of a party's origins are in fact capable of exerting a weight on its organizational development even decades later."

5. *Sovetskaya Rossiya*, 23 July 1991, p. 1; reproduced in Zyuganov (2000).

6. Decree of 20 July 1991, *Izvestiya*, 22 July 1991, and for Gorbachev's condemnation, see *Pravda*, 26 July 1991.

7. At the 23 August 1991 session of the Russian Supreme Soviet, with Gorbachev looking on, Yeltsin suspended the CPSU in Russia (confirmed on 29 August by the USSR Supreme Soviet for the country as a whole); a decree of 25 August declared that all the CPSU's property belonged to the state; and on 6 November Yeltsin banned the party in Russia. The three decrees are reproduced in Rudinskii (1998).

8. The debates and materials submitted to the Constitutional Court are presented and analyzed in the fascinating work by Rudinskii (1998). A day-by-day account of the issues raised and debates has been produced by Kantanyan (1999).

9. The judgement is reproduced in full by Rudinskii (1999): pp. 475–492 and 402–431.

10. The figure given by Zyuganov, *Pravda Rossii*, 15 April 1997.

11. According to Zyuganov in late 1994, only some 20,000 of the party's half million membership were new, "Lyubaya diktatura besperspektivnaya: boyarskaya, proletarskaya, presidentskaya," *Oppozitsiya*, No. 11 (1994). In Moscow *oblast'*, for example, 1,500 were former members and 90 new.

12. As Zyuganov noted, Stalin on 28 March 1945 had stressed the similarities between Soviet and Slavophile policies: "We are new Slavophile-Bolsheviks," in Stalin's words, Zyuganov (2000): p. 251.

13. Vladimir Razuvaev, *Nezavisimaya gazeta*, 27 November 1996: pp. 1, 2.

14. The two main newspapers are *Pravda* and *Pravda Rossii*.

15. The Second Plenum of the Central Committee on 24 March 1995 established thirteen commissions covering socioeconomic questions: work with youth, international links, and so on. V. Zorkal'tsev was head of the commission responsible for links with social organizations, N. Bindyukov for ideological work, G. Seleznev for informational policy, and I. Mel'nikov for international links. *Pravda Rossii*, No. 2 (16), 30 March 1995, p. 1.

16. Yegor Ligachev, Gorbachev's right-hand man before perestroika became radicalized, is perhaps the best representative of this tendency. See (Ligachev, 1996).

17. Zyuganov's views are developed at considerable and repetitive length in his numerous books. See Zyuganov (1993; 1994, 1995, 1996a, 1997).

18. The theme of the "two parties" and the two traditions in the CPSU run as an almost obsessive theme in Zyuganov's writings. It is mentioned repeatedly, for example, in his collection of articles and speeches. See Zyuganov (2000): pp. 44, 55–56, 94–96, 238 and 289.

19. Bruce Clark, "Nationalist Ideas Move From the Margins," *The World Today*, May 1996, p. 120.

20. "Za nashu sovetskuyu rodinu! Predvybornaya platforma KPRF," adopted by the Third All-Russian KPRF Conference on 26 August 1995 (Moscow, 1995); *Pravda Rossii*, no. 16 (7 September 1995): p. 2.

21. Zyuganov's own "nationalistic" thinking at this time, moving ever further from Marxist orthodoxy, can be found in *Sovetskaya Rossiya*, 24 October 1995: pp. 1–2.

22. *Sovetskaya Rossiya*, 18 November 1995.

23. In its statement of 26 October 1993, a special KPRF conference noted the strength of those calling for "a boycott of this electoral farce," but insisted that the political opportunities of participation outweighed the negative aspects. See Zyuganov (2001): pp. 36–39.

24. Chernomyrdin voiced a common frustration about the character of the election campaign as "a choice between systems" rather than simply "the choice of a president," *OMRI Press Survey*, no. 14, 5 July 1996. For the argument that these elections were the last polarized ones, see McFaul (1997).

25. The Fourth KPRF Conference on 15 February 1996 anointed Zyuganov the candidate of the left. See Belin (1996): pp. 12–15; *Nezavisimaya gazeta*, 5 April 1996, p. 1.

26. For an analysis of these contradictions, see Sergei Markov, "Ekonomicheskaya programma Zyuganova do sikh por ne obnarodovana," *Nezavisimaya gazeta*, 22 May 1996, pp. 1, 2; and his "Kuda mogut privesti blagie namereniya kommunistov," *Kapital*, 29 May–4 June 1996, pp. 15–18.

27. For details of the conference and the programmatic statements adopted, see http://www.KPRF.ru/blok

28. Sergei Baburin, "Oppozitsiyu ne dolzhny vozglavlyat' kommunisty," *Nezavisimaya gazeta*, 14 August 1996, p. 5.

29. *Moskovskaya pravda*, 15 January 1997.

30. The issue is debated, for example, by Andrei Fedorov in, "KPRF v postel'tsinskuyu epokhu," *Nezavisimaya gazeta*, 30 November 2000, p. 8.

31. Anna Zakatnova, "Kommunistam nuzhna legal'naya tribuna: NPSR mozhet sozdat' mediakholding," *Nezavisimaya gazeta*, 11 October 2000, p. 3.

32. Listed at the KPRF's website: http://www.KPRF.ru/workfr/KPRFgd.htm

33. Only 66 percent of the electorate that had voted for the KPRF in December 1999 intended to cast their votes for Zyuganov in March, while 22 percent planned to vote for Putin. From a VTsIOM poll released on 28 February 2000, in Tacis, The European Union's Project for Capacity Development in Election Monitoring, *Weekly Report*, 8 March 2000.

34. ORT, *Vremya*, 5 March 2000.

35. Even here Zyuganov was inconsistent, conceding after the 1995 elections that the typical communist voter remained older, less-educated, and more provincial than average, usually employed in a state enterprise, *Sovetskaya Rossiya*, 16 January 1996.

36. *Moskovskie novosti*, no. 77 (5–12 November 1995), p. 6.

37. For example, Myagkov (2000) cites evidence that about half of all pensioners supported the KPRF.

38. Turnout exceeded 70 percent in 35 of the 225 single-member constituencies, and leftists won 27; in 23 turnout was between 65–70 percent and leftists won two-thirds; but leftists did not win a single seat where turnout fell below 55 percent. Viktor Trushkov, see *Pravda Rossii*, 14 March 1996, pp. 1, 3.

39. The KPRF overall gained 22.3 percent of the 64.4 percent turnout. In regions where turnout was 50–55 percent, the KPRF won 12 percent of the vote, but where turnout was 75–80 percent, the KPRF won 32 percent, Zyuganov (2001, p. 63).

40. A point made, for example, by Kagarlitsky (1996, p. 17).

41. *Segodnya*, 18 January 1996, p. 1.

42. See Ol'ga Gerasimenko, "Vertikal' kompartii-ot TsK do raikoma-oplachena iz karmana nalogoplatel'shchika," *Komsomol'skaya pravda*, 26 March 1996.

43. *Voronezhskie vesti*, 3 March 2000, in EastWest Institute, *Russian Regional Report*, vol. 5, no. 9, 9 March 2000.

44. TACIS, The European Union's project for Capacity Development in Election Monitoring, *Briefing Document* no. 7, 14 March 2000.

45. EastWest Institute, *Russian Regional Report*, vol. 6, no. 4, 31 January 2001.

46. This provoked a split, with a small group trying to retain its independence from Moscow. Interview with President Mintimer Shaimiev's political adviser Rafail Khakimov, Kazan, 8 April 1997.

47. Michael McFaul characterized their performance as "ineffective and marginal," *New York Times*, 22 July 1997.

48. Sergei Baburin, *Nezavisimaya gazeta*, 28 May 1997.

49. This did not prevent Zyuganov from employing his most purple rhetoric for the occasion, "Otvergaem 'pravitel'stvo katastrofy'!," *Zavtra*, no. 11 (380), March 2001, p. 1; his more sober speech on the day of the vote is in *Pravda*, 15 March 2001, p. 1.

50. strana.ru, 21 February 2001.

51. For example, VTsIOM poll, reported in *Sovetskaya Rossiya*, 20 March 2001, p. 2.

52. The argument against sociological determinism in comparative party development and survival is made by Rose and Mackie (1988, pp. 546, 557).

53. John Ishiyama has correlated initial regime type with postcommunist party trajectories, arguing that parties emerging out of "patrimonial communism" have to traverse more stages than those coming out of systems based on greater national consensus (Ishiyama 1997a).

54. *Nezavisimaya gazeta*, 15 March 2001, p. 3.

55. Mikhail Vinogradov, "KPRF budet umirat' eshche let dvadtsat' pyat," *Izvestiya*, 14 March 2001, p. 4.

56. Sergei Chugrov, *Izvestiya*, 21 March 1996, p. 5.

57. *Johnson's Russia List*, No. 5025/2.

58. About which Seleznev complained at the Seventh Congress, Anna Zakatnova, "Sed'moi S"ezd KPRF: tot zhe lider, te zhe tseli," *Nezavisimaya gazeta*, 5 December 2000, p. 3.

59. See Anna Zakatnova, "Kommunisty opyat' vozrodili NPSR," *Nezavisimaya gazeta*, 26 September 2000, p. 3.

60. Lisitsyn et al. *Gennadii Zyuganov*, p. 231.

61. V. P. Peshkov, *Oppozitsiya i vlast': obshchestvennoe vospriyatie* (Moscow, ITRK, 2000).

62. Boris Kagarlitsky, "Communists Seek a Place under Putin," *Moscow Times*, 23 December 2000.

63. Sergei Baburin, "Naivnost' 1993 goda ne povtoritsya!," *Sovetskaya Rossiya*, 27 March 1997, p. 2.

64. Viktor Aksyuchits, "Poslednii shans dlya reform, kotorye eshche ne nachinalis," *Nezavisimaya gazeta*, 25 March 1997, p. 2.

65. Alexander Lebed, for example, argued that Zyuganov and Yeltsin were both descended from the "old communist *nomenklatura*" and were far more similar than their rhetoric suggested. See *Izvestiya*, 25 April 1996.

66. Anna Zakatnova, "Karmannyi komsomol zyuganova," *Nezavisimaya gazeta*, 31 October 2001, p. 3.

67. Sergei Kislitsyn, "Predislovie," in S. Kislitsyn et al. *Gennadi Zyuganov*, p. 6.

68. The argument made, for example, by Viktor Peshkov in a talk with the present author, 21 March 2001.

69. For example, the "Appeal to the Citizens of Russia," *Sovetskaya Rossiya*, 24 June 1997, calling for an all-Russia protest strike. Once again, in February 2001 the KPRF collected signatures to introduce a no-confidence motion on Mikhail Kasyanov's government.

Part III

Theoretical and Comparative Considerations

13

A Typology of Communist Successor Parties

An Overview

John T. Ishiyama

Although a considerable body of work has emerged on the evolution of party systems in the post-communist world, there has been surprisingly little systematic comparative work done on the organizational development of political parties, even for those parties that clearly "qualify" as parties—the communist successor parties. Why do certain organizational types of parties emerge as opposed to others?[1] More specifically, what explains the variety of organizational configurations exhibited by the communist successor parties?

To begin to address these questions, I will first develop a theoretical framework that identifies the factors that affect party organizational development. For the purposes of this chapter, a sample of seventeen communist successor parties were used to test these hypotheses. These parties include: the Socialist Party of Albania (PSSH), the Social Democratic Party of Bosnia-Hercegovina (SDPBiH), the Bulgarian Socialist Party (BSP), the Social Democratic Party of Croatia (SDPH), the Communist Party of Bohemia and Moravia (KSCM) in the Czech Republic, the Estonian Social Democratic Labor Party (ESDTP), the Hungarian Socialist Party (MSZP), the Latvian Socialist Party (LSP), the Lithuanian Democratic Labor Party (LDDP), the Social Democratic Union of Macedonia (SDSM), the Democratic Left Alliance (SLD, formerly the Social Democracy of the Republic of Poland party, SdRP), the Party of Social Democracy of Romania (PDSR), the Communist Party of the Russian Federation (KPRF), the Party of the Democratic Left in Slovakia (SDL), the United List of Social Democrats in Slovenia (ZLSD), the Communist Party of the Ukraine (KPU), and the Socialist Party of Serbia (SPS).

These parties were selected for two reasons. First, unlike "new parties," these communist successor parties, when they first emerged from the remains of their former regimes, were not merely groups of notables, but by any definition represented "real" political parties. Second, these cases fit the following criteria, which make them roughly comparable: (1) in each of the seventeen states, all had at least one reasonably competitive election between 1992 and 1995, and have arguably progressed into the period of democratic consolidation; (2) in all seventeen states the communist successor parties faced new competitive conditions and a party system in the earliest stages of development (thus excluding the Party of Democratic Socialism in Germany).

To test various theoretical explanations for party organizational development, I will first briefly review the existent explanations for the organizational development of the communist successor parties. Second, I will propose one way of measuring party organizations based upon the *degree of personnel overlap* between *the organs of the extraparliamentary party, the party in public office,* and *organizational density.* Finally, I will examine which of the often cited factors affecting party organizational development best explains variations found among the communist successor parties.

Party Organizational Models

Much of the literature on party organizational development is based upon the assumption that parties primarily seek to win elections; as such, party organizational change is seen as a product of the party's desire to survive electorally (Duverger 1954; Kirchheimer 1966; Downs, 1957; Epstein, 1967; Janda, 1980). Thus, industrial society produced the mass party which superseded the cadre or caucus party as the dominant organizational form, because of the former's ability to more effectively mobilize newly enfranchised voters. In turn, the former cadre parties were compelled to adapt the organizational features of mass parties in order to survive (Duverger 1954).

In order to identify the kinds of organizational changes that occurred as the result of this process of adapting to new political environments, scholars have traditionally focused on the "three faces of the party": the party in office, the party as organization, and the party as electorate (Schlesinger 1984) or for Katz and Mair (1994) *the party in public office, the party in central office, and the party on the ground.* According to earlier cross national research on party organization in Western Europe (Katz and Mair 1990, 1992), the party in public office is understood as the representative of the party in parliament and/or government, and the party in central office is "the national leadership of the party organization which at least in theory, is organizationally distinct from the party in public office, and which, at the same time, organizes and is usually the representative of the party on the ground" (Katz and Mair 1993, p. 594). Historically, different party organizations have generally been characterized by different sorts of relations between these three components (Koole 1994; Ignazi 1996). In particular, several indicators have been used to measure the relationship between these "faces," most notably the relative size of official membership, and the relationship between the party's officeholders and the party's activists in the central office.

There have also been several attempts to predict the kinds of parties that will emerge in Eastern Europe. For instance, Lewis (1996) notes the persistent appeal of the "traditional mass party" model. For Lewis the success of the parties like the Polish SLD and the Hungarian Socialist Party resulted from the main strengths of the "traditional mass party: a high membership in terms of the post-communist context, strong finances, and material resources and a high degree of organizational development"—virtues of a model that still seem of "considerable importance in post-communist . . . Europe" (Lewis 1996, pp. 16–17). Padgett (1996) in his analysis of the development of political parties in the former East Germany suggests another model: parties as associations of sympathizers run by a political elite and a professional party apparatus as subordinate while important organizations provide political services to a loosely constituted electoral clientele.

Kopecký (1995), Van Biezen (2000), and Kitschelt (1995a) have also investigated the development of party organizations in post-communist Eastern Europe. For Kopecký the most likely organizational forms are those "formations with loose electoral constituencies, in which a relatively unimportant role is played by the party membership, and the dominant role by party leaders" (Kopecký 1995, p. 517). This is because (1) parties are likely to be forced to appeal to a wide clientele of voters, largely because the parties cannot count on voters having preexisting party loyalties, since under authoritarian rule such loyalties between party and individual simply did not exist; (2) parties are likely to favor relatively small memberships because parties do not depend on members for financial resources (rather they rely on the state), and smaller membership limits the probability of the emergence of potentially powerful challenges to the existing leadership; (3) finally, the depoliticized citizenry in post-communist systems are unlikely to identify intensively with all-encompassing ideologies and party symbols; rather, citizens are more likely to identify with strong personalities. Thus, Kopecký argues that what is most likely to exist in post-communist politics is something like a "catchall" or "electoral professional" party where the party leadership plays the dominant role and the party organization is subordinate.

Van Biezen (2000) also argues that parties are not likely to resemble the "mass" model. Rather she views parties largely dominated by officeholders, with rather weak party organization. Indeed, the relationship between the party in central office and the party in public office in the new democracies is likely to be characterized by the dominance of the party in public office. She offers three reasons why this is likely to be the case. First, most parties in new democracies are newly created. Since they were founded only shortly before the first democratic elections they acquired parliamentary representation early on. Thus, it was only natural that the parties are dominated by the party in public office. However, this dominance is likely to continue it is expected that the party in public office will subsequently control organizational development. Second, competition in new democracies is not organized based upon distinct social interests but on the basis of "politicized attitudinal differences regarding institutional issues—namely the desirability, degree, and direction of regime change" (Van Biezen 2000, p. 397).

Third, parties in new democracies will likely concentrate on a relatively less time-consuming and labor-intensive strategy of electoral mobilization rather than attempt to channel societal demands through extra-parliamentary organization. Thus, concentrating on the party in public office is a more cost-effective strategy in party organization building.

Kitschelt (1995) also provides some theoretical guidelines for analyzing party organization in Eastern Europe and the former Soviet Union. He identifies three "ideal types" of parties (*charismatic, clientelistic,* and *programmatic*) and specifies the conditions under which these parties might emerge. The charismatic party is characterized by "not much more than an unstructured mass of people rallying around a leader" (1995, p. 449). Such parties are inherently unstable given that in order to maintain the allegiance of their followers leaders must sooner or later provide selective incentives to their constituencies and enter upon trajectories of organizational development that result in either clientelistic or program parties. Clientelistic parties are characterized by an emphasis upon personal patronage, and invest much into creating an organization that effectively disburses resources to followers. These parties, however, avoid the costs of coordinating the activities of followers since the role of the member is not to believe in a set of ideological goals, but to be personally loyal. Program parties, on the other hand, are built to advertise ideals "about a desirable society as the collective good they promise to produce and to attract activists and leaders ready to propagate and to implement these ideas" (1995, p. 449). Program parties are relatively harder to build than either of the other types, yet are "more likely to reinforce the consolidation and stability of democratic regimes than the two alternative modes" of party organization (1995, p. 450).

Beyond identifying the different organizational types, Kitschelt also provides a heuristic model by which to explain the emergence of different types of parties in post-communist politics (1995, p. 457). In general, Kitschelt explains the likelihood of the emergence of programmatic parties to be a function of four factors: the timing of industrialization, institutional features such as the existence of a presidential as opposed to a parliamentary system, the type of democratic transition that occurred, and the amount of system-time passed (in terms of the number of free elections) since the first free elections. From this model, Kitschelt predicts that program parties are most likely to emerge in the Czech Republic, Hungary, Poland, and Slovenia, less so in Slovakia, the Baltic States, and Croatia. In Bulgaria, Romania, and most of the republics of the former Soviet Union and Yugoslavia, clientelistic parties are most likely to emerge.

Conceptualizing and Measuring Party Organization

A useful starting point in classifying parties in post-communist politics is the distinction made by Kitschelt (1995) between "programmatic" and "clientelistic" parties.[2] The programmatic party shares some of the features of the historic mass party, particularly the continued influence of the party organization and party activists. However, the role of the party in office is important in the programmatic party, and relations between the party organization and the political elite are mutually supportive as opposed to the historic mass organizational form, where the party in office merely acted as delegates for the party organization. Although the role of the membership as the primary source of electoral support is less than in the historic mass party, the membership continues to play an important role. The clientelistic party, on the other hand, may have features that resemble mass parties in form, but which in practice emphasize the independence of the party in office. These parties, like the past historic cadre parties, are run by political elites, and the party organization is subordinate to the party in office. However, in these parties the role of the membership is very much deemphasized. Further, the role of the membership, particularly as the primary source of electoral support, is much less important in the clientelistic party than the programmatic party. Although some of these parties have fairly large memberships, what binds the members to these organizations is the existence of patron-client ties and an interest in electoral victory as opposed to ideological program (Koole, 1994).

As Van Biezen (2000) notes, post-communist parties more generally resemble the clientelistic party model than the programmatic type, particularly as parties in the new democracies are more likely to be dominated by their officeholders. One of her principal explanations for this is that because parties focus on organizing parliamentary and governmental institutions in the early period of new democracies, they are to compelled to "concentrate their activities around the party in public office," thus significantly strengthening that face of the party in the organization as a whole (Van Biezen 2000, p. 397). Moreover, parties in new democracies are more likely to concentrate on the relatively less time-consuming and labor-intensive strategy of electoral mobilization rather than attempting to channel societal demands through extraparliamentary organization. Thus, concentrating on the party in public office is a more cost-effective strategy in party organization building, particularly in the early stages of party building. However, this dominance is likely to continue since it is expected that the party in public office will control subsequent organizational development.

To create a party organization index, I will first measure the relationship between the central organization and the party in public office using the degree of personnel overlap between the organs of the extra-parliamentary party and the party in public office. Using Van Biezen's (2000) measure, I have gauged the actual extent of the personnel overlap between the narrow executives (the narrow executive is the smallest statutory extra-parliamentary organ) and the party in public office in the first half of the 1990s. Indeed, as Van Biezen argues, the crucial period in a party's development is the early period, "especially given the parliamentary origins of most parties and their relatively early acquisition of government responsibility. A significant representation of public officeholders within the extra-parliamentary organs are more likely to be interpreted as a sign of predominance of the party in public office, enabling this face to preserve its leading position with the party and to maintain control over the extra-parliamentary structures as the organization develops" (Van Biezen 2000, p. 398). To measure the degree of personnel overlap, I calculated the proportion of the members of the smallest statutory party executive body who were also members of Parliament or the government.

Second, I measured the extent to which the party membership is important to the party's political support. The first indicator employed is organizational density which is defined as the proportion of estimated official party members over the number of votes a party receives. This measure was first developed by Duverger (1954), and has been employed elsewhere as well, and measures the relative importance of the party's membership as a proportion of its electoral support (Duverger 1954; Kopecký 1995). Parties that are more clientelistic are likely to rely less heavily on membership for their support than parties that are more programmatic. For the seventeen parties, the average estimated membership figures are used and divided by the average vote received by the party over the course of the legislative elections from 1990–1995. This, in turn, is subtracted from the number one to yield an organizational density score where the high value indicates less reliance on the party membership for political support.

To construct a measure of party organization, a principal components factor analysis technique was employed taking into account the degree of personnel overlap between the organs of the extra-parliamentary party and the party in public office as well as the organizational density score for each party. The two items were illustrated on a unidimensional scale and are highly correlated with a principal component score of .79. The derived factor scores or the *party organization score*, were taken as measures of the dependent variable, where a high score indicates a party where officeholders dominate the party executive and where there is less reliance on the party membership for political support.

Measurement of Independent Variables

Several scholars have noted that party politics in general in Eastern Europe and FSU countries have been affected by the degree to which there is popular trust in parties as institutions, presidential power, the degree to which labor is unionized, and the previous regime type. Thus, scholars have argued that the transformation of a political movement depends on what Tarrow (1989; 1996) and Schlesinger (1984) refer to as the "opportunity structure." The "opportunity structure" represents the "set of opportunities and constraints that discourage or encourage movement behaviors and lead movements toward certain forms of collective action over others" (Young 1997, p. 231). The opportunity structure comprises a number of factors, but some of the most commonly cited include institutional features of the political system (such as parliamentary versus presidential systems and the election law) as well the "political environment" that the party faces.

Previous Regime Type and Organizational Transition

One type of explanation for the evolution of the communist successor parties focuses on the legacy left by the previous communist regime (Ágh 1995; Waller 1995; Evans and Whitefield 1995; Racz 1993). From this perspective, the nature of the previous regime affects the type of transition that occurs, which in turn structures the character of politics in the period following the transition. Welsh (1994) finds such a connection in Eastern Europe, where regime type affected the extent to which bargaining and compromise took place during the transition period; countries that had an extended period of bargaining and compromise were more likely to produce a trained cadre of politicians within the contending political parties, politicians who had learned how to play according to the rules of democratic competition and electoral politics. The more extended the period of transition the greater the likelihood that the parties (and hence the party systems) emerging from communist rule became more institutionalized and structured. The more institutionalized the parties the more likely relations within the party would become structured and hierarchical, ultimately producing pressures to develop along more mass rather than cadre-like lines (Ágh 1995, pp. 492–493).

To measure the differences between regime types in Eastern Europe and the former Soviet Union, Kitschelt (1995) constructed a useful three-part typology of communist regimes: *patrimonial, bureaucratic-authoritarian,* and *national consensus* communism. The first, patrimonial communism, relied heavily on hierarchical chains of personal dependence between leaders and followers, with low levels of inter-elite contestation, popular interest articulation, and rational-bureaucratic professionalization. Moreover, these systems were characterized by a heavy emphasis on "democratic centralism" which fit well with the hierarchical structure of dependence between leaders and the led. In this category Kitschelt placed Serbia, Romania, Bulgaria, Russia, Ukraine, Belarus, and most of the rest of the former Soviet Union (coded as 0).

In the second type, bureaucratic authoritarian communism, inter-elite contestation and interest articulation were circumscribed, but the level of rational-bureaucratic institutionalization was high. In this category Kitschelt placed the former German Democratic Republic, the Czech Republic, and Slovakia (coded as 1). The third type of system (coded as 2) was national consensus communism, where levels of contestation and interest articulation were permitted, and there was a degree of bureaucratic professionalization. In essence, the communist elites allowed for a measure of contestation and interest articulation in exchange for compliance with the basic features of the existing system. In this category Kitschelt places Poland and Hungary, as well as Slovenia and Croatia. Also within this category, as "borderline" cases, were the three Baltic states: Estonia, Latvia, and Lithuania. Although these states had been absorbed by the Soviet Union, there was a remarkable degree of intraregime contestation and the tolerance of the demands of the national independence movements, at least far more so than in other parts of the USSR (Kitschelt 1995). In sum, Kitschelt argues that the features of previous organizational legacies vitally affected the character of political party development, and hence explain to a large extent the different organizational trajectories followed by the communist successor parties.

An argument related to the effects of previous regime type is the kind of organizational transition that took place for each successor party. Such organizational transitions may independently affect the kind of party organizations that emerge later. Indeed as Ishiyama (1995) notes, each communist successor party underwent very different kinds of organizational transformations, defined by the extent to which they followed what Huntington (1991) referred to as "standpatter," "liberal," or "democratic reformist" paths of internal leadership transformation between 1990 and 1993.

In reviewing the organizational transitions that Ishiyama (1995) identified, I scored each transition type for the period 1990–1993 from 0–2 with zero representing a leadership dominated by standpatters (those who preferred retaining party organization based upon Marxist-Leninist norms). The number one represents a leadership controlled by liberals (or those who favored democratic but "controlled" competition), and two represents a leadership controlled by democratic reformists (or those who favored transforming the party into a fully competitive organization). Each year from 1990–1993 was coded separately because it often occurred that in one year democratic reformists dominated only to be replaced by liberals later (such as in Estonia). Further, half points were scored for years in which democratic reformists and liberals or liberals and standpatters coexisted in a rough balance. A total *organizational transition score* was calculated by adding all the individual yearly scores for each party and dividing by the total number of years. The resulting score ranges from 0–2 with the high score indicating an organizational transition controlled by democratic reformists within the successor party.

Presidential Power

In addition, there are pressures generated by the existence of a powerful presidency. Linz (1990) notes that the existence of a powerful presidency provides an incentive for the party to win that office, dwarfing all other political goals. This applies not only to directly elected presidencies but also to indirectly elected ones (such as via the legislature). This situation tends to deemphasize campaigns based upon ideological principles and emphasize campaigns based upon personality. In particular, it has been argued that powerful presidencies act as a major impediment to the development of political parties (Huskey 1997; Colton 1995; Roeder 1994; Fish 2000). For instance, White, Wyman, and Kryshtanovskaya (1995) have argued that the existence of a strong presidency is inimical to the development of political parties. By concentrating authority in the hands of a single individual, the politics of personality prevails, making it more difficult for parties to develop coherent programs and identities (White, Wyman, and Kryshtanovskaya 1995; Moser 1998). Fish (2000, p. 23) contends that this effect is exhibited throughout the states of the former Soviet Union where powerful presidencies chill "party development in part by holding down incentives for important political and economic actors to invest in politics." In such a system candidates have relatively little incentive to associate with political parties, when the legislature (the principal arena for party politics) has such little say in policy. Rather, individuals tend to focus on forming personal attachments with presidential hopefuls, bypassing association with political parties. Thus, the more powerful the presidency the greater is the tendency toward clientelistic politics.

To measure the strength of the presidency, I have employed the measure developed by Hellman (1996), the *Index of Formal Presidential Powers*.[3] This value takes into account the constitutional powers invested in the hands of the president and provides a standard measure by which to evaluate the relative strength of different presidencies cross-nationally in Eastern Europe and the former Soviet Union. The value ranges from zero to 27 with a high score indicative of a powerful presidency and a lower score a less powerful presidency.

Average District Magnitude

In addition to previous regime type and the degree of presidential power, another factor that is cited as affecting the organizational development of parties is the electoral system, in particular the *district magnitude* for elections to the lower (and more powerful) house of the legislature. Average district magnitude has been labeled as the most crucial element of the electoral system in affecting the evolution of party politics (Taagepera and Shugart 1989; Schlesinger 1984). The average district magnitude is defined as the number of seats allocated in an electoral district on average and operationally defined as the total number of seats in the lower house of the legislature, divided by the number of electoral districts. The lowest average district magnitude is one for legislatures entirely elected by the single member district system, and highest where the entire country represents a single electoral district (as is the case in pure list proportional representation [PR] systems), with mixed systems and PR systems, using regional lists, occupying intermediate positions.

Estimated Percent Labor Force Unionized

An additional environmental variable is the strength of the trade union movement. As Duverger (1954) has noted, the mass parties of the past grew out of the trade union movement, and the trade unions represented a continual source of support for mass parties. This has been one of the principal arguments offered by Waller (1995) as to why the communist successor parties in Eastern and Central Europe have enjoyed the political success they have. For Waller, these parties have successfully forged ties with the post-communist trade unions, providing them with invaluable organizational and electoral support (Mahr and Nagle 1995). In essence, the success that parties like the Hungarian Socialist Party and the Polish Social Democrats have enjoyed derives from the organizational and electoral support the unions have mobilized at the local levels. Of course, this connection could only exist where the labor unions are relatively strong. This would, in turn, suggest that in systems where labor unions are strong there would exist an incentive for the parties to form a political alliance with them, thus pushing the party in the direction of more mass party-like organizational characteristics.

To assess the relative strength of trade unions, I have used data (see Table 13.1) from the International Labor Organization (ILO) to measure the degree of union membership as a proportion of the nonagricultural labor force (ILO, 1998).

In sum, based upon the literature discussed above, the following hypotheses can be derived:

- Hypothesis 1: Previous communist regimes that were characterized by the greatest levels of inter-elite contestation and open interest articula-

Table 13.1

Successor Parties' Reported Memberships and Average Narrow Executive Sizes for Seventeen Post-Communist Countries

Country	Successor Party	Member-ship	Size of Narrow Executive
Albania	Socialist Party of Albania (PSSH)	110,000	15
Bosnia	Social Democratic Party (SDP)	40,000	12
Bulgaria	Bulgarian Socialist Party (BSP)	330,000	16
Croatia	Social Democratic Party of Croatia (SDP)	2,000	20
Czech Republic	Communist Party of Bohemia and Moravia (KSCM)	21,1000	8
Estonia	Estonian Social Democratic Labor Party (ESDTP)	300	3
Hungary	Hungarian Socialist Party (MSZP)	40,000	15
Latvia	Latvian Socialist Party (LSP)	360	7
Lithuania	Lithuanian Democratic Labor Party (LDDP)	9,000	20
Macedonia	Social Democratic Union of Macedonia (SDSM)	40,000	21
Poland	Democratic Left Alliance (SLD)	62,000	40
Romania	Party of Social Democracy of Romania (PDSR)	309,000	8
Russian Federation	Communist Party of the Russian Federation (KPRF)	554,000	15
Slovakia	Party of Democratic Left (SDL)	48,000	7
Slovenia	United List of Social Democrats (ZLSD)	27,000	5
Ukraine	Communist Party of Ukraine (KPU)	142,000	20
Yugoslavia	Socialist Party of Serbia (SPS)	70,000	37

Sources: Vocea Romaniei, November 24, 1995, pp. 1–2 in *Foreign Broadcast Information Service-Eastern Europe* (hereafter referred to as FBIS-EEU)-95-230, pp. 60–61; Day, German and Campbell (1996); *Eastern Europe and the Commonwealth of Independent States 1997* (1998); Glubotskii (1993). Various party web sites.

tion are likely to produce communist successor parties with more mass party-like characteristics.

- Hypothesis 2: Significant differences should exist between parties in which democratic reformists dominated the transition process as opposed to liberals or standpatters.
- Hypothesis 3: The greater the power of the constitutional presidency, the greater the emphasis on personality in politics and hence the less likely the emergence of communist successor parties with more mass party-like characteristics.
- Hypothesis 4: The greater the average district magnitude, the greater the pressure for the development of communist successor parties with more mass party-like characteristics.
- Hypothesis 5: The greater the strength of labor unions the greater the support for the development of mass parties.

Analysis

Table 13.2 summarizes the values of the independent variables for the seventeen cases. An interesting finding from Table 13.2 results from comparing parties in terms of scores on the party organization index.

A high score on this index is indicative of parties whose organizations are dominated by the party in public office, and which rely less on mass membership for political support. These features approximate, at least organizationally, the clientelistic model. Interestingly, the parties that score highest on this index are the MSZP (1.66), KPU (1.30), SLD (1.28), and KPRF (1.22). This is somewhat surprising, given the marked differences between these parties. On the one hand the MSZP and the SLD have often been identified as the model "pragmatic-reform" type successor parties, whereas the KPRF and KPU have been characterized as "leftist retreat" or "nationalist-Socialist." However, it should be remembered that the index measures organizational characteristics and not identity characteristics. What these results indicate is that, first, organization and identity may be quite independent from one another, and, second, that the MSZP, SLD, KPRF, and KPU have much more in common than is often claimed. All of these parties share in common the powerful position of the party in public office, and a lessened reliance on mass membership, although the party organization is still important, particularly during campaigns. However, these parties have evolved beyond the bloated and mass-based models retained by so many other parties (such as the KSCM and the BSP) and have become fairly effective organizations designed to serve the "party in public office" and win elections.

Turning to the hypotheses mentioned above, Table 13.3 illustrates the Spearman bivariate correlation coefficients using the variables specified above.[4] As indicated in Table 13.3, the single independent variable that exhibits a strong and statistically significant relationship with *Party Organization* is *Presidential Power* (.63). The positive sign of the coefficient indicates that the more powerful the presidency, the more the successor party was dominated by the party in public office and the less reliant it was on mass membership. This finding is consistent with the literature that has suggested that powerful presidencies tend to weaken political parties as organizations by highlighting the role played by individuals. However, I would contend that a powerful presidency does not weaken parties, but provides incentives for the development of clientelistic rather than programmatic parties. This finding is also consistent with earlier work that suggested that institutional incentives were the most important factors in explaining party organizational development in postcommunist Eastern Europe (Ishiyama, 1999a).

On the other hand, *Regime Type* (.15), *Organizational Transition Type* (.21), *Average District Magnitude* (−.39), and *Percent Nonagricultural Labor Force Unionized* (−.51) were not systematically related to the dependent

Table 13.2

Values of Variables

Country	Degree of personnel overlap in narrow executive	Organizational density score (1–[members/ votes])	Party organi- zation score	Average district magnitude	Presidential power score	Organiza- tional transition type	Previous regime type	% Non– agricultural labor force unionized
Albania	0.73	0.83	0.03	1.22	4.75	3	0.0	
Bosnia	0.66	0.89	0.05			5	0.0	
Bulgaria	0.38	0.82	-1.07	7.74	9.00	3	0.0	51.4
Croatia	0.55	0.98	0.57	3.72	14.00	5	2.0	
Czech Republic	0.50	0.68	-1.70	25.00	5.25	2	1.0	36.3
Estonia	0.33	0.90	-0.62	9.18	5.25	4	1.5	25.4
Hungary	0.93	0.98	1.66	1.95	5.25	6	2.0	52.5
Latvia	0.14	0.99	-0.53	20.00	3.75	2	1.5	
Lithuania	0.50	0.93	0.05	1.96	9.50	6	1.5	27.0
Macedonia	0.38	0.86	-0.77	1.00	3.25	5	0.0	
Poland	0.80	0.98	1.28	8.68	9.00	6	2.0	27.0
Romania	0.34	0.92	-0.43	8.17	10.00	3	0.0	40.5
Russian Federation	0.80	0.97	1.22	1.99	13.50	2	0.0	74.8
Slovakia	0.43	0.98	0.22	37.5	5.50	5	1.0	52.3
Slovenia	0.40	0.79	-1.20	9.00	4.50	6	2.0	
Ukraine	0.80	0.98	1.30	1.95	16.00	6	0.0	74.2
Yugoslavia	0.41	0.96	0.01	3.83		1	0.0	

Sources: Hellman (1996); Kitschelt (1995); *Foreign Broadcast Information Service–Central Eurasia* (hereafter referred to as FBIS–SOV) – 94–066, pp. 60–61; Ishiyama 1995.

Table 13.3

Spearman's Correlation Coefficients for Party Organization

Variable	Coefficient
Previous regime type	0.15
Organizational transition type	0.21
Presidential powers	0.63**
ln (average district magnitude)	−0.39
Percentage of non-agricultural labor force unionized	0.51

Source: Author's compilation.
Notes:
 *p≤ .05
 **p≤ .01

variable party organization. Although the sign of average district magnitude was negative (in the predicted direction), indicating that larger average district magnitude was associated with more mass-like parties, the coefficient size was not particularly large (−.39). However, no such relationship was uncovered when considering the previous regime and organizational transition score. Indeed, the sign of the coefficients were opposite to those predicted. In other words, this would indicate that the more open the previous regime and the more democratic reformists dominated the organizational transition process from 1990 to 1993, the more likely the party would exhibit clientelistic rather than mass party-like characteristics. However, these relationships are not statistically significant. Thus, Hypotheses 1 and 2 were not supported, i.e. there was no systematic evidence that the previous regime type nor the process of organizational transition, especially in terms of who controlled that process, was related to how the successor parties have evolved as organizations.

The most interesting findings relate to the relationship between party organizational type and the strength of labor unions. As indicated, it appears that no relationship exists between estimated strength of the labor unions and the organizational form of the communist successor party. However the positive sign of the coefficient (.51) suggests that this relationship is contrary to that expected in Hypothesis 5; the result indicates that stronger labor unions are associated with the emergence of a more clientelistic communist successor party. Although this appears to contradict the argument that labor union strength is related to party organizational development, further research is still required. It is quite possible that labor union strength is not particularly important, but based on the kind of linkages established between party and union, as has been suggested with the cases of the MSZP and the Polish SLD. However, these findings would suggest that explanations which focus largely on party-union linkage may be less generalizable when venturing outside of Eastern and Central Europe.

Conclusions

The analysis above represents an initial investigation into the development of party organizations represented by the communist successor parties emerging in Eastern Europe. The primary goal of this chapter was to test some of the propositions derived from western party organizational theory in light of the evidence from the communist successor parties in Eastern Europe and the former Soviet Union. It was found that among the most frequently cited factors affecting party organizational development, structural factors, especially the strength of the constitutional presidency, were the best predictors of party organization, conceived in terms of the dominance of the party in office and the party's reliance on mass membership.

How does this finding relate to the survival strategies outlined in chapter 1 of this volume? In general I contend that the face the party puts forth to the electorate is a dimension independent from party organizational development per se. Indeed, parties that have adopted pragmatic reformist strategies (such as the MSZP and the SLD) have also exhibited clientelistic organizational characteristics which they share with parties like the KPRF and KPU, both of which have opted for national leftist retreat/national patriotic strategies. Indeed, not only are these dimensions independent from one another, but they are also shaped by different dynamics. Thus, as Ishiyama and Bozoki (2001) point out, the type of survival strategy selected is largely a function of internal factors, such as the extent to which the party is ideologically coherent. However, organizational characteristics and adaptations appear to be largely a result of external incentives, particularly institutional incentives.

The development of the successor parties into competitive organizations dominated by the party in public office indicates that they have come a long way, although this clearly varies across the parties in Eastern Europe. As the evidence from the successor parties addressed above illustrates, even parties that were generally cut from the same organizational cloth have evolved along very different lines in post-communist politics. How these parties develop will not only shed a considerable amount of new light on identifying the reasons why parties develop into the organizations that they become, but provide insight into the future shape of politics and democracy in the post-communist world.

Notes

1. To be sure, there have been a number of studies that have investigated individual cases (Ágh, 1995; Zubek, 1994; Roper, 1995; Zudinov, 1994) and a few works that have compared several countries in Eastern and Central Europe (Kopecký, 1995; Lewis, 1996; Wightman, 1995; Novopashin, 1994; Segert and Machos, 1995).

2. These types are different from the historic cadre or elite parties. The cadre or "elite" parties of the nineteenth century were basically "committees of people who jointly constituted state and civil society" (Katz and Mair, 1995, p. 9; Duverger, 1954). Parties then, were merely "groups of men" pursuing the public interest, with little need for formal or highly structured organizations or large formal membership. The parliamentary component or the party in office dominated, and the resources required for election often involved local connections and personal political notability. The *mass party*, unlike the cadre party, was characterized by a large, active membership. This is because the mass party arose "primarily among the newly activated and often disenfranchised elements of civil society" (Katz and Mair, 1995, p. 10). Whereas the old cadre party had relied on the quality of supporters (personal attributes), the mass party relied on the quantity of supporters, attempting to make up in membership what it lacked in terms of individual patronage. As the political instrument of the disenfranchised, the mass parties were naturally dominated by those whose political base was in the party rather than in government; moreover, given their activist political agenda, and the life experiences of their supporters, these parties were more amenable to enforced party cohesion and discipline than were the cadre parties (Duverger, 1954). Thus, mass parties were characterized by large memberships, internal hierarchy, and elite homogeneity, and the dominance of the party organization. Representatives of the party were merely delegates representing the view of the party as organization (Neumann, 1956, p. 403).

3. Another measure is McGregor's (1994) the *Weighted Presidential Power Score*. Unfortunately, this score by itself does not take into account whether the president is directly or indirectly elected, nor whether the system is a parliamentary or presidential one.

4. The Spearman bivariate correlation procedure was employed because (1) in order to test whether a systematic relationship exists between any of the independent variables and the dependent variable of *Party Type* when constrained by a very small number of cases, a simple bivariate correlation reduces the degrees of freedom problem that is faced when using small samples in multivariate models; (2) the Spearman's procedure is the appropriate technique for both interval variables which do not fulfill the "normality assumption" and/or categorical variables.

14

Doomed to be Radicals?

Organization, Ideology, and the Communist Successor Parties in East Central Europe

Daniel F. Ziblatt and Nick Biziouras

This chapter begins with a puzzle: why have some of the Leninist successor organizations in Eastern and Central Europe been capable of ideologically distancing themselves from the past while others have continued to be burdened with an ideological commitment to Marxism? In the face of clear and decisive electoral incentives across parts of the postcommunist world to adopt a more social democratic profile, some ex-communist parties have quickly dropped their Marxist rhetoric to act as "European-style" pragmatic social democrats while others have remained tied to their ideological roots.[1] If one lesson is clear from the postcommunist setting, it is that despite sharing a history as Leninist organizations in a Moscow-centered world until 1989–1990, the successor parties to these organizations have followed divergent trajectories of reform during the past ten years.

In the following, we will undertake a comparative analysis of the paths of ideological adaptation pursued by six successor parties to the former ruling communist organizations of six formerly communist Eastern and Central European countries: the SdRP/SLD in Poland, the KSČM in the Czech Republic, the SLD in Slovakia, the PSRD in Romania, the MSZP in Hungary, and the PDS in East Germany. We study these six cases because, according to the growing literature on ex-communist parties, they offer a complete sample of the types of ex-communist parties in Eastern and Central Europe ten years after communism's fall, including those that have pursued a pragmatic path of "social democratization," those that have remained committed to a Marxist path of leftist retreat, and those, finally, that have adopted a "patriotic" social democratic path of ideological change (Ishiyama, 1999b).

To understand this array of ideological outcomes, our analysis shifts away from explanations that focus solely on the external determinants of change in order to adopt a perspective that seeks to link the macro legacies of communism and modes of transition with micro-level organizational challenges facing the communist successor parties. More precisely, we argue that different communist legacies as well as different paths of transition left the former ruling organizations of Eastern and Central Europe facing variations on a critical organizational challenge: how to transform themselves from Leninist political organizations into electorally minded political parties. A centerpiece of this transformation process was the effort to develop new systems of party finance. The different responses of different parties to this challenge shaped the subsequent ideological developments of each party. In the following, we argue that in response to different modes of transition, the former communist parties adopted different types of party financing which have affected the chances for successor party ideological adaptability in the postcommunist electoral setting. To summarize the argument: Successor parties that have largely retained their resources after 1989–1990 or that rely to a greater extent on the state for party funding have a greater chance for ideological adaptability. For such parties, less of a reliance on members for financial support results in an ability to engage in the attraction of new voters by taking more center-oriented ideological positions. Conversely, successor parties that cannot reduce their material reliance on their existing members, remain "captured" by their membership and hence have significantly less chances for ideological adaptability.

Macro-Level Explanations of Ideological Adaptation

Few areas of postcommunist political life have been as striking as the degree to which former communist parties have not only survived but also thrived after the collapse of communist regimes in 1989. A central part of the saga of the reconstruction of former communist parties has been the uncanny ability of some parties to redefine themselves in ideological terms as reform-oriented, social democratic, European-style organizations that seek to bring the countries of Eastern and Central Europe into the community of a broader, modern Europe.

In the postcommunist setting, analysts have identified three paths of reform for former communist parties: *pragmatic reform, leftist retreat,* and *national patriotic* (Ziblatt 1999; Ishiyama 1999). To understand why some of the Leninist organizations that governed the communist world have been able to redefine themselves as western-oriented social democratic parties while others have maintained a reconstituted commitment to Marxist ideals, analysts have tended to emphasize a set of inter-related macro-level political and economic conditions that run as themes throughout this volume (1) the structural legacies of the precommunist and communist era; (2) the mode of postcommunist transition; (3) the postcommunist environment. At first glance the legacies of the past seem to have a high degree of explanatory leverage as analysts usually tell two parallel analytical narratives. In countries with a highly mobilized and large working class in the precommunist era, the ex-communist party in the postcommunist era seems to have maintained its commitment to its socialist ideals (East Germany and Czech Republic). By contrast, in countries with a larger agrarian population in the precommunist era, communist parties have had an easier time in abandoning their communist pasts (Poland and Hungary).[2] Finally, in states that were almost entirely agrarian before the communist era, the ex-communist parties have tended to adopt a nationalist social democratic agenda (Bulgaria and Romania).

In parallel fashion, the nature of the postcommunist transition appears decisive: countries that experienced a regime implosion in 1989 have been left with a more leftist ex-communist party in the postcommunist setting (East Germany and the Czech Republic), while countries that experienced a negotiated exit from communism have generated more social democratic ex-communists (Poland and Hungary). And finally, in countries that experienced a transition from above where the ruling communists rapidly reformed and immediately installed themselves in power between 1989 and 1990, it appears that ex-communist parties have tended to adopt a nationalist social democratic ideological profile.

Such macro-level explanations provide a set of reinforcing arguments that over-determine the paths of adaptation that ex-communist parties have followed since 1989. Likewise, though there is an intuitive appeal to such explanations, the precise causal mechanisms of how these structural conditions result in the divergent ideological profiles of central European ex-communist parties remains unclear. Indeed as Ishiyama (1995) has argued, "in reviewing the empirical evidence thus far, it is clear that reference to environmental factors alone does not sufficiently explain the evolution of the ex-communist parties during the course of democratic transition and consolidation" (Ishiyama 1995, 163). To complement macro-level approaches to ideological adaptation and to provide a potentially new research agenda, we shall shift our focus to a different level of analysis; we will seek to understand how the communist-era legacies and the mode of postcommunist transition shape systems of party finance, which in turn shape efforts at ideological adaptation. Our work complements earlier work by Ishiyama that showed that the regime type of the pretransition communist regime, the strength of the constitutional presidency, and the average district magnitude were the best predictors of successor party organizational types (Ishiyama 1999a). If, as Ishiyama (1999b) and Kitschelt et al. (1999) have argued, the type of communist regime, the mode of postcommunist transition, as well as the political conditions of the postcommunist setting shape the organizational attributes of ex-communist parties, then an important question for students of postcommunism and for students of party organization in general remains unanswered; in the postcommunist setting, what is the impact of party organization on party ideology?

Overview of Our Argument: The Impact of Organizational Capacity on Ideological Adaptation

Studies of the postcommunist party systems in Eastern Europe have focused on a variety of themes:

(1) the rapid proliferation and disintegration of nascent political party organizations (Toole 2000);[3]
(2) the increased differentiation of the underlying ideological dynamics, highlighting the emergence of pro- and antimarket currents in the Eastern and Central European countries and the emergence of nationalist tendencies in the Southeast European and post-Soviet countries (Krause 2000; Markowski 1997; Roskin 1993);
(3) the increased institutionalization of these nascent political parties and the emergence of a new political class (van Biezen 2000);
(4) the continued persistence and transformation of the ex-communist political parties.

This chapter will focus its analysis on the internal organizational aspects of these successor parties. It examines the relationship between the degree of organizational centralization and the potential for successor party ideological adaptability. More explicitly, we will argue that the institutional setting of successor party financing, i.e. the type and the context of resource dependency, affects the parties' ability to adapt ideologically to a new electoral environment.

Based on the work of Orenstein (1997), Grzymala-Busse (1999), Waller (1995), Ágh (1995), and Kopecky (1995), it is important to note the legacies of the transitional period. In essence, the successor parties had a variety of differences both within their ranks as well as vis-à-vis their competitors. In terms of their competitors, the successor parties emerged from the communist setting with a variety of important organizational tools and resources. First, despite the huge reductions in their member ranks, they still had a reservoir of committed and locally organized members who could be electorally mobilized.[4] Such membership structures provided the successor parties with the ability to move beyond the loosely affiliated membership associations of other parties.[5] Second, such membership structures provided successor parties with organizational nonmaterial resources that did not have to be created *de novo*, such as local branches, regional councils, and central commissions. Third, and perhaps most importantly, the organizational material resources of ex-communist parties meant that the successor parties could compete electorally by focusing on their ideological message, while relying on their existing and deployed national mass organization structures, without engaging in a simultaneous construction of both ideology and organization.[6]

However, the successor parties of Eastern and Central Europe differed in their actual material resource levels, i.e. not all of them exited the transitional period with the same set of resources. The Hungarian, Czech, and East German parties exited with significantly reduced fund bases, whereas the Polish and Romanian parties exited with more monetary resources.[7] This legacy differentiation assumes an important level of explanatory power in our argument because it provides the catalytic link between organizational capacity and ideological adaptability. More explicitly, the successor parties with significantly reduced resources were forced to engage in an active process of fund-raising, which often left them with primarily two choices: to increasingly rely on their membership base or to engage in the creation of state-based political party systems. We treat the creation of state-based party financing systems as an important intervening variable because it altered the internal organizational dynamics of these successor parties. In countries where the state-based party financing system created adequate resources for electoral mobilization and routine party maintenance, the successor party elites were more capable of reducing their reliance on local party branches, insulating themselves from recalcitrant members, and thus were able to increase the ideological adaptability of their parties. By contrast, in countries where a state-based party financing system did not create adequate resources for these successor parties, the parties were forced to rely on their local party branches for material support; thus, they were not capable of pursuing the same degree of ideological adaptation.

This argument is particularly relevant in the postcommunist party system setting because of a variety of underlying structural factors (1) these countries lack the Lipset Rokkan (1967) electoral cleavages where voter-party identification has been solidified; (2) these countries are undergoing a significant amount of rapid economic restructuring which has left their electorates increasingly unstable, fluid, and intent upon securing material benefits in exchange for votes. Hence, given the emergence of an ideological space where voters choose parties on the basis of the benefits that they receive, the need arises for parties to become public organizations that have to increase the material resources at their disposal if they are to succeed electorally. Even though our analysis does not subscribe wholeheartedly to the rational choice explanations for the malleability of ideological platforms, we agree that because of the increased chances for becoming part of the governing coalition, the paramount concern of the successor party leader is electoral success.

However, we argue that the degree to which successor party leaders achieve the ideological adaptation of these parties is governed by the aforementioned types of party financing. Hence, our argument complements existing arguments on the relationship between ideology and party organization.

Ideological Adaptation: Concepts, Measures, and Findings

The systematic empirical study of political ideology is notoriously difficult. Yet, to compare the divergent paths of ideological adaptation of different ex-communist parties, we will undertake precisely this task. To that end, we will utilize a concept of *ideological adaptation* that can be understood as the extent to which a political party transforms the shared conceptions held by party leaders and activists regarding their vision of society and the accompanying vision of what role their political party ought to play in society. A political party's ideology contains multiple content themes or multiple threads of concern.[8] Additionally, a political party's ideology, like any organization's, is "operationalizable" in the sense that it links an abstract set of ideas to the more concrete everyday problems confronted by the organization.[9] In our account we will borrow from an approach originally developed by Budge et al. (1987), previously utilized in the postcommunist setting by Ishiyama and Shafqat (2000), to examine content themes expressed in party programs. In so doing, our conception of a political party's ideology allows for a nuanced grasp of the possibly multiple threads of concern within a single organization.

Studies of party ideology have used a wide array of methodological strategies. In his work on party systems in Eastern Europe, Kitschelt et al. (1999) conducted surveys of party activists and electorates to place parties on a left-right axis. Without the resources at hand to undertake this type of analysis, content analysis offers itself as a useful mode of research. In a case study of the East German ex-communist party, Ziblatt (1998) utilized content analysis techniques on a very broad range of party documents, speeches, advertisements, and programs to provide an account that assessed all of the fine-grained ideological distinctions within the East German ex-communist party of the mid-1990s. However, in order to develop reliable and valid measures of ideological adaptation that can be used systematically to compare the ideological adaptation of several political parties across different countries, it is useful to focus exclusively on political party election programs. We conducted a content analysis of the complete texts of the most recent party programs of the Romanian PDSR (1997), the Polish SdRP (1999), the Czech KSČM (1999), the East German PDS (1993), the Slovak SDL (1996), and utilize Ishiyama's and Shafqat's findings on the Hungarian MSZP (1994).[10] Like Budge et al., we utilized "sentences" and "quasi-sentences" as our units of analysis since, as Budge et al. argue, sentences "form the natural grammatical unit in most languages" (1987, p. 24). We adopted the identical methodology used by Ishiyama and Shafqat (2000) in their recent study that coded each sentence according to a set of 32 categories grouped in seven domains. In their work, Ishiyama and Shafqat utilized these categories to examine the Hungarian, Polish, and Russian ex-communist parties (see Appendix A for a complete listing of themes and domains).

As in Ishiyama and Shafqat's (2000) account, we have created proreform and antireform cumulative indices that include all references to the political identity of the party and country. To comprise the proreform index, we follow Ishiyama's lead to code, for example, all positive references to social democracy, markets, capitalism, private property/privatization, enterprise, incentives, NATO, and the European Union as well as negative references to Marx, Lenin, Stalin, communism, and nationalism. By contrast, all positive references to communism, controlled economy, state control, nationalization, and national greatness and negative references to NATO, the European Union, markets, privatization, and social democracy constituted the components of the antireform index.[11] After coding each complete party program, we calculated a composite score for each party by dividing the total number of pro-reform "units" by a total of units coded to arrive at a proreform score (0–100): the higher the score, the more proreform the rhetoric of the party; the lower the score, the less proreform the rhetoric of the party.[12]

In Table 14.1, we present our findings.[13] In our sample of cases, the Hungarian (MSZP) and Polish ex-communist party (SdRP) have the highest proreform scores; the Slovak SDL has the third highest score, closely followed by the Romanian PDSR. The two lowest scoring parties, both with scores of less than 60, are the German PDS and the Czech KSČM. The findings largely confirm the conventional wisdom on the divergent trajectories of ex-communist parties, with one exception; the high score of the Romanian successor party. According to most accounts, the PDSR has made very few changes from the past (Murer, 1999). Still, under the leadership of Ion Iliescu, the party tended to be viewed as a "reform laggard" among the universe of ex-communist parties. However, since he was voted out of office in 1996, the party undertook a major and rapid overhaul of its ideology, embracing the causes of NATO and EU expansion and adopting the rhetoric of a European social democratic party. The extent to which this ideological change will actually translate into political change has been tested with the return of the PDSR to office in the fall of 2000.

Several additional observations are important. First, the top four ranked parties all explicitly adopt a "social democratic" agenda that advocates a "mixed" economy. By contrast, the two laggards—the East German and Czech parties—explicitly argue for increased state control over the economy, the nationalization of certain key sectors, and reject—in very strong language— the "neoliberal hegemony" of globalization. While the first four parties have reconciled themselves to the concept of the free market, the two lowest scoring parties by and large reject the notion of the free market. Second, the Hungarian, Polish, Romanian, and Slovak ex-communists are enthusiastic supporters of membership in NATO and the European Union. The Czech and East German party programs, however, are not. These parties alterna-

Table 14.1

Proreform Score for Most Recent Party Programs, 1990s

Party	Pro-reform score for 1999 party program
Hungarian MSZP	100 (1994), n=19
Polish SdRP/SLD	80.6 (1999), n=219
Slovak SDL	75.9 (1999), n=133
Romanian PDSR	72.6 (1999), n=270
East German PDS	63.2 (1993, n=139
Czech KSČM	33.5 (1999), n=141

Source: Authors' analysis. See Appendix A for coding procedure.

tively call for the withdrawal of the Czech Republic from NATO or for the complete elimination of NATO. In respect to the European Union, both parties in fact accept the supranational body but do so critically; the Czech party program rejects "one-sided" accession negotiations, and the East German party program calls for major reforms of the European Union. Despite these important differences, all five of the parties explicitly embrace democratic elections, reject (in varying degrees) the pre-1989 regimes, and seek to provide an alternative to "capitalism" on the one hand, and pre-1989 "communism" on the other. In short, in the ten years since communism's collapse, despite some minimal similarities, there are quite a range of postcommunist outcomes that require explanation.

Explanation: Organization, Resources, and Ideology

In our analysis, the type of successor party financing determines the degree of successor party ideological adaptability. The successor parties that participated in the creation of state-based party financing systems or those that maintained a significant part of their communist-era material resources have a greater amount of ideological adaptability because their elites are less reliant on their members for material support.[14] Conversely, the successor parties that were faced with state-based financing systems and that did not effectively decrease their members' share in their internal budgets did not allow their elites to effectively implement the same processes of ideological change.

In Table 14.2, we present the main contours of our argument and how it links to more traditional macro-level arguments. Our analysis begins with the distinctive modes of transition that Kitschelt et al. (1999) among others have identified: revolution from above, negotiated transition, and implosion. All of the regimes of Eastern and Central Europe experienced one of these types of regime change. The different paths of regime transition left each successor organization with a different level of material and nonmaterial re-

Table 14.2

Determinants of Ideological Adaptation in Six Postcommunist Countries

	National Patriotic (Romanian PDSR)	Pragmatic Reform (Hungarian-MSZP, Polish-SLD, Slovak SLD)	Leftist Retreat (Czech-KSČM, German PDS)
Mode of transition	From above	Negotiation	Implosion
Amount of resources left to successor party after transition	High	Medium	Low
Party financing strategy	Clientalism	State-centered funding	Membership-centered funding
Reliance on membership	Low	Low	High
Ideological adaptability	High	High	Low

sources. Those that led a revolution from above maintained greater control over party-state resources; those that imploded were left with the lowest level of resources; and those that negotiated their way out of power maintained moderate control over their resources. In response to these different postcommunist paths of change, successor parties in 1990–1991 supported the establishment of different systems of party financing: in countries where the party had maintained control over resources, clientalism emerged as the dominant form of party finance. In countries where the party exited communism with few resources, the party was forced to rely on party member contributions; and in parties that exited communism with a moderate level of resources, less reliance on membership was required. These varying party finance responses to the challenges of party competition left the leadership of some parties insulated from party members and free to respond to electoral incentives. In contrast, the leadership of other parties were captured by their party membership and were incapable of responding to similar electoral incentives for reform. In short, the ideological adaptability of former communist parties is a function of different systems of party finance and organization.

At one side of the extreme, as presented in Table 14.2, lies the Romanian successor party (PDSR) that benefited enormously from the protracted nature of the transition (Stevenson-Murer, 1999). The inability of the anticommunist forces to remove the ex-communists from power in the immediate post-transition period meant that the implemented laws concerning the successor party's resources were toothless when compared to the experience of the other successor parties. Hence, even in its first term of opposition, the Romanian successor party remained by far the most resource-endowed party in the country. Even more importantly, the absence of an effective change in the personnel of party leadership meant that the Romanian successor party could maintain the centralized structure of its communist past as well as its highly hierarchical internal organizational structure.

In the case of Hungary, the MSZP was stripped of the vast majority of its material resources, both in terms of real estate holdings as well as in terms of actual funds during the transitional period, finally releasing up to 90 percent of its communist-era assets (Waller 1995, 482). As part of the negotiated transition, the HSP cooperated with its political competitors in the creation of a state-centered financing system that provided campaign electoral assistance to parties based on their entrance into Parliament as well as on the number of seats that each party achieved. In comparison to other national systems, such as the Czech or German systems, the Hungarian system of party finance assured all parties a disproportionately high degree of public resources for the purposes of party finance. As a result, beginning in 1990, the winning parties in Hungary gained almost all of their funding from the state. In 1990, the Independent Smallholders Party received 93 percent of its financing from the state, the Christian Democratic People's Party gained 88 percent of its funding from the state, and even the Hungarian Socialist Party after gaining only 10.9 percent of parliamentary vote was assured 24 percent of its finances from the state (Lewis, 1998, 141). With the MSZP's reversal of electoral fortunes in 1994, 51 percent of the Hungarian Socialist Party's income came from the state and only 3 percent came from membership dues (Lewis, 1998, 139). Although a variety of analysts, including Ágh (1995), Waller (1995), and Ishiyama (1997a) have stressed the degree of internal party democracy and the degree of independence afforded to local party organizations in the MSZP, Lomax (1996) has shown the increased tendencies of the party's leadership toward centralization, especially in terms of parliamentary candidate selection; a tendency that has increased since the 1994 parliamentary elections and has provided the MSZP with a significant increase of state-based funds. In short, even as early as 1990, a party finance system was formalized in Hungary that insulated party leaders from their members; parliamentary representation was highly rewarded with increased material resources and the MSZP relied less on its members for material resources. As a result, the incentives for ideological adaptation were higher and the organizational constraints on adaptation were less, making ideological adaptation possible for the MSZP beginning in 1990.

Likewise, in Poland and Slovakia, the creation of a state system of party financing operated as a catalyst for the creation of increasingly centralized successor parties. Much like Hungary, these two countries rewarded electoral campaign resources on the basis of parliamentary representation. In Poland, as Waller (1995) has shown, the SdRP was able to retain a significant part of its assets, under the strong protection afforded by the Solidarity government. In terms of party financing this development meant that SdRP did not face the post-transition political environment without resources, as their Czech and East German counterparts did. As a result, the SdRP party leadership was also less reliant on its members. However, much like their Hungarian counterparts, the SdRP leaders developed a party financing system which rewarded more electorally successful parties, since it allocated state funds for the reimbursement of campaign expenses, on the basis of parliamentary representation. Given the use of a 5 percent electoral threshold and the use of the d'Hondt system of proportional representation for determining the final apportionment of seats, the SdRP, as Lewis (1998) has shown, was able to recoup twice its electoral outlay (Lewis 1998, 143), as part of the Union of the Democratic Left coalition. This institutional mechanism for the allocation of state resources for party financing increased the transformation of the SdRP from a member-based successor party to an electoral-professional party. By the end of the 1994 elections, which ushered the SdRP into the governing coalition, center-local and elite-based internal party relationships in Poland were being changed in favor of the party's elites (Lewis and Gortat 1995, 601). This increase in organizational centralization was compounded by an increase in the independence of the party's parliamentary members; as Gebethner has shown, the SdRP was not capable of effectively controlling the voting records of its parliamentary members (1996, 124–25).

In Slovakia, the SDL intentionally and strategically participated in the creation of a state-based system of party financing that shifted the burden of party financing away from member contributions alone. As Grzymala-Busse (1999) has shown, the aim of the SDL leadership in the early stages of the post-transition period has always been the organizational centralization of the successor party as well as the creation of a party membership that was biased against the inclusion of radical ex-communist activists. Hence, the creation of a state-based system of financing mirrored the Hungarian system, but provided for increased monetary contributions from firms and individuals.

In Germany, the imposition of the West German state-based system of party financing did not effectively change the PDS's reliance upon its members for material resources because the state allocation of party financing was dependent upon nationwide political participation. Beginning in 1991, 24 percent of the PDS total income was based on membership contributions. During the 1990s this figure has only grown, reaching a high of 63 percent in 1992 and leveling out to 46 percent in 1997 (PDS, 2001). Given the highly localized amount of political support for the PDS and the continued ideological rigidity of its more affluent West German members, this meant that even though PDS party elites were attempting to transform the PDS ideologically, they were organizationally thwarted by their members. This tension within the PDS became most striking at the Party Congress of May 2000. Moderate leaders of the party pushed for a new party program that would reject the "dogmatism" of young party members in western and eastern Germany. With the aim of subverting some of the more "radical" elements of the party program such as the inclusion of Germany in NATO, and the nationalization of industry, the party leadership sought to move the PDS closer to the political center in order to attract western voters. The aim was, as party leaders themselves admitted, to attract enough West German voters to guarantee the PDS more than the 5 percent national parliamentary threshold. All such efforts, however, foundered as a result of an entrenched membership that exerted great control over the finances and agenda of the party. Two of the reform leaders in the PDS announced their resignation from the party immediately following their programmatic failure in May 2000. Unlike the Hungarian, Polish, and Slovak cases, the East German ex-communist leaders remained "captured" by their members.

Similarly, the Czech Republic successor party's reliance upon membership for financial resources resulted in the nonimplementation of ideological adaptation. Despite the creation of a modest state-based system of party financing in the early 1990s, in comparison to other communist successor organizations, the KSČM still relied extensively upon its members for material resources. This reliance was formalized as a fixed proportion of member incomes (0.5 percent of their annual earnings) and increased in proportion to their parliamentary representatives. After the first round of elections, the Civic Movement (OD) victors gained only 77 percent of their income from the state (in contrast to the higher figure of 93 percent for the election victor in Hungary). More importantly, the KSČM received only 8.5 percent of its funding from the state and 36.7 percent of its funding from membership dues (Lewis, 1998, 138). As a result, the active KSČM membership has a high degree of programmatic authority within the party. Likewise, Kopecky (1996) has shown how the KSČM has enforced a high degree of parliamentary discipline, itself a result of an organizational structure that has explicitly codified "party in public office" with "party in central office" consultations on a variety of matters. In this sense, party members can even exert influence at the parliamentary level. The resulting dispersion of authority among party members has also been noted by Kroupa and Kostelecky (1996), who show how the KSČM's membership is spread throughout the country, and not just isolated in urban areas like the majority of its competitors. Partly as a result of the leaders' increased reliance upon membership dues since the early 1990s, the marginalized KSČM has helped push for legislation to increase state subsides for parties and has sought a lowering of the threshold for access to state funds. Beginning in March 2001, new legislation has been approved that increases the proportion of state funds to parties. This development, if our analytical framework has in fact identified a key explanatory variable, portends the potential de-radicalization of the Czech KSČM. Hence, even in an ideological space where promarket issues had the greatest amount of relevance (and Czech voters had consistently demonstrated that they were the most promarket voters in the postcommunist Eastern European setting), the KSČM leadership could not alter its ideological preferences.

Conclusions

Our account has sought to provide a new analytical lens through which to examine the postcommunist adaptation strategies of the formerly dominant Leninist political organizations in Eastern and Central Europe. As these organizations have attempted over the past ten years to transform themselves from Leninist organizations to electorally minded parties, one of the key but understudied features of that transformation has been the development of systems of party financing. As a result of divergent historical legacies, each of the former ruling organizations of the postcommunist world were left with different resource legacies, including different levels of membership, varying degrees of organizational capacity, and varying levels of financial resources. Taken together, each of these internal organizational factors in turn have shaped how each party responded to the new stimulus of electoral competition.

In order to understand why and how successor parties are capable of responding to the incentives for ideological adaptation, an analysis of electoral conditions often misses important efforts at ideological adaptation that have failed. A focus solely on the structural conditions of the communist legacy and the paths of postcommunist transition does not identify some of the critical causal mechanisms that have allowed some parties to adapt and have prevented other parties from doing so. Furthermore, structural accounts do not account for change. Are ex-communist parties, once on divergent paths of reform, permanently "locked in" to their trajectories of development? Our analysis has examined how the resources available to each party at communism's demise have affected the extent to which each party's leadership has been either captured or insulated from its membership to freely pursue ideological adaptation. Such an approach identifies the causal mechanisms of ideological adaptation. Furthermore, such an approach can help to identify the conditions of change; though the Czech and East German parties exited communism with fewer political resources than their Hungarian, Polish, Slovak, and Romanian neighbors, these two "resource poor" parties are not doomed to radicalism. If the Czech and East German parties could shift the internal balance of power away from their members and toward their party leadership, ideological adaptation would be possible. In short, in the postcommunist setting, social democracy involves an irony that Roberto Michels himself might perhaps recognize; to be a "successful" social democrat in postcommunist Eastern and Central Europe requires the removal of authority from party members and the centralization of authority under party leaders.[15]

APPENDIX A

Appendix A. Issue Domains and Theme Codes

Domain 1: Attitudes about the Past
101   Pro-Marxism, Pro-Leninism
102   Soviet, Communism
103   Anti-Marxism, anti-Leninism
104   Controlled/planned economy
105   Nationalization

Domain 2: External Relations with the West
201   Foreign contacts with Europe, the West or the world, neutral military
202   Military
203   Foreign contacts with the USSR, the Soviet Union, and the CMEA (Council for Mutual Economic Assistance)

Domain 3: Political Structure
301   Freedom, political and human rights
302   Social democracy, social democratic, democratic socialism
303   Government decentralization and local autonomy
304   Current government efficiency and inefficiency
305   Current government corruption
306   Current government effectiveness

Domain 4: Evaluations of Current Economic Situation
401   Enterprise
402   Private property/privation
403   Incentives
404   Capitalism, market
405   Inflation
406   Unemployment

Domain 5: Welfare and Quality of Life
501   Environment, environmental protection
502   Social security
503   Social welfare, social equality, and social justice
504   Education/cultural promotion

Domain 6: Nation, National Way of Life, Security
601 Defense of national way of life, patriotism
602 Promotion of national traditions, culture
603 Law and order
604 National social harmony

Domain 7: Social groups
701 Labor
702 Agriculture and farmers
703 Other noneconomic social groups
704 Defense of national ethnic minorities

Notes

1. A potential criticism of the framing of this puzzle could be the claim that some parties do not pursue social democratization not because they are "incapable" of it but rather because they do not want to reform. Indeed, analysts have correctly argued the electoral conditions in each country vary, perhaps suggesting that in comparison to Hungary, Poland, Slovakia, and Romania, there are simply less electoral incentives for the Czech KSČM and the German PDS, for example, to move closer to the "ideological center." Yet, some evidence suggests precisely the opposite. In Germany, during the Spring of 2000, the PDS party leadership self-consciously and explicitly sought to drop some of the more leftist elements of its program. Party leaders such as Andre Brie and Gregor Gysi defended this failed attempt to move the party away from the far left with the justification that in order to guarantee more than the 5 percent electoral threshold required by German electoral law, the PDS had to moderate their message to attract West German voters. Unlike the fates of efforts at ideological adaptation in Hungary and Poland, this effort failed. Similarly, in the Czech Republic, the KSČM faces an electorate that in most surveys displays a significantly more promarket orientation than either Hungary or Poland (Markowski, 1997). Given the absence of a viable competitor to their left, the KSČM party elites could easily move closer to the center, especially in terms of issues concerning the pace and the scope of market-oriented reform, without being worried that they would lose electoral support. If anything, such a change in terms of ideological position would increase their electoral results and thereby increase their chances for participation in the governing coalition. In short, linking national electoral conditions to ideological adaptability finds at best mixed empirical support.

2. Indeed, as Ishiyama (1997) has argued, successor parties that have evolved from "national consensus" communist regimes, such as Poland and Hungary, are more likely to survive over time than successor parties that have emerged from different types of communist regimes.

3. Bielasiak (1997) argues that Eastern and Central European party systems have moved closer toward pluralization and have not yet reached consolidation because the "weakness of party institutionalization prevents the final shift of the political structure to a consolidated equilibrium rooted in a close interrelationship between society and polity" (Bielasiak 1997, 41).

4. As Szczerbiak (1999) has shown, the SdRP entered the post-transition period of party competition not only with significantly higher levels of national membership, vis-à-vis its competitors, but also with a national organizational infrastructure that included local party branches complete with the material resources that make party organization and voter mobilization effective (telephones, faxes, copiers, and computers).

5. We focus intentionally on the mobilizational attributes of large-scale, nationally-dispersed organizations of the successor parties because as Bohrer et al. (2000) have shown, between 1990 and 1999, increased voter turnout benefited the electoral fortunes of the successor parties in the postcommunist countries that we are analyzing.

6. Following Janda and Colman (1998), we argue that the organizational resources of the successor parties differed from those of their competitors and that these organizational resources were relatively immobile in the time period under consideration.

7. It is important to note at this point that although the Polish party emerged as more financially capable than the other parties, it had nowhere near the financial resources that the Romanian party had.

8. Our conception of political ideology and the methodology of analyzing content themes is borrowed from an approach originally developed by Nathan Leites (1953) but further developed by Alexander George (1969) and Walker (1990, 1995).

9. See Alexander George (1969, 191).

10. Our analysis relied on English translations of the most recent party programs of each of the parties under study with the exception of the Hungarian HSP's program. The English translations of the Polish SdRP program and the Slovak SLD program can be found at the Friedrich Ebert Stiftung in Bonn, Germany. The English translations of the East German PDS program and the Czech KSČM programs have been provided by the respective parties themselves. Our data on the Hungarian HSP come from Ishiyama and Shafqat's (2000, 451) study of the HSP.

11. A complete listing of the themes and domains appears in Appendix A.

12. For a more complete description and discussion of this methodology, see Ishiyama and Shafqat (2000, 450–451).

13. Calculated as the number of references to proreform terms, divided by the number of proreform + antireform terms. A test of the reliability of these findings was conducted using two coders to assess the intercoder reliability of the results. Of the five party programs analyzed here, the intercoder reliability score was 0.88 for all the cases.

14. We utilize the term "resources" to refer to (1) party membership; (2) expertise; (3) material resources (e.g. property), and (4) nonmaterial organizational resources (e.g. local and regional offices).

15. Robert Michels, *Political Parties: A Sociological Study of the Oligarchical Tendencies of Modern Democracy* (Glencoe: Free Press, 1958).

15

The Return of the Left and Democratic Consolidation in Poland and Hungary

Valerie Bunce

> . . . from an ideological point of view I was never a communist in Poland, I've seen very few communists, especially since the 1970s. I met a lot of technocrats, opportunists, reformers, liberals."
>
> —*Aleksander Kwasniewski,*
> *President of Poland (elected in November, 1995)*
> *and leader of the Social Democratic Party*
> *(quoted in Perlez, 1995: A3).*

In the immediate aftermath of 1989, Hungary and Poland appeared to be two countries in the postsocialist region with the strongest case for a rapid and successful transition from dictatorship to democracy. In particular, in comparison with their neighbors, these two Central European states began the process of democratization with a number of distinctive assets. They were old, not new states; they were relatively homogeneous in their national and religious composition, and publics and elites alike within these two states tended to concur on all those thorny issues surrounding the definition of/and membership in the nation. Moreover, their transition to democracy had been preceded for a decade and more by liberalized politics (and economics) during the socialist era. Their claims to having civil and political societies, therefore, were, by regional standards at least, compelling. These countries were also advantaged in several other ways. Poland and Hungary were the leaders in the events of 1989; their transitions to democracy involved pacting between the opposition and the communists; and their first competitive elections produced a clear victory for the opposition forces. Whether judged by the standards of new democracies within or outside the postsocialist region, therefore, Poland and Hungary seemed to be unusually well-positioned to both put their socialist pasts behind them and to build sustainable democratic orders (see, for example, Karl, 1990; Snyder and Vachudova, 1997; Linz and Stepan, 1996; Bunce, 1999a, 1999b, 1998b).

The optimists, however, were in for a surprise. In the second competitive parliamentary elections held in Hungary in 1994, the ex-communists registered a decisive victory. In a similar fashion (though with a smaller political mandate), the ex-communists returned to power in Poland—by coming in first in the parliamentary elections of 1993 and by capturing the office of the presidency in 1995. With the ex-communists returning to power in both Poland and Hungary, many analysts began to revise their rosy predictions. In particular, several concerns came to the fore. In all those countries in the postsocialist region where the ex-communists had been able to maintain political power through more or less genuinely competitive elections, the transitions to democracy and capitalism had both been compromised (Bunce, 1994; Fish, 1998). Another worry was whether public support for the ex-communists might reflect either nostalgia for the socialist past, deep dissatisfaction with democratic politics and capitalist economics, or some combination of the two. Finally, there was a temptation to draw a parallel with Weimar Germany, wherein polarization among parties had been the first step in the road to democratic breakdown. That this was also the story throughout much of interwar Eastern and Central Europe by the end of the 1920s, only reinforced the seeming applicability of the Weimar scenario.

The purpose of this chapter is to look more closely at the return of the left in Poland and Hungary and to assess its impact on the consolidation of these two new democracies. In order to do so, I will analyze:

1) the various reasons why democracies seem to break down;
2) the reasons why the left returned to power in Poland and Hungary;
3) the behavior of the left in power, and
4) the impact of the Polish parliamentary elections of 1997 and the Hungarian parliamentary elections of 1998 (both of which shifted the left from government to opposition).

As we will discover, the return of the ex-communists to power in Hungary and Poland was not a problem for democracy. Indeed, its impact was quite the opposite. The return of the left—at least in these cases—functioned as an *investment* in democratic governance. This conclusion, moreover, is only reinforced by the recent return to power of rightist forces in both Poland and Hungary.

Why Young Democracies Fail or Endure

There is, unfortunately, no ready list of factors that can be cited to explain why some new democracies endure, whereas others fail to take root or, in the extreme, collapse. However, there are three bodies of literature that provide some useful ideas. The first is the work on democratic consolidation in postwar Germany and Italy and, more recently, southern Europe and Latin America (see, for example, Baker, Dalton, and Hildebrandt, 1981; Putnam, 1993; Higley and Gunther, 1992; Gunther, 1995; Tarrow, 1995; Mainwaring and Scully, 1995; O'Donnell, 1993 and 1994; Linz and Stepan, 1996). The focus of this work is, among other things, concerned with the process by which new and uncertain democracies, following the period of transition (that is, the period extending from the break with authoritarian rule to the holding of the first competitive elections), become rooted, routinized, and, thus, durable. Second, there is the literature on the breakdown of democracy. Here, the focus has been primarily on the collapse of democracy in interwar Europe and postwar Latin America (see, for example, Bermeo, 1994; Linz, 1990; Valenzuela and Linz, 1994; Linz and Stepan, 1978). Finally, there is a growing body of work on the problems and possibilities surrounding transitions from state socialism in eastern Europe. While this overlaps to some degree with the other two bodies of literature, it also points to some distinctive problems and possibilities arising from the nature of the postcommunist context (see, especially, Bunce, 1995a, 1995b; Osa, 1995; Ost, 1995).

When combined, these three families of research suggest two very different lines of argument. One begins with the assumptions that new democracies are fragile and that democratic consolidation is a long and difficult process. This then leads to a goal of identifying all those factors that have the potential for derailing democracy—for example, angry and mobilized publics; low levels of economic development and/or deteriorating economic performance (especially when expressed through growing levels of unemployment); deficits in social capital and other aspects of a democratic political culture; political polarization; and institutional problems, such as presidential (as opposed to parliamentary) government, incomplete civilian control over the military, and easily invoked emergency powers.

The other approach begins by assuming that democracy can take root under a variety of circumstances and that democratic consolidation is best understood in the minimalist sense of the survival of the democratic rules of the game. This then leads to the argument that threats to democratic rule are those developments—and only those developments—that tempt publics and, especially, elites to opt out of the democratic game (see, especially, Przeworski, 1986, 1991). The concern in this approach, therefore, is with the establishment of democratic rules, the degree to which democracy functions as a political monopoly, and the incentives available to publics and elites to play by the democratic rules.

There are, of course, costs and benefits attached to adopting either of these approaches. While the first approach has the advantage of providing a concrete list of threats, it has three major disadvantages. One is that it provides in effect a long list of challenges to democracy, rather than a shorter list of threats to democracy. Another is that it is easily misinterpreted. Some so-called threats to democracy—for example, the stresses posed by economic liberalization—can under some circumstances function as assets in the process of democratic consolidation (see, for example, Bunce, 1994 and 1998a; Schamis, 1997). A final problem is that this approach under-predicts democratic survival; that is, it seems to generate a lot of false negatives. The gaming approach also has assets, as well as liabilities. Its major assets are that it is parsimonious, it accounts for the high survival rate of new democracies, and it focuses our attention directly on the issue at hand—the disruption of democratic rule. Its major liability is that it borders on the tautological. What is being argued is in effect that threats to democracy are those developments that lead to nondemocratic politics.

The way out of this problem is to use the first approach to fill in the blanks of the second approach. More specifically, we can argue the following: First, the key question in democratic governance is whether democracy functions as a political monopoly. Second, whether this happens depends upon two factors: whether democratic institutions and a set of rules are in place and whether elites are playing by those rules. Finally, whether elites choose to play within rather than outside the democratic game depends upon the incentives generated by economic and political developments over the course of democratization (including those suggested by the first approach). Thus, what interests us in this analysis is the extent to which the return of the left in Poland and Hungary has created incentives and disincentives for elites to play the democratic game.

Why the Left Won

Let us now set the stage for answering this question by reviewing the electoral results.[1] In Hungary, the Hungarian Socialist Party (HSP) won 54 percent of the seats in the May 1994 parliamentary elections. This involved a considerable increase in their seats from the May 1990 elections, where they won a mere 10.89 percent of the seats. The Alliance of Free Democrats (AFD) came in second (as they had in 1990), with 18 percent of the seats. The sharpest decline in support in 1994 was for the Democratic Forum—the dominant party in the previous government, which had ruled from 1990 to 1994. It received 9.5 percent of the vote in 1994, sharply down from 42.2 percent in 1990.

In the Polish parliamentary elections of October 1993, the Democratic Left Alliance (DLA) won 20.41 percent of the vote (up from 11.89 percent in 1991) and was awarded 37 percent of the seats in the Sejm (as compared with 13 percent in 1991). The second-place party was the Polish Peasant Party (PPL), which received 15.4 percent of the vote and 29 percent of the seats. This election was then followed by the Polish presidential election[2] of No-

vember 1995 (which involved a runoff between the top two vote-getters in
the first round, since no candidate received a majority). In this election,
Aleksander Kwasniewski (the candidate of the ex-communists, or the DLA)
received 51.5 percent of the vote and the incumbent, Lech Walesa, received
48.5 percent.[3]

Before we move on to an explanation of these electoral outcomes, several
points need to be made. First, the most dramatic electoral shift in favor of the
ex-communist left was in Hungary from 1990 to 1994 (see, for example,
Girnius, 1995a, 1995b, 1995c; Lewis, 1994; Barany, 1995a and 1995b; Racz
and Kukorelli, 1995). Second, only in Hungary did the ex-communist left—
that is, the HSP[4]—win an absolute majority. Here, it is important to note, by
contrast, the following for Poland:

1) the actual percentage of the vote won by the DLA was only 20.4
   percent in 1993 (and 7 percent higher in 1997);
2) the new Polish electoral system introduced in 1993 worked in effect
   to leave 35 percent of those voting without representation in the
   Sejm in 1993, and
3) a mere shift of 1.5 percent of the vote, plus one, in the direction of
   Lech Walesa would have led to his reelection as president
   (Osiatynski, 1995; Ash, 1996).

Thus, the actual mandate of the newly empowered left was much smaller
in Poland than in Hungary.

The end result of both the Hungarian and Polish elections, however, was
the same; the formation of a coalition government. In Hungary, the HSP and
the AFD (the party of the former intellectual opposition) formed a government. This was unnecessary, given the size of the left's victory, but it was an
action that was strongly supported by the public and by the HSP (which saw
it as a mechanism to enhance their legitimacy and to ward off fears of a
"communist return"). While every member of the HSP parliamentary delegation supported the idea of the coalition, members of the AFD were more
divided. The size of the coalition—72 percent of the seats—also meant that
all kinds of important legislation, requiring by law a two-thirds majority,
could be passed. This is particularly the case, since the 150 page agreement
forming the coalition laid out, among other things, strict rules enforcing
intraparty discipline (see, especially, Racz and Kukorelli, 1995; Pataki, 1994).

In Poland, a coalition was also formed between the top two vote-getters,
the DLA and the PPL (the latter, it must be remembered, was also a political
survivor of the communist era). This gave them just under two-thirds of the
seats in the Sejm—65.9 percent. Thus, fully one-half of the PPL deputies
could defect, and the coalition government would still have a majority of the
seats. It is also important to note that the coalition government formed was

the first relatively stable parliamentary majority to develop in postcommunist Poland. This reflected the ways in which the new electoral law of 1993 worked to reduce sharply the number of parties in the Sejm—from 29 to 6.[5] However, from 1993 to 1997, there were, nonetheless, three different governments (see Karpinski, 1997).

Let us now turn to the key question: why did the left win? We can begin to locate some answers to this question by comparing Poland and Hungary with the Czech Republic. This is a useful comparison, because, while these three countries are widely understood as being quite similar to each other in the sense of being "ahead" in the race to democracy and capitalism, they diverge in the variable that concerns us. Thus, while the ex-communists have returned to power in Poland and Hungary, they have failed to do so in the Czech Republic—even after the June, 1996 elections.[6] This comparison, as Zoltan Barany (1995a) has argued, reveals several important points. Namely, it hints at the importance of economic stress in predisposing voters to support the ex-communists. The contrast between these three countries on this dimension is clear, whether we examine indicators of economic performance (such as economic growth or trends in industrial output, income per capita, inflation, and unemployment), or public evaluations of their economic situation around the time of the election,[7] which reveal economic downturns in Hungary and Poland far more dramatic than those registered during the Great Depression (Greskovits, 1998; Bakos, 1994).

Another important contrast between Poland and Hungary, on the one hand, and the Czech Republic, on the other, is in the nature of communist party rule during the last years of state socialism. For a variety of reasons, Poland and Hungary were the most liberalized countries in Eastern Europe, or to borrow Barany's phrase (1995b), the "happiest barracks in the bloc." By contrast, the Czechoslovak regime was much more hard-line—both before and after the Prague Spring. This contrast is evident, whether we examine the issues of economic reform, the size and institutionalization of the dissident community, the exercise of political freedoms, or the degree of conformity to Soviet political, economic, and military dictates. These differences had two important implications. In Hungary and Poland, reformers dominated the Communist Party, whereas in Czechoslovakia dominance by hard-liners was the rule. Once state socialism collapsed, therefore, the transition to a social democratic party was much easier to make—and more believable—in Hungary and Poland than in Czechoslovakia (a point to which we shall return later in this chapter).[8]

This also meant that publics in Hungary and Poland had a more positive view of their communist parties than did publics in Czechoslovakia.[9] While in the first two cases, the communists oversaw significant economic and political liberalization during the last decade of communist party rule, in Czechoslovakia hard-line politics and Stalinist economics remained the order of the day. While it is certainly true that the Poles were far less supportive of "their" communists than were the Hungarians (which helps us understand why the Hungarian Socialists did so much better than their Polish counterparts in their recent parliamentary elections), Polish voters were also influenced by the facts that:

1) martial law and not "party law" was declared in Poland in December, 1981 (and was widely understood to be a choice that the Soviets made);

2) one-third of the members of the Polish United Workers Party—the Polish communists—had in fact joined Solidarity between 1980 and 1981 (Wasilewski, 1995a), and

3) with the lifting of martial law in 1982 came economic reforms and a search throughout the rest of the decade for a workable compromise between communist party rule and significant economic and political liberalization.

A third difference—and one that follows from the previous point—is the mode of transition from authoritarian rule. In Poland and Hungary in 1989, an economic and political crisis (the latter caused in part by Gorbachev and his reforms) led the communists to propose a roundtable between themselves and the opposition on the future contours of the system. This led to the end of their political hegemony and to competitive elections that they lost—the latter an outcome they did not expect (especially in Poland), but which they nonetheless accepted. This was a crucial stage in the transition and, especially in the Polish case (because it was June 1989 and not a year later), set a region-wide precedent. By contrast, the end of communist party rule in Czechoslovakia occurred not because the communists struck deals with the opposition, but rather because hundreds of thousands of citizens mobilized in a matter of days against the regime. Thus, the Czechoslovak communists did not put their power on the line and did not participate in developing the new order. Instead, they were forced from power, and the new rules of the game were developed without them—and, to some degree, against them. They were placed, in short, in the position of defending the old order—a position that undermined their potential for playing a political role in the new order that followed.

The contrast between the Czech Republic, on the one hand, and Hungary and Poland, on the other, allows us, therefore, to identify some key factors explaining the return of the left in the latter two countries. In particular, what seemed to benefit the left was economic stress, relatively positive public views of the left (especially in Hungary), and the legitimacy of the left's claim to being a social democratic party that played by the democratic rules of the game.

Let us now turn to a more intensive look at why the left won in Poland and Hungary. There are a number of reasons. First, the left won because there were a large number of voters who supported their platform; that is, a strong commitment to capitalism, democracy, and joining Europe (which echoed the position of the liberal parties). This was coupled with a call for reducing the human costs of the transition to capitalism (which distinguished the left from the liberals) (see Bunce, 1998a).[10] This position, of course, invited a number of jokes—for example, Ryszard Bugaj (one of the leaders of the Union of Labor Party—the other left party in the 1993 elections and one of the spinoffs of Solidarity), commented with respect to the Democratic Left Alliance in Poland that: "Not only are they still communists, now they're capitalists, too!" (quoted in Tymowski, 1994: 99).

However, it was also a popular position, because it managed to resonate with a broad range of people, including those who were losers in the economic transition, or who were likely to be losers in the near future (for example, workers in large state enterprises, clerical workers dependent upon a large state, pensioners and those living outside large metropolitan centers); those who supported the economic and political transition, but were dissatisfied with the prevailing approach; those who wanted fewer politicians and more professionals running things (which was a particular concern in Hungary); and those who were ideological leftists as a consequence of the cultural residues of state socialism (see, for example, Mason, 1995).[11] Indeed, it is here where we find yet another reason for the much higher levels of support for the ex-communists in Hungary than in Poland; that is, greater political support in Hungary for the leftist ideology.[12]

At the same time, the ex-communists enjoyed a virtual political monopoly on the left. In Hungary and to a lesser extent, Poland (since there we find the Union of Labor—a new party in 1993), there is no well-developed leftist party, aside from the ex-communists. This is primarily because (1) the left as a political ideology has been tainted by all the years of communist rule and thus has drawn few political entrepreneurs in its direction since the collapse of communist party hegemony (a factor which was only reinforced by the poor showing of the left in the first postcommunist elections), and; (2) the nature of the economic transition in Poland and Hungary—with its twin emphases on structural economic adjustment and a rapid transition to capitalism—left little room for leftist ideology, while concentrating the terms of elite political debate on the right end of the political spectrum. When combined, these two factors suggest a very simple explanation. The left won because of high demand and limited political supply.

To this explanation we can add two more factors.[13] One is that the communists won because their primary concern was winning the election, whereas other concerns seemed to have preoccupied their competitors. As Andrzej Tymowski (1994: l02) put it: Despite the handicap of its PZPR (the Polish acronym for the communist party) past, the SLD (or DLA, as we have termed it) never lost sight of the simple rule that elections are won by getting out the vote in the hustings, not by arguing in Warsaw salons over high moral principles. This insight into electoral arithmetic escaped most of the post-Solidarity parties.

A similar point was recently made by Timothy Garton Ash (1996: 10), when he argued that: "Former communists . . . also have the habits and discipline of doing patient, boring political groundwork, which former dissidents and intellectuals generally do not."

Thus, as is often the case in democratic politics, one party won primarily because the other parties lost—or, put into our particular context, the left won in part because the right lost. If the right in Hungary and Poland was hurt by its failure to practice electoral rationality, it was also undermined by its previous political success. In the Hungarian case, four years of rule by a coalition dominated by the Democratic Forum had left voters hostile to this party and, more generally, to parties on the right. In this sense, as Bela Greskovits (1998) has argued, the vote for the HSP was a protest vote against the Forum—just as the vote for the Forum in 1990 was a protest vote against the ex-communists. In the Polish case, the weakness of the right was less a matter of what it did while in office (though the instability of governing coalitions from 1991 to 1993 did not help) than its more general tendency toward fragmentation following the breakup of the Solidarity movement (see, especially, Lewis, 1994; Osiatynski, 1995; Tymowski, 1994; Millard, 1994; Zubek, 1994). As Jacek Wasilewski and Edmund Wnuk-Lipinski (1996: 16) so elegantly express the dilemma of Solidarity in a postcommunist setting:

> Solidarity—like a character from an ancient tragedy—created the situation that led to its unavoidable annihilation. Subverting communism, promoting democracy, pluralism and the market economy; it fundamentally changed social reality, the perception of that reality, and even the language in which this reality was described. And all these changes questioned its identity, and negated the very justification of its existence: solidarity.
>
> What all this meant in the Polish context was that rightest parties spent a great deal of time killing each other off, while the left stood back and reaped the benefits. The left was advantaged in this process, no doubt, by both its tradition of democratic centralism and the departure from its intraparty environs of particularly troublesome leaders and followers who had opted to build their future on the basis of economic, not political capital (Tarkowski, 1990).[14]

We can now put the pieces of these electoral puzzles together. The ex-communists returned to power in Poland and Hungary because of (1) the economic stress of the transition (which made leftist claims appealing, while predisposing voters to throw the incumbent rascals out—which in these two cases were rightest parties); (2) the left had some historical support for its claim to being a social democratic party (see, in particular, Seleny, 1994); (3) there was a sizeable left constituency demanding representation, and the ex-communists were the only party willing and able to respond to that demand; and (4) because the political right, fragmented and closely tied to the traumas of transition, proved to be a weak political opponent. The question now becomes: what does this suggest about Polish and Hungarian democracy? On the one hand, it suggests two worrisome possibilities. One is political polarization, a common prelude to the breakdown of democracy (see Linz and Stepan, 1978; Kaufman, 1986). However, the electoral results do not show a polarized electorate. In Hungary, the left won, its platform was social democratic, and the moderates, or the Free Democrats, which had a program relatively similar to that of the left came in second. The extreme right—for example, Istvan Çsurka's Hungarian Path Party—did not even get enough votes to be represented in Parliament.

Moreover, the government that formed was composed of two parties—the HSP and the DF—that were located on the moderate left and the moderate right of the political continuum, respectively. Thus, in Hungary, it could be argued that neither the extreme left nor the extreme right did well in the elections. In the Polish case, the left won, once again, on a social democratic platform, and a series of moderate right parties followed in their vote tallies. As in Hungary, moreover, the extreme right did very poorly and is not represented in Parliament. All this would seem to suggest that the victory of the left in these two cases did not lead to or reflect political polarization, and that the victory of the left in fact worked to drain support from the extreme right (on this point, see Bunce, 1994).[15] The lesson for all to learn, then, was that democracy had managed to tame the left as well as the right—a lesson that is considered crucial for democratic consolidation (see Di Palma, 1990).

The other concern is that the victory of the left points to a great deal of public dissatisfaction with the postcommunist experience, particularly in Hungary, given the size of the leftist vote. But is this a problem for democracy? It would be if (1) voters were rejecting democracy and capitalism by voting for the left and rejecting the right, and; (2) voters thought they were supporting a return to authoritarian politics. However, there is no empirical support for these interpretations. First, public opinion surveys in Poland and Hungary point to strong and widespread support for democratic institutions and procedures—support that also appears in public opinion polls in some of the other postcommunist states, including Russia (see, especially, the sophisticated distinctions drawn by Whitefield and Evans, 1994). The protest vote, in short, was against rightest politicians and policies, not democratic politics, and it was about ideological readjustment, not ideological transformation. Second, there is no evidence that the public viewed the left as communist; rather, the sense was that the ex-communists were social democrats and were members of a party that was not appreciably different from other political parties (see, especially, CBOS, April, 1994: 2).

On the other hand, there are a number of reasons to see the victory of the left as an investment in democratization. Here, one can note that the left won for what could be termed "good democratic reasons." The election was fair; the left used appeals that presented a particular variation on the economic and political transition, but without rejecting the process in any way and without resorting to various sensationalist appeals, such as nationalism; the left ran by all accounts a clean as well as an efficient campaign (see, for example, Jasiewicz, 1994; Karpinski, 1996) and appealed to a broad constituency that had not been well-represented in the previous election.

The final point is crucial. Rather than viewing these elections as a contraction of democratic rule, they should be viewed as an expansion of democracy. A wide variety of people and their political perspectives, excluded from political influence in the first round of elections, were brought into the democratic process (see Mason, 1995, for a different interpretation).[16] Democracy, in short, was broadened. This is important, whether we focus on publics or elites. In the public case, we can point to increasing turnout over the course of these parliamentary elections, as well as the participation of a large number of voters who did not vote the first time around. In the elite case, we can remind ourselves of one precondition for a successful transition from authoritarian to democratic rule. As Robert Kaufman reminds us:

> . . . the formation of durable polyarchies requires, at least during the formative periods, accommodation with the still powerful economic and political forces on which the old authoritarian order was based (Kaufman, 1986: 100, quoted in Kaminski and Kurczewska, 1995: 6n).

This leads to one more advantage to be gained from the return of the ex-communists to political power: turnover in governing parties. As a number of specialists have argued, one key test of democratic consolidation is the capacity of democracy to survive a change in ruling parties. Thus, many specialists pronounced Germany a stable democracy, once the long-ruling Christian Democrats shared power with the Social Democrats in 1965 and then became the opposition in 1969. So too, many analysts have made the same argument when viewing the victory of the Socialists in Spain in 1982 (see, especially, Maravall and Santamaria, 1986; Share, 1989).[17] What is important about party turnover can be stated succinctly. Losers learn that they can win, and winners learn that they can lose. If losers can win, then the incentives for the "outs" to play the democratic game increase. At the same time, if winners can lose, the uncertainty that defines democratic politics is institutionalized. Another important implication is that democratic institutions are shown to be successful in managing political change. Finally, turnover means that a larger circle of elites will become "implicated" in the democratic process—which means, among other things, that more will be exposed to democratic experiences and thus to the cognitive changes necessary for authoritarians to become democrats (see Bermeo, 1992: 275).

Elections, of course, are one thing, and governing often another. Let us now turn to an assessment of the left in power.

Ex-Communists in Office[18]

Evaluating the impact of the left in office on democratic governance can be reduced to a simple question. Have the ex-communists been the social democrats they have claimed to be, or have they functioned, instead, as Leninists with new names? Embedded in this straightforward question, however, is a series of complex issues. First, at the level of values, have the ex-communists rejected authoritarian politics and embraced capitalism and democracy? Second, at the level of behavior, have they been playing by the democratic rules of the game? Third, have they pursued policies that further the transition to democracy and capitalism? Finally, to what degree have existing democratic institutions functioned to constrain the ex-communists?

The first question is a difficult one to answer. Elites rarely reveal their true sentiments—especially in a democratic order, with the tendency to say things that will please the public. Moreover, the historical burden of the ex-communists makes them unusually aware of the costs of revealing any authoritarian sentiments they might hold. In this sense, their professed commitments to capitalist liberal democracy during their campaigns for office could simply mean that they know what they need to do to win votes.[19]

Even more important is the question of whether it is valid to assume that the communists during their years in power were authoritarians, rejected capitalism and democracy, and, thus, had to undergo a dramatic shift in their ideological perspectives, following the dramatic events of 1989. As Anna Seleny (1994) has argued in her careful analysis of reform discourse in Hungary during the last decade of communist party rule, the communists in fact underwent a series of changes—in values, membership, and leadership—that served as a prelude for the end of their hegemony and for their full participation in a liberalized economic and political context. Similar arguments, moreover, have been made about the Polish communists (see Wasilewski and Wnuk-Lipinski, 1995). As Jacek Wasilewski (1995a: 117–118) has summarized:

> . . . the new elite was not formed in a spontaneous way, at the moment when the ancien regime breathed for the last time. Rather, the elite passed through a long process during which it absorbed various ideological influences, worked out operational strategies, and established organizational

structures. . . . All this occurred during the time when communism was still vital in Poland.

Indeed, this is a major reason why we see pacted transitions in Poland and Hungary and why the transition to a new order, despite the loss of the ex-communists in the first competitive elections, was peaceful. To revise Marx: ruling classes do give up power willingly, especially when they see no alternative and when their concern is less one of holding onto the past, which is widely understood as bankrupt, than jockeying for position in the future (see, especially, Urban, 1991).

Finally, there is some question as to whether "deauthoritarianization" of the elites is a relevant issue when considering the process of democratization. As Dankwart Rustow (1970) argued long ago and Barrington Moore (1966) even before that, democracy does not in fact require democratic-minded elites. Indeed, how could it, since the engineers of democracy are so often those who once wielded authoritarian powers (see also Di Palma, 1990). Thus, just as a democratic political culture at the mass level is perhaps understood best as an effect rather than as a cause of democracy (see, especially, McDonough, Barnes and Pina, 1986), so the same can be said for elites. A democratic elite political culture, in short, probably emerges—if it emerges at all—as the result of socialization within a longstanding democratic system, and as a result as well of incentives, alternatives, and learning.

This leads us to the second issue: the behavior of the ex-communists. Here, one can observe that the ex-communists in Hungary and Poland, when outside the government in the parliaments of 1990–1994 and 1991–1993, respectively, played by the democratic rules of the game. This says something, among other things, about how they had changed in the last years of state socialism, how they saw their future, and, thus, how they calculated their interests (Grzymala-Busse, 1998a). Moreover, their behavior during the most recent elections points to their willingness to play within rather than outside democratic politics (despite the fact that polls prior to these elections, especially in Poland, understated the extent of socialist party support). Indeed, what is striking about the Hungarian and Polish cases in particular is the extent to which the electoral campaigns of the ex-communists did not just embrace democracy and capitalism, but also refrained from the kinds of divisive appeals that one found in some of the other parties competing with them for power (for instance, the incumbent Democratic Forum in Hungary) and, elsewhere, in other former communist parties, as in Bulgaria, Romania, Belarus, Russia, and Serbia. Third, since forming governments, the ex-communists have behaved in ways that conform closely to democratic practices (see, for instance, Ágh and Kurtan, 1995; Pataki, 1994; Oltay, 1995; Grzymala-Busse, 1998a).

At the same time, there are clear indications that the ex-communists are committed to the transition to a democratic and capitalist order, or at least as committed as their rightest predecessors.[20] This is most evident if we focus on their foreign policies. The leftist governments recently in power have been quite active in building cooperative relations with their neighbors, in pushing for admission of their countries to NATO, and in pressing the European Union for full membership (see Bunce, 1998b). Indeed, one could argue that there is a correlation between leftist governments and support for regional cooperation, if one compares the recent foreign policies of the Czech Republic versus Poland and Hungary. This correlation, moreover, follows directly from the policy platforms of the rightest ruling party of the Czech Republic versus the leftist ruling parties of Poland and Hungary.

Trends in domestic policy, moreover, suggest a commitment to proceeding with the transition begun by their predecessors. For example, the coalition government in power in Hungary from 1944–1998 moved slowly at first when addressing the pressing need for economic austerity measures and for cutting back on an increasingly burdensome welfare state. However, by early 1995, after the departure of a socialist finance minister who fought hard for an austerity budget, the Socialist-Free Democratic coalition finally bit the bullet (see Gedeon, 1995; Szilagyi, 1995), a bullet their rightest predecessors, it must be noted, dodged for four years. Thus, ironically, it was the ex-communist-led Hungarian government, facing a tension endemic throughout the postcommunist region between attracting support and introducing unpopular economic measures, that carried out the unpalatable and quite rightest policies of economic stabilization.

This leads to the final question. To what degree are the democratic institutions now in place functioning to constrain the powers of the ex-communists? It could be argued that the institutional limits on their powers are minimal—most generally, because these institutions are too new to be strong and, more specifically, because these parties enjoy such a large percentage of the seats. To this can be added the problem that, since the fall of 1997, political power in Poland is divided between an ex-communist president and a rightest coalition government. This is a sure recipe, of course, for deadlock—a development that has been closely linked to democratic breakdown in presidential and mixed presidential-parliamentary systems, as in much of Latin America and Weimar Germany, respectively (see, especially, Linz and Stepan, 1996; Berman, 1997).

There is no indication, however, that democratic governance has suffered in either Poland or Hungary. Non-Socialist parts of the government in both countries have in fact proved to be quite assertive in making their political presence felt, and the Socialists, whether in the government or in the presidential office, have operated according to the democratic rules of the game. Second, the stability of the Hungarian Parliament since 1990 has generated a series of well-established institutional constraints (see, especially, Ágh and

Kurtan, 1995; Kukorelli, 1995; Soltez, 1995)—constraints that seem to be developing, albeit more slowly, in Poland as well (and aided by the final approval of a new constitution in 1997). Third, while socialist parties in Poland and Hungary have the legitimacy and thus the power that comes from placing first in competitive elections, that legitimacy and thus the power it generates is severely circumscribed, not just by institutions, but also by their very abuse of power during the communist period. The past has given postcommunist parties a burden of proof—just as the past, particularly in Hungary, worked to free—one could argue—the right from justifying what they did and how they did it following their election to power in 1990.

One must also recognize the crucial role of intraparty constraints. It is all too easy—and certainly wrong—to view the ex-communist parties of Poland and Hungary as Leninist parties; that is, as highly disciplined vanguards ready to carry out the policy directives of their leadership. It is not just that Leninist parties in power were in practice quite divided organizations (especially in Poland and Hungary) and were, as a consequence, constrained (at least from within) in what they could do; it is also that their postcommunist successors are, if anything, even more divided and operate within a political and policy climate that. both encourages and reinforces intraparty conflict (see, especially, Osiatynski, 1995). As Tabajdi Csaba, the assistant to the prime minister of Hungary, argued in an interview I conducted in Budapest in January, 1995, the HSP is a party with a very big tent, within which it includes a moderate and dominant social democratic wing and a radical, but minority trade unionist wing. As Csaba argued at that time, this division has assumed political importance, given two issues in particular: the need to carry through on economic austerity measures and the size of the electoral victory. While the first factor alienated the left constituency within and outside the HSP (causing some defections in voting for the austerity legislation), the second energized every faction to try to get a piece of the policy action. In the process, the Socialists were severely constrained from within— just as democratic institutions and their alliance with the Free Democrats constrained them from without. This, describes in a larger sense the normal life of political parties in democratic orders.

Conclusions

The major conclusion to be drawn from this chapter is that the return of the left in Poland and Hungary has been less a threat to, than an investment in democracy. This seems to be the case, first, if we focus on the question of why the left won. Here, we find the absence of many of those factors that seem to preface democratic breakdown—for instance, political polarization and a sharp decline in public support for democratic institutions. At the same time, through their role as an ideological corrective, their inclusion of once excluded publics and their generation of party turnover in government, the most recent elections in Poland and Hungary could be said to have contributed to a deepening of democracy. An examination of the left in power reveals a similar favoring of costs over benefits. Simply put, the left has played by the democratic rules of the game; it has supported policies that enhance democracy, and it has been constrained by itself and other institutions. This is primarily because there now exists in Poland and Hungary powerful incentives for the ex-communists to play within, rather than outside the new democratic order.

We can now step back from these details and return to the larger issue concerning the relationship between democratization and political parties. What seems to emerge as critical for the future of democracy after communism is two contrasting models of political sequencing. One model, which tends to describe the politics of most of the postcommunist region, is where the ex-communists won the first competitive elections and were then subjected to varying degrees of political competition in subsequent electoral rounds. The other model, which is represented by Poland and Hungary (along with Lithuania, for instance), is where the ex-communists lost the first election and then won a subsequent election.

This distinction is crucial for our purposes, because it seems to have important consequences for the development of democracy, and, to return to our specific concern here, the impact of the return of the left on that process. These consequences are best understood if we remember that the transition from authoritarianism to democracy requires, at the minimum, relatively quick action on three fronts: decisive breakage with the authoritarian past, introduction of democratic institutions, and cooptation of authoritarians (O'Donnell and Schmitter, 1986). If we apply this list to the postcommunist states, we can observe the following. In most of the postcommunist world, the problem was that the break with the authoritarian past was incomplete, given the outcome of the first competitive elections. That affected, in turn, the kind of constitutional order that was crafted, since the ex-communists used their powers to develop constitutions that could function in effect as their "democratic business cards" (to use Stanislaw Gebethner's phrase, quoted in Dreijmanis and Malajny, 1995; also see Easter, 1997). At the same time, the continued power of the ex-communists compromised as well the process of economic reform, thereby producing in effect an incomplete break with the economic, as well as the political past (see, especially, Bunce, 1994; Fish, 1998). As an end result the victory of the left in the first competitive elections undermined the transition to both capitalism and democracy. The cooptation of the ex-communists, therefore, was "too complete"—to the clear detriment of the other tasks involved in moving from dictatorship to democracy. The many concerns about democratization in the postcommunist south, therefore, are well founded, and they speak in part to the costs of the left maintaining political power during the shift from state socialism to a more liberalized political environment (see Pusic, 1997).

By contrast, the sequence of the left losing, then winning, in most of northeastern Europe, including Poland and Hungary, has proven to be an ideal way to realize in short order the three main tasks of transition. In particular, with the loss of the left in the first elections, a sharp break was made with the authoritarian past[21]—a break that allowed for the construction of democratic rules of the game and a rapid transition to capitalism. The remaining task— that is, to attach authoritarians to the new order—seemed to be a problem, however, precisely because of the success in instituting a sharp discontinuity with the state socialist past. A closer look, though, reveals a solution to this problem. The rapid transition to capitalism, which had been made possible by the defeat of the left, provided rapidly expanding opportunities for the ex-communists to convert their political capital into economic capital. At the same time, the harshness of the economic transition, which was the product, in part, of rightists in power pursuing rightist policies, created a sizeable electoral constituency for the left. This, plus the historical claims in these particular cases of the left as social democrats, and, thus, as forces allowing for a certain continuity with the past within a larger process of breaking with that past, meant that the ex-communists had the possibility of winning elections in a democratic order. As a result, the loss of the left in the first competitive elections set in motion a complex dynamic, wherein rapid progress in building capitalism and democracy laid the groundwork for the return of the left to power, which in turn furthered the process of consolidating democratic politics.

Thus, with institutions in place and functioning and with clear benefits to be had from participating in democratic politics, the sequence of the left losing, then winning, proved to be an optimal solution in the postcommunist context to balancing the seemingly contradictory tasks of building and consolidating a democratic order. The concerns about the return of the left, as discussed in the introduction, therefore, are misplaced. Democracy in northeastern Europe, in short, has been well served by the loss, then the victory of the ex-communists.

Notes

1. Here, we should note the design of the electoral systems in Hungary versus Poland. The Hungarian system (see Racz and Kukorelli, 1995) is a variation on the German system; that is, it combines single member districts with party lists. Each voter has two votes: one for individual candidates (176 seats) and one for county or territorial lists (152 seats). In addition, there are 58 national list seats (based on 19 counties or provinces, plus Budapest city), which are calculated from fragments of the vote. Mandates for these seats are determined proportionally, with the conditions that (1) turnout must be 50%, plus 1; (2) the winning list must have 5%, plus 1 of the

national list vote (with each member of a party coalition required as well to get 5% of the vote). All this produces a total of 386 seats in parliament. Finally, there is a runoff election in the individual districts when (1) the turnout is less than 50%, plus 1, and/or; (2) no candidate receives an absolute majority. All candidates receiving 15% or more of the vote can participate in the runoff election, with the stipulation that at least three candidates must run. The outcome of the runoff election is determined by a plurality of the vote, and the turnout must be 25%, plus 1 to validate the election. In the Polish case, a new electoral law passed just before the dissolution of the Sejm in 1993 created a proportional representation system with a 5% threshold (based on nationwide party support) required for representation. The calculation of seats is such as to boost considerably the seats of parties receiving the most votes (see Millard, 1994).

In contrast to Hungary, which has a parliamentary system (with a weak president elected, at least at this time, by the Parliament), Poland has a mixed presidential-parliamentary system, similar to that of the French Fifth Republic (and, for that matter, Weimar Germany). The powers of the president are not terribly well specified, but are less than those of, say, either the French president or, certainly, the Russian president (according to the 1993 Russian constitution).

2. In the fall of 1997, there was yet another Polish parliamentary election. Once again, the vote of the ex-communists increased, moving up to 27.1 percent of the vote (though electing seven fewer deputies). However, the DLA was unable to form a government for two reasons. First, the PPL, their former coalition partner and a party that was, like the DLA, a holdover from the communist era, collapsed as an electoral force in the 1997 elections. Second, the parties on the right (especially Solidarity Electoral Action, or SEA) did surprisingly well, and succeeded after much wrangling to form a rightest coalition. Thus, with its rightest government and its ex-communist president (and its large ex-communist opposition within the Sejm), Poland has at present a divided government—a common problem in mixed presidential-parliamentary systems. However, as I will argue later in this chapter, the ideological gap between the left and right in Poland, as in Hungary, is quite small.

3. For reasons of clarity, the party acronyms used in this paper will conform to the English names of the parties, not the Hungarian or Polish names of the parties.

4. This is in sharp contrast to Hungary, where the six parties represented in the Parliament elected in 1994 are the very same parties represented in the 1990 Parliament.

5. In fact, the ex-communists received 13 percent of the vote in the June 1990 elections in Czechoslovakia, thereby coming in second and doing better than their counterparts in Poland and Hungary. However, since that time, they have been besieged by political divisions. However, recent public opinion surveys and most recent election show that the Social Democrats—the successor to the interwar social democratic party of Czechoslovakia (and *not* the successor to the Czech and Slovak Communist Party)—have closed in on the current ruling party, the Civic Democratic Party led by Prime Minister Vaclav Klaus.

6. The importance of looking at parties as the product of their historical evolution, rather than as mere vote-maximizers responding to the electoral cues of the moment, has also been emphasized by analysts examining the Spanish transition and the Spanish Social Democrats (see Share, 1989).

7. For example, public opinion polls conducted by the *New York Times* (and carried out by Gallup, Hungary, Ltd.) in the Czech Republic, Hungary, and Poland during June–July 1994, reveal a sharp contrast in evaluations of personal economic situations. When asked to compare one's economic situation today with five years ago,

32 percent of the Czech respondents said they were better off, while 12 and 18 percent of the Hungarians and the Poles, respectively, said the same. When asked to assess trends in the next few years in their personal economic circumstances, 18 percent of the Czechs expected deterioration; 44 percent of the Hungarians; and 26 percent of the Poles. Finally, when asked about unemployment, 16 percent of the Czech respondents said they were very concerned, in contrast to 36 percent of the Hungarians and the Poles.

8. One indicator of this contrast is that it was in the Czech Republic—and not in Poland and Hungary—where we see the strongest lustration legislation. Indeed, there is some evidence that anger about the proposal to introduce lustration in Poland led to some additional support for Kwasniewski (see Osiatynski, 1995).

9. See, especially, Luan Troxel, 1993 on the complexity of defining left and right in the postcommunist context. In this analysis, left refers to support for state intervention in the economy to support socioeconomic equality, whereas right—or liberal, in the European sense—refers to support for policies that envision socioeconomic inequalities as natural and as good for efficiency and growth and that allow markets considerable flexibility in distributing labor, goods, and services.

10. This also helps explain the common pattern throughout Eastern and Central Europe of communists doing better in the countryside and in small towns than in the major cities (see, for instance, Osiatynksi, 1995; Barany, 1995; Racz and Kukorelli, 1995; Krause, 1995). It is not just that the ex-communists have the organizational and financial capacity to penetrate less urban areas, or that the intellectuals leading the liberal parties lack the time, patience, and, in some cases, interest to develop grassroots political organization, or that most of the beneficiaries of the economic transition are in medium and large cities. It is also that highly urbanized areas offer a broader menu of ideological alternatives; given the focus of most liberal parties, the relative diversity of the media, higher overall levels of education, and greater access to foreign travel and travel abroad.

11. For example, in a poll conducted by Gallup for the *New York Times* in July, 1994, 60 percent of the Hungarians polled selected equality over freedom, whereas the comparable figure for the Czech republic was 20 percent, and for Poland, 42 percent. Similarly, in the New Democracies Barometer, conducted in November 1993 by Paul Lazarsfeld-Gesellschaft fur Sozialforschung, 37 percent of the Poles approved of the communist regime (that is, the pre-1989 regime); 23 percent of the Czechs; and 58 percent of the Hungarians. It is also telling that the Socialists also came in first in the local elections following the parliamentary elections in Hungary in 1994 (though the biggest winners were the independents—see Oltay, 1995).

12. There are two other factors that are important. One is that voters for the left appear to be less fickle than voters for the right. The left, in short, has a consistent base (see, for example, Osiatynski, 1995; Tymowski, 1994). Second, the shift to the left in the Polish (but not the Hungarian) case from 1991 to 1993 reflects in part differences in turnout. Thus, a large percentage of those who voted in 1993, but not in 1991, voted for the Democratic Left Alliance.

13. By the 1997 parliamentary elections, however, the right seemed to have learned from the experiences and the success of the left and was able to forge greater unity in pursuit of votes. Indeed, this is one advantage of party turnover in general; it creates incentives for both winners and losers to change their organizations, policy orientations, and political behavior in order to maximize public support. And Solidarity, once considered defunct, was in 1997 the major beneficiary of these political lessons.

14. It is interesting to note in this regard that there is a correlation in the postcommunist experience between the speed of the economic transition and the political support of the extreme right. Thus, the faster the economic transition, the less popular are extreme right parties. There is little empirical support, then, for the argument, often voiced in discussions about shock therapy in Poland and Russia (the latter evidencing, I would argue, shock but without much therapy), that a rapid transition to capitalism would produce severe economic stress which in turn would create constituencies supporting the extreme right.

15. However, it should also be noted that in the Polish case in particular, the fragmentation of the party system, in combination with the biases built into the new electoral law of 1993, meant that a full 35 percent of the voters in the 1993 election chose parties that did not get represented in the Sejm (see Millard, 1994).

16. The parallels between the Spanish and Hungarian cases are striking. They were both pacted transitions, and the left in both cases won big, after having been excluded from political power following the first competitive elections. It is interesting to note in this regard that, in the Spanish case, these characteristics are considered testimony to the process of democratic consolidation (see Maravall and Santamaria, 1986).

17. Because the results of the Polish presidential elections are so recent, this discussion of the impact of the left in power will concentrate primarily on the left-dominated governing coalitions in Hungary and Poland.

18. However, it must be noted that there are considerable cross-national variations in the rhetoric ex-communists have used during and between elections. To put the matter bluntly, Gennadi Zhuganov is not Gyula Horn, and this says something about differences in the political cultures of Russia versus Hungary and, thus, about differences in everything from electoral tactics to the beliefs of these two leftist political leaders.

19. Here, I refer to the questionable actions at times of the Hungarian government of 1990–1994, led by the Democratic Forum, especially with respect to political control over the media.

20. The contrast between the north and the south also affected patterns of membership recruitment and turnover in the ex-communist parties. For example, compare the statistics presented by Wasilewski and Wnuk-Lipinski, 1996 on the Polish ex-communists versus those reported on the Bulgarian ex-communists by Kuntchhev, 1995.

16

The Effects of Communist Party Transformation on the Institutionalization of Party Systems

Anna Grzymala-Busse

The persistence of the communist parties and their successors after the collapse of their rule in Eastern and Central Europe in 1989 remains one of the most salient continuities from the previous regime. In all cases, these parties survived, and often regained power.[1] As scholars searched for reasons for the parties' survival and electoral success, a major strand of the literature focused on the transformation of the communist parties after 1989 (Ishiyama, 1995; Kovacs, 1995; Szelenyi et al. 1997; Waller, 1995; Zubek, 1994). However, there has been less focus on the *effects* of these actors on the new democratic political party systems. On the one hand, scholars have argued that the initial balance of power between communist and opposition forces would determine the kind of electoral institutions that were likely to arise (Kitschelt 1995a; Colomer, 1995; Geddes 1995; Ishiyama 1997a).[2] On the other, there has been no examination of the communist parties' effects on the substance of party competition.

This chapter will focus on the broad decisions of the communist parties and their successors, and the effects they had on the institutionalizing of political party systems after 1989 in Eastern and Central Europe. As the literature on both the "new institutionalism" and "the renewed role of the state" has shown, it is often fruitful to trace the effects of a particular independent variable. Such an analysis cannot explain all facets of political development in the new democracies of Eastern and Central Europe, but it can fill in some of the gaps by examining how the incumbent authoritarian political actors affected the subsequent institutionalization of party systems.

Across the region, the ruling communist parties and their successors went on to participate in the new political system. Some were forced to exit from power: the Hungarian, Polish, Czechoslovak, and East German parties met this fate. Others retained their hold on power, as the Albanian, Romanian, and Bulgarian communist parties had done. Some transformed themselves radically, into moderate social democratic parties that were accepted democratic competitors and managers of economic reforms. Thus, the Polish SdRP, Hungarian MSzP, and Slovenian ZSLD were all re-elected to power on the strength of their commitment to democracy and managerial expertise. Others retained many of their old appeal and organization. These include the Czech KSČM, the Albanian PSSH, the Romanian PDSR, and to a lesser extent, the Bulgarian BSP.

Much as the communist parties followed diverging trajectories, the decade-old party systems have not institutionalized uniformly after the collapse of the communist regimes in 1989. The rapid development of these party systems was both necessary for modern democracy, and an enormous challenge to these new actors. Institutionalization, defined as the stabilization of competitors and competition to such an extent that "political actors have clear and stable expectations about the behavior of others" (Mainwaring, 1997), became both an empirical and theoretical concern. In parliamentary systems, such institutionalization comprises both the *character* of the competition (free and fair competition that does not privilege any players *ex ante*, and the control of the political process by the political parties) and its *contents* (competition that centers around public policy issues, rather than on fundamental questions of system choice and legitimacy).

The variation ranges from the fully pluralist competition, consolidated around policy questions (as in the Czech Republic), to limited competition that has not yet fully resolved basic questions of system legitimacy, seen in Albania or Romania. Two broad clusters emerged; in the Czech Republic, Poland, and Hungary, free elections favored no competitors *a priori*, political parties largely controlled the political process, and parties competed on policy programs, rather than relying on populism or patronage. By contrast, in the second group, consisting of Bulgaria, Romania, and Albania, party competition was more likely to favor the incumbents, and elections were often marred by intimidation and corruption. Parties tended to compete on populist programs and nationalist appeals, and once elected, were often hindered in controlling the political process. Slovakia, for its part, moved from the second cluster to the first over the course of the late 1990s.

Thus, the degree to which the elections were free varied, as Table 16.1 shows. The control of the political process by the parties also differed. This control consisted both of the nomination of candidates for parliamentary office, and the parties' ability to formulate and legislate policies. It meant that competition was more likely to be robust; the electorate was offered a meaningful choice, and when a given party won the vote, its victory could translate into policy changes. In countries such the Czech Republic or Hungary, political parties both exercised full control over candidate nomination and dominated the policy process. In contrast, in others, such as Romania,

Table 16.1

Freedom House Rating of Fairness in Elections and Political Freedoms

Albania	Bulgaria	Czech Republic	Hungary	Poland	Romania	Slovakia
4.5	3.5	1.25	1.25	1.25	3.25	3.5 until 1998– 2.0 after

Source: *Nations in Transit*. 1998. Washington, D.C., Freedom House.

only parties could nominate candidates but the country was governed chiefly by presidential decrees until 1996. In Slovakia and in Albania, individual politicians were also able to take over the political process. See Table 16.2 and 16.3 for lower party fragmentation.

These two measures thus divide the parties into two clusters. In the first, consisting of the Czech Republic, Hungary, and Poland, both freedoms and political control by parties is high. Slovakia may join this group, depending on whether it can minimize the possibility that a dominant political party such as the HZDS monopolizes the political process. In the second cluster, consisting of Bulgaria, Romania, and especially Romania, both freedom of competition and political control are far lower.

If these characteristics constitute one dimension of party institutionalization, a second dimension consists of the content of competition—the broad issues on which the parties compete. Each of these countries faced the "triple transition" (Offe 1991) to democracy, to new redistributive policies, and to new definitions of the citizenship. In more consolidated party systems, questions of the new political system and its boundaries were settled quickly. Parties now debated which policies to implement, and who could best administer these policies. In the less institutionalized party systems, the very nature of the political system was disputed, as parties debated the desirability of democracy and the free market, vague promises of direct material incentives, and nationalist exclusion of ethnic minorities.

Thus, in Poland, Hungary, and the Czech Republic, economic issues, and which party could best implement economic reform policies, became the chief structuring dimension of political competition (Kitschelt et al., 1999). Secondary dimensions of competition also included secularism in Poland (specifically, Church-related issues such as abortion and religion in the schools), and "western" vs. "traditional" values in Hungary. These occasionally reduced political debates to personal recriminations, but economic issues dominated both political appeals and voting decisions.

In Albania, both the former communists and the new democrats com-

Table 16.2

Control of Political Process by Parties

Albania	Bulgaria	Czech	Hungary	Poland	Romania	Slovakia
Low. Parties have low role in policy-making. PSSH monopoly until 1996.	Medium. Only parties can field candidates, but policy control problematic.	High. Parties both field candidates and control policy fully.	High. Parties both field candidates and control policy fully.	High. Parties field candidates, control policy.	Medium. Only parties can nominate candidates. Country ruled by decree until 1996.	Medium. Parties field candidates. HZDS monopolized politics until 1998.

Source: Author's compilation.

Table 16.3

Fragmentation, as Measured by the Number of Effective Electoral Parties

	Albania	Bulgaria	Czech Republic	Hungary	Poland	Romania	Slovakia
# of effective parties in first election*	2.1	2.75	3.4	6.8	13.5	2.25	4.8
Average	2.4	3.5	5.2	5.7	9.7	5.3	5.4

Note: As measured by $1/\Sigma \, V_i^{\,2}$, where V_i is the vote share of each individual party i competing. Since electoral institutions, such as thresholds and districting, mitigate the effects of party fragmentation, this analysis uses party vote shares, rather than party seat shares.

peted together on populist promises of painless reform and foreign aid (Pano, 1997). Nationality issues became more prominent over time.[3] In Bulgaria, the main divide ran along attitudes to the former communist regime, and the presence of its representatives in political life (Kitschelt et al., 1999). Both the Bulgarian Socialist Party and the Union of Democratic Forces, the two main political forces, consistently engaged in populist out-bidding (Karasimeneov, 1995). In Romania, the main communist successor, the National Salvation Front, blended populism and nationalism with a patronage network that exchanged material benefits for political support.[4] Finally, in Slovakia, the populism of the Movement for a Democratic Slovakia successfully divided Slovak parties into two groups until 1998: those promoting standard democratic competition and cleavages, and those emphasizing populism, nationalism, and even authoritarianism. In these cases, political debates were often dominated by nationalist attacks and the questioning of democracy.

The resulting "index" of institutionalization combines political freedom, party control, and dimensions of political competition. As we can see from Table 16.4, the Czech Republic achieves the highest score, and Albania, the lowest.

This variation matters, for several reasons. The institutionalization of political party competition has been found to determine the success of economic reform (Hellman, 1997), since it determines the stability and turnover of coalition governments. Second, party institutionalization determines how effective rules and institutions guiding parties are in promoting strategic voting and rational party decision-making (Moser, 1999.) Most importantly, political party systems also influence the legitimacy and effectiveness of

Table 16.4

Index of Party System Institutionalization

Country	Political Freedom (1=free, 7=fully repressive)	Party Control of Political Process (1=high, 5=low)	Policy-Based Party Competition (1=high, 5=low)	Overall Score (range: 3–17)
Czech Republic	1.25	1	1	3.25
Hungary	1.25	1	2	4.25
Poland	1.25	2	2	4.75
Slovakia	3.5/1.5 after 1998	3	4/2 after 1998	10.5/6.5
Bulgaria	3.5	3	4	10.5
Romania	3.25	4	5	12.25
Albania	4.5	4	5	13.5

Source: Author's compilation.

governance (Huntington, 1968). Thus, where the parties are not institution-alized, voters have resorted to mass protests (as in Albania after the collapse of the pyramid schemes in 1996–97) or to referenda and mass mobilization against the ruling party (as in Slovakia in 1998).

Communist Party Decisions and Their Effects

One of the most salient differences between new democratic systems and established ones is the endogeneity of the latter institutions and the political competition to earlier decisions of the participants. Specifically, negotiations ensue between the old rulers and their opposition regarding the new electoral systems, constitutional arrangements, and political guarantees. Even where the system "collapses" (as it did in GDR and Czechoslovakia), some form of such negotiations took place (Przeworski, 1992, Huntington, 1991, Elster, 1996). Thus, the very actors who stand to participate, compete, and benefit in this new party system also participate in setting up the initial rules of the game. This initial ability to play to competitive strength means that neither political institutions nor societal preferences are truly independent of these actors. If actors in regime transitions shape their own environment, then their strategic decisions and interactions will shape both the formal electoral rules and the subsequent institutionalization.

It follows, then, that we should take into account both the strategic deci-sions of the participants and their positions. Those already in power can wield the most influence. Thus, future moves depend on the willingness or ability of communist parties and their successors to negotiate and to leave power. First, they are the indispensable negotiating partners—the opposition could take many forms, but it faced the ruling party in all cases. Thus, even where the former rulers appear discredited and marginalized (as the commu-nist parties did in 1989), they had a considerable role to play. As a result, communist parties actively engaged in formal negotiations that brought an end to their rule (as in the case of Poland), in *post facto* handover negotia-tions (as in the former Czechoslovakia), or in leading the transition them-selves (as in Romania.)

To demonstrate the persistent influence of these authoritarian actors, we turn to three representative cases: the Czech Republic, Poland, and Roma-nia, to demonstrate how communist parties influence party-system institu-tionalization. These three countries show a range of outcomes: from full institutionalization of the party system (the Czech Republic), to the increas-ingly highly institutionalized (Poland), to tenuous institutionalization (Ro-mania, as late as 1996). By tracing the communist party decisions, the eventual outcomes, and the mechanisms that led from one to the other, we can gener-ate hypotheses that are then tested on other cases in the region.

Two key decisions of the communist parties shaped the subsequent democratic system. First, whether or not the parties exit from power during the transition determined the character of political competition, i.e. how freely it can be conducted and how much access political parties had to governance and political control. Second, how these parties chose to adapt to democracy influenced the content of political competition; whether or not it revolved around policy issues, or whether it instead centered around unsettled questions of system choice, defining the nation, or populist appeals.

First, where the communist rulers leave power and agree to compete in elections without any special privileges, all the competitors stand a fairer chance. Since this uncertainty of outcome is so central to democratic consolidation, the departure of the ruling authoritarian party is a prerequisite for the institutionalization of the political party system. Thus, when the communist party and its regime collapsed in Czechoslovakia in November 1989, it opened the way for fully free elections. The Czech communist party negotiated from a relatively weak bargaining position, especially once Václav Havel was elected president in December 1989. As a result, the June 1990 elections were fully free and greatly reduced the communist presence in the legislature. Such an early and complete exit from power meant that no competitor had the built-in advantages of media control, access to state funding, the electoral boards, or the electoral outcomes. State bureaucrats also had less time to convert their political power into economic assets, which can also be a further source of patronage.

Conversely, the longer the communist party stays in office, the more it can entrench itself, extracting privileges and resources that help it to stay in power. The first preference of communist parties is to stay in power, continuing their clientelist relationships to society (Colomer and Pascual, 1994). If they cannot retain power, their next preference is to try to undercut programmatic parties, given that their advantage lies in patronage and side payments (Kitschelt, 1995a). A communist party that stayed in power thus could continue to draw material and political benefits from office, especially since the communist state and the party were fused (Fish, 1998). Such a party can then build in competitive advantages for itself, such as institutions favoring big parties, state funding based on organizational strength, etc. For example, in Poland, the Round Table negotiations of 1989, designed to liberalize the communist system enough to ensure its survival, resulted in 65 percent of the seats in the lower house (Sejm) reserved for the communist party and its satellites, as was the presidency. The freely elected Senate was chosen under majoritarian formulas, to better represent the communists.[5] Other communist parties also tended to prefer strong presidencies, since they perceived (often incorrectly, as it turned out) that these institutions would favor their prominent personalities and strong organizations (Geddes, 1995; Colomer, 1995).[6] Such strong presidencies would limit party control of the political process. Thus, in Poland's semi-presidential system, parties remained divided, unable to agree on policies, and the president's office, filled by Lech Walesa in 1990, attempted to wrest further policy control.

The more completely a communist party dominated the transition, the more able it was to favor itself not only through formal institutions but also through fraud. In Romania, the communist National Salvation Front initially promised it would not stand in the June 1990 free elections and announced a proportional representation system with a 3 percent threshold, which would ostensibly benefit the weak opposition (Crampton, 1997). However, the NSF then reneged on this promise, insisted on a strong presidency, and used both physical intimidation and isolation by the official state media of the competition to ensure a communist victory. State funding was given to parties only if they received 5 percent of the vote (with a 3 percent threshold to enter Parliament), and parliamentary parties received twice as much media time as nonparliamentary parties. This combination of democratic rhetoric and authoritarian actions skewed the field (Tismaneanu, 1997). Not surprisingly, the communist presidential candidate and leader of the NSF, Ion Iliescu, won 85 percent of the presidential vote, and the NSF, 66 percent of the vote. Iliescu then began to rule the country by diktat (Tismaneanu, 1997).

Second, communist party decisions also affected the content of party competition. Whether or not the cleavages would revolve around "standard" issues of policy and its implementation, rather than around questions of system choice, populism, and defining the nation, depended on the communist successors' clear choice of its ideological profile and mobilizational methods—the ways in which the party hoped to convince the electorate to support it. The communist successor parties had three options:

1) to exit from power and transform themselves, attempting to gain new voter support with new appeals,
2) to exit from power and retain their old appeals and constituencies, or
3) to attempt to negate this choice by holding onto power either as a party or as individuals.

The first two profiles are associated with clear policy-based debates, while the third favors populist and nonpolicy competition.

The degree to which the communist party would clearly profile itself, in turn, depended on the configurations of the political alternatives at the time, the conflict between the rulers and the opposition tends to structure future electoral cleavages (Powers and Cox, 1997). The anti-communist opposition, where it existed, had as its chief preference a clear break with the past. To that end, the articulation of reform policy proposals would be its first and most credible signal of its intentions. Therefore, if a strong opposition emerged before or during the negotiations, the communist parties were forced to orient their appeals to policy stances, either to defend their past policies or to propose new ones. They could not rely on their previous clientelism. Thus, the balance of power between these two forces also influenced the strategic considerations of the communist party itself, which subsequently have an impact on the institutionalization of the party systems.

Where the parties clearly profiled themselves and the kind of policies they advocated (that is, whether the communist party and its successors would converge on pro-democratic, pro-reform appeals, or whether it would retain its communist orthodoxies) depended on the extent of the parties' earlier experience with reform under communism. Thus, the Polish party, with its experience in negotiation, policy innovation, and reform implementation, parlayed these elite resources into moderate appeals, organizational stream-lining, and new acceptance as a social democratic party. In contrast, the successor to the stagnant and orthodox Czech communist party retained much of its old appeals and organization, becoming a marginal political player in Parliament. In neither case, however, did the communist parties set the agenda; they had to respond to the opposition and choose their new identities.

Where the opposition was relatively weak, in contrast, there was no need for the communist party to formulate a clear policy profile. Communist parties wanted to avoid policy discussions, both because of their earlier policy failures, and because their comparative advantage lay with patronage disbursement. There was little incentive to formulate clear policy alternatives, since the opposition could then easily point to the parties' continuing stranglehold on power as a key reason for the need to reform. In these cases, political debates revolved around populist promises and nationalist mobilization, rather than policy choice within a democratic framework (Vachudová and Snyder, 1997). For example, in Romania, no clear policy stances emerged, due to the parties' lack of knowledge and experience (Pasti, 1997). Policy issues were obscured by Iliescu, as populism and clientelism dominated the political discourse (Tismaneanu, 1997).

Testing the Explanation

To test this explanation, we move to a broader examination of post-communist party institutionalization, including the cases of Albania, Bulgaria, Hungary, and Slovakia. First, where the communist party rapidly admitted its defeat and exited the political arena, both the integrity of competition and party control over the political process is considerably higher. Thus, in Hungary, parties have not only dominated the fielding of candidates, but have coopted civic society and ensured a weak presidency. (Bruszt and Stark, 1991). By leaving, the communist party allowed both unfettered competition, and the consolidation of meaningful democratization. A rejection of the communist system in these first elections was associated both with greater democratic consolidation and with free market reforms (Fish, 1998).[7]

In contrast, where the communist party managed the transition, it was able to privilege its position, often under the guise of electoral laws designed to "stabilize" competition. The fairness of elections was often disputed, and parties *per se* developed less control over the political process. At worst, local strongmen could wrest control over policymaking, monopolize the administration of the country, and weaken the political capacities of political parties by denying them funding and media access, or by overriding their decisions or eliminating them from policymaking (Pano, 1997).

Thus, in Albania, President Ramiz Alia controlled policymaking and administration. Non-communist parties were not given access to the media.[8] State funding had to be returned by parties with less than 3 percent of the vote. And, in both 1992 and 1996, the proportion of seats in Parliament elected by majoritarian rules increased.[9] All these moves favored the incumbent communists, who were able to not only remain in power through the transition, but win the first few elections as a result. Subsequently, the system was ripe for abuse by the incumbent; the democratic party's flagrant violations of the spirit and letter of the electoral law skewed the 1996 elections, much as the communists had done earlier (CSCE, 1997; Biberaj, 1998).

The situation was less severe in Bulgaria, where the communists had not controlled the transition as fully. Electoral laws did favor major parties (such as the communist successors) with a half-PR, half-majoritarian system, and state funds were given only to parties with more than 50,000 votes (loans were given to the rest). A 4 percent threshold and the party nomination of electoral commission candidates further ensured an advantage for the larger parties (Pano, 1997). As the opposition gained in strength, compromises with the communists in the spring of 1990 led to more PR seats and to the parliamentary elections of the president.

The content of party competition was affected by the extent to which the parties adopted a clear policy-based profile. In Hungary, the communist party was forced to exit from power and began to metamorphose into a moderate leftist party, the Hungarian Socialist Party (MSzP). It could neither depend on its former patronage networks, nor could it make populist appeals, given its newly declared direction. Instead, forced to compete on programmatic issues, the party continued to critique the government of the Hungarian Democratic Forum (MDF) from 1990 to 1994 on the basis of its competence in implementing economic and political reform.

Moreover, the MSzP in Hungary made a dramatic turnaround, changing its organization, appeal, and behavior to that of moderate social democrats, much as the communist party in Poland did. As a result, these parties contributed in two ways to the general policy consensus on democracy and market reform. First, their campaign appeals and programs did not question the need for democracy and market reform. Secondly, once they returned to govern in 1993–94, this time freely elected, these parties further stabilized both the political party system and the policy consensus by continuing the economic and administrative reforms of their predecessors (Bartlett, 1995 and Blazyca and Rapacki, 1995).

In contrast, where the communist parties managed to avoid exiting from power fully, the structuring of party competition around clear policy alternatives was weak. In Albania, Bulgaria, and to a lesser extent, in Slovakia, a weak opposition did not force the communist party's hand. In Albania, not only did the Communist Party not exit from power, but it hesitated in making any clear decision regarding their new role and ideology. Instead, the Socialist Party of Albania (PSSH, as the communist heir was known) turned to clientelism and patronage, preventing the rise of clear policy-structuring of party competition. Because they retained their power and continued to draw benefits from the status quo, they had no incentive to promote economic reform. In Slovakia, the dispersal of communists into several parties meant that the new elites consisted of a "combination of dissidents and 'laundered communists'" (Innes, 1997, p. 406). Such dispersal meant that there would be fewer actors in whose interest it would be to consistently and credibly critique the communist record or the party itself.[10] Many politicians instead chose to exploit national grievances and populist appeals, instead of clear policy divisions. Most notably, Vladimir Mečiar crossed over from the communist party to the opposition Public Against Violence in 1989, and then founded the ironically named Movement for a Democratic Slovakia (HZDS), which managed to dominate Slovak politics from 1991 to 1998 with a mixture of nationalism, populism, intimidation, and a disrespect for minority and civic rights.

Nonetheless, the existence of an opposition, even if weaker than in the Czech Republic, Hungary, or Poland, meant that the communists were forced to profile themselves to a degree in Slovakia and in Bulgaria. In the case of Slovakia, one group of communists remade the rump Slovak Communist Party into the Party of the Democratic Left (SDL'), while the Bulgarian communists remade themselves into the Bulgarian Socialist Party (BSP). The Slovak SDL then went on to become one of the antipopulist "democratic" parties (although it changed its views and appeals several times), while the BSP, for all its vague ideology, ceased to rely on patronage once it was ousted in the 1991 elections. By that point, however, the chief dimensions of competition were already established as demagogic populism and nationalism (Bell, 1998). The belated profiling of both the Slovak and Bulgarian parties thus did little to structure the political debates around policy; the SDL was too weak, and the BSP, too vested in populism and patronage.

Accounting for Communist Party Strategies

Why, then, would some communist parties be more likely to exit from power? Why would the opposition grow strong enough in some cases to force the communist parties to profile themselves clearly? Finally, why would the communist parties transform their appeals and organization in some cases but not in others? To answer these questions, it is helpful to move back one analytical level, to the historical record of the relationship between the ruling communist parties and society prior to 1989, and specifically, to the record of popular mobilization and the communist response to this opposition.

First, where there was no record of popular mobilization against the communist regime, or of widespread attempts to reform this system, no set of potential opposition elites formed, and no record of past mobilization could serve as a template for the organization or mobilization of popular protest in 1989. As a result, no mass opposition arose to challenge the communist parties in 1989, and these parties could remain in power, largely by default. This is the pattern of communist parties retaining their rule, as observed in Albania, Bulgaria, and Romania.

Where the populace had earlier mobilized against communist rule, this historical record led both to sustained (if not necessarily widespread) dissent against the communist regime. It produced both a cohort of potential opposition leaders and the popular memory of previous mobilization. In these countries, the communist parties were forced to exit as a result of popular mobilization, the subsequent popular upsurge (in the former Czechoslovakia and East Germany) or elite negotiations (in Hungary and Poland). Ironically, then, the existence of a societal opposition was partly dependent on the decisions of the communist party itself; the degree to which it tolerated, however intermittently and ambivalently, the rise of such an opposition.

Second, the communist parties' response to these societal demands determined their choice of ideological and mobilizational profiles after 1989. Where the parties had attempted to engage the populace, through negotiation or policy reform and its implementation, the communist elites had gained the personal experience and skills needed to transform the communist parties into moderate, centrist political competitors that could succeed in a democratic system. We observe this pattern in Poland and in Hungary. Where they had not engaged society, they were unable to transform their appeals or organizations into credible, moderate, democratic competitors, for lack of elite skills and experiences. As a result, if they were forced to exit from power, as in Czechoslovakia and the former East Germany, they retained their old appeals. If they were not forced to exit from power, as in Albania, Bulgaria, and Romania, they retained their old strategies of patronage and populism. Where they were forced to exit from power, but faced little opposition and had few resources, the communists largely dispersed into other parties, and then used the familiar patrimonial mobilization methods, as in Slovakia. Table 16.5 summarizes these historical records and communist party strategies.

Therefore, rather than looking at a broad "regime type," it may be more useful to disaggregate more recent communist party practices, and how they affected both the set of potential elite strategies, and the record of state-

Table 16.5

The Historical Record of Opposition/ Engagement with Society and Communist Party Strategies

	Pre-1989 engagement with society, skilled communist elites	No engagement, fewer elite skills.
Pre-1989 higher societal mobilization and opposition.	Communist parties exit in 1989, reject old appeals and transform. (Hungary, Poland)	Communist parties exit, retain old appeals. (Czech Republic, GDR)
Lower societal mobilization and opposition.		Communist parties do not exit fully, retain populist appeals and patronage structures. (Albania, Bulgaria, Romania, [Slovakia])

Source: Author's compilation.

society relations. This alternative can explain the differences broad regime-type explanations cannot; for example, the Czech and Slovak outcomes. The Czechoslovak regime collapsed in 1989, so the same opportunity existed for free competition. But, the stronger opposition in the Czech Republic (the Civic Forum) forced the communist party to clearly profile itself. Its lack of elite resources led it to adopt an orthodox communist profile. In Slovakia, meanwhile, the opposition party, Public Against Violence, was considerably weaker, all the more so since its representatives did not fully participate in the handover negotiations conducted by the Czech Civic Forum on their behalf in Prague between late 1989 and early 1990. While some Slovak communists remained in the party and transformed it from within, most instead dispersed into other parties. Unchallenged by a strong opposition, many of these communists then began to structure the political debates around populist and nationalist appeals.

Alternative Explanations

In explaining party institutionalization, one set of explanations has focused on "democratic innovations." These emerged from the uncertainty of the transition, exacerbated by the scope of the transformation (Bunce and Csanadi, 1993). First, the new parties now faced a new set of political institutions. Thus, the differences in the new electoral laws and institutions may be responsible for the variation (Bielasiak, 1997). The major institutional choices were similar: parliamentary or semipresidential systems, with mostly proportional representation. The more detailed institutions varied, however, and so electoral thresholds, district magnitude, and party lists offered distinct incentives for party behavior, and could thus determine the differences in party institutionalization (Moser, 1999).

The lower the electoral thresholds, and the higher the district magnitude, the greater the likelihood of party proliferation (Taagepera and Shugart, 1989). The more numerous the parties, the lower the chance of establishing stable political control. And as these parties attempt to distinguish themselves, the risk of highly ideologized and polarized politics increases, making antisystem and populist parties more likely (Katz, 1980). Higher electoral thresholds and lower district magnitude, on the other hand, tend to lower the number of competing parties and promote the stabilization of the axes of competition, at the price of greater disproportionality (Moraski and Lowenberg, 1997). Closed party lists also promote institutionalization, giving parties greater control over candidate nomination, since the voters cannot override the parties' prioritization of candidates on the ballot. Therefore, we would expect that in countries with low thresholds, high district magnitudes, and open party lists, party systems have greater difficulties institutionalizing, since political party control and policy-based debates are not promoted.

Second, another democratic innovation was the articulation of *electoral cleavages*. In Western Europe, democratic stability resulted from clearly defined and identified social cleavages, with strong linkages between groups and parties (Evans and Whitefield, 1993). In contrast, even a strong electoral system may be unable to exert a reductive influence when the cleavages are vague, since electoral systems interact with, but do not override, underlying societal cleavages (Ordeshook and Shvetsova, 1994). As electoral cleavages stabilize and become more apparent, political parties stand to better anticipate the voters and to better predict their competitors' strategies (Kitschelt, 1992, Evans and Whitefield, 1993). If parties faithfully reflect their constituencies, then electorates may be responsible for the patterns of party consolidation we observe.[11]

The third set of explanations for party institutionalization have emphasized *historical continuities* as responsible for the patterns of party competition and its stabilization. Scholars identified numerous communist legacies, and their effects on post-communist politics, economy, and society (Kitschelt, 1999; Jowitt 1992; Hanson, 1995; Pridham and Lewis, 1996). One prominent explanation argued that the type of communist regime (itself predicated on prewar configurations of socialist and bourgeois parties) could determine the subsequent quality of party democracy; the Czech "bureaucratic-authoritarian" regime better prepared it for programmatic party cleavages than the Albanian, Bulgarian, and Romanian form of "patrimonial" communism, or the Polish and Hungarian "national-accommodative" type (Markowski, 1997; Kitschelt et al., 1999).[12]

Prewar configurations of political forces thus influenced the communist regimes, which in turn affected the post-communist cleavages and their representation. If this explanation holds, we should see similar levels of party institutionalization where the communist regimes shared these characteristics.

However, it is not clear that these explanations are fully satisfactory. First, it is not clear that political institutions alone, however powerful, account for party institutionalization. Thresholds did not necessarily reduce the number of parties, and thus could not increase party control. For example, the number of effective electoral parties in Poland shrank from 13.5 to 9.8 with the introduction of a 5 percent threshold in 1993. However, this number shrank even further, to 4.6, under the same threshold in 1997.[13] Similarly, district magnitude varied with little respect to institutionalization—Slovakia had the highest district magnitude, with 37.5 seats per district. The Czech Republic followed with 25 seats per district; in the 1991 elections Poland had 10.6 seats and in the 1993 elections, 7.5 seats per district (Stanclik, 1997). Hungary's seats varied from 4 to 28, for a mean of 6. Yet the Czech and Hungarian party systems, on the opposite ends of this scale, have been among the first to institutionalize. Finally, party lists were a relatively weak factor. Thus, in Poland, open party lists have not precluded individual parties from exercising considerable discipline over their candidates, while the closed party lists of the Czech Republic, Romania, and Hungary have not necessarily promoted greater control over candidates. Recent research has reversed these causal arrows, arguing that party institutionalization itself determines whether or not these electoral institutions will have the expected effect (Moser, 1999).

Second, since the links between voters and parties are relatively weak, popular cleavages have less power to structure political competition and the institutionalization of the party systems (Millard, 1994; Racz, 1993). This relationship holds across the region—in even the most institutionalized systems, the voters had considerable difficulties clearly aligning themselves with individual parties. The interaction between party elites and potential constituencies only occasionally gave rise to parties that better represented social cleavages (Ágh, 1994; Lewis, 1994). Thus, while elite cleavages are salient and structure party politics (Toka, 1996), these divisions do not necessarily reflect popular differences in political opinion. Newly competitive party politics took place on a national, not local level, and were characterized by the primacy of parliamentary representation, low electoral turnout, and low popular identification with parties (Lomax, 1995; Korosenyi, 1996).[14] Instead, across the region, parties "floated" above societies and did little to encapsulate electorates (Racz, 1993). Therefore, electoral cleavages had few transmission mechanisms that would translate popular divisions into political party institutionalization.

Third, the legacies of the interwar period are highly ambiguous; not only were the societies radically changed by World War II itself, but the parties themselves took on several different organizational and ideological forms during this time.[15] Moreover, "regime type" seems too broad an analytical category, since these regimes changed over time; the Czechoslovak communist regime during the brief interlude of the Prague Spring in 1968 was very different from the Stalinist repression of 1953 (or the post-1968 "normalization").[16] Finally, this characterization does not explain the variation between Slovakia and the Czech Republic, which shared a bureaucratic-authoritarian communist regime, yet diverged in outcome of party institutionalization.

Conclusions

As the continuing influence of communist parties on democratic party system institutionalization shows, historical continuities affect democratic innovations. Brand-new pluralist structures are fundamentally shaped by institutions and agents of the eradicated *ancien regime*. This influence is neither all-determinant nor indiscriminate; rather, how communist parties affected the democratic party systems was conditioned on the configurations of elite resources within the party, and the constellations of political alternatives that were allowed to arise prior to 1989. Paying closer attention to the dynamics of institutional creation, the timing and sequencing of political change, and the decisions that led to these transformations allows us to better understand how political party systems institutionalize after transitions to democracy. The post-transition environment is neither the result of ahistorical and acontextual bargaining between opposition and communist forces, nor is it a simple and direct response to political institutions. Rather, the institutionalization of political party systems shows how earlier communist practices translated into communist elite resources and opposition strength. The two interacted to alter communist party decisions to exit from power and to form programmatic profiles. These decisions, in turn, shaped the ability of other political parties to compete freely, to control the political process, and to debate policies rather than populist promises.

Notes

1. The successors were re-elected into power in Poland in 1993, in Hungary in 1994, and joined government coalitions in Slovakia in 1994 and 1998.
2. Most of these scholars argued that the communists would want SMD districting, majoritarian systems, and strong presidencies, which would reduce the salience of parties and allow the discredited communists to win on the basis of individual personalities. However, these findings have been disputed, most recently by (Bernhard, 2000).
3. Ethnic parties were banned in 1992, chiefly hindering the Greek minority.
4. The NSF split into two smaller parties; the dominant one is now known as the Social Democratic Party of Romania, PDSR.
5. These were also the first negotiations to take place in the region between the

communist party and the opposition, and as such, were marked by hesitation on both sides, lest the Soviet Union intervene. See (Bernhard, 2000).

6. However, SMD was also favored by the stronger parties in the Hungarian opposition in 1989 (Bernhard, 2000, p. 324).

7. This is a necessary, but not sufficient condition—communist exit does not guarantee democratic success, as evidenced by Russia.

8. Subsequently, parties in Albania gained access to the media, in proportion to the number of candidates.

9. Starting out with a mixed PR-SMD system in 1991, the communist successors reduced parliamentary seats from 250 to 140, with 100 selected by majoritarian rules. By 1996, 115 seats were single-member.

10. The one party to claim noncommunist "purity" were the Christian Democrats, who were hampered by their leader, Jan Čarnogurský, who frequently managed to alienate potential allies and supporters.

11. Thus, Evans and Whitefield (1993) argue that ethnic diversity and established statehood may determine whether the cleavages that result will be the standard economic ones, or whether they will revolve around ethnic divisions or valence issues.

12. According to Kitschelt et al. (1994) parties prior to World War II led to a bureaucratic-authoritarian communism, characterized by repression and bureaucratization. This in turn led to the primacy of the economic-distributive cleavage after 1989. Where socialist parties were weak and bourgeois ones strong prior to World War II, national-accommodative communism arose, with greater willingness to respond to society and bargain with the opposition. Parties after 1989 supported economic change, and so social, national, or ethnic divisions trumped other cleavages. Finally, where both socialist and bourgeois parties were weak, patrimonial communism arose, with its repression, cooptation, and intolerance of dissent. The regime cleavage was deeper than elsewhere, and because economic reform was more badly needed, parties tended to resort to social protectionist policies.

13. Similarly, the number of parliamentary effective parties, where the influence of the thresholds would be strongest, shrank from 10.2 to 3.9 between 1991 and 1993, and continued to shrink to 3.0 in 1997. In contrast, Russia has had a 5 percent threshold and a mixed electoral system for all three elections, yet the number of effective electoral parties has ranged from 7.6 in 1993, to 10.7 in 1995, to 7.2 in 1999.

14. For example, 68 percent of Poles polled saw no local party activity. (*Rzeczpopolita*, 28–9 August, 1993).

15. For example, the Communist Party of Czechoslovakia went from being a moderate, mass-party organization close to the Social Democrats prior to 1925 to a "bolshevized" cadre-party after 1926.

16. Similarly, the Hungarian orthodoxy of the Stalinist period has little in common with the relatively liberal "goulash communism" after 1960.

17

Changing Cleavage Structure and the Communist Successor Parties of the Visegrád Countries

Michael Bauer

This chapter focuses on a comparison of the development of the communist successor parties in the four countries of the Visegrád Group (the Czech and Slovak Republics, Poland and Hungary). Unlike many other post-communist countries in transition, their course of reform toward a market economy and pluralist democracy was established very early on (Crome 1992, p. 716). Many regarded them, with the exception of Slovakia, as shining examples of success among the post-communist countries in transition. The reforms they undertook caused rapid and profound political, economic, and social changes, and the communist parties had to face these new circumstances. If they wanted to survive and not end up on the political scrapheap, the communist parties were forced, on the one hand, to come to terms with their post-communist legacies and, on the other hand, adapt to the new, fundamentally different conditions.

Political Orientations and Adaptation Strategies of the Communist Successor Parties in the Four Visegrád Countries–Some Significant Differences

Today, more than twelve years after the start of the transition, the adaptation strategies of the communist successor parties in the four Visegrád countries can be described as very successful. Not only did the successor parties without exception survive as important parliamentary parties, but for certain periods they even returned to power to affect the course of the transition. In Poland from 1993 to 1997 and from 2001 onwards, and in Hungary from 1994 to 1998, they acted as leading parties in the governing coalition. However, at present, the successor parties in the Visegrád countries represent a party-type only formally (see in detail, Stöss and Segert 1997). Empirically, there are many differences that distinguish them. The Polish United Worker

Party (PZPR) evolved into the social democracy of the Republic of Poland (SdRP) in January 1990, becoming a reformed, non-transmuted, social-democratic party. The social-democratic orientation of the SdRP can be characterized as a moderate concept of modernization, compariable to the liberal parties. While the SdRP clearly support the market economy in general, it stresses political redistribution and state intervention with a strong emphasis on social justice (Stöss and Segert 1997, p. 404). The SdRP rejected nationalistic aspirations and supported the integration of Poland with the West, especially toward an EU and NATO membership. It became a full member of the Socialist International (SI) in 1996 and received observer status in the Party of European Socialists (PES).

Concerning the change of political orientations and the location within the programmatic party families, almost the same is true for the Hungarian Socialist Party (MSZP) founded in October 1989 as the successor of the Hungarian Socialist Workers' Party (MSZMP).

In contrast, the Communist Party of Bohemia and Moravia (KSCM) remains a non-reformed and non-transmuted successor of the Communist Party of Czechoslovakia (KSC). The neo-communist orientation of KSCM leans toward the "old" state socialism. Anti-liberalism, anti-universalism, collectivism, authoritarianism, and centralism are important elements of the party's identity (Stöss and Segert 1997, p. 404). Without nationalistic aspirations, however, they seek an anti-Western path toward democracy and transformation of the economy.

The Party of the Democratic Left (SDL) in Slovakia—the other successor of the KSC—could be characterized as pragmatically reformed and as semi-transmuted. The social-democratic orientation of the SDL is combined with an obviously populist, sometimes nationalistic stance. Although one can find intraparty divisions and splinter groups in all of the successor parties of the Visegrád countries, the struggle between the "moderate" and the "conservative" camps within the SDL is most apparent. While the moderates tend to prefer a path of social democratization similar to that followed in Poland and Hungary, others tend to defer toward the model of the KSCM. In spite of many disagreements, both camps within the SDL clearly support the integration of Slovakia into the West. The SDL became a full member of the Socialist International in 1996 and received observer status in the Party of European Socialists (PES).

Despite some similiarities, the conditions in the Visegrád countries were very different, which called for different adaptation strategies on the part of the successor parties. The party programs, the political strategies, and identities of the successor parties had to develop in accordance with national circumstances and with different organizational and programmatic starting points. A uniform strategy was unthinkable. The successor parties also shifted strategies during the course of the transition in the face of new political issues, new cleavages, and new opponents. In sum, one might argue that the SdRP and MSZP owe their rise to a break with their own past and a clear acknowledgment of democracy and the market economy, as well as to a gradual and finally successful social-democratization. This course is less pronounced in the case of the SDL. On the one hand the SDL distanced itself from its communist past and by doing so adopted a social-democratic identity. On the other hand, and much more than in Poland and Hungary, the SDL relies on political nostalgia and national populism to mobilize voters.

The KSCM, in contrast, has survived because it hangs on to elements of the old system and follows a "strategy of leftist-retreat," i.e. rejects free market economy and stresses the (in their eyes mostly negative) outcome of the transformation. In this sense it plays the role of "an anti-system opposition party and attacks bourgeois democracy and capitalist exploitation" (see the chapter by Gryzmala-Busse in this book).

Theoretical Issues

How did such different thematic-programmatic orientations of the successor parties in the V4 countries arise? Which factors triggered the change in political identities? It is obvious that the successor parties followed differing strategies to ensure their post-communist survival, but when and why did the parties choose or change their strategies?

Concerning the explanation of the development of post-communist party systems in general, and therefore of the communist successor parties in particular, one can find three main approaches in the literature (Stöss and Segert 1997, p. 387) (1) institutional settings of the course in the context of systemic change as determinants of party development (Babst 1992, Dellenbrant and Berglund 1992, Grotz 2000); (2) pre-democratic cleavages developed in the modernization process of the countries as determinants of party development (Körösényi 1992, Mangott 1992, G. Márkus 1994); (3) cleavages developing in the process of systemic change in connection with different interests, political aims and value orientations as determinants of party development (Kitschelt 1992, 1995b, Kitschelt et al. 1999, Lindström 1991, Meyer 1997).

To be able to analytically ascertain both the persistent influences (including the legacies of the communist past and the structural resources of the successor parties) and the change of the conditions and strategies of the communist successor parties, I will, in the following, focus on a third approach, or the argument that "parties and voters, elites and social groups in Eastern and Central Europe differ mainly along certain cleavages representing important issues, interests, and value orientations in the transition processes" (Meyer 1997, p. 152). The new parties have the potential to permanently mobilize and politicize the population in the context of the post-communist transition on the basis of these cleavages. Since we are faced with the development of new party systems, two aspects of cleavage theory, namely, "mobilization" and "politicization" (Lipset and Rokkan 1967, pp. 2–5), are of central importance. "With the introduction of the democratic vote . . . the post-communist situation . . . can be viewed as a phase of politicization of the social structures by parties, as a historic epoch, which can be rightfully compared to those of the first mobilizations of social groups by parties" (Steinwede 1997, pp. 22–23). In contrast to "classical" cleavage theory, I argue that this process mainly took place from top down. Which cleavages have the potential to mobilize permanently? How do the cleavages change in the course of the transition? Which of them are suited for mobilization and politicization, and which parties are in a position to take advantage of certain cleavages? Indeed, the "challenge is to understand the relationship between the process of defining choice and the content of choice afforded at different stages of development. The electoral market, in short, is defined by both the transformation of the socioeconomic environment that gives rise to more pronounced cleavages in society, and the translation of the social division into politically salient forces through the filter of party organization, elections, and parliamentary action" (Bielasiak 1997, p. 29).

Periods of Transition and Periods of Party System Development

It is useful to divide party system development into distinct phases. This division enables us to identify similar stages in the process, even if they do not take place at the same time in the respective countries. It also helps to uncover similarities and differences concerning the changing significance of certain cleavages or changes in strategy. In the following I will distinguish these features, using the phases identified by Bielasiak (1997).

The *hegemonic* phase is characterized by the actual single party rule of the communist parties. The *polarized* phase that follows is characterized by the dichotomy between the opposition movements and the communists. The *fragmented* phase is marked by the disintegration or paralysis of the (ruling) oppositional alliances and by the development of new parties. It begins with the inauguration of the first freely elected Parliaments and ends with the second elections. The *pluralist* phase is marked by the concentration of political party competition. It starts after the second elections (in the Czech and Slovak Republics, respectively, after the third election) and continues until today. A consolidated party system following the Western example would be achieved if the parties were profoundly rooted in society. (For further criteria for a consolidated party system see Beyme 1997, Segert 1997). Until now, however, this has not been the case in any of the four countries. The party systems of the Visegrád countries have remained in flux.

The parliamentary elections themselves act as points that delineate these phases. In the following, I will focus on the development of the successor parties in the four Visegrád countries in the context of the changing cleavage structure and in terms of the different stages. Other parties will generally remain unconsidered, unless they are important to the development of the successor parties. This framework allows for some basic comparisons to be made.

The Hegemonic Party System

In this stage, the Soviet Union is the hegemonic leading power. The centralized authority under the leadership of the communist "vanguard party" is the main guiding principle of this stage. Based upon this "historical role," the communist parties claim an absolute leading role in politics. Pluralistic political competition is not allowed. The interests of the citizens and of the political actors are hardly taken into consideration. The intermediary structures at best serve as "transmission belts" that link society to the official state structures. Participation and mobilization of the citizens is ritualized and generally independent of individual or group-specific interests.

Beside the dynamics of the transition period, the legacies of the communist regimes affect the later performance of the successor parties. A comparison of the communist parties in the Visegrád countries helps illustrate this point. As Ishiyama notes, "the particular history of each communist party affected whether or not a tradition of tolerance and internal pluralism existed, which in turn affected the strength of the democratic reformist impulse within the party during the transition period" (Ishiyama 1995, p. 158, Ishiyama 1997a). Indeed, there were fundamental differences between the KSC in Czechoslovakia and the MSZMP and PZPR in Hungary and Poland.

Right from the start of their rule, the MSZMP and PZPR lacked legitimacy and domestic roots in the population. Both were viewed as alien elements, controlled by Moscow. In Poland and Hungary there was a deep cleavage between "them" (the communists) and "us" (the general public). This lack of legitimacy "resulted in a greater willingness on the part of the Polish and Hungarian parties to engage in economic and political reforms. There emerged a historical tradition of tolerance for some measure of intraparty political pluralism and moderate reform, a tradition which was especially important in explaining the greater willingness to accept the movement toward democratic reform" (Ishiyama 1995, p. 159). This shows especially in Hungary, where, from its beginning in the 1970s, the legitimacy of the Kádár regime was to be increased by well-administered doses of (less) political and (more) economic reforms. The comparatively high standard of living in particular made Kádár's "goulash communism": the state socialism most popular with its own population within the region" (Machos 1994,

p. 31). Despite all of the above, this hidden pluralism was not the same as interest pluralism in the West. The monopoly of rule established in the constitution and the claim to leadership were not called into question by the communists themselves until 1989.

In Czechoslovakia, on the other hand, the KSC could refer to a long tradition and a social rootedness of the communist movement. It was only in the wake of the Prague Spring of 1968 that the people distanced themselves from the communists. In the time between Dubcek's nomination as secretary general of the KSC in January 1968 and the intervention of the Warsaw-Pact troops in August, far-reaching reforms of the socialist system were attempted. Dubcek's goal of creating "socialism with a human face" resonated with a large part of the population. In order to prevent the liberalization and reformation of the socialist system, the Warsaw Pact invaded. With Husák's entry into office in October 1968 the Prague Spring reformers were removed from office and replaced by party followers loyal to Moscow while any kind of intra-party pluralism was terminated. As a result, "no tradition of internal pluralism and political tolerance emerged, nor in turn did a strong party constituency for democratic reform develop" (Ishiyama 1995, p. 159). The popular support for Dubcek's reforms does indicate however, that in Czechoslovakia there was a deeply rooted support for socialism "with a human face" and a significant number of supporters for a "third way."

The Polarized Party System

The beginning of this phase is marked by the public appearance of the opposition movements and ends with the founding elections. When the communist parties gave up the monopoly of power, post-communist party system development began. Strongly molded by a retrospective orientation, the central cleavage is that between supporters of the old system, represented by the communists, and supporters of the new, represented by the opposition movements.

In Poland, this period began in 1976 with the foundation of the Committee for the Defense of the Workers (KOR). The appearance of the independent trade union Solidarity in 1980, the first serious opposition mass movement within the communist bloc, marked the beginning of the end of communist rule (Ziemer 1997a, p. 176). Although Solidarity was banned from December 1981 to April 1989, no other influential opposition movement to the PZPR or competitor with Solidarity could emerge, nor did one take part in the negotiations with the PZPR. Solidarity was the only opposition movement in the V4 countries that could claim an actual monopoly on opposition activities (Grotz 2000, p. 97). The key actors of the opposition were a small number of intellectuals associated with the Committee of Citizens led by Lech Walesa.

The legitimacy deficit of the PZPR became even more evident after the events of 1981 and the proclamation of martial law. Neither the foundation of the National Trade Union Alliance (OPZZ), as a replacement for the banned Solidarity, nor the half hearted institutional reforms of the political system (together with a policy of extensive inclusion of the population and strategic exclusion of the oppositional elites) would change this. From 1987 onwards, in the context of a deteriorating economic situation, the population's critical attitude toward the regime manifested itself in the form of strikes and the call for a re-legalization of Solidarity. When in November 1987 a referendum on planned economic reforms (which originally were intended to create some legitimacy for the regime) failed to gain the necessary 50 percent of votes, the Messner administration resigned. Consequently, the PZPR under the new Rakowski cabinet was ready to enter into talks with the leadership of the Citizens' Committee. At the Tenth Plenary Session of the Central Committee in January 1989, after intense disagreements between the conservatives and the reformers, the PZPR by its own accord gave up the constitutional claim to a monopoly of power. In July 1989, after the semi-free elections, it was removed from the constitution. Poland then became the first country in the Eastern Bloc where the communists met the opposition in the round-table talks of February to April 1989.

The main goals of the opposition were the legalization of Solidarity, free parliamentary elections, and the transformation of the political and economic system in the direction of a pluralist democracy and market economy. The strategy of the PZPR, on the other hand, was to secure and legitimize their own position by including Solidarity in the decision-making process and to arrange a number of institutional reforms, without giving up power and without fundamentally altering the communist system as such. Besides other results, the PZPR finally allowed semi-competitive elections. The result of the semi-competitive elections of June 1989 showed the failure of the PZPR strategy. Although the voting system was originally designed to secure the victory of the communists, all the freely eligible seats went to Solidarity. The legitimacy of the PZPR had hit rock bottom. In September 1989, as a result, the communist government resigned and the first government led by former dissidents took office in the communist world. Obviously, the communists had misjudged the situation completely and had chosen the wrong strategy. They lost the elections and consequently their claim to power. Shortly after Wojciech Jaruzelski was re-elected president, he resigned as party chairman. After that, the struggle between the reformers and the conservatives within the PZPR escalated. While the extra-parliamentary conservative leadership of the PZPR under the new chairman Rakowski tried to hold together the Communist Party without having a clear strategy, new splinter groups within the PZPR surfaced. The most important initiatives were driven by members of the Parliament who faced the new demands of the transition process.

The dynamics of the transition and the appearance of transitional cleavages forced the PZPR parliamentarians to find answers for the most pressing questions of the early transition period, such as a strategy for economic transformation. This power struggle ended with the Eleventh PZPR Party Conference in January 1990. The PZPR dissolved and broke up into three major groups: the Polish Social Democratic Union (PUS), the SdRP, and the Parliamentary Club of the Democratic Left, which was later incorporated into the SdRP. The PUS tried to adopt a strategy of radical anticommunism, a strategy that ultimately failed. The anticommunist end of the communism/anticommunism cleavage was already occupied by the Solidarity camp. In 1992 PUS dissolved. The SdRP stood much closer to becoming the successor of the PZPR. It was founded on the broad financial, organizational, and logistic resources of that party. With the newly elected chairman Kwasniewski, the SdRP chose a strategy of pragmatic intra-party reforms. SdRP dissociated itself from its communist past but without a radical break. As for the transition process, they stood for a gradual transformation of the economy (instead of the shock therapy preferred by the government) and a basic democratization of the political system. But neither the SdRP nor any other party, including Solidarity, had a clear program or long-term strategy at this stage of the transition. In order to avoid a setback like that experienced in the first real free elections of October 1999, the post-communist camp opted for an alliance, the SLD, to marshal their forces. Besides the leading SdRP the alliance was made up of the trade union OPZZ and twenty-six minor successor organizations of the PZPR (Ziemer 1997b, pp. 60–61).

The strategy of the leaders of the SLD was to set themselves apart from the fragmented Solidarity camp. There were also signs of social-democratization occurring within the party. Although the SLD was not able to join the government after the 1991 election, their strategy was rather successful; in a totally fragmented Parliament, the SLD had become the second strongest party with 11.99 percent of the votes after the Democratic Union (UD), which had 12.32 percent. In Poland, the fragmented phase had already begun.

In Hungary, the polarized phase began in the summer of 1985 with the first formal meeting of the opposition groups. The second meeting of 1987 (with the participation of some MSZMP reformers, e.g. Imre Pozsgay, but with the exclusion of the more radical wing of the opposition) was followed by the founding of the three most important opposition groups in 1988: the Hungarian Democratic Forum (MDF), the Alliance of Free Democrats (SZDSZ), and the Federation of Young Democrats (Fidesz). While in Poland there was a bipolarity between the PZPR and Solidarity, in Hungary some programmatic and organizational alternatives already existed within the opposition camp in the run up to the founding election. Due to the comparatively relaxed regime of János Kádár and the stable "second economy" in that country, the legal formation and articulation of the opposition was comparatively easy. In addition, the economic process stimulated the social and economic differentiation of society, especially at the elite level. Nevertheless, the main cleavage was the one between the MSZMP and the opposition groups, which were able to hide their conflicts as long as a common enemy ruled the country. The key actors of the opposition were again a small number of intellectuals associated with the most important opposition groups.

Parallel to the organization of the opposition, the articulation and formation of intra-party reform forces within the MSZMP took place. Beginning in 1987, the old leadership around Kádár started to struggle with the radical and moderate reformers. In May 1988, at the MSZMP national conference, Kádár and several of his supporters were voted out of the Politburo. Kádár became honorary chairman but lost his influence. While the moderate reformer Károly Grósz became the new secretary general, the radical reformers, Imre Pozsgay and Rezsö Nyers, joined the Politburo. In 1988, the struggle between reformers and conservatives in the MSZMP deepened. Besides the prominent national elite groups, numerous local and regional reformist circles were also among the pacemakers of internal democratization. During the summer Grósz maintained efforts to carefully reform the MSZMP, to preserve its unity in conflict with a dissatisfied population, an increasingly well-organized opposition, and the reformist forces within the party. In November 1988, Grósz stepped down as prime minister. The radical reformer Miklós Németh took office, but until May of 1989 was forced to rule with the former Grósz cabinet and without a government program of his own. In the winter of 1988–89, disagreements between the former MSZMP leaders under Grósz, the reformist wing under Pozsgay, as well as the head of government under Németh, increased.

The break within the Communist Party became evident, when Pozsgay, much to the dismay of the party leadership, publicly stated that the events of 1956 had not been a counterrevolution but a people's uprising. Pozsgay's strategy to secure the population's support for the intra-party struggle for power worked out. A few days later the conservative MSZMP leadership adopted his position reluctantly and cleared the way for comprehensive institutional reforms. On 21 February 1989, the "leading role" clause of the MSZMP was removed from the constitution, which paved the way for multiparty competition. By March of 1989, the MSZMP had already presented the draft of a new democratic constitution, by its own accord and without participation of the opposition. After the increasingly lessened role of the party in the government, and the party's reformation during the spring of 1989, Grósz was removed from office as secretary general of the party in June of that year. Nyers, as the speaker of a four-person committee (which included himself, Pozsgay, Németh, and Grósz), became the new chairman. Kádár, who had been seriously ill, lost his position as honorary chairman, and died in July 1989. Following the Polish example, Hungarian communist elite groups made a pact with the most important elite circles of the opposition and the communist mass organizations as the controversial "third side." From June to September 1989 trilateral "roundtable talks" took place among those political groups. Those involved agreed on a peaceful transition toward a pluralistic, parliamentary democracy, a market economy, and free elections in the spring of 1990.

At the MSZMP Party Congress in October 1989, the MSZMP was dissolved and a successor party, the Hungarian Socialist Party (MSZP), was established. Whereas formally the MSZP was the legal successor of the MSZMP, its leaders wanted to radically distance themselves from the past regime. Unlike almost all other successor parties, the MSZP renounced the financial resources of the MSZMP. Although MSZMP members were invited to join the MSZP, only 1.5 percent, or about 10,000 members, did so (Grotz 2000, p. 219). Because of the strategy of a radical renunciation of the communist past the communism vs. anticommunism cleavage in Hungary lost importance very early on. Grósz had tried to provide a political home for orthodox communists by refounding the MSZMP shortly after its dissolution, but essentially dropped the plan due to lack of voter support. Distancing themselves from their past and their general support of democracy and a market economy alone was not enough to gain the electoral victory the MSZP had hoped for in the founding elections of March-April 1990. After the MDF, the SZDSZ, and the Independent Smallholders' Party (FKGP), the MSZP finished fourth in the polling of 1990 and was not included in the government.

In Czechoslovakia, political polarization had only started in November 1989, even though there were some older roots of the opposition, like the Charter 77 or the Movement for Civil Liberty (HOS). In this country all opposition activities were suppressed by the system until 1989. At the beginning of 1989, the Club for Socialist Reform (Obroda) formed. Obroda recruited its members mainly among the former reform-communists of 1968. They declared their support for socialism, but strived for political and economic reforms based on the Gorbachev model. Whereas in Poland and Hungary such currents could form within the communist parties, this was not possible in Czechoslovakia because of the absolute dominance of the hard-liners in the KSC. Until 1989 it was mainly intellectuals who, on the side of the opposition, made demands upon the regime. The participation of the citizens, however, gradually increased by the beginning of 1989. In August 1989, 3,000 members of the opposition demonstrated on the anniversary of the Warsaw Pact invasion. The brutal action of the police against the protesters reflected the dominance of the hard-liners. In the KPC there were no prominent reformers, and no rupture in the power structure was discernible.

In September 1989 one of the opposition groups, the Democratic Initiative (DI), renamed itself the Party of the Czechoslovakian Democratic Initiative and adopted a program that included a return to democracy and a market economy. Although initially this represented in essentially only a change of name, this action could be seen as the founding of the first party before the collapse of the system. The polarized phase, however, began with the founding of the Civic Forum and the Public Against Violence. The Civic Forum (OF), in which all renowned Czech opposition groups and opponents of the regime joined together, was founded on 19 November 1989 as "the voice of the opposition." In the Slovakian part of the country, the opposition alliance Public Against Violence (VPN) was also founded on 20 November 1989. With the foundation of the OF and the VPN for the first time after forty-one years, opponents of the KPC entered the political stage. Although, in this phase other political groups also came into existence, the OF and the VPN dominated the side of the opposition. As in Hungary, there was no bipolarity between the KPC on the one hand and the opposition movements on the other. While in Hungary the opposition differentiated along first, somewhat vague, cleavages, in Czechoslovakia there was one specific cleavage that was to eclipse all others until the division of the country in January of 1993—the Czech-Slovak contrast. Until after the founding elections, however, the "communism vs. anticommunism" cleavage remained the most important.

Whereas in Poland and Hungary the establishment of the opposition and that of the reformers within the communist parties was roughly a parallel process, this was not the case in Czechoslovakia. In December 1987 Husák stepped down as secretary-general, and his successor was Milos Jakes. Jakes was not burdened with the stigma of 1968, but within the KSC he was considered an uncompromising hard-liner. On 16 November 1989 Gorbachev called the 1968 invasion an unlawful act. The KSC still legitimized the event, however, as the suppression of counterrevolutionary actions. On 17 November 1989 the first mass protest occurred in Prague. Once more a large number of security forces were used to suppress the demonstration. The brutal actions of the police caused the international isolation of the orthodox communist regime in Prague. Meanwhile, the ongoing transition in Poland and Hungary continued, and the opening of the Berlin Wall on 9 November 1989 foreshadowed the end of communist rule in the GDR. The erosion of the power of the Socialist Unity Party of Germany (SED) especially illustrated the isolation of the KPC. Romania, however, was the only other country besides Czechoslovakia in the disintegrating Eastern Bloc that steered a similarly hard course toward the opposition. On 18 November 1989, Prime Minister Adamec approved an investigation of the brutal police action of the day before. This marked a decisive turning point. A schism in the KSC was in the offing, although there were no signs of a democratic opening. On 23 November 1989, the Soviet ambassador refused to grant Jakes military support. Jakes had to abandon his last hope of saving the authoritarian system. The strategy of the party committee to secure power with force had proved wrong. International isolation and internal erosion of power only allowed one consequence; on 24 November 1989 Secretary General Jakes and the whole party leadership of the KPC stepped down.

At this point, Jakes was already discredited as a political partner for carrying on a dialogue with the opposition. The moderate "reformer" Urbánek became the new secretary general. After the general strike of 27 November 1989, mass demonstrations ceased; there followed a period of negotiations between the opposition and representatives of the regime. The first meeting between Václav Havel (speaker of the OF) and the communist moderate Adamec on 26 November 1989, marked the start of a dialogue between the KSC and the opposition. For the first time there were public discussions about democratizing the political system and about how this was to be achieved. As a first step, on 29 November 1989 the leading role of the KSC was removed from the constitution. The KSC then tried—much too late—to distance itself from its authoritarian past by replacing all party leaders. Their goal and new strategy was to not lose too much support in the beginning process of transformation. On 7 December 1989 Adamec resigned as prime minister. Marián Calfa took on the formation of a government, with the Prague roundtable in December 1989 advising. At the roundtable were the isolated and discredited KSCs, other organizations of the communist dominated National Front, as well as the OF, the VPN, and further citizens' initiatives.

The most important outcome of the roundtable talks was the scheduling of the first free elections. With the resignation of Husák as head of state on 10 December 1989, the last hard-liner and protector of the authoritarian system lost his position of power. Under Prime Minister Calfa a "Government of National Accord" was formed; the KSC provided nine ministers, the bloc parties four, and the OF and the VPN seven in this government. At the end of December 1989 the KSC publicly apologized for its past wrongs. Twenty-eight leading members were excluded from the party, including Husák and Jakes. In spite of this strategy of purging leaders from the past, the KSC never really parted from its past.

In order to account for general trend toward a federalization of the institutions (Hatschikjan and Weilemann, 1994, p. 93), the KSC was subsequently divided into Czech and Slovakian organizations. The founding of the Communist Party of Bohemia and Moravia (KSCM) on 31 March 1990 in the Czech region of the country sealed the division of the KSC. In Slovakia, the Communist Party of Slovakia (KSS) evolved into the KSS-SDL in October 1990 and then turned into the Party of the Democratic Left (SDL) in January 1991. Whereas the KSCM viewed itself as the successor of the KSC, the election of Peter Weiss as party chairman of the KSS in

January 1990 marked the Party's concerted effort to break with the legacy of its communist past.

The founding elections in Czechoslovakia were not really an election of alternatives, "the voters in Czechoslovakia could not clearly determine a defined political and economic course in June of 1990" (Hatschikjan and Weilemann 1994, p. 94). The election was much rather a referendum about the communist system and in this sense a ratification of the new reforms. Whereas the SdRP/SLD and the MSZP had the opportunity to reform and to reposition themselves before the founding elections and made use of this chance, this was not possible in Czechoslovakia due to the rapid implosion of the communist regime and the rigid position of the KSC. Predictably, the communists were the losers in the elections; the KSC/KSCM in the Czech portion of the country gained 13.24 percent of the votes, while the KSC/KSS in the Slovakian part gained 13.43 percent.

The short period between the start of a party competition and the founding elections was still strongly shaped by the legacy of authoritarian rule. Neither the communists nor the opposition movements were able to develop clear, differentiated political positions. The opposition movements stood against communism and for some unspecified "something else." They were melting pots for people of most diverse world views. The emphasis was on common values instead of diverging interests. At this time, in contrast to Hungary, no real party system format was discernible, especially in terms of coherent programs. The polarized phase was characterized by abstract debates about the past and the future, rather than about policies. At the beginning of the party development, elite groups appeared as the main actors on the side of the regime as well as on that of the opposition. They were the driving forces behind the initial development of parties. The role of the population was for the most part limited to supporting the opposition elite. The polarization of the elites, however, reflects the main social and political cleavage in that phase, e.g. the old vs. new system. Solidarity and unity were considered more important than the articulation of different interests. The diffuse aims of "democracy" and "market economy" had been put on the banners of all relevant parties, with the exception of the KSCM. Additionally, rudimentary socioeconomic and structural-regional cleavages were further blurred by the insecurities of the first transitional phase, or at least strongly eclipsed by them. The polarization of existing interests and conflict patterns was very low (Bielasiak 1992, p. 201), and their (institutionalized) articulation weak (Bielasiak 1997, p. 36). The social homogeneity of the population helps explain the lack of differentiated expectations toward politics. The "weakness of political society" (Bielasiak 1997, pp. 24–25) as well as their political apathy also meant that that there were hardly any concrete foundations for the mobilization of political attitudes. Melanie Tatur (1991, p. 235) refers to these as barriers to "the politicization of the public."

The MSZP and the SdRP/SLD initially followed the strategy, or rather hoped that by engaging in internal change and constructive cooperation in the transition process, they could secure their hegemonic position within the party system, or at least be part of the government. The KSC, on the other hand, tried—until the implosion of its rule—to maintain this power position by force. Both strategies eventually failed. The communists were the big losers of the first elections.

Concerning the ideological-programmatic development of the communist parties, and thus their later positioning along certain political cleavages, who won the internal struggle within the party was decisive. If the reformers, who sought to discard the ideological ballast of the past, dominated, then they were very likely to support democracy and the market economy and to choose the road of social-democratization. If, on the other hand, the conservative hard-liners dominated (as with the KSCM) then some other strategy was adopted. Discredited in the eyes of the population, still dominated by a conservative leadership, acting as an anti system-opposition seemed almost predetermined. Nonetheless, whether a party followed a reformist or hard-line strategy seems not to have made much difference (at least initially). Indeed, all the successor parties gained between 10 and 13 percent of the votes in the initial elections.

The Fragmented Party System

The transition period in the post-communist states opened up opportunities for new actors to compete for power and influence. As there were hardly any firm bonds between parties and society, new actors could position themselves wherever they felt they could potentially mobilize political support (Beyme 1997, p. 42, Glaessner 1994, p. 260, Kitschelt 1992, p. 17). The weak party bonds, the insecurity and inexperience of the voters provided actors with many opportunities to solicit votes.

Over time, new cleavages emerged. The communism vs. anticommunism cleavage dominant in the first phase lost its importance. Since the conflict axis "old vs. new system" was already overpopulated, and the issue was seen as settled by many after the first elections, new actors had to choose new cleavages for themselves. Political cleavages, brought about by quarrels to do with the right policy as well as political-cultural cleavages or even "cultural wars," became dominant in the second phase (Timmermann 1994, p. 5, Glaessner 1994, p. 253, Meyer 1997, pp. 152–153, Márkus 1996). Concerning this, an analytical distinction between the culture of the elites and the mass culture has to be taken into consideration. The transitional and cultural politics were very much driven by elites. The readiness to participate and support the parties by part of the population was rather limited after the experiences of forced participation and ritualized politicization in the times of state socialism. In contrast to the transitional and cultural conflicts of the elites, "bread-and-butter" questions became the focus of much of the population (Stöss and Segert 1997, p. 389).

However, the elites still played the decisive role. Conflicts between elites within the opposition camp and the emergence of new elite groups using parties as a means to gain power were instrumental in causing political fragmentation. The conflicts between the parties equalled the conflicts between the elites, but in this phase, these conflicts "were based on no or at best rudimentarily consolidated social cleavage structures" (Glaessner 1994, p. 253). The lack of trust in the parties was furthered still by the top-down process of party development.

Popular condemnation of the successor parties because of their communist past began to lose its force. Those that railed most against the mistakes of the past were increasingly seen as incompetent, egotistical, and corrupt. Competence and professionalism became highly valued and many reformers in the successor parties thus gained greater respect (such as Prime Minister Horn in Hungary, President Kwasniewski in Poland, and Representative Weiss in Slovakia).

Although the lack of intra-party organizational structures as well as a stable voter basis characterized the numerous proto- or pseudo-parties that developed during this phase (Beyme 1994, p. 279), the successor parties were the exception. They were among the parties with the most loyal members and voters and a nationwide, uniform organization (Stöss and Segert 1997, pp. 418–420). They possessed considerable financial and logistic resources, an effective bureaucracy, and good connections with the mass media. The MSZP and the SDL especially presented themselves as united, fresh alternatives to the unstable and splintered governments of the conservative-bourgeois, Christian Catholic, and nationalist camp. The strategic connection with the trade unions in Poland (SLD-OPZZ) and Hungary (MSZP-MSZOSZ) were further structural advantages of the ex-communists. However, the image of stability and unity belied the conflicts between the pragmatic-technocratic, social-democratic, leftist-socialist, social-liberal, and national-populist wings of the successor camp.

Nonetheless, electoral defeats in the founding elections compelled the party leaders to a change of strategy and to reposition themselves along new political cleavages. In Poland and Hungary, countries with weak competition from other left-wing parties, this strategy involved social-democratization, largely because there was an absence of other social democratic alternatives. Indeed, "contrary to the SLD and MSZP, other, genuinely social-democratic groups had no professional, prominent leadership and were estranged among themselves and inadequately organized" (Meyer 1997, p. 156). In Poland only the Union of Labor (UP) and the Polish Peasant

Party (PSL) competed with the SLD on the left. In Hungary, only the SZDSZ competed besides the MSZP for left-wing votes.

Besides social-democratization, however, party leaders followed a strategy of developing political-cultural bonds with the voters (Fenner 1984, Meyer 1997, Miller and White 1998). This strategy included distancing the party from the Marxist-Leninist ideology as well as promoting their image as West European–orientated parties of experts, technocrats, and pragmatists. In Hungary, a high-brow "cultural war" between the center-right parties alienated the voters. The strategy of the MSZP and SLD was to depict themselves as more competent, more professional, and more in touch with the people than the competition, with popular top candidates as crisis managers (Eyal, Szelényi, and Townsley 1998). They stressed cooperation instead of confrontation, announced that they would take the concerns of the little man seriously, and distinguished themselves from the other parties as morally upright and incorruptible.

In Hungary, the MSZP cultivated the image of early reformers and credible democrats. MSZP wanted a calmer, safer, more predictable, and most of all more socially tolerable transformation. The emphasis lay on more social security, equality of opportunity, and justice. Because of the disappointment that the new elite groups had so far (only) brought upon them, the losers of the economic transition gathered around the successor parties; these strata were about 40–50 percent of the electorate. (For an overview of winners and losers, see Meyer 1997, p. 156.) Without programmatically tying themselves down to a strictly social-democratic course, they also managed to present themselves as a competent alternative to the fragmented or paralyzed center-right camp. This image made the post-communists also attractive to the winners of the transition. In Poland "the SLD under Kwasniewski managed to gain a relative majority among all major socioeconomic groups with exception of the devoted Catholics over 55 years of age" (Meyer 1997, p. 156). The support from all walks of life showed that at this point in time a (structural) socioeconomic cleavage was less momentous than political-cultural or transition-related political cleavages. This is also true of Hungary where "the lack of a sharp profile of support probably helped the Socialist Party toward its election victory" (Miller and White 1998, p. 209).

Both in Poland and in Hungary the strategies of the ex-communists were successful. They were the winners of the second free parliamentary elections in 1993 and 1994, respectively (partly due to the distortion caused by the electoral system and the splintering of the competition). The SLD obtained 20.4 percent of the votes and 37.2 percent of the seats, while the MSZP won 32.9 percent of the votes and 54.15 percent of the seats. Both parties filled the positions of the new prime ministers and were the leading parties in the ruling coalitions.

In the Czech Republic the KSCM had difficulty developing a strategy for adaptation after the sudden loss of power. The party leadership vacillated between neo-communism and democratic socialism, and failed to put together a coherent party platform or to set a forward-looking course as the Polish and Hungarian successor parties had. Between 1990 and 1993 (perhaps, even longer), the KSCM was consumed with internal factional infighting. In order not to lose even more ground as an anti-system party, the KSCM finally made up its mind to generally support political (party) pluralism, parliamentary democracy and economic transformation. It defined itself as the party of the underprivileged and of the common man. It was skeptical toward NATO and, in part, toward the EU. While comparable non-reformed successor parties in other post-communist countries transmuted into a nationalistic direction, the KSCM remained definitely non-transmuted, perhaps because of the ideological internationalism as a legacy of the communist past. More likely it was because the national camp was already occupied by the nationalistic Coalition for the Republic-Republican Party of the Czech Republic (SPR-RSC), founded in February 1990. Further the moderate left-wing, social-democratic position on the Czech party scale was occupied by the historic Czech Social Democratic Party (CSSD), refounded in December 1989. The CSSD developed into the strongest force within the Czech party system up to the 1998 parliamentary elections. Even if the KSCM had been able to decide upon social-democratization, they would have been faced with a powerful, historically unburdened rival.

In January 1992 the KSCM together with a few unimportant leftist splinter groups formed the election coalition Left Bloc. Whereas the SLD strategy of the SdRP worked (to gain control over potential competitors) and led to more unity within the post-communist camp, the KSCM and the Left Bloc failed to do so. Factional disputes in the KSCM were worsened by conflicts in the Left Bloc and due to the insignificance of the splinter groups, not even the potential voter base was increased.

The second democratic election in the Czechoslovak Federated Republic (CSFR) on 24 June 1992 was, on the one hand, the first election involving real alternatives, on the other a referendum on the future of the CSFR as a nation-state (Nohlen and Kasapovic 1996, p.150). The predominant relevant political cleavage was that of the future unity of the country. This cleavage was primarily represented by the Civic Democratic Party (ODS) in the Czech region and by the Movement for Democratic Slovakia (HZDS) in the Slovak area. The opposition parties were not included in the ensuing negotiations. This was especially true of the KSCM in the Czech region, which was mainly concerned with its own survival (Kitschelt 1989, pp. 1–74).

In the CSFR the pluralist phase did not begin until after the second election of 1992. Unresolved problems between Czechs and Slovaks prevented a consolidation of the political system and of the party system. As a matter of fact, there were two party systems after the 1992 election. Only the division of the CSFR on 1 January 1993 provided the opportunity to consolidate the now separated, autonomous party systems. However new elections were held much later. In Slovakia elections took place in 1994, in the Czech Republic only in 1996. The developments as of 1992 were thus the starting point of party system development in the respective states. The separation brought about no qualitative changes; it only intensified existing trends. Kitschelt states that generally at this time, "Czech politics tended to be (aimed) toward libertarian-promarket policies, [whereas] Slovak politics primarily appeal(ed) to more authoritarian and antimarket sentiments" (Kitschelt 1992, p. 30).

The libertarian, pro-market climate in Czech politics only pushed the KSCM further toward the margins of the party system and increased internal tensions. The party convention of the KSCM in December 1992 indicated a growing influence of the conservative wing within the party. But it was not until the party congress of June 1993 that a break occurred between the old-school Stalinist wing surrounding Miroslav Stepan, the reform-socialist wing around party head Jiri Svoboda, and the conservative-communist middle around Milos Grebenícek. After Grebenícek was elected the new party chairman, strengthening the conservative-communist wing, the Stalinists left for the Party of Czech Communists and the reform-socialists left for the Party of the Democratic Left. The KSCM did become more internally homogenous; at the same time a tough competition developed with three parties fighting for the same voter basis. After the division into two states the cleavages concerning the adequate strategy for the transition and the winner-loser cleavage moved to the center of the party competition in the Czech Republic. While the successor parties in Poland and Hungary managed to (in addition to the losers of the transition) appeal to young, successful voters with their programmatic and strategic redirection and their modern image, both camps denied the KSCM their support. The disappointed losers of the transition found a political home with the CSSD, the contented winners with the ODS. In the third democratic parliamentary elections of 1996, the first in the sovereign Czech Republic, the KSCM had to endure their worst result yet, polling only 10.33 percent of the votes. However, they still qualified for third place in the competition (after ODS and CSSD). Thus, despite the split the KSCM could still count on a core of loyal voters.

In Slovakia, the strategy of the SDL at first appeared to be similar to the paths followed by the SLD and MSZP. The reform course initiated under Weiss was continued after the elections. However, the SDL was faced with an additional challenge; the HZDS presented an ideological-programmatic competitor with similar political strategies. Promotion of a socially tolerable policy of transformation, and a paternalistic, partly national-populist empathy for the worries of the common man became the latter party's hallmarks. The SDL had great difficulty distinguishing itself from the HZDS. The two parties were in agreement on many issues, both programmatic and strategic as well as tactical. Yet the SDL often appeared to be a more moderate, less authoritarian copy of the original.

The parliamentary elections of 1992, which further strengthened the HZDS, showed the gap between the SDL and the HZDS. The SDL obtained a mere 14.7 percent of the vote, while the HZDS won almost 35 percent. After the division into two states, the political cleavages concerning the adequate strategies of transition and political-cultural conflicts moved into the spotlight in Slovakia. In this context, conflicts between the HZDS camp and the "anti-Mečiar-parties" developed rapidly. Yet until their inclusion in the government in March 1994, the SDL maintained their social-democratic and, in contrast to the HZDS, clearly pro-Western image, despite performing poorly in the 1992 elections.

This situation changed when the SDL joined a coalition government that replaced the HZDS in 1994. The SDL wanted to both distance itself from the coalition partners of the center-right government and from the HZDS. However this touched off intraparty conflicts. A first indicator of factional dispute was the departure of the radically leftist Workers' Union of Slovakia (ZRS) in April 1994, from the ranks of the SDL. With the emergence of the ZRS, another competitor for the SDL arose in the leftist camp. To compensate for this, before the 1994 election, the SDL entered into an electoral alliance entitled the "United Vote" (SV) with the Social Democratic Party of Slovakia (SDSS), the Peasant Movement (HP), and the Green Party (SZS). Instead of the development of a common (campaign) strategy under SDL leadership, conflicts with the smaller parties led to a further loss of SDL prominence, including the worst electoral result that the SDL had yet experienced: a mere 10.4 percent of the votes.

The Pluralist Party System

Of the large number of new parties that entered the competition in the new democracies of Eastern and Central Europe, only a few were able to formally constitute themselves before their countries' second parliamentary elections and only about 20 to 40 per country were registered for the elections. The outcomes of the elections acted as an important filter for future party system development. The number of the relevant parties was reduced, and the remaining parties were forced to clarify their positions and programs and to put clear emphasis on certain issues.

The years after the second elections brought about a structuring of the political and social space. The election winners stood for relatively clear positions and positions on left-right axes which, in turn, reinforced these axes and kept the voters aware of differences between the parties. The election losers had lost because they had positioned themselves along cleavages that were less important. The losers either dissolved after a short time or tried to reenter the political competition by retooling their identities or by joining forces with other parties. In this way, extra-parliamentary parties had to choose niches by which to compete with parties of similar programs. Transition-related political cleavages lost importance and were less and less appropriate as a basis of party competition. Voters gradually found their new position in the social structure. Their objective and subjective self-classification within the new system helped develop individual and collective interests, identities, and value orientations. Political-cultural conflicts still remained an important starting point for the party competition, due to the continuous mobilization and politicization of these cleavages by the parties and their elite groups.

The development of specific identities was a prerequisite for the development of a more specific process of interest articulation. This process formed the basis for the emergence of new intermediary structures corresponding to the new situation of market-economic transformation and democratic consolidation. The programmatic and strategic integration of intermediary structures and political elites/parties still remained the exception. In addition to collective interests, the voters also developed a more pronounced political ability to judge. Vague ideas and hopes about the perspectives of the transformation were replaced by more differentiated judgments. A broad basis of information and the first experiences with political programs implemented a "retrospective evaluation of policies" (Bielasiak 1997, p. 39). The population, increasingly aware of their own position within the social structure, learned to assess the effects of different political programs on their lives, especially economic policies.

The dominance of political-cultural and socioeconomic cleavages in this phase did not mean the disappearance of others. Indeed, there occurred a movement away from merely political cleavages toward increasingly structural social ones. Even though the voters could now distinguish the parties and their programs and more clearly understood how the parties' policies affected their own socioeconomic status, this did lot lead to strong bonds between the parties and the populace. Also in this phase, the parties remained for the most part elite-dominated with relatively few members. There was little in the way of a move toward mass parties with distinct intra-party structures. The roots of the parties were generally stronger in the Parliament than in the constituencies (Bielasiak 1997, p. 40). Essentially, the function of interest articulation/aggregation/representation only weakly developed. It seems appropriate to speak of "top-down politics" in this phase.

The organizational weakness of the parties also influenced the consolidation of the party systems. Parties are very much dependent on the course of the political filtering process and on the transformation. This weakness is expressed in the continuing process of new party formation, party restructuring, and party disintegration. In this situation, extra-parliamentary parties can still hope to enter the Parliament in the next elections. The stabilization of the party systems in the Visegrád countries remains uncertain for the time being.

In Poland and Hungary, the ruling successor parties were faced with ever more contradictory expectations because of their heterogeneous voter base. They had won the elections with votes from workers, pensioners, managers, administration clerks, artists, members of economic elites, winners and losers of the transformation, and votes from the urban and rural population alike. They gained support from the trade unions as well as the goodwill of international and national financial institutions. However, it became increasingly difficult to offer a cohesive identify (G. Márkus 1996, p. 24). The responsibility for the setting of the course in the transition process also posed a great challenge to the internal unity of the SLD and the MSZP.

In Hungary, the MSZP continued with their course of reform, evident in their coalition with the decidedly anticommunist SZDSZ. In Hungary, the MSZP unambiguously positioned itself as a consensus-orientated, cosmopolitan, pro-Western party, a party that identifies with the basic values and principles of Western social-democratic parties (G. Márkus 1996, p. 24). After coming to power, the tensions in the MSZP were mainly caused by debates over economic policy. The strategy of continuing internal social-democratization and intra-party compensation progressively came into conflict with the requirements of a fundamental reform of the economy and the social security systems. Because of the economic "shock therapy" the different political-ideological currents within the party became more and more evident. As a compensation for the planned reforms, Horn suggested the appointment of MSZOSZ-chairman Sándor Nagy as deputy prime minister in charge of overseeing the economy. This strategy eventually failed because of the resistance of the MSZP's coalition partner. After approving the Bokros package in March 1995, and against the backdrop of a worsening economic crisis, tensions mounted, leading to an identity crisis of the MSZP. The left-wing of the party (trade unionists, the nationalist and Marxist left, representatives from the province, etc.) clashed with the social-liberals and the non-ideological technocrats of the MSZP right-wing. Only with great effort did Horn manage to avoid the breakup of the party into mass protests by disappointed voters. Within the MSZP, however, now, despite continuing tensions, the course of the powerful technocratic center of the party has prevailed and prevented programmatic changes (Bozóki 1997).

During the runoff to the parliamentary election of 1997, the formerly estranged opposition camp of the center-right parties in Hungary managed to form an electoral alliance. Consequently, the 1998 campaign became increasingly polarized, pitting the Fidesz-Hungarian Civic Party (Fidesz-MPP) and the MDF on one side and the MSZP on the other. The non-ideological and substance-free campaign was rather surprising considering the contenders. It proves, however, that the party competition in Hungary was still strongly determined by the tactical strategies of the elite groups and not so much by established political-ideological positions or the orientation toward a particular voter base. The outcome of the 1998 parliamentary elections was just as surprising as the campaign. Although the MSZP, with 43 percent of the vote, actually won the election, because of the unusual Hungarian electoral system they actually only received 30.7 percent of the seats (Grotz 2000, pp. 268–274), and thus returned into the opposition. Nonetheless, the MSZP continued to act as a social-democratic, Western-style party and did not fundamentally change after the election. Both the tactical vote against constitutional change in favor of Hungary's entry into NATO in December 1998, and Horn's refusal to ally with the national-populist FKGP (who resigned in favor of László Kovács in September 1998) are noteworthy. In June 2001, the MSZP elected its candidate for prime minister, Péter Medgyessy, a former member of the Grósz and Németh cabinets of 1987–89 and a representative of the technocratic wing, but interestingly not an official member of the MSZP.

In Poland, as in the case of Hungary, the economic and political pragmatism of the liberal wing of the successor party SdRP prevailed against the trade-union wing of the OPZZ. Prior to the 1995 presidential election the communism-anticommunism cleavage was reactivated, but was eventually eclipsed by political-cultural conflicts. It was the candidate of the Solidarity camp, Walesa, who revived the communist-anticommunist cleavage and accused the SLD of representing the "old" system. The election victories of the popular SLD candidate Kwasniewski in the presidential elections of 1995 and 2000 prove, however, that this conflict was not suited to mobilize voters for Walesa. In June 1996 the foundation of the Solidarity Electoral Action (AWS) brought about a decisive change in the Polish party system. By forming the AWS, the formerly fragmented Solidarity camp managed to unify. In the runoff to the 1997 parliamentary elections the campaign became polarized mainly along political-cultural cleavages, e.g. nationalist vs. cosmopolitan, Catholic vs. secular, and traditional vs. modern value orientations. These divisions became increasingly prominent in the struggle between the AWS and the SLD. In terms of the socioeconomic cleavage (hardly politicized in the campaign) the AWS was positioned decisively "left" of the SLD. In traditionally Catholic Poland, the 1997 elections showed that the "right-wing" political-cultural views represented by the AWS could mobilize a slightly larger voter base. The assessment of the election outcome is nevertheless ambivalent. On the one hand, the SLD came in only second with 27.1 percent of the vote (slightly behind the AWS with 33.8 percent) and thus returned into the opposition. On the other hand, the SLD had managed to improve their proportion of the votes by 7 percent in comparison to 1993, so the voter mobilization strategy of the SLD could also be rightfully described as successful. The election result and, in part, the stabilization of the demographic and regional voter base of the respective parties and alliances, confirm the trend of the formation of political camps. In addition to the heterogeneous Solidarity camp, including the conservative-nationalistic

Movement for the Reconstruction of Poland (ROP), there is also room for the much more homogenous SLD-camp. The table on page 364 summarizes the main ideological components of the two competing camps.

In addition, there was the smaller neo-liberal camp of the Freedom Union (UW) and the less important agricultural, rural, and clientelistic PSL. The formation of camps was institutionalized by the post-communists upon the "founding congress" of the SLD in December 1999. The SdRP had dissolved in June, thus after members of the groups involved agreed by a large majority, the SLD alliance became the SLD party. According to party chairman Miller, "the SLD henceforth wants to be a mass party, not a class or cadre party [to] win over people who belong to the political center as well as depoliticized non-voters with a non-ideological and undogmatic course" (quoted in Lang 2000, p. 2). Accordingly, the goal of the new SLD was to become "a pragmatic, center-left mass party with a social basis not restricted to certain classes" (Lang 2000, p. 2). The recent SLD victory at the parliamentary elections in September 2001 made clear that the adopted strategy was quite successful.

In Slovakia, the factional dispute in the SDL worsened after the party's poor electoral performance in the 1994 elections. Increasingly, two camps formed within the SDL, that of the "moderates" and that of the "conservatives." Whereas the moderates around party chairman Weiss were still in favor of a pro-Western, social-democratic course of the party and against cooperation with the HZDS, the conservatives wanted go back to the leftist roots of the party in combination with a nationalistic-populist strategy. They were also in favor of cooperation with the HZDS. The fundamental conflicts within the party reflected the dominant cleavages in Slovakian society. The main question was that of cooperation with the HZDS and thus of support for their authoritarian-populist and nationalistic style of politics and their leftist economic policies of redistribution. After the well-respected and popular party chairman Weiss resigned unexpectedly in November 1995, a breakup of the SDL seemed possible. Weiss's successor, the compromise candidate Josef Migas, who was voted into office with only a small majority, managed to prevent the split of the party. He also profited from the campaign for the 1998 parliamentary elections. Against the backdrop of the main cleavages sketched above and that of the campaign, "the parliamentary party system polarized less according to political-programmatic differences but rather according to the diverging concepts of democracy of the respective parties" (Grotz 2000, p. 392). The 1998 election turned out to be a referendum on Prime Minister Mečiar. The SDL benefited from its refusal to cooperate with the HZDS, and, because of this, they appealed to voters who supported the economic and social policy of the HZDS but did not agree with Mečiar's anti-democratic style of politics. Moreover, by nominating young, modern, and competent candidates, the SDL managed to attract new potential voters. With 14.7 percent of the votes in the 1998 elections, the SDL was compara-

Table 17.1

Comparative Attributes of Poland's SLD and Solidarity Parties

	"Solidarity"-camp	SLD-camp
Culturally:	National, traditional, Catholic	Westernized, modern, secular
Economically:	Leftist-redistributionist	Technocratic and liberal

Source: Author's compilation.

tively successful. They could establish themselves as the third strongest force and, after a four year hiatus, reenter government. A promising young member of Parliament, Róbert Fico, became vice party head, and for a short time the paralyzing internal factional dispute seemed to be a thing of the past.

But the conflict soon reemerged. The SDL did not find a clear profile in the heterogeneous government coalition. While the policies of the SDL minister of finance were too market-economic and too liberal for the conservative wing, the national-populist conflicts with the Hungarian minorities were a thorn in the flesh of the moderates. The SDL failed to find a clear strategy and could not position itself clearly on the dominant conflict axes. Since Fico's departure from the party in December 1999 and Weiss's failure to regain the party leadership at the July 2000 party convention, support for the SDL has dwindled. While Slovakia, despite the rule of Mečiar, steers toward democratic consolidation, the SDL has failed to establish itself as a modern, social-democratic party clearly distanced from the authoritarian, leftist-populist HZDS.

In the Czech Republic, as in all the other Visegrád countries, the fragmentation of party systems decreased dramatically after the 1996 elections. After the 1996 elections, the ODS remained the strongest force, but only barely. The performance of the CSSD, which increased its share of the vote from 6.5 percent to 26.4 percent in the 1996 election, challenged the ODS victory. The two dominant and almost equally strong parliamentary parties, ODS and CSSD, both needed (several) coalition partners to form a government. Because of mounting conflict between the center-right parties, and especially because of personal quarrels focusing on the respective party elites, the minority government of ODS, Christian Democratic Union (KDU-CSL), and Civic Democratic Alliance (ODA) that was formed came under increasing pressure. The CSSD rejected any cooperation with the KSCM, even though there was no other potential coalition partner on the left.

While the KSCM began to consolidate internally in 1993 and managed to further consolidate their voter base after that, year all strategies aimed at broadening their voter base or at attracting new voters had heretofore failed. The KSCM was seen as an extremist left-wing, anti-system party with which no party would form a coalition. The economic crisis of 1997 and 1998 and escalating personal quarrels (additionally fueled by corruption and party donation scandals) between and within the parties led to the disintegration of the formerly stable right-wing camp. The decline of the coalition had already begun with the defection of the Freedom Union (US) from the ODS in January 1998. These difficulties facing the center-right camp ultimately led to the resignation of prime minister Klaus because of a party donations scandal. Fanned by the interim appointment of Czech National Bank head, Josef Tosovsky, as prime minister in the caretaker government, the quarrels continued up until the parliamentary elections of July 1998. The left-right cleavage dominant in the Czech Republic both on the level of the parties and that of the voters (Klima 1998, p. 76) was strongly eclipsed by personal conflicts among party elites in the 1998 elections. As Grotz notes, "the configuration of the party-political elites was even more paradoxical after the 1998 elections than two years before; on the one hand, the parliamentary party system was more concentrated than before; on the other hand the formation of a government had become [even] more problematic" (Grotz 2000, p. 378).

Despite the difficulties facing their competitors, the KSCM only slightly improved upon its previous electoral showings with 11 percent of the vote in 1998. In July 1998, the CSSD and the ODS, who had acrimoniously fought each other during the campaign, agreed on a controversial "Opposition Contract." This cleared the way for a minority government by the CSSD, with the toleration of the ODS who had, for the first time, by a narrow margin been defeated by the CSSD. The enduring stalemate between the CSSD and the ODS led to a stagnation in the political decision process and to an increasing loss of trust in the parties. Numerous scandals involving ministers and members of Parliament further lessened the public trust in the major parties. The great beneficiary of this situation was the KSCM, which "has, in some polls, become the most popular party, with up to a quarter of the electorate willing to vote for them" (Lang 1999, p. 1). The KSCM owed its current popularity to a number of positional advantages it held since 1998. As Lang notes, "after the formation of the Zeman government, the KSCM is the only relevant leftist opposition party . . . the only radical opposition party with an anti-systemic direction [and] after the CSSD took on responsibility in the executive [branch] the only parliamentary party that has not yet ruled and thus could not discredit themselves by that" (Lang 1999, p. 4).

Conclusions

All communist successor parties managed to secure a place for themselves on the post-communist political stage. The SLD achieved this most easily, on the eve of again taking power as a unified, dynamic, and undogmatic party of the left-center with a broad and relatively stable voter base. The

MSZP was not quite as successful. It has developed into a stable Western-style social-democratic party with by far the best results in the last elections, but its strategy seems slightly confused and in comparison to Poland the voter base has yet to become consolidated. To the surprise of many, the neo-communist KSCM has recently established itself as a third power in the party system, and it seems possible that it may even overtake the CSSD in the next elections. It remains an open question which thematic programmatic consequences this could have for the fundamental-oppositional KSCM which has up to now been isolated in the party competition. The future of the internally estranged and programmatically hazy SDL is just as uncertain.

In order to explain the different level of success experienced by the parties, I focused on the interaction of the changing cleavage structure and party competition. With the possible exception of the KSCM, the defeat of the communist parties in the founding elections, dominated by the "communism-anticommunism" cleavage, illustrated that ex-communists as discredited representatives of the authoritarian systems could not rely on the existence of a secure voter base. They were forced, just like the newly founded parties, to face the political competition and to position themselves in the new political space. How they positioned themselves in terms of the predominant political cleavages depended heavily on which wing of the party gained the upper hand. If the reformists managed to take control, as in Poland and Hungary and to a lesser extent in Slovakia, a course of social-democratization followed later on. Conversely, if the structural-conservative hard-liners dominated, an anti-system opposition strategy was more likely. The questions as to which cleavages emerged, which of them could be used for mobilization and politicization, and which parties aligned themselves with these cleavages were just as decisive. Since there were hardly any pronounced structural cleavages, the communist successor parties, just like all other parties, could position themselves top-down along a multitude of cleavages potentially suited for mobilization and politicization. While the fundamentalist-oppositional KSCM holds an exceptional position by remaining isolated in the party competition, the SLD and MSZP managed, by a predominantly political-cultural mobilization of the voters, to appeal to both losers and winners of the transformation. They also profited from the weak competition presented by other leftist parties and from the logistical and organizational advantages they also held. In sum, the future of the SLD and the MSZP, as the only relevant social-democratic, center-left parties appears to be permanently secured. The KSCM can at least count on a stable voter potential of 10 to 14 percent and hope for a broadening of their voter base. The SDL's programmatic weakness however, seems to be the greatest obstacle in its way toward a continuous existence in the Slovakian party system.

18

Mainstreaming Extremism

The Romanian PDSR and the Bulgarian Socialists in Comparative Perspective

Jeffrey Stevenson Murer

In November and December of 2000, the Party of Democratic Socialism in Romania [PDSR] won electoral victories against the Party of Greater Romania [PRM], a party described as nationalistic, xenophobic, anti-Semitic, and anti-Hungarian. The Western news media depicted the victories for the PDSR's leader Ion Iliescu as a triumph over extremism. While this may have been an accurate assessment by comparison, such depictions gloss over many of the policy positions of the PDSR, and certainly minimize the importance of the anti-democratic and anti-liberal positions trumpeted by the PDSR in the past. Since the revolutions of 1989, most political science research about Romania has been cast in terms of a tripartite political struggle oriented along a traditional left-right spectrum. Yet evidence to date suggests that in the wake of the Ceauşescu regime's collapse, and in the context of a global neo-liberal project, this familiar framework might obscure as much as it elucidates. Specifically, the four election cycles in Romania since 1990 indicate that parliamentary coalitions frequently transgress the regular boundaries of political alliances. Rather than viewing these developments as an anomaly specific to Romania *qua* exception, this chapter seeks to (a) illuminate these political developments with respect to the recent Romanian experience of global capitalism and neo-liberalism; (b) link these tendencies to trends occurring elsewhere, particularly in Bulgaria; and (c) develop an alternative modeling of contemporary politics in Romania which can be applied to European politics in general and to common market integration in particular.

This chapter will analyze in historical perspective the confluence of political rhetoric of the Party of Democratic Socialism in Romania and the Party of Greater Romania produced within the past ten years. It will also assess the implications of the PDSR's continuing electoral successes in relation to the ongoing economic and political transformations in Romania. It will examine the PDSR's relationships with the PRM in the past, and conclude with an assessment of the PDSR's victories in the broader context of

Central European political transformations. Specifically, this chapter will investigate the role of communist successor parties as the public face of opposition to globalization and neo-liberalism in southeastern Europe through a comparison of the PDSR and the Bulgarian Socialist Party (BSP).

The PDSR and the BSP in a Comparative Perspective

In their introduction to this book, Bozóki and Ishiyama refer to the PDSR as a "partly reformed" and "transmuted" party. This is in contrast to the non-transmuted, non-reformed Communist Party of Bohemia and Moravia [KSCM] of the Czech Republic or the non-transmuted, reformed socialist parties of Hungary, Poland, and Slovenia. In this instance, Bozóki and Ishiyama use the label "reformed" to refer to the degree that a communist successor party has abandoned its Marxist-Leninist past. Indeed, both the Hungarian Socialist Party [MSzP] and Poland's Party of the Democratic Left [SLD] have greatly "reformed" themselves since the beginning of the changes of 1989. They have advocated privatization and integration into the European Union, and have contributed significantly to each country's accession into NATO. In order to remain relevant and to attract new constituents, both of these parties, as well as other "reformed socialist" parties described in this book, depict themselves as parties of "experts." The claim suggests that these parties "know how to govern." They are experienced in developing budgets, assigning and delegating civil service projects, and making the difficult decisions required of governments. The implication of these claims is to counter opposition parties by portraying them as collections of amateurs, inexperienced in the difficult charges of governing. In many ways, the description of these parties as "reformed" stresses the "normalization" that they have undergone. The implication is that the Hungarian Socialist Party is much like the German Social Democratic Party or the French Socialist Party. The irony is that these Western European parties may yet retain leftist elements to a much greater degree than their reformed East European counterparts. The presence of figures like Oskar La Fountaine and Joska Fischer in the German SDP government shines a small light into the hidden, left-leaning ideological corners of such mainstream Western parties. As we shall see below, not all communist successor parties have taken this reform path, mainly because anti-market, anti-capitalist rhetoric remains a powerful force upon a large segment of the electorates in Romania and southeastern Europe.

In addition, Bozóki and Ishiyama describe the Romanian PDSR as a "transmuted" party. They use this term to signify a "rightist" turn in the political rhetoric employed by these successor parties. Such a "rightist turn" would be marked by the abandonment of international socialist solidarity, the lack of commitment to egalitarian wealth redistribution, and the elimination of other forms of "Marxist liberation." Moreover, the loss of these leftist politi-

MAINSTREAMING EXTREMISM 369

cal aims is replaced with an attention to nationalism, programs that smack of xenophobia, and the promotion of ethno-chauvinism. Often the combination of "leftist" political values with "rightist" values is described as a red-brown coalition or as the meeting of the two extreme ends of the political spectrum. In this case, the term "transmuted" presumes two distinct sets of assumptions (a) that nationalism, xenophobia and interethnic conflict were not part of the political programs of communist parties during the reign of "realized socialism"; (b) that these political sentiments are the preserve of the "right." Under the conditions of global neo-liberalism, the traditional conceptions of left and right may no longer yield meaningful categories. The depiction of liberalism as a centrist force between the opposite poles of communism and fascism obscures the political struggles against liberal forces. In this way, successor parties like the PDSR have not so much "transmuted" to the "right," or been co-opted by "rightist" politics, as the political landscape itself has changed. Thus, nationalism may be dangerous and repugnant, but it may also be a political expression of opposition to globalization. Likewise, xenophobia and anti-immigrant sentiments may generate hostility and insult the principle of political tolerance, but may also represent an expression of opposition to the portability of capital as much as the portability of labor. Therefore, it may be useful to discard the traditional conceptualization of the political continuum along a "left" and "right" axis and replace it with a new conceptualization that orients the political continuum along a liberal/anti-liberal axis.

Such a reconceptualization would not only elucidate some of the seemingly contradictory positions of a party like the PDSR, but would also alter our understanding of other political parties in Central and Eastern Europe. Specifically, a party like the Party of Greater Romania [PRM], often described as being on the "extreme right," would be seen more as a potential ally of the PDSR rather than as an adversary representing the opposite end of the political spectrum. What makes the PDSR different from the PRM—or other parties in Europe like István Csurka's Hungarian Truth and Justice Party [MIÉP], Jorg Heider's Freedom Party in Austria, or Jean Marie LePen's *Front Nationale* in France—is not so much the content of the political rhetoric, but the form in which it is delivered. The division between these parties is not the breadth of the political spectrum, but the degree to which these parties may be considered extreme—the degree to which they advocate violence as a form of political action.

In contrast, Bozóki and Ishiyama describe the Bulgarian Socialist Party [BSP] as "partly-reformed" and "non-transmuted." The emphasis of their description focuses on the BSP's continued adherence to "leftist" political principles while not succumbing to a "rightist turn." Indeed, the BSP remains committed to leftist politics. In preparation for the 2001 parliamentary elections, the BSP has made an electoral alliance with the Bulgarian Social

Democratic Party to form the Alliance of the Democratic Left. Moreover, in its 1998 party platform, the BSP declared that it remained committed to "Marxist values" and the fight against inequities and injustices in Bulgarian society (BSP Party Platform 1998). Curiously, this continued commitment to leftist principles is expressed by the BSP despite a resounding electoral defeat in 1997. The expectation that parties would change their "public face" after such a defeat suggests that parties attempt to maximize their public appeal. Yet, such an expectation discounts the unequal economic effects on a given polis. Much like in Romania, the election of self-proclaimed liberals has not brought economic success to all sectors. Many in Bulgaria remain impoverished and have become disillusioned by the economic transitions to liberal capitalism. The BSP commitment to minimize the adverse effects of capitalism does not appear to be just an unwillingness to break with the past. Rather, it appears to be a political message with powerful resonance for a society struggling within the framework of a liberal economic transition.

Unlike Romania, where the successor party has united with traditionally described "rightist" parties to confront the liberal nature of the transition, the BSP is currently facing stiff opposition from a coalition of "rightist" forces united under the banner of the former king Simeon II. Because of the relationship between the communists and the monarchy immediately after World War II, reconciliation between the Alliance of the Left and the Simeon II movements appears impossible. Yet, the presence of the two forces represents a strong opposition to the path taken throughout 1997 to 2001 by the liberal Union of Democratic Forces [SDS], which renamed itself in 2000 the United Democratic Forces [ODS]. A comparison of the BSP and the PDSR and their respective courses since 1989 reveals an often overlooked theme in post-communist politics: continued opposition to advanced capitalism.

The PDSR as Political Force

The PDSR is perhaps the most powerful political force in Romania. Its electoral victories in 2000 mark the third time that this party will lead the government since 1989. It is also the third time that its leader, Ion Iliescu, will hold the presidency. The party is recognized as the successor to Nicolae Ceauşescu's Romanian Communist Party, but in terms of policy, the PDSR is a bit of an enigma. It is often described as a left-wing party, retaining its communist roots and arguing for the protection of workers. Its self-declared priorities are accession to NATO and the European Union, and its parliamentary leader, Prime Minister Adrian Nastase, has called for new negotiations with the International Monetary Fund, the European Union, and the International Bank for Reconstruction and Development [IBRD] (RFE/RL *Newsline*, December 14, 2000). Yet Iliescu often rails against the demands of the World Bank and the IMF, and Nastase himself is critical of both of these institutions. In a February interview with a *New York Times* reporter, Nastase said of economic reform advocated by the IMF, "You cannot just come in here with these words, with everything taken form the international dictionary. The previous government[1] used the words 'economic reform' for four years and the result was an important economic decline" (*International Herald Tribune*, February 12, 2001). Earlier, Nastase said the PDSR's economic plan would be a "Romanian one," suggesting the pursuit of some third way. Yet, according to Ion Caramitru, the outgoing Democratic Convention culture minister: "Iliescu says he is democratic and pro-European; they are empty phrases" *(The Daily Telegraph*, December 16, 2000). These contradictions and competing sentiments make it difficult to position the PDSR.

The PDSR came to the political fore as the National Salvation Front [NSF] in 1989. During the contentious and dangerous days of the 1989 revolution, a number of high-ranking Communist Party officials pushed aside the student revolutionary leadership in Bucharest, declaring themselves as the "Supreme Leadership of the Revolution" (Gilbert 1990). After the Christmas Day execution of the Communist Party premier, Nicolae Ceauşescu, the Supreme Leadership transformed itself into the National Salvation Front and declared that it was the "steering committee of the nation." Perturbed by their ouster and exclusion from any post-revolutionary political bodies, student protestors began mass demonstrations in Bucharest in January 1990. The students also protested against the presence of Communist Party leaders in the NSF, including Ion Iliescu, Peter Roman, and Dimitri Maziku. In a move that would signal a frequently used tactic, the NSF broke up the student protests with police forces and with mine workers bussed into the capital city.

To protect its newfound power, the NSF began harassing competing political groups. Newly founded opposition organizations frequently found themselves the targets of attacks by "rampaging workers," and the NSF recruited mine workers and former members of the state security forces to "protect the new post-revolutionary order." These working-class elements came mainly from heavy industrial sectors, such as the steel, coal mining, and other metallurgical enterprises. These workers were employed by state-owned firms which were threatened with disbandment by many of the new democratic organizations. In addition, these sectors were highly prized by the Communist Party, and many workers readily threw in their lot with former communists leading the NSF. This commitment included attacks on ethnic Hungarians in Tîrgu Mures and other Transylvanian cities in March of 1990. In February of 1990, Ion Iliescu, then the chairman of the NSF, called for multiparty parliamentary elections in May, but used the NSF's power to tightly control access to media, thereby handicapping all other political groups. The short election cycle, threats of intimidation, and the use of violence by the NSF and its supporters thrust the NSF into the new Parliament with a huge mandate.

The *de facto* successors of the Communist Party won four times as many seats as its nearest rival, and landed Iliescu the presidency for the first time. Yet this was a weak façade of multiparty parliamentarianism. Iliescu showed little inclination to engage in political or economic reform. The NSF government supported the return of communist officials and apparatchiks to the local level bureaucracy and restructured the feared and notorious state security service—the *Securitate*—into an equally powerful domestic intelligence force within the Interior Ministry—the Romanian Intelligence Services [SRI] (Ratesh 1993). Many student leaders, believing Iliescu was nullifying the sacrifices of the revolution, began a series of sit-down strikes at the University of Bucharest. Repeating the successful tactics of January, Iliescu and the NSF recruited mine workers from eastern Romania to physically confront the protestors and silence them (Murer 1999). *Le Monde Diplomatique* described this as a "bloody march which was openly welcomed by Ion Iliescu" (*Le Monde Diplomatique*, February 1999). Through these tactics a new partnership was forged. The NSF's reliance on working-class elements to preserve its power and to quash any demonstrations of opposition led to an alliance of former communists and those elements least interested in reform. The NSF painted liberal reformers as highly threatening to the Romanian "nation." It attempted to discredit any scheme for privatization by suggesting that market reforms were the functional equivalent of selling the country off to foreigners (Ratesh 1993).

Feeling secure in his party's ability to retain power, Iliescu called for parliamentary elections to be held in the autumn of 1992. This was not, however, to be a repeat of the overwhelming victory of 1990 for the NSF. Changing its name to the Party of Democratic Socialism in Romania, the PDSR faced an alliance of liberal and monarchist parties, unified as the Democratic Convention of Romania [CDR]. Additionally, one of Iliescu's former allies, Peter Roman, broke with the PDSR and joined the Social Democratic Union [USD], giving this party (which failed to receive even one percent of the vote in 1990), a much higher public profile. Both the CDR and the USD ate into the PDSR's 1990 electoral gains, and although the PDSR again won control of the Parliament, retaining control in both the lower House (the Chamber of Deputies) and the upper House (the Senate), it was forced to enter into a coalition in order to form a government. That coalition was an odd assortment of parties that does not easily fit into Western ideas as to what constitutes "left" and "right" along the political spectrum.

The Red Quadrangle

Although the 1992 elections brought an opening for politically liberal parties which were determined to engage in economic and political reform, it also brought to the fore small extremist political parties, particularly the Party of Greater Romania [PRM] and the National Unity Party [PUNR]. Both of these parties claimed to be rooted in the extreme left, but espoused a brand of brazen nationalism and xenophobic politics usually associated with the extreme right (Ratesh 1993). Taken together these two parties accounted for barely thirteen percent of the electoral vote for the Chamber of Deputies, landing them a scant forty-six of the 343 seats. Yet rather than form a government of national unity with either the Democratic Convention or even Peter Roman's Social Democratic Union, Iliescu's PDSR formed a minority government with the extremist PRM and PUNR, and the smaller Socialist Labor Party [PSM]. Thus, the "red quadrangle" was forged.

Corneliu Vadim Tudor, the head of the PRM, was a poet and hymnwriter for the Ceauşescu regime. From its inception his party was a strange mix of nostalgia for the Ceauşescu era and its anti-capitalist rhetoric, and vehement nationalism, calling for Romania's reincorporation of the Bukovina in the Ukraine and Bessarabia in Moldova. As a member of the Marshal Ion Antonescu League (which celebrates the exploits of Romania's World War II fascist military dictator), Tudor also called for the official political rehabilitation of this "Romanian hero." Tudor has vehemently denied that Antonescu was in way responsible for the deaths of hundreds of thousands of Jews in the Holocaust. Rather, Tudor claimed that "hundreds of thousands of Jews . . . owe their lives [to the Marshal]." He continued by noting that he found it "outrageous for Jews to claim restitution or compensation . . . for an invented Holocaust" (Shafir 2000). Antonescu is held in such high regard by the PRM that its weekly *Politica* once suggested that Tudor was "the Righteous, only he can be tomorrow's Marshal Antonescu, who would make order in Romania" (*Politica* July 15, 1995; Shafir 2000).

More recently the PRM has called for the political rehabilitation of Nicolae Ceauşescu. PRM Senator Florea Preda praised Ceauşescu for his display of "courage" and claimed that his "natural intelligence" transformed him into "one of the world's great statesmen" (*Mediafax,* October 3, 2000). Preda continued by suggesting that Ceauşescu had been executed in order to undermine his efforts to consolidate Romania's independence. This theme of Romanian resistance to "foreign forces" is one of the mainstays of PRM rhetoric. Tudor insists that Romania has been "humiliated" and turned into a "colony" by traitors and gangsters serving foreign interests, who were forcing the country to "endlessly mime a so-called democracy, copied in a parrot-like manner from the West" (Shafir 2000). One of the most oft-cited sources of such "treason" is the Hungarian minority living in the Bánát and in Transylvania. Shortly before the 1990 elections, Tudor told a crowd of supporters that should the "present serious situation" of Hungarian minorities living in Romania continue, he would "propose that a military, serious national governance be established for two years, for the purpose of saving Romania" (*Romania Mare,* December 14, 1990). "Two Years of

Authoritarian Rule" would be one of the PRM's main campaign slogans through the mid-1990s.

The personal relationship between Tudor and Iliescu has been quite contentious. In many ways, Iliescu and the PDSR assisted in the formation of the PRM, mainly by bestowing its blessing on the extremist party. Michael Shafir suggests that the political alliance between the two parties is a "perfect display of Iliescu's 'utilitarian anti-Semitism'" (Shafir 2000). Nevertheless, in 1995 the alliance broke down over the government's decision to sign a Basic Treaty with Hungary, guaranteeing certain basic human rights to ethnic minorities living in both countries. At the urging of the European Union, the Organization for Security and Cooperation in Europe, the North Atlantic Treaty Organization, and its associated program the Partnership for Peace, President Iliescu felt he had no choice but to sign the agreement. For this Tudor accused Iliescu of "being a 'Gypsy,' a former KGB agent, put in power and kept there by Jews, and an atheist who did not hesitate to order Ceauşescu's execution on the 'Holy day of Christmas' 1989" (Shafir 2000). Yet their political alliance was renewed again in 1996, only to be severed by 1999.

The National Unity Party [PUNR] had a similar political disposition to the PRM. Its first party chairman, Radu Contea, shared with Tudor the opinion that Romania's government should be an authoritarian one. Following the first election cycle of 1990, he stated simply that "the country's president must have very extensive powers, and should rule with an iron hand" (Baricada January 8, 1991; Shafir 2000). To demonstrate this commitment many PUNR supporters were involved in the violent attacks upon ethnic Hungarians in Tîrgu Mureş throughout March of 1990. These attacks were organized in part by the PUNR mayor of Cluj-Napoca, Ghorghe Funar. Funar has made attacking the ethnic Hungarian minority in Transylvania a centerpiece of his political repertoire. In 1997, after the Hungarian government opened a consulate in Cluj, Funar order city employees to remove a Hungarian flag from the front of the building. Corneliu Vadim Tudor and the PRM then awarded the employees one million lei ($143 at the then current exchange rate) and further offered three million lei to anyone who would burn the flag in public (Shafir 2000). Funar has made regular charges that the presence of the consulate represents Hungarian "imperial intentions" (Mediafax, September 3, 2000). Funar also shares with his PRM counterpart an affection for Ion Antonescu, and in 1993 erected a statue of the Marshal in central Cluj.

After the PUNR's poor showing in the 1990 elections, Funar replaced Contea as party chair. The PURN made significant gains, increasing its number of seats in the Chamber of Deputies from ten to thirty-one in 1992. That same year Funar ran for president and finished third behind Iliescu and the CDR candidate Emil Constantinescu, receiving more than one million votes, or nearly eleven percent. Funar also made inroads with Romanian irredentist nationalists in Moldova. In 1992 seven MPs in Chişinău belonged to the PUNR. Since 1992 however, the PUNR has seen a reversal of fortune, partially due to the success of Tudor's PRM. In 1996, Funar received only three percent of the presidential vote in the first round, and his party garnered a mere four and half percent for the Chamber of Deputies, representing eighteen seats. The PUNR felt that it had such little electoral potential by the 2000 election cycle that Funar decided to enter an "unofficial electoral" alliance with Ion Iliescu. PUNR candidates ran on PDSR lists.

The ties between PDSR, PRM, and PUNR are quite close, the personal relationship between Ion Iliescu and Corneliu Tudor notwithstanding. The memberships of the three parties often overlap with the membership roles of the vehemently anti-Hungarian and anti-Roma "cultural organization" *Vatra Romaneâsca* (Romanian Cradle). This organization has been supportive of the activities of the PRM and Corneliu Tudor, often asking him to address its rallies and meetings. In 1999 Ion Iliescu revealed that not only was he a *Vatra* sympathizer, but also one of its founding members (Shafir 2000b). This relationship is important, for it reveals some of the personal sentiments of the PDSR leader, even when that party's official rhetoric shies away from the antagonistic vulgarisms employed by the *Vatra*. Throughout the reign of the second government, the "red quadrangle" worked to prevent any legislation that might promote the rights of ethnic minorities, particularly those of Hungarians and Roma. On the other hand, the four parties did promote what many PRM partisans claimed to be a "mixed economy," with the "state holding a preponderate position in strategic economic sectors" (Shafir 2000). The continuation of these state-centric economic strategies would have dire consequences.

The PDSR and the Economy

Throughout its second government the PDSR remained reluctant to engage in economic reform. Before the autumn elections inflation was already reaching a hyperactive level at 200 percent. By the end of 1993 inflation climbed to an incredible 254.8 percent, unemployment stood at nearly fifteen percent, and industrial production fell to one half of its 1989 level. Total external debt grew to $4.25 billion and the private sector represented only fifteen percent of GDP by the end of 1993 (World Bank 1996). Under pressure from external forces like the International Monetary Fund, the World Bank, and the International Bank for Reconstruction and Development, the PDSR government introduced a privatization scheme in 1994 designed on the Czech model of vouchers. However, the PDSR was reluctant to relinquish control of the largest state firms and to lay off thousands of workers dependent on the state sector—workers who were also potential PDSR voters (Murer 1999). Thus, the PDSR government never implemented the privatization plan and continued to subsidize loss-making industries in an attempt to placate PDSR constituencies (*European Forum*, October 1997). As a result of the PDSR's reluctance to privatize the economy, Romania received very little in the way of foreign direct investment. Between 1989 and 1996 Hungary received $13 billion and Poland $5 billion, while Romania received a scant $1.4 billion during the same period. By 1996, the PDSR did privatize eighty percent of the assets involved in agricultural production, raising the private sector share of total GDP to fifty-five percent, and the agricultural share of total GDP to twenty percent (*European Forum*, October 1997). Yet by the conclusion of the PDSR mandate, total external debt grew to a burdensome $6.65 billion, with debt service payments alone equaling nearly three percent of GDP.

The continuing stagnation of the economy had significant consequences for the PDSR. Exasperated by the lack of economic opportunities and the apparent lack of change in the structure of the economy since the 1998 Revolution, many urban dwellers actively rallied for the Democratic Convention [CDR] and its 1996 presidential candidate, Emil Constantinescu. Although Iliescu won the first round of the presidential contest, the PDSR could not hold back the support for the CDR candidate in the second round runoff. Similarly, the CDR edged out the PDSR in both houses of Parliament, wresting control away from Iliescu for the first time since the 1989 revolution. It was hoped that CDR could bring about sweeping liberal change. To accomplish its goals of European Union and NATO accession, the new CDR government planned a radical restructuring of the economy, to be guided by compliance with the precepts of the International Monetary Fund. Its first goals were to reduce budget and trade deficits, cut governmental social spending, and eliminate "non-profitable" state sector enterprises, either through privatization sales or through outright closures.

Even the CDR found this ambitious program to be a tremendous challenge. In order to form a government, the CDR formed a coalition with Peter Roman's Social Democratic Union [USD] and the Hungarian Democratic Alliance of Romania [UDMR or in Hungarian RMDSz]. The presence of an ethnic Hungarian political party in the government so incensed Corneliu Tudor that he was able to form an "unofficial" opposition alliance with the PDSR. The "red quadrangle" was now the opposition. Within the government, the CDR and its coalition partners represented a broad range of political perspectives. The CDR itself was a coalition of smaller parties including the National Peasant Christian Democratic Party [PNȚCD], the National Liberal Party [PNL], the National Liberal Party–Democratic Convention [PNL-CD], and the Democratic Party [DP]. The task of holding all of the parties in government together was not an easy one, and infighting and bickering soon broke out among the many partners.

Beginning in 1997 the CDR government under Prime Minister Victor Ciorbea began a mass privatization scheme, first eliminating state agroindustrial facilities. He then began to eliminate jobs in heavy industrial sectors by offering cash payments to workers to accept redundancies. However, many workers in the steel and mining industries would not accept the state redundancy reimbursements. In 1998, with the privatization scheme stalled, Radu Vasile replaced Ciorbea. The international lending community, which had welcomed the CDR's arrival, began to grow impatient with the slow course of market reform. By the end of 1998, total GNP growth fell by more than five percent, domestic prices had increased by nearly sixty percent, and total debt stood at more than ten billion dollars (World Bank 1999). Current accounts, as a percentage of GDP, fell by more than seven percent, total debt represented nearly one quarter of GDP, and overall foreign investments continued to decline, down seven percent (as a percentage of GDP) from the pre-revolutionary level. The International Monetary Fund threatened to suspend the payment of macro-stabilization loans if the CDR government did not hasten its economic reform program. Vasile announced to great public fanfare that the government would close thirty-eight coal mines as proof to the IMF and the IBRD that reform would proceed. Heralded by the IMF as a success, Vasile moved forward with the plan, targeting two mines in the Jiu Valley region. Yet the previous government had recently invested three million dollars into one of the mines (*Le Monde Diplomatique*, February 1999). With that investment the coal miners felt that their jobs were secure. The fact that these revitalized mines were on the CDR's list for closure incensed the workers there.

As the program accelerated, Vasile announced, just prior to Christmas 1998, the closure of nearly 140 coal mines and forty-nine other state owned enterprises, a five year restructuring program of the steel industry, and the elimination of nearly seventy thousand jobs in the heavy industrial sectors (*The Economist*, February 6, 1999). Originally nationalized following World War II, the mining sector had proved difficult to privatize. On the one hand, the mines represented a strategic national economic asset that the previous PDSR government had been reluctant to relinquish. Similarly, the miners represented a loyal political following to the PDSR. On the other hand, the mines were technologically antiquated and produced a heavily sulfurous, highly polluting coal. They proved to be so inefficient that the Minister of Industry claimed in November of 1998 that it would be cheaper to import Polish coal than it would be to use Romanian coal produced by state-owned mines. The failure of the previous redundancy scheme, and the political relationship between the coal miners and the PDSR and PRM, set the stage for a dramatic confrontation. On January 19, 1999 nearly ten thousand miners set out from the Jiu Valley to march on Bucharest to express their opposition to the government plan. Fearful of the possibility of a repetition of the sort of confrontations that occurred between miners and students in 1990, the government hoped to prevent the miners from arriving in the capital. With the government having prohibited their use of mass transportation, the miners slowly made their way on foot, arriving in the city of Costeşti on January 21. With their ranks swelled by sympathizers, nearly fifteen thousand miners encountered a police cordon, broke it after a violent clash, and marched on to Ramnicu Valcea where they took the governor of Valcea hostage. Alarmed at the confrontation, President Constantinescu traveled to the city to negotiate with the miners. It was agreed that the mines would be reopened and that the workers would receive a pay increase. In order to avoid bloodshed, Constantinescu suspended Vasile's closure scheme, much to the chagrin of the International Monetary Fund, which then suspended the extension of a new $500 million macro-stabilization credit. *Le Monde Diplomatique* stated that "the recent events will inevitably increase the IMF's distrust of a government which has so far delivered on [few] of the . . . agreements it has signed" (*Le Monde Diplomatique*, February 1999). The *London Financial Times* put it sharply when it declared that the settlement with the miners was a "devastating setback to the government's flagging efforts to push through market reforms" (*London Financial Times*, January 24, 1999).

With such an inauspicious beginning, 1999 proved to be another year of troubling economic performance. Domestic prices increased by forty-five percent; direct investments did not even top one billion dollars—reaching instead only a dismal $949 million. Perhaps more importantly, portfolio investments not only fell, but actually represented a $700 million loss. While total indebtedness decreased slightly, the total debt still stood at more than nine billion dollars, more than half of which ($4.968 billion) was owed to private lenders. This put the government in a very tight situation. By suspending the macro-stabilization loan, the IMF had deprived the Romanian government of desperately needed funds to pay the debt service on private loans. Further, Romania was now indebted to the IMF for nearly one half of a billion dollars, and owed the IBRD $1.7 billion (World Bank 2000). Current accounts continued to run a one billion dollar deficit, and the overall external trade imbalance crept ever closer to a two billion dollar deficit (-1.8 billion Euros for 1999) (EU 2000).

Much of the economic news in 2000 continued to be bad. In August, the privately held National Investment Fund—part of the nation's largest savings bank (the *Casa De Economi Si Consemnnatiuni* [CEC])—collapsed, wiping out nearly $170 million in private savings (RFE/RL *Newsline*, September 2000). This was but one example of the state of the banking industry, which was in a terribly precarious position. Crowded with "popular banks" or credit cooperatives, the banking industry was a new and unregulated economic sector rife with fraud. Erik D'Amato of the *Budapest Business Journal* quotes a local IMF official who calls the co-ops "functionally illiquid." Such a condition would place some $200 million of private deposits at risk (*Euromoney*, September 2000). This situation remains one of the central problems cited by the European Union as preventing Romanian accession. Gunter Verheugen, European Union Commissioner for Enlargement Affairs, stated that Romania has the weakest democratic institutions of all of the applicants for membership. He cited the presence of weak financial institutions, a poor commitment to reform, the lack of a financial system, falling investments, and the lack of progress on privatization as the five largest hurdles that Romania must clear to be seriously considered for EU membership (Synovitz 2000). The European Union *2000 Report on Romanian Acquis* concluded that the "Romanian authorities have not elaborated a comprehensive policy framework of internal financial control. . . . A number of crises in the banking industry demonstrate that the effective supervision of financial services still has to be considerably strengthened" (EU 2000).

For liberals and market advocates, the election of the Democratic Convention brought the possibility of economic reform and the possible fulfillment of aspirations for European institutional membership. It is significant that throughout its four-year tenure the CDR was unable to accomplish its stated goals and Romania found itself at the bottom of these institutional accession lists rather than at the top. In an article for the London *Daily Telegraph* foreign editor Alec Russell quoted an unnamed Western diplomat as saying, "Romania is not just in the last carriage of the train to the EU, but in the back of the last carriage" (*Daily Telegraph*, December 16, 2000). Romania either needed to make "improvements" or "substantial improvements" with respect to nearly every criterion for European Union *acquis*. Regarding market reforms, the European Union *Report on Acquis* stated simply: "[Romania] has not yet fully implemented any of the Accession Partnership Priorities concerning the internal market" (EU 2000: 91). In an ironic twist, the failures of the CDR government to achieve progress in European Union integration became a central platform in the PDSR's preparation for the 2000 election cycle. Notwithstanding its earlier resistance to market and institutional reform, the PDSR was now poised to assume the mantle of leadership to integrate Romania in the EU.

The 2000 Romanian Elections

In its preparations for the 2000 elections, the PDSR proclaimed that it was a "European, social democratic party, committed to joining the European Union and NATO" (PDSR Party Platform, 2000). At the same time however, a close reading of the party's platform reveals a tone of animosity toward market capitalism and the market structures of the West. In fact, the platform comprises a mix of nationalist rhetoric amid vague calls to restructure the economy. In his candidacy announcement, Iliescu promised to raise living standards, boost investments, and eliminate corruption. He also insisted upon the need to "return to Romanian values," mentioning the Church and the army as the "pillars" of those values (*Mediafax*, October 6, 2000). In another example the PDSR party platform states that "mistakes were made in the field of economic reform" and that Romania must "integrate into the world economy." Yet it also states that the economy is "dominated by the control of transnational corporations and international financial bodies" which are to be resisted (PDSR 2000). Thus, while economic reforms are a "national imperative," because it is a "center-left party," the PDSR has tried to "correlate the pace of reform with the degree of people's endurance, rejecting the recklessness and dilettantism specific to previous governings [CDR], as well as the temptations of aggressive liberalism" (PDSR 2000). The party platform further states that under the conditions of the CDR's government:

> ... there have proliferated a series of phenomena specific to wild capitalism: extension of subterranean economy, fraudulent privatization, speculative practices, and the plundering of public [wealth]. The wave of infringements, illegalities and corruption gave to citizens a feeling of insecurity and affected their trust in the institutions of democracy (PDSR 2000).

The document concludes by calling for a dialogue between government and trade unions to address problems of social protection, unemployment, and manpower reconversion. It states frankly: "we lost lots of electors in November 1996," admitting that economic growth during that period was not reflected in the people's standard of living, causing the "deterioration of our party image." With the economy in shambles and the CDR government plagued by failure, the stage was set for a PDSR comeback.

Early polls showed great support for the PDSR and for Iliescu's candidacy for president. As early as September 2000 polls had Iliescu leading the CDR candidate (then Prime Minister Mugur Isarescu) by nearly twenty percentage points. By October that lead had narrowed to fifteen points. With less than two months remaining before the November 24 elections, it appeared that the two major parties from the 1996 election would face off once again. Although Corneliu Tudor had announced his candidacy in March of 2000, polls showed him lagging in third position, while the PRM as a party was polling at about ten percent, or in fourth position in a widening field of parliamentary contenders. Yet a number of incidents were to change PRM's fortunes.

Just as the National Unity Party had fielded candidates in Moldova before, the PRM invited the Moldovan MP Ilie Ilascu to run on the PRM list, but as a senate candidate in Romania.[2] What should have been normal nationalist fare from the PRM within Romania became an international *cause celebre* when the Moldovan government expressed "surprise" that Romania would allow the candidacy of a man who Tiraspol authorities had imprisoned since 1992 on charges of terrorism (*Reuters*, October 6,

2000). Moldovan irredentism had worked its way into the Romanian election debate.

The PRM had also benefited from the September 2000 murder of trade union leader Virgil Sahleanu. The ongoing investigation revealed that the director of an oil company with whom Sahlenau had been negotiating might have contracted the murder. Asserting that this crime was evidence of the brutality of capitalism, many trade unionists shifted their support to PRM. Tudor then launched a tirade against foreigners, and particularly against foreign capital, claiming that "the world was facing an attempt to impose 'globalization' by 'brutality'" (Shafir 2000).

Although this anti-globalization theme continued throughout the campaign, it is significant that Tudor also appears to have accepted the need for European integration, suggesting that "a small country like Romania has no other choice" (Shafir 2000). This stance, like one taken by the PDSR, is underwritten by animosity. Tudor advocated European integration as a means of protection to "successfully oppose the danger of enforced Americanization and the loss of identity." Similarly, Tudor peppered his new embrace of EU membership with his continued endorsement of irredentism in Moldova and the Bukovina. The PRM daily *Romania Mare* suggested that EU must understand that Romania is a "Latin country that is still bleeding territorially. . . [whose] brethren in Bessarabia and Bukovina had reached the limit of endurance" (*Romania Mare,* March 10, 2000; Shafir 2000). It was the Europeans' "duty" to aid Romania in saving this "brethren," and this duty went beyond human rights monitoring. Tudor stated that Europe's borders "must move from the River Prut to the River Dniester" (Radio Bucharest, March 17, 2000).

Other events seemed to propel the PRM forward and hurt the CDR presidential candidate Isarescu. In November 2000 the chairman of the Ion Tiriac Bank called on the government and the public to "prevent the destruction of the banking system" (RFE/RL *Newsline,* November 28, 2000). Rumors of liquidity problems had caused a run on the bank by depositors; such runs occurred at other institutions throughout the summer and autumn. It was widely believed that the rumors and public discussions of the vulnerability of the banking industry were part of an effort to discredit Isarescu, who was the governor of the Romanian Central Bank from 1991 to 1999. These events highlighted the economic and structural problems facing Romania, summarized by a report from the European Parliament indicating that progress for European membership "still had a long way to go." The report stated that Romania's economic situation was "worrying" (RFE/RL *Newsline,* October 5, 2000). By the end of October, the PRM had moved into second place, and Tudor was now following Iliescu in the race for president.

When the dust settled after the elections of November 26, 2000, the PDSR had won a resounding 155 mandates in the Chamber of Deputies and sixty-five seats in the Senate. Surprisingly, the PRM finished in second place with eighty-four seats in the Lower House and thirty-seven seats in the Upper House. With respect to the liberal parties, the Democratic Party [DP] secured thirty-one seats, the National Liberal Party [PNL] thirty seats, and the Hungarian Democratic Federation [UDMR] twenty-seven seats. In the Senate, the DP and PNL took thirteen seats and the UDMR took twelve seats. The Democratic Convention was ousted from Parliament and its presidential candidate received less than ten percent of the vote in the first round. This was an incredible showing by the PRM. In the presidential race, Tudor received more than twenty-eight percent of the vote, forcing a runoff with Iliescu, who received thirty-six percent in the first round.

Immediately following the parliamentary elections the PRM stated that it wanted to form a coalition with the PDSR. If such a coalition did not occur, the PRM threatened that the PDSR would assume a grave responsibility "if it allies itself with political forces that have repeatedly proved their incompetence and inclination toward treason" (RFE/RL *Newsline,* November 30, 2000). The PRM animosity toward the liberal parties was further expressed by Gheorghe Funar, who said that should the PRM come to power (with a Tudor victory in the second round of presidential voting), the UDMR would be outlawed in twenty-four hours. Funar also felt that UDMR leaders would have nothing to fear because Tudor is a "Christian soul who can wrong no one" (*Mediafax*, November 30, 2000). Continuing in this venomous mode, PRM MP Anghel Stanciu said that journalists who had "sold out to the West" by writing that Tudor was an extremist, could work in the future on the Bucharest-River Danube Canal, a reference to the 1950 communist labor camp.

Throughout the campaign period before the presidential runoff, the leadership of the liberal DP and PNL parties called upon their supporters to "reject extremism" and back Iliescu's bid to become president again. In contrast, the PDSR stated that it would consider a one-year pact of cooperation with the two parties only if they proved to be prepared to support the government's "national priorities." Although the PDSR appeared to be willing to cooperate with the DP and PNL at the expense of the PRM, the PDSR did make it clear that they would form a minority government and would not cooperate with the UDMR. With the expressed support of the DP and PNL Iliescu won the December 10 runoff with 66.83 percent to Tudor's thirty-three percent. Tudor ranted that the PDSR had bribed election officials and committed "the greatest fraud in this century's Romanian history," and that Iliescu's triumph was a "victory for the antichrist" (RFE/RL *Newsline,* December 11, 2000). Iliescu, on the other hand, called on the public to display "unity in an effort to struggle against poverty, corruption, and crime." He then pledged to punish those who "plundered national wealth." He further expressed hope that international lenders would understand Romania's difficult situation.

The situation certainly is a difficult one. In preparation for renewed negotiations with the new Romanian government, the World Bank announced that forty percent of Romania's citizens lived below the international poverty line of one U.S. dollar per day. Iliescu expressed hope that the International Monetary Fund would take notice of this situation and relax the terms of the macro-stabilization loans that it had canceled in 1999. Meanwhile, the IMF issued a report that was highly critical of the situation in Romania. It stated that successive governments had failed to reduce state budget arrears, privatize the banking industry, and reduce the governmental deficit to less than three percent of GDP. Upon taking office the new PDSR prime minister, Adrian Nastase, stated that the government hoped the IMF would reduce the deficit threshold to four and one half percent of GDP. In February 2001, after Nastase met with IMF officials, the international lender's chief negotiator, Neven Mates, stated that IMF could not accept the PDSR offer. Mates further stated that the IMF would grant no further loans until Bucharest had solved some of the economy's main problems (*Mediafax*, February 26, 2000). In a show of good faith Nastase announced that the government would sell off five state-owned companies in the coming weeks. This proposal from the PDSR prime minister was far more modest than the Vasile proposal of 1998.

In February 2001 the PDSR government also signed an agreement with the country's leading trade unions to raise real wages by four percent and increase the minimum wage by ten percent. These pledges were made in exchange for the unions' agreement not to conduct any strike action for one year (RFE/RL *Newsline*, February 20, 2001). This agreement was followed by the government's announcement that seventeen more state-owned firms would be privatized in cooperation with the World Bank, and that a commission would be established to privatize Galati Sidex, the country's largest steel mill. Yet Nastase's announcement also advised that privatization would be done "without harming the social equilibrium" of the country. The PDSR government appears to be set on maintaining social protections for workers even if it slows privatization and troubles relationships with international lending institutions in the process.

If the PDSR appears to be maintaining its slow pace of economic reform, it also continues to express some of its previous tendencies regarding the Hungarian minority. Although the PDSR presented and passed a new law allowing ethnic minorities to use their own language in communities where they constitute more than twenty percent of the population, President Iliescu stated that he continues to oppose a separate Hungarian language university in Romania. He also stated that other claims of the Hungarian minority could only be addressed once Romania's economy can afford it (*Magyar Hirlap*, February 20, 2001). Such sentiments were likewise expressed in the opposition to a Hungarian demand that the constitutional definition of Romania as a "national state" be amended. MP Valeriu Stocia stated that the "myth of the national state is the cornerstone of the modern world," and that "its dismemberment would also mean the dismemberment of that world" (RFE/RL *Newsline*, February 12, 2001). It would appear that even with the trappings of a renewed commitment to the European Union and to NATO, the PDSR continues to express political rhetoric that is wholly in line with its post-revolutionary past. The decision to accept European integration as inevitable certainly allows room for continued nationalist rhetoric as Tudor and the PRM have demonstrated. Similarly, Nastase's ability to reach an agreement with the trade unions that have supported the PDSR in the past should come as no surprise. It is significant that the government's newly announced privatization scheme is so small in scope. It would appear that rather than going through a significant transformation, the PDSR may have simply become more media savvy.

The BSP as a Political Force

Perhaps the most telling difference between Romania and Bulgaria has been the cooperation shown to international monetary institutions by successive governments. Both the Bulgarian Socialist Party [BSP] and the Union of Democratic Forces [SDS] have cooperated with international funding institutions like the IMF, World Bank, and the European Bank of Reconstruction and Development. Yet for all of their cooperation and for all of the macro-stabilization funds provided these successive governments, the Bulgarian economy remains weak. Since the mid-1990s, the BSP position regarding protecting citizens against the ravages of capitalist social displacement has strengthened. However, when the BSP first came to power, it was the party that reached out to the IMF. In addition, unlike the Romanian PDSR, the BSP came to power following communism's demise in what might be called a "palace coup."

Although in the late 1980s the Bulgarian Communist Party (BKP) followed Mikhal Gorbachev's "new thinking" by introducing a series of reforms under the rubric of "the July Concept," many reformers within the party sought even greater change. After the 1989 collapse of the Hungarian Socialist Worker's Party [MSzMP], the Minister of Foreign Affairs Petar Mladenov and Minister of Defense Dobri Dzsurov planned the ouster of leading party figures in favor of more reform-minded party members. On November 10, the day after East German officials "opened" the Berlin Wall, reformist elements within the BKP removed Todor Zhivkov, who had been the Communist Party chief since 1956. The reformers then called for Roundtable Talks, modeled on those held in Hungary, to begin in January 1990. In the interim, the BKP passed a number of amendments to the constitution to make way for multiparty elections. It is significant that there were no active dissident movements in Bulgaria at the time (Kolarova 1996). Most critics of the Zhivkov regime were either reformers within the BKP or part of the independent trade union *Podkrepa* [Support], founded in February 1989. Thus, independent-minded political activists were forced to scramble to create new organizations or revive old political parties to participate in the discussions. However, the non-communist participants of the Roundtable lacked political and economic experience and therefore were not seen as equal partners. Nevertheless, elections were declared for November 1990, and following the end of the talks on February 8, 1990, the Bulgarian Communist Party changed its name to the Bulgarian Socialist Party. As an additional sign of the party's commitment to change, a new prime minister, Andrei Lukanov, was appointed.

Immediately Lukanov began initiating reforms. Even before Bulgaria was admitted into the International Monetary Fund, he implemented an economic reform package in line with expressed IMF wishes (Troxel 1993). The prime minister made ready for currency convertibility, price increases and liberalization, wage controls, demonopolization, and the privatization of state enterprises and assets. In a bold step, taken to impress both the IMF and the public in its commitment to change, the government announced price increases of forty percent on goods and sixty percent on services, a mere three months before the elections. However, the government also froze prices on food staples, providing government subsides to keep the basics affordable for everyone.

In the runoff to the 1990 elections, numerous groups competed for the historical party names such as "democratic, agrarian, or social democratic" in an attempt to invoke the legacy of the "traditionally strong social democratic party" (Kolarova 1996). A number of these groups decided to forgo any struggle among them, unite under the umbrella of the Union of Democratic Forces [SDS], and lay claim that they alone were the legitimate opposition to the BSP. The SDS took great pains to stress its links to the past and its anti-communist stance, and began to label the BSP as the "enemy" of the Bulgarian nation. It made constant reference to communist excesses in the past and claimed retribution would be a major part of the SDS political platform. Yet, the BSP managed to hold its own quite well by appealing directly to its membership. In the late 1980s, the BKP had one million members in a country with slightly more than nine million people, and the BSP emphasized to them its experience and its demonstrated concerns for both economic reform and social welfare (Bell 1990). The message resonated with many voters as the BSP won a slight majority in the 1990 elections. However, this was a special parliamentary session, declared as a Grand National Assembly, with the sole charge of devising a new constitution and political system. In a show of goodwill, the BSP invited the SDS into a grand coalition government of national unity and appointed an independent, Dimitar Popov, as prime minister.

Even as the Lukanov and Popov governments attempted to meet all IMF directives and implement widespread economic reforms, the Bulgarian economy was being devastated. Much of this was a result of the collapse of the communist economic structure and trading patterns. In 1988, eighty percent of all Bulgarian exports went to the Council of Mutual Economic Assistance [CMEA or COMECOM] trading partners; sixty-three percent of that to the Soviet Union alone. When CMEA collapsed in early 1991, Bulgaria lost its trading partners. Further, Bulgaria lost its main supplier of materials when the newly formed Russian Federation began demanding hard currency for items the Soviet Union provided for trade. In addition, Bulgaria relied on the Soviet Union for a majority of its oil and gas. Unfortunately, the timing of these economic transitions could not have been worse for Bulgaria. To abide by IMF directives, Bulgaria honored the United Nations sanctions in place against Iraq following the Persian Gulf War. Thus, Bulgaria surrendered nearly one billion dollars worth of oil in kind and any hope of repayment in cash. Similarly, Bulgaria honored UN sanctions against Libya, also foregoing both oil supplies and any prospect of repayment. In all, other CMEA members—particularly Iraq, Syria, and Libya—owed Bulgaria $2.36 billion in hard currency or oil. On top of this, Bulgaria honored the UN embargo on Yugoslavia, thus losing an additional $1.2 to 2.0 billion in trade (Troxel 1993).

In 1991, Bulgaria was running a $750 million trade deficit, a $1.15 billion balance of payment deficit, a domestic budgetary deficit of thirteen percent of GDP, and a $10 billion foreign debt with only $125 million in foreign exchange reserves. For all of Bulgaria's international cooperation, it was on the verge of utter financial collapse. On top of this, in February 1991, the IMF declared the Bulgarian currency, the lev, convertible, causing prices to leap by 123 percent. Although the IMF disbursed $550 million in loans, and a special $109 million to specifically offset Bulgaria's energy crisis, real gross domestic production fell by twenty-three percent and inflation ran at an astonishing 330 percent. When the November 1991 elections were held, SDS won largely because of economic issues. Frightened by the economic conditions caused by the socialist reform initiatives, many voters hoped the Union of Democratic Forces could do better. However, SDS won only a marginal number of seats more than the BSP. SDS thus formed a coalition government with the Turkish ethnic party, the Movement for Rights and Freedoms (DPS).

The 1991 campaign became an economic referendum on the government, and the electorate demonstrated that they wanted relief, and quickly. According to Rumyana Kolarov, "The 1991 election result proved that the majority of the public was obviously demanding a radical and quick economic reform" (1996). However, true to its word, the SDS was more concerned with retribution than pluralist democracy, and gave priority to restitution over privatization. The first law passed by the new SDS government was the confiscation of all Communist Party property. Then the SDS banned all former communist officials from serving in governing bodies of banking institutions, and restricted pensions paid to former communist officials. The government began investigating former party officials, and even voted to revoke the immunity of the former prime minister, Andrei Lukanov, who was arrested in 1992 for crimes against the Bulgarian nation. Additionally, the government continued its restitution program by voting to return agricultural lands to the owners who held these properties before 1947. While this may sound laudable, this measure would result in the reversal of massive land reform initiatives, returning property into the hands of a few large landholders. The scheme would affect any privatization program in two ways. First, such a scheme would deprive the state of numerous assets that it could sell for capitalization, and thus fund government welfare programs. Second, such a scheme would make widespread privatization impossible. By returning large tracks of agricultural land to a limited number of holders, the SDS would preclude individual landholders from selling deeds or receiving rent payments for leases. This threat to the effective restructuring and "marketization" of agriculture and rural production was but a symptom of the highly anti-democratic and even "authoritarian" approaches of the anti-communist coalition.

The BSP turned to the institutions of pluralist democracy. By appealing to the Constitutional Court, the BSP was able to overturn much of the SDS legislation, particularly the banking and pension laws affecting former communist officials. It was also able to forestall any property restitution in favor of widespread property redistribution. Such "backward-looking" policies of SDS in general led to a no-confidence vote in the Parliament and the defection of the Turkish ethnic party (DPS) from the coalition. The SDS government fell, and BSP and DPS formed a minority government under the leadership of another independent prime minister, Lyuben Berov, who ruled until the next round of elections could be held. This new government represented a slight shift for the BSP, highlighted by a cautious stance concerning the IMF.

After Berov became prime minister, the new Socialist government was able to slow the economic bleeding. By early 1993, the government had stabilized the lev, inflation came in check, and exports started to pick up. By the autumn of 1993, exports had grown such that Bulgaria was able to enjoy a $425 million balance of payments surplus (Troxel 1993). However, the BSP government challenged the IMF and asserted that the circumstances demanded that Bulgaria be allowed to run a domestic budget deficit at eight to ten percent of GDP. Although the IMF insisted that the deficit be lower, it did not penalize Bulgaria for running higher than normally tolerated deficits. The BSP had won a small victory and portrayed itself as the economic defender of the state. The BSP was ready for the next elections.

Just as the 1991 elections were about economics, so too were the parliamentary elections of 1994, only this time the results were reversed. The BSP enjoyed a near landslide victory. The socialists similarly stressed their ability to manage economic reforms, but also their interest in protecting social welfare. The BSP received nearly twice as many seats as the SDS. The socialists also invited members of the "green" Ecoglasnost Movement (DE) to join them in coalition. While this party did not win any seats on their own, some BSP candidates also ran on the DE ticket. Much of the rhetoric from this party can be found in the platforms of other Green parties in Europe. The major concern for the DE was environmental degradation and the lack of concern for this problem expressed by the IMF and other European institutions. This message fit well with the BSP campaign in the countryside, which appealed to rural voters affected by the SDS plans for property restitution. The BSP dominated the rural municipalities and in rural regions bordering cities and towns, largely by capitalizing on their message of protecting agricultural interests (Creed 1995). This support for the BSP in the countryside largely parallels that of the PDSR and the PRM. However, the Bulgarian Socialists proved that it is possible to advocate rural economic policy without resorting to traditionalism or nationalist-populism.

The socialists were getting everything they wanted. After their 1991 defeat, there was a significant change in the party leadership, culminating with a new party chair, the young charismatic Zhan Videnov. Videnov led the BSP in an aggressive economic restructuring program that brought inflation down from 120 percent to sixty-six percent. Domestic production grew by two percent, and the currency remained stable. However, the plan was firmly rooted in principles of social democracy (Kolarova 1996). This was not a liberal economic restructuring program, particularly demonstrated by commitments to state economic planning and price controls. Thus, the government became deeply involved in macro-economic initiatives. In late 1995, however, two significant cracks in the new economic program appeared; production began to fall again and the government had to intervene in order to save two private banks from insolvency.

In May 1996, the dam broke. Five large banks simultaneously declared bankruptcy, including the largest private bank in all of Bulgaria, First Private Bank. Domestic production quickly fell by eight percent, interest rates jumped from an already high 39 percent to 108 percent by June, and the lev fell in value by half against the U.S. dollar. The state was forced to announce its insolvency to the IMF (Kolarova 1996). Prime Minister Videnov agreed to any and all requirements of the IMF and the World Bank. The BSP social democratic experiment of 1995 had ended terribly. Videnov was removed as prime minister at the end of December 1996, and an independent caretaker government was formed. After a month of public demonstrations calling for new elections, the socialists conceded and returned their mandate to form a government while new parliamentary elections were called for April 1997.

The BSP defeat in 1997 was as resounding as their victory was in 1994. Although the SDS took a majority of the popular vote, they again formed a coalition with DPS, this time for a large parliamentary majority.

Immediately, the SDS took to implementing economic reforms and macroeconomic restructuring. The new government engaged in a massive asset sell-off, advocating the privatization of all sectors. Most importantly, the SDS government returned to the agricultural privatization scheme that they were forced to abandon in 1994. By 1999, ninety percent of all agricultural land, eighty-five percent of the food industry, and fifty-five percent of total agricultural assets had been privatized. During the same period, 1997 to 1999, the SDS government oversaw the privatization of $882.9 billion in state assets equaling nearly seventy-seven percent of all assets sold. In addition, the government pegged the currency, the lev, to the German Deutschmark. Combined with an extensive austerity program the government slashed inflation to single digits, from 578.6 percent in 1997 to 6.6 percent in 1999 (World Bank 1999). With additional support coming from international lending institutions, including a $600 million macro-stabilization loan from the IMF, SDS proclaimed that for the first time the government would show a surplus representing 1.6 percent of GDP in 1998. This was in contrast to the planned annual deficit for 1998 that would have equaled 2.6 percent of GDP (World Bank 1999). However, by the end of 1998, the governmental deficit still stood at two percent of GDP. Moreover, total external debt was cut from 114 percent of GDP in 1997 to only eighty-six percent of GDP in 1998 (Bulgarian Investment Guide 2000). While this was still extremely high, it was a significant accomplishment. Finally, real GDP growth was experienced for the first since 1993. The international lending institutions of the West were duly impressed, and Bulgaria was invited to join CEFTA—the Central European Free Trade Association. Other framework agreements were settled with the EU, the European Free Trade Association (EFTA), and Macedonia and Turkey, giving Bulgaria access to needed markets.

While the SDS government was making Bulgaria more attractive to Western financial institutions, there were costs associated with the austerity program. Unemployment remained steady at thirteen percent of the workforce. When long-term unemployment was included, nearly half of all Bulgarian adults were out of work (Ministry of Statistics 1999).[3] Further, while inflation was cut, consumer prices rose in 1998 by nineteen percent, placing a difficult financial burden on Bulgaria's already hard-hit workers. Other important indicators demonstrated that the economic situation was not all what it seemed from the declarations of the SDS government. The trade deficit grew from a surplus of $350 million in 1997 to nearly one billion dollars in 1999 (*Bulgarian Investment Guide* 2000). Moreover, like Romania, foreign direct investment remained low; a steady $600 million in 1997 through 1999 (*Bulgarian Investment Guide* 2000). This is an important statistic, for it demonstrates that, while the government was successful in privatizing many assets, additional investment has not been forthcoming. These trends led the Ministry of Finance to conclude in 2000, that gains delivered by the austerity program in 1998 and 1999 would have only a limited duration of approximately two years. Specifically, the ministry cited that the government macroeconomic policy and restructuring imposed by the currency board—the body that pegged the lev to the Deutschmark—would have only a limited effect. It predicted that current and trade deficits would continue to rise, making Bulgaria increasingly dependent on imports, thus further increasing consumer prices (Ministry of Finance 2000).

In November of 2000, the BSP organized a rally at which 10,000 people marched decrying the effects of the SDS austerity program. The BSP organizers declared that the SDS government contains only "poverty, unemployment and corruption" (RFE/RL *Newsline*, November 3, 2000). While the European Union has looked favorably upon the SDS government and its restructuring program, it too agreed that corruption was running rampant in Bulgaria and represented a major obstacle to EU accession (RFE/RL *Newsline*, January 7, 2001). The BSP has accentuated the charges of corruption in the run up to the 2001 parliamentary elections, suggesting that the SDS has created two Bulgarias: a wealthy and urban one in Sophia's business community, the other impoverished and neglected in the countryside. This division is demonstrated by the weak public support for the SDS in 2000 and 2001. Georgi Lazonov, a professor of political science at Sophia University, declared that the SDS goals of accession to the European Union and NATO have "little domestic support" (RFE/RL *Ten Years After*, December 9, 1999). Similarly, by the spring of 2001, SDS was polling at only twenty-three percent support (RFE/RL *Newsline,* April 17, 2001). In a distinct move, the BSP proclaimed that it will protect those most adversely affected by the SDS macro-stabilization scheme and will attempt to create a more egalitarian society. It is worth noting however, that in the spring of 2001, the BSP was still only polling equal to the SDS. Nevertheless, the BSP has demonstrated its continued commitment to opposing the excesses of capitalism in Bulgaria. This message is in direct response to the conditions created by the SDS and appears to retain a degree of resonance. This is not the case of a party not changing with the times. Quite to the contrary, it would appear that the BSP appeals to a particular constituency hard hit by the economic transformation.

The PDSR and the BSP as "Successor Parties"

Since the beginnings of the Central European political transitions, political scientists have scrutinized the former communist parties, often searching for some commonality among them. Vladimir Tismaneanu has claimed that most former communist officials are "cynical pragmatists, chameleon-like survivors, ready to espouse any creed with lightening speed . . . if it only upholds their stay in power" (Tismaneanu 1999: p. 52, as cited in Shafir 1999). Yet this paints the former communists with a brush so wide it covers the entire canvas. Other attempts to place the former ruling communist parties in a comparative perspective have focused on the electoral dynamics of these parties. These efforts have followed two tendencies: The first examines party structures and party formation, evaluating the significance of party type. It then places the former communist parties within a structural typology. Ágh (1995) and Kitschelt (1992) have articulated this emphasis on party type. This work is significant because it challenges assumptions that were prevalent at the time of the transitions—namely, that the former communists would disappear. The second tendency focuses on the impact of continued political participation by the former communists, particularly their impact on democratic processes. According to this perspective, it is significant that across Central Europe, multiparty, free and fair, and contested parliamentary elections have become normal. Elections in countries from the Baltic to the Black Sea, at least in those states that were not part of the Soviet Union, have demonstrated a commitment to pluralist parliamentarianism. One effect described by these writers has surfaced in certain political environments. Gerhard Mangott warned that the "rapid return of communist positions of power could result in a 'distorted interpretation of the communist past'" (Ziblatt 1999; Mangott 1995). While the Romanian example appears to confirm this prediction, it also appears that it is the presence of non-communist parties in power that inspires nostalgia for the communist past. Democratic consolidation has taken place even with, or in part because of, the participation of the former communist parties. Karen Dawisha has stated that part of this has to do with a most minimalist definition of democracy (Dawisha 1999: 256). If democracy is understood as a process of regular elections, then democracy has indeed taken root. Both Romania's PDSR and Bulgaria's BSP are committed to open, free and fair, contested parliamentary elections.

A third wave of scholarship has focused on how former communist parties have remained relevant. This work has focused on electoral performance and programmatic strategy. Evans and Whitefield (1995) as well as Ishiyama (1995, 1997a, and 1999a) particularly articulate this perspective. Among these authors Daniel Ziblatt has also suggested that former ruling communist parties will take one of two paths in their need to find a new purpose: practical ideology or leftist retreat (Ziblatt 1999). He has compared the former East German Communist Party (the Party of Democratic Socialism [PDS]) and the former Hungarian Communist Party (the Hungarian Socialist Party [MSzP]). As examples of these two tracks Ziblatt argues that the PDS, unable to carve out a social democratic niche because of the strength of the German Social Democratic Party, was forced to play a "peripheral left-wing

role in German politics." The PDS thus engaged in a "leftist retreat," emphasizing its Marxist ideology in order to remain part of the political landscape
with particular appeal to disaffected workers in East Berlin. The Hungarian
Socialist Party by contrast moved toward a political center, espousing social
democratic programs, and shed all semblances of its Marxist ideological past.
By doing so, Ziblatt argues that the MSzP adopted a "practical ideology." Yet
Ziblatt's proposition suggests a stasis to post-communist politics. The recent
political history of Romania and Bulgaria suggest that the PDSR and BSP
are responding to constituencies that oppose the effects of liberal economic
transformation. Rather than needing to find a purpose or niche, these two
successor parties have remained relevant within the context of the transitions
in their respective countries.

The PDSR has not taken the path of a "leftist retreat," nor has it adopted
a "practical ideology" for the sake of survival. Iliescu's defense of working-class elements and the PDSR's alliances with heavy industrial sector
workers appears to be a party-constituency linkage. However, the defense
of local workers against transnational corporations and international high
finance is couched more in the rhetoric of populism than in Marxist-
Socialist ideology. This is not a "leftist retreat" but rather the continued
use of Ceaușescu-style "national communist" rhetoric. On the other hand,
the PDSR has not engaged in the adoption of "practical ideology." Although it has continually professed to support the concepts of European
Union and NATO accession, the party has not created the most favorable
conditions to accomplish those goals. The latest round of election rhetoric
would suggest that the PDSR has not taken a radically new position. Moreover, the PDSR has not adopted conservative campaign slogans to fill a
void along the political spectrum. Quite to the contrary, the PDSR has argued that the liberal parties would "sell off the nation's treasures" and that
the liberalism they champion should be regarded with suspicion. To ensure
that the liberals would not force Romania to submit to transnational capitalist power, the PDSR has asserted that it should be they who shepherd the
country through this arduous task. In this way, the PDSR may accept European integration as an inevitable course for Romania, but it has always
stressed that this should be a course taken with the protection of workers in
mind. This is what Adrian Nastase means when he refers to maintaining
the "social equilibrium" during the course of privatization.

The BSP has behaved in much the same way. It has not engaged in a
"leftist retreat" but steadily advocated that Marxist principles remain relevant in contemporary Bulgarian society. In this way the BSP is not trying to
carve a political niche for itself, but remains one of the two largest parties in
Bulgaria and represents a sizable constituency. Similarly it has not engaged
in a program of "pragmatic ideology." Like the PDSR, the BSP has softened
its language concerning the European Union and NATO accession, declar-

ing these to be goals of the party. However, as in the case of the PDSR, such actions appear to be a recognition that EU accession is the only game in town. Ultimately, however, any softening of the rhetoric on EU accession and market reform by these parties appears to be more for the benefit of the international community than for domestic political consumption.

If Iliescu and Nastase support the use of the Hungarian language in Hungarian ethnic communities, they continue to stress that they will not support autonomous cultural institutions, such as a Hungarian language university. Similarly, Iliescu cautions the Hungarian minority that they must wait until the economy improves before any other demands will be considered. This is an important statement, for it means that the Hungarians must wait until Romanian workers' needs are satisfied. At the same time, Iliescu and the PDSR clearly understand that EU and NATO accession are impossible if the West continues to believe the Romanian government is denying the Hungarian minority its civil and human rights.

Likewise, it is clear that the Romanian government will have great difficulty settling budget arrears without capital inflows. At present, the quickest access to this capital is through IMF and IBRD stabilization loans. The PDSR's announcement to these institutions that it is both willing to negotiate on loan terms as well as implement a privatization scheme is part of that access to needed capital. However, the PDSR was not willing to promise a reduction of the government deficit to below three percent of GDP, nor did it announce a privatization scheme until it won the support of trade unions and promised a wage increase. These movements do not appear to be a willing descent into the "valley of sorrows" in order to stabilize the economy. Rather it appears that the PDSR understands what it must do to communicate effectively with the Western and international communities. By telling the West what it wants to hear while keeping campaign promises, the PDSR appears reactive to both internal and external audiences. This is not merely an adoption of a program to stay in power, but reflects a tightrope walk many governments confront between internal and external forces influencing policy.

Assuming that a programmatic bankruptcy was inevitable, Andrew Janós has suggested that former communist parties make strategic choices from three traditions: the liberal/civic tradition, the technocratic tradition, and the neo-populist tradition (Janós 1994: 21). Janós suggests that upon their inception former communist parties must choose between the "idiom of universalism and particularism." Michael Shafir describes such a choice as similar to Kenneth Jowitt's distinction of the civic versus the ethnic (Shafir 1999). This suggests that in order to remake themselves, former communists were forced to make a choice. Yet the populist nationalism espoused by the PDSR bears affinities and continuities with the program of the former Ceauşescu regime. Janós' proposition of a "choice" suggests that the communist regimes were not populist or nationalist before the political changes that may have driven them from power. Moreover, the populist, nationalist rhetoric employed by Corneliu Tudor and the PRM was probably closer to the rhetoric employed by the Ceauşescu regime. Yet the PRM is nearly universally described as an extreme "rightist" party. The connection between it and the PDSR is not a red-brown coalition, or the conflation of two extreme ends of the political spectrum. Rather, these parties appear to be cut from the same bolt of cloth. Both share an animosity toward the processes of globalization and advanced capitalism, and both share hostility toward liberalism.

Janós describes the neo-populist tradition as an "aggressive anti-liberalism" coupled with a resistance to Westernization or globalism (Janós 1994: 24). While such a description can be seen as part of the radical tradition of rejecting individualist values, it is significant to note that neither the PDSR nor the BSP reject the values of democratic elections or parliamentarianism. This is in contrast to the slippery slope posited by Vladimir Tismaneanu, according to which the rejection of individualist values equals a rejection of democracy and parliamentarianism (Tismaneanu 1999: 78). For Tismaneanu the neo-populist tradition would reject Western-liberal definitions of democracy. But that is not the only possible form of democracy.

What is at stake in Romania is not a "left-right" split, with the PDSR at the "extreme left" end of the spectrum, the PRM at the "extreme right," and liberal parties in the middle. Rather, Romanian politics can be described as a "collective-individualist" cleavage, with the PDSR and the PRM sharing the same side of the spectrum. This requires not only a realignment of the dominant political spectrum, but also a redefinition of anti-liberalism. These parties prove that parliamentary democracy can function in its most limited definition in a non-liberal environment. Thus, the West must recognize that its desired goal for Central Europe should not simply be its democratization but its liberalization. These achievements are not one in the same.

Similarly, the BSP uses "leftist" language not in an attempt to recreate the past, but in opposition to the adverse conditions created by capitalism in the present. This opposition is more like the position of the PDSR in spirit, if not in language and rhetoric. The BSP remains committed to parliamentary democracy, even if it opposes liberalization of the economy.

I would like to propose that the distinction of "extreme" is an organization's willingness to employ violence to accomplish its political ends. In Romania, both the PRM and the PDSR have shown such a willingness to use violence, and the PDSR has indeed deployed coal miners on a number of occasions to confront physically the party's political opponents. The question facing Romania today is whether the PDSR, in its most current incarnation, remains as willing. Thus, it appears possible to place parties like the PDSR and the PRM along the same end of a political spectrum, differentiated by degree, rather than situating them as polar opposites. Along the same end of the new conceptual spectrum, the BSP would appear as a communitarian party opposed to liberalism. However, unlike the PDSR or the PRM, it is not extreme, as it has never advocated the use of violence for political ends.

This political situation has profound implications for the institution of democracy. Both liberalism and communitarianism can be constructed in a democratic fashion; likewise each can be constructed in an anti-democratic or authoritarian fashion. While it is often taken for granted that the structure of government is reflected in the structure of the economy, numerous examples prove this not to be the case. Liberal economies can be overseen by anti-democratic, authoritarian regimes, just as illiberal economies may be governed by participatory democracies. The political contests engendered by globalization require an analysis of "democracy" beyond its classic definition of free and fair, contested multiparty elections.

In the cases of Romania and Bulgaria, resistance to globalization not only raises questions about the social "costs" of entering the global economy, but about the role of history in politics. The rhetoric typically used by both the PDSR and the PRM to frame their rejection of neo-liberalism evokes the past. The PRM is especially similar to Romania's interwar society. For the PRM, resistance to "global high finance" parallels the romantic notions of the interwar fascist conception of a "third" economic path. Similarly, the PDSR argues that limited privatization can serve the "national interest," yet its rationale for privatization appears to conflict with that of neo-liberal projects. Additionally, the PDSR utilizes many arguments based on Ceaușescu's "National Communism," which resisted international markets. Throughout the countryside, particularly in areas hardest hit by recent economic downturns, a Ceaușescu nostalgia movement has appeared. Eleven years after its violent overthrow, Romania has yet to come to terms with the significance of the Ceaușescu regime. Any discussion regarding globalization and participation in the world economy requires a parallel discussion of reconciliation regarding the fascist and communist pasts.

In the case of Bulgaria, the BSP similarly represents a force opposing liberalization. It evokes a rural egalitarian political movement that has long been present in Bulgarian politics. What makes Bulgaria different from Romania is an apparent lack of extremist or radical parties. However, the continued success of the BSP and the PDSR to mobilize voters and represent vast constituencies may say less about post-communist politics than it says about the new struggles and forces opposing globalization and neoliberal capitalism.

Notes

1. Nastase is making reference to the Democratic Convention–led government of 1996–2000. See below.
2. When the PURN fielded candidates in Moldova in 1992, they ran for the

396 JEFFREY STEVENSON MURER

Moldovan Parliament. The PRM's candidacy of Ile Ilascu was for the Romanian Senate. This had important implications for the irredentist Romanian organizations in Moldova, who had been campaigning for integration with Romania. Throughout the region irredentist nationalist organizations pose a threat to the stability of state borders. In the early 1990s, the Hungarian Prime Minster Jozsef Antal proclaimed that he represented all fifteen million Hungarians. The implication of this statement was that he represented the interests of the five million Hungarians living outside of the Republic of Hungary. Many read this statement as an indication that Antal desired an alteration of borders. The PRM's example would appear to have the same implication. By running a Moldovan citizen living in Moldova, the PRM stressed that Ilascu was "really" a Romanian, entitling him to a seat in the Parliament.

3. Long-term unemployment as defined by the World Bank includes those no longer seeking work, or those no longer able to work. This calculation includes elderly pensioners and the disabled.

19

Organizational Strength Divorced from Power

Comparing the Communist Parties of the Russian Federation and Ukraine

Barbara Ann Chotiner

Before the Union of Soviet Socialist Republics dissolved on December 25, 1991, the Russian and Ukrainian national subdivisions of the Communist Party of the Soviet Union (CPSU) had been rendered illegal (Prezident RSFSR 1991, pp. 369–379; Chebanenko 1997, p. 95). Consequently, the political landscape of the two largest Soviet successor states originally lacked large mass parties that continued the organizational life of the central institution of the Soviet state. Members of the Communist Party of the Russian Soviet Federated Socialist Republic (CPRSFSR) and the Communist Party of Ukraine (KPU) that had existed until 1991 were forced to seek recognition of their rights to associate and contest elections (Konstitutsionnyi Sud Rossiiskoi Federatsii 1992, p. 378; Chebanenko 1997, p. 97). Once these sanctions had been granted, party members and leaders had to rebuild and/or reknit the party formations, learn to contest elections effectively and orient the organizations not only to the dilemmas of the post-communist transitions but also to the heritage of the past. In addition, party elites and officials, elected on communist slates, faced the challenge of using governmental structures in super-presidentialist systems to translate programmatic statements into policy and to extract rewards for constituents.

Since their reconstruction and official recognition by the Ministries of Justice in their respective countries (Ministerstvo iustitsii Rossiiskoi Federatsii 1993, p. 379; Andrushchak et al. 1999, p. 90), the Communist Party of the Russian Federation and the Communist Party of Ukraine have achieved some notable successes. The Communist Party of the Russian Federation (KPRF) is the largest party in Russia with 570,000 members, reported by an officially sanctioned book published in 2000. With 142,000 members in 1999, the KPU appears to be the second largest electoral association in its state—ranking behind the presidentially-inspired Agrarian Party with 172,000 members (Kholmskaia 2000, p. 5; Andrushchak et al. 1999, p. 90; Luts'kyi 2000, p. 2).

In national elections, both partisan formations have polled well. The KPU slate received 24.65 percent of the vote in the 1998 elections, with its nearest competitor, Rukh, garnering 9.4 percent. A communist candidate, First Secretary Petro Symonenko, participated in the presidential balloting in 1999, and he gained 37.8 percent of the vote in the second round (Marchenko and Telemko, 1998, n.p.; Central Election Commission of Ukraine 1999, p. 1). Likewise, KPRF Chairman Gennadii Ziuganov ran second to Vladimir Putin in the second round of the 2000 presidential voting. Ziuganov acquired the support of 29.21 percent of the electorate. The Russian communists had their best party list showing to date in the 1999 State Duma contest, while the KPRF placed first with 24.29 percent of the ballots (Tsentral'naia izbiratel'naia komissiia Rossiiskoi Federatsii, 2000; Tsentral'naia izbiratel'naia komissiia Rossiiskoi Federatsii 1999b). Thus, both parties have established themselves as significant political actors with genuine popular support.

Nonetheless, the KPRF and the KPU have had mixed success in parleying their following into influence in either the legislature or the executive. While Gennadii Seleznev is serving his second term as Duma Speaker, in February 2000 the communist faction he represents commanded only seven more seats than Putin's Edintsvo (Unity) Party. From the early months of the lower house's third convocation in 1999, the potential was noted for Edinstvo leaders to construct majority coalitions without the KPRF (Babichenko and Iur'ev 2000, p. 2; Belonuchkin 1996, p. 191; Belonuchkin 2000, pp. 229, 233; Iur'ev 2000a, p. 4). A communist entered the cabinet for the first time when Iuri Masliukov accepted the portfolio of Minister of Trade and Industry under Prime Minister Evgevii Primakov. However, any negotiations about Masliukov's possible inclusion in Mikhail Kasianov's government did not lead to a formal bid (Iur'ev 1998a, p. 1; Masliukov 2000, p. 2). In the elected Rada of 1998, Communist Vice Speaker Adam Martyniuk was displaced in a parliamentary upheaval when the majority met in another building and elected new officers (Razumovskii and Chubanenko 2000, p. 2; Desiatnikov 2000, p. 1). KPU deputies elected on the party's slate chaired five committees (Andrushchak, Marchenko, and Telemko 1998, pp. 31–37).

Since 1993, the parties' approaches have evolved divergently, so that the KPU and the KPRF present different faces to one another, the public, and other elites. In the terminology selected in the introduction of this book, the KPU is neither *reformed* nor *transmuted*. At the same time, the KPRF may have evolved somewhat towards the direction of *reformed* but may be facing questions about the efficacy of *transmutation*. The relative programmatic stasis of the KPU and shifts from Soviet communist orthodoxy in the KPRF have occurred within organizations that, themselves, manifest a mixture of similarities and dissimilarities in structure, membership, and operations. The two electoral associations appeal to constituencies that are somewhat unlike, and the parties have oriented themselves somewhat differently toward political allies.

Communists in Russia and Ukraine have had to negotiate electoral systems that developed out of sync with one another as well as to learn to function within multiparty legislatures. Partisans in both countries also face the constraints of super-presidential systems that limit the impact of parliaments on policy and in administrative oversight. Thus, there are systemic obstacles to the KPRF and the KPU's ability to translate electoral success into policies that carry out platforms or reward supporters. Of course, both activities contribute to any party's capability to increase its electoral following. Impediments to making these translations may thus deprive the KPU and the KPRF of resources to facilitate or undercut some kind of metamorphosis and may create a disconnect between performance and calculations about ideological change (Ishiyama and Bozoki, forthcoming; Crawford and Lijphart 1995, p. 177; Kubicek, 1994; Linz, 1994, pp. 34–35; Shugart 1998; Kitschelt et al. 1999; Fedotkin 2000, p. 2).

Party members and leaders react to external signals and parameters on the basis of legacies (Jowitt 1992, p. 286; Crawford and Lijphart 1995, p. 172; Ishiyama and Bozóki, 2001) from past history. Hence, choices, lessons, and personnel from the defunct CPSU and Soviet Union continue to shape preferences, opportunities, and assets for stability and change in partisan identities.[1] This chapter will assess the impact of various factors on the KPU and the KPRF through their countries' presidential elections in 1999 and 2000, respectively.

The Soviet Legacy and Its Aftermath

While the KPRF and the KPU have their roots in the republican formations of the CPSU, their histories as organizations and their responses to the politics of the Gorbachev era diverge in significant ways. Over the decades that the Soviet Union existed, the Communist Party of Ukraine had a distinct institutional life. The Ukrainian Central Committee (CC) decided a range of questions affecting the republic. Two national leaders—Leonid Brezhnev and Nikita Khrushchev—spent formative periods of their professional careers in the Ukrainian Communist Party, with Khrushchev serving as its first secretary. He and his successor's clients from Ukraine served in other republics and in prominent all-Union posts. When the office of deputy secretary general of the CC CPSU was created by the Twenty-eighth Party Congress in 1990, KPU First Secretary Volodymyr Ivashko was tapped to fill the job (Kommunisticheskaia partiia Sovetskogo soiuza 1991, v. 2, p. 392).

In contrast, no separate Communist Party entity for the Russian Soviet

Federated Socialist Republic (RSFSR) existed until 1990. Party committees (*partkoms*) of oblasts, krais, and autonomous republics in Russia reported directly to the CC CPSU. There was no Russian party congress to formulate and direct demands or concerns for the union republic as a whole to the top national party bodies. Hence, when the CPRSFSR was formed with claims that its establishment would remediate neglect of Russian interests (Gill 1994, pp. 93–94, 124, 129, 137; Brown 1997, p. 208; Urban and Solovei 1997, p. 39), the constituent units, as well as their leaders and members, may have been less politically integrated than their Ukrainian counterparts. Moreover, emphasis on the formulation and expression of Russian views meant that proponents could find that portraying the successor KPRF as "patriotic" was not impossible (Urban and Solovei, 1997; Ishiyama and Bozóki 2001; Ziuganov 2000a, p. 2; Ziuganov 2000b, p. 1).

Instead of reinforcing the coalescence of an organization that manifested some hallmarks of institutionalization (Huntington 1968, pp. 12–24; Panebianco 1988, pp. 55–56), Ukrainian communist elites responded divisively to the nationalist movement. Leonid Kravchuk, the republican CC Secretary for ideology during the Gorbachev era and the first post-independence president, supported "nation-building" as an ex-communist. Former party member Oleksandr Moroz helped found the Socialist Party as a one-time advocate of Ukrainian communist separatism (D'Anieri, Kravchuk, and Kuzio 1999, pp. 59–62; Wilson 1997a, p. 1297; Wilson 1997b, pp. 25, 114, 104). Yet many who remained loyal to the KPU qualified their acceptance of national autonomy and continued to value the USSR (D'Anieri, Kravchuk, and Kuzio 1999, p. 161; Wilson 1997a, p. 1300; Chebanenko 1997, p. 106; Kommunistychna partiia Ukrainy 1999a, pp. 93, 1013). This history and the continuity of negative attitudes later gave opponents grounds for requesting the banning of the KPU as subversive of the constitutional order (Kuzio 1997, p. 124; Wilson 1997a, p. 1301; Mel'nichuk 2000, p. 2). The party's long organizational continuity may have rendered metamorphosis more difficult (Huntington 1968, p. 13; Panebianco 1988, pp. 49, 53, 54; Sartori 1976, p. 244).

Before the dissolution of the Soviet Union in December 1991, Ukrainian and Russian communists were, of course, highly involved in debates between conservatives and reformers over the whole gamut of Soviet domestic and foreign policy. While a degree of continuity in conservative leadership from the Soviet past can be observed in the Ukrainian successor party, this linkage is not so clear in the KPRF. The final Ukrainian first secretary within the CPSU was Politburo member Stanislav Hurenko. He expressed concern about a range of policies on the reform agenda under Gorbachev as well as little support for Ukrainian nationalism. Today, he retains a position as counselor to the Presidium of the CC of the revived KPU; and a journalist has identified Hurenko as one of the party's major financiers (Wilson 1997b, pp. 102–103, 108; Kommunisticheskaia partiia Sovetskogo Soiuza 1991, v. 1, pp. 286–290; Andrushchak, Marchenko, and Telemko 1998a, p. 100; Rakhmanin 2000, p. 5). In contrast, Vladimir Kuptsov was elected first secretary of the CPRSFSR in August 1991 after working as secretary of the CC CPSU under Gorbachev. As the only deputy chairman that the KPRF has ever had, Kuptsov administers the party and has provided liaison to the local *partkoms* (Gill 1994, p. 152; Urban and Solovei 1997, pp. 42–43, 127–128; Sakwa 1998, p. 139; Svechnikov 1997, p. 2; Kuptsov 1990, p. 99). Thus, he serves as a connection to Soviet-era efforts at partisan adaptation. Once again, the legacy of the USSR to the KPRF seems to afford more resources for change than does the inheritance of the KPU.

After the abortive 1991 coup by the State Committee for the State of Emergency, the Supreme Soviet of the USSR interdicted CPSU activities across the country on August 29. The next day, the Supreme Rada in Kiev followed suit for the KPU. By a decree of November 6, 1991, President Boris Yeltsin "dissolve[d]" the CPRSFSR—along with other all-Union Communist Party agencies in Russia (Gill 1994, p. 175; Tsikora 1991, p. 2; Prezident RSFSR 1991, p. 369). Hence, unlike the histories of many Central European successor parties, a structural caesura provided the opportunity for the reshuffling of personnel and the adoption of a different mix of ideas. The parties' banning could also provide reinforcement for holding on to views that had been considered orthodox at various times in Soviet history.

The Revival of Communist Parties in Russian and Ukraine

Relatively large, mass membership communist parties were reestablished in Russia and Ukraine in 1993, pursuant to different types of governmental authorization. Activists, with a limited number of former members of the CPSU elite, instigated these foundings. Between 1991 and 1993, dissimilar parties were created in the two countries to substitute for the banned CPSU subdivisions, and adherents of these alternative formations did not always reaffiliate with the KPU and the KPRF. Consequently, the alternative organizations were placed disparately on the left of the political spectra in Russia and Ukraine (Chebanenko 1997, p. 101; Matsuzato, 1997; White and McAllister 1996, pp. 106–107; Wilson 1997a; Wilson 1997b, p. 114; Sakwa 1998, pp. 131–132; Sartori 1976, pp. 342–350; Ishiyama 1995, p. 134; Ishiyama 1997a, p. 303; Kitschelt et al., 1999a, pp. 69–77).

Those parties succeeding the KPU and the KPRF provided important resources for political activities as well as a reservoir of expectations about policy orientations and elite behavior in the national arena. To the extent that participants harbored nostalgia for the Soviet past, they could also inhibit partisan reform. Yet, relationships of local communists with elites, groups, and organizations in their areas could undercut aversion to change

(Panebianco 1988, pp. 26–27, 205, 242–247; Ishiyama 1999b). Some evidence suggests that—to at least an extent—subnational components of the KPU and the KPRF may also be situated differently in their socioeconomic and political environments.

Without clear legality, the Communist Party of Ukraine returned to the political scene in the new country. Delegates from every province assembled on March 6, 1993 for the All-Ukrainian Conference of Communists, to try to reestablish their organization. Slightly more than two months later, the Presidium of the Supreme Rada legalized formation of communist-type parties. Representatives from across the national territory gathered for the First (Nineteenth) Congress of the KPU on June 19, 1993. To head the association, they elected Petro Symonenko, whose last CPSU position had been the relatively junior role of second secretary of the Donetsk Obkom. In October, the Ministry of Justice registered the organization, which declared itself heir to the original KPU (Chebanenko 1997, pp. 96–98; Kommunistychna partiia Ukrainy 1999b, p. 91; Wilson 1997a, p. 1300).

While it was disallowed, several entities continued the KPU's traditions. Both the Socialist Party, led by Oleksandr Moroz, and the Rural or Agrarian Party of Ukraine were founded as proxies for the communist formation. The two new parties advocated the KPU's revival, but the socialists and ruralists continued their independence and advocated programs closer to the political center (Potichnyi 1994, p. 25; Chebanenko 1997, p. 95; Bojcun 1995, pp. 238–239; Wilson 1997a, pp. 1297–1301, 1306–1310; Wilson 1997b, p. 114; Urban 1999, p. 10). Nevertheless, the communists backed Moroz for the first round of the 1994 presidential race. He not only spoke at the Fourth KPU Congress in 1999 but was also an invited visitor to the Fifth Congress in June 2000 (Chebanenko 1997, p. 98; Andrushchak et al. 1999, p. 90; *Pravda Ukrainy* 2000, p. 1).

Despite this continued comity, the socialist and rural parties created their own electoral bloc for the 1998 parliamentary campaign. The KPU—which had performed better than its precursors in the 1994 Rada elections with 25.4 percent of all deputies' mandates—also resolved to run independently in 1998 (D'Anieri, Kravchuk, and Kuzio 1999, pp. 158–159; Wilson and Birch 1999, p. 1040; Chebanenko 1997, p. 100). This decision was rewarded with still greater success, for the communists won 27.11 percent of the seats in the Rada, while the socialist-rural alliance acquired 7.56 percent (Wilson and Birch 1999, p. 1040). After this showing, the communists ran Symonenko as their presidential contender in 1999. The party's negotiators with the socialists and ruralists were apparently unwilling to subordinate the KPU's vote-getting capability to another attempt by Moroz to gain national executive office (Central Election Commission of Ukraine 1999a; Simonenko 2000, p. 2). Hence, a better showing at the polls seems to have impelled the communists to greater self-assertion, and perhaps to further encapsulation. Neither move contributed toward transformation or transmutation but may have, instead, been conducive to a reaffirmation of traditional beliefs (Ziblatt 1999).

While the presence of competitors affirming Ukrainian nationhood on the right might be another factor expected to limit transformation or transmutation (Urban 1999, pp. 9–10; Sartori 1976, pp. 342–350; Ishiyama 1995, p. 134; see Wilson 1997a), a reformist impulse has existed in the KPU. At the Third Party Congress, the first secretary mentioned disparagement of delegates, in his words, for "revisionism" and "nationalism" (Urban 1999, p. 11). Joan Barth Urban reports a conversation with the Donetsk Obkom first secretary who advocated Gennadii Ziuganov's formula of going "not back to socialism but forward to socialism" (Urban 1999, p. 11). However, resistance to liberalization may be seen in Symonenko's criticisms, at the May 1997 CC plenum, of efforts to move the party in a "social democratic" direction. The program currently in force contains a similar warning (Chebanenko 1997, Kommunistychina partii Ukrainy 1999a, p. 100, 104).

A small number of parliamentarians in Ukraine and Russia were participants in the effort to resurrect communist parties. Rada delegate Evhen Marmazov was a prominent figure and with Deputy Oleksandr Kotsiuba became a member of the CC Secretariat chosen in 1993. Somewhat in contrast, Ivan Rybkin served as a liaison between representatives in the Russian Supreme Soviet and other organizers of the project who wished to create a new national communist party. Rybkin, who later served as speaker of the First State Duma, later complained that his group was marginalized at the convocation that established the KPRF (Wilson 1997b, p. 114; Andrushchak et al., 1999, p. 90; Urban and Solovei 1997, pp. 46, 48, 50, 54–55). This development may actually have provided greater legitimacy and a larger opening for the development of parliamentary influences in the KPRF, for the communist deputies' corpus in the Duma and Federation Council was largely comprised of individuals whose adherence to the party predated their elections.

Reconstitution of the Russian communist organization took place after the Constitutional Court ruled that local party bodies had a right to exist, guaranteed by the country's basic law (Konstitutsionnyi Sud Rossiiskoi Federatsii 1992, p. 378). The KPRF thus appears to have a firmer guarantee for its activity than its Ukrainian counterpart. Recognition of the Russian party's regular status as a political actor has been reinforced by President Putin's comments acknowledging some aspects of the Soviet past. Moreover, the textbook on the Russian party system approved by the Ministry of General and Professional Education describes the KPRF as a "systemic . . . opposition" (Kholmskaia 2000, p. 560). First Deputy Chairman Kuptsov has also employed the term to describe what he perceives to be a significant role for the KPRF (Kuptsov 2000, p. 2).

The organization formally reconstituted itself at its Second Extraordinary Congress on February 13–14, 1993. According to a compendium of official documents, "more than 650 delegates . . . represent[ed] half a million communists who had already registered in the Com[munist] Party that was being revived" (Kommunisticheskaia partiia Rossiiskoi Federatsii 1999b, p. 6). The Central Executive Committee elected by the congress chose Gennadii Ziuganov as its Chairman and Vladimir Kuptsov as its deputy chairman (Kommunisticheskaia partiia Rossiiskoi Federatsii 1999b, p. 6). As in Ukraine, former activists took a significant role in restarting party operations. However, leaders of several radical associations founded as alternatives to the defunct CPRSFSR and officials of "patriotic" groups participated in the Second Congress. Other conservative substitutes, including the Russian Communist Workers' Party, did not affiliate (Ziuganov 1998, p. 1; Urban and Solovei 1997, pp. 24–25, 81, 110; Sakwa 1998, pp. 131–132; Kholmskaia 2000, p. 559).

These circumstances may have set some parameters to organization modification. The existence of backward-looking groups outside the Communist Party of the Russian Federation might have reduced the leverage of conservatives within the formation (Sakwa 1996, p. 13; Ishiyama 1997a, p. 303; Sartori 1976, pp. 342–350). Symptomatic of these limitations might have been the failure, in 1998, of Central Committee members Leonid Petrovskii, Albert Makashov, and Teimuraz Avaliani to create a "Leninist-Stalinist Platform" within the structure of the KPRF. Forestalled, they established a free-standing "National Communist Movement" the following year. The inhospitable climate that neo-Stalinists came to face may be highlighted by the recollection that General Makashov urged Ziuganov's selection as KPRF Chairman in 1993 (Korguniuk 1999, p. 369; Kholmskaia 2000, p. 578; Belonuchkin 1996, p. 190; Urban and Solovei 1997, p. 54).

Nationalist involvement in the Second Extraordinary Congress helped to lay the organizational groundwork bolstering Ziuganov's own policy preferences (Urban and Solovei; Chotiner 1999, pp. 112–113; Sakwa 1998, pp. 139–141) and facilitating the creation in 1996 of a rather inclusive umbrella organization—the National Patriotic Union of Russia. Under the movement's aegis, the Communist Party campaigned in the 1996 presidential elections; and the NPUR nominated Ziuganov for the presidency in 2000 (Oleshchuk and Pavlenko 1997, pp. 21, 170; Ziuganov 2000d; "NPSR poderzhivaet Gennadiia Ziuganova" 2000, p. 1). Yet in the aftermath of the KPRF's first-place showing in the 1995 State Duma elections and the chairman's receipt of more than 40 percent of the vote in the 1996 contest for Russian chief executive (Belonuchkin 1996, p. 191; White, Rose, and McAllister 1997, p. 267), party leaders decided to reemphasize organizational identity. In October 1998, a CC plenum decided that the KPRF would present candidates under its own name for the proportional section of the 1999 Duma balloting. The party's list would subsume at least some allies in the NPUR (Kuptsov 2000, p. 1;

Tsentral'nyi komitet Kommunisticheskoi partii Rossiiskoi Federatsii 1998b, pp. 354–355), but they—and their parties or groupings—might be subordinated. In another move that affected the KPRF's relations with nationalist partners in the Patriotic Union, the party fraction in the lower house of Parliament ended its ties to Alexei Podberezkin (Korguniuk 1999, p. 368). As the head of "Spiritual Heritage" and a co-chairman of the NPUR, he shared a nationalist approach with Ziuganov and had supported him over the years (Urban and Solovei 1997, pp. 161, 168–169, 185; Sakwa 1998, p. 141; Oleshchuk and Pavlenko 1997, p. 23). This step may have somewhat weakened the party chairman's ability to promote his preferred variety of "patriotic" Marxism.

However, these steps to demarcate the KPRF from its coalition partners may have had unintended consequences. Some Russian specialists note that after the KPRF's decision to campaign separately from the agrarians, a group of longtime communist associates reevaluated their options. Mikhail Lapshin and other agrarians agreed to run for office as part of the Fatherland-All Russian formation. Spiritual Heritage also mounted a separate effort to win Duma seats. After the voting, Kemerovo governor Aman Tuleev—who was placed near the top of the Communist Party's country wide list—called for Ziuganov's replacement, and sought the presidency himself. Ziuganov accused NPUR co-chair Aleksandr Rutskoi of cooperating with Putin during his bid for the chief executive's post. The KPRF leader addressed the dissidence within the National Patriotic Union as one cause of his defeat (Korguniuk 1999, p. 368; Belonuchkin 2000, pp. 232, 247; Grachev 2000, p. 73; Tsentral'naia izbiratel'naia komissiia Rossiiskoi Federatsii 2000, p. 3; Tuleev 2000b, p. 21; Tuleev 2000a, p. 1; Ziuganov 2000d, pp. 5–7).

The NPRU was built on existing party organizations, but in the aftermath of the 2000 presidential election, the Central Committee's Department of Party Organizational and Cadre Work reported questions about this nexus (Ziuganov 2000d, p. 7; Kommunisticheskaia partiia Rossiiskoi Federatsii, Otdel organizatsionno-partiinoi i kadrovoi raboty TsK 2000, p. 4). Therefore, the NPUR's weakening might have reduced the salience and influence of the Ziuganov line at the lower levels of the Communist Party. Further diluting the advantages bestowed on the chairman was Duma Speaker Gennadii Seleznev's involvement with the extra-legislative group Rossiia (Kamyshev 2000c, p. 2). Because the two leaders kept jockeying for position within the KPRF's structure, the expanded number of collateral organizations to which a party member could belong helped provide elements of heterogeneity within the party. They served as a further impetus to change.

Party Organizations and Their Linkages

While conditions of partisan reestablishment and the evolution of alliances rooted in these efforts contribute different influences upon the stability of the

KPU and the KPRF, their subnational branches also affect the likelihood of change. Limited evidence suggests the possibility that at least some Ukrainian local party organizations may be relatively inflexible and unlikely to cooperate with other political actors. In addition, the Party Statute gives lower-echelon officials and rank-and-file members a degree of leverage over both the central councils and the Rada faction. Having a broader perspective and/ or government responsibilities might conduce national party elites to moderate doctrinaire positions inappropriate to Ukraine's changed status. KPU activists might, however, wish to brake such adaptation. In contrast, Russian communists in republics and regions seem to have crafted a variety of alliances and arrangements of convenience. These not only provide electoral advantage but also help to realize programmatic goals. Information suggests that beyond the formal consultative mechanism of the Central Committee, there are practices by which the National KPRF officers and the Duma fraction exchange views with their party constituents. The range of subunit involvement as well as channels for interchange about disparate experiences may add to the political flexibility of the Russian Communist Party.

Communists in Western Ukraine and the Donbas found themselves at odds with the dominant political forces. In Lviv, oblast government agencies legally disestablished the KPU provincial association and then refused the local party representation on referendum commissions (Mel'nichuk 2000, pp. 1–2). In Luhansk, the oblast organization purged two Rada deputies, as well as its own first secretary, P. Kupin. He refused to resign from the position, to which President Kuchma had named him, as deputy chairman of the Customs Committee of Ukraine. Kupin's views seem to have been somewhat progressive; for in an interview with Joan Urban in 1995 he had argued for compromise in the Rada and for "economic reform" (Chebanenko 1997, pp. 103–104; Urban 1999, p. 11). In partial contrast, the Crimean republican party organization diverged from the national in the first round of the 1994 presidential race, by backing the original winner, Kuchma, in preference to Oleksandr Moroz. However, the Crimean communists wanted their preferred candidate to state that he favored stronger economic ties with former Soviet republics —and, eventually, the re-creation of the USSR (Kuzio 1997, p. 58).

Should the views of a large number of KPU adherents diverge from the positions of the national leaders, the party statute provides a mechanism of accountability. Before the date for a regularly scheduled congress, oblast-level associations comprising at least a third of all activists may require convocation of such an authoritative body, to set new courses of action and choose new officers. Two-thirds of all adherents or a third of the provincial-level communist formations can, likewise, request "a general party referendum or internal party discussion" (Kommunistychna partiia Ukrainy 1999b, p. 91). Since those parliamentary deputies who held a place on the party's electoral roster can be recalled for failure to follow the organization's line

(Kommunistychna partiia Ukrainy 1999b, p. 92), ordinary communists may have the possibility of influencing legislative activity. Conservatism at the grassroots can be translated into a degree of stasis in official statements and policy endeavors.

Accounts of local party and legislative efforts in Russia suggest a variety of types of cooperation between communist associations and other formations. Over the years in the provinces, KPRF organizations have fielded candidates in electoral alliances not only with such leftist entities as the agrarians, the Russian Communist Workers' Party, and the Socialist Party of Labor but also with the Congress of Russian Communities (Moser 1998, pp. 403, 407, 412; Golosov 1999, pp. 1336, 1339; "Dogovor skrepili podpisiami 2000," p. 1). NPUR co-chairman Rutskoi's nationalist movement "Derzhava" (The Great Power) and the Liberal Democratic Party of Russia were allied with local KPRF groups (Moser 1998, p. 403; Matsuzato 1997, p. 64). For local elections, communists in Kemerovo Oblast in 1994 joined in a coalition with the Democratic Party of Russia; and in the Leningrad area, individual party members campaigned on a slate with their ideological opponents. In a municipality in Tambov Oblast, the KPRF supported local businessmen for the council, so that it could in turn require the new legislators to carry out activities favored by the communists (Matsuzato 1999, pp. 1385–1386).

Yet organizational cohesion could also be a problem in political contests. Seeking the mayor's job in Uvarovo were the official KPRF nominee and one of his fellow members in the formation. Referring to a lack of party discipline, First Deputy Chairman Kuptsov noted that in six "oblasts and okrugs . . . we lost votes and mandates [because] . . . them were advanced communists by twos and threes" (Matsuzato 1999, p. 1389; Kuptsov 2000, p. 2). Competition within the party, should, of course, create the possibility for the emergence of a broader spectrum of publicly voiced opinions. In addition, winning candidates of different persuasions would gain new resources to promote their ideas. Following organizational discipline could limit the emergence and viability of alternatives. Utilizing different alliance strategies could also introduce heterogeneous influences and, therefore, more varied ideas about policy and the Russian system (See Huntington 1968, pp. 18–19; Panebianco 1988, p. 63).

Informal practices and rules about coordination provide for interchange between the local KPRF agencies and the central party organs, and these arrangements could also contribute to adaptation. Golosov argues that the lower-level party bodies exercise preponderant influence in naming representatives to campaign for subnational offices. Urban reports consultations by members of the Communist Party faction with the KPRF organizations across the country during the 1997 confidence crisis over the Viktor Chernomyrdin government. First Deputy Chairman Kuptsov has met regularly with the obkom first secretaries (Golosov 1999, pp. 1348–1349; Urban

1999, pp. 6, 17; Svechnikov 1997, p. 2). Thus, influences and new approaches derived from the party organizations' responses to different environments could spread to those deliberative bodies—the CC and the Presidium—where programmatic changes and new tactics would first be decided.

On the other hand, ranking party leaders are somewhat insulated from efforts by the rank-and-file or subordinate officers to accelerate or contain change. Unlike the arrangements in the KPU, the Statute of the Russian Communist Party provides no way for activists and republican, krai, or oblast associations to force discussions that the central KPRF authorities do not want to conduct (Kommunisticheskaia partii Rossiiskoi Federatsii 1999b, pp. 253–255). Hence, the national elite is perhaps better situated than its Ukrainian counterparts to respond to broader experiences and a different set of expectations than their constituents know.

Elections and the Electorate

Both the Russian and Ukrainian communist parties have nationwide constituencies (Wilson and Birch 1999, p. 1055; Colton 2000, p. 28), but the two electoral organizations have differentiated bases of support and dissimilar histories at the polls. The geographic and ethnic bases of the KPU vote may provide an underpinning for the party's stance on the orientation and character of the Ukrainian state. In Russia, efforts to link nationalist and socioeconomic "protest" appeals may have been challenged by limited gains in the 1999 Duma balloting and by Vladimir Putin's election as president. The rural bedrock of the KPRF in the agricultural "Red Belt" seems to have eroded in the 2000 presidential contest—perhaps on account of better incentives available from the incumbent administration. However, in 1999, the KPU gained its largest vote totals for Petro Symonenko outside the heavy industrial areas that provide a dependable base of party support. Initially, the KPU and the KPRF competed under different electoral systems; the Ukrainian formation gained the advantage of running candidates on a party list only for the 1998 Rada elections (Kubicek 1994, p. 438; Birch 2000, p. 15; Bojcun 1995, pp. 231–232), while half of the lower house of the Russian parliament had been chosen on the basis of proportional representation since 1993. The Ukrainian communists fielded a presidential candidate for the first round only in the 1999 balloting. Gennadii Ziuganov's second attempt to head the national executive was less effective than his first.

The Ukrainian communists' record in the three elections in which they have participated since the fall of communism is one of an increasing share of vote totals (as shown above) and of rising support outside the Western oblasts. In both the 1994 and 1998 legislative elections, the KPU has won the largest fraction of all ballots cast (Birch 2000, p. 84; Wilson and Birch 1999, pp. 1039, 1056). In the single-member district contests by which the

1994 Rada was constituted, "two-thirds" of all victorious KPU candidates came from the nine jurisdictions in the "south" and "east" of Ukraine (Bojcun 1995, p. 242). Four years later, in the party-roster portion of the parliamentary elections, the Communist Party received "a plurality in all but one non-western" province (Kubicek 2000, p. 286). However, the organization did not amass 10 percent of all citizens' choices in the Lviv, Volyn,' Ivano-Frankivsk, Ternopil', and Transcarpathian provinces (Wilson and Birch 1999, p. 1055). In the 1999 presidential runoff, Symonenko achieved a majority in the Crimea and one-fourth of all oblasts, but between 4.48 and 5.15 percent in the three Galician regions. His highest levels of support, however, were not in such usual centers of communist activism as the Donbas or the Crimean Republic but in Vinnitsia Oblast, followed by the Chernihiv region (Central Election Commission of Ukraine 1999b, p. 1).

Of course, Western Ukraine was a cradle of nationalism and has been a bastion of Rukh (Birch 2000, pp. 112, 139; Kubicek 2000, p. 287; Wilson and Birch 1999, p. 1049), while the more industrialized areas like the Donbas or Dnipropetrovsk were part of an integrated web of production and supply in Soviet times. Crimea had only become part of the Ukrainian Soviet Socialist Republic under Khrushchev. The geographical dimension of orientations toward the KPU and pro-independence involvement with Russia is echoed by the ethnic aspect of partisan selection; Russians are more likely to vote for the KPU and its candidates (Birch 2000, pp. 112–113, 139).

Therefore, the Ukrainian Communist Party's programmatic strictures about the lost advantages of the Soviet state, the need for integration with other members of the Commonwealth of Independent States, and making Russian a language of official business (Kommunistychna partiia Ukrainy 1999a, pp. 93, 100–102; Communist Party of Ukraine 1998, p. 3) may respond to voters' interests. While these policy preferences can be viewed as legacies from the conservative tradition within the Soviet-era KPU, the appeals may be functional for attracting and maintaining a base of supporters. Rukh received just over 10 percent of the vote in 1998 (Birch 2000, p. 106), and President Leonid Kravchuk was seen as significantly more nationalist and interested in promoting Ukrainian language and culture when he lost to Kuchma in 1994. Hence, there would seem to be no reason for the Communist Party to jettison its statements about cross-border ties or language parity. On the other hand, emphasis on the re-creation of a "new union" to replace the USSR (Kommunistychna partiia Ukrainy 1999a, p. 101; Communist Party of Ukraine 1998, pp. 1, 2) would seem counterproductive. Such a stance would obviously raise doubts among those, potentially responsive to some KPU appeals, who valued Ukrainian independence. A poll undertaken in the early years of Ukrainian statehood showed respondents attentive to their country's "security" and interactions with Russia (Bojcun 1995, p. 234).

Economic appeals may find resonance: communist voters are likely to have suffered economically since 1991; they are elderly and have smaller incomes. These citizens do not favor the establishment of a market economy (Wilson and Birch 1999, p. 1060; Birch 2000, pp. 112, 114). As a consequence, the communists' claims that they would restore jobs and the social safety net (Kommunistychna partiia Ukrainy 1999a, pp. 100–101; Communist Party of Ukraine 1998, p. 2) are likely to be attractive to the party's constituency. The KPU's calls for substantial social and public ownership—and even nationalization may have also been attractive to supporters. The program still in force advocates collective farming. In order to better realize national economic performance, the KPU prescribes extensive governmental direction and control. Preferred mechanisms include state price-fixing and banking (Kommunistychna partiia Ukrainy 1999a, pp. 100–101).

The Russian communists have developed a substantial base of support since they garnered 12.4 percent of the list vote in the 1993 Duma elections. Several surveys taken in the mid-nineties indicated that more Russians felt a sense of connectedness with the KPRF than other parties (White, Rose, and McAllister 1997, pp. 123, 137; Colton 2000, pp. 115, 124). However, as noted above, the 1999 and 2000 balloting dealt the organization a setback. Although the association's list was chosen by nearly one-quarter of the citizenry and the communists won the largest number of contests in single-member districts in the Duma elections, more parties cleared the 5 percent threshold for representation. Therefore, the communist delegation that began the 2000 session of the Duma numbered 139, rather than the 159 who had been chosen in 1995 (Kuptsov 2000, p. 1; Tsentral'naia izbiratel'naia komissiia Rossiikoi Federatsi 1999b, pp. 18–19; Belonuchkin 1996, p. 191). In the 2000 presidential race, Chairman Ziuganov received 29.21 percent of the ballots—about 11 percent and 2.3 million votes less than in the second stage of his 1996 contest with Yeltsin (Tsentral'naia izbiratel'naia komissiia Rossiiskoi Federatsii 2000, p. 3; "Nekotorye itogi uchastii KPRF v vyborakh Prezidenta Rossiiskoi Federatsii 2000, p. 29).

In contrast to Ukraine, the KPRF had more backing in the southern agricultural area than in the industrial regions of Russia (Birch 2000, p. 138), but in the 1999 and 2000 elections, the distribution of communist support altered somewhat. In both instances, the party bettered its showing in Siberia and some of the more northern parts of the country. An "analytical memorandum" made available in connection with the May 2000 Plenum declared that "the main electoral conclusion about the results of the . . . presidential campaign . . . is the shift to the left of urban, industrial Russia" (Kuptsov 2000, p. 1, "Nekotorye itogi uchastiia KPRF v vyborakh Prezidenta Rossiiskoi Federatsii 2000, p. 39). Thus, to a degree, the KPRF's electoral course paralleled that of the KPU with a diffusion and diversification of voter interest. However, the presidential balloting also marked an erosion of support in many regions of the "Red Belt," where high ballot totals for the communists had come to be expected. In nine southern agricultural oblasts that had delivered dependable KPRF victories in the past, Ziuganov lost from 6 to 41 percentage points of his 1996 first round totals. In Voronezh Oblast alone, he lost 200,000 votes ("Nekotorye itogi uchastiia KPRF v vyborakh Prezidenta Rossiiskoi Federatsii, pp. 33, 35–37; Ziuganov 2000d, p. 5). Both the party chairman and the authors of the May memorandum attributed some of the decline in areas of KPRF strength to incentives from the central government. Even the communist Speaker of the Federation Council was accused of acquiescing to such pressures (Ziuganov 2000d, p. 6; "Nekotorye itogi uchastiia KPRF v vyborakh Prezidenta Rossiiskoi Federatsii 2000, p. 40).

If the attrition of party influence in agricultural regions were to continue, the KPRF leaders and members might lose some concrete incentives for their opposition to private ownership of most cultivable land (Kommunisticheskaia partiia Rossiiskoi Federatsii 1999a, pp. 240, 241; Kommunisticheskaia partiia Rossiiskoi Federatsii, VI [vneocherednyi] s"ezd 2000, p. 1). Likewise, if the KPRF did succeed in expanding support in areas where manufacturing is important, several programmatic strands might be reinforced. In his campaign to become the president, Gennadii Ziuganov spotlighted the issue of workers' rights in business, as did the Sixth Congress ("Dumali, shto kombinat 'plokho lezhit'" 2000, p. 1; Kommunisticheskaia partiia Rossiiskoi Federatsii, VI [vneocherednyi] s"ezd 2000, p. 1). This party body also attached importance to the development and "modernization" of manufacturing. In partial contrast to their Ukrainian colleagues, Russian communists envisaged parts in this process not only for private banking but also for planning (Kommunisticheskaia partiia Rossiiskoi Federatsii, VI [vneocherednyi] s"ezd 2000, p. 1). Yet this public intervention would appear to be more limited than the government "planning, regulation, coordination . . . and centralized administration of the state sector of the economy" preferred by the KPU (Kommunistychna partiia Ukrainy 1999a, p. 101). According to presidium member Viktor Zorkal'tsev, the KPRF goal is the "transfer to a socially oriented market economy" (Zorkal'tsev 2000, p. 2).

Concerns about industrial development would likely be of interest to citizens in areas dependent upon various plants and factories, but the KPRF's package of social measures is likely to remain important to voters and to the organization's image. The program addresses social "justice." Mentioned under this rubric in the document are access to jobs, fair wages, provision of education and health care without cost, as well as housing, "rest," and "social insurance" (Kommunisticheskaia partii Rossiiskoi Federatsii IV s"ezd 1999, p. 230). This emphasis—which parallels a theme of the Ukrainian communists—was also well-developed in the Ziuganov campaign with its promises about pensions, minimum wages, family support, schooling, and medical services (Ziuganov 2000c, p. 1; Kommunisticheskaia partiia Rossiiskoi Federatsii, VI [vneocherednyi] s"ezd 2000, p. 1).

Such appeals would appear to be well founded and less likely to change. In 1996, as Timothy Colton shows, a Russian citizen whose salary or "social benefits" were further behind was more likely to vote communist (Colton 2000, p. 130). By highlighting safety-net issues, the KPRF had the opportunity to link itself to personalized and specific dissatisfactions with the performances of Yeltsin and Putin. Indeed, the authors of the 2000 report on the party's electoral showing looked forward to the chance that continued poor socioeconomic conditions might create more interest in KPRF ("Nekotorye itogi uchastiia KPRF v vyborakh Prezidenta Rossiiskoi Federatsii 2000, p. 39).

Besides emphasis on access to entitlements taken for granted in the Soviet era, another dimension of the KPRF's identity has been nationalism. This orientation—which sets the organization apart from its Ukrainian counterpart—has included concerns about preserving Russian culture, enhancing state capacity, and strengthening the international position of Russia (Kommunisticheskaia partiia Rossiiskoi Federatsii 1999a, p. 242; Kommunisticheskaia partiia Rossiiskoi Federatsii, VI [vneocherednyi] s"ezd 2000, p. 1; Ziuganov 2000d, p. 4). Communist electoral campaigns employed these themes in 1995 and 1996, when the party's candidates ran under the aegis of the NPUR. Presidential candidate Ziuganov's "Appeal" to the voters in 2000 mentioned the Russian Federation's contribution to the "revival of the balance of interests in the world" and "a special role for the Russian Orthodox Church" (Ziuganov 2000a, p. 2).

There has long been disagreement over the "patriotic" aspect of the KPRF's platform and presentation of itself (Urban and Solovei 1997; Urban 1999, pp. 3–4; Kholmskaia 2000, pp. 565, 568, 575). However, in the wake of Edinstvo's second-place showing in the 1999 Duma races and the erosion of Ziuganov's support—vis-à-vis 1996—in the 2000 presidential campaign, dissension continued. At the third phase sessions of the Sixth KPRF Congress, CC Secretary Nikolai Bindiukov seemed to feel that the party's nationalist credentials had been clouded by the decision to run independently in the Duma elections. He also seemed to suggest that the Chechen War allowed Putin to compete effectively along the nationalist dimension. While Kuptsov defended what he called the KPRF's "correct strategy," Ziuganov argued for the continued relevance of devotion to Russian power and values at the May 2000 Plenum (Bindiukov 2000, p. 2; Kuptsov 2000, p. 1; Ziuganov 2000d, pp. 2–3).

Yet analysts of his race pointed out that Putin was viewed as more "patriotic" than Ziuganov and that the Chechen War had allowed the acting president to make significant inroads into traditional areas of communist support ("Nekotorye itogi uchastiia KPRF v vyborakh Prezidenta Rossiiskoi Federatsii 2000, pp. 6, 39–40). If competition along the nationalist cleavage continues, the KPRF may seek to mobilize voters along other fault lines of public opinion (Ishiyama and Bozoki, forthcoming; Sartori 1976, pp. 342–50; Shefter 1994; Kitschelt et al. 1999, pp. 69–77).

Yet for party leaders to recraft their appeals in response to electoral results, and for members to accept these changes, there would have to be confidence that officially reported outcomes convey true information about voters' choices. In both Ukraine and Russia, for example, there have been allegations of fraud in recent balloting. In Ukraine, Prime Minister Valerii Pustovoitenko was reported to have insisted that his party receive "40 percent of the vote" in Donetsk (Wilson and Birch 1999, p. 1058). If the controversial Melnichenko tapes correctly convey President Kuchma's exact words, threats to local officials were intended to produce his victory in the 1999 presidential race (Tyler 2001, p. A6). Communist figures in Russia accused the Putin administration of producing incorrect totals in both the 1999 parliamentary race and the 2000 presidential contest (Kamyshev 2000b, p. 2; Levchenko 2000, p. 1; Kuptsov 2000, p. 2). Belief that one's party in fact performed better is not likely to moderate views of the system and may produce doubts about what alterations in a party's message might be effective.

The Parties in Parliament

The Ukrainian and Russian communist parties have established noteworthy presences in their respective legislatures, with large delegations, multiple committee chairmanships, and members in leading posts. Participation in the Federal Assembly and the Rada provides parliamentarians with opportunities to act on their programs and to publicize their associations' positions. In addition, representation in the legislature can yield resources for organizational development. However, involvement in government can also influence party members to change their views or to become more receptive of post-Soviet political arrangements (Dahl 1966, pp. 338–339; Sakwa 1996). Such influences, or alternatively, modification of existing stances might be disseminated throughout the parties as a result of the leaderships' parliamentary engagement and the manner in which fractions' endeavors are coordinated with other associational work.

In the KPU, involvement in Rada operations seems to be more concentrated at the upper levels of the formation. National First Secretary Petro Symonenko heads the party fraction in Parliament, and Second Secretary Adam Martyniuk attained the highest leadership position there of any organization member. As of 1999, all the secretaries of the Central Committee, as well as 88.2 percent of all Presidium members, were People's Deputies of Ukraine. (The exceptions were Borys Novikov, a dean at Kiev Polytechnical Institute, and Leonid Hrach, who chairs the Crimean Rada.) However, only 58.3 percent of the obkom first secretaries and the leader of the Kiev City party organization were elected to the Supreme Rada of the country, and only three additional CC delegates on the KPU list were selected by voters (Andrushchak, Marchenko, and Telemko 1998b; *Spysok narodnykh deputativ Ukrainy* 1998; Andrushchak et al., 1999; Marchenko and Telemko 1998). As a result, top KPU officers have some positional resources at their disposal to try to ensure that the deputies' corpus take positions in accord with the party line. At the same time, nearly 40 percent of the regional and republican leaders who are not people's deputies at the national level may be less likely to transmit cross-pressures to compromise on reform and to work within the new institutional order to the rank and file. Concerns about such influences toward transformation may have underlaid First Secretary Symonenko's criticism of the party's Rada delegation the Fifth Congress. The program warns against efforts to make the KPU "an appendix of the fraction in the Supreme Rada" (*Pravda Ukrainy* 2000, p. 1; Kommunistychna partiia Ukrainy 1999a, p. 103).

At important junctures, communist legislators took confrontational stances. In 1996, a group of Rada deputies proposed repossession of "larg[er] . . . enterprises [and] commercial banks" (Chebanenko 1997, p. 99). The same year, the communist faction tabled a constitutional proposal that failed to provide for an independent chief executive. The KPU deputies refused to help constitute a quorum to discuss the version of the basic law favored by Kuchma. In 2000, they did not vote on his version of the suggested constitutional amendments (Kuzio 1997, pp. 123–124; "V Konstitutsionnom sude" 2000, p. 1). Such stands perhaps reinforce perceptions of the KPU as an anti-system opposition and, no doubt, create barriers to the use of existing institutions to attain the party's ends.

Parliamentarians of the KPRF have worked within Russian governmental structures and have compromised with proponents of the Yeltsin and Putin regimes. In the spring 2000 legislative session, negotiations with Edintsvo yielded a second term for Gennadii Seleznev as Duma Speaker and the communists combined with most other factions to support former prime minister Sergei Stephashin's appointment as head of the Duma's Accounting Chamber. The communist deputies' corpus supported two of President Putin's bills to strengthen national governmental control over lower-level legislative and executive bodies. Despite the fact that the KPRF has claimed its opposition to a powerful presidency, the faction argued that the proposed legislation accorded with the party's own preference for a strong state (Kamyshev 2000a, p. 1; "Ne ishchite koshku . . ." 2000, p. 1; Iur'ev 2000b, p. 1; Seleznev 2000, pp. 7–8; Kommunisticheskaia partiia Rossiiskoi Federatsii, VI [vneocherednyi] s"ezd, 2000 p. 1).

At important junctures in Yeltsin's administrations, the communists also cooperated with the government. Members of the central committee deadlocked over whether to ensure that the Duma would remain in session by confirming Sergei Kirienko as premier, when his candidacy received its scrutiny. Despite the fact that the CC Plenum directed party members in the legislature not to approve the nomination, some deputies were believed to have done so (Goriacheva 1998, p. 3; Tsentral'nyi komitet Kommunisticheskoi partii Rossiiskoi Federatsii 1998a; "Kto kak golosoval?" 1998, p. 2; Iur'ev 1998a, p. 1; Slavin 1998, p. 1). Party (and faction) chairman Ziuganov removed a proposal of "no confidence" against Prime Minister Viktor Chernomyrdin from the parliamentary agenda after receiving promises of more consultation (Urban 1999, p. 6). KPRF leaders continued to invoke the achievements of Evgenii Primakov's cabinet, in which Iurii Masliukov served as first deputy premier (Ziuganov 2000d, p. 4; Bindiukov 2000, p. 2; Masliukov 2000, p. 2). Bargaining with the Communist Party's opponents as well as shared pragmatic advocacy or acquiescence for specific measures demonstrated a certain degree of acceptance of the post-Soviet political system. Moreover, the communists' involvement in give-and-take over specific bills (Seleznev 2000) and, in more limited measure, in administrative issues have created opportunities to rethink and refine policy theses in accord with evolving circumstances.

Nevertheless—at least in the short run—the results of the 1999 balloting may have reduced the impact of parliamentary service and participation in governance as influences for change throughout the KPRF. Within the central party organs that existed when the Duma elections were held, the percentage of members who were people's deputies fell after the voting. Before 2000, 83.3 percent of the party Presidium served in the Duma; in the new legislative session, only 80.9 percent continued as parliamentary delegates. The percentage of the Secretariat members with seats in the State Duma dropped from 88.8 percent in the Second Convocation to 77.7 percent in the Third. Of the party Central Committee's voting personnel, 52.4 percent served as people's deputies elected in 1995; following the 1999 election, only 36.1 percent of the full members of the committee held seats in the lower house of the Federal Assembly ("Sostav fraktsii KPRF v Gosudarstvennoi Dume RF FS sozyva 2000–2003 godov; Chotiner 1999, p. 119; "Prezidium TsK KPRF" 1998; "Sekretariat" 1998; "Tsentral'nyi komitet KPRF 1998; Belonuchkin 2000, pp. 191–195; Kasianenko 2000, pp. 24–26). These percentages were lower than those of leading communist party bodies in Ukraine. Similarly, the proportion of Russian obkom, kraikom, and republican first secretaries in Parliament was lower than the share of their Ukrainian peers who belonged to the Rada (Sostav fraktsii KPRF v Gosudarstvennoi Dume RF FS sozyva 2000–2003 godov; "Pervye sekretari regional'nykh komitetov KPRF 2000; Kasianenko 2000, pp. 24–26). Hence, the Ukrainian communist leaders' structural assets for transmitting legislative influences were greater than the Russian party elites; experiences of intransigence and conflict with reformers and nationalists might be organizationally magnified to a larger extent than a record of engagement and a significant degree of acceptance of the concrete political situation. However, the KPRF officers had the possibility of using the Seventh Congress to redress the situation somewhat.

Including more parliamentarians in the Russian Central Committee could magnify possibilities for adjustment to the evolving situation in the country, because of the way in which communists participate in the Duma. While Ziuganov and Kuptsov are chairman and deputy chairman of the party delegation in the lower house (Belonuchkin 2000, p. 231), Presidium member Gennadii Seleznev has carved out a more independent role as speaker. He is not listed as a member of the faction, and his connections with the executive branch might be better than the ties of other KPRF leaders. Seleznev received a decoration from Boris Yeltsin and the backing of Vladimir Putin in his campaign to become governor of Moscow Region. In company with Iurii Masliukov and against nearly all the rest of the communist representatives in the lower chamber, the speaker voted for reduction of the second Strategic Arms Reduction Treaty (Sostav fraktsii KPRF v Gosudarstrennoi Dume RF FS sozyva 2000–2003 godov; Makarkin and Smirnov 2000, p. 4; Sukhova 2000, p. 2; "Rezul'taty golosovaniia deputatov Gosudarstvennoi dumy RF po ratifikatsii Dogovora SNV-2" 2000, p. 1). His counsels in intraparty discussions and the weight of his very prominent national position could thus provide further impetus towards KPRF evolution in a reformist direction (Urban 1999, p. 7; Urban and Solovei 1997).

The Russian communists' presence in the Duma should also engender a diversity of currents within the party. This aspect in the secondment of communist deputies to other groups is seen to give the party an advantage in the business of the chamber (Urban and Solovei 1997, p. 167). In the Duma of the Second Convocation, KPRF members also belonged to "Narodovlastie" (People's Power) and the Agrarian Deputies' Group. Although the Narodovlastie faction no longer exists, there are still communist representatives among the agrarians (Belonuchkin 2000; Kasianenko 2000, pp. 24–26; "Tsentral'nyi komitet" 1998). Through interactions with them, the communist representatives may gain new insights into Russia's rural problems and assist in providing effective solutions. Cooperation might therefore also contribute to greater heterogeneity within the KPRF.

Conclusions

The Communist Party of the Russian Federation functions and is structured in ways that make it more open to change than the Communist Party of Ukraine. However, the former was refounded with a more diverse constituency. The Russian organization seems to operate in an environment in which there are a range of opportunities for cooperation with different political forces. Although leaders of both parties opted to sharpen their image after electoral successes, the outcome for the KPU may be a reinforcement of orthodoxy. For the KPRF, the results of this gambit may call its "patriotic" approach into question at the same time that a plethora of groups on the left make a return to pre-Gorbachevian positions difficult.

While characteristics of the KPU's electorate to date seem to suggest that the party's platform does speak to some citizens' concerns, the Ukrainian communists may in the future encounter incentives for evolution. If the party were to gain an increasing following outside the industrial areas with ties to Russia, the leadership might want to moderate its anti-nationalist stance and develop policy suggestions more concretely responsive to farmers' actual situations. The smaller share of the vote totals gained in the 1999 elections by the socialists and the Rural Party may mean that barriers to a rightward move by the KPU may weaken.

In the wake of Putin's victory at the polls in 2000, the KPRF faces questions about more than cleavage mobilization. The party's reduced universe of potential allies in Parliament, the president's greater powers vis-à-vis regional and republican authorities, and the repertoire of rewards and penalties he can exact may make some of the communists' political resources irrelevant. On the other hand, the maneuverability of many local party organizations may provide an alternative source of political capital. Finally, there are no appreciable extra-organizational barriers for a move by the KPRF to the more moderate left.

Thus, both Russian and Ukrainian communist parties may face chances and pressures for change. The organizational legacies and arrangements— as well as the recent history of entrepreneurship by political leaders— would seem to suggest that the KPRF is better endowed to respond. On the other hand, it may face a more challenging environment in the future than the KPU.

Note

The author thanks Ann B. Chotiner for her assistance in the translation of portions of the Statute and Program of the Communist Party of Ukraine. This chapter is indebted to Chotiner, 1999.

1. The large literature on partisan transformation includes Kitschelt, 1992; Kitschelt et al., 1999; Ishiyama, 1995; Ishiyama, 1996a; Ishiyama, 1997a; Ishiyama, 1999a; Ishiyama, 2000; Evans and Whitefield, 1993; Waller, 1995; Pridham and Lewis, 1996, Belasiak, 1997; McAllister and White, 1995, Sakwa, 1996; Sakwa, 1998; and Hashim, 1999.

Part IV

Conclusions

20

An Unfinished Story

Toward Explaining the Transformation of the Communist Successor Parties

John T. Ishiyama and András Bozóki

Throughout this book two consistent themes have been emphasized. First, that the development of the communist successor parties in post-communist politics not only has important implications for the development of theories of political party development, but that the activities of these parties have an important effect upon the development of democracy. Indeed, the experience of the communist successor parties offers a unique opportunity to test first-hand longstanding (western-based) theories on party development so painstakingly formulated by scholars and analysts, as well as assess whether the successor parties are a positive or negative force in post-communist politics.

However, the primary focus of this volume has been on explaining why the successor parties developed the way they did in the first ten years after the collapse of communism. In the introductory chapter, three questions were posed regarding the evolution and development of the communist successor parties in the decade following the collapse of communism in Eastern Europe and the former Soviet Union. These included:

(1) To what extent did the legacy of the communist past impact upon the adaptation strategies adopted by the successor parties? Did the relatively more "open" communist regimes give birth to successor parties that were more apt to adopt a "reformist" strategy, as opposed to more repressive regimes? Did the legacy of the past impact upon the kind of competition the successor parties faced, which in turn affected the performance of the successor parties?

(2) To what extent did the dynamics of the transition process impact upon the composition of the successor parties, and how did this in turn affect the kind of adaptation strategy that was adopted?

(3) To what extent did the electoral performance of parties affect the

choice of adaptation strategy and subsequent changes (if any) in strategy? Did poor electoral performance result in changes to fundamentally alter the "public face" of the party, or did poor electoral performance embolden the "hard-liners" within the party?

How do the preceding chapters address these questions? In the first place many of the preceding chapters have pointed to the importance of the legacies of the previous communist regime. This is certainly an important focus of the arguments in the chapters by Herbert Kitschelt, Radoslaw Markowski, Daniel Ziblatt and Nick Bizourias, Valerie Bunce, Barbara Chotiner, János Ladányi and Iván Szelényi. The effects of the legacies of the past regime can be differentiated in terms of (1) effects upon the development of the successor parties as organizations; and (2) effects upon the political environment facing the successor parties. Indeed, as Kitschelt points out, the skills, experiences, and expectations of successor party leaders, as well as initial resource endowments, were powerfully shaped by past political developments. In some of the communist regimes a measure of political pluralism existed, a legacy that gave rise to the political tolerance and "maturity" that would serve the leaders of the successor parties so well later. In his study of the SLD in Poland, Markowski points to the difference between the Polish communist regime and the regimes in other Soviet satellite countries, a differnce due perhaps more importantly to the existence and the role of the Catholic Church, which played a much more important role during Polish communist rule than elsewhere and provided for a political "pluralism" absent from other communist regimes. Valerie Bunce, in her comparative analysis of the SdRP/SLD and the MSZP, and Anna Gryzmala-Busse in her comparative chapter on the KSCM in the Czech Republic and the SDL in Slovakia have also pointed to the organizational assets possessed by the successor parties that assisted in their political successes later.

The organizational effects of the communist past are the primary foci of the chapter by Ziblatt and Bizourias who contend that because the successor parties emerged with a variety of important organizational tools, they did not have to create *de novo* local branches, regional councils, and central commissions. This meant that the successor parties could compete electorally by focusing on their ideological message, rely on their existing and deployed national mass organization structures, and avoid engaging in a simultaneous construction of both ideology and organization.

Ziblatt and Bizourias also point out the important link between the legacies of the past and the adaptation strategies adopted. Indeed, as they note, not all of the successor parties exited the transitional period with the same set of resources. For instance, the Hungarian, Czech, and East German parties exited with significantly reduced fund bases, whereas the Polish and Romanian parties exited with more monetary resources. These different endowments had an important effect on the ability of the parties to adapt to changing political circumstances. More explicitly, the successor parties with significantly reduced resources were forced to engage in an active process of fund raising, which left them with primarily two choices: to rely increasingly on their membership base or to engage in the creation of state-based political party systems. In countries where a state-based party financing system existed, the successor parties were more capable of reducing their reliance on local party branches. Thus they were able to insulate themselves from recalcitrant members, and increase the ideological adaptability of their parties. In countries where a state-based party financing system did not create adequate resources for these successor parties, the parties were forced to rely on their local party branches for material support, and thus they were not capable of pursuing the same degree of ideological adaptation.

The legacies of the communist past also have benefited the successor parties in other ways. Alina Mungiu-Pippidi directly points to the effect of the authoritarian legacy of Ceauşescu in affecting the kind of competition faced by the Romanian successor party. Indeed, the fact that the left competitors to the successor PDSR were weak and disorganized, rather than the organizational strengths of the successor party remains one of the primary reasons that the PDSR has been electorally successful. (See also the chapter by Srbobran Brankovic on the Serbian Socialist Party and that by Jeffrey Murer on the PDSR and the Bulgarian socialists.) Such was also the case in Bulgaria, where the primary opposition to the Bulgarian Socialist Party (BSP)— the Union of Democratic Forces (SDS)—was initially a highly fragmented and loosely organized coalition of groups whose only common bond was opposition to the communists (see chapter 18).

On the other hand, legacies regarding the performance of the successor parties can also be quite constraining. Indeed, as Ladányi and Szelényi point out, the legacy of the overgrown welfare state that characterized communist societies prevented the development of a true social democratic movement in Central and Eastern Europe. Further, as Sharon Fisher points out in regard to the Slovakian case, part of the reason why the SDL has been unable to match the success of its Hungarian and Polish counterparts is undoubtedly historical. In former Czechoslovakia, which had one of the most severe communist regimes during the "normalization" period of 1968–89, it was difficult for any communist successor party—no matter how reformed it might be—to gain the equivalent electoral support of its counterparts in Poland and Hungary (see also a reference to this point in chapter 7). Taken together, these findings support some of the observations made by Ishiyama (1997a) regarding how the legacies of the communist past have impacted on the electoral success of the communist successor parties. The first was that patrimonial communist systems (such as the aforementioned KPRF and the BSP, the ex-communist parties of Belarus and the Ukraine, as well as Moldova, Albania, Macedonia, and Romania, which were based upon hierarchical patron-client ties and relatively low degrees of bureaucratic professionalization) had two effects (1) the successor parties in these systems have remained primarily conglomerate parties, made up of very different and at times incompatible political viewpoints, a carryover from the patronage networks that existed in the past regime; (2) the success of these parties is largely due to the organizational weakness and greater incoherence (relative to the successor parties) of the competitors that the successor parties face, rather than the transformation of the latter into coherent political organizations with distinct political platforms. The existence of only weak competitors is the primary reason why the successor parties have been successful in post-patrimonial communist politics.

The political environment facing the successor parties that emerged from national consensus systems has been quite different when compared to the political environment facing those parties that emerged from patrimonial systems. The legacy of national consensus systems exerted two cross-pressures. On the one hand, the degree of internal elite contestation and political pluralism within the old regime contributed to providing the ex-communist parties with organizational resources and a pool of political talent which enabled them to quickly adopt characteristics akin to a "modern European left" party. This was clearly the case with the Hungarian socialists, but also the Polish SLD and to a much lesser extent, the LDDP. Where a relatively high degrees of professionalization in the bureaucracy and a pre-transition technocratic opposition existed within the national consensus regimes, the dissolution of the old regime led to the emergence of relatively strong competitors to the ex-communists.

Yet in no way should the relationship between the communist legacy and the political performance of the successor parties be seen as deterministic, a point that is made quite clearly in the chapters by both Kitschelt and Bunce. Indeed, as Kitschelt reminds us, the legacies of the past do not prevent political learning nor negate the political skills of the leaders when adapting to changed political circumstances. As Dieter Segert notes in Chapter 8, despite the fact that the PDS has one of the most conservative and least pluralistic political regimes in Soviet-dominated Eastern Europe, its leadership is well on the way to a moderate leftist understanding of post-communist realities. The story of the PDS is, however, not entirely similar to that of the Hungarian or Polish socialists, because the German Democratic Republic has ceased to exist. This pushed the PDS toward transmutation rather than technocratic or social democratic reform. This was largely due to the energetic efforts of the party's leadership, especially its ability to maintain a working balance between reformist and hard-line orientations within the party (see also chapter 17).

In her comparative chapter on the KPRF and KPU, Barbara Chotiner also argues that leaders make a crucial difference in the development of the successor party. For instance, although in many ways the KPRF and the KPU started with the same kinds of political resource endowments, the Communist Party of the Russian Federation functions and is structured in ways that make it more open to change than the Communist Party of Ukraine. This is largely due to the entrepreneurial skills of the KPRF leaders who have consciously sought to broaden the appeal of the party (via calls for "patriotism") and who have sought cooperation with different political forces. Although leaders of both parties opted to sharpen their image after electoral successes, the KPU's evolution has been very different, indeed toward the development of greater rather than less communist orthodoxy.

The question of whether the dynamics of the transition process impacted upon the kind of adaptation strategy that was adopted, was clearly scrutinized in the chapters on the Czech and Slovak successor parties (by Grzymala-Busse), the LDDP (by Diana Janusauskiené), and the KPRF and KPU (by Chotiner). Indeed, as each of these chapters note, the effects of the dynamics of the transition process were an important part of the legacies left by previous communist regimes, particularly the resolution of the struggle over control of the party that pitted democratic reformists against more conservative elements within the successor parties. According to Grzymala-Busse, this is precisely what differentiated the Czech and Slovak successor parties, with the reformists seizing control of the SDL very early on in the transition process as opposed to the KSCM, which remained controlled by party conservatives. Similarly in Lithuania, Janusauskiené also points to the early seizure of power by the reformists as the key to explaining the reformist strategy later adopted by the LDDP. For Chotiner, a key factor of contrast between the KPRF and KPU was that the former had experienced at least a partial transformation of the leadership, where some reformists were incorporated into top positions (unlike the KPU), thus explaining the KPRF's attempt to redefine itself.

As to the third question noted in the introductory chapter, many scholars have also argued that political performance vitally affects the extent to which parties change their political identities. Indeed, the greater the external challenges to a party (either in the form of increased competition or electoral defeat) the more likely the party will seek to establish a new political identity for itself. András Bozóki's chapter on the evolution of the Hungarian MSZP clearly illustrates this relationship, especially following the party's initial defeat in 1989–90—which led the party leadership to reevaluate its identity —and again later, after the party's defeat in the legislative election of 1998. (For a broader, historical framework, see Bozóki 2001a.) Such a process is also evident in the Polish SLD, where Markowski points to the effect of early defeat upon the revitalization of that communist successor party, as well as in the case of the German PDS (as argued by Segert).

Yet, there are limits to which parties can alter their identities. Indeed, as

Ishiyama (2000) has pointed out, internal organizational configurations act as a powerful brake upon the ability of a party's leadership to change their movement's identity at will. Rather, changing identities has had more to do with the internal configuration of political forces within the party, particularly the extent to which "democratic reformists" have won the battle for control of the successor party over more "hard-line elements." Successor parties in which the democratic reformists "won" the internal struggle were more likely to change the parties' identities, regardless of electoral performance.

When there is no clear-cut victor in this internal struggle, the successor party is faced with the problems illustrated by Richard Sakwa's account of the KPRF. On the one hand, the party cannot adapt fully to new political circumstances given the continued existence of hard-line elements within the party. Indeed, as he points out, the KPRF today is faced by problems of organizational closure and partial adaptation. As a result, the party adopted a vague and confusing oppositional stance, fearing that too active opposition would provoke confrontation with the authorities and reduce opportunities to benefit from the current regime. Unelectable yet the main electoral alternative, an opposition but an organic one, adapted to both democratic and regime politics, the KPRF is beset by internal contradictions.

Ishiyama also focuses on adaptation, but more specifically organizational adaptations. In general, he contends that the face the party puts forth to the electorate is a dimension independent from party organizational development per se. Indeed, parties that have adopted pragmatic reformist strategies (such as the MSZP and the SLD) have also exhibited clientelistic organizational characteristics that they share with parties like the KPRF and KPU, which have both opted for national leftist retreat/national patriotic strategies. Indeed, not only are these dimensions independent from one another, but they are also shaped by different dynamics. Thus, as Ishiyama and Bozóki (2001a) point out, the type of survival strategy selected is largely a function of internal factors, such as the extent to which the party is ideologically coherent. However, organizational characteristics and adaptations appear to be largely a result of external factors, particularly institutional incentives.

Toward a Model of Successor Party Change and Adaptation

Taken together the above chapters point to several key factors that explain the development of the successor parties. In the introductory chapter, we identified several different adaptation processes (see Table 1.1 in Chapter 1). How do the three factors identified in the questions posed at the beginning of this book (and reiterated at the beginning of this chapter) combine to produce the observed adaptation processes?

In Figure 20.1, we outline a tentative model of interaction between communist legacies, transition processes, and electoral performance, thus producing the kinds of adaptation strategies we have observed among the communist successor parties. First, adhering to Kitschelt's (1995a) formulation, it is possible to identify three different types of former communist regimes. The first was the *patrimonial* communist system. This system relied heavily on hierarchical chains of personal dependence between leaders and followers, with low levels of inter-elite contestation, popular interest articulation, and rational-bureaucratic professionalization. Moreover, these systems were characterized by a heavy emphasis on "democratic centralism" which fit well with the hierarchical structure of dependence between leaders and the led. In this category we can place Serbia, Romania, Bulgaria, Russia, Ukraine, Belarus, and most of the rest of the former Soviet Union (except possibly the Baltic States). The second type, *bureaucratic authoritarian* communism, was characterized by a circumscription of inter-elite contestation and interest articulation, but the level of rational-bureaucratic institutionalization was high. In this category can be placed the former German Democratic Republic, the Czech Republic, and Slovakia. The third type of system, *national consensus* communism, was characterized by relatively higher levels of contestation and interest articulation and a degree of bureaucratic professionalization. In essence, the communist elites allowed for a measure of contestation and interest articulation in exchange for compliance with the basic features of the existing system. This final category includes Poland and Hungary, as well as Slovenia and Croatia. Within this category Kitschelt also placed the three Baltic states: Estonia, Latvia, and Lithuania. Indeed, although all three states had been absorbed by the Soviet Union, there was a remarkable degree of intra-regime contestation and tolerance for the demands of national independence movements, at least far more so than in other parts of the USSR (Kitschelt, 1995a).

These systemic legacies in turn affected the development and performance of the communist successor parties in three ways. First, different system legacies left different organizational endowments for the successor parties. Some parties simply were better endowed in terms of physical resources (such as buildings, membership, money) than others. As Ziblatt and Bizourias note, some were left with substantial membership resources, but little money. Second, the previous regime also affected the kind of competitive environment (i.e. the structure of competition) facing the successor parties. In countries that evolved from patrimonial communist systems (such as in Russia, Ukraine, Bulgaria, and Romania), the early development of opposition parties was severely retarded by the oppressive nature of the system. This meant that the successor parties did not have to face stiff competition—heightening their ability to be electorally competitive, but instead had little incentive to adopt reformist measures (since none were needed to compete). On the other hand, for successor parties emerging from national consensus regimes and bureaucratic authoritarian systems where relatively high degrees of professionalization

Figure 20.1

The Process of Communist Successor Party Change and Adaptation

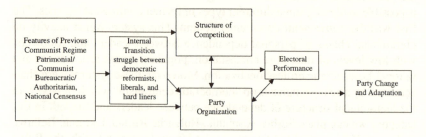

Source: Author's compilation.

in the bureaucracy and a pre-transition technocratic opposition existed, the dissolution of the old regime led to the emergence of relatively strong competitors to the communist successor parties. This provided additional incentives for these parties to reform their identities in response to stiff electoral competition.

A third legacy of the communist past was based upon who won out in the transition struggles that occurred internally within each of the successor parties. The previous regime had a direct impact on who ultimately won the contest between democratic reformists and more conservative elements with the parties. Parties that evolved from national consensus regimes were particularly likely to produce leaders that were sensitive to the demands of a new politically competitive environment. Indeed, the degree of internal elite contestation and political pluralism within the old regime contributed to providing the successor parties with the pool of political talent that enabled them to quickly adopt characteristics akin to a "modern European left" party. This was clearly the case with both the Hungarian and Polish socialists.

However, such organizational transitions may independently affect the kind of party organizations that emerge later. Indeed as Ishiyama (1995) notes, each communist successor party underwent very different kinds of organizational transformations, defined by the extent to which they followed what Huntington (1991) referred to as "standpatter," "liberal," or "democratic reformist" paths of internal leadership transformation between 1990 and 1993. According to Huntington these three groups were defined by their basic attitudes toward democratic transition, the promotion of popular participation, and political competition. For Huntington, the key to the kind of transition that took place depended heavily on the internal struggle between democratic reformists, liberals, and standpatters within the communist party. In reviewing the organizational transitions that Ishiyama (1995) identified, we identified three types of internal leadership transitions for the period 1989–1993. The first represented a leadership dominated by standpatters (those who preferred retaining party organization based on Marxist-Leninist norms).

The second represented a leadership controlled by liberals (or those who favored democratic but "controlled" competition), and the third represented a leadership controlled by democratic reformists (or those who favored transforming the party into a fully competitive organization).

Taken together, both the results of the internal transition (who won the struggle for control of the party) and the organizational resources left by the previous regime affected the kind of party organization that initially "succeeded" the old communist parties. The interaction between the party as an organization and the structure of competition also affected how well the party performed electorally. In some cases, as in Hungary and Poland, the existence of well-endowed organizations, led by leaders who sought to transform these parties into electorally competitive organizations, coupled with strong competition (leading to the early electoral defeats of the Hungarian and Polish socialists), prompted these parties to move very quickly to a western-oriented social democratic identity. On the other hand, successor parties, such as the KPRF in Russia, with relatively weak competition (and fairly successful electoral performance) has provided little incentive for the party to transform itself. The KPRF's further inability to resolve internal contradictions between moderate reformists and more conservative elements within the party is likely to prevent it from transforming any further. However, electoral performance alone does not determine change. In the case of the KSCM, which faces both strong competition (particularly from the leftist Czech Social Democratic Party, or CSSD) there has been little move in the direction of a change in party identity. This is because the leadership of the party has essentially remained in the hands of party conservatives, who continue to cling to the orthodox communist past—thus electoral performance alone. However, even if a party's leadership may lean toward change (which is at least partially the case with the KPRF in Russia) the internal constraints placed on such leaders can affect, for instance, the extent to which external political incentives promote or dampen party identity change. Indeed, one can imagine the situation where an external incentive to moderate a party's political position may have little effect upon a party leadership whose range of movement is constrained by the presence of a significant number of "hard-liners" in the ranks of the organization.

Table 20.1 summarizes the characteristics of each of the communist successor parties discussed in this volume, in terms of the variables illustrated in Figure 20.1. In addition, the type of party adaptation process is also listed. From the table some discernible patterns emerge. In the case of parties that followed a social democratic/modernizationist adaptation process, such as the Polish SLD and Hungarian MSZP, the fact that they emerged from the transition process led by democratic reformists, coupled with the fact that they faced strong opposition and suffered early electoral defeats, prompted these parties to completely abandon communist orthodoxy and embrace something akin to a western social democratic identity. For parties that were non-

Table 20.1

Summary of Variables Affecting Successor Party Change and Adaptation

Country(party)	Previous regime type	Who won the internal leadership struggles 1989–93	Structure of competition	Electoral performance in first post-communist legislative elections (percent of seats won)	Transformation type
Bulgaria(BSP)	Patrimonial Communist	Liberals	Weak opponents	44.17%	Partly reformed/partly transmuted
Czech Republic(KSCM)	Bureaucratic authoritarian	Liberals/Standpatters	Strong opponents	17.50%	Non-reformed/non-transmuted
Germany(PDS)	Bureaucratic authoritarian	Liberals/Reformists	Strong opponents	3.57%	Non-reformed/partly transmuted
Hungary(MSZP)	National consensus	Reformists	Strong opponents	8.55%	Reformed/non-transmuted
Lithuania(LDDP)	National consensus	Liberals/Reformists	Strong opponents	51.77%	Partly reformed/partly transmuted
Poland(SLD)	National consensus	Reformists	Strong opponents	13.04%	Reformed/non-transmuted

Romania(PSDR)	Patrimonial Communist	Liberals/Stand-patters	Weak opponents	67.96%	Partly reformed/ Transmuted
Russia(KPRF)	Patrimonial Communist	Liberals/ Standpatters	Weak opponents	13.78%	Non-reformed/ transmuted
Serbia(SPS)	Patrimonial Communist	Standpatters	Weak opponents	40.40%	Non-reformed/ Transmuted
Slovakia(SDL)	Bureaucratic authoritarian	Reformists	Strong opponents	19.33%	Reformed/partly transmuted
Ukraine(KPU)	Patrimonial Communist	Standpatters	Weak opponents	27.83%	Non-reformed/ non-transmuted

Source: Author's compilation.

reformed and non-transmuted (akin to the orthodox communist type) like the KPU and KSCM, the adaptation process appeared to be determined by whether the democratic reformists were defeated in the transition stage. Indeed, although both the KPU and the KSCM were faced with different structures of competition (with the KPU facing only weak opposition and the KSCM facing very strong competition) and performed poorly in the initial elections, they have fairly similar patterns of development. On the other hand, the national communist type of adaptation (illustrated by the KPRF and the SPS) also appears to share some of the same factors that produced the orthodox communist type of adaptation. A primary example of differentiation between national communist adaptation and the orthodox communist type is the historically strong and entrenched sense of nationalism that characterized both the Serbian and Russian communist parties (especially prior to the collapse of communist systems), as opposed to the KSCM and the KPU. In addition, although there is no case that perfectly fits the national populist type of successor party adaptation (the closest is probably the Romanian PSDR or the Slovakian SDL), what differentiates this type from the social democratic/modernizationist type is the historical emphasis upon nationalism that characterized both the Romanian and Slovakian communist parties.

In a recent study on Southern European communist (successor) parties, Anna Bosco offered an ideal model indicative of the process of democratic integration of former anti-regime parties. This process includes the following stages (1) the communist party accepts the democratic regime; (2) the "inner system" of already democratic parties recognize the communist party's new, pro-regime identity; and finally, (3) the (former) communist party "manages to play a significant political role, possibly in government, within the new democratic regime" (Bosco 2001, p. 384).

In Central and Eastern Europe, democratic change occurred in a sweeping way between 1989 and 1991 which underlines the importance of the "demonstration effect," i.e. the impact of external, international forces (Pridham 2000). This situation made it practically impossible for communist successor parties not to accept the new, democratic regime, even in the case of the Czech KSCM, and the German PDS. However, as Table 20.1 shows, the composition of communist elite groups varied, which determined the adaptation potential of the given party accordingly. Therefore, the internal constellation of power elite, and the unity and division of political forces did, indeed, matter in shaping the dynamics of transition and the consolidation of democracy. In those countries where internal party struggles had been won by reformers, or mixed groups of reformers and liberals, the communist party could quickly adapt to sudden change, sometimes even initiating it (as in Poland and Hungary). Here, the likelihood for peaceful elite-settlements (Burton and Higley 1987) was higher, and the type of democratic change in those two countries was frequently described in the literature as a "roundtable-type" of transition process (Arato 2001, Bozóki 1996, 2001b, Colomer 2000, Elster 1996, Kis 1998, Munck and Leff 1999, Tōkés 1996). Where changes occurred quickly (and the opposition was rather weak while the ruling communist party were dominated by reformists), either a process of elite-convergence took place, as in Slovakia, or the reformist wing of the communist party made a successful coup against the incumbent hard-liners (and was able to catch up the tempo of change), as in Bulgaria. In some countries, the communist party did not just accept the democratic regime but helped to create it; nationwide democratization and party transformation were therefore parallel processes. Countries where standpatters dominated the communist parties were slow to democratize themselves to prove their democratic credentials. The Czech KSCM and the German PDS parties subjectively accepted the democratic regime since they took part in the democratic procedure. However, other parties did not include the successor organizations into the family of democratic parties so quickly; instead, they were strongly stigmatized and sometimes marginalized by the mainstream parties.

In countries with a smooth transition to democracy, communist successor parties had to reform themselves in order to be competitive and return to government (as the Polish SLD, the Hungarian MSZP, and the Lithuanian LDDP). Those communist successor parties that did not fully undertake the process of internal reform could not be equally accepted players by the mainstream democratic parties, or the "inner system" (Morlino 1986, p. 229) in the democratic game (as the German PDS or the Czech KSCM), therefore they could not return to government. In countries of slower transition to democracy or transition to semi-democracy, communist successor parties were not necessarily forced to reform themselves, so they could successfully adapt themselves to the new regime by modes of transmutation (as the Romanian PSDR, the Bulgarian BSP, and the Russian KPRF). In contrast to southern Europe, semi-reformed successor parties could return to power in Central and Eastern Europe because the regime itself was not everywhere fully democratic. In the countries of slower, belated transition (Romania, Bulgaria) and of semi- or pseudo-democracies (Russia, Ukraine, Serbia) communist successor parties could either return to government or remain the strongest party in opposition by assuming a transmuted or partly reformed character as well. Democracy requires reformed, democratized successor parties, but semi-democracy tolerates transmuted successor parties returning to, or staying in, power. Adaptation strategies are shaped by the past and the mode of transition, but also by post-communist conditions. Moreover, some transmuted communist successor parties had a chance to shape the post-communist condition first in order to successfully "adapt" themselves to it later on. (As the chapter by Brankovic demonstrates, this was clearly the case in the new Yugoslavia where the SPS, led by Milošević, not only adapted to but determined the framework of the political game.)

Finally, have the successor parties had a positive effect upon the development of democracy in post-communist politics? As Bunce has argued, the
return of the ex-communists to power has not been a problem for democracy.
Indeed, its impact has been quite the opposite. The return of the left, particularly in the cases of Hungary and Poland, functioned as an *investment* in
democratic governance. (It is important to note, however, that *return* means
defeat in the previous elections, which should be differentiated from those
cases where the communist successor party could manage to stay in power
continuously.) Further, as Sakwa argues, the shape of Russian democratic
evolution will also strongly depend upon how the KPRF evolves.

Ishiyama (1999a) has further argued that not all of the communist successor parties have promoted the process of democratic consolidation, at least in
terms of promoting the acceptance of democracy among their supporters in
occupational groups most hurt by the political and economic transition. Indeed, the degree to which the communist successor parties appear to have a
positive impact on democratic consolidation (at least in terms of drawing
those who lost out in the transition into acceptance of democracy) depends
on the kind of party it has become and whether that party enjoyed some
degree of success early on in the democratic transition. Successor parties
that have enjoyed electoral success in the 1990s and those who have experienced real power (such as the MSZP and the SLD) appear to be better able to
draw their supporters into accepting democracy than are parties that remain
marginalized or worse yet, treated as significant oppositions and almost completely excluded from real power (such as the KPRF).

This is not to say that parties like the KPRF, KSCM, or KPU will never be
able to act as agents promoting democratic consolidation. The fact that they
have continually participated in elections and have generally recognized the
legitimacy of democratic competition is a testimony to their potential as actors
promoting democratic consolidation. They are not anti-regime parties as defined by Morlino (1980) as parties that "wish to change the regime and do not
accept the norms and structures of authority of the current regime" (Bosco
2001, p. 331; for other approaches to anti-regime or "disloyal" political forces,
see Sartori 1976, p. 133, or Linz 1978, pp. 27–31). However, two factors will
continue to impede their evolution from what Gunther et al. (1995) have referred to as *semi-loyal* opposition parties (1) while these parties continue to
cling to their pre-transition political identities and organizational practices (i.e.
Marxism-Leninism and mass party organization) it is unlikely that they will be
able to resocialize their followers into the acceptance of democracy; (2) this
transformation is made even more unlikely with the continued demonization
of the communist successor parties in these states, and their continued exclusion from the centers of political power. Indeed, continued exclusion is likely
to reinforce anti-democratic sentiment in these parties, and lead to the growing
alienation of the social and political groups they represent.

Bibliography

Ágh, Attila. (1994). "The Hungarian Party System and Party Theory in the Transition of Central Europe." *Journal of Theoretical Politics* 6: 217–238.
———. (1995). "Partial Consolidation of the East-Central European Parties: The Case of the Hungarian Socialist Party." *Party Politics* 1: 491–514.
———. (1996). "New Political Elites in East Central Europe." In G. Pridham and P. Lewis, eds. *Stabilizing Fragile Democracies Comparing New Party Systems in Southern and Eastern Europe*. London: Routledge.
———. (1998a). *The Politics of Central Europe*. Thousand Oaks: Sage Publications.
———. (1998b). *Emerging Democracies in East-Central Europe and the Balkans*. Cheltenham: Edward Elgar.
Ágh, Attila, József Géczi, and József Sipos, eds. (1999). *Rendszerváltók a baloldalon* [Transformers on the Left]. Budapest: Kossuth.
Ágh, Attila and Sandor Kurtan. (1995). "The 1990 and 1994 Parliamentary Elections in Hungary: Continuity and Change in the Political System." In Ágh and Kurtan, eds. *The First Parliament (1990–1994)*. Budapest: Hungarian Center for Democracy Studies.
Altmann, Franz-Lothar and Edgar Hösch, eds. (1994). *Reformen und Reformer in Osteuropa*. Regensburg: Pustet Verlag.
Andrushchak, Hryhorii, Iurii Marchenko, Oleksandr Telemko, and Diana Charishvili. (1999). *Politychni partii Ukrainy*. Kiev: Ukladeannia "K.I.S."
Andrushchak, Iu., Iu. Marchenko, and O. Telemko. (1998a). *Khto ie khto v ukrainskii politisi*. 4th ed. Kiev: TOV "K.I.S."
Andrushchak, Iu., Iu. Marchenko, and O. Telemko. (1998b). *Oftisiina Ukraina S'ohodni*. Kiev: Vydavnitsvo "K.I.S."
Angelusz, Róbert and Róbert Tardos. (1995). "A választói magatartás egy mögöttes pillére: az egykori MSZMP-tagság szerepe" [A Background Pillar of Voting Behavior: The Role of Former MSZMP Membership]. *Politkatudományi Szemle* 4: 5–18.
Antonic, Slobodan. (1993). "Democracy in Serbia—The Actual and the Possible." *In Serbia Between Populism and Democracy*. Belgrade: Institute for Political Studies.
Apter, David E. (1965). *The Politics of Modernization*. Chicago: The University of Chicago Press.
Arato, Andrew. (2001). "The Roundtable Talks, Democratic Institutions and the Problem of Justice." In Bozóki, ed. *The Roundtable Talks of 1989: The Genesis of Hungarian Democracy*. Budapest-New York: Central European University Press.
Ash, Timothy Garton. (1996). "'Neo-Pagan' Poland." *New York Review of Books* 43 (1): 10–14.
Babichenko, Denis and Evgenii Iur'ev. (2000). "Kremlevsvkaia neozhidannost.'" *Segodnya*, 20 January, 1–2, p. 1.
Babst, Stefanie. (1992). "Wahlen in Ungarn, der CSFR und Polen: Erschweren Wahlgesetze die Regierbarkeit?" *Zeitschrift für Parlamentsfragen* 23: 69–83.

Bahrmann, Hannes and Christoph Links. (1994). *Chronik der Wende. Die DDR zwischen 7. Oktober und 18. Dezember 1989*. Berlin: Links Verlag.

Baker, Kendall, Russell Dalton and Kai Hildenbrandt. (1981). *Germany Transformed: Political Culture and the New Politics*. Cambridge: Harvard University Press.

Bakos, Gábor. (1994). "Hungarian Transition After Three Years." *Europe-Asia Studies* 46: 1189–1214.

Barany, Zoltan. (1995a). "Political Transitions and the Return of the Left in East-Central Europe." Unpublished manuscript, University of Texas.

———. (1995b). "Socialist-Liberal Government Stumbles through Its First Year." *Transition* 1 (13): 64–69.

Baricada (Bucharest), January 1991, p. 1.

Barker, Peter, ed. (1998). *The Party of Democratic Socialism in Germany: Modern Post-Communism or Nostalgic Populism?* Amsterdam: Rodopi.

Bartlett, David. (1996). "Democracy, Institutional Change, and Stabilisation Policy in Hungary." *Europe-Asia Studies* 48: 47–83.

Bartolini, Stefano. (2000). *The Political Mobilization of the European Left, 1860–1980: The Class Cleavage*. Cambridge: Cambridge University Press.

Bauer, Tamás. (1996). "Válságoktól a konszolidációig: Az MSZP-SZDSZ kormánytöbbség 1995–ben" [From Crises to Consolidation: The MSZP-SZDSZ Governing Majority in 1995]. In *Magyarország politikai évkönyve* [The Political Yearbook of Hungary]. ed. Kurtán et al. Budapest: DKMKA.

Beck, Ulrich, Anthony Giddens and Scott Lash. (1994). *Reflexive Modernization: Politics, Tradition, and Aesthetics in the Modern Social Order.* Cambridge: Polity Press.

Belasiak, Jack. (1997). "Substance and Process in the Development of Party Systems in East Central Europe." *Communist and Post-Communist Studies* 30: 23–44.

Belin, Laura (1996). "Zyuganov Tries to Broaden an Already Powerful Left-Wing Coalition." *Transition* 2 (5): 12–15.

Bell, David S. (1993). *Western European Communists and the Collapse of Communism.* Oxford: Berg.

Bell, Janice. (1997). "Unemployment Matters: Voting Patterns During the Economic Transition in Poland, 1990–1995." *Europe-Asia Studies* 49: 1263–1292.

Bell, John, ed. (1998). *Bulgaria in Transition*. Boulder, CO: Westview Press.

———. (1990). "Post-Communist Bulgaria." *Current History* 89 (551): 35–45.

Bell, Laurence. (1997). "Democratic Socialism." In Hood and Bell, eds. *Political Ideologies in Contemporary France*. London: Pinter.

Belonuchkin, Grigorii Vladimirovich. (2000). *Federal'noe Sobranie: Sovet Federatsii. Gosudarstvennaia Duma*. Moscow: Fond razvitiia parlamentarizm v Rossii.

———. (1996). *Federal'noe Sobranie: Sovet Federatsii. Gosudarstvennaia Duma: Spravochnik po sostoianuiu na 5 noiabria 1996*. Moscow: Fond razvitiia parlamentarizma v Rossii.

Benjamin, Michael, Uwe-Jens Heuer and Winfried Wolf. (1999). "Votum zu den Thesen der Programmkommission der PDS vom November 1999." In: www.sozialisten.de7download7dokumente7minderheitenvotum.pdf.

Bericht, B. (1998). "Bericht von der Bundeskonferenz der PDS am 7. November 1998 in Berlin." *Pressedienst PDS* 8 (46): 2–6.

Berman, Sheri. (1997). "Civil Society and the Collapse of the Weimar Republic." *World Politics* 49: 401–429.

Bermeo, Nancy. (1994). "Democracy in Europe." *Daedalus* 123: 159–178.

———. (1992). "Democracy and the Lessons of Dictatorship." *Comparative Politics* 24: 273–291.

Bernhard, Michael. (2000). "Institutional Choice after Communism: A Critique of Theory-Building in an Empirical Wasteland." *East European Politics and Societies* 12: 316–347.

Bernstein, Eduard. (1961). *Evolutionary Socialism.* New York: Schocken Books.

Beyme, Klaus von. (1997). "Parteien im Prozess der demokratischen Konsolidierung." In Merkel and Sandschneider, eds. *Systemwechsel 3. Parteien im Transformationsprozess.* Opladen: Westdeutscher Verlag.

———. (1994). *Systemwechsel in Osteuropa.* Frankfurt/M.: Suhrkamp Verlag.

Biberaj, Elez. (1998). *Albania in Transition.* Boulder, CO: Westview Press.

Bielasiak, Jack. (1992). "The Dilemma of Political Interests in the Post-Communist Transition." In Connor and Ploszajski, eds. *Escape from Socialism: The Polish Route.* Warsaw: IfiS.

———. (1995). "Substance and Process in the Development of Party Systems in East Central Europe." Paper presented at the Fifth World Congress of the International Council of Central and East European Studies, Warsaw, Poland.

———. (1997). "Substance and Process in the Development of Party Systems in East Central Europe." *Communist and Post-Communist Studies* 30: 23–44.

Bigio, Isaac. (1998). "The Successor Parties in Eastern Europe: Between Social Democracy and National Communism." *Labour Focus on Eastern Europe* 61: 31–62.

Bihari, Mihály. (1990). "Az állampárt végórái: egy pártkongresszus szociológiája" [The Last Hours of the State-Party: Sociology of a Party Congress.] In Bihari, ed. *Demokratikus út a szabadsághoz* [Democratic Road to Freedom]. Budapest: Gondolat. *Pravda.* (2000). "Revansh osoboi tretei sily." 27 January, p. 2.

Birch, Sarah. (2000). *Elections and Democratization in Ukraine.* New York: St. Martin's Press.

Bisky, Lothar. (1998). "Chancen für und Herausforderungen an die Politik der PDS nach den Wahlerfolgen 1998" (report at the Federal conference of PDS at 7 November, 1998). *Pressedienst PDS* 8 (46): 7–16.

———. (2000). "Manchmal waere es besser, ein Bild zu malen." (interview) *Neues Deutschland*, 13 October 2000, p. 3.

Black, Cyril E. (1967). *The Dynamics of Modernization: Study in Comparative History.* New York: Harper and Row.

Blair, Tony, and Gerhard Schröder. (2000). "The Third Way / Die Neue Mitte" (with the annotation of Joanne Barkan) *Dissent* 1: 51–65.

Blazyca, George, and Ryszard Rapacki. (1996). "Continuity and Change in Polish Economic Policy: The Impact of the 1993 Elections." *Europe-Asia Studies* 48: 85–100.

Bloze, M. (1997). "Politiniu Partiju Susikurimas ir Veikla Nepriklausomoje Lietuvoje." In Jankauskas, Kuris, Novagrockiene, eds. *Lietuvos Politines Partijos ir Partine Sistema.* 2 vols. Kaunas: Naujasis Lankas.

Bobbio, Norberto. (1987). *Which Socialism? Marxism, Socialism and Democracy.* Minneapolis: University of Minnesota Press.

Bohrer, Robert, Alexander Pacek and Benjamin Radcliff. (2000). "Electoral Participation, Ideology, and Party Politics in Post-Communist Europe." *Journal of Politics* 62: 1161–1172.

Bojcun, Marko. (1995). "The Ukrainian Parliamentary Elections in March–April 1994." *Europe-Asia Studies* 47: 229–249.

Böröcz, József. (1999). "Reaction as Progress: Economists as Intellectuals." In Bozóki, ed. *Intellectuals and Politics in Central Europe.* Budapest: Central European University Press.
Bortfeldt, Heinrich (1999). "Eine Partei im Aufwärtstrend-zugleich sehr verwundbar." *Disput,* November, at www.pds-online.de/disput/9911/bortfeldt.html.
———. (1992). *Von der SED zur PDS. Wandlung zur Demokratie?* Bonn-Berlin: Bouvier.
Bosco, Anna, and Carlos Gaspar. (2001). "Four Actors in Search of a Role: The Southern European Communist Parties." In Diamandouros and Gunther, eds. *Parties, Politics, and Democracy in the New Southern Europe.* Baltimore: The Johns Hopkins University Press.
Botez, Mihai. (1978). *Romanii despre ei insisi.* Bucharest: Litera.
Bozóki, András. (1996). "Building Democracy: Institutional Transformation in Hungary." In Nagel et al., eds. *Political Reform and Developing Nations.* Greenwich, CT, London: JAI Press.
———. (1996). "Intellectuals in a New Democracy: The Democratic Charter in Hungary." *East European Politics and Societies* 10: 173–213.
———. (1997). *Between Modernization and Nationalism: Socialist Parties under Post-Socialism.* Working Paper, Dept. of Political Science, Budapest: Central European University.
———. (1997). "The Ideology of Modernization and the Policy of Materialism: The Day After for the Socialists." *Journal of Communist Studies and Transition Politics* 13: 56–102.
———. (1999). "Rhetoric of Action: The Language of the Regime Change in Hungary." In *Intellectuals and Politics in Central Europe.* Bozóki, ed. Budapest: Central European University Press.
———. (2000). "The Roundtable Talks of 1989: Participants, Political Visions and Historical Preferences." *Hungarian Studies* 1: 1–25.
———. (2001a). "Globalists vs. Localists: A Historic Debate and the Position of the Left in Hungary." *Central European Political Science Review* 2: 175–199.
———, ed. (2001b). Introduction to *The Roundtable Talks of 1989: The Genesis of Hungarian Democracy.* Budapest-New York: Central European University Press.
Bozóki, András, et al., eds. (1999–2000). *A rendszerváltás forgatókönyve: kerekasztal-tárgyalások 1989–ben* [The Script of the Regime Change: Roundtable Talks in 1989]. Vols. 1–4. Budapest: Magvető. Vols. 5–8. Budapest: Új Mandátum.
Bozóki, András, and John T. Ishiyama. (2002). "Introduction and Theoretical Framework." In Bozóki and Ishiyama, eds. (2002). *A Decade of Transformation: Communist Successor Parties in Central and Eastern Europe.* Armonk: ME Sharpe.
Bozóki, András, and Gergely Karácsony. (2001). "The Making of a Political Elite: Participants of the Roundtable Talks." In Bozóki, ed. *The Roundtable Talks of 1989: The Genesis of Hungarian Democracy.* Budapest: Central European University Press.
Bozóki, András and Bill Lomax. (1996). "The Revenge of History: The Portuguese, Spanish and Hungarian Transitions–Some Comparisons." In Pridham and Lewis, eds. *Stabilizing Fragile Democracies.* London: Routledge.
Brankovic, Srbobran. (1995). Serbia at War with Itself: Political Views of the Citizens of Serbia. Belgrade: The Sociological Society of Serbia.
Brazauskas, A. (1999). "LKP 20TH Suvaziavimo Desimtmetis." In Masilionis, ed. *Lemties Posukis. Prisiminimai ir Pamastymai.* Vilnius: Gaires.

Brie, André. (2000). "PDS in Ost und West-Fakten und Argumente statt Vermutungen."
At www.pds-online.de/partei/aktuell/0008/brie-studie.html.
Brie, André, and Uta Schulze-Lessel (1998). "Zum Plus und Minus des Bundestag-
swahlkampfes der PDS 1998 und zu einigen Schlußfolgerungen (Vorschläge)."
Brie, Michael, Martin Herzig and Thomas Koch, eds. (1995). *Die PDS.*
*Postkommunistische Kaderorganisation, ostdeutscher Traditionsverein oder linke
Volkspartei? Empirische Befunde und kontroverse Analysen.* Cologne: PappyRossa.
Brie, Michael. (1995). "Das politische Projekt PDS–eine unmögliche Möglichkeit."
In Brie et al. eds.
Brown, Archie. 1997. *The Gorbachev Factor.* Oxford: Oxford University Press.
Bruszt, Laszlo, and David Stark. (1991). "Remaking the Political Field in Hungary."
Journal of International Affairs 1: 201–245.
Budge, Ian, David Robertson and Derek Hearl, eds. (1988). *Ideology, Strategy, and
Party Change: Spatial Analyses of Post-War Election Programmes in 19 Democ-
racies.* Cambridge: Cambridge University Press.
Bukowski, Charles, and Barnabas Racz, eds. (1999). *The Return of the Left in Post-
Communist States: Current Trends and Future Prospects.* Northampton, MA: Ed-
ward Elgar.
Bulgarian Ministry of Finance. (2000). *Overview of the Bulgarian Economy,* Sofia.
Bulgarian Investment Guide. (2000). *The Economic Situation in Bulgaria.* Sofia,
Bulgaria.
Bulgarian Socialist Party Platform. (1998). Sophia: BSP.
Bull, Martin J., and Paul Heywood, eds. (1994). *West European Communist Parties
After the Revolutions of 1989.* New York: St. Martin's Press.
Bunce, Valerie. (1991). "Democracy, Stalinism and the Management of Uncertainty."
In Szoboszlai, ed. *Democracy and Political Transformation: Theories and East-
Central European Realities.* Budapest: Hungarian Political Science Association.
———. (1994). "Sequencing Political and Economic Reforms." In Hardt and Kaufman,
eds. *East-Central European Economies in Transition.* Washington, DC: U.S. Congress, Joint Economic Committee.
———. (1995a). "Comparing East and South." *Journal of Democracy* 6: 87–100.
———. (1995b). "Should Transitologists Be Grounded?" *Slavic Review* 55: 111–
127.
———. (1998a). "Regional Cooperation and European Integration in Postcommunist
Europe: The Visegrad Initiative." In Katzenstein, (ed). *Mitteleuropa: Between
Europe and Germany.* Providence, RI: Berghahn Books.
———. (1998b). "Regional Differences in Democratization: The East Versus the
South." *Post-Soviet Affairs* 14: 323–354.
———. (1999a). "The Political Economy of Postsocialism." *Slavic Review* (forthcoming).
———. (1999b). *Subversive Institutions: The Design and the Destruction of Social-
ism and the State.* Cambridge: Cambridge University Press.
Bunce, Valerie, and Maria Csanadi. (1993). "Uncertainty in Transition: Post-
Communists in Hungary." *East European Politics and Societies* 7: 240–273.
Burnell, Peter, and Alan Ware, eds. (1998). *Funding Democratization.* Manchester:
Manchester University Press.
Burton, Michael G., and John Higley. (1987). "Elite Settlements." *American Socio-
logical Review* 52: 295–307.
Butorova, Zora, ed. (1994). *Aktualne problemy Slovenska.* Bratislava: Focus.

Butorova, Zora, ed. (1998). *Slovensko pred volbami: ludia-nazory-suvislosti.* Bratislava: Institut pre verejne otazky.

Butorova, Zora, Olga Gyarfasova and Miroslav Kuska. (1996). *Aktualne problemy Slovenska na prelome rokov, 1995–1996.* Bratislava: Focus.

Buzgalin, Aleksandr. (1997). "Russia's Communist Party." *The Jamestown Foundation Prism.* 3 (11): 1–2.

Byulleten' Tsetral'noi izbiratel'noi kommissii (TsiK) Rossiiskoi Federatsii. (1994). no. 12, p. 67.

Castex, Michel. (1990). *Un mensonge gros comme le siecle Roumanie, histoire d'une manipulation,* Paris: Albin Michel.

CBOS (Polish Opinion Research Center) Reports. (1994). "Polish Public Opinion." April, Central Election Commission of Ukraine. (1999a). "Elections of the President of Ukraine October 31, 1999." At http://195.230.157.53/vpl/webproc17e?kodvib=100; Internet, accessed 21 January 2001.

Central Election Commission of Ukraine. (1999). "Unified all-state single-mandate election constituency: Elections result 14.11.99." At http://195.230.157.53/vpl/webproc11oe?kodvib=200; Internet. Accessed 21 January 2001.

Central Europe Online. (2000). "ODS and CSSD Pass Electoral Act Amendments, Citizens Abroad to Vote." *Central Europe Online,* 5 June, http://www.centraleurope.com/czechtoday/localpress/carolina.php3?id=166005.

Chebanenko, S.V. (1997). *Politicheskie partii Ukrainy. Politicheskie partii Luganshcheny.* Luhansk: Fond Sotsial'no-ekonomicheskikh issledovanii "Initsiativa."

Chelemendik, Sergej. (1996). "Socialista-Technokrat: Politicky portret Petra Weissa." In *Superslovak Vladimir Meciar: portrety Slovenskych politikov.* Bratislava: Slovansky dom.

Chirot, Daniel, ed.(1986). *The Origins of Backwardness in Eastern Europe.* Berkeley: University of California Press.

Chotiner, Barbara Ann. (1999). "The Communist Party of the Russian Federation: From the Fourth Congress to the Summer of 1998 Government Crisis." In Ishiyama, ed. *Communist Successor Parties in Post-Communist Politics.* Huntington, NY: Nova Science.

Clark, Bruce. (1996). "Nationalist Ideas Move From the Margins." *The World Today* May: 120.

Cohen, Lenard J. (1997). "Embattled Democracy: Postcommunist Croatia in Transition." In Dawisha and Parrott, eds. *Politics, Power and the Struggle for Democracy in South-East Europe.* Cambridge: Cambridge University Press.

Colomer, Josep M. (2000). *Strategic Transitions: Game Theory and Democratization.* Baltimore: The Johns Hopkins University Press.

———. (1995). "Strategies and Outcomes in Eastern Europe." *Journal of Democracy* 6: 74–85.

Colomer, Josep M., and Margot Pascual. (1994). "The Polish Games of Transition." *Communist and Post-Communist Studies* 27: 275–294.

Colton, Timothy J. (1995). "Superpresidentialism and Russia's Backward State." *Post-Soviet Affairs* 11: 144–148.

———. (2000). *Transitional Citizens: Voters and What Influences Them in the New Russia.* Cambridge: Harvard University Press.

Commission on Security and Cooperation in Europe. (1997). *Albania's Parliamentary Elections of 1997.* New York: OSCE.

Communist Party of Ukraine. (1998). "Pre-Election Program of the Communist Party of Ukraine." At http://www.ifesukraine.org/english/Elections1998/ Programs.party11.html; Internet, accessed 25 July 2000.

Cox, Gary W. (1987). "Electoral Equilibrium under Alternative Voting Institutions," *American Journal of Political Science* 31: 35–50.

Crampton, R. J. (1997). *Eastern Europe in the Twentieth Century and After.* London: Routledge.

Crawford, Beverly and Arend Lijphart. (1995). "Explaining Political and Economic Change in Post-Communist Eastern Europe: Old Legacies, New Institutions, Hegemonic Norms, and International Pressures." *Comparative Political Studies* 28: 171–199.

Creed, Gerald. (1995). "The Politics of Agriculture in Bulgaria." *Slavic Review* 54: 843–869.

Crick, Bernard. (1987). *Socialism.* Milton Keynes: Open University Press.

Crome, Erhard. (1992). "Osteuropaforschung und politikwissenschaftlicher Vergleich. Problemfelder und aktuelle Fragen" *Osteuropa* 42: 716.

CTK (News Agency) Various Issues, Various Years.

Czech Social Democratic Party (1995). *Protokol XXXVI. Sjezdu ČSSD.* Prague: CSSD [Transcript of 1993 CSSD Congress].

D'Anieri, Paul, Robert Kravchuk, and Taras Kuzio. (1999). *Politics and Society in Ukraine.* Boulder, CO: Westview Press.

de Weyenthal, Jan B. (1978). *The Communists of Poland: An Historical Outline.* Stanford: Hoover Institution Press.

Di Palma, Giuseppe. (1990). *To Craft Democracies: An Essay on Democratic Transitions.* Berkeley: University of California Press. *Pravda.* "Dogovor skrepili podpisiami." 20–21 June 2000, p. 1.

Dos Santos, T. (1976). "The Crisis of Development Theory and the Problem of Dependence in Latin America." In Bernstein, ed. *Underdevelopment and Development: The Third World Today.* Harmondsworth: Penguin.

Dahl, Robert A., ed. (1966). *Political Oppositions in Western Democracies.* New Haven: Yale University Press.

———. (1971). *Polyarchy.* New Haven: Yale University Press.

The Daily Telegraph (2000), London.

Damus, Martin. (1991). "Malerei der DDR. Funktionen der bildenden Kunst im Realen Sozialismus." Reinbek b. Hamburg: Rowohlt.

Darnolf, Staffan, and Yonhok Choe. (1997). "Free and Fair Elections: What Do We Mean and How Can We Measure Them?" Paper presented at the 17th World Congress of the International Political Science Association (IPSA), August 18–21, Seoul, South Korea.

Dawisha, Karen. (1999). "Electoracies and the Hobbesian Fishbowl of Postcommunist Politics." *East European Politics and Societies* 13: 256–270.

Day, Alan J., Richard German and John Campbell, eds. (1996). *Political Parties of the World.* 4th ed. London: Cartermill.

Degutis, M. (1997). "Politines Partijos ir Rinkiminio Elgesio Dinamika 1992–1996 m." In Jankauskas, Kuris, Novagrockiene, eds. *Lietuvos Politines Partijos ir Partine Sistema.* Kaunas: Naujasis Lankas.

Dellenbrant, Jan, and Sten Berglund. (1992). "The Evolution of Party Systems in Eastern Europe." *The Journal of Communist Studies* 8: 148–157.

Delletant, Dennis. (1995). *Ceausescu and the Securitate.* London: Hurst and Company.

Der Standard, Various issues, Various years.

Desai, A. R. (1976). "Need for Revaluation of the Concept." In Black, ed. *Comparative Modernization*. New York: Free Press.

Desiatnikov, Viktor. (2000). "Parlamentarii tozhe plachut." *Pravda Ukrainy*, 1 February, p. 1.

Downs, Anthony. (1957). *An Economic Theory of Democracy*. New York: Harper and Row.

Dreijmanis, John, and Malajny, Ryszard M. (1995). "Managing Constitutional Change: Post-Communist Experiences." Paper presented at the International Workshop on Managing Constitutional Change, Pretoria, So. Africa, January 19–20.

Dunleavy, Patrick. (1991). *Democracy, Bureaucracy and Public Choice*. New York and London: Harvester Wheatsheaf.

Duverger, Maurice. (1954). *Political Parties*. London: Methuen.

East-West Institute. *Russian Regional Report*, Various Issues, Various Years.

Easter, Gerald. (1997). "Preference for Presidentialism: Postcommunist Regime Change in Russia and the NIS." *World Politics* 49: 184–211.

Eastern Europe and the Commonwealth of Independent States, 1997. 3rd ed. (1996). London: Europa.

Eberhadt, P. (1996). *Przemiany Narodowosciowe na Litwe*. Warsaw: Preglad Wschodni.

The Economist (1999) London.

Eisenstadt, Shmuel N. (1966). *Modernization: Protest and Change*. Englewood Cliffs, NJ: Prentice-Hall.

Elster, Jon, ed. (1996). *The Round Table Talks and the Breakdown of Communism*. Chicago: University of Chicago Press.

Emmerich, Wolfgang (1997). *Kleine Literaturgeschichte der DDR. Erweiterte Neuausgabe*. Leipzig: Gustav Kiepenheuer.

Enyedi, Zsolt. (1996). "Organizing a Subcultural Party in Eastern Europe: The Case of the Hungarian Christian Democrats." *Party Politics* 2: 377–396.

Epstein, Leon N. (1967). *Political Parties in Western Democracies*. New York: Praeger.

Estrin, S., and J. LeGrand, eds. (1989). *Market Socialism*. Oxford: Clarendon Press.

Euromoney. (2000). London.

European Bank of Reconstruction and Development. (1999). *Transition Report*. London: EBRD.

European Forum. (1997). London.

The European Union. (2000). *2000 Report on Romanian Acquis Progress and Membership*. Brussels: European Union.

Evans, Geoffrey, and Stephen Whitefield. (1995). "Economic Ideology and Political Success: Communist-Successor Parties in the Czech Republic, Slovakia and Hungary Compared." *Party Politics* 1: 565–578.

———. (1993). "Identifying the Bases of Party Competition in Eastern Europe." *British Journal of Political Science* 23: 521–548.

Eyal, Gil (2000). "Anti-Politics and the Spirit of Capitalism: Dissidents, Monetarists, and the Czech Transition to Capitalism." *Theory and Society* 29: 50–92.

Eyal, Gil, Iván Szelényi and Eleanor Townsley. (1998). *Making Capitalism Without Capitalists: The New Ruling Elites in Eastern Europe*. London: Verso.

Fedotkin, Vladimir Nikolaevich. "Esli ne mozhete obespechit 'narodu dostoinuiu zhizn'. . . ." Interview by Iurii Makhrin. *Pravda*. 28–29 March (2000), p. 2.

Fenner, Christian. (1984). "Parteiensysteme und Politische Kultur. Ein Vorschlag zur systematischen Verortung von Parteien in der Politischen Kulturforschung." *Österreichische Zeitschrift für Politikwissenschaft* 13: 37–52.

Firdmuc, Jan. (2000). "Political Support for Reform: Economics of Voting in Transition Countries." *European Economic Review* 44: 1491–1514.

Fischer, Mary Ellen. (1997). *Establishing Democracies.* Boulder, CO: Westview.

Fish, M. Steven. (2000). "The Executive Deception: Superpresidentialism and the Degradation of Russian Politics." In Sperling, (ed). *Building the Russian State: Institutional Crisis and the Quest for Democratic Governance.* Boulder, CO: Westview.

———. (1998). "The Determinants of Economic Reform in the Post-Communist World." *East European Politics and Societies* 12: 31–77.

Fisher, Sharon. (1996). "Meciar Retains Control of the Political Scene." *Transition* 2 (16): 32–36.

Földes, György. (2000). "Az új többség" [The New Majority]. *Népszabadság*, December 6.

Frank, Andre. (1978). *Dependent Accumulation and Underdevelopment.* London: Macmillan.

Friedman, Milton. (1962). *Capitalism and Freedom.* Chicago: The University of Chicago Press.

Friedrich-Ebert-Foundation. (1997). "Die Perspektiven der Sozialdemokratie in Ostmitteleuropa. Politikinformation Osteuropa, 72" *Online*: http://www.fes.de/fulltext/id/00112.html#sozi [access 04.04.2001].

Frunza, Victor. (1990). *Originile stalinismului.* Bucharest: Humanitas.

Gaidys, V. (1999). "Lietuvos gyvetoju politiniu vertybiu raida: stabilumas versus Labilumas." In Mitrikas, ed. *Vertybes permainu metais.* Vilnius: Lietuvos filosofijos ir sociologijos institutas.

———. (1995). "Political Preferences in Lithuania: Why the 1992 Elections Was a Surprise." In Taljunaite, (ed). *Lithuanian Society in Social Transition.* Vilnius: Institute of Philosophy, Sociology and Law.

Gamble, Andrew, and Tony Wright, eds. (1999). *The New Social Democracy.* Oxford: Blackwell.

Gebethner, Sebastian. (1996). "Parliamentary and Electoral Parties in Poland." In Lewis, ed. *Party Structure and Organization in East-Central Europe.* Aldershot: Edward Elgar.

Geddes, Barbara. (1995). "A Comparative Perspective on the Leninist Legacy in Eastern Europe." *Comparative Political Studies* 28: 239–274.

Gedeon, Peter. (1995). "Hungary: Social Policy in Transition." *East European Politics and Societies* 9: 433–458.

George, Alexander. (1969). "The Operational Code: A Neglected Approach to the Study of Political Leaders and Decision-Making." *International Studies Quarterly* 13: 190–222.

Gerschenkron, Alexander. (1979). *Economic Backwardness in Historical Perspective.* Cambridge, MA: Harvard University Press.

Giddens, Anthony. (1994). *Beyond Left and Right: The Future of Radical Politics.* Stanford: Stanford University Press.

———. (1998). *The Third Way: The Renewal of Social Democracy.* London: Polity Press.

Gilbert, Trond. (1999). "Romania: Will History Repeat Itself?" *Current History* 89: 23–30.

Gill, Graeme. (1994). *The Collapse of a Single Party System: The Disintegration of the Communist Party of the Soviet Union*. Cambridge: Cambridge University Press.

Girnius, K. (1991). "The Party and Popular Movements in the Baltic." In Trapans, ed. *Towards Independence. The Baltic Popular Movements*. Oxford: Westview Press.

Girnius, Saulius. (1995a). "Learning toward the Right—For Now." *Transition* l (12): 52–55.

———. (1995b). "State Takes the High Moral Ground." *Transition* 1 (7): 18–20.

———. (1995c). "A Tilt to the Left." *Transition* l (9): 28–35.

Glaessner, Gert-Joachim. (1994). *Demokratie nach dem Ende des Kommunismus. Regimewechsel, Transition und Demokratisierung im Postkommunismus*. Opladen: Westdeutscher Verlag.

Glubotskii, Alexei. (1993). *Estoniia, Latviia, Belorussiia: Politicheskie partii I organizatsii (Estonia, Latvia, Belorussia: Political Parties and Organizations)* Moscow: Panorama.

Gohde, Claudia. (1997). *Die PDS in Westdeutschland: eine Studie zur inneren Verfaßtheit der PDS im Auftrag des PV der PDS*. Berlin: Mimeo.

Golosov, Grigorii V. (1999). "From Adygeya to Yaroslavl: Factors of Party Development in the Regions of Russia." *Europe-Asia Studies* 51: 1333–1365.

González Enriquez, Carmen. (1998). "Elites and Decommunization in Eastern Europe." In Higley, Pakulski and Wesolowski, eds. *Postcommunist Elites and Democracy in Eastern Europe*. Basingstoke: Macmillan.

Goodwin, Barbara. (1987). "Socialism." in B. Goodwin, *Using Political Ideas*. Chichester-New York: John Wiley and Sons.

Goriacheva, Svetlana. (1999). "'Ne priemliu politku dvoinoi morali.'" *Nezavisimaia gazeta*, 6 May, p. 3.

Gosolov, Grigorii V. (1997). "Russian Political Parties and the 'Bosses.' Evidence from the 1994 Provincial Elections in Western Siberia." *Party Politics* 3: 5–21.

Götzová, Jitka. (2000a). "Grebeníček: Vedení KSČM chce zrušit organizace dogmatikům.'" *Právo*, 9 March 2000, p. 1.

———. (2000b). "Komunisté podporují rozchod s lidmi, kteří volají po minulosti." *Právo*, 13 March, p. 3.

Grachev, Mikhail Nikolaevich. (2000). *Parlamenskie vybory v Rossii: god 1999: Izbiratel'nye ob "edinenia i bloki, ikh lidery i programmnye dokumenty, rezultaty vyborov*. Moscow: NOU MELI.

Grebeníček, Miroslav. (1992). "Kde je perspektiva našeho hnutí a budoucnosti naší vlasti," *Naše pravda* 98: 1.

———. (1993a). "Přání je otcem myšlenky." *Haló noviny*, 12 March, p. 1.

———. (1993b). "Předseda M Grebeníček se obrací na členy a příznivce' KSČM a Levého bloku." *Haló noviny*, 29 June, p. 2.

———. (1993c). "Jsem přesvědčen, že lidé potřebují stranu našeho typu." *Naše pravda*, 21: 3.

———. (1993d). "Žádnému diktátu nebudeme ustupovat." *Naše pravda* 34: 3–4.

———. (1998). "Klepší budoucnosti ČR můžeme přispět svými volebními výsledky." *Haló noviny*, 23 March, Supplement *Společnost, ekonomika. politka*, p. 3.

———. (1999). "Vystoupení předsedy ÚV KSČM Miroslava Grebeníčka na programové konferenci KSČM v Praze dne 30. 1. 1999." Speech at KSČM Program Conference, 30 January. At http://www.KSČM.cz/dokument/gre30199.htm#návestí1.

Gregg, Richard B. (1971). "The Ego-function of the Rhetoric of Protest." *Philosophy and Rhetoric* 4: 72–82.

Greskovits, Béla. (1998). *The Political Economy of Protest and Patience*. Budapest: Central European University Press.

Grotz, Florian. (2000). *Politische Institutionen und post-sozialistische Parteiensysteme in Ostmitteleuropa. Polen, Ungarn, Tschechien und die Slowakei im Vergleich*. Opladen: Westdeutscher Verlag.

Grzymala-Busse, Anna. (1998a). "Political Legacies and Communist Party Adaptation in East Central Europe." Paper presented at the Eleventh Conference of Europeanists, Baltimore, Md. February 26–28.

————. (1998b). "Reform Efforts in the Czech and Slovak Communist Parties and Their Successors, 1988–1993." *East European Politics and Societies* 12: 442–471.

————. (1999a). "Czech and Slovak Communist Successor Party Transformations After 1989: Organizational Resources, Elite Capacities, and Public Commitments." In Ishiyama, ed. *Communist Successor Parties in Post-Communist Politics*. Commack, NY: Nova Science.

————. (1999b). "Redeeming the Past: The Regeneration of Communist Successor Parties in East Central Europe after 1989." Revised Ph.D. thesis, Department of Government, Harvard University.

Guilhot, Nicolas. (2001). "'The Transition to the Human World of Democracy': Notes for a History of the Concept of Transition from Early Marxism to 1989." *European Journal of Sociology* (forthcoming).

Gunther, Richard, ed. (1995). *The Politics of Democratic Consolidation: Southern Europe in Comparative Perspective*. Baltimore: Johns Hopkins University Press.

Gyafarsova, Olga, Miroslav Kuska, and Marian Velsic. (1999). "First-time Voters." In Bútora, Mesežnikov, Bútorová and Fisher, eds. *The 1998 Parliamentary Elections and Democratic Rebirth in Slovakia*. Bratislava: Institute for Public Affairs.

Gyurcsány, Ferenc. (2000). "A győzelemnél kevesebb" [Less Than Victory]. *Népszabadság*, 16 November, p. 1.

Gysi, Gregor (2000). "Speech on the party congress in Muenster, 9 April 2000." At www.pds-online.de/parteitage/0603/gysi.html.

Gysi, Gregor and Thomas Falkner (1990). *Sturm aufs Große Haus. Der Untergang der SED*. Berlin: Edition Fischerinsel.

Hába, Zdeněk. (1993). "Má KSČM vlastní ekonomický program?" *Haló noviny*, 15 April, p. 5.

Hadjiisky, Magdaléna. (1996). *La fin du Forum civique et la naissance du Parti démocratique civique (janvier 1990–avril 1991)*. Prague: Documents du travail du CEFRES no. 6.

"Za socialismus." (1993a). *Haló noviny*, 27 March, p. 5.

"J. Svoboda oznámil svou rezignaci." (1993b). *Haló noviny*, 11 March, p. 1.

"III Sjezd KSČM skončil rozštěpením strany." (1993d). *Haló noviny*, 28 June, p. 1.

Hankiss, Elemér. (1990). *East European Alternatives*. Oxford: Clarendon Press.

Hanson, Stephen. (1995). "The Leninist Legacy and Institutional Change." *Comparative Political Studies* 28: 306–314.

Harmel, Robert and Kenneth Janda. (1994). "An Integrated Theory of Party Goals and Party Change." *Journal of Theoretical Politics* 6: 259–287.

Harsanyi, Nicolae. (1999). "From Red Star to Roses: The Left in Post-Communist Romania." In Bukowski and Racz, eds. *The Return of the Left in Post-Communist States: Current Trends and Future Prospects*. Northampton, MA: Edward Elgar.

Hasche, Christa, Traute Schölling, and Joachim Fiebach (1994). *Theater in der DDR. Chronik und Positionen*. Berlin: Henschel-Verlag.

Hashim, Syed Mohsin. (1999). "KPRF ideology and its implications for democracy in Russia." *Communist and Post-Communist Studies* 32: 77–89.

Hatschikjan, Magarditsch, and Peter Weilemann, eds. (1994). *Parteienlandschaften in Osteuropa. Politik, Parteien und Transformation in Ungarn, Polen, der Tschecho-Slowakei und Bulgarien 1989–1992*. Paderborn: Schöningh.

Hegedüs, András, Ágnes Heller, Mária Márkus and Mihály Vajda. (1976). *The Humanisation of Socialism: Writings of the Budapest School*. London: Allison Busby.

Hellman, Joel. (1996). "Constitutions and Economic Reform in the Postcommunist Transitions." *East European Constitutional Review* 5: 46–56.

———. (1998). "Winner Take All: the Politics of Partial Reform in Postcommunist Transitions." *World Politics* 50: 203–234.

Higley, John, and Richard Gunther, (eds). (1992). *Elites and Democratic Consolidation*. Cambridge: Cambridge University Press.

Higley, John, Judith Kullberg and Jan Pakulski. (1996). "The Persistence of Post-Communist Elites." *Journal of Democracy* 7: 133–147.

Holsti, Ole. 1977. *The Operational Code as an Approach to the Analysis of Belief Systems*. Final Report to the National Science Foundation, Durham, NC: Duke University.

Huber, John, and Ronald Inglehart. (1995). "Expert Interpretations of Party Space and Party Locations in 42 Societies." *Party Politics* 1: 73–112.

Huntington, Samuel. (1968). *Political Order in Changing Societies*. New Haven: Yale University Press.

———. (1991). "How Countries Democratize." *Political Science Quarterly* 106: 579–616.

———. (1996). *The Clash of Civilizations and the Remaking of World Order*. New York: Simon & Schuster.

Huskey, Eugene. (1997). "Kyrygyzstan: The Fate of Political Liberalization." In Dawisha and Parrott, eds. *Conflict, Cleavage and Change in Central Asia and the Caucasus*. Cambridge: Cambridge University Press.

Ignazi, Piero. (1996). "The Crisis of Parties and the Rise of New Political Parties." *Party Politics* 2: 549–66.

Iliescu, Ion. (1992). *Revolutie si reforma, redactia publicatiilor pentru strainatate*. Bucharest: PDSR.

Innes, Abby. (1997). "The Breakup of Czechoslovakia: The Impact of Party Development on the Separation of the State." *East European Politics and Societies*. 11: 393–435.

International Herald Tribune (2001), London.

International IDEA. (1997). *Democratia in Romania*. Bucharest: Humanitas.

International Labor Organization (ILO). (1998). *World Labor Report*. At url <www.ilo.org/public/english/dialogue/publ/wlr/annex/tab12.htm >.

Ionita, Sorin. (1998). *Sistemele de partide in Europa de Est*. Bucharest: Center for Institutional Reform, Romanian Academic Society.

Ishiyama, John T. (1995). "Communist Parties in Transition: Structures, Leaders and Processes of Democratization in Eastern Europe" *Comparative Politics* 27: 147–166.

————. (1996a). "The Russian Proto-Parties and the National Republics: Integrative Organisations in a Disintegrating World?'" *Communist and Post-Communist Studies* 29: 395–411.

————. (1996b). "Red Phoenix: The Communist Party in Post-Soviet Russian Politics." *Party Politics* 2: 147–175.

————. (1997a). "The Sickle or the Rose? Previous Regime Types and the Evolution of the Ex-Communist Parties in Post-Communist Politics." *Comparative Political Studies* 30: 258–274.

————. (1998). "Strange Bedfellows: Explaining Political Cooperation between Communist-successor Parties and Nationalists in Eastern Europe." *Nations and Nationalism* 4: 61–85.

————. (1999a). "The Communist Successor Parties and Party Organizational Development in Post-Communist Politics." *Political Research Quarterly* 52: 87–112.

————, ed. (1999b). *Communist Successor Parties in Post-Communist Politics.* Commack: Nova Science.

————. (1999c). "Sickles into Roses: The Communist Successor Parties and Democratic Consolidation in Comparative Perspective." *Democratization* 6: 52–73.

————. (2000). "Candidate Recruitment, Party Organization and the Communist Successor Parties: The Case of the MSzP, the KPRF, and the LDDP." *Europe-Asia Studies* 52: 875–896.

Ishiyama, John T., and Andras Bozoki. (2001). "Adaptation and Change: Characterizing the Survival Strategies of the Communist Successor Parties." *Journal of Communist Studies and Transition Politics* 17: 32–51.

Ishiyama, John and Matthew Velten. (1998). "Presidential Power and Democratic Development in Post-Communist Politics." *Communist and Post-Communist Studies* 31: 217–234.

Ishiyama, John, and Sahar Shafqat. (2000). "Party Identity Change in Post-Communist Politics: The Cases of the Successor Parties in Hungary, Poland and Russia." *Communist and Post-Communist Studies* 33: 439–455.

Iur'ev, Evgenii. (1998a). "Muzhskoe nachalo vozobladelo nad kommunisticheskim." *Segodnia*, 24 July, p. 1.

————. (1998b). "Ziuganov poigral prezidentskie vybory." *Segodnia*, 25 April, p. 1.

————. (2000a). "Lishnie liudi: Dumski kommunisty vlasti ne uzhny." *Segodnia*, 4 April, p. 4.

————. (2000b). "Stepashin–starshii po palate." *Segodnia*, 20 April, p. 1.

Izvestiya, Various Issues, Various Years.

Janda, Kenneth. (1980). *Political Parties: A Cross-National Survey.* New York: Free Press.

————. (1990). "Toward a Performance Theory of Change in Political Parties." Paper presented at the 12th World Congress of the International Sociological Association, Madrid, Spain, July.

Janda, Kenneth, Robert Harmel, Christine Edens and Patricia Goff. (1995). "Changes in Party Identity: Evidence from Party Manifestos." *Party Politics* 1: 171–196.

Janda, Kenneth and Tyler Colman. (1998). "Effects of Party Organization on Performance During the 'Golden Age' of Parties." *Political Studies* 46: 611–632.

Jankauskas, A., E. Kuris, and J. Novagrockiene, eds. (1997). *Lietuvos Politines Partijos ir Partine Sistema.* 2 vols. Kaunas: Naujasis Lankas.

Janós, Andrew. (1994). "Continuity and Change in Eastern Europe: Strategies of Post-Communist Politics." *East European Politics and Societies* 8: 25–40.

Jasiewicz, Krzysztof. (1994). "My Name is President: Lech Walesa and the Future of Presidentialism in Poland." Paper presented at the annual meeting of the American Association for the Advancement of Slavic Studies, Philadelphia, PA, Nov. 17–20.

Jelavich, Charles, and Barbara Jelavich. (1977). *The Establishment of the Balkan National States, 1804–1920.* Seattle: University of Washington Press.

Johnson's Russia List, Various Issues, Various Years.

Jones-Luong, Pauline. (2000). "Sources of Institutional Continuity. The Soviet Legacy in Central Asia." Paper presented at the Annual Meeting of the American Political Science Association, Washington, DC, August 31–September 3.

Joseph, Detlef. (2000). "Gegen einen Richtungswechsel-fuer eine starke PDS." At: www.pds-online.de/partei/aktuell/0004/joseph.html.

Jowitt, Ken. (1992). *New World Disorder: The Leninist Extinction.* Berkeley: University of California Press.

Juza, Peter. (1994). "Formovanie koalicie Spolocna volba a jej volebny vysledok." In Szomolanyi and Meseznikov, eds. *Slovensko: Volby 1994.* Bratislava: Slovak Political Science Association and Friedrich Ebert Foundation.

Kagarlitsky, Boris. (1996). "Russia Between Elections." *Labour Focus on Eastern Europe* 53: 17.

Kalenská, Renata. (1998). "Vojtěch Filip: I kdybychom ve volbách vyhráli . . ." *Lidové noviny,* 2 April, p. 3.

Kaminski, Antoni, and Joanna Kurczewska. (1995). "Strategies of Post-Communist Transformations: Elites as Institution-Builders." Unpublished manuscript, University of Warsaw.

Kamyshev, Dmitrii. (2000a). "Staroe litso novoi Dumy." *Kommersant,* 18 January, p. 1.

———. (2000b). "Ziuganov khochet snimat'sia s Putinym." *Kommersant,* 29 January, p. 2.

———. (2000c). "'Rossiia' Selezneva protiv Rossii Ziuganova." *Kommersant,* 16 May, p. 2.

Kapital, Various Issues, Various Years.

Kaplan, Karel. (1987). *The Short March: The Communist Takeover in Czechoslovakia, 1945–48.* London: Hurst.

Karasimeneov, Georgi. (1995). "Parliamentary Elections of 1994 and the Development of the Bulgarian Party System." *Party Politics* 1: 579–587.

Karl, Terry. (1990). "Dilemmas of Democratization in Latin America." *Comparative Politics* 23: 1–22.

Karpinski, Jakub. (1996). "In the Wake of Presidential Elections, a Crisis of Authority." *Transition* 2(2): 56–59.

———. (1997). "Poland's Phoenix Rises." *Transition* 4 (15): 62–65.

Kasianenko, Zhanna. (2000). "Dvadtsat' sed'moi priem dziu—do." *Sovetskaia Rossia.* At http://udb.eastview.com/00/SRS/04/data/043sr21.htm; accessed 16 August 2000.

Katanyan, Konstantin. (1999). *Konstitutsionnyi 'protsess veka' v Rossii: poslednie stranitsy istorii KPSS.* Moscow: Tsentr Konstitutsionnykh Issledovanii, Moskovskii Obshchestvennogo Fonda.

Katz, Richard S. (1980). *A Theory of Parties and Electoral Systems*. Baltimore: Johns Hopkins University Press.

Katz, Richard S., and Peter Mair. (1995). "Changing Models of Party Organization and Party Democracy: The Emergence of the Cartel Party." *Party Politics* 1: 5–28.

———. (1993). "The Evolution of Party Organizations in Europe: Three Faces of Party Organization." In Crotty, ed. *Political Parties in a Changing Age*. Special issue of the *American Review of Politics* 14: 593–596.

———. (1992)."The Membership of Political Parties in European Democracies, 1960–1990." *European Journal of Political Research* 22: 329–45.

Katzenstein, Peter J. (1985). *Small States in World Markets*. Ithaca, New York: Cornell University Press.

Kaufman, Robert R. (1986). "Liberalization and Democratization in South America: Perspectives from the 1970s." In O'Donnell, Schmitter and Whitehead, eds. *Transition from Authoritarian Rule: Comparative Perspectives*. Baltimore: Johns Hopkins University Press.

Keep, J. (1996). *Last Empires. A History of the Soviet Union. 1945–1991*. Oxford: Oxford University Press.

Kholmskaya. M.R. (2000). "Kommunisti Rossiii mezhdy ortokokal'nost'iu i reformizm." In *Politicheskie partii Rossii: Istoriya i Sovermennost'* Zhevelev, Shelokaev, Sviridenko, Tiumiukin, and Sorokin, eds. 551–579. Moscow: ROSSPEN.

King, Anthony, ed. (1998). *New Labour Triumphs: Britain at the Polls*. Chatham, NJ: Chatham House.

Kirchheimer, Otto. (1966). "The Transformation of West European Party Systems." In Lapalombara and Weiner, eds. *Political Parties and Political Development*. Princeton, NJ: Princeton University Press.

Kis, János. (1998). "Between Reform and Revolution." *East European Politics and Societies* 12: 300–383.

Kislitsyn, Sergei, V. Krikunov, and V. Kuraev. (1999). *Gennadi Zyuganov*. In the series *Sled v istorii*. Moscow, n.p.

Kitschelt, Herbert. (1989). *The Logics of Party Formation*. Ithaca, NY: Cornell University Press.

———. (1992). "The Formation of Party Systems in East Central Europe." *Politics and Society* 20: 7–50.

———. (1994). *The Transformation of European Social Democracy*. New York: Cambridge University Press.

———. (1995a). "Formation of Party Cleavages in Post-Communist Democracies: Theoretical Propositions." *Party Politics* 1: 447–472.

———. (1995b). "Party Systems in East Central Europe: Consolidation or Fluidity?" *Studies in Public Policy*, no. 241. Glasgow: University of Strathclyde.

———. (1999a). "Accounting for Outcomes of Postcommunist Regime Change. Causal Depth or Shallowness in Rival Explanations." Paper presented at the 1999 Annual Meeting of the American Political Science Association, Atlanta, GA, September 3–6.

———. (1999b). "Verfassungsdesign und postkommunistische Wirtschaftsreform." In Hinrichs, Kitschelt and Wiesenthal, eds. *Kontingenz und Krise. Institutionenpolitik in Kapitalismus und postsozialistischen Gesellschaften*. Frankfurt: Campus Verlag.

———. (2000). "Linkages Between Citizens and Politicians in Democratic Politics." *Comparative Political Studies* 33: 845–879.

———. (2001). "Accounting for Postcommunist Regime Diversity. What Counts as a Good Cause?" In Ekiert and Hanson, (eds). *Time, Space, and Institutional Change in Central and Eastern Europe* (forthcoming).

Kitschelt, Herbert, and Edmund Malesky. (2000). Constitutional Design and Postcommunist Economic Reform. Paper presented at the Midwest Political Science Association Meeting in Chicago, IL, April 28.

Kitschelt, Herbert and Regina Smyth. 2000. "Programmatic Party Cohesion in Emerging Post-Communist Democracies. Russia in Comparative Context." Unpublished manuscript.

Kitschelt, Herbert, Zdenka Mansfeldova, Radoslaw Markowski and Gabor Toka. (1999). *Post-Communist Party Systems. Competition, Representation, and Inter-Party Cooperation.* Cambridge: Cambridge University Press.

Klíma, Michal. (1998). "Consolidation and Stabilization of the Party System in the Czech Republic." In Hofferbert, ed. *Parties and Democracy. Party Structure and Party Performance in Old and New Democracies.* Oxford: Blackwell.

Koch, Thomas. (1993). "'Die DDR ist passé, aber die Zeiten des naiven Beitritts auch.' Von der Renaissance des ostdeutschen Wir- und Selbstbewußtseins." In Misselwitz, ed. *Die real existierende Postsozialistische Gesellschaft.* Berlin: Wissenschaftsverlag Berliner Debatte.

Kóczián, Péter. (2000). "Kovács és Németh" [Kovács and Németh] *Élet és Irodalom* 47: 1–5.

Kolarova, Rumyana. (1996). "Bulgaria: Could We Regain What We Have Already Lost?" *Social Research* 63: 543–558.

Kommentar. (1997). *Zur Programmatik der Partei des Demokratischen Sozialismus. Ein Kommentar.* Foundation Gesellschaftsanalyse und Politische Bildung, Berlin: Dietz-Verlag.

Kommunalpolitik. (2000). "Figures on local politics on the website of the PDS." At www.pds-online.de/politik/kommunalpolitik/madate/index.html.

Kommunisticheskaia partiia Rossiiskoi Federatsii. (1999a). *Kommunisticheskaia partiia Rossiiskoi Federatsii v rezoliutsiiakh i resheniiakh s"ezdov, konferentsii, i plenumov TsK (1992–1999),* Comp., V. F. Gryzlov. Moscow: Izdatel'stvo ITRK.

———. (1999b). "Ustav obshche rossiiskoi obshchestvennoi organizatsii 'Kommunisticheskaia partiia Rossiiskoi Federatsii.' In *Kommunisticheskaia partiia Rossiiskoi Federatsii v rezoliutsiiakh i resheniiakh s"ezdov, konferentsii, i plenumov TsK,* Comp. V.F., Gryzlov. Moscow: Izdatel'stvo ITRK.

———, IV s"ezd. (1999c). *Programma Kommunisticheskoi partii Rossiiskoi Federatsii (dopolneniia i izmeneniia priniaty IV S"ezdom KPRF 20 apreliia 1997 goda.* In *Kommunisticheskaia partiia Rossiiskoi Federatsii v rezoliutsiiakh i resheniiakh s"ezdov, konferentsii, i plenumov TsK,* Comp., V.F., Gruzlov. Moscow: Izdatel'stvo ITRK.

Kommunisticheskaia partiia Rossiiskoi Federatsii, Otdel organizatsionno-partiinoi i kadrovoi raboty TsK. (2000). "Zapiska o nekotorykh itogakh provedeniia otchetnovybornykh konferentsii regional'nykh organizatsii KPRF v mae-iiule 2000 goda." In "Otchetno-vybornye konferentsii KPRF v respublikakh, kraiakh i oblastiakh i Rossiiskoi Federatsii," KPRF website. At www.kprf.ru/arhiv/congre7/preddv_conf.htm., Internet, accessed 30 August 2000.

Kommunisticheskaia partiia Sovetskogo soiuza. (1991). *XXVIII s"ezd Kommunisticheskoi partii Sovetskogo soiuza: Stenograficheskii otchet.* 2 vols. Moscow: Izdatel'stvo politicheskoi literatury.

Kommunistychna partiia Ukrainy. (1999a). "Programa." In Andrushchak, Marchenko, Telemko, and Charishvili, (eds). *Politychni partii Ukrainy*. Kiev: Ukladannia "K.I.S."

———. (1999b). "Statut (vytiag)." In Andrushchak, Marchenko, Telemko, and Charishvili, eds. *Politychni partii Ukrainy*. Kiev: Ukladannia "K.I.S."

Komsomol'skaya pravda, Various Issues, Various Years.

Konrád, George, and Iván Szelényi. (1979). *The Intellectuals on the Road to Class Power*. New York: Harcourt, Brace, Jovanovich.

Konstitusionnyi Sud Rossiiskoi Federatsii. (1992). Postanovlenie Konstitutsionnogo Suda Rossiiskoi Federatsii po delu o proverke konstitutsionnosti Ukazov Prezidenta Rossiiskoi Federatsii ot 23 avgusta 1991 goda. "Ob priostanovlenii deiatel'nosti Kommunisticheskoi partii RSFSR" ot 25 avgusta 1991 goda, Ob imushchestve KPSS i Kommunisticheskoi partii RSFSR, i ot 6 noiabria 1991 goda "O deiatel'nosti KPSS i KP RSFSR," a takzhe o proverke konstitutsionnosti KPSS i KP RSFSP." In Gyzlov, ed. (1999). *Kommunisticheskaia partiia Rossiiskoi Federatsii v rezoliutsiiakh i resheniiakh s"ezdov, konferentsii i plenumov TsK (1992–1999)*, comp. V. F. Gyzlov, 376–379. Moscow: Izdatel'stvo ITRK.

Koole, Ruud. (1994). "The Vulnerability of the Modern Cadre Party in the Netherlands." In Katz and Mair, (eds). *How Parties Organize: Change and Adaptation in Party Organizations in Western Democracies*. London: Sage.

———. (1996). "Cadre, Catch-all, or Cartel? A Comment on the Notion of the Cartel Party." *Party Politics* 2: 507–523.

Kopecky, Petr. (1995). "Developing Party Organizations in East-Central Europe: What Type of Party is Likely to Emerge?" *Party Politics* 1: 515–534.

———. (1996). "Parties in the Czech Parliament: From Transformative Towards Arena Type of Legislature." In Lewis, ed. *Party Structure and Organization in East-Central Europe*.

Kopstein, Jeffrey, and David Reilly (2000). "Geographic Diffusion and the Transformation of the Post-Communist World." *World Politics* 53: 1–37.

Korguniuk, Iurii Grigor'evich. (1999). *Sovremennaia rossiiskaia mnogopartiinost'.* Moscow: Regional'nyi obshchestvennyi fond INDEM "Informatika dlia demokratii."

Kornai, János. (1980). *The Economy of Shortage*. Amsterdam: North Holland.

———. (1992). *The Socialist System: The Political Economy of Communism*. Princeton: Princeton University Press.

Körösényi, András. (1992). "Revival of the Past or New Beginning? The Nature of the Post-Communist Politics." In Bozóki, Körösényi and Schöpflin, eds. *Post-Communist Transition. Emerging Pluralism in Hungary*. London: Pinter.

———. (1993). "Stable or Fragile Democracy? Political Cleavages and Party Systems in Hungary." *Government and Opposition* 28: 87–104.

Kostelecký, Tomáš(1994). "Economic, Social and Historical Determinants of Voting Patterns in the 1990 and 1992 Parliamentary Elections in the Czech Republic." *Czech Sociological Review* 2: 1–20.

———. (1995). "Changing Party Allegiances in a Changing Party System: The 1990 and 1992 Parliamentary Elections in the Czech Republic." In Wightman, ed. *Party Formation in East Central Europe*. Aldershot: Edward Elgar.

Kostelecký, Tomaš and Aleš Kroupa (1996). "Party Organization and Structure at the National and Local Level in the Czech Republic since 1989." In Lewis, (ed). *Party Structure and Organization in East-Central Europe*. Aldershot: Edward Elgar.

Kostelecký, Tomáš, Petr Jehlička and Ludek Sýkora. (1993). "The Czechoslovak Parliamentary Elections of 1990: Old Patterns, New Trends and Lots of Surprises." In O'Lôughlin and van der Wursten, (eds). *The New Political Geography of Eastern Europe*. London: Belhaven Press.

Kovács, András. (1995). "Two Lectures on the Electoral Victory of the Hungarian Socialists." *Constellations*. (January): 72–75.

————. (1996). "Did the Losers Really Win? An Analysis of Electoral Behavior in Hungary in 1994." *Social Research* 63: 1–20.

Krause, Kevin. (2000). "Public Opinion and Party Choice in Slovakia and the Czech Republic." *Party Politics* 6: 23–46.

Krickus, Richard J. (1997). "Democratization in Lithuania." In Dawisha and Parrott, eds. *The Consolidation of Democracy in East Central Europe*. Cambridge: Cambridge University Press.

Krisch, Henry. (1998). "Searching for Voters: PDS Mobilisation Strategies, 1994–97." In Barker, ed. *The Party of Democratic Socialism in Germany: Modern Post-Communism or Nostalgic Populism?* Amsterdam: Rodopi.

Kroupa, Ales, and Tomas Kostelecky. (1996). "Party Organization and Structure at the National and Local Level in the Czech Republic since 1989." In Lewis, ed. *Party Structure and Organization in East-Central Europe*. Cheltenham: Edward Elgar.

KSČM. (1990). *Dokumenty I. Sjezdu KSČM*. ÚV KSČM [KSČM Central Committee], Prague.

————. (1992). *Dokumenty II. Sjezdu KSČM*. ÚV KSČM [KSČM Central Commitee], Prague.

————. (1993). *Dokumenty III. Sjezdu KSČM*. ÚV KSČM [KSČM Central Committee], Prague.

————. (1995a). *Dokumenty IV. Sjezdu KSČM*. ÚV KSČM [KSČM Central Committee], Prague.

————. (1995b). "Úvod do analýzy příčin a dùsledků 17. listopadu 1989." Unpublished congress material. A version of this document was posted on the party's website in December 1999 at http://www.KSČM.cz/dokument/17list89.htm.

————. (1996). *Za občanskou a sociální spravedlnost*. Ústřední volební štáb KSČM [KSČM Election Headquarters], Prague.

————. (1998). *Jiní o lidech, my s lidmi*. ÚV KSČM [KSČM Central Committee], Prague.

————. (1999). "Draft report of the Central Committee of the Communist Party of Bohemia and Moravia (KSČM), on the Party's work in the period between the Fourth and Fifth Congresses." Published on-line at http://www.KSČM.cz/dokument/zpr4–5sje.htm.

Kto est' chto: politicheskaya Rossiya, 1995–1996. (1996). Moscow: Ministerstvo ekonomiki RF.

Kto je kto na Slovensku 1991. (1991). Bratislava: Konzorcium Encyklopedia.

Kubicek, Paul. (1994). "Delegative Democracy in Russia and Ukraine." *Communist and Post-Communist Studies* 27: 423–441.

————. (2000). "Regional Polarisation in Ukraine: Public Opinion, Voting and Legislative Behavior." *Europe-Asia Studies* 52: 273–294.

Kubilius, J. (1999). "Esminis Zingsnis Kelyje i Nepriklausomybe." In Masilionis, ed. *Lemties Posukis. Prisiminimai ir Pamastymai*. Vilnius: Gaires.

Kubín, Lubos, et al. (1993). *Dva roky politickej slobody—ex post*. Bratislava: RaPaMaN.

Kukorelli, István. (1995). "The Parliamentary Cycle of 1990–1994." In Ágh and Kurtán, eds. *The First Parliament, 1990–1994*. Budapest: Hungarian Center for Democracy Studies.

Kunc, Jiří (1996). "The Fall and Rise of Social Democracy in the Czech Republic." Unpublished paper presented at the "Liberalism, Social Democracy in Central Europe Past and Present" conference, Sandbjerg, Denmark, November 15–18.

Kuptsov, V.A. (1990). "Shto bespokoit Kommunistov." *Izvestiia TsK KPSS*, 10 October, p. 1.

———. (2000). "Rossiya na poroge peremen: Doklad pervogo zamestitelia Predsedatelia TsK KPRF V. A. Kuptsova," *Pravda*, 18–19 January, pp. 1–2.

Kusin, Vladimír. (1978). *From Dubček To Charter 77*. Edinburgh: Q Press.

Kuzio, Taras. (1997). *Ukraine Under Kuchma: Political Reform, Economic Transformation and Security Policy in Independent Ukraine*. New York: St. Martin's Press.

Ladányi, János, and Iván Szelényi. (1996). "Jenseits Wohlfahrtstaat und Neokonservativismus. Für einen Neuen Gesellschaftsvertrag" [Beyond the Welfare State and Neo-Conservatism: Toward the empowering state and a new New Deal]. *Transit* 12:1–20.

Lagerspetz, Mikko. (1999). "Postsocialism as a Return: Notes on a Discoursive Strategy." *East European Politics and Societies* 13: 377–390.

Laitin, David. (1998). *Identity in Formation. The Russian-Speaking Populations in the Near-Abroad*. Ithaca, New York: Cornell University Press.

Land, Rainer, and Ralf Possekel (1995). "PDS und Moderner Sozialismus." In Brie et al.

Lang, Jürgen P., Patrick Moreau and Viola Neu. (1995). *Auferstanden aus Ruinen . . . ? Die PDS nach dem Super-Wahljahr 1994*. Saint Augustin, Germany: Konrad Adenauer Foundation.

Lang, Kai-Olaf. (1999). "Die tschechischen Kommunisten in der Offensive." *Aktuelle Analysen des Bundesinstitutes für ostwissenschaftliche Studien* 55: 1–15.

———. (2000). "Polens Demokratische Linksallianz–eine post-kommunistische Partei?" *Aktuelle Analysen des Bundesinstitutes für ostwissenschaftliche Studien* 4: 1–10.

Lapeikis, P., P. Masilionis, and V. Paulauskas, eds. (1999). *Nepriklausomybes ir Demokratijos Zingsniai, 1989–1999 Metu Kronika*. Vilnius: Gaires.

Le Monde Diplomatique, Various Issues, Various Years.

Lehman, David, ed. (1979). *Development Theory: Four Critical Studies*. London: Frank Cass.

Leites, Nathan. (1951). *The Operational Code of the Politburo*. New York: McGraw Hill.

———. (1953). *A Study of Bolshevism* Glencoe, IL: Free Press.

Lerner, Daniel, James S. Coleman and Ronald P. Dore (1968), "Modernization." In Sills, ed. *International Encyclopedia of the Social Sciences*. London: Macmillan.

Levchenko, Mikhail. (2000). "Vremia sobirat' urozhai: A est' li on?" *Pravda*, 4 May, p. 1.

Levy, Marion J. (1966). *Modernization and the Structure of Societies*. Princeton: Princeton University Press.

Lewis, Paul G. (1994). *Central Europe Since 1945*. Harlow: Longman.

————. (1994). "Political Institutionalization and Party Development in Post-Communist Poland." *Europe-Asia Studies* 46: 777–799.

————. (1996) "Introduction and Theoretical Overview." In Lewis, ed. *Party Structure and Organization in East Central Europe.* Cheltenham: Edward Elgar.

————. (1998). "Party Funding in Post-Communist East-Central Europe." In Burnell and Ware, eds. *Funding Democratization.* Manchester: Manchester University Press.

————. ed. 1996. *Party Structure and Organization in East-Central Europe.* Cheltenham: Edward Elgar.

Lewis, Paul G., and Radzislawa Gortat. (1995). "Models of Party Development and Questions of State Dependence in Poland." *Party Politics* 1: 599–608.

Lidové noviny. (1998a). "KSČM nedokáže oslovit mladé lidi, proto postupně "vymírá." 2 April, p. 3.

————.(1998b). "Gottwalda baví práce s lidmi." 2 April, p. 3.

————.(1998c). "Stalinisté viní Ransdorfa, že je příliš vstřícný ke kapitalismu." 2 April, p. 3.

————.(1998d). "Politici kritizují, že odbory nejsou nadstranické." 23 April, p. 3.

————.(1998e). "US a DŽJ mají nejmenší voličské jádro." 2 April, p. 4.

————.(1998f). "Důchodci za životní jistoty se nijak neliší od komunistů." 29 April, p. 4.

————.(1999a). "Voliči ČSSD přecházejí ke komunistům." 21 July, p. 1.

————.(1999b). "Komunisté se stali nejoblíbenější stranou v zemi." 22 October, p. 1.

Liekis, A. (1995). *Nenugaletoji Lietuva.* Vol. 3. Vilnius: Valstybinis leidybos centras.

————. (1996). *LKP Agonijos Kronika.* Vol. 1. Vilnius: Lietuvos mokslas.

Ligachev, Yegor. *Inside Gorbachev's Kremlin.* Boulder, CO: Westview Press, 1996.

Lijphart, Arend. (1977). *Democracy in Plural Societies.* New Haven: Yale University Press.

Lindström, Ulf. (1991). "East European Social Democracy: Reborn to be Rejected." In Karvonen and Sundberg, eds. *Social Democracy in Transition.* Aldershot: Dartmouth.

Linz, Juan J. (1977). "The Totalitarian Regime." In Greenstein, ed. *Handbook of Political Science.* New York: Macropolitics.

————. (1978). *The Breakdown of Democratic Regimes: Crisis, Breakdown and Reequilibration.* Baltimore: The Johns Hopkins University Press.

————. (1990). "The Perils of Presidentialism," *Journal of Democracy* 1: 51–69.

————. (1994). "Presidential or Parliamentary Democracy: Does It Make a Difference?" In Linz and Valenzuela, eds. *The Failure of Presidential Democracy.* Baltimore: The Johns Hopkins University Press.

Linz, Juan J., and Alfred Stepan. (1996). *Problems of Democratic Transition and Consolidation: Southern Europe, South America, and Post-Communist Europe.* Baltimore: Johns Hopkins University Press.

Lipset, Seymour M. (2001). "The Americanization of the European Left." *Journal of Democracy* 12: 74–87.

Lipset, Seymour, and Stein Rokkan, (eds). (1967). *Party Systems and Voter Alignments: Cross-National Perspectives.* New York: The Free Press.

Liptak, Zostavil L. (1992) *Politica* (1995) Bucharest. *Politicke Strany na Slovensku: 1860–1989.* Bratislava: Archa.

Lomax, Bill. (1995). "Impediments to Democratization in East-Central Europe." In Wightman, ed. *Party Formation in East Central Europe.* Aldershot: Edward Elgar.

———. (1996). "The Structure and Organization of Hungary's Political Parties." In Lewis, ed. *Party Structure and Organization in East-Central Europe*. Cheltenham: Edward Elgar.

London Financial Times. (1999). London.

Lukac, Milan. (1992). "Sluby nic nestoja. . . ." *Plus 7 dni*, 18 May, p. 1.

Lukes, Steven. (1974). *Power: A Radical View*. London: Macmillan.

Lukosaitis, A. (1997). "Moderniosios Partines Sistemos Formavimosi Etapai Lietuvoje." In Jankauskas, Kuris, Novagrockiene, eds. *Lietuvos Politines Partijos ir Partine Sistema*. 2 vols. Kaunas: Naujasis Lankas.

Luts'kyi, O. (2000). "Zakon pro politychni partii: krok do demokratii chy muntsiuvannia na mistsi? *Pravda Ukrainy* 31 March, p. 2.

McAllister, Ian, and Stephen White. (1995). "Democracy, Political Parties and Party Formation in Postcommunist Russia." *Party Politics* 1:49–72.

McAuley, Mary. (1997). *Russia's Politics of Uncertainty*. Cambridge: Cambridge University Press.

McDonough, Peter, Sam Barnes, and Antonio Lopez Pina. (1986). "The Growth of Democratic Legitimacy in Spain." *American Political Science Review* 80: 735–760.

McFaul, Michael. (1997). *Russia's 1996 Presidential Election: The End of Polarised Politics*. Stanford, CA: Hoover Institution Press.

McGregor, James. (1994). "The Presidency in East Central Europe." *RFE/RL Research Report* 3(2): 23–31.

McKay, Joanna. (2000). "Keeping the Red Flag Flying: The Electoral Success of the PDS in East Berlin." *Journal of Communist and Transition Politics* 16: 1–20.

Machonin, Pavel. (1997). *Social Transformation and Modernization—Sociální transformace a modernizace*. Prague: SLON.

Machonin, Pavel, Pavlina Št'astnová, Aleš Kroupa and Alice Glasová. (1996). *Strategie sociální transformace české společnosti*. Brno: Doplněk.

Machos, Csilla. (1994). "Kádárismus und politische Stabilität in Ungarn." In Segert, ed. *Konfliktregulierung durch Parteien und politische Stabilität in Ostmitteleuropa*. Frankfurt: M. Lang.

———. (1997). "Elitenbildung und Elitenwandel in der Ungarische Sozialistischen Partei, 1989–1996." *Südosteuropa* 46: 65–89.

———. (1999). "A magyar pártok szervezeti struktúrájának vázlatai" [Outlines of the Organizational Structures of Hungarian Political Parties]. *Budapest Papers on Democratic Transition* no. 63. Budapest: DKMKA.

———. (2000). *A magyar parlamenti pártok szervezeti felépitése, 1990–99* [The Organizational Structures of Hungarian Political Parties, 1990–99]. Budapest: Rejtjel.

Magyar Hirlap. (2001). Budapest.

Mahr, Alison, and John Nagle. (1995). "Resurrection of the Successor Parties and Democratization in East-Central Europe." *Communist and Post-Communist Studies* 28: 393–409.

Mainwaring, Scott. (1997). "Rethinking Party Systems Theory in the Third Wave of Democratization: The Importance of Party System Institutionalization." Paper presented at the APSA Annual Meeting, Washington, DC, August 28–31.

Mainwaring, Scott, and Scully, Timothy, eds. (1995). *Building Democratic Institutions: Party Systems in Latin America*. Stanford: Stanford University Press.

Mair, Peter. (1996). "What is Different about Post-Communist Party Systems?" *Studies in Public Policy*, no. 259. Glasgow: Center for the Study of Public Policy, University of Strathclyde.

Makarkin, Aleksei, and Andrei Smirnov. (2000). "Bol'shoi sgovor" *Segodnia*, 19 January, p. 4.

Mangott, Gerhard. (1992). "Parteienbildung und Parteiensysteme in Ost-Mitteleuropa im Vergleich." In Gerlich, Plasser, and Ulram, eds. *Regimewechsel. Demokratisierung und politische Kultur in Ost-Mitteleuropa*. Vienna: Böhlau.

———. (1995). *When Ballot Boxes Turn Red: The Return of Former Communists – A Threat to the Consolidation of the New Democracies of the East?* Vienna: Austrian Institute for International Affairs.

Maravall, José María, and Julián Santamaria. (1986). "Political Change in Spain and the Prospects for Democracy." In O' Donnell, Schmitter and Whitehead, eds. *Transitions from Authoritarian Rule: Southern Europe*. Baltimore: Johns Hopkins University Press.

March, Luke. (2001). "For Victory? The Crises and Dilemmas of the Communist Party of the Russian Federation." *Europe-Asia Studies* 53: 263–290.

———. (2000). "The Russian Communist Party in 2000: A Cosmetic Opposition?" *Analysis of Current Events* 12 (7–8): 15–19.

Marchenko, Iurii, and Oleksandr Telemko (1998). *Vybori '98: Iak holosuvala Ukraina.* Kiev: Ukladannia KNTM "ANOD."

Markovic, Mihalo. (1982). *Democratic Socialism*. Brighton: Harvester.

Markowski, Radoslaw. (1997). "Political Parties and Ideological Spaces in East Central Europe." *Communist and Post-Communist Studies* 30: 227–254.

Markowski, Radoslaw, and Gábor Tóka. (1995). "Left Turn in Poland and Hungary Five Years After the Collapse of Communism." *Sisyphus* 9: 75–99.

Márkus, György. (1994). "Parties, Camps and Cleavages in Hungary." In Waller, Coppieters and Deschouwer, eds. *Social Democracy in a Post-Communist Europe*. Newbury Park, CA: Frank Cass.

———. (1996). "Party System and Cleavage Translation in Hungary." Budapest: Working Papers of the Institute for Political Science of the Hungarian Academy of Sciences.

Marody, Mira. (1995). "Three Stages of Party System Emergence in Poland." *Communist and Post-Communist Studies* 28: 263–270.

Martin, Peter. (1990). "New Challenges For the Czechoslovak Communist Party," *Report on Eastern Europe* 4 May, pp. 9–13.

Masliukov, Iurii. (2000). "Masliukov boitsia dvoevlastiia v regionakh." Interview by Konstantin Smirnov. *Kommersant*, 20 May, p. 2.

Mason, David. (1995). "Attitudes toward the Market and Political Participation in the Postcommunist States." *Slavic Review* 54: 385–406.

Masopust, Zdeněk, and Josef Mečl. (1993a). "Česká politika: prostor a výzva." *Haló noviny*, 5 March, p. 7.

———. (1993b). "Proč KSČM transformovat?" *Haló noviny*, 19 June, p. 3.

Matějů, Petr, and Blanka Řeháková. (1996). *Turning Left or Class Realignment? The Changing Relationship between Class and Party in the Czech Republic 1992–96.* "Social Trends" Working paper 1. Prague: Institute of Sociology, Prague, Czechoslovakia.

Matějů, Petr, and Klará Vlachová. (1998). "Values and Electoral Decisions in the Czech Republic," *Communist and Post-Communist Studies* 31: 249–269.

Matoušková, Markéta. (1995a). "Řady KSČM údajně nejpočetnější." *Lidové noviny*, 24 November, p. 1.

———. (1995b). "Rozpory mezi členy a příspěvky." *Lidové noviny*, 30 November, p. 1.

Matsuzato, Kimitaka. (1997). "The Split and Reconfiguration of Ex-Communist Party Factions in the Russian Oblasts: Chelyabinsk, Samara, Ulyanovsk, Tambov, and Tver (1991–1995)." *Demokratizatsiya* 5: 53–88.

———. (1999). "Local Elites Under Transition: County and City Politics in Russia 1985–1996." *Europe-Asia Studies* 51: 1357–1400.

Mediafax. (2000). Bucharest.

Melis, Frantisek. (1995). "Opozicne odpustky pre SDL." *Praca*, 17 October, p. 1.

Mel'nichuk, Yaroslav. (2000). "Zapretili Kompartiyu." *Pravda Ukrainy*, 29 February, p. 2.

Meseznikov, Grigorij. (1995). "Vnutropoliticky vyvoj SR a slovenska politicka scena v prvom polroku 1995." In Butora and Huncik, eds. *Slovensko v siestom roku transformacie: Suhrnna sprava o stave spolocnosti v 1. polroku 1995*. Bratislava: Sandor Marai Foundation.

———. (1997a). "Domestic Political Developments and the Political Scene in the Slovak Republic." In Butora and Huncik, eds. *Global Report on Slovakia*. Bratislava: Sandor Marai Foundation.

———. (1997b). "Postoje a cinnost politickych stran a hnuti." In Meseznikov and Butora, eds. *Slovenske referendum '97: zrod, priebeh, dosledky*. Bratislava: Institut pre verejne otazky.

Meyer, Gerd. (1997). "Parteien, Wählerverhalten und politische Kultur." *Der Bürger im Staat. Landeszentrale für politische Bildung Baden-Württemberg* 47: 150–163.

Mihailovic, Srecko. (1995). *The Parliamentary Elections of 1990, 1992, and 1993: The Challenges of Parliamentarism*. Belgrade: Institute for Social Science.

Miladinovic, Slobodan. (1998). "On the Relativity of the Terms: The Left and the Right." *Serbian Political Thought* 1: 1–10.

Millard, Frances. (1994). "The Shaping of the Polish Party System." *East European Politics and Societies* 8: 467–494.

Miller, William L., and Stephen White. (1998). "Political Values Underlying Partisan Cleavages in Former Communist Countries." *Electoral Studies* 17: 197–216.

Miller, William L., Stephen White and Paul Heywood. (1998). *Values and Political Change in Postcommunist Europe*. Basingstoke: Macmillan.

Minar, Imrich. (1994). "Zamyslenie sa nad pricinami volebnej porazky Strany demokratickej lavice." In Szomolanyi and Meseznikov, eds. *Slovensko: Volby 1994*. Bratislava: Slovak Political Science Association and Friedrich Ebert Foundation.

Ministerstvo iustitsii Rossiiskoi Federatsii. (1993). "Svidetel'stvo o registratsii ustava obshchestvennogo ob"edineniia 24 marta 1993." In Gryzlov, ed. (1999). *Kommunisticheskaia partiia Rossiiskoi Federatsii v rezolyutsiiakh i resheniiakh s"ezdov, konferentsii i plenumov TsK, 1992–99*. Moscow: Izdatel'stvo ITRK.

Minnerup, Günter. (1994). "German Communism, the PDS, and the Reunification of Germany." In Bull and Heywood, eds. *West European Communist Parties After the Revolutions of 1989*. New York: St. Martin's Press.

Misiunas, R., and R. Taagepera. (1993). *The Baltic States. Years of Dependence. 1940–1990*. London: Hurst and Company.

Misselwitz, Hans, ed. (1993). *Die real existierende Postsozialistische Gesellschaft*. Berlin: Wissenschaftsverlag Berliner Debatte.

Mitrofanov, Alexander. (1998). *Za fasádou Lidového domu-Česká sociální demokracie 1989–1998: lidé a události.* Prague: Aurora.
Mladá fronta Dnes. (1997). "Nástupnické strany KSČ se mají rády asi jako zhrzení Milenci." 5 July, p. 1.
———. (1998a). "Odborová centrála volí sociální demokracii." *Mladá fronta Dnes,* 26 March, p. 3.
———. (1998b). "Půrzkum veřejného mínění. . ." 25 April, p. 3.
———. (1998c). "Jak volili lidé nad 60 let." *Mladá fronta Dnes,* 21 June, p. 7.
———. (1999a). "STEM: Preference ODS a komunistů se vzrovnaly." 22 December, p. 2.
Mlynář, Zdeněk. (1996). *Proti srsti: politické komentáře 1990–1995.* Prague: Periskop.
Molnar, A. (1998). "The History of the Terms Left and Right, and the Serbian Case." *Serbian Political Thought* 1: 10–20.
Moore, Barrington (1966). *Social Origins of Dictatorship and Democracy.* Boston: Beacon Press.
Moraski, Bryon, and Gerhard Loewenberg. (1997). "The Effect of Legal Thresholds on the Revival of Former Communist Parties in East-Central Europe." Paper presented at the Annual Meeting of the American Political Science Association, Washington, DC, August 28–31.
Moreau, Patrick. (1992). *PDS. Anatomie einer postkommunistischen Partei.* Bonn: Bouvier.
Morlino, Leonardo. (1980). *Come cambiano i regimi politici.* Milan: Franco Angeli.
———. (1986). "Consolidamento democratico: definizione e modelli." *Rivista italiana di scienza politica* 16: 197–238.
Mosca, Gaetano. (1968). Teoria dei governi e governo parlamentare. Milano: Giufre.
Moser, Robert. (1998a). "The Electoral Effects of Presidentialism in Post-Soviet Russia." In Lowenhardt, ed. *Party Politics in Post-Communist Russia.* London: Frank Cass.
———. (1998b). "Sverdlovsk: Mixed Results in a Hotbed of Regional Autonomy." In Colton and Hough, eds. *Growing Pains: Russian Democracy and the Election of 1993.* Washington, DC: Brookings Institution Press.
———. (1999). "Electoral Systems and the Number of Parties in Postcommunist States." *World Politics* 51: 359–384.
Moskovskaya Pravda, Various Issues, Various Years.
Moskovskie Novosti, Various Issues, Various Years.
MSZP. (1990). "Programnyilatkozat" [Program Declaration]. In Kurtán, ed. *Magyarország politikai évkönyve* [The Political Yearbook of Hungary]. Budapest: Aula-OMIKK.
———. (2000). "Magyarország mindannyiunké! A Magyar Szocialista Párt távlati programja" [Hungary Belongs to All of Us! The Long-Term Program of the Hungarian Socialist Party]. *Hírlevél kongresszusi különszáma* [Special Issue for the Congress]. Budapest: August 24.
MSZP. Left Wing Platform. (2000). "Esélyegyenlőség–az emberért: Az MSZP 15 éves programtervezete [Equality of Opportunity–For Humans: Draft Program of MSZP for the Next 15 Years] Budapest, August 17.
Mudde, Cas. (2000). "Populism in Eastern Europe." *RFE/RL Perspectives.* Vol. 2, no. 5. At www.rferl.org.
Munck, Gerardo L., and Carol Skalnik Leff. (1999). "Modes of Transition and Democratization: South America and Eastern Europe in Comparative Perspective." In Anderson, ed. *Transitions to Democracy.* New York: Columbia University Press.

Mungiu, Alina. (1996). *Die Rumanen nach '89*. Timisoara: Intergraph.

Murer, Jeffrey S. (1999). "Challenging Expectations: A Comparative Study of the Communist Successor Parties of Hungary, Bulgaria, and Romania." In Ishiyama, ed. *Communist Successor Parties in Post-Communist Politics*. Commack, NY: Nova Science.

Myagkov, Yu. (2000). "Effekt prestizhnykh imen v sotsiologicheskikh oprosakh," *Polis* 6: 87–90.

Nagle, John, and Mahr Alison. (1999). *Democracy and Democratization*. London: SAGE.

Nalewajko, Ewa. (1997). *Protopartie i protosystem? Szkic do obrazu polskiej wielopartyjnosci* Warszawa: Instytut Studiów Politycznych PAN.

Narodna Obroda, Various Issues, Various Years.

Naše Pravda. (1992). "Sebevědomě vstříc voličm." 10 April, pp. 1, 8.

———. (1995). "V Praze po komunistech nikdo křapky neházel." 3 May, p. 1.

"Nekotorye itogi uchastiia KPRF v vyborakh Prezidenta Rossiiskoi Federatsii." 2000. KPRF website. At http://www.kprf.ru/workfr/kckvl_1.htm, Internet, accessed 7 September 2000.

Nelson, Daniel, (ed). (1981). *Romania in the '80s*, Boulder, CO: Westview.

Neu, Viola. (2000). *Am Ende der Hoffnung: Die PDS im Westen*. Saint Augustin: Konrad Adenauer Foundation.

Neugebauer, Gero, and Richard Stöss. (1996). *Die PDS. Geschichte, Organisation. Wähler. Konkurrenten*. Opladen: Leske + Budrich.

Neumann, Sigmund. (1956). "Towards a Comparative Study of Political Parties." In Neumann, ed. *Modern Political Parties*. Chicago: Chicago University Press.

New York Times, Various Issues, Various Years.

Nezavisimaya Gazeta, Various Issues, Various Years.

Nicholson, Tom. (2000). "SDL fights retreating battle." *The Slovak Spectator*, 5–11 June, pp. 1–2.

Niedermayer, Oskar, ed. (1995). *Intermediäre Strukturen in Ostdeutschland*. Opladen: Leske und Budrich.

Nohlen, Dieter, and Mirjana Kasapovic. (1996). *Wahlsysteme und Systemwechsel in Osteuropa. Genese, Auswirkungen und Reform politischer Institutionen*. Opladen: Westdeutscher Verlag.

Novak, Adam. (1992). "The Last Communist Party in Europe." *East European Reporter* 5 (May–June): 28–29.

Novák, Vratislav (1993). "O nebezpečích ohrožujících stranu," *Haló noviny*, 28 April, p. 1.

Novopashin, S. (1994). *Politicheskie Partii I Dvishzheniia Vostochnoi Evropy* [Political Parties and Movements in Eastern Europe]. Moscow: Institut Slavyanovedeniia I Balkanistiki.

Nyirö, András, et al., eds. (1989). *Segédkönyv a Politikai Bizottság tanulmányozásához* [Guidebook for the Study of Politburo]. Budapest: Aula.

O'Donnell, Guillermo. (1993). "On the State, Democratization and some Conceptual Problems." *World Development* 212: 1355–1369.

———. (1994). "Delegative Democracy." *Journal of Democracy* 5: 55–69.

O'Donnell, Guillermo, and Phillipe C. Schmitter. (1986). *Tentative Conclusions about Uncertain Democracies*. Baltimore: The Johns Hopkins University Press.

O'Neil, Patrick H. (1998). *Revolution from Within: The Hungarian Socialist Worker's Party and the Collapse of Communism*. Northampton, MA: Edward Elgar.

Obrman, Jan. (1990). "Communist Party Changes Its Structure." *Report on Eastern Europe*, 2 February, 1–2.
———. (1993). "Czech Opposition Parties in Disarray." *RFE/RL Research Report* 2(16): 1–7.
Offe, Claus. (1991). "Capitalism by Democatic Design? Democratic Theory Facing the Triple Transition in East Central Europe." *Social Research* 33: 865–902.
Oleshchuk, V.A., and V.B. Pavlenko. (1997). *Politicheskaia Rossiia: Partii, Bloki, Lidery: Spravochnik.* Moscow: Izdatel'stvo Ves' mir.
Olson, David. (1993). "Compartmentalized Competition: The Managed Transitional Election System of Poland." *Journal of Politics* 55: 415–430.
Oltay, Edith. (1995). "New Election Dynamics." *Transition* 1 (7): 22–25.
Oppositsiya, Various Issues, Various Years.
Ordeshook, Peter, and Olga Shvetsova. (1994). "Ethnic Heterogeneity, District Magnitude, and the Number of Parties." *American Journal of Political Science* 38: 3–28.
Orenstein, Michael. (1998). "A Genealogy of Communist Successor Parties in East Central Europe and the Determinants of Their Success." *East European Politics and Societies* 12: 472–499.
Osa, Maryjane. (1995). "Collective Protest and Democratic Consolidation in Poland (1989–1993): Labor's Opposition to Economic Reforms." Paper presented at the annual meeting of the American Political Science Association, Chicago, IL, August 31–September 3.
Osiatynski, Wiktor. (1995). "After Walesa." *East European Constitutional Review* 4 (4): 35–44.
Ost, David. (1995). "Labor, Class and Democracy: Shaping Political Antagonisms in Post-Communist Society." In Crawford, ed. *Markets, States and Democracy: The Political Economy of Post-Communist Transformation.* Boulder, CO: Westview.
Otáhal, Milan. (1992). "Der rauhe Weg zur samtenen Revolution. Vorgeschichte, Verlauf und Akteure der antitotalitären Wende in der Tschechoslowakei." *Bericht des Bundesinstitutes für ostwissenschaftliche Studien* 25: 1–25.
Padgett, Stephen. (1996). "Parties in Post-Communist Society: The German Case." In Lewis, ed. *Party Structure and Organization in East-Central Europe.* Cheltenham: Edward Elgar.
Panebianco, Angelo. (1988). *Political Parties: Organization and Power.* Translated by Marc Silver. Cambridge: Cambridge University Press.
Pano, Nicholas. (1997) "The Process of Democratization in Albania." In Dawisha and Parrott, eds. *Politics, Power, and the Struggle for Democracy in South-East Europe.* Cambridge: Cambridge University Press.
"Paradox Explained." (1996). *The Economist*, 22 July, p. 52.
Parsons, Talcott. (1964). "Evolutionary Universals in Society." *American Sociological Review* 29: 339–357.
Party of Democratic Socialism in Romania. (2000). *The Political Programme of the PDSR.* Bucharest: PDSR.
Pasti, V.M. Mirou, and C. Codita. (1997). *Romania-Starea de fapt.* Bucharest: Nemira.
Pataki, Judith. (1994). "Hungary's New Parliament Inaugurated." *RFE/RL Research Report* 3(29): 7–11.
Patton, David F. (1998). "Germany's Party of Democratic Socialism in Comparative Perspective." *East European Politics and Societies* 12: 500–526.

Paul, David W. (1979). *The Cultural Limits of Revoultionary Politics: Change and Continuity in Socialist Czechoslovakia*. New York: Columbia University Press.

PDS. (1993). Berlin: PDS.

PDS Programm. (1998). Beschlossen von der 1. Tagung des 3. Parteitages.

PDSR Party Platform. (2000). Bucharest: PDSR.

Pehe, Jiří. (1990a). "Communist Party Faces Growing Pressure." *Report on Eastern Europe*, 6 July, pp. 11–13.

———. (1990b). "The Communist Party at a Crossroads." *Report on Eastern Europe*, 28 September, pp. 13–17.

———. (1990c). "Changes in the Communist Party." *Report on Eastern Europe*, 30 November, pp. 1–5.

———. (1991). "Divisions in the Communist Party of Czechoslovakia." *Report on Eastern Europe*, 26 July, pp. 10–13.

Pelinka, Anton. (1983). *Social Democratic Parties in Europe*. New York: Praeger.

Perryman, Mark, ed. (1996). *The Blair Agenda*. London: Lawrence & Wishart.

"Pervye sekretari regional'nykh komitetov KPRF." 2000. KPRF website. At http:// www.kprf.ru/rukorg/region.htm; Internet; accessed 21 September 2000.

Phillips, Ann L. (1994). "Socialism with a New Face? The PDS in Search of a Reform." *East European Politics and Societies* 8: 495–530.

Pierson, Paul. (2000). "Big, Slow Moving and . . . Invisible: Macro-Social Processes in the Study of Comparative Politics." Paper presented at the Comparative Historical Analysis Workshop, New York, November 10–11.

Plakans, Andrejs. (1997). "Democratization and Political Participation in Postcommunist Societies: the Case of Latvia." In Dawisha and Parrott, eds. *The Consolidation of Democracy in East-Central Europe*. Cambridge: Cambridge University Press.

Plus 7 dni, Various Issues, Various Years.

Pop-Eleches, Grigore. (1999). "Separated at Birth or Separated by Birth? The Communist Successor Parties in Romania and Hungary." *East European Politics and Societies* 13: 117–147.

Potichnyj, Peter J. (1994). *Berichte des Bundesinstituts für ostwissenschaftliche und internationale Studien*, no. 1. "Formation of Political Parties in Ukraine." Cologne: Bundesinstitut für ostwissenschaftliche und internationale Studien.

Powers, Denise, and James H. Cox. (1997). "Echoes from the Past: The Relationship between Satisfaction with Economic Reforms and Voting Behavior in Poland." *American Political Science Review* 91: 617–634.

Pozitsiya Kommunisticheskoi partii Rossiiskoi Federatsii po vyvodu strany iz ekonomicheskogo krizisa. (1999). Moscow: ZAO *Gazeta Pravda*.

Pravda (Bratislava), Various Issues, Various Years.

Pravda (Moscow), Various Issues, Various Years.

Pravda Rossii, Various Issues, Various Years.

Pravda Ukrainy, Various Issues, Various Years.

Pravda Ukrainy. (2000). Photograph caption, untitled. 27 June, p. 1.

———. (2000). "V Konstitusionnom sude." 14 July, p. 1.

Pravda. (2000). Kommunisticheskaia partiia Rossiiskoi Federatsii, VI (vneocherednyi) s"ezd. "Zachem nado idti vo vlast': Nakazy delegatov VI s"ezda Kommunisticheskoi partii Rossiiskoi Federatsii kandidatu v Prezidenty Rossiiskoi Federatsii Ziuganovu Gennadiiu Andreevichu." 15–16 February, p. 1.

———. (2000). "NPSR podderzhivaet Gennadiia Ziuganova." 29–31 February, p. 1.

————. (2000). "Ne ishchite koshku. . . ." 28–31 January, p. 1.

Právo. (1998). "Ètvrtina nìkdejãch voliëì ODS by nyní podpoøla US." 29 April, p. 3.

————. (2000). "Vetãna lidí proti izolaci KSÈM." *Právo,* 11 January, p. 1.

Pressedienst. (1998). *Pressedienst der PDS, 25 June.* At: www.pds-online.de/ pressedienst/ 9826/25065.html.

————. (1999). *Pressedienst der PDS,* 16 April, p. 9.

————. (2000). *Pressedienst der PDS,* 18 February, p. 9.

Prezident RSFSR. 1991. "Ukaz Presidenta Rossiiskoi Sovetskoi Federativnoi Sotsialisticheskoi Respubliki. O Deiatel'nosti KPSS i KP RSFSR." In *Kommunisticheskaya partiya Rossiiskoi Federatsii v resoliutsiiakh i reshenniiakh s"ezdov, konferentsii i plenumov TsK (1992–1999),* com V.F. Gryzlov, 369–370. Moscow; Izdatel'stvo ITRK, 1999.

"Prezidium TsK KPRF." (1998). KPRF website. At http://www.kprf.ru/htm/ prezid.htm.

Pridham, Geoffrey. (2000). *The Dynamics of Democratization: A Comparative Approach.* London: Continuum.

Pridham, Geoffrey, and Paul Lewis, eds. (1996). *Stabilising Fragile Democracies in Southern and Eastern Europe.* London: Routledge.

Programm der PDS zur Bundestagswahl 1998. (1998). Berlin: PDS electoral office. Rudolph: Hedwig.

Programma Kommunisticheskaya partii Rossiiskoi Federatsii Prinyata III s"ezdom KPRF (1995). Moscow: KPRF.

Przeworski, Adam. (1985). *Capitalism and Social Democracy.* Cambridge: Cambridge University Press.

————. (1986). "Some Problems in the Study of the Transition to Democracy." In O'Donnell, Schmitter and Whitehead, eds. *Transitions from Authoritarian Rule: Comparative Perspectives.* Baltimore: The Johns Hopkins University Press.

————. (1991). *Democracy and the Market.* Cambridge: Cambridge University Press.

Pusic, Vesna. (1997). "Mediteranski Model na zalasku autoritarnih drzava." *Erasmus* 20: 2–18.

Putnam, Robert. (1993). *Making Democracy Work: Civic Traditions in Modern Italy.* Princeton: Princeton University Press.

Quirk, Paul J., and William Cunion. (2000). "Clinton's Domestic Policy: The Lessons of a New Democrat." In Campbell and Rockman, eds. *The Clinton Legacy.* New York: Chatham House.

Rácz, Barnabás. (1999). "Left Politics in Post-Communist Hungary." In Bukowski and Racz, eds. *The Return of the Left in Post-Communist States: Current Trends and Future Perspectives.* Northampton, MA: Edward Elgar.

————. (1993). "The Socialist-Left Opposition in Hungary." *Europe-Asia Studies* 45: 647–670.

Rácz, Barnabás, and Istvan Kukorelli. (1995). "The 'Second-Generation' Post-Communist Elections in Hungary in 1994." *Europe-Asia Studies* 47: 251–279.

Radio Bucharest, Various Issues, Various Years.

Rakhmanin, Sergej. (2000). "Prikupite Kommunista. Bystro-Bystro, Ochen' Bystro." *Zerkalo nedeli,* 24 July 2000. At http://www.integrum.com/artefact3/ia/ ia3dll?lv=8&si=bgrf3E&qu=2&bi=70&nd=15&f=0.

Ramet, Sabrina Petra. (1997). "Democratization in Slovenia—the second Stage." In Dawisha and Parrott, eds. *Politics, Power, and the Struggle for Democracy in South-East Europe.* Cambridge: Cambridge University Press.

Ransdorf, Miroslav. (1992). "Naše rozcestí," *Naše pravda*, no. 89–94 (Parts I–VI).
———. (1993a). "Nesvoboda pod Svobodou." *Naše pravda*, no. 12.
———. (1993b). "Chybí koncepční politika." *Haló noviny*, 6 March, pp. 1, 4.
———. (1993c). "Strana na rozcestí," *Haló noviny*, 30 April, p. 2.
———. (1998). "'Jen blázen by se vzdával hodnot spojených s ekonomikou politikou a kulturní pluralitou' říká Miroslav Ransdorf," *Právo*, 5 December 1998, p. 16.
———. (2000a). "Strana pro třetí tisíciletí." Paper presented at the KSČM Conference marking tenth anniversary of party's foundation, 27 May. At http://www.KSČM.cz/aktuel/index.htm.
———. (2000b). "Some Thoughts Concerning Present Stage of the World." Paper presented at KSČM Conference marking tenth anniversary of party's foundation, 27 May. At http://www.KSČM.cz/aktuel/index.htm.
Ratesh, Nestor. (1991). *The Entangled Revolution*. New York: Praeger.
———. (1993). "Romania: Slamming on the Breaks" *Current History* 93: 23–29.
Raun, Toivo U. (1997). "Democratization and Political Development in Estonia, 1987–1996." In Dawisha and Parrott, eds. *The Consolidation of Democracy in East-Central Europe*. Cambridge: Cambridge University Press.
Razumovski, Kirill, and Yuri Chubanenko. (2000). "Parlamentskii krizis na Ukraine." *Kommersant*, 22 January, p. 2.
Reisinger, W.M., A.H. Miller, V.L. Hesli and K.H. Maher. (1994). "Political Values in Russia, Ukraine and Lithuania: Sources and Implications of Democracy." *British Journal of Political Science* 24: 183–224.
Reuters, Various Issues, Various Years.
RFE/RL *Newsline*, Various Issues, Various Years.
Ripp, Zoltán. (2000). "A tévedésnél több" [More Than a Mistake]. *Népszabadság*, 24 November, p. 1.
Roeder, Philip G. (1994). "Varieties of Post-Soviet Authoritarian Regimes." *Post-Soviet Affairs* 10: 61–101.
Roman, Petre. (1994). *Libertatea ca datorie*. Cluj-Napoca: Dacia.
Romania Mare, Various Issues, Various Years.
Roper, Steven D. (1995). "The Romanian Party System and the Catch-All Party Phenomenon." *East European Quarterly* 28: 518–532.
Rose, Richard. (1996). "Ex-Communists in Post-Communist Societies." *The Political Quarterly* 67: 14–25.
Rose, Richard, and Thomas T. Mackie. (1988). "Do Parties Persist or Fail? The Big Trade-off Facing Organisations." In Lawson and Merll, eds. *When Parties Fail*. Princeton: Princeton University Press.
Roskin, Michael. (1993). "The Emerging Party Systems of Central and Eastern Europe." *East European Quarterly* 27: 47–64.
Rossiya v tsifrakh. (2000). Moscow: Goskomstat.
Rothschild, Joseph. (1974). *East Central Europe Between the Two World Wars*. Seattle/London: University of Washington Press. (1992). "Miloš Zeman za Realistický blok." *Rudé právo*, 12 February.
Rudinskii, F.M. (1998). "Delo KPSS v Konstitutsionnom Sude: zapiski uchastnika protsessa." Moscow: Bylina.
Rupnik, Jacques. (1981). *Histoire du parti communiste tchécoslovaque*. Paris: Presses de la Fondation nationale des sciences politiques.
Rustow, Dankwart. (1970). "Transitions to Democracy: Toward a Dynamic Model." *Comparative Politics* 2: 337–363.

Rzeczpopolita, Various Issues, Various Years.

Sakwa, Richard. (1996). *The Communist Party of the Russian Federation and the Electoral Process.* Studies in Public Policy, no. 265. Glasgow: Center for the Study of Public Policy.

———. (1998). "Left or Right? The KPRF and the Problem of Democratic Consolidation in Russia." In Lowenhardt, ed. *Party Politics in Post-Communist Russia.* London: Frank Cass.

Sartori, Giovanni. (1966). "European Political Parties—The Case for Polarised Pluralism." In LaPalombara and Weiner, eds. *Political Parties and Party Development.* Princeton: Princeton University Press.

———. (1976). *Parties and Party Systems: A Framework for Analysis.* Cambridge: Cambridge University Press.

Schamis, Hector. (1997). "Collective Action, Institution Building and the State: The Politics of Economic Reform in Latin America." Unpublished manuscript, Cornell University, January.

Schlesinger, Joseph. (1984). "On the Theory of Party Organization." *Journal of Politics* 46: 369–400.

Schwarz, O. (1993). "Co je vlastni ESOP?" *Haló noviny,* 7 April, p. 1.

Segert, Dieter. (1993). "Politische Visionen im Zerfallsprozeß der DDR–das Beispiel des Sozialismusprojekts." *Utopie kreativ* 4: 87–108.

———. (1995). "Aufstieg der (kommunistischen) Nachfolgeparteien?" In Wollmann, Wiesenthal and Bönker, eds. *Transformation sozialistischer Gesellschaften: Am Ende des Anfangs.* Special edition of Leviathan no. 15. Opladen: Westdeutscher Verlag.

———. (1997). "PDS und SdRP: Historische Wurzeln ihrer Verschiedenheit." *WeltTrends* 5: 125–137.

Segert, Dieter, and Csilla Machos, eds. (1995). *Parteien in Osteuropa: Kontext und Akteure.* Opladen: Westdeutscher Verlag.

Segodnya, Various Issues, Various Years.

"Sekretariat." (1998). KPRF website. At http://www.kprf.ru/htm/sekretar.htm.

Seleny, Anna. (1994). "Constructing the Discourse of Transformation: Hungary, 1979–1982." *East European Politics and Societies* 8: 439–466.

Seleznev, A. (2000). "Informatsiia o rabote fraktsii v period vesennei sessii 2000 god." KPRF website. At http://www.kprf.ru/workfr/workfroo.htm.

Severin, Adrian. (1996). *Lacrimile diminetii.* Bucharest: Scripta.

Shafir, Michael. (1999). "Radical Politics in East-Central Europe: Reds, Pinks, Blacks and Blues." *East European Perspectives* 1: 1–2.

———. (2000). "Radical Politics in East-Central Europe: Radical Continuity in Romania, The Greater Romania Party." *East European Perspectives* 2: 1–2.

Share, Donald. (1989). *Dilemmas of Social Democracy: The Spanish Socialist Workers Party in the 1980s.* New York: Greenwood Press.

Shefter, Martin. (1994). *Political Parties and the State. The American Historical Experience.* Princeton, NJ: Princeton University Press.

Shevtsova, L.F. (1996). "Dilemmy postkommunisticheskoi obshchestva." *Polis* 5: 80–91.

Shugart, Matthew Soberg. (1998). "The Inverse Relationship Between Party Strength and Executive Strength: A Theory of Politicians' Constitutional Choices," *British Journal of Political Science* 28: 1–29.

Šimíček, Vojtěch. (1995). "Poznatky k financování politických stran." *Politologický časopis* 2 (1): 15–26.

Simon, G. (1991). *Nationalism and Policy Towards the Nationalities in the Soviet Union. From the Totalitarian Dictatorship to Post-Stalinist Society*. Boulder, CO: Westview Press.

Simonenko, Petr. (2000). "Kompartiia Ukrainy prodolzhaet bor'bu." Interview by Anton Kolesnikov. *Pravda*, 15–16 February, p. 2.

Simonsen, Sven Gunnar. (1996). "Gennadii Zyuganov: Hankering for the Good Old Days." In *Politics and Personalities: Key Actors in the Russian Opposition*. Oslo: PRIO.

Slavin, Boris. (1998). "Krizie pravitel'stva zakonchilsia Nachnetsia 1: Krizis oppozitsii." *Pravda piat,'* 28 April, p. 1.

Slovakia and the Slovaks: A Concise Encyclopedia. (1994). Bratislava: Goldpress Publishers.

Sme, Various Issues, Various Years.

Smena, Various Issues, Various Years.

Smith, Anthony D. (1976). *Social Change: Social Theory and Historical Processes*. London: Longman.

So, Alvin Y. (1990). *Social Change and Development: Modernization, Dependency and World-System Theories*. London: Sage.

Soltész, István. (1995). "Controlling the Government by Parliament." In Ágh and Kurtan, eds. *The First Parliament 1990–1994*. Budapest: Hungarian Center for Democracy Studies.

Sopel, Jon. (1995). *Tony Blair, the Modernizer.* London: Bantam Books.

"Sostav fraktsii KPRF v Gosudarstvennoi Dume RF FS sozyva 2000–2003 godov." (2000). KPRF website. At http://www.kprf.ru/workfr/kprfgd.htm.

Sovetskaya Rossiya, Various Issues, Various Years.

Spysok narodniky deputativ Ukrainy. 1998. n.p.

Stanclik, Katarzyna. (1997). "Electoral Law and the Formation of Political Party Systems in the New East European Democracies." Paper presented at the Annual Meeting of the American Political Science Association, Washington, DC, August 28–31.

Stedman, Jones. (1998). *Culture, Ideology and Politics*. London: Routledge.

Steinwede, Jacob. (1997). *Entwicklungschancen sozialdemokratischer Parteien. Polen, Ungarn, die Tschechische und Slowakische Republik im Vergleich*. Opladen: Westdeutscher Verlag.

Stewart, Charles J. (1991). "The Internal Rhetoric of the Knights of Labor." *Communication Studies* 42: 67–82.

Stöss, Richard, and Dieter Segert. (1997). "Entstehung, Struktur und Entwicklung von Parteiensystemen in Osteuropa nach 1989–Eine Bilanz." In Stöss and Segert, eds. *Parteiensysteme in Postkommunistischen Gesellschaften Osteuropas*. Opladen: Westdeutscher Verlag.

Stuikys, V. (1999). "Lukesciu Issipildymo Metai." In Masilionis, ed. *Lemties Posukis. Prisiminimai ir Pamastymai*. Vilnius: Gaires.

Suda, Zdenek. 1980. *Zealots and Rebels. A History of the Communist Party of Czechoslovakia*. Stanford, CA: Hoover Institution Press.

Sukhova, Svetlana. (2000). "Seleznev poigryvaet Gromovu," *Segodnia*, 11 January, p. 2.

Svechnikov, Valentin Aleksandrovich. (1997). "Biografia obychnaia—Sovetskaia." Interview by Valentina Nikolaeva, *Pravda Rossii*, 15 April, p. 2.

Svoboda, Jiří. (1993a). "S kým jít a s kým se rozejít." *Haló noviny*, 27 January, p. 3.

———. (1993b). "Obhajujeme a rozvíjíme občanskou společnost." *Naše pravda*, no. 4, 29 January, pp. 2–3.

———. (1993c). "O jedno prosím." *Haló noviny*, 23 February, p. 5.

———. (1993d). "O straně, která je na rozcestí." *Haló noviny*, 24 February, p. 5.

———. (1993e). "Strana na rozcestí." *Naše pravda*, no. 9, 5 March, p. 2.

———. (1993f). "Všechny důvody k ofensivní činnosti." *Haló noviny*, 8 March, pp. 4–5.

———. (1993g). "Kdo si přeje zákaz strany." *Haló noviny*, 2 April, p. 2.

———. (1993h). "Mýlil jste se někdy?" *Haló noviny*, 23 June, p. 1.

———. (1993i). "Dopis delegátům." *Haló noviny*, 26 June, p. 2.

Svobodné slovo. (1990a). "Z rozhovoru s Miroslavem Štěpánem." 15 May, p. 5.

———. (1990b). "Co chystají komunisté." 25 June, p. 3.

———. (1997). "Zeman proti Svobodovi nic nemá." 20 June, p. 3.

———. (1998a). "Předčasné volby v číslech." 22 June, p. 1.

———. (1998b). "Nejvíc hlasů nepomohlo Zemanovi k vítžství." 22 June, p. 1.

Synovitz, Ronald. (2000). "Romania and Bulgaria Lag on the European Union Card." *RFE/RL Year in Review*, pp. 24–26.

Szabó, Miklós. (2000). *Viszonylag békésen* [Relatively Peacefully]. Budapest: Helikon-Mozgó Világ.

Szalai, Erzsébet. (1990). *Gazdaság és hatalom* [Economy and Power]. Budapest: Aula.

Szczerbiak, Aleks. (1999). "Testing Party Models in East-Central Europe: Local Party Organization in Postcommunist Poland." *Party Politics* 5: 525–537.

Szelényi, Iván. (1983). *Urban Inequalities Under State Socialism*. Oxford: Oxford University Press.

Szelényi, Iván, Éva Fodor and Eric Hanley. (1997). "Left Turn in Post-Communist Politics: Bringing Class Back In?" *East European Politics and Societies* 11: 190–224.

Szilágyi, Zsófia. (1995). "A Year of Economic Controversy." *Transition* 1: (21): 62–66.

Szomolanyi, Sona. (1994). "Old Elites in the New Slovak State and Their Current Transformations." In Szomolanyi and Meseznikov, eds. *The Slovak Path of Transition—to Democracy?* Bratislava: Slovak Political Science Association.

Szporluk, Roman. (1988). *Communism and Nationalism: Karl Marx versus Friedrich List*. New York: Oxford University Press.

Sztompka, Piotr. (1993). "Civilizational Incompetence: The Trap of Post-Communist Societies." *Zeitschrift für Soziologie* 2: 85–95.

———. (1996). "Looking Back: The Year 1989 as a Cultural and Civilizational Break." *Communist and Post-Communist Studies* 29: 115–129.

Taagepera, Rein, and Matthew Shugart. (1989). *Seats and Votes: The Effects and Determinants of Electoral Systems*. New Haven: Yale University Press.

TACIS. (2000). "The European Union's Project for Capacity Development in Election Monitoring." *Briefing Document* 7 March.

Taras, Raymond. (1992). *From Critical Marxism to Post-Communism in Eastern Europe*. Armonk, NY: M.E. Sharpe.

Tarkowski, Jacek. (1990). "Endowment of Nomenklatura, or Apparatchicks Turned into Entrepreneurchiks, or from Communist Ranks to Capitalist Riches." *Innovation* 3: 89–105.

Tarrow, Sidney. (1995). "Social Movements and Democratic Development." In Gunther, et al. *The Politics of Democratic Consolidation: Southern Europe in Comparative Perspective*. Baltimore: The Johns Hopkins University Press.

Tatur, Melanie. (1991). "Zur Dialektik der 'civil society' in Polen." In Deppe, Dubiel and Rödel, eds. *Demokratischer Umbruch in Osteuropa.* Frankfurt: Edition Suhrkamp.

Thesen zur programmatischen Debatte vom November 1999. (1999). At: www. sozialisten.de/download/ dokumente/programmthesen.pdf.

Thompson, Wayne C. (1996). "The Party of Democratic Socialism in the New Germany." *Communist and Post-Communist Studies* 29: 435–452.

Timmermann, Heinz. (1994). "Die KP-Nachfolgeparteien in Osteuropa. Aufschwung durch Anpassung an nationale Bedingungen und Aspirationen." *Berichte des Bundesinstituts für ostwissenschaftliche und internationale Studien* 31: 1–21.

Tismaneanu, Vladimir. (1988). *The Crisis of the Marxist Ideology in Eastern Europe.* London: Routledge.

———. (1992). *Reinventing Politics, Eastern Europe from Stalin to Havel.* New York: The Free Press.

———. (1997). "Romanian Exceptionalism?" In Dawisha and Parrott, eds. *Politics, Power, and the Struggle for Democracy in South-East Europe.* Cambridge: Cambridge University Press.

———. (1999). *Fantasies of Salvation: Democracy, Nationalism and Myth in Post-Communist Europe.* Princeton: Princeton University Press.

Tóka, Gábor. (1994a). "Who Is Satisfied with Democracy?" In Bozóki, ed. *Democratic Legitimacy in Post-Communist Societies.* Budapest-Tübingen: T-Twins.

———. (1994b). "Pártok és választóik 1990–ben és 1994–ben" [Parties and Their Voters in 1990 and 1994]. In Andorka et al., eds. *Társadalmi riport* [Social Report]. Budapest: Tárki.

———. (1996). "Electoral Choices in East-Central Europe." In Pridham, Geoffrey and Lewis. *Stabilising Fragile Democracies: Comparing New Party Systems in Southern and Eastern Europe.* London: Routledge.

———. (1997). "Political Parties and Democratic Consolidation in East Central Europe." Studies in Public Policy, no. 279. Glasgow: Center for the Study of Public Policy, University of Strathclyde.

Tökes, Rudolph L. (1996). *Hungary's Negotiated Revolution: Economic Reform, Social Change, and Political Succession, 1957–1990.* Cambridge: Cambridge University Press.

Toole, James. (2000). "Government Formation and Party System Stabilization in East Central Europe." *Party Politics* 6: 441–461.

Treisman, Daniel. (1998). "The Causes of Corruption: A Cross-National Study." Department of Political Science. University of California: Los Angeles.

Troxel, Luan. (1993). "Bulgaria: Stable Ground in the Balkans?" In *Current History* 92: 577–580.

Tsebilis, George. (1990). *Nested Games: Rational Choice in Comparative Politics.* Berkeley, CA: University of California Press.

Tsentral'naia izbiratel'naia komisiia Rossiiskoi Federatsii. (1999a). "Obshchie itogi vyborov deputatov Gosudarstvennoi Dumy Federal'nogo Sobraniya Rossiiskoi Federatsii tret'ego sozyva po federal'nomy izbiratel'nomy okrugu." *Rossiiskaia gazeta,* 31 December, p. 18.

———. (1999b). "Spisok izbrannykh deputatov Gosudarstvennoi Dumy Federal'nogo Sobraniia Rossiiskoi Federatsii tret'ego sozyva: Prilozhenie k postanovleniiu Tsentral'noi izbiratel'noi komissii Rossiiskoi Federatsii ot 29 dekabria, No. 65/ 764–3." *Rossiiskaia gazeta,* 31 December, pp. 18–19.

————. (2000). "O rezul'tatakh vyborov Prezidenta Rossiiskoi Federatsii: Postanovlenie Tsentral'noi izbiratel'noi komissii Rossiiskoi Federatsii ot 5 aprelya 2000
goda No. 98/1110–3 g. Moskva." *Rossiiskaia gazeta*, 7 April, p. 3.

"Tsentral'nyi komitet KPRF." (1998). KPRF Website. At http://www.kprf.ru/htm/
sovtavck.htm.

Tsentral'nyi komitet Kommunisticheskoi partii Rossiiskoi Federatsii. (1998). "O
zadachakh partiinykh organizatsii po podgotovke vyborov v Gosudarstvennuyu
Dumu, ispolnitel'nye i zakonodatel'nye organy sub"ektov federatsii Prezidenta
Rossiiskoi Federatsii: Postanovlenie." In *Kommunisticheskaia partiia Rossiiskoi
Federatsii v rezoliutsi'akh i resheniiakh s"ezdov, konferentsii i plenumov TsK
(1992–1999)*. Moscow: Izdatel'stvo ITRK.

————. (1989). "Postanovlenie VI (vneocherednogo) Plenuma TsK KPRF, in VI plenum TsK KPRF." KPRF website. At http://www.kprf.ru/archiv/plenum5/5.htm.

Tsikora, Sergei. (1991). "Ministerstvo oborony sozdano, ministra-net." *Izvestiia*, 2
September, p. 2.

Tucker, Robert C. (1969). *The Marxian Revolutionary Idea*. New York: W.W. Norton.

Tuleev, Aman. (2000a). " 'Zyuganov nechego delat' v prezidentskoi gonke.'" Interview by Svetlana Ofitova. *Segodnya*, 25 January, p. 1.

————. 2000b. "Levym nuzhen novyi lider." Interview by Igor Ivanov. *Rossiiskaia
gazeta*, 30 June, p. 21.

Týden. (1998). "Co si lidé myslí o stranách. . ." no. 9, p. 11.

Tyler, Patrick E. (2001). "New Tapes Appear With Threats By Ukraine's President."
New York Times, 19 February, p. A6.

Tymowski, Andrzej W. (1994). "Left Turn in Polish Elections?" *New Politics* 16: 99–
107.

Urban, Joan Barth. (1996). "The Communist Movement in Post-Soviet Russia."
Demokratizatsiya: The Journal of Post-Soviet Democratization 4: 173–184.

————. (1999). "The Communist Parties of Russia and Ukraine on the Eve of the
1999 Election." *Demokratizatsiya* 7 (Winter) available from Expanded Academic
ASAP at Article 67. At http://web5.infotrac.galegroup.com/itw/i. . .
_A59624690&dyn=25!ar_fmt?sw_aep=naal_uat.

————. (2000). "Zyuganov's Communists at Odds." *The New Leader*, September/
October, p. 14.

Urban, Joan Barth, and Valerii Solovei. (1997) *Russia's Communists at the Crossroads: Leninism, Fascism, or Social Democracy*. Boulder, CO: Westview.

Urbán, László. (1992). "The Hungarian Transition from a Public Choice Perspective." In Bozóki, Körösényi and Schöpflin, eds. *Post-Communist Transition: Emerging Pluralism in Hungary*. New York: St. Martin's Press.

————. (1991). "Why Was the Hungarian Transition Exceptionally Peaceful?" In
Szoboszlai, ed. *Democracy and Political Transformation: Theories and East-
Central European Realities*. Budapest: Hungarian Political Science Association.

VII S"ezd Kommunisticheskoi Partiie Rossiiskoi Federatsii (2001). Moscow: KPRF.

VII S"ezd Kommunisticheskoi Partii Rossiiskoi Federatsii, 2–3 dekabrya 2000 goda
(2001). Moscow: ITRK.

Vachudová, Milada Anna. (1993). "Divisions in the Czech Communist Party." *RFE/
RL Research Report* 2 (37): 28–33.

Vachudová, Milada, and Timothy Snyder. (1997). "Are Transitions Transitory? Two
Types of Political Change in Eastern Europe Since 1989." *East European Politics
and Societies* 11: 1–35.

Valenzuela, Arturo, and Juan Linz, eds. (1994). *The Failure of Presidential Democracy*. Baltimore: The Johns Hopkins University Press.

Van Biezen, Ingrid. (2000). "On the Internal Balance of Party Power: Party Organizations in New Democracies." *Party Politics* 6: 395–418.

Večerník, Jiří. (1996). "Už vím koho volit: Jak poslední čtyři roky změnily voliče a jejich strany." *Respekt*, 17 (22–8 April): 9–11.

Vermeersch, Jan. (1993). "Social Democracy in the Czech Republic and Slovakia." In Waller, Coppieters and Deschouwer, eds. *Social Democracy in a Post-Communist Europe*. London: Sage.

Vestnik TsIK, Various Issues, Various Years.

Vilhelm, Petr. (1990). "Zůstat, vystoupit, přestoupit?" *Tvorba* no. 3, 17 January, p. 23.

Vocea Romaniei, Various Issues, Various Years.

Volebny program SDL, 1992.

Voronezhskie vesti, Various Issues, Various Years.

Votova, Vratislav (1993). "Aktivní sociální sebeobrana," *Naše pravda*, 20 January, p. 3.

Vremya, Various Issues, Various Years.

Vujacic, Veljko. (1992). "Gennadiy Zyuganov and the "Third Road." *Post-Soviet Affairs* 12: 118–154.

Wade, Larry L., Peter Lavelle and Alexander J. Groth (1995). "Searching for Voting Patterns in Post-Communist Poland's Sejm Elections." *Communist and Post-Communist Studies* 28: 411–425.

Wagner, Peter. (2000). "Rational Choice: The Default Mode of Social Theorizing." In Archer and Tritter, eds. *Challenging Rational Choice*. London: Routledge.

Walker, Stephen. (1990). "The Evolution of Operational Code Analysis." *Political Psychology* 11: 403–418.

———. (1995). "Psychodynamic Processes and Framing Effects in Foreign Policy Making: Woodrow Wilson's Operational Code." *Political Psychology* 16: 697–717.

Waller, Michael. (1995). "Adaptation of the Former Communist Parties of East Central Europe: A Case of Social Democratization." *Party Politics* 1: 473–490.

———. (1996). "Party Inheritances and Party Identities." In Pridham and Lewis, eds. *Stabilising Fragile Democracies: Comparing new party systems in southern and eastern Europe*. London: Routledge.

Wasilewski, Jacek. (1995a). "The Crystallization of the Post-Communist and Post-Solidarity Elite." In Wnuk-Lipinski, ed. *After Communism: A Multidisciplinary Approach to Radical Social Change*. Warsaw: Institute of Political Studies, Polish Academy of Sciences.

———. (1995b). "The Forming of the New Elite: How Much Nomenklatura is Left? *Polish Sociological Review* 2: 113–123.

Wasilewski, Jacek, and Edmund Wnuk-Lipinski (1995). "Poland: Winding Road from the Communists to the Post-Solidarity Elite." *Theory and Society* 25: 669–696.

Weber, Max. (1990). *Wirtschaft und Gesellschaft*. Cologne and Berlin: Kiepenheuer-Witsch.

Weiner, Myron, ed. (1966). *Modernization: The Dynamics of Growth*. New York: Basic Books.

Welsh, Helga. (1994). "Political Transition Processes in Central and Eastern Europe." *Comparative Politics* 26: 379–391.

White, Stephen. (1994). "Communists and their Party in the Late Soviet Period." *Slavonic and East European Review* 72: 644–663.

White, Stephen, and Ian McAllister. (1996). "The CPSU and Its Members: Between Communism and Postcommunism." *British Journal of Political Science* 26: 105–122.

White, Stephen, Richard Rose, and Ian McAllister. (1997). *How Russia Votes.* Chatham, NJ: Chatham House.

White Stephen, Matthew Wyman and Olga Kryshtanovskaya. (1995). "Parties and Politics in Post-Communist Russia." *Communist and Post-Communist Studies* 25: 185–202.

Whitefield, Stephen, and Geoffrey Evans. (1994). "The Russian Election of 1993: Public Opinion and the Transition Experience." *Post-Soviet Affairs* 10: 38–60.

Wightman, Gordon, ed. (1995). *Party Formation in East Central Europe.* Aldershot: Edward Elgar.

Williams, Kieran. (1997). The Prague Spring and Its Aftermath: Czechoslovak Politics 1967–1970. Cambridge: Cambridge University Press..

Wilson, Andrew. (1997a). "The Ukrainian Left: In Transition to Social Democracy or Still in Thrall to the USSR." *Europe-Asia Studies* 49: 1293–1316.

———. (1997b). *Ukrainian Nationalism in the 1990s: A Minority Faith.* Cambridge: Cambridge University Press.

Wilson, Andrew, and Sarah Birch. (1999). "Voting Stability, Political Gridlock: Ukraine's 1998 Parliamentary Elections." *Europe-Asia Studies* 51: 1039–1068.

Wittich, Dietmar. (1995). "Mitglieder und Wähler der PDS." In Brie, Herzig and Koch, eds. *Die PDS. Postkommunistische Kaderorganisation, ostdeutscher Traditionsverein oder linke Volkspartei? Empirische Befunde und kontroverse Analysen.* Cologne: PappyRossa.

Wolchik, Sharon. (1997). "Democratization and Political Participation in Slovakia." In Dawisha and Parrott, eds. *The Consolidation of Democracy in East-Central Europe.* Cambridge: Cambridge University Press.

World Bank. *Statistical Overview: Romania.* (1996) Washington, D.C.: World Bank.

———. *Statistical Overview: Bulgaria.* (1999) Washington, D.C.: World Bank.

———. *Statistical Overview: Romania.* (2000) Washington, D.C.: World Bank.

Wrobel, Janusz. (1999). "Young, Westernized, Moderate: The Polish Left After Communism." In Bukowski and Racz, eds. *The Return of the Left in Post-Communist States: Current Trends and Future Prospects.* Northampton, MA: Edward Elgar.

Yeltsin, Boris. (2000). *Midnight Diaries.* London: Weidenfeld & Nicolson.

Young, Lisa. (1996). "Women's Movements and Political Parties: A Canadian-American Comparison." *Party Politics* 2: 229–250.

Zavtra, Various Issues, Various Years.

Zeman, Miloš. (1993). "Byli bychom aktivní opozicí, která jde vládě po krku." *Rudé právo*, 5 February, pp. 1, 25.

Ziblatt, Daniel. (1998). "The Adaptation of Ex-Communist Parties to Post-Communist East Central Europe: a Comparative Study of the East German and Hungarian Ex-Communist Parties." *Communist and Post Communist Studies* 31: 119–137.

———. (1999). "Two Paths of Change? How Former Communist Parties Remade Themselves After Communism's Collapse." In Ishiyama, ed. *Communist Successor Parties in Post-Communist Politics.* Commack, NY: Nova Science.

Zielonka, Jan. (1989). *Political Ideas in Contemporary Poland.* Aldershot: Avebury.
Ziemer, Klaus. (1997a). "Polen hat die Maßstäbe gesetzt. Polen nach sieben Jahren, Dritter Republik.'" *Der Bürger im Staat. Landeszentrale für politische Bildung Baden-Württemberg* 47: 176–180.
Ziemer, Klaus. (1997b). "Das Parteiensystem Polens." In Stöss, Segert and Niedermayer, eds. *Parteiensysteme in Postkommunistischen Gesellschaften Osteuropas.* Opladen: Westdeutscher Verlag.
Zorkal'tsev, Viktor. (2000). "Shto dast izbranie Gennadiia Zyuganova." *Pravda,* 23 March 2000, p. 2.
Zubek, Vojtech. (1994). "The Reassertion of the Left in Post-Communist Poland." *Europe-Asia Studies* 46: 801–837.
———. (1995). "The Phoenix out of the Ashes. The Rise to Power of Poland's Post-Communist SdRP." *Communist and Post-Communist Studies* 28: 275–306.
Zudinov, Yu. F. "Bolgarskaya Sotsialisticheskaya Partiya: Ukhod b Oppositsiyu." In Novopashin, (1994) *Politicheskie Partii I Dvishzheniia Vostochnoi Evropy* [Political Parties and Movements in Eastern Europe]. Moscow: Institut Slavyanovedeniia I Balkanistiki.
Zverev, Alexei. (1998) "Qualified Sovereigny: The Tatarstan Model for Resolving Conflicting Loyalties." In Waller, Coppieters and Malashenko, eds. *Conflicting Loyalties and the State in Post-Soviet Eurasia.* London: Frank Cass.
Zyuganov, Gennadii. (1993). *Drama vlasti: stranitsy politicheskoi avtobiografii.* Moscow: Paleya.
———. (1994). *Derzhava.* 2nd ed. Moscow: Informpechat'.
———. (1995). *Za gorizontom.* Moscow: Informpechat'.
———. (1996). *Rossiya: Rodina moya.* Moscow: Informpechat'.
———. (1997). *Geografiya pobedy: osnovy Rossiikoi geopolitiki.* Moscow: Informpechat'.
———. (1998). "K pyatiletka KPRF." *Sovietkaia Rossiia,* 17 February, p. 1.
———. (2000a). *Postizhenie Rossii.* Moscow: Mysl'.
———. (2000b). "Obrashchenie k narodu Gennadiia Zyuganova, kandidata v Prezidenty Rossii." *Pravda,* 10 February, p. 2.
———. (2000c). "Proshu poverit' mne." Interview by Aleksandr Il'in. *Pravda,* 24 March, p. 1.
———. (2000d). "Sud'ba Rossii v vashikh rukakh!" *Pravda,* 24 March, p. 1.
———. (2000e). "Politicheskie itogi Parlamentskikh i Prezidentskikh vyborov I ocherednye zadachi partii: Doklad plenumu TsK KPRF," 20 maia 2000g. *Sovetskaia Rossiia,* 23 May 2000. At udb.eastview.com/oo/SRS/05/data/058sr21.htm.

Appendices

Appendix 1

Successor Parties Estimated Memberships for 17 Post-Communist Countries

Country	Successor Party	Estimated Membership the 1990s
Albania	Socialist Party of Albania (PSSH)	110,000
Bosnia	Social Democratic Party (SDP)	40,000
Bulgaria	Bulgarian Socialist Party (BSP)	330,000
Croatia	Social Democratic Party of Croatia (SDP)	20,000
Czech Republic	Communist Party of Bohemia and Moravia (KSČM)	211,000
Estonia	Estonian Social Democratic Labor Party (ESDLP)	300
Hungary	Hungarian Socialist Party (MSZP)	40,000
Latvia	Latvian Socialist Party (LSP)	360
Lithuania	Lithuanian Democratic Labor Party (LDDP)	9,000
Macedonia	Social Democratic Union of Macedonia (SDUM)	40,000
Poland	Democratic Left Alliance (SLD)	62,000
Romania	Party of Social Democracy of Romania (PDSR)	309,000
Russian Federation	Communist Party of the Russian Federation (KPRF)	554,000
Slovakia	Party of Democratic Left (SDL)	48,000
Slovenia	United List of Social Democrats (SLSD)	27,000
Ukraine	Communist Party of Ukraine (KPU)	142,000
Yugoslavia	Socialist Party of Serbia (SPS)	70,000

Sources: Vocea Romaniei, November 24, 1995, pp. 1–2 in *Foreign Broadcast Information Service-Eastern Europe* (FBIS-EEU-95–230) pp. 60–61; Day, German and Campbell. *Eastern Europe and the Commonwealth of Independent States, 1997,* 3rd edition. London: Europa Publications, 1996; Glubotskii, Alexei, (1993) *Estoniia, Latviia, Belorussiia: Politicheskie partii i organizatsii* (Estonia, Latvia, Belorussia: Political Parties and Organizations) Moscow: Panorama. Also various political party web sites.

Appendix 2

Proportion of Votes and Seats in Lower House of the Legislature Won by Successor Parties in Three Most Recent Legislative Elections

	Third Most Recent Election		Second Most Recent Election		Most Recent Election	
	% Vote (year of election)	% Seats (number of seats in lower house of legislature/ total number of seats in legislature)	% Vote	% Seats	% Vote	% Seats
Socialist Party of Albania (PSSH)	20.4% (1996)	7.14% (10/140)	52.8% (1997)	70.7% (99/140)	41.5% (2001)	54.3% (76/140)
Bulgarian Socialist Party (BSP)	43.5% (1994)	52.1% (125/240)	22.0% (1997)	24.2% (58/240)	17.1% (2001)	20.0% (48/240)
Social Democratic Party of Croatia (SDP)	5.5% (1992)	7.2% (11/151)	8.9% (1995)	6.6% (10/151)	40.6%** (1999)	47.0% (71/151)
Communist Party of Bohemia and Moravia (KSCM)	14.0% (1992)	17.5% (35/200)	10.3% (1996)	11.0% (22/200)	11.0% (1998)	12.0% (24/200)
Hungarian Socialist Party (MSZP)	33.0% (1994)	54.2% (209/386)	32.9% (1998)	46.9% (134/286)	42.1% (2002)	46.1% (178/386)
Latvian Socialist Party (LSP)	5.6% (1993)	7.0% (7/100)	5.7% (1995)	5.0% (5/100)	Merged with Tautas Saskanas Partija (TSP) Party of People's Harmony (1998)	—
Lithuanian Democratic	42.6% (1992)	51.8% (73/141)	9.5% (1996)	8.5% (12/141)	**31.1% (2000)	36.2% (51/141)

Labor Party (LDDP)						
Social Democratic Union of Macedonia (SDSM)	48.3% (1994)	48.3% (58/120)	25.2% (1998)	25 (22.5%)	(2002)	
Polish Democratic Left Alliance (SLD)	20.4% (1993)	37.2% (171/460)	27.1% (1997)	35.7% (164/460)	***41.0% (2001)	47.0% (216/460)
Party of Social Democracy of Romania (PDSR)	27.7% (1992)	35.7% (117/328)	21.5% (1996)	27.8% (91/328)	36.6% (2000)	47.3% (155/328)
Communist Party of the Russian Federation (KPRF)	12.4% (1993)	13.8% (62/450)	22.3% (1995)	34.9% (157/450)	24.3% (1999)	25.1% (113/450)
Slovak Party of Democratic Left (SDL)	14.7% (1992)	19.3% (29/150)	**** (1994)	12.0% (18/150)	14.7% (1998)	16.0% (24/150)
United List of Social Democrats of Slovenia (SLSD)	13.6% (1992)	15.6% (14/90)	9.0% (1996)	10.0% (9/90)	12.1% (2000)	12.2% (11/90)
Communist Party of Ukraine (KPU)	12.7% (1994)	19.1% (86/450)	25.4% (1998)	27.1% (122/450)	20.0% (2002)	14.7% (66/450)
Socialist Party of Serbia (SPS)	(1993)	49.2% (123/250)	(1997)	44.0% (110/250)	13.5% (2000)	14.8% (37/250)

Source: Parties and Elections in Europe at http://www.parties-and-elections.de/indexe.html.

Notes:

*   Ran in coalition with Croatian Social Liberal Party

**   Ran in coalition with Lithuanian Social Democratic Party

***   Ran in coalition with Union of Labor

**** Ran in coalition with Slovak Social Democratic Party and Greens

Index

Vatican, 136
Vatra Romaneâsca (Romanian Cradle), 375
Velten, Matthew, 9–10
Velvet Revolution (1989), 121, 143, 162, 309, 329, 330, 335
Verdet, Ilie, 199, 202
Verheugen, Gunter, 379
Videnov, Zhan, 388
Visegrád Group, 341–66
  conclusions about, 365–66
  differences in political orientations and adaptation strategies of, 341–43
  periods of transition and periods of party system development of, 344–65. *See also* party system development
  theoretical issues for, 343–45
Voiculescu, Voican, 192
VPV. *See* Public Against Violence
Vucelic, Milorad, 211

Wagner, Peter, 114*n.4*
Walesa, Lech, 57, 307, 330, 346, 362
Walker, Stephen, 302
Waller, Michael, 55, 280, 296
Warsaw Pact, 99, 346, 350
Wasilewski, Jacek, 311, 314–15, 322*n.20*
Weber, Max, 212, 217
Weighted Presidential Power Score, 286*n.3*
Weiss, Peter, 119–25, 127–31, 133–34, 138, 140*n.5*, 352–53, 355, 363, 364
welfare state, 48, 109, 112, 113, 226, 423
  workfare state vs., 45–46
Welsh, Helga, 277
Western Europe, crisis of the political Right in, 48
White, Stephen, 264*n.2*, 279
Whitefield, Stephen, 340*n.11*, 391
Wnuk-Lipinski, Edmund, 311, 322*n.20*
"Word to the People, A" (manifesto), 241
Workers' Association of Slovakia (ZRS), 20

"workers self-management," 213
Workers' Union of Poland (UP), 31, 76
Workers' Union of Slovakia (ZRS), 359
workfare state vs. welfare state, 109
"Working Russia" movement, 248
World Bank, 63, 140*n.9*, 375, 383, 384, 388, 396*n.3*
World War I, 8
World War II, 17, 18, 24, 226, 338, 340*n.12*, 373
Wyman, Matthew, 279

Yabloko (Apple) Party, 254
Yakovlev, Aleksandr, 243
Yeltsin, Boris, 6, 241–42, 247, 249–51, 253, 262, 264*n.7*, 401, 412, 414, 416
Young Democratic Left, 131
Yugoslavia, 91, 275, 386
  regime legacy in, 18, 35, 213
Yugoslav Left (JUL), 206–7, 211

Zajedno (Together) Coalition, 221
ZChN. *See* Christian National Union
Zeman, Milos, 149, 161, 365
Zhivkov, Todor, 384
Zhuganov, Gennadi, 322*n.18*
Zhukov, Marshal Gheorgii, 6
Ziblatt, Daniel, 5, 6, 292, 391–92, 422–23, 427
Zimmer, Gabi, 181
Ziuganov, Gennadii, 241, 242, 244–54, 257–61, 263, 265*n.11*, 266*n.33*, 398, 403, 404, 405, 408, 411, 412, 416
  ideology of, 245–46
ZLSD. *See* United List of Social Democrats in Slovenia
Zorkal'tsev, Viktor, 265*n.15*, 411
Zor'kin, Valerii, 242
ZRS. *See* Association of Workers of Slovakia; Workers' Union of Slovakia
Zselenak, Jozef, 123, 129
ZSL, 54, 86*n.3*, 88*n.25*
ZSLD, 324